Marketing for Tourism and Hospitality

A Canadian Perspective

Second Edition

Simon Hudson

Haskayne School of Business
University of Calgary

NELSON / EDUCATION

NELSON / EDUCATION

**Marketing for Tourism and Hospitality:
A Canadian Perspective, Second Edition**

Simon Hudson

**Associate Vice President,
Editorial Director:**
Evelyn Veitch

Editor-in-Chief:
Anne Williams

Senior Acquisitions Editor:
Kevin Smulan

Marketing Manager:
William de Villiers

Developmental Editor:
Elke Price

**Photo Researcher/Permissions
Coordinator:**
Sheila Hall

Content Production Managers:
Carrie McGregor
Karri Yano

Production Service:
GEX Publishing Services

Copy Editor:
Madeline Koch

Proofreader:
GEX Publishing Services

Indexer:
GEX Publishing Services

**Senior Manufacturing
Coordinator:**
Charmaine Lee-Wah

Managing Designer:
Katherine Strain

Cover Design:
Johanna Liburd

Cover Image:
Straw hat on chair at beach:
Jacobs Stock
Photography/Photographer's
Choice/Getty Images

screen on back of airplane seat:
Steve Craft/Masterfile

Compositor:
GEX Publishing Services

Printer:
Edwards Brothers

**Library and Archives Canada
Cataloguing in Publication**

Hudson, Simon
    Marketing for tourism and
hospitality: a Canadian
perspective / Simon Hudson. —
2nd ed.

Includes bibliographical references
and index.
ISBN 13: 978-0-17-644047-3
ISBN 10: 0-17-644047-X

    1. Tourism—Canada—
Marketing—Textbooks. 2.
Hospitality industry—Canada—
Marketing—Textbooks. I. Title.

G155.C2H82 2008
338.4'79171040688
C2007-905105-7

Brief Contents

Contents

Special Interest Boxes

MARKETING IN ACTION

PROFILES

SNAPSHOTS

Preface

Tourism is a powerful economic force providing employment, foreign exchange, income, and tax revenue for countries all over the world. The number of international arrivals has risen from just 50 million in 1950 to 842 million in 2006. While this represents an annual growth rate of 6.5 percent over more than half a century, the receipts generated by these tourists have increased nearly twice as fast. This growth rate for tourism far outstrips the world economy as a whole, and tourism now represents a quarter of all exports of services. In Canada, tourism is an increasingly important sector of the economy. In 2006, Canada attracted over 18 million international overnight visitors who spent nearly $13 billion, making tourism one of Canada's top foreign exchange earners. More than 10 percent of Canada's labour force works in tourism, accounting for approximately 1.7 million jobs. The United Nations World Tourism Organization (UNWTO) ranks Canada as the 12th most popular destination in the world.

Alongside the growth of the tourism industry, tourism education has expanded rapidly over the last few decades, reflecting the growing recognition of tourism (and the travel and hospitality industries that serve it) as one of the world's most significant economic, social, and environmental forces. Tourism education and training have been developed at various levels, ranging from highly vocational courses to higher research degrees. The growth reflects the widely held belief that one of the major challenges the industry faces is to recruit, develop, and retain employees and managers who have appropriate educational backgrounds.

Yet despite this obvious interest in the subject of tourism, until now there has been no text that specifically deals with tourism and hospitality marketing in Canada. There are many tourism marketing books, the majority of which are aimed at the American or European markets, but none of them is relevant to Canadian students in particular. There is also very little material available for the marketing practitioner in relation to marketing tourism and hospitality products in Canada. The second edition of *Marketing for Tourism and Hospitality: A Canadian Perspective* fills this void. Marketing is a subject of vital concern in tourism because it is the principal management influence that can be brought to bear on the size and behaviour of this major global market. The main sectors of the tourism industry — travel organizers, destination organizations, transportation, and various product suppliers — combine to manage visitors' demands through a range of marketing influences.

HIGHLIGHTS

Real-World Canadian and International Examples and Case Studies

This very readable text's unique focus on Canada makes it suitable for use in both educational and professional contexts. More than 70 up-to-date examples and case studies from all over Canada, and overseas are included, covering all sectors of tourism and hospitality. Case studies at the end of each chapter examine the marketing of diverse tourism products, such as sport and adventure tourism, nostalgia tourism, space tourism, wine tourism, urban ecotourism, and native tourism. Readers will be fascinated to learn why Roots Air failed while WestJet Airlines succeeded, why Four Seasons Hotels and Resorts has such a successful positioning strategy, how Canadian Mountain Holidays sells heli-skiing trips with no advertising, and how the Sheraton Suites Calgary Eau Claire consistently wins awards for service excellence. Indeed, they will be interested to know how Canada has re-branded itself to compete for international tourists, why the backpacker is getting older and richer, and why the Calgary Stampede is known as the Greatest Outdoor Show on Earth.

Comprehensive Marketing Coverage

As well as offering numerous Canadian examples, the book provides comprehensive coverage of essential marketing principles, such as developing a marketing plan, understanding consumer behaviour, doing marketing research, and implementing the marketing mix. The text also includes sections on contemporary marketing issues such as integrated marketing communications, Internet marketing, responsible marketing, and internal marketing.

ORGANIZATION

Marketing for Tourism and Hospitality: A Canadian Perspective begins with a chapter dedicated to the tourism and hospitality environment in Canada. **Chapter 1** starts by providing an introduction to tourism and hospitality marketing in general by discussing the definition and role of marketing and its importance in tourism. A synopsis of services marketing theory highlights the unique characteristics of services and introduces important service marketing models, such as the services marketing triangle and the services marketing mix. The chapter then focuses on tourism in Canada and analyzes the key players in Canada's tourism industry. The remainder of the chapter examines the marketing environment's microenvironmental and macroenvironmental forces, and the ways in which they affect an organization's ability to serve its customers.

Chapter 2 considers behavioural trends in tourism by reviewing tourism motivational studies, examining typologies of tourists, and discussing the external factors that influence consumer behaviour. The chapter includes a section devoted to organizational buying behaviour, as well as an analysis of current trends in consumer behaviour that are affecting tourism marketing today.

Successful marketing in tourism and hospitality requires careful planning and execution. **Chapter 3** focuses on the development of a marketing plan in the tourism and hospitality industry by discussing the eight key steps in the marketing planning process. Practical examples from various sectors of the tourism industry are also provided.

Chapter 4 covers marketing research and it begins with a description of the type of applied research conducted in tourism, followed by a discussion of the various stages in the research process. The chapter then describes the various methodologies available to researchers and discusses the relative merits of primary and secondary research. The next part of the chapter looks at sampling and highlights five common research problems. The final section discusses effective use of research in decision making.

Chapter 5 begins by introducing the peculiarities of the tourism product and the idea that tourism and hospitality products are a group of selected components or elements brought together in a "bundle" to satisfy needs and wants. The chapter includes sections on the different product levels, product planning, the product life cycle model, and the positioning strategies available to organizations in the tourism and hospitality fields. The final three sections of the chapter discusses the concepts of branding, packaging, and new product development.

The pricing chapter, **Chapter 6**, begins by looking at the impact of various corporate objectives on pricing. The key factors determining an organization's pricing decisions are discussed, along with the contribution of economics to pricing. The basic approaches to pricing are then examined, and an important discussion on yield management follows. The difference between strategic pricing and tactical pricing is then explained, and the final section of the chapter looks at the specific characteristics of the tourism and hospitality industry that affect pricing policy.

Chapter 7 examines the various ways of distributing a tourism and hospitality product. It begins by looking at the nature and types of distribution channels and the different functions of a distribution system. The key intermediaries involved in the tourism distribution system are then discussed, and a consideration of channel conflict and organization follows. Finally, the process of designing an organization's distribution system and ensuring the effective execution of the distribution strategy is examined.

The next three chapters explore the various marketing communications methods used by tourism and hospitality providers. **Chapter 8** begins with an introduction that explains the role and types of promotion tools used in tourism and hospitality, and a section on the communications process follows. The chapter then discusses the rise of integrated marketing communications — the recognition that advertising can no longer be crafted and executed in isolation from other promotional mix elements. The communication techniques of advertising and sales promotion are then considered.

Chapter 9 begins by focusing on public relations. It examines the roles and functions of public relations and the main public relations techniques used in tourism and hospitality. Personal selling is the subject of the next section, which discusses the roles and objectives of personal selling, the sales process, and the roles of a sales manager. The key advantages of direct marketing are discussed in the following section of this chapter, as are the major direct marketing tools. The chapter then concludes with a section on word-of-mouth communication — an important but often misunderstood form of promotion in tourism.

Chapter 10 looks at an important and growing area of tourism and hospitality marketing: Internet marketing. The first section describes the growth of Internet generally and how it has affected the marketing of tourism. The tourism and hospitality industry is using the Internet to perform six key marketing functions: direct e-mail marketing, advertising, distribution and sales, provision of information, customer service and relationship marketing, and marketing research. These are discussed in turn.

Chapter 11 begins by defining internal marketing and describing the four key steps in the internal marketing process. The next section, on service quality, includes segments on the "gaps model" of service quality, methods of measuring service quality, and behavioural consequences of service quality. The third section discusses loyalty and relationship marketing. Various customer retention strategies are introduced, as are the benefits of relationship marketing to both company and customer. The final part of the chapter discusses service recovery and offers guidelines for tracking and handling complaints.

Chapter 12 examines both the opportunities and challenges inherent in marketing destinations. It begins by discussing the principles of destination marketing and defining, characterizing, and classifying destinations. A small section also examines the scope of visitor attractions. A summary of the objectives and benefits of destination marketing is followed by a more in-depth look at the role of destination marketing organizations. The next two sections focus on destination branding and destination promotion. Finally, the chapter looks at the marketing of two particularly important sectors for destinations: events and conferences, and all-inclusive resorts.

Chapter 13 covers marketing trends and focuses on some of the key contemporary tourism marketing issues. An analysis of tourism marketing trends is followed by a discussion about tourism marketing in the experiential economy. The next section looks at the responsible marketing of tourism, and then examples of cause-related marketing in tourism are outlined. The final two sections of the chapter look at the marketing of sport and adventure tourism, and the role of marketing tourism in crisis management.

WHAT'S NEW AND IMPROVED

- **Chapter 10, Internet Marketing** — The important subject of marketing via the Internet has been given a dedicated chapter of its own. Topics covered include direct e-mail marketing, advertising on the Internet, distribution and sales on the Internet, customer service and relationship marketing via the Internet, and marketing research online, and travel blogs.
- **Chapter 13, Contemporary Issues in Tourism and Hospitality Marketing** — This new chapter covers contemporary tourism marketing issues such as trends in tourism and hospitality marketing, experiential marketing, responsible marketing, cause-related marketing in tourism, and marketing tourism in times of crisis.
- **Stronger international coverage** — While the focus is on the marketing of tourism and hospitality in Canada, more cases from around the world have been added, such as "The Influence of Politics on Tourism: The Case of Myanmar" (Chapter 1) and "Marketing After a Crisis: Recovering from the Tsunami in Thailand" (Chapter 13).

- The topic of **consumer behaviour** is now covered earlier (now Chapter 2) as requested by reviewers. Coverage of VALS and the accompanying illustration has also been thoroughly revised and updated.
- **Expanded photos and advertisements throughout** — more than 20 new photos and advertisements have been added and the majority of the existing photos have been replaced.
- **More real-life examples** — In addition to the chapter opening *Spotlight* and final *Case Study,* each chapter now contains a consistent number of boxed features that effectively illustrate the concepts and strategies covered in the chapter. There is now one *Profile,* one *Marketing in Action,* and two *Snapshots* in every chapter.
- **New and updated statistics on Canadian tourism —** New statistics on Canadian tourism have been added, such as international tourism arrivals to Canada and provinces visited, and all of the existing statistics have been updated.

PEDAGOGICAL FEATURES

The objective of all the chapters in this text is to cover the basic tourism and hospitality theories well while omitting unnecessary detail. Careful selection of topics, appropriate depth of coverage, and concise writing help to achieve this objective. Current examples from all types and sizes of tourism and hospitality businesses are used in the text discussion.

Each chapter contains the following pedagogical features:

- *Spotlights:* These stories that begin each chapter have been designed to draw students into the chapter by presenting a real-life example that is carefully linked to the material covered in the chapter.
- *Objectives:* Objectives are provided at the beginning of each chapter to identify the major areas and points covered in the chapter and to guide the learning process.
- *Chapter Overview:* A brief introductory section at the beginning of each chapter summarizes the material that is to be presented.
- *Chapter Summary:* Each chapter ends with a summary that distils the main points of the chapter. This synopsis serves as a quick review of important topics covered and as a helpful study guide.
- *Key Terms:* Throughout each chapter, key terms appear in boldface in the text and have corresponding definitions in the margins. A list of these terms, including page numbers, appears at the end of each chapter and also in the glossary at the back of the book, making it easy for students to check their understanding of important terms throughout the text.
- *Discussion Questions and Exercises:* Each chapter ends with discussion questions that provide students with an opportunity to review how well they have learned the material in the chapter.
- *Case Studies:* Each chapter contains an up-to-date and relevant case study. As a collection, these studies cover a variety of tourism and hospitality sectors and regions. Designed to foster critical thinking, the case studies illustrate actual business scenarios that stress several concepts found in the chapter. Questions at the end of each case study encourage students to spot issues, analyze facts, and solve problems.

- *Websites:* Web addresses of organizations discussed in the chapter are provided for students who wish to further explore topics presented in the text.
- *Endnotes:* Bibliographical references for sources cited within each chapter are provided in a numbered list at the end of the chapter.

SPECIAL INTEREST BOXES

Boxed features in each chapter help students to connect principles to practice more easily. Three types of feature boxes are interspersed throughout the text.

Marketing in Action:

Each chapter has one Marketing in Action box that provides an in-depth example of the practical application of the tourism and hospitality marketing theory discussed in each chapter.

MARKETING IN ACTION

"IT'S OUR PLEASURE!" — SERVICE EXCELLENCE AT THE SHERATON SUITES CALGARY EAU CLAIRE

The Sheraton Suites Calgary Eau Claire has a reputation for service excellence. The hotel was awarded the Sheraton Brand Highest Guest Satisfaction from 2001 straight through to 2006 continuously. This Sheraton award recognizes exceptional levels of hospitality, service, and attention to detail, as well as upscale facilities and variety of amenities. The Sheraton Suites was also the winner of the Alberta Tourism Award (Alto) for Service Excellence in 2002 and 2005. This particular award honours an organization in the tourism industry that demonstrates a commitment to service excellence, delivering outstanding customer service to their visitors, employees, suppliers, and other stakeholders.

Profiles

One profile per chapter highlights the achievements of successful individuals or organizations in the tourism and hospitality industry. Those profiled in these boxes were chosen for their expertise in specific areas related to the chapter material.

PROFILE

AN ADVENTURE WITH BRUCE POON TIP

In 1990, Bruce Poon Tip withdrew every last penny in his bank account to open his own travel company specializing in taking tourists to emerging countries in Central and South America. Due to the risky nature of the travel industry at that time, caused by the first Gulf War, the banks were unwilling to lend him any money. Poon Tip would not be discouraged and, as a result, he stretched the limit of his credit card to follow his vision. Today, G.A.P Adventures is one of the largest adventure companies in the world. At 21, Poon Tip found his G.A.P concept when he travelled in Thailand for $10 a day and stayed with the hill tribes. "It wasn't my first visit, but it was my most genuine," says Poon Tip, who has consulted on *Survivor*. "That was when I knew others would want authentic travel experiences." Just as baby boomers were maturing and realizing the detrimental effects of their hedonistic youth, Poon Tip positioned his company as a vehicle to do some good while travelling via environmentally friendly, experience- and adventure-oriented tourism.

Snapshots

Two snapshots in each chapter provide examples of real-life cases. These are used to illustrate a particular concept or theoretical principle presented in the chapter.

SNAPSHOT

INTERNAL MARKETING AT FAIRMONT HOTELS AND RESORTS

Fairmont Hotels and Resorts is a good example of a company that aims its marketing efforts toward its employees. Fairmont is the largest luxury hotel management company in North America and has achieved great success since it opened in 1907. The company now operates 51 hotels in 12 countries with 20 in development. The company sees internal marketing as critical in achieving guest satisfaction, and consequently Fairmont is world renowned for its excellent guest service. The company measures the success or failure of its internal marketing programs through employee turnover rate — currently running at about 20 percent, with industry averages five or six times higher. Staff loyalty in turn encourages customer loyalty; repeat guests make up 60 percent of Fairmont's business.

SUPPLEMENTS

Instructor's Resource CD (0-17-647341-6)

Managing classroom resources is easier than ever. The comprehensive Instructor's Resource CD contains all of the key instructor supplements.

- **Instructor's Manual:** The Instructor's Manual contains detailed lecture outlines with supporting text figures and discussion questions organized by chapter learning objectives. The manual also contains suggested answers to all of the discussion questions and exercises and case studies in the second edition text.
- **Microsoft PowerPoint Slides:** A comprehensive of PowerPoint slides to accompany the second edition of *Marketing for Tourism and Hospitality: A Canadian Perspective.* These slides are designed for classroom presentation and are also available for downloading from the textbook's dedicated website at www.hudson2e.nelson.com.
- **Test Bank:** The test bank contains a comprehensive set of multiple-choice, true/false, and short answer questions.
- **Computerized Test Bank:** The Examview computerized testing program contains all of the questions in the test bank. Examview is easy-to-use software for creating tests that is compatible with both the Microsoft Windows and Macintosh platforms. Instructors can add or edit questions, instructions, and answers, and select questions

by previewing them on the screen, selecting them randomly, or selecting them by number. Instructors can also create and administer quizzes online, whether over the Internet, a local-area network, or a wide-area network.

- **Hudson Website at (www.hudson2e.nelson.com):** This rich online resource to accompany the second edition of *Marketing for Tourism and Hospitality: A Canadian Perspective* provides resources for both the student and instructor. The student resources include true/false, multiple-choice, and matching questions as well as Internet exercises, web links, PowerPoint slides, career information, and more. The instructor site includes the Instructor's Manual and PowerPoint slides available for downloading.

ACKNOWLEDGMENTS

I am grateful to the many individuals who helped to make the second edition of *Marketing for Tourism and Hospitality: A Canadian Perspective* a reality. In particular, I would like to thank the team at Nelson Education Ltd., especially Elke Price, senior developmental editor; Kevin Smulan, senior acquisitions editor; William DeVilliers, marketing manager; Sheila Hall, permissions researcher; Carrie McGregor and Karri Yano, content production managers; and Madeline Koch, copy editor.

This book has benefited tremendously from the people in the tourism industry who took the time to talk to me and to provide me with valuable material for the book. Those people are too numerous to list, but I thank them all. I would also like to thank my wife, Louise, for her editorial assistance, and my secretary, Joyce Twizell, for all her help with the tables and diagrams. Finally, I am indebted to the reviewers who participated in the reviewing of this second edition and those who reviewed the first edition and its original proposal. They provided encouragement, criticism, ideas, and enthusiasm and this is a better book because of their input. I would like to extend my gratitude to Julie Aumais, Mohawk College; Candace Blayney, Mount Saint Vincent University; Marc Bussiéres, St. Lawrence College; Mark Elliott, Douglas College; Brenda Hodgins, Red Deer College; Marion Joppe, University of Guelph; Georgina King, Seneca College; Ian McVitty, Algonquin College; Iain Murray, University of Guelph; Sue Nickason, Georgina College; Jan Procter, Medicine Hat College; Steve Renton, Assiniboine Community College; Margaret Shaw, University of Guelph; Arlene Shieven, British Columbia Institute of Technology; Marc Simard, Nova Scotia Community College; Anne Terwiel, Thompson Rivers University; Michael Tittel, Vancouver Community College; and David Wright, Seneca College.

About the Author

Simon Hudson Ph.D, MBA, BA, DipM

Simon Hudson is a Professor in Tourism and Marketing at the University of Calgary in Canada. He has held previous academic positions at universities in England, and has worked as a visiting professor in Austria, Switzerland, Spain, Fiji, New Zealand, the United States, and Australia. Prior to working in academia, Dr. Hudson spent several years working in the tourism industry in Europe, and he now consults for the industry in Alberta and British Columbia. This is Dr. Hudson's third book. His first, written in 2000 called *Snow Business*, was the first book to be written about the international ski industry, and *Sports and Adventure Tourism* was published in 2003. The marketing of tourism is the focus of his research and he has published numerous journal articles and book chapters from his work. He is frequently invited to international tourism conferences as a keynote speaker.

The Tourism Marketing Environment

1

Spotlight
CANADIANS JUST LOVE TO TRAVEL

Over the past few years Canada has experienced significant growth in outbound travel. In 2006, Canadians took more trips abroad than ever before and spent more money than they ever have while away. In total, Canadians took an estimated 22.7 million overnight trips in 2006, spending a record $20.1 billion in the process. Mexico surpassed the United Kingdom as the most visited country by Canadians, following the United States. Healthy economic growth, a strong Canadian dollar, and strong consumer confidence have all supported demand for travel.

About 6.7 million trips, just under one third of the total, were to destinations other than the U.S., up 8.2 percent from 2005. This was the fourth consecutive annual increase and a new record for overseas travel. Canadians spent a record $9.9 billion on these trips. Choosing a destination for pleasure travel is very important for Canadians; commitment to their main destination is higher than commitment to which brand of soft drinks, beer, cigarettes, or gasoline to use.

Travel increased to every overseas region, except South America. On a regional basis, Europe was still the most popular destination, accounting for nearly 4 million overnight visits in 2006. The Caribbean was second, with almost 1.6 million overnight visits. Canadian tourists made an estimated 842 000 overnight visits in Mexico, up 6.0 percent from 2005. This was despite the publicity generated by the murder of a Canadian couple in early 2006. At the same time, travel to the UK fell 13.4 percent to only 778 000 overnight visits. This was due partly to a noticeable decline in visits during the third quarter, coinciding with a major security threat at London's Heathrow Airport in August 2006.

France, Cuba, and the Dominican Republic were in third, fourth, and fifth place respectively. Visits to China surged 55.7 percent, the largest increase among the top 10 overseas countries visited by Canadians. This was perhaps a reflection of an increase in the number of flights between the two countries.

Overnight travel by Canadians to the U.S. rose 7.6 percent and reached the 16 million mark in 2006, the highest level since 1993 (see Table 1.1). While on their trips, Canadians spent an estimated $10.2 billion, up 7.2 percent from 2005. New York State remained the most popular overnight destination for Canadians, with more than 2.6 million visits to the state, up 10.8 percent. Travel for pleasure remained the most popular reason for overnight travel by Canadians to the U.S., as 9 million such trips were made, up 9.9 percent.

Although the number of Canadians travelling abroad continues to rise, fewer visitors are coming to Canada. In 2006, Americans took fewer trips to Canada and spent less as well. The number of overnight trips from the U.S. fell 3.7 percent to only 13.9 million. American tourists spent about $7.3 billion, down 2.6 percent. However, travel from overseas countries to Canada rose for the third straight year in 2006 after declining for three consecutive years. The number of overnight trips to Canada from countries other than the U.S. increased 1.2 percent to almost 4.3 million. These overseas tourists spent an estimated $5.7 billion on these trips, down 1.1 percent from 2005. The UK retained its status as the most important overseas market for Canada in 2006, although the number of overnight trips to Canada declined 5.2 percent to 842 000. Major sources of rising foreign visitors include China, Mexico, Australia, and Europe.

The fact that more Canadians are travelling abroad while the number of visitors to Canada is stagnating presents a challenge to the Canadian Tourism Commission (CTC), whose mandate is to market Canada as a tourist destination. Canadians continue to spend abroad more than foreigners do in Canada so Canada remains a net importer of tourism activity, creating a travel deficit as highlighted in the table below. So how do you persuade more international and domestic tourists to take their holidays in Canada?

Table 1.1

Overnight Travel between Canada and Other Countries

	TRIPS			EXPENDITURES		
	2005	2006	2005 to 2006	2005	2006	2005 to 2006
	thousands		% change	$ millions		% change
Canadian trips abroad	**21 091**	**22 731**	**7.8**	**18 965**	**20 146**	**6.2**
To the United States	14 862	15 992	7.6	9 537	10 228	7.2
To other countries	6 229	6 739	8.2	9 428	9 919	5.2
Travel to Canada	**18 612**	**18 126**	**–2.7**	**13 229**	**12 972**	**–1.9**
From the United States	14 390	13 855	–3.7	7 463	7 268	–2.6
From other countries	4 222	4 271	1.2	5 766	5 704	–1.1

Source: Statistics Canada. (2007). Characteristics of international travellers. *The Daily*, May 29. www.statcan.ca/Daily/English/070529/d070529a.htm (retrieved September 2007).

Objectives

On completion of this chapter, readers should understand:

- the meaning of tourism and hospitality marketing;
- the unique characteristics of services;
- who the key players are in Canada's tourism industry; and
- how various micro- and macroenvironmental forces are shaping the tourism industry world-wide.

Chapter Overview

The opening *Spotlight* shows how important travel has become for many Canadians and highlights some of the challenges facing tourism marketers in Canada. The explosion in world tourism is one of the most remarkable economic and social phenomena of the last half-century and tourism is now one of the world's largest industries. This book begins with a chapter dedicated to the current tourism marketing environment. The chapter starts with an introduction to tourism and hospitality marketing in general by discussing the definition and role of marketing and its importance in international tourism. A synopsis of services marketing theory reviews the unique characteristics of services and introduces important services marketing models, such as the services marketing triangle and the services marketing mix. The marketing environment is made up of microenvironmental and macroenvironmental forces, and the remainder of the chapter examines the major environmental forces that affect an organization's ability to serve its customers.

INTRODUCTION TO TOURISM AND HOSPITALITY MARKETING

tourism

the activities of persons travelling to and staying in places outside their usual environment for not more than one year for leisure, business, or other purposes not related to the exercise of an activity remunerated from within the place visited

Tourism is a powerful economic force providing employment, foreign exchange, income, and tax revenue. For the purposes of this book, the United Nations World Tourism Organization's (UNWTO) definitions of tourism and visitors have been adopted. UNWTO define **tourism** as comprising the activities of persons travelling to and staying in places outside their usual environment for not more than one consecutive year for leisure, business, and other purposes not related to the exercise of an activity remunerated from within the place visited. A **visitor** is defined as any person travelling to a place other than that of his or her usual environment for less than 12 months and whose main purpose for the trip is other than exercise of an activity remunerated from within the place visited. The **tourism market** reflects the demands of consumers for a wide range of travel and hospitality products, and it is generally claimed that this total market is now being serviced by the world's largest industry. The number of international arrivals in Canada has risen from just 50 million in 1950 to 842 million in 2006. While this represents an annual growth rate of 6.5 percent over more than half a century, the receipts generated by these tourists have increased nearly twice as fast (see Figure 1.1). Excluding air tickets, revenue from domestic tourism reached $780 billion dollars in 2005. Including air tickets, the figure is more than $920 billion.[1]

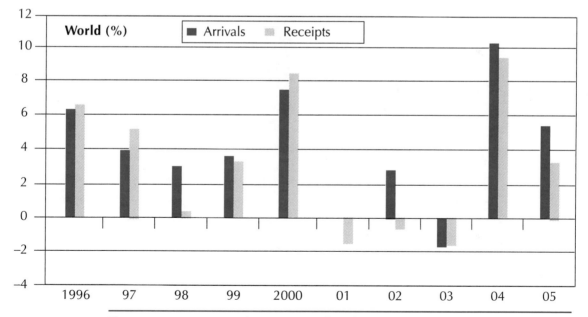

Figure 1.1 International Tourist Arrivals and Receipts (percent change)

Source: United Nations World Tourism Organization. (2006). Tourism is a socio-economic driver. *UNWTO News* 20(3): 4. www.unwto.org/newsroom/magazine/archives/news3_06_e.pdf (retrieved September 2007).

visitor

any person travelling to a place other than that of his or her usual environment for fewer than 12 months and whose main purpose for the trip is other than exercise of an activity remunerated from within the place visited

tourism market

a market that reflects the demands of consumers for a wide range of travel and hospitality products and services

This growth rate for tourism far outstrips the world economy as a whole, and tourism now represents a quarter of all exports of services. In 2005 employment in the travel and tourism economy accounted for more than 200 million jobs or 8.2 percent of total employment. The UNWTO Tourism 2020 Vision forecasts that international arrivals will reach more than 1.56 billion by 2020.[2] Of these 1.18 billion will be intra-regional and 377 million will be long-haul travellers. The top three receiving regions are expected to be Europe, East Asia and the Pacific, and the Americas, followed by Africa, the Middle East, and South Asia.

The impact of tourism goes far beyond enrichment in purely economic terms, helping to benefit the environment and culture and the fight to reduce poverty. Over the past decade, the annual growth rate of tourists to developing countries was higher than the world average, with 326 million arrivals generating $235 in revenue. In 2005, arrivals to least developed countries (LDCs) were up 48 percent compared with the world as a whole, while receipts grew 76 percent against 40 percent (see Figure 1.2). Tourism can serve as a foothold for the development of a market economy where small and medium-sized enterprises can expand and flourish. And in poor rural areas, it often constitutes the only alternative to subsistence farming, which is in decline.

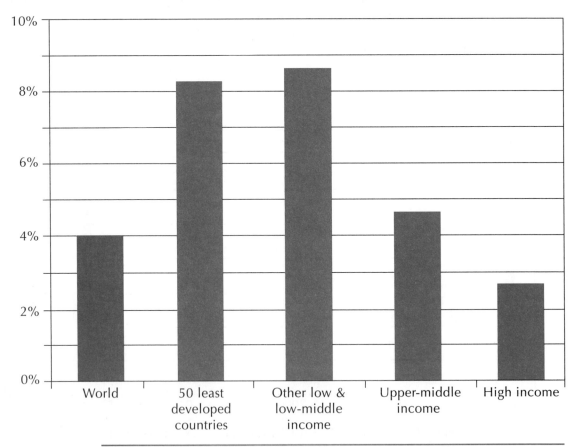

Figure 1.2   Annual Growth in International Tourist Arrivals 1990–2005 (percent)

Source: United Nations World Tourism Organization News Issue 3 p. 5. (2006). Growing faster in poorest countries. *UNWTO News,* 20(3), 5. www.unwto.org/newsroom/magazine/archives/news3_06_e.pdf (retrieved September 2007).

In Canada, tourism spending totalled $62.7 billion in 2005, a 7.2 percent increase compared to 2004. Canadian residents accounted for 72.1 percent or $45.2 billion, while foreigners spent $17.5 billion or 27.9 percent. Figure 1.3 shows the number of tourism arrivals in Canada since 1995. The chart indicates a fall in U.S. visitors between 2003 and 2006, whereas the number of international arrivals has been steadily increasing. Table 1.2 shows how Canada is fairing compared to competitors in its efforts to attract international tourists. In 2006, half of the top overseas markets for Canada recorded declines in the number of trips to Canada. Among these, travel from Japan fell 8.7 percent, the largest drop, while travel from China rose 22.8 percent, the biggest gain. *Marketing in Action* in this chapter shows how Canada is preparing for the increase in the number of Chinese travellers.

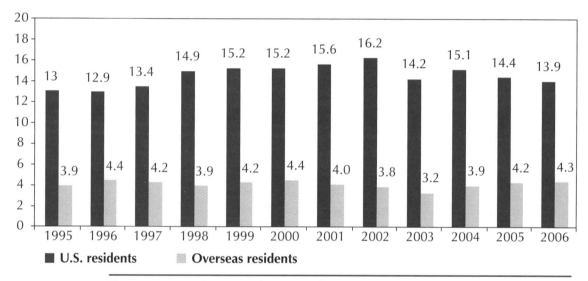

■ U.S. residents　　▨ Overseas residents

Figure 1.3　Tourism Arrivals to Canada 1995–2006 (000 000)

Source: Canadian Tourism Commission. (2006). *Tourism snapshot: 2005 year review,* 5(1), 4. http://www.corporate.canada.travel/docs/research_and_statistics/stats_and_figures/YearReview_2005_eng_Web_letter.pdf (retrieved September 2007).

Table 1.2

International Tourism Arrivals: Canada and Selected Competitors, 2006

DESTINATION								
	Canada		**United States**		**Australia**		**United Kingdom**	
Trips from:	**Number of visitors (000)**	**Change from 2005 to 2006 (%)**	**Number of visitors (000)**	**Change from 2005 to 2006 (%)**	**Number of visitors (000)**	**Change from 2005 to 2006 (%)**	**Number of visitors (000)**	**Change from 2005 to 2006 (%)**
Total International	18 175	–3	43 502	6	5 532	1	32 136	7

TABLE 1.2 *continued*

DESTINATION

Trips from:	Canada		United States		Australia		United Kingdom	
	Number of visitors (000)	Change from 2005 to 2006 (%)	Number of visitors (000)	Change from 2005 to 2006 (%)	Number of visitors (000)	Change from 2005 to 2006 (%)	Number of visitors (000)	Change from 2005 to 2006 (%)
United States	13 765	–4	—	—	456	2	3 694	7
Other Key Markets								
United Kingdom	866	–4	4 176	–4	734	4	—	—
Japan	386	–9	3 673	–5	651	–5	324	–2
France	370	4	790	–10	67	6	3 714	12
Germany	302	–7	1 386	–2	148	1	3 398	3
Mexico	211	11	5 841	27	—	—	81	5
Australia	200	–1	603	4	—	—	911	–1
S. Korea	194	8	758	8	261	4	—	—
China	144	23	458	13	309	8	128	–2
Canada	—	—	15 995	8	110	7	845	6
Total Key Markets	16 438	–4	17 685	5	2 736	2	13 095	6

Source: Adapted from Canadian Tourism Commission. (2007). Tourism snapshot February 2007. *Tourism, 11*(3), 5.

In 2005, the most visited Canadian provinces by international tourists were Ontario, British Columbia, and Quebec (see Table 1.3). Tourists from the U.S. made up the majority of these visitors (14.39 million), while other core markets were the UK, Japan, France, and Germany. Total tourism gross domestic product (GDP) reached $26.1 billion in 2005 or 2 percent of Canada's GDP. In 2005, a total of 1.65 million people were employed in the tourism sector in Canada — 37 percent in Ontario, 17 percent in British Columbia, 11 percent in Alberta, 6 percent in Atlantic Canada, 4 percent in Manitoba, and 3 percent in Saskatchewan. This represented 10.2 percent of the Canadian labour force.

Table 1.3

International Tourism in Canada: Provinces Visited

PROVINCE VISITED	NUMBERS (000s)	PERCENTAGE OF TOTAL (%)
Ontario	9203	43.0
British Columbia	4983	23.3
Quebec	3258	15.1
Alberta	1782	8.3
Nova Scotia	564	2.6
New Brunswick	434	2.0
Manitoba	365	1.7
Yukon	277	1.3
Saskatchewan	228	1.1
Prince Edward Island	206	1.0
Newfoundland	77	0.4
Northwest Territories	37	0.2

Source: Adapted from Canadian Tourism Commission. (2006). *Tourism snapshot: 2005 year review, 5*(1), 2. www.corporate.canada.travel/docs/research_and_statistics/stats_and_figures/YearReview_2005_eng_Web_letter.pdf (retrieved September 2007).

MARKETING IN ACTION

PLANNING FOR THE GROWING CHINESE TRAVEL MARKET

According to many reports, China's tourism industry holds massive potential. Due to the rising levels of affluence, particularly among the expanding middle class, the number of outbound tourists from China grew nearly 50 percent in 2004, reaching 28.9 million. In the same year, 15 European countries were granted approved destination status (ADS) by China, which is predicted to lead to a sharp increase in the number of Chinese nationals

MARKETING IN ACTION *continued*

visiting the continent. At the end of 2005, the number of countries granted ADS by China was more than 90. It is predicted that China's outbound sector will grow 20 percent annually. According to the Economic Intelligence Unit, the number of Chinese travellers is forecast to rise to 49 million by 2008, 60 million by 2010, and 100 million by 2015. At that point, China will be the world's biggest source of outbound tourism.

At the time of writing, Canada did not have ADS, but even without ADS, the number of Chinese visitors is rising, and Canada expects to see growth of 15 percent annually. In 2006, an estimated 140 000 Chinese visited Canada, up 23 percent from 2005. Based on research showing there is a high demand for Canadian tourism products in China, the Canadian Tourism Commission (CTC) is reaching out to Chinese consumers with every marketing tactic that is allowed by the Chinese government. The CTC opened a national marketing office in Beijing in 2006 to leverage opportunities in the market, and is engaging in activities such as travel agent training, media familiarization tours to Canada, trade shows, and the development of publications. The CTC has also launched a dedicated website for Chinese consumers, which they can access through the www.Canada.travel Internet portal.

In January 2007, representatives from the CTC, Tourism British Columbia, Travel Alberta, and the Ontario Tourism Marketing Partnership Corporation (OTMPC) took part in a series of media orientation workshops in China's three main cities: Beijing, Shanghai, and Guangzhou. The workshops were held to strengthen the media's knowledge and understanding of each participating province. Thirty tourism businesses and 95 journalists from 85 media outlets attended the workshops. "We held the workshops in these key three cities because we felt the need to establish a clear and informative communication platform for the media and provinces," noted Derek Galpin, managing

director, CTC China. "We are delighted with the attendance figures, which go to show how popular Canada and news about Canada is becoming in this market."

But Canada is not alone in targeting this potentially lucrative market. New York City for example, employs a multi-pronged approach to the Chinese market. The tourism bureau participated in the China International Travel Mart for the first time in 2005, but earlier sent sales missions to Shanghai and Beijing to meet with tour operators, airlines, government, and trade organizations. Additional components of the program include relationship building with both U.S. and Chinese news media, and cultivating the large Chinese population in New York City. The bureau also added Chinese-language pages to its website and provides market intelligence and educational seminars for its members. A specialist in Asia tourism development was brought on board to address the market in 2001.

Chinese travellers are somewhat conservative in their travel behaviour. Most travel with tour groups, making the trip as comfortable as possible. Not until they have embarked on multiple trips do they shun the tour group and take on more individual travel itineraries. A recent study of Chinese travellers by Synovate Hong Kong showed that they were technologically up to date, with most owning computers, mobile phones, and MP3 players. Sightseeing, visiting friends and relatives, and shopping were the main purposes for leisure travel and the average leisure visit lasted about five days. The study also showed the need for international hotels to build brand loyalty in the Chinese market. Very few hotels obtained an overwhelming percentage of unaided awareness among Chinese travellers. Synovate suggests that the best way to build such loyalty among the younger generation of future Chinese travellers may be through the Internet.

According to a survey by Goldman Sachs Global Investment Research, Chinese travellers spend twice as much on luxury items abroad

MARKETING IN ACTION *continued*

as they do at home. In the short term, Hong Kong is likely to attract most of this spending by mainland tourists due to its proximity and attractive prices. However, Europe, particularly France and Italy, will lure an increasing number of Chinese tourists in the future. "Travelling overseas has already become the hot new lifestyle choice for modern Chinese," said Willie Fung, senior vice-president and general manager, Greater China, for MasterCard International. From research, his firm has concluded that the Chinese regard travel overseas as a way of expressing pride in their achievements, improvements, and social status, and proving that they are indeed becoming "world travellers."

Sources: Alberta Economic Development. (2005, April 15). Tourism Issues Update. Business Information & Research. industry.travelalberta.com/Research/archives (retrieved September 2007); Synovate Research. (2005, September 28). Study shows Chinese travellers are a market force to be reckoned with. www.synovate.com/current/news/article/2005/09/study-shows-chinese-travelers-are-a-market-force-to-be-reckoned-with.html (retrieved September 2007).

THE GLOBALIZATION OF THE TOURISM INDUSTRY

In our globalizing world, people, places, and countries are increasingly interdependent. Countries once considered inaccessible to western tourists because of geographical, cultural, or political barriers are now not only becoming accessible — their very remoteness makes them an attractive choice for travel today. An example is Tibet, one of the most impoverished parts of the world, where the opening of a new Chinese railway in 2006 across the Himalayas is expected to double tourist revenue, with more than a million people a year predicted to use the line.

The globalization of tourism has cultural, political, and economic dimensions. Cultural globalization is characterized by cultural homogenization as western consumption and lifestyle patterns spread throughout the world, a process facilitated by the flow of travellers from the West to the developing world. Travel also enhances friendships among people and facilitates cultural exchange. Political globalization involves the undermining of the roles and importance of nation-states as borders are opened up to free trade and investment. Economic globalization has both positive and negative effects. On the one hand, it could be argued that a key aspect of economic globalization has been the increasing power in the hands of a small number of travel organizations, leading to oligopolistic control in the industry. On the other hand, tourism brings with it economic rewards and opportunities for host communities in particular, to benefit from foreign exchange and enhance their livelihood options.

There are many examples of tourism and hospitality companies operating in a global environment. Disney is one, and a *Snapshot* later in the chapter focuses on Disney's latest theme park in Hong Kong. Another example is the Hard Rock brand, a favourite on tourists' T-shirts the world over. The chain was founded by music lovers Isaac Tigrett and Peter Morton with one London restaurant in 1971, and in 2007 included 138 venues in more than 42 countries.[3] Hard Rock International, now owned by the Seminole Tribe of Florida, had worldwide sales in 2005 of $566 million and profit of $75 million in 2006.[4] The rock 'n' roll diners, which carry the motto "Love All, Serve All," own the world's most comprehensive collection of rock memorabilia. The collection has grown from Pete Townsend's and Eric Clapton's guitars, donated during the 1970s, to include the doors of the Beatles' Abbey Road recording studios and one of Madonna's trademark bustiers.

THE INFLUENCE OF MARKETING ON TOURISM

Marketing

marketing

the process of planning and executing the conception, pricing, promotion, and distribution of ideas, goods, and services to create exchanges that satisfy individual (customer) and organizational objectives

Marketing has been defined as "the process of planning and executing the conception, pricing, promotion, and distribution of ideas, goods, and services to create exchanges that satisfy individual (customer) and organizational objectives."[5] The marketing concept is a business philosophy that defines marketing as a process intended to find, satisfy, and retain customers while the business makes a profit. Central to both these definitions is the role of the customer and the customer's relationship to the product, whether that product is a good, a service, or an idea. The tourism and hospitality sector, like other service sectors, involves a combination of tangible and intangible products. A hotel is a mixture of goods (beds, food, telephone, and communication systems) that are linked with a range of services (front desk, housekeeping, room service, finance, and accounting). A tourist attraction such as a national park is a combination of facilities (hotels, shops, visitor centres) situated within a physical attraction (the mountains, forests, or rivers, for example), offering a range of services (guided tours, interpretation, education, etc.). This whole package of tangible and intangible products is perceived by the visitor as an experience, and represents the core of the tourism product.

International Marketing

international marketing

business activities designed to plan, price, promote, and direct the flow of a organization's goods and services to consumers in more than one country for profit

International marketing is defined as the business activities designed to plan, price, promote, and direct the flow of a organization's goods and services to consumers in more than one country for profit.[6] The important difference between this definition and the one given earlier for marketing in general is that international marketing activities take place in more than one country. The uniqueness of foreign marketing comes from the range of unfamiliar problems and the variety of strategies necessary to cope with different levels of uncertainty encountered in foreign markets. It is important to acknowledge that tourism is an invisible export industry, and often a highly unstable one. As in the case of banking and insurance, there is no tangible product that is shipped from one place to another. It is one of the few industries in which the consumer actually collects and consumes the service from the place where it is produced. In consequence, the exporting destination incurs no direct freight costs outside its own boundaries except where the transportation facilities used by the tourist are owned by the destination. However, for most destinations, there are substantial costs involved in marketing to an international clientele.

Figure 1.4 illustrates the environment of an international marketer. The inner circle depicts the domestic controllable elements that constitute a marketer's decision area, such as product, price, promotion, distribution, and research decisions. The second circle encompasses those environmental elements at home that have some effect on foreign-operation decisions, and the outer circles represent the elements of the foreign environment for each of the foreign markets in which the marketer operates. As the outer circles illustrate, every foreign market in which the organization operates can present separate problems involving certain uncontrollable elements. Examples of uncontrollables include political instability, economic climate, cultural problems, and the level of technology. To adjust and adapt a marketing program to foreign markets, marketers must be able to interpret effectively the influence and impact of each of the uncontrollable elements on the marketing plan for each foreign market in which they hope to do business. The *Snapshot* on Disneyland Hong Kong later on in the chapter illustrates how Disney's management was insensitive to cultural differences in Hong Kong, and therefore experienced some teething problems. More market research and better environmental scanning would have helped make some of the hiccups at least foreseeable, if not entirely controllable.

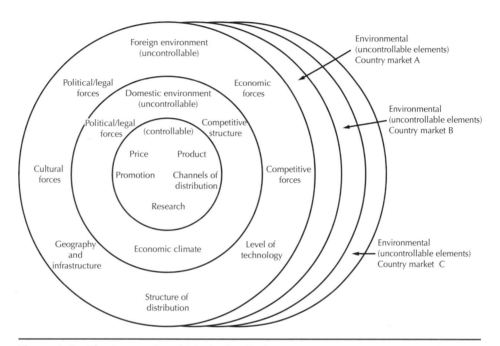

Figure 1.4   The International Marketing Task

Source: Cateora, P. R., & Graham, J. L. (2005) *International marketing* (12th ed.). New York: McGraw-Hill Irwin, 10.

self-reference criteria (SRC)

an unconscious reference to one's own cultural values, experiences, and knowledge as a basis for decisions

ethnocentrism

notion that one's own culture knows best how to do things

Key obstacles facing international marketers are not limited to environmental issues. Just as important are difficulties associated with the marketer's own **self-reference criteria (SRC)** and ethnocentrism. SRC is an unconscious reference to one's own cultural values, experiences, and knowledge as a basis for decisions. Closely connected is **ethnocentrism**, which is the notion that one's own culture knows best how to do things. Both limit the international marketer's ability to understand and adapt to differences prevalent in foreign markets. A global awareness and sensitivity are the solutions to these problems. In recent years, Americans have been accused of ethnocentrism, and this has led to the country developing a poor image overseas. In order to try and tempt back both business and tourist travellers, the American tourism industry has partnered with government to launch an aggressive and highly competitive marketing campaign to revive U.S. figures. The campaign targeted visa, passport, and security procedures to make international visitors feel more welcome. In 2006, both the Travel Industry Association of America and the Travel Business Roundtable supported the establishment of a Presidential Advisory Council on Travel and Tourism to promote the U.S. in major travel destinations around the world.

Tourism Marketing

Marketing is a subject of vital concern in tourism because it is the principal management influence that can be brought to bear on the size and behaviour of this major global market. All sectors of the tourism industry — travel organizers, destination organizations, transportation, various product suppliers — combine to manage visitors' demand through a range of marketing influences. However, the influence of this marketing activity is likely to vary according to visitors' interests and circumstances. For example, domestic visitors travelling by car to stay with friends or relatives may not be influenced by destination marketing in any way, whereas first-time buyers of package tours to exotic destinations may find that almost every aspect of their trip is influenced by the marketing decisions of the tour operator they choose. In between these two examples, a business traveller will select a destination according to business requirements, but may be influenced as to the choice of airline or hotel.

Knowledge of the customer, and all that it implies for management decisions, is generally referred to as consumer or marketing orientation. A detailed understanding of consumer characteristics and buying behaviour is central to the activities of marketing managers, and therefore consumer behaviour is the topic of Chapter 2.

UNIQUE CHARACTERISTICS OF SERVICES

The tourism and hospitality sector incorporates both goods and services. Goods are easier to measure, test, and evaluate, while services provide a greater challenge. Service products are commonly distinguished from goods products by four unique characteristics: intangibility, inseparability, heterogeneity, and perishability. These are described in Table 1.4. A useful way to distinguish between goods and services is to place them on a spectrum from tangible-dominant to intangible-dominant. Very few products or services are purely intangible or totally tangible. However, services tend to be more intangible than manufactured products. For example, the fast-food industry, while classified as a service, also has many tangible components such as the food and the packaging.

Table 1.4

The Four Unique Characteristics of Services

CHARACTERISTIC	DESCRIPTION
1. Intangibility	Service products cannot be tasted, felt, seen, heard, or smelled. Prior to boarding a plane, airline passengers have nothing but an airline ticket and a promise of safe delivery to their destination. To reduce uncertainty caused by service intangibility, buyers look for tangible evidence that will provide information and confidence about the service.

CHARACTERISTIC	DESCRIPTION
2. Inseparability	For many services, the product cannot be created or delivered without the customer's presence. The food in a restaurant may be outstanding, but if the server has a poor attitude or provides inattentive service, customers will not enjoy the overall restaurant experience. In the same way, other customers can affect the experience in service settings.
3. Heterogeneity	Service delivery quality depends on who provides the services. The same person can deliver differing levels of service, displaying a marked difference in tolerance and friendliness as the day wears on. Lack of consistency is a major factor in customer dissatisfaction.
4. Perishability	Services cannot be stored. Empty airline seats, hotel rooms, daily ski passes, restaurant covers—all these services cannot be sold the next day. If services are to maximize revenue, they must manage capacity and demand since they cannot carry forward unsold inventory.

SERVICES MARKETING MODELS

Several models and frameworks have been developed over the years to assist in making services marketing and management decisions at both the strategic and implementation levels. Two of these will now be discussed: the services marketing triangle and the services marketing mix. Both of these frameworks address the challenges inherent in services, and each of them can be used to assess and guide strategies, as well as provide a roadmap for implementation planning.

The Services Marketing Triangle

services marketing triangle

a model that illustrates the three interlinking groups that work together to develop, promote, and deliver services: the company, the customer, and the provider

The **services marketing triangle** (see Figure 1.5) shows the three interlinked groups that work together to develop, promote, and deliver services. These key players — the company, the customers, and the providers — are labelled on the points of the triangle. Among these three points there are three types of marketing that must be successfully carried out for a service to succeed: external, interactive, and internal marketing. For all services, especially for tourism and hospitality services, all three types of marketing activities are essential for building and maintaining relationships. Through its external marketing efforts, a organization makes promises to its customers regarding what they can expect and how it can be delivered. Traditional marketing activities (such as those discussed in Chapters 8, 9, and 10) facilitate this type of marketing, but for services, other factors such as the servicescape and the process itself help to establish customer expectations.

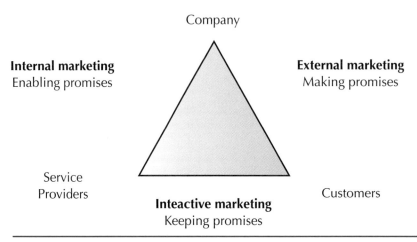

Figure 1.5 The Services Marketing Triangle

Source: Zeithaml, V. A., & Bitner, M. J. (2000). *Services marketing: Integrating customer focus across the firm.* New York: McGraw-Hill, 16.

Keeping promises, or interactive marketing, is the second kind of marketing activity captured by the triangle. Interactive marketing occurs in the "moment of truth" when the customer interacts with the organization and the service is produced and consumed. From the customer's point of view, the most vivid impression of service occurs in the service encounter or the moment of truth. It is in these encounters that customers receive a snapshot of the organization's service quality, and each encounter contributes to the customer's overall satisfaction and willingness to do business with the organization again.

Finally, internal marketing takes place through the enabling of promises. Promises are easy to make, but unless providers are recruited, trained, provided with tools and appropriate internal systems, and rewarded for good service, the promises may not be kept. Internal marketing is discussed in more depth in Chapter 11.

The Marketing Mix for Services

services marketing mix

the original four Ps of the marketing mix — product, place, promotion, and price — plus the people, the physical evidence, and the process

Another way to begin addressing the challenges of services marketing is to think creatively about the **services marketing mix** — through an expanded marketing mix for services. The marketing mix may be defined as "the mixture of controllable marketing variables that the firm uses to pursue the sought level of sales in the target market."[7] The traditional marketing mix is composed of the four Ps: product, place, promotion, and price.[8] Because services are usually produced and consumed simultaneously, customers are often part of the service production process. Also, because services are intangible, customers will often look for any tangible cue to help them understand the nature of the service experience. These facts have led service marketers to conclude that they can use additional variables to communicate with and satisfy their customers. Acknowledgment of the importance of these additional variables has led service marketers to adopt the concept of an expanded marketing mix for services, shown in Table 1.5. In addition to the traditional four Ps, the services marketing mix includes people, physical evidence, and process.

Table 1.5

Expanded Marketing Mix for Services

	PRODUCT	PLACE	PROMOTION	PRICE

Traditional Four P's of Marketing	Physical good features
	
	Quality level
	Accessories
	Packaging
	Warranties
	Product lines
	Branding
		Channel type
		
		Exposure
		Intermediaries
		Outlet locations
		Transportation
		Storage
		Managing channels
			Promotion blend
			
			Salespeople
			  number
			  selection
			  training
			  incentives
			
			Advertising
			  targets
			  media types
			  types of ads
			  copy thrust
			
			Sales promotion
			Publicity
				Flexibility
				
				Price level
				Terms
				Differentiation
				Discounts
				Allowances

	PEOPLE	PHYSICAL EVIDENCE	PROCESS

Additional Three P's of Services Marketing	Employees
	  recruiting
	  training
	  motivation
	  rewards
	  teamwork
	
	Customers
	  education
	  training
		Facility design
		Equipment
		Signage
		Employee dress
		
		Other tangibles
		  reports
		  business cards
		  statements
		  guarantees
			Flow of activities
			  standardized
			  customized
			Number of steps
			  simple
			  complex
			
			Customer involvement

Source: Booms, B. H., & Bitner, M. J. (1981). Marketing strategies and organizational structures for service firms. In J. H. Donnelly & W. R. George (Eds.), *Marketing services* (pp. 47–51). Chicago: American Marketing Association.

The people element includes all human actors who play a part in service delivery and thus influence the buyer's perceptions — namely the firm's personnel, the customer, and other customers in the service environment. The physical evidence is the environment in which the service is delivered and where the firm and customer interact, and any tangible components that facilitate performance or communication of the service. Table 1.5 gives some examples of tangible evidence or cues used by service organizations. Finally, the process is the actual procedures, mechanisms, and flow of activities by which the service is delivered. The three new marketing mix elements are included in the marketing mix as separate elements because they are within the control of the firm and any or all of them may influence the customer's initial decision to purchase a service and the customer's level of satisfaction and repurchase decisions. The traditional elements as well as the new marketing mix elements are explored in depth in later chapters.

KEY PLAYERS IN CANADA'S TOURISM INDUSTRY

The key players in Canada's tourism industry are outlined in Figure 1.6. They include private and nonprofit sector services, public sector services, suppliers (transportation, accommodations, food and beverage services, attractions, events and conferences, sport and adventure tourism), intermediaries, and the visitors (tourists/travellers) themselves. Each will be discussed in turn below.

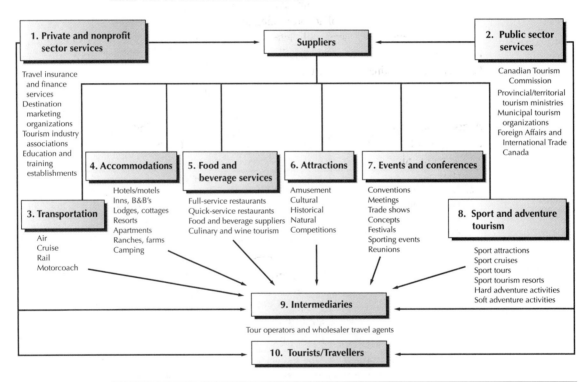

Figure 1.6   Key Players in Canada's Tourism Industry

1. Private and Nonprofit Sector Services

In Canada, the private and nonprofit sector includes tourism industry associations such as the Association of Canadian Travel Agents (ACTA), Canadian Standard Travel Agency Registry (CSTAR), financial and banking services, educational institutions, the media, such as the *Canadian Travel Press*, and insurance services.

2. Public Sector Services

Public sector involvement in Canada is led by the CTC, a Crown corporation representing provincial and regional tourism associations, government agencies, hoteliers, tour operators, airline companies, and attractions owners. The key role of the CTC is to design, deliver, and fund marketing and research initiatives in partnership with the above groups. The government of Canada contributes about $85 million annually to the CTC. Public sector involvement also comes from provincial tourism ministries, regional organizations, and municipal tourism organizations. Other important tourism groups in the public sector include those responsible for national parks and for national heritage.

Under the umbrella of each provincial tourism organization, there are a number of public, quasi-public, and independent organizations, which work independently and in cooperation to create more attractive tourism products and services. For example, Ontario has the Niagara Economic Tourism Development Corporation (NECTOR), the Niagara Parks Commission (park-based), and Niagara Falls Tourism (city-based). At a state or provincial level, marketing agencies spend millions of dollars promoting tourism. Their marketing programs target both individual travellers and travel trade intermediaries. Often they enter into cooperative marketing with suppliers, carriers, intermediaries, and other destination marketing organizations. Chapter 12, on destination marketing, explores these issues in more detail.

3. Transportation

A good transportation infrastructure is crucial for the tourism industry to thrive in any country, and transportation accounts for about a third of tourism expenditure in Canada. Major companies that operate in the transportation sector include Air Canada, Transat, WestJet, and VIA Rail. Passenger-related revenues for these four companies combined account for about 80 percent of total transportation revenues.

a) The Airline Industry

Despite the impacts of high-profile terrorism acts and natural disasters over the last decade, the world's airlines are experiencing increasing demand. Rising economic growth is spurring travel demand in Asia and Europe, where airlines were expected to be profitable in 2006.[9] North American carriers meanwhile were expected to have lost $5.2 million in 2006 as several major U.S. airlines restructured under bankruptcy protection. Airline deregulation around the world has led to the development of no-frill, low-cost airlines, operating mainly out of secondary airports. The Snapshot in Chapter 6 focuses on this development. There is also a trend in airlines toward "bigger and better." Airbus's new 560-tonne jet, the A380, carries up to 800 passengers and has become the world's biggest commercial airliner. After the demise of Concorde, which epitomized speed and luxury, the new super-jumbos have redirected the industry toward size, facilities, and economies of scale.

Canada is a signatory to the Open Skies Policy, which has opened the borders and allowed foreign carriers greater access to Canadian customers, allowing customers greater choice. The Open Skies Policy took effect in 1995, with the result that airlines and not governments now decide which transborder routes they can fly. More than 90 new scheduled routes have been added by Canadian and American carriers since the signing of the agreement, with 40 percent added in Toronto alone. However, Canada has only signed two open skies accords, with the U.S. and the UK. The U.S., by contrast, has nearly 70 such accords in place.

Airports play a vital role in keeping the tourism sector growing in many countries and are continually investing to keep up with growing demand. London's Heathrow, for example, expected to become the leading hub for the new A380 with 10 million more passengers each year predicted by 2016, is investing more than $966 million over the next decade to handle the aircraft. And airports in Paris, Amsterdam, Washington, and Hong Kong are also catering for the A380. In Canada, Toronto's Lester Pearson International Airport is undergoing a multi-phased $2 billion expansion. The entire project, which is expected to be completed in 2010, includes the construction of a new terminal to replace existing terminals 1 and 2, a new parking garage, a "people mover" to connect the new terminal with Terminal 3, an interim passenger facility known as an infield holdroom, and various other facilities including new fuelling stations and administrative offices.

b) The Cruise Industry

The cruise ship industry has been growing for many years, with more than 12 million people around the globe taking a cruise each year in this $40 billion industry. Cruises will continue to be one of the fastest-growing segments in the tourism industry. Bigger and better-equipped ships are being built in order to provide more varied facilities for the different age groups and cultures and also to appeal to wider income brackets. Since 1998, when 223 cruise ships carried 10 million passengers, the industry has grown by an average of 10 percent annually.

Traditionally cruises were the preserve of the rich and famous who travelled in luxury with no financial or time restraints on such vessels as the *Lusitania* and the *Queen Elizabeth 2*. Nowadays, bigger ships can improve company profits, since economies of scale in purchasing and operating expenses reduce overhead costs. Thus cruise lines with the latest 3000-passenger mega-ships can offer all-inclusive fares for about $100 per person per day, less than half the cost on most small ships and comparable to resorts on shore. More information on trends in the cruise industry is given in the *Snapshot* titled "Cruising Trends: Bigger Is Better!" in Chapter 13.

c) Railways

With the rising cost of fuel around the world, many countries are turning to their railways to solve their transportation problems. In continental Europe and Japan, for example, governments have invested massive sums in dedicated high-speed lines and trains offering city-to-city services at speeds in excess of 200 kilometres per hour. In Britain, high-speed trains were even put forward as a solution to current environmental concerns and as a means of boosting the country's economy. Major new projects are also planned in many other countries, including China and the United States. A high-speed network is being developed in South Africa to be ready in time for the 2010 World Cup.

Luxury train travel is another important component of the transportation sector. According to international travel agents, Canada offers the best experience in the world. Royal Canadian Pacific won the world's leading luxury train award at the 2006 World Travel Award ceremony, held in the Turks and Caicos Islands. The other nominees were the Blue Train (South Africa), the Eastern and Orient Express (Asia), Pride of Africa-Rovos Rail (Africa), Palace on Wheels (India), and the Venice Simplon Orient Express (Europe). At the same ceremony, Eurostar was named the world's leading rail service, beating out VIA Rail, Amtrak, SNCF, Die Bahn, and Rail Europe.

In Canada, a single carrier, VIA Rail Canada, dominates the passenger rail industry. VIA serves more than 3.8 million passengers annually, and of those, 3.2 million ride the train between Toronto and Quebec City. The flagship of the industry is The Canadian, which runs from Toronto to Vancouver, attracting more than 150 000 passengers a year, most of them tourists. VIA claims to have been the world's first railway to provide interactive online access to timetables and fares, followed by ticket reservation and payment capability. The Rocky Mountaineer is another Canadian success story (see the *Spotlight* in Chapter 9). However, there are many more railway operators in Canada. In British Columbia, for example, the Pacific Wilderness Railway takes people to the top of Malahat Mountain on Vancouver Island. There is also the Okanagan Valley Wine Train, which provides excursions into the province's wine-growing regions. In Winnipeg, tourists can take the Prairie Dog Central, a steam train that runs into the prairies, and in Ontario they can choose between the Polar Bear Express, which runs through the wilderness from Cochrane to Moosonee, and the Agawa Canyon Train out of Sault Ste. Marie. In Hull, Quebec, the Hull-Chelsea-Wakefield Steam Train takes visitors for a five-hour journey into the past, and in the Yukon, the historic White Pass & Yukon Route Railway takes tourists between White Pass, Yukon, and Skagway, Alaska.

4. Accommodations

The accommodation sector consists of a great variety of types of accommodation facilities to meet the consumers' needs. Among these, the subsector of hotels is the most important, and hotel chains are particularly significant in large cities. In London and Paris, for example, their share of the bed capacity amounts to 50 percent. An example of the global nature of the hotel sector is the Hilton group. Hilton has nearly 2800 hotels in 80 countries and has plans to spread its traditional U.S. brands such as Conrad, Doubletree, Embassy Suites, Hampton Inn, and Hilton Garden to other parts of the world. Aiming for growth of 7 percent a year across the group, Hilton is focusing its main international expansion on China, India, and Eastern Europe for the high-demand mid-price market.[10] Hilton will tailor the brand for different parts of the world, for instance increasing the range of food and beverage offering in India to attract western travellers.

Other types of accommodation, such as bed and breakfast, tourist residences, holiday dwellings, timeshare apartments, and campsites, are showing considerable growth. In the U.S., one of the country's largest privately held companies, Utah-based Flying J, is transforming the highway hospitality and service business. Targeting mainly long-haul drivers, the company operates about 220 travel plazas in America for truckers, RV owners, and the public. The plazas feature showers, a lounge, laundry facilities, Internet, and phone and banking services. The company has recently expanded into Canada, with plans for 15 plazas built in partnership with Shell Canada at a cost of $200 million.

The accommodation sector in Canada is dynamic and characterized by fast-paced change. In 2005, there were more than 15 000 accommodation establishments, with 53 percent of these being hotels and motels. Major Canadian participants include Fairmont Hotels and Resorts, Legacy Hotels, and Four Seasons Hotels and Resorts. Large foreign-based chains with a significant presence in Canada include Cendant, Marriott International, and Accor. Hotel ownership has shifted dramatically, resulting in the concentration of hotel assets in the hands of a few portfolio investors. Three real estate investment trusts (REITs), including Legacy Hotels, Canadian Income Hotel Properties (CHIP), and Royal Hosts, own more than 80 hotels with over 17 000 rooms. Similar to global trends, acquisitions are expected to continue across North America, and branding has become increasingly important. In Canada, 76 percent of hotels with 100 rooms or more are attached to a brand. The larger hotel brands operating in Canada include Best Western, Choice, Fairmont (see Chapter 11), Four Seasons (Chapter 3), Delta, Hilton, Holiday Inn, Howard Johnson, Hyatt, Marriott, Radisson, Ramada, Sheraton, and Westin.

Second-home ownership has been growing in Canada, with 10 percent of Canadians owning recreational properties. Companies such as Intrawest, which are developing four-season resorts, are investing heavily in real estate development and profiting from vacation ownership. For example, in Whistler, BC, building investment has exceeded $2 billion since the establishment of this municipality in 1975. Now, with more than 55 000 beds, and 18 000 of those within 500 metres of the lifts, Whistler boasts the most ski-in/ski-out beds of any mountain recreation resort in North America.

5. Food and Beverage Services

The food and beverage industry comprises establishments primarily engaged in preparing meals, snacks, and beverages, as ordered by customers, for immediate consumption on and off the premises. Major Canadian companies in the industry include Cara Operations and Priszm. Foreign companies with a presence in Canada include Compass Group, McDonald's, and Wendy's International. These large operations account for a minority share of revenues in the industry. In fact, a 2005 survey by the Canadian Restaurant and Foodservices Association (CRFA) found the largest 50 chains in Canada accounted for only 53 percent of revenues. The key reason for the low level of concentration is that the industry has very low barriers to entry. The food services industry reported a modest profit of $39 million in 2005, but the profit margin was very low, estimated to be only 0.6 percent.

Worldwide, statistics on the size of this sector are hard to come by, but there is considerable growth in developing countries. For example, the food and beverage sector in China and India grew by 20 percent and 9 percent respectively in 2005. A fair share of that growth can be attributed to multinational corporations expanding into those countries. An example is Starbucks. At the end of August 2006, Starbucks had 12 142 stores around the world, about 70 percent of them in the United States. The company's target is 30 000 stores globally, and chair Howard Schultz is aiming to open more locations in areas where the company remains under-represented, including parts of the U.S., China, and India. Starbucks expects to have 2400 new stores in 2007, opening on average six new stores a day.[11]

6. Attractions

As with other sectors of the tourism industry, attractions are increasingly polarized between a few large attractions and thousands of small and micro-sized enterprises. Within the range of visitor management techniques available to attractions, marketing is increasingly seen as fundamental to success. It is recognized as the best way of generating revenue to contribute to the cost of operation and maintenance of the resource base, to develop and sustain satisfying products, to create value for money, and to influence the volume and seasonality patterns of site visits.

Tourist attractions can be classified as natural or human-made, and Canadians are extremely proud of their 39 national parks, 3 marine conservation areas, and over 850 natural historic sites. Experiencing these special places is a top motivator of both domestic and international travel, and a vital component of Canada's multi-billion dollar tourism industry. Increasingly consumers are attracted to attractions that provide entertainment. For example, throughout the world, 253 million people visited theme parks in 2005, up 2.2 percent from 2004. No fewer than 176 million attended the most popular parks in North America, in part due to investments made by the big players such as Disney and Six Flags. However, the growth in the industry is expected to come outside of the U.S., particularly in China and India, where the middle classes are growing rapidly and are undersupplied with entertainment opportunities. Theme parks revenues are forecast to grow 3.7 percent in the U.S. between 2005 and 2009, whereas revenues will grow 5 percent in Europe, the Middle East and Africa, and 5.7 percent in the Asia/Pacific region.[12]

7. Events and Conferences

Events and conferences often play a key role in bringing business and leisure travellers to destinations. These events can vary from conventions and exhibitions for the business market to huge sporting events like the Olympics or soccer's World Cup, which attract millions of sport tourists. From the destination's perspective, event tourism is the development and marketing of events to obtain economic and community benefits. To the consumer, it is travel for the purpose of participating in or viewing an event. The average event in Canada generates more than $11 million in taxes and creates nearly 700 full-time jobs, mostly in the hospitality sector. The marketing of events and conferences is discussed more fully in Chapter 12.

8. Sport and Adventure Tourism

The marketing of sport and adventure tourism, also covered in more detail in Chapter 13, is a fast-growing segment of the Canadian tourism industry. The Canadian Sport Tourism Alliance (CSTA) estimates that sport travel generates more than $2.4 billion in domestic spending in Canada. There are about 200 000 sport events that occur annually in this country, and nearly 40 percent of travellers participate in, or are spectators at, a sport event every year. Adventure tourism is also on the increase. This type of travel brings together travel, sport, and outdoor recreation, and three key factors have facilitated its growth: a deferring of control to experts; a proliferation of promotional media, including brochures; and the application of technology in adventurous settings. Adventure tourism is often classified according to activity, where "hard" adventure tourism activities include mountaineering, white-water rafting, scuba diving, and mountain biking, and "soft" adventure activities include camping, hiking, biking, animal watching, horseback riding, canoeing, and water skiing.

9. Intermediaries

The key intermediary players in the tourism industry are tour operators, destination marketing companies, travel agents, travel specialists, and web-based intermediaries (a detailed analysis of intermediaries can be found in Chapter 7). Both tour operators and wholesalers are organizations that offer packaged vacation tours to the general public. These packages can include everything from transportation, accommodation, and activities, to entertainment, meals, and drinks. Destination marketing companies (DMCs) are private sector companies that also act as inbound tour operators. Travel agents are the most widely used marketing intermediaries in the tourism industry, but the emergence of new and cheaper distribution tools such as the Internet has challenged the future role of travel agents. This is explored more in depth in Chapter 10.

10. The Visitor

The final key player in the tourism industry is the visitor. As mentioned earlier in the chapter, international visitor arrivals reached an all-time record of 842 million in 2006. The majority of arrivals corresponded to trips for the purpose of leisure, recreation, and holidays (52 percent), while business travel accounted for about 16 percent of the total. A further 24 percent covered travel for other motives, such as visiting friends and relatives (VFR), religious purposes, and health treatment. For the remaining 8 percent of arrivals the purpose of visit has not been specified. As the *Spotlight* at the beginning of the chapter indicated, the number of visitors to Canada appears to have stagnated, whereas outbound travel from Canada has been growing. Asia has been growing in popularity for Canadian travellers, and the *Snapshot* focuses on an attraction in Hong Kong that is very popular with overseas visitors: Hong Kong Disneyland.

SNAPSHOT

DISNEY EXPANDS GLOBAL EMPIRE TO HONG KONG

Despite financial and cultural difficulties in Paris, Disney expanded its global empire to Hong Kong opening its fifth theme park in the fall of 2005. The Hong Kong government offered financial incentives to attract Disney to the island as part of its marketing strategy to boost tourism and assuage business fears about the return of the island to China from its former UK control. The government invested around $3.4 billion, providing 90 percent of the investment as well as providing the site on Lantau Island, formerly a semi-rural paradise inhabited by fishermen and Buddhist monks. According to its promotional website, the partnership will inject $22 billion into the island's economy over the next 40 years and create 18 000 jobs.

Hong Kong Disneyland is Disney's first step in challenging the Chinese market and there are tentative plans to expand to the mainland, with a focus on Shanghai. However, there have been some hitches.

Hong Kong residents (anglicized after a hundred years of British rule and education) were outraged by mainland Chinese visitors walking barefoot, smoking in non-smoking areas, and urinating in public. There were also food poisoning issues as well as fish farm claims to settle in relation to toxic construction damage to fish stocks. Another unforeseen problem was the overwhelming success of a discount-ticket promotion in 2006 that, in conjunction with the Chinese Lunar New Year, led to huge numbers of mainland families being turned away at the gates despite having valid tickets. Shark fin soup served at the park has also caused an animal rights outcry. Critics point out Disney's hypocrisy in promoting nature in films such as *Finding Nemo* and, at the same time, condoning the wholesale annual slaughter of millions of sharks for their fins and wasting the rest of the meat.

Disney has been forced to make dozens of changes to make the experience more understandable to Chinese, many of whom seemed more confused than amused during visits. The "Jungle Cruise" attraction, for example, has separate queues for three languages, so riders can hear the narration in their native tongue. But Mandarin speakers were regularly hopping into the often-shorter English line, eager to get to the front faster — only to be perplexed by the English-speaking guide. There are now three separate signs to make it clear to guests that there is no point moving to a different queue. The addition of Mandarin speakers to the park's staff of guides has been accompanied by Mandarin reading materials and subtitles added to shows such as "Festival of the Lion King" and the "Golden Mickeys," because Disney noticed that audiences were missing their cues to laugh or applaud. "The subtitles are very helpful," said Lu Ming, a 34-year-old finance worker from Zhe Jiang province who went to the park with her husband as part of a tour group. However, she expressed a common complaint: "The park is too small, even smaller than the parks in our province. We have all sorts of theme parks at home so there is really nothing more exciting here."

Ocean Park with its 28-year history of education, entertainment, and animal conservation (notably, two giant pandas) is Disney's competition in Hong Kong. It attracts three million visitors a year and the entrance fee is nearly half the price of the new Disneyland. Overseas, Disney is, of course, competing against itself. The more established and larger branches in the U.S., Europe and, Japan have between 44 and 65 attractions at their sites, whereas Hong Kong can only boast 22, making the cost per item the highest. However, the Hong Kong government has already allocated $3.3 billion for future expansion to provide more attractions and satisfy local opinion and tourist needs.

Michael Eisner, CEO of the Walt Disney Co. during construction, claimed that the "turbulence" caused by the project helped create a better product. "Life is turbulence. Life isn't only Disneyesque. Disneyesque is the end result of trying to do it better," he asserted. He also explained that although Asia has never been a "castle-oriented environment" and did not really know the Disney product, Hong Kong Disneyland would become, over time, one of Disney's biggest properties with about 40 percent of the customer demographic being Chinese because of their love of family entertainment.

Sources: Foreman, W. (2005, December 9). Life not always "Disneyesque." *Globe & Mail*, B8; Hutchinson, B. (2004, 23 October). The next Hong Kong. *National Post*, P11; Disneyland in hot water over plan to serve shark's fin soup. (2005, 24 May). *National Post*, A13; Marr, M. & Fowler, G. A. (2006, June 12). Chinese lessons for Disney at Hong Kong Disneyland: park officials learn a lot from their past mistakes. *Wall Street Journal*, B1.

MICRO- AND MACROENVIRONMENTS

Microenvironment

microenvironment

forces close to the organization that can affect its ability to serve its customers: the organization itself, marketing channel firms, customer markets, and a broad range of stakeholders or publics

The marketing environment is made up of a microenvironment and a macroenvironment. The **microenvironment** consists of forces close to the organization that can affect its ability to serve its customers: the organization itself, marketing channel firms, customer markets, and a broad range of stakeholders or publics (see Figure 1.7). For a tourism marketer, these factors will affect the degree of success in attracting target markets, so it is important to understand their importance. This book discusses most of these components in detail: customers in Chapter 2, competitors in Chapter 3, intermediaries in Chapter 7, and the various publics in Chapter 9. However, it is important to acknowledge the influence that the organization and its suppliers will have on achieving marketing objectives.

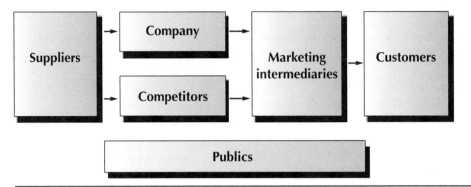

Figure 1.7 Major Components in a Company's Microenvironment

Marketing managers need to work closely with other departments in the organization, as all of these departments will have some impact on the success of marketing plans. Every tourism organization will differ as to how many departments it has and what they are called. However, finance is normally responsible for finding and using the funds required to carry out marketing plans, accounting has to measure revenues and costs in order to evaluate marketing objectives, and human resources will be crucial in supporting a services marketing culture (see Chapter 11). Suppliers also have an important role to play in supporting marketing objectives. Suppliers are firms and individuals that provide the resources needed by the organization to produce its goods and services. Marketing management must pay close attention to trends and developments affecting suppliers, and to changes in supply availability and supply costs. At one level, hotels and exhibition centres contract with restaurant companies to supply food and beverage services. In turn, these restaurants will have their own favoured suppliers of produce. On another level basis, tourist destinations will need suppliers in the form of airlines, hotels, restaurants, ground operations, meeting facilities, and entertainment.

Macroenvironment

macroenvironment

the larger societal forces that affect the microenvironment: competitive, demographic, economic, environmental and natural, technological, political, cultural and social, and legal forces

The **macroenvironment** comprises the larger societal forces that affect the entire microenvironment, and shapes opportunities and pose threats. There are eight major forces as shown in Figure 1.8, and tourism businesses need to take into consideration the fact that they operate in a competitive national and international environment. Although an organization cannot control many of these external factors, they should never be allowed to come as a total surprise. A planned response to potential environmental issues allows for a balanced, thoughtful reaction — a process often referred to as "environmental scanning." Chapter 13 looks in more detail at how some tourism organizations have responded to environmental influences outside of their control. The *Profile* on Bruce Poon Tip is an example of a Canadian success story in the tourism industry. By understanding and adapting to a changing environment, G.A.P Adventures has become one of the largest adventure companies in the world.

Figure 1.8   Major Forces in a Company's Macroenvironment

AN ADVENTURE WITH BRUCE POON TIP

In 1990, Bruce Poon Tip withdrew every last penny in his bank account to open his own travel company specializing in taking tourists to emerging countries in Central and South America. Due to the risky nature of the travel industry at that time, caused by the first Gulf War, the banks were unwilling to lend him any money. Poon Tip would not be discouraged and, as a result, he stretched the limit of his credit card to follow his vision. Today, G.A.P Adventures is one of the largest adventure companies in the world. At 21, Poon Tip found his G.A.P concept when he travelled in Thailand for $10 a day and stayed with the hill tribes. "It wasn't my first visit, but it was my most genuine," says Poon Tip, who has consulted on *Survivor*. "That was when I knew others would want authentic travel experiences." Just as baby boomers were maturing and realizing the detrimental effects of their hedonistic youth, Poon Tip positioned his company as a vehicle to do some good while travelling via environmentally friendly, experience- and adventure-oriented tourism.

Born in Trinidad, Poon Tip runs his company based on his ethical commitment to developing mutually beneficial international relationships, incorporating values and respect for local cultures, and promoting ecotourism. His $100 million business, which sells 1000 different trips to 100 destinations through its many offices worldwide, does more to promote sustainable tourism than any other company in the business.

Toronto-based G.A.P Adventures and Bruce Poon Tip himself have been recognized by many organizations as leaders in business practices and leadership. In 2006, Poon Tip won Entrepreneur of the Year in Canada for the second time at the 13th Annual Ernst & Young Entrepreneur of the Year Awards. In addition to receiving an award as one of Canada's top 40 Canadians Under 40, Poon Tip has also been honoured as one of Canada's top five entrepreneurs by *Canadian Business* and as one of Canada's 100 leaders of tomorrow. Poon Tip also received the Global Traders Leadership award from the government for his groundbreaking ideas in exporting services. He has also spearheaded a postgraduate diploma program for Humber College on Ecotourism and Adventure Travel. Recently, he was asked by the World Bank and UNESCO to be on a team visiting China to lecture on sustainable development. In January 2002, Poon Tip was the only Canadian operator invited to attend the United Nations' launch of the Year of Ecotourism in New York.

In 2005 and 2006, G.A.P was selected as one of Canada's Best Managed Companies as well as Canada's Top 100 Employers and one of the Top 10 Employers for Young People. The company's enthusiasm for the product is instrumental, too, in creating customer and staff loyalty. Poon Tip explains: "We are a company of travellers and our employees share a true passion for the industry. We are a work hard/play hard company that is dedicated to our entrepreneurial spirit."

In a world where people are living longer and staying fit and healthier later in life, the company is targeting those who are "young at heart." For "adventure with a bit of comfort" G.A.P offers the traveller small-group excursions throughout South and Central America, Africa, Asia, North America, and Europe, plus expeditions to the Antarctic, the Arctic, and the Panama Canal onboard the ship *M/S Explorer*. With a slant toward wildlife, culture, history, and the environment, these expeditions put leisure and entertainment in an educational package, using small-scale lodging and local transportation. The company also supports locally owned businesses and incorporates community-based ecotourism projects into most of its tours.

Newspaper advertising focuses attention on the company's differentiation within the travel industry. No glossy photos of perfect hotels or idyllic beaches, but, instead, pictures of indigenous people and text that says "our impact is low and sustainable tourism is at the forefront of our agenda." Instead of listing resorts, the ads promote adventures in every corner of the globe for the "New Traveller" in small groups. Accommodation is advertised not as a star rating, but as "local" and "full of character," with activities described as "unique and off the beaten track." This innovative targeting stresses the company's authenticity and experience-based, cultural tourism.

Poon Tip believes that ecotourism does not have to be small-scale. "Most people say ecotourism means 'leave only footprints,' " he says. "I disagree with that. I think that we've got to get those 10 000 people off the cruise ships and into 200 small groups. I think that tourists can leave behind a huge impact." To that end, Poon Tip has worked with the World Bank to help impoverished villages finance tourist lodges and teach communities to profit through tourism. Six communities in Bolivia, for example, now sustain themselves through such initiatives, which help reduce their

PROFILE *continued*

dependence on logging and the drug trade. This aspect of G.A.P's philosophy puts the company into the cause-related tourism category as well as making a stand against the typical, profit-oriented tourism operations. G.A.P Adventures was recently included in *Condé Nast Traveller*'s 12th annual Green List. Top candidates are chosen for their commitment to environmental initiatives, contributions to local communities, and quality of guest experience.

Despite the obvious advantages to ecotourism, which brings sustainable prosperity to locals as well as cultural exchanges between the travellers and the inhabitants, the concept has detractors. Some think that ecotourists

travel on low budgets (and G.A.P emphasizes the good value for the traveller's dollar in its advertising) and contribute less to local economies. However, Poon Tip contends that ecotourists generally stay longer than five-star hotel guests and the money they spend goes directly to the community rather than into the coffers of a western-run hotel chain.

Sources: Baginski, M. (2002). GC acquisition fills large G.A.P. *Tourism.* www.canadatourism.com/ en/ctc/ctx/ctxnews/search/newsbydateform.cfm (retrieved October 2002); G.A.P Adventures. (2006). www.gapadventures.com; B. Poon Tip, personal communication, December 15, 2006; Travel for the Fifty Plus, *Travelweek magazine* (2005, May 26), 16.

Competitive Forces

Being aware of who the competition is, knowing their strengths and weaknesses, and anticipating what they may do are important aspects for understanding the macroenvironment. The marketing concept states that to be successful a company must satisfy the needs and wants of consumers better than its competitors. Furthermore, competitive advantage is now widely accepted as being centrally important to the success of organizations, regions, and countries. Although competition occurs among hotels, airlines, tour operators, travel agents, and other tourism services, this inter-enterprise competition is dependent upon and derived from the choices tourists make between alternative destinations. Competition therefore centres on the destination. Countries, states, regions, and cities now take their role as tourist destinations very seriously, committing considerable effort and funds toward enhancing their touristic image and attractiveness. As a consequence, destination competitiveness has become a significant part of tourism literature, and evaluation of the competitiveness of tourism destinations is increasingly recognized as an important tool in the strategic positioning and marketing analysis of destinations.

As a result of globalization, a growing number of countries are aware of the importance of tourism to their economies. These countries have therefore increasingly targeted international tourism markets, augmenting their investment in marketing to attract international visitors and increase foreign earnings. Canada's major competitors in overseas markets are the U.S., Australia, New Zealand, and South Africa. While revenues related to overnight international travel to Canada have grown in recent years, Canada's competitive position in this sector has eroded (see Table 1.2). There has been a decline in the number of tourists coming from the U.S., Japan, France, and Germany over the last decade. Competition is also intensifying for larger share of the expected growth in outbound travel from China (see *Marketing in Action*). UNWTO expects that by 2020, China will become one of the world's major outbound tourism markets, generating globally 100 million tourists, or 6.2 percent of the world total. Competitive product, price, and quality, as well as access to and delivery of tourism goods and services will be the major success factors in attracting new Chinese outbound tourists and encouraging repeat travellers in the next decade and beyond.

Demographic Forces

Demographics are statistics that describe the observable characteristics of individuals, including our physical traits, such as gender, race, age, and height; our economic traits, such as income, savings, and net worth; our occupation-related traits, including education; our location-related traits; and our family-related traits, such as marital status and number and age of children. According to David Foot, author of *Boom, Bust, & Echo*, demographics explain about two thirds of everything.[13] For example, the dramatic increase in popularity of golf over the last 25 years is explained by golf's popularity among aging baby boomers who are entering a stage of life that enables them to spend more time on the golf course.

In fact, the single most notable demographic trend in many western countries including Canada is the aging population. The over-50 segment, sometimes referred to as the maturing or greying market, is nearly 30 percent of the population, and this market has a keen interest in travel and leisure services. By 2026, one out of very five people in Canada will be a senior. Other demographic trends affecting the marketing of tourism in Canada include the relatively slow population growth, the continued increase in education and service sector employment, increasing ethnic diversity, the demise of the traditional family, and the geographic mobility of the population. In addition to understanding general demographic trends, marketers must also recognize demographic groupings that may turn out to be market segments because of their enormous size, similar socioeconomic characteristics, or shared values. Such segments are discussed in Chapter 3.

Economic Forces

Economic forces in the environment are those that affect consumer purchasing power and spending patterns. Total purchasing power depends on current income, prices, savings, and credit, so marketers must be aware of major economic trends in income and of changing consumer spending patterns. For example, newly rich Russians, Indians, and Chinese and a wider rise in disposable income are expected to boost the luxury goods market over the next decade. As a consequence, the luxury travel market will grow considerably. The market is already a lucrative one. In 2005, Virtuoso, a network of more than 6000 travel consultants that specialize in the luxury travel segment, booked more than $4.8 billion in travel for its clients.

Price changes and exchange rates can also have a significant impact on tourism. The upward pressure on the prices of travel packages has eroded Canada's competitiveness in major overseas markets. Since 1995, the travel price index in Canada has increased by over 20 percent, much more than the consumer price index. The situation has been aggravated in several markets as a result of a drop in the rate of currency exchange, the U.S. is an example. As a direct result, travel packages to Canada from these countries became more expensive. On the other hand, favourable exchange rates with countries such as the United Kingdom have worked to Canada's advantage.

Environmental and Natural Forces

The last four decades have witnessed a dramatic increase in environmental consciousness worldwide. Media attention given to the climate change, acid rain, oil spills, ocean pollution, tropical deforestation, and other topics has raised public awareness about environmental issues. This environmental awareness has had an impact on the tourism industry. International leisure travellers are increasingly motivated by the quality of destination landscapes, in terms of environmental health and the diversity and integrity of natural and cultural resources. Studies of German and U.S. travel markets indicate that environmental considerations are now a significant element of travellers' destination-choosing process, down to — as in the case of the Germans — the environmental programs operated by individual hotels.[14] The *Snapshot* shows how increased environmental awareness has affected tourism in Banff National Park in Alberta.

The growing concern among consumers for the protection of the environment has clearly attracted the attention of companies seeking to profit from environmentally sound practices. Surveys have shown that consumers are more likely to choose one brand over another if they believe the brand will help the environment, and environmental quality is a prevailing issue in making travel-related decisions. This has led to the "greening" of attractions, hotels, and even resorts, and to an increase in the number of environmentally friendly tourism products. An increasing emphasis is also being placed upon evaluating the likely environmental impacts of any tourism development, with environmental audits, environmental impact analysis, and carrying capacity issues being taken more seriously. A 2005 report from the UK suggested that there are a growing number of concerned individuals in Britain who have begun to turn away from international travel because of its environmental price.[15]

Finally, uncontrollable natural forces can have a negative impact on the tourism industry. For example, the South Asian tsunami of 2004, due to the number of victims among foreign visitors and among workers of the tourism sector, constitutes the greatest catastrophe ever recorded in the history of tourism. Before the tsunami, tourism was at an all-time high in many of the affected countries. A two-year ceasefire between the Sri Lankan government and the Tamil Tigers had helped produce an 11 percent increase in the number of tourists. Thailand was continuing its strong growth with a 20 percent rise from the previous year. Even Bali, which was unaffected by the tsunami, had seen almost a complete recuperation of tourism revenues, almost equalling its numbers prior to the al Qaeda bombings in October 2002. The tsunami devastated tourism in many of these countries. Due to its magnitude and repercussions the disaster took on a global scale, reflecting the world-wide reach tourism has today.

SNAPSHOT

TOURISM AND THE ENVIRONMENT IN BANFF NATIONAL PARK

An example of how government policies and increasing environmental awareness have affected tourism in Canada comes from Alberta's Banff National Park. In 1885, Sir John A. Macdonald's government established the initial federal land reserve in the Bow River Valley, creating Canada's first national park. Banff Park was then established as a tourist zone catering to a largely British elite. In 1909, the park boundaries were expanded, a Banff warden service was established, and hunting was banned. The park superintendent had to approve all building plans, and the preservation and repopulation of wildlife began with a buffalo paddock and the importation of moose from Ontario. As a reaction to the growing number of day visitors who had come along with the first road in 1911, conservation and preservation became a popular cause. It was taken up by two early conservation groups, the

SNAPSHOT *continued*

Alpine Club of Canada and the National Parks Association of Canada, and became enshrined in the National Parks Act of 1930. This original Parks Act placed the use and enjoyment of the park by the human population first and foremost, and this encouraged the first alpine ski resort at Sunshine in 1932. By the late 1960s, Sunshine had been joined by the ski resorts of Lake Louise and Mount Norquay, as Banff became a playground for the masses.

However, the environmental movement worldwide was gathering speed, and in 1996, the minister of Canadian Heritage appointed the Banff–Bow Valley (BBV) Task Force to assess the cumulative environmental effects of development in the park. The task force for the Banff–Bow Valley Study made over 400 recommendations, including stricter limits to growth, creative visitor management programs, the refocusing and upgrading of the role of tourism, and improvements in education, awareness, and interpretation programs for tourists and residents. For ski resorts in particular, it recommended capping skier numbers and prohibiting night use of ski hills. In response to the BBV report, Ottawa took a much more active role in the park's future. In 1998, the government imposed controversial limits on commercial development in the Banff town site. Then, in the spring of 2000, Sheila Copps, the heritage minister, introduced legislation in Parliament outlining new rules for restrictive development in Banff and other national parks. These new policies would cut back ski area operations, cap daily skier capacity, and restrict future expansions in Banff and Jasper national parks.

The new Act moves ecological integrity to the top of the park's management agenda. However, owners of the ski areas in the park are far from happy with this new legislation, and have pursued legal action against Parks Canada over these new policies, saying that the government measures were taken without consulting them and without obtaining the environmental assessment required under the Canadian Environmental Assessment Act. They say that their 30-year leases allow them to build lifts, clear trees, and cut glades, but the government is now prohibiting them from doing so. The conflict is still going on.

Source: Hudson, S. (2002). Environmental management in the Rockies: The dilemma of balancing national park values while making provision for their enjoyment. *Journal of Case Research, 22*(2), 1–14.

Technological Forces

The most dramatic force shaping the future of tourism and hospitality is technology. The accelerated rate of technological advancement has forced tourism organizations to adapt their products and services accordingly, particularly in terms of how they develop, price, distribute, and promote their offerings. Technology facilitates the continual development of new systems and features that improve the tourism product. Technology has allowed for extra security in hotels and resorts, thanks to security systems and safety designs. It has also created new entertainment options for travellers, such as in-room movies and video games. Increasingly, hotels, and even airplanes, are offering Internet services to cater to the technological needs of today's consumer.

The Internet fits the theoretical marketing principle in the travel industry because it allows suppliers to set up direct links of communication with their customers. Travellers are turning in increasing numbers to the Internet to plan and book their travel (see Chapter 10 for more on this subject). Technology is also beginning to have an impact on consumer research, as tourism organizations realize the potential of database management and the value of relationship marketing. Databases of customer profiles and customer behaviour are the basis for effective direct marketing. In tourism, the collection and analysis of data streams that now flow continuously through distribution channels and booking systems provide the modern information base for strategic and operational decisions of large organizations. The rate of technological change as databases connect and interact indicates that the speed and quality of information flows will be further enhanced in the coming decade.

Political Forces

Marketing decisions are strongly affected by developments in the political environment. This environment is made up of government agencies and pressure groups that influence and limit the activities of various organizations and individuals in society. Government policies can have far-reaching implications for the tourism industry. For example, the nation of Myanmar (formerly called Burma) receives very few tourists because of the turbulent political situation in the country (see the *Case Study* at the end of this chapter). In Fiji, tourism is often influenced by political forces. A military coup in December 2006 — the country's fourth in 20 years — had a negative impact on the tourism arrivals.

Terrorism can also have a devastating impact on tourism around the world. Since September 11, 2001, there have been more than 3000 major terrorism attacks worldwide, most of which have affected the tourism industry. Media attention to these attacks is usually enough to sway many international travellers to reconsider their vacation plans. The terrorists themselves target tourist destinations in order to force governments to rethink and abandon specific policies, or to deny governments the commercial and economic benefits of tourism.

Political actions can also have a positive impact on tourism. In some parts of the world, the relaxing of political barriers is making areas more accessible to tourists. An example is Mongolia, where Soviet influence smothered Mongolia's cultural traditions and closed off outside access until recently. But now, adventurous westerners are exploring central Asia's vast wilderness of grasslands, deserts, and alpine terrain.

Cultural and Social Forces

Marketing's consumer focus relies on an understanding of who the markets are, what motivates them, and how to appeal to them. Understanding the cultural environment is thus crucial for marketing decision making. This **cultural environment** includes institutions and other forces that affect society's basic values, perceptions, preferences, and behaviour. Cultural values influence consumer behaviour, and marketers tend to concentrate on dominant cultural values or core values. A grouping technique that is used to track trends in cultural values is psychographics, which determines how people spend their time and resources (activities), what they consider important (interests and values), and what they think of themselves and the world around them (opinions). Psychographics is discussed more fully in Chapter 2. Core values are slow and difficult to change, but secondary values are less permanent values that can sometimes be influenced by marketers.

Major cultural trends in Canada that affect the tourism industry include

1. calls for increased responsibility on the part of those who drink as well as those who sell and serve alcoholic beverages;
2. the desire to develop individuality in order to be seen and treated as different from others (egonomics);
3. the tendency to act and feel younger than one's age (down-aging);

cultural environment

institutions and other forces that affect society's basic values, perceptions, preferences, and behaviour

4. the urge to change one's life to a slower but more rewarding pace (cashing out);
5. the refusal to tolerate shoddy products and poor service (the vigilant consumer);
6. acceptance of the gay and lesbian community;
7. concerns for the environment;
8. an increasing desire for smoke-free restaurants and hotels; and
9. the desire to regularly eat out.

Legal Forces

The tourism industry has witnessed an increase in legislation and regulation that affects business, enacted to protect companies and consumers from unfair business practices. Government regulation also aims to protect society's interests against unrestricted business behaviour, as profitable business activity does not always improve the quality of life within a society. Hence the regulations in many parts of the world that restrict smoking in restaurants and hotels. In fact, government agencies have become involved in the regulation of everything from food-handling practices in restaurants to fire codes for hotels. Travellers are seen as good sources of revenue by politicians, as witnessed by the increasing number of cities, provinces, or states that implement hotel taxes. Some governments are also imposing international taxes on air travel to help alleviate poverty in Africa, such as France, or to mitigate climate change, as in the UK.

Most countries have laws that permit governments to restrict foreign trade when such trade could adversely affect the economy of the country or when such trade is in conflict with foreign policy. There are laws about the level of foreign investment permitted and the amount of money that can be transferred out of the country, and immigration laws affect the transfer of staff internationally from one multinational property to another. All laws have an impact on investment and development in the tourism industry. More specifically, laws regarding landing taxes for aircraft, health regulations, gaming licences, and visa and entry permits all affect the tourism industry in one way or another.

New visa and customs regulations introduced in 2007 are expected to have a negative affect on tourism in Canada. As of January 2007, the Western Hemisphere Travel Initiative (WHTI) required all travellers, including U.S. citizens, to present a passport when entering the United States. The Canadian Tourism Research Institute estimates that by 2008, implementation of the new regulations could decrease potential U.S. visitation by 12.3 percent, resulting in a shortfall of tourism receipts of $1.6 billion.[16] The Tourism Industry Association of Canada was particularly concerned about the impact of the legislation on day trips for purposes such as shopping, visiting casinos, attending or participating in sporting events, and other leisure activities.[17]

CHAPTER SUMMARY

Service products are commonly distinguished from goods products by four unique characteristics: intangibility, inseparability, heterogeneity, and perishability. The services marketing triangle shows the three interlinked groups that work together to develop, promote, and deliver services. These key players are the company, the customers, and the providers. The triangle also suggests that three types of marketing must be successfully carried out for a service to succeed: external, interactive, and internal marketing. The expanded marketing mix for services includes the traditional four P's — product, price, place, and promotion — as well as the more recently added people, physical evidence, and process.

The key players in the tourism industry are private and nonprofit sector services, public sector services, suppliers (transportation, accommodation, food and beverage services, attractions, events and conferences, and sport and adventure tourism), intermediaries, and the visitors (tourist/travellers) themselves.

The marketing environment is made up of a microenvironment and a macroenvironment. The microenvironment consists of forces close to the organization that can affect its ability to serve its customers: the organization itself, marketing channel firms, customer markets, and a broad range of stakeholders or publics. The macroenvironment comprises the larger societal forces that affect the entire microenvironment and shape opportunities and pose threats. The macroenvironment consists of eight major forces: competitive, demographic, economic, environmental and natural, technological, political, cultural and social, and legal.

KEY TERMS

cultural environment, p. 33
demographics, p. 30
economic forces, p. 30
ethnocentrism, p. 13
international marketing, p. 12
macroenvironment, p. 26

marketing, p. 12
microenvironment, p. 25
self-reference criteria (SRC),
    p. 13
services marketing mix, p. 16

services marketing triangle,
    p. 15
tourism, p. 5
tourism market, p. 6
visitor, p. 6

DISCUSSION QUESTIONS AND EXERCISES

1. Why do managers in tourism and hospitality need to understand the services marketing triangle and the services marketing mix?

2. Choose one key player in the tourism industry and suggest how it should deal with the unique characteristics of services outlined in Table 1.4. For example, how do airlines overcome the perishability of their product?

3. Which of the key players in the tourism industry outlined in Figure 1.7 are more vulnerable to external influences such as terrorist attacks and tsunamis?

4. Choose one of the transport sectors discussed in this chapter (airlines, cruises, railways, or motorcoach operators) and update the material presented in the text. How is this sector performing in today's environment?

5. What are the key challenges facing Canada's tourism and hospitality industry today? Which of these are controllable and which are uncontrollable?

CASE STUDY

THE INFLUENCE OF POLITICS ON TOURISM: THE CASE OF MYANMAR

Canadian tourists contemplating a visit to any country with a history of human rights abuses are confronted with a similar ethical dilemma: keep yourself and your tourist dollars away, or go and bear witness, facilitate the exchange of ideas, and support local businesses. Visitors to Myanmar are faced with such a dilemma and some profound political and ideological decision making. Tourism marketing strategies in Myanmar have focused on a picturesque and idyllic landscape, imbued with spirituality as a consequence of its Buddhist traditions, and inhabited by peaceful people whose traditional culture has been preserved. However, this image of a country at peace denies the harsh realities that underlie such representations, and Myanmar has been referred to as the "land of fear." Under allegations of human rights abuse, the generals running the country spend about 40 percent of the county's budget on the military, while most of the people live in poverty and disease. The Burmese health system is ranked 190th out of 190 countries by the World Health Organization. Aung San Suu Kyi, leader of the elected Democratic Party, and winner of the Nobel Peace Prize in 1991, remains under house arrest, while more than 1800 political prisoners are held in jail.

Tourism to Myanmar has been both promoted and deterred. On one side, the State Peace and Development Council (SPDC), the ruling elite, opens its arms to foreign visitors. For more than 25 years, tourism has been accepted as an industry of potential importance and a major foreign exchange generator. In 1990 a tourism law recognized tourism as a significant economic activity and ended the state monopoly, allowing local and foreign private operators to run hotels, transport businesses, and tour guiding services. A hotel and tourism law in 1993 affirmed official support, setting out objectives related to the growth of the hotel and tourism sector. Myanmar's cultural heritage and scenic beauty were to be exploited, maximizing employment opportunities, while fostering international friendship and understanding. In short, the SPDC saw tourism as an opportunity to disseminate a favourable picture of Myanmar to the rest of the world.

But the high-speed growth in tourism infrastructure did not come without a price. It caused mass upheaval, with millions of labourers required to erect the suitable tourism infrastructure and to restore cultural sites as tourist attractions (often crudely, according to archeologists and conservationists). Tourism development was directly linked to human rights violations, and there were reports in the 1990s of the government conscripting labour to complete infrastructure and tourism projects. People were also displaced from their homes to make way for tourism. For example, people in Palaung were reportedly uprooted and moved into "ethnic villages" built for tourism purposes. Whether the members of these ethnic groups object to their cultural identities being commodified for tourism purposes was not a concern of the SPDC.

In reaction, many groups, both inside and outside Myanmar, have opposed tourism, including Suu Kyi, and her party. They have urged travellers to refrain from visiting Myanmar until there is a political transition to democracy. In 2002 she said: "Burma will always be here, and when it is democratic it will be a place that I think tourists will enjoy visiting with no qualms and guilty feelings." Her anti-tourism campaign has proved to be successful, with travellers and their dollars staying away. Whilst tourism has expanded rapidly in neighbouring Asian countries, Myanmar still receives relatively few tourists. In 2006, 263 000 tourists (about 3000 of them Canadian) visited Myanmar, compared to neighbouring Thailand, which attracted more than 10 million.

Non-government organizations (NGOs) that support Myanmar's pro-democracy movement, such as Canadian Friends of Burma (CFOB), are also raising the call to world travellers, urging them to avoid travel to Myanmar and thus prevent the SPDC from obtaining the hard currency and global legitimacy it needs to survive. "Tourism money is not as beneficial to the people as it is to the junta," said Tin Maung Htoo, CFOB executive director. These NGOs stress that tourism fosters an illusion of peace and regularity while providing foreign exchange to pay for arms that strengthen the military. It thus fortifies the regime whose members may benefit personally and politically from any increase in arrivals. The Burma Campaign UK — which, like CFOB, refers to the country by its former name — has lined up politicians and celebrities to back its "I'm not going" campaign. In February 2005 Tony Blair, the British prime minister, joined such stars as Susan Sarandon and Ian McKellen in pledging not to vacation in Myanmar and urging others to do the same.

In Canada, the government has condemned the country's human rights situation but does not discourage travel to Myanmar for purely political reasons. In fact, there are some outside analysts that believe tourism should be encouraged in Myanmar, despite the political situation. The opportunities to engage in cross-cultural communication form the basis of the ethical arguments put forward by some of those in favour of tourism in Myanmar. These protagonists argue that tourism can break down barriers and accelerate economic progress that improves the lives of local people; that tourism provides a rare channel of communication for the Burmese, because it provides jobs and it allows foreigners to learn about the culture; and that travel enhances friendships between peoples and facilitates cultural and political exchange. In the case of repressive countries such as Myanmar, it may also allow visitors to bear witness to local conditions. Such arguments fall under the umbrella of "citizen diplomacy" — the cross-national interactions between people of different cultures that can have a positive impact on society.

To conclude, the recent fortunes of Myanmar's tourism are clearly tied to various manifestations of its politics. The instability of the military regime has been a deterrent to travel, and unattractive images of its leaders, associations of political repression and arguments that tourism is partly responsible for human rights abuses represent strong disincentives in certain markets. The features and actions of Myanmar's government seem to have hindered tourism and prevented the country from realizing its potential as a popular tourism destination. Until the underlying political tensions are resolved and new policies put in place leading to improvements both in realities and perceptions, Myanmar's tourism industry is unlikely to thrive.

Source: Hudson, S. (2007). To go or not to go? Ethical perspectives on tourism in an "Outpost of Tyranny." *Journal of Business Ethics* (Online First).

QUESTIONS

1. Explain how political factors have influenced the growth of tourism in Myanmar.
2. Do some research to find out what the political situation in Myanmar is today and how this is affecting tourism arrivals.
3. Do you think boycotting tourism in Myanmar will have any effect on government policies in the country? Why?
4. Give examples from other countries around the world where politics is having a negative impact on tourism.
5. Apart from political factors, what other factors are influencing tourism in Myanmar?

WEBSITES

www.hongkongdisneyland.com
Hong Kong Disneyland

www.cruising.org
Cruise Lines International Association

www.world-tourism.org
United Nations World Tourism Organization

www.myanmar-tourism.com
Myanmar Tourism Promotion Board

www.gapadventures.com
G.A.P Adventures

ENDNOTES

1. United Nations World Tourism Organization. (2006). Tourism is a socio-economic driver. *UNWTO News, 20*(3), 4–5.
2. World Tourism Organization. (2003). Tourism Highlights 2003. www.world-tourism.org (retrieved April 2003).
3. Hard Rock International. (2007). The Hard Rock Café story: A brief history of a global phenomenon. www.hardrock.com/corporate/history (retrieved September 2007).
4. Allen, K. (2006, July 5). Rank may roll hard rock off its wagon, *Guardian*, 25.
5. Kotler, P. (1984). *Marketing management: Analysis, planning, implementation and control* (8th ed.). Upper Saddle River, NJ: Prentice Hall, 92.
6. Cateora, P. R., & Graham, J. L. (2005). *International marketing* (12th ed.). New York: McGraw-Hill Irwin.
7. McCarthy, E. J. (1981). *Basic marketing: A managerial approach* (7th ed.). Georgetown, ON: Irwin.
8. AMA board approves new marketing definition. (1985, March 1). *Marketing News, 1*, 1.
9. Suga, M. (2006, September 1). Rising travel demand lifts world's airlines. *National Post*, FP3.
10. Blitzin, R. (2006, September 15). Hilton set to make move. *Financial Post*, FP8.
11. Starbucks raises the bar on national, global expansion plans. (2006, September 20). *Financial Post*, FP4.
12. Cetron, M. (2006). Seven trends directly affecting theme parks. *Hospitality Sales & Marketing Association International, 23*(1).
13. Foot, D. (2000). Boom, bust, & echo: Profiting from the demographic shift in the 21st century. Toronto: MacFarlane Walter & Ross, 313.
14. Ayala, H. (1996). Resort ecotourism: A paradigm for the 21st century. *Cornell Hotel & Restaurant Administration Quarterly, 37*(5), 1–9.
15. Kesterton, M. (2005, May 16). Social Studies: A Daily Miscellany of Information. *Globe & Mail*, A14.

16. Conference Board of Canada (2005, July 20). The potential impact of a Western Hemisphere Travel Initiative passport requirement on Canada's tourism industry. Report prepared for the Canadian Tourism Commission.

17. Tourism Industry Association of Canada (2007). Western Hemisphere Travel Initiative latest developments. www.tiac-aitc.ca/english/whti.asp (retrieved September 2007).

Consumer Behaviour

2

Spotlight
VACATIONS FROM THE HEART: TRAVELLER PHILANTHROPY

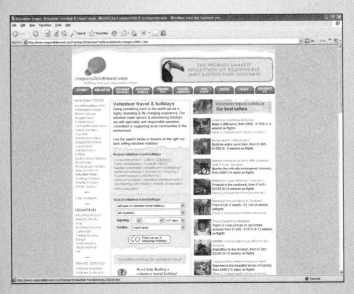

In all regions of the world, a new source of international development aid called "Traveller Philanthropy" is evolving. Civic-minded travellers and travel businesses are giving time, talent, and financial resources to further the well-being of the places that they visit. The phenomenon is expected to grow exponentially, benefiting from trends in giving, travel, and globalization.

Philanthropic initiatives have a number of benefits. Destinations obviously benefit from increased funds for conservation, given that lack of money to sustain tourism destinations is a growing problem worldwide. Travellers themselves also benefit. Travel provides the rare opportunity to witness firsthand the beauty and fragility of other societies, cultures, and natural systems. Such experiences generate strong philanthropic impulses. The majority of travellers agree that their travel experience is better when the destination preserves its natural, historical, and cultural sites and attractions.

Tourism organizations also benefit from traveller philanthropy. Philanthropic initiatives have been shown to offer a number of strategic benefits to corporations, including brand differentiation, enhanced image, higher sales, and increased brand loyalty. Travellers exhibit a high degree of commitment to travel that protects the local environment, engages visitors in the local culture, and returns benefits to the community. Previous research shows that travel companies can gain competitive advantage by adopting ethical policies.

Scores of travellers' philanthropy programs now exist around the globe, representing every sector of the travel and tourism industry. In many of the programs, a foundation has been established that channels donations and charitable funds to address environmental and social needs. An example is the Yasawa Island chain of Fiji, where resort owners have created the Yasawas Community Foundation, which directs charitable funds to village chiefs to address many social needs. The foundation typically receives $23 000 to $35 000 annually in donations from guests, who are primarily American.

How guests are asked to contribute to these philanthropic efforts tends to vary. For the Galapagos Conservation Fund created by Lindblad Expeditions, guests are provided with a direct solicitation envelope the night before landing, and offered a discount coupon of $250 on future Lindblad excursions in return for charitable contributions of $250 or more. Since 1997, guests have contributed close to $1 million. Another example is the New Orleans Metropolitan Convention and Visitors Bureau, which enlists large convention groups to forgo dessert and donate the saved money to local nonprofits.

Many schemes exist whereby the travel company makes a "per booking" contribution on behalf of their customers. For example, in 2002 Sunvil Africa brought together 19 operators that committed to donating £50 per person booking a trip to Zambia or Malawi. Alternatively, a travel company might include an optional additional item on invoices that is then donated to support work in the destination. Gambian Expeditions, for example, match donations by clients with equal or greater contributions to assist schools in the Gambia.

Other schemes ask travellers (or corporations) to make quite significant payments to support a very specific project or activity. The name of the sponsor may then be linked to the project. The gift may be in the form of a one-time payment or a pledge to give support over a number of years. Another method is to invite visitors to join a club that supports a conservation cause. Payment is usually by annual subscription. Typical examples are "friends" schemes for national parks.

Finally, a growing form of traveller philanthropy comes in the form of what has been labelled "voluntourism," whereby travellers contribute time and effort to philanthropic initiatives. Visitors may get involved in practical tasks, such as restoring old buildings or wildlife habitats, or undertake research. Activities may take place for a few hours, like an organized beach cleaning, or form the basis of a complete working eco-tourism package holiday. One company that specializes in offering this type of package is responsibletravel.com. Based in the United Kingdom, Justin Francis and Harold Goodwin co-founded responsibletravel.com in April 2001. The idea was to create a place for tourists to find and book holidays from tour companies and accommodations that were committed to more responsible travel. They launched with 20 holidays from just four tour companies that met their criteria for responsible travel. Since then they have turned away far more tourcompanies than they accept, but at the end of 2006 had more than 2000 holidays from 220 tour companies. The web page above gives some examples of the type of volunteer holidays the company offers.

Sources: Centre on Ecotourism and Sustainable Development. (2004). Travellers' philanthropy. www.ecotourismCESD.org (May 2004); Goodwin, H. (2004). Visitor payback in the outbound UK tourism industry. www.responsibletourismpartnership.org/payback.pdf (September 2007); Tearfund (2000). A tearful guide to tourism: Don't forget your ethics. London: Tearfund.

Objectives

On completion of this chapter, the readers should understand

- the importance of consumer behaviour within tourism marketing;
- the major factors influencing consumer behaviour;

- some of the typologies of tourist roles;
- the underlying principles of organizational buying behaviour; and
- some of the trends in consumer behaviour influencing tourism marketing today.

Chapter Overview

The *Spotlight* on travel philanthropy is an excellent example of changing behavioural patterns among tourists — in this case the increasing desire of tourists to give time, talent, and financial resources to further the well-being of the places that they visit. This chapter looks at behavioural trends in tourism and begins by reviewing the factors that influence consumer behaviour. The second part of the chapter focuses on typologies of tourists, and the third section in the chapter examines the external factors that influence consumer behaviour. The fourth section looks at the stages of the buying process, and this is followed by a section devoted to organizational buying behaviour, as tourism marketers need to understand both the decision-making criteria used and the process of decision making that groups and organizations go through in buying tourism services. The final section looks in-depth at some of the trends in consumer behaviour affecting tourism marketing today.

CONSUMER BEHAVIOUR AND TOURISM MARKETING

consumer behaviour analysis

the study of why people buy the products or services they do and how they make decisions

The cornerstone of marketing theory is the satisfaction of the consumer. Therefore, the marketer needs to understand three related aspects of **consumer behaviour analysis**: consumer motivations, consumer typologies, and the consumer purchasing process. Most tourism and hospitality organizations have an imperfect picture of their customer, and few monitor patterns of consumer behaviour at the level of detail necessary to remain competitive. Many organizations consider that they are sufficiently close to their visitors and therefore do not commit resources to more formal consumer studies. Others are constrained by limited marketing budgets and by the fact that researching consumer motivation and the buying process can be a time-consuming and difficult procedure. In fact, most organizations rely almost entirely on the scanning of secondary consumer data, combined with management observation and judgment. However, in a rapidly changing environment, conclusions drawn from secondary data can be out of date in no time. Consumer patterns recorded in 2007, for example, will most likely have changed by 2014, but many companies might still be using this type of information as a benchmark.

FACTORS INFLUENCING CONSUMER BEHAVIOUR

Figure 2.1 shows the seven key factors that influence a consumer's behaviour. Motivation is often seen as a major determinant of consumer behaviour, but cultural, personal, and social influences will also have an important effect on consumer purchases. Each of the influences in Figure 2.1, including motivation, culture, age and gender, social class, lifestyle, life cycle, and reference groups, will be discussed here in turn.

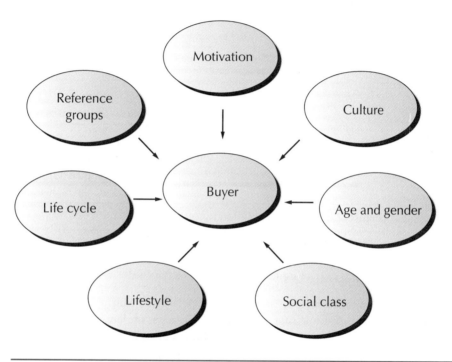

Figure 2.1   Factors Influencing Behaviour

Motivations

motivations

inner drives that cause people to take action to satisfy their needs

needs

the gaps between what people have and what they would like to have, seen as the force that arouses motivated behaviour

Motivations are inner drives that cause people to take action to satisfy their needs. Understanding consumer motivation is one of the most effective ways of gaining competitive differential advantage. Understanding the key triggers that lead to the purchase of a tourism or hospitality product or service, such as a visit to an attraction or a hotel booking, is recognized as one of the main factors in the success of competitive organizations. Central to most content theories of motivation is the concept of need. **Needs** are seen as the forces that arouse motivated behaviour, and it is assumed that, to understand human motivation, it is necessary to discover what needs people have and how they can be fulfilled. Maslow, in 1943, was the first to attempt to do this with his needs hierarchy theory, now the best-known of all motivation theories (see Figure 2.2).

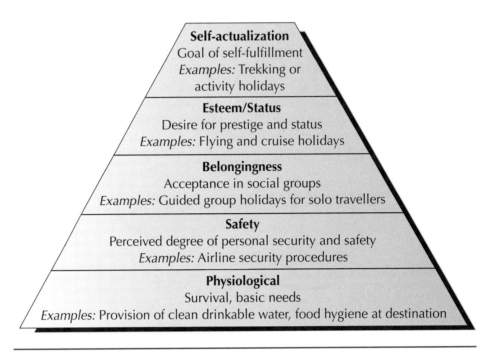

Figure 2.2   Maslow's Hierarchy of Needs

Source: Maslow, A. H. (1943). A theory of human motivation. *Psychological Review, 50,* 370–396.

Maslow's hierarchy of needs

One of the main reasons for the popularity of **Maslow's hierarchy of needs** is its simplicity. Maslow suggested that human needs are arranged in a hierarchy, from the most pressing to the least pressing. In order of importance, these needs are physiological needs, safety needs, social needs, esteem needs, and self-actualization needs. A person tries to satisfy the most important need first. When that need is satisfied, it will stop being a motivator, and the person will then try to satisfy the next most important need. Maslow's theory was originally developed in the context of his work in the field of clinical psychology, but it has become widely influential in many applied areas such as industrial and organizational psychology, counselling, marketing, and tourism.

Other factors that influence motivation and purchase include learning, beliefs and attitudes, and perception. **Learning** refers to the way in which people receive and interpret a variety of stimuli. In the context of tourism, people gain experience through taking holidays, by listening to others, and through a variety of other sources. From these experiences a consumer will develop a mental inventory of expectations about places — a catalogue of good and bad holiday experiences. These form the basis of learned criteria that will be recalled when selecting future holidays and destinations. **Beliefs** refer to the thoughts that people have about most aspects of their life. As far as tourism is concerned, consumers will have beliefs about companies, products, and services, including tourism offerings and destinations. Such thoughts can be positive, such as trust or confidence in a certain hotel or tour guide, or negative, such as a feeling about lack of security on airlines, or fear of injury on the ski slopes. **Attitudes** are more difficult to change, and many organizations have discovered it can be expensive to try to change an attitude. However,

learning

the way in which people receive and interpret a variety of stimuli

beliefs

the thoughts that people have about most aspects of their life

attitudes

ingrained feelings about various factors of an experience

changing attitudes is possible. Many people have a negative attitude toward flying, so airlines have converted non-flyers into flyers by holding special flying educational days for those in fear of flying. Similarly, theme parks hold seminars on combating the fear of roller coaster rides — a session one psychologist described as helping people cope with their "weaker self."[1]

perception

an overall mind-picture of the world, shaped by information that people filter and then retrieve

Finally, **perception** is an overall mind-picture of the world, shaped by information that people filter and then retrieve. Thus, perception is inextricably bound to the concepts of bias and distortion. People choose to interpret different stimuli in different ways, ignoring some factors while enhancing others. This is known as selective perception. People often perceive tourism offerings in a way that compliments their self-image. In this way tourism products and services are viewed as bundles of benefits that are personal to the consumer. It is, however, through the technical factors (which are called "significative stimuli") that the marketer can seek to change perceptions.

perceptual mapping

technique used to identify the relationship between the level of perceived importance of certain aspects of a product or service on the part of the consumer and the actual performance on the part of the supplier

Marketers sometimes use a technique known as **perceptual mapping** to identify the relationship between the level of perceived importance of certain aspects of a product or destination on the part of the consumer and the actual performance on the part of the supplier. Figure 2.3 shows how key long-haul destinations are positioned relative to each other in the minds of Chinese travellers on two dimensions that motivate travel in this market: outdoor adventure and indulging.[2] The perceptual map shows that Canada is solidly positioned on the *Outdoor Adventure* dimension. However, Australia is a major competitive threat, while Switzerland and the U.S. are also fairly well positioned. On the *Indulging* dimension, Canada is out-ranked by all five competitors, with the U.S. being the clear winter on this front, offering the casinos, entertainment and first-class hotels that these travellers seek.

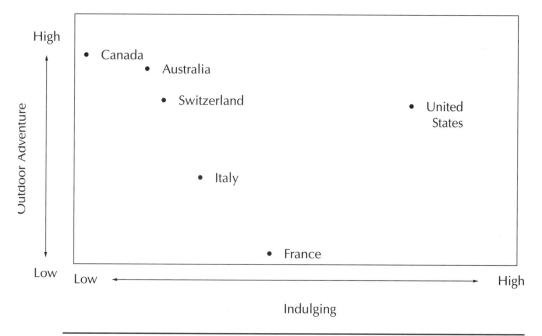

Figure 2.3 Perceptual Map of Competitive Positioning of Key Long-Haul Destinations

Source: Decima Research Inc. (2006, April 24). Consumer and travel trade research in China: Quantitative report. 102. www.tourism.bc.ca/PDF/China%20Consumer%20Research%20(2006).pdf (September 2007).

consumer attitudes

a consumer's enduring favourable or unfavourable cognitive evaluations, emotional feelings, and action tendencies toward some object or idea

Consumer attitudes are a consumer's enduring favourable or unfavourable cognitive evaluations, emotional feelings, and action tendencies toward some object or idea. As these evolve, travel industry organizations must try to stay ahead without venturing too far off course. Some changes are evident years in advance — for example, few failed to anticipate the impact the aging baby boomers would have on the industry. Other changes, however, are unforeseeable. After September 11, 2001, many in the hospitality industry had to adapt strategies quickly to suit customers whose perceptions, needs, and attitudes changed literally overnight. Destinations began to focus more on domestic tourism. Restaurants, too, had to adapt to changing needs. Ed Michalski, president of Management Insight, a hospitality consulting firm, says that "for some, comfort food had a new appeal, while for others, suddenly it seemed the time to try something new and be more adventurous."[3] Michalski also says that people are increasingly demanding high-quality ingredients, service, and presentation, whether they are eating pork chops or prime rib. "There's so much access to information about fine foods, with the popularity of food magazines, the food channel and cooking shows on television, that people are much more knowledgeable than they used to be, and restaurants have to upgrade their products and services."

The *Marketing in Action* is an example of an attraction that has responded to changing attitudes to travel. After September 11, 2001, U.S. tourists began taking shorter vacations and were apprehensive about leaving their home country. Domestic vacation facilities therefore became more attractive. In addition, the desire for spiritual enlightenment on a vacation (see trends later in this chapter) has led to a boom in religious tourism. The Holy Land Experience in Florida has been developed as a response to these changes in consumer behaviour.

MARKETING IN ACTION

MARKETING RELIGION: THE HOLY LAND EXPERIENCE

The Holy Land Experience theme park in Orlando, Florida, is just one of a series of religious entertainments in the United States that bring together the spiritual world and corporeal amusement. Alongside biblical movies such as *The Passion of the Christ* and the new Kentucky-based Creation Museum, both religious tourists and entertainment seekers are being invited to experience religion outside of the more conventional settings of church, mosque, and temple. The park was opened in 2001 to capitalize not only on the tens of millions of tourists who flock to nearby Disney World every year, but also to take advantage of the growing Christian market in the United States. The market for Christian products — including books, movies, and music — is worth $8.5 billion a year, and may be even larger for services.

The emergence of a distinctly Christian market in the U.S. has paralleled a political and cultural coming out. In George W. Bush, Americans had their first born-again president. Bush, who often speaks in overtly religious language, told a group of Conservatives in 2006 that the U.S. was in the midst of a "third awakening" of religious fervour, not unlike the periods 1730–60 and 1800–30. "After 9/11, people are beginning to realize that life isn't just fun and games," says Dan

MARKETING IN ACTION *continued*

Hayden, executive director of the 15-acre theme park. "They are looking for meaning that knowledge of God brings." At Holy Land, the quest for knowledge comes in the form of re-enactments of the crucifixion, plus scale models of Jerusalem, Herod's Temple, and Christ's tomb. The destination now draws more than 200 000 visitors a year. "We thought that if we put flesh and blood on biblical stories, it would be a way to capture the interest of people," Hayden explained.

For the past two decades, Gallup polls in the U.S. have shown that approximately 45 percent of Americans believe that God created humans sometime within the past 10 000 years. The not-for-profit evangelical Christian ministry, Zion's Hope, capitalized on this pool of potential believers by building the $18.4 million theme park in conjunction with ITEC Entertainment in 15 acres of prime real estate near to Universal Studios and Walt Disney World in Orlando. In counterpoint to its rival parks, Holy Land Experience does not offer rides. However, it does provide 100 authentically clad actors recreating biblical episodes in Israel circa 1450 BC to AD 66 in an educational, inspirational, theatrical, and historical environment. Even camel hoofprints are noticeable on dusty Jerusalem streets (although apparently actual camels were considered unnecessary to the staged authenticity).

The Holy Land website (www.holylandexperience.com) says it aims "to demonstrate the living truths of the Bible in innovative ways." Perhaps the visitors contemplate those truths whilst munching on Goliath Burgers and Centurion Salad in the site's many refreshment facilities.

Alongside more frivolous attractions such as Calvary's Garden Tomb, the Qumran Dead Sea Caves, and the Temple of the Great King, the theme park houses a separate $14 million Scriptorium, and a museum and archive for serious religious scholars, with the largest private collection of biblical texts and artifacts in the United States.

With Las Vegas providing the U.S. tourist with mini experiences of Paris, Venice, Egypt, and New York all conveniently along the same street, the Holy Land Experience is doing much the same thing for Christianity by saving tourists the anxieties and expense of foreign pilgrimage. Unlike Vegas, however, the Holy Land Experience does not seem to have targeted its customer very distinctly. Its doors are open to religious scholars, general theme-park fanciers, spiritually lost pilgrims, and anyone who happens to be in Orlando to experience its vacation product range. However, it does cater to children, with a KidVentura area where they can meet biblical characters and scale a rock-climbing wall. One dramatic presentation portrays the biblical account of Jesus greeting the children. The audience's reaction to the actors tends to vary: "Some of the children run and jump into my arms, but others are shy," said Steve Bleiler, a Methodist at the Baptist Church in Orlando, who is one of the cast members who portray Jesus.

Sources: Alford, H. (2005). It's a surreal world after all. *Travel & Leisure*, 111–115; McKenna, B. (2006, September 25). The prophet motive: U.S. faithful form rich market. *Globe & Mail*, B1; Holloway, L. (2006, June 1). Orlando's Holy Land experience theme park offers guests a living museum feel with dramas, exhibits. *Alabama Baptist Online*. www.thealabamabaptist.org/ip_template.asp?upid=10955 (September 2007).

Culture

The second key factor from Figure 2.1 that influences a consumer's behaviour is culture. **Culture** can be defined as the norms, beliefs, and rituals that define a group of people or a way of life. These different factors influence how we live, communicate, and think about

culture

the norms, beliefs, and rituals that define a group of people or a way of life

certain things; culture can also often dictate how a person will act in a certain situation. In terms of self-image and the satisfaction of underlying tensions, most people seek to satisfy their desires in a way that fits into societal norms. For example, today it is acceptable to be a green consumer in tourism, but sex tourism is viewed disparagingly. Awareness of cultural shifts is equally important. Another example is the way smokers are increasingly prohibited from smoking in social places, especially on transport carriers and in restaurants.

A complete and thorough appreciation of the origins (geography, history, political economy, technology, and social institutions) and elements (cultural values, rituals, symbols, beliefs, and ways of thinking) of culture may well be the single most important goal for a marketer in the preparation of international marketing plans and strategies.[4] One of the most accepted theories in cross-cultural and marketing research was developed by Gert Hofstede.[5] He defined culture as "the collective mental programming of the people in an environment," and stated that "culture is not a characteristic of individuals; it encompasses a number of people who were conditioned by the same education and life experience." It was mentioned in the opening chapter of this book that cultural globalization is characterized by cultural homogenization as western consumption and lifestyle patterns spread throughout the world, a process facilitated by the flow of travellers from the West to the developing world. However, it is still critical for tourism marketers to understand the different cultures in the markets in which they operate. For example, Koreans are one of the most homogenous peoples in the world, with few cultural or racial variations and virtually no ethnic minorities among them. In Myanmar, on the other hand, there are an estimated 135 ethnic minority groups with more than 100 languages and dialects spoken in the country.

Other aspects of culture that are appropriate to motivational studies include languages, societal practices, institutions, and subcultures. The transmission of culture is primarily through the spoken and written word, but also through symbolic gestures, including the ways in which people are expected to be greeted by others. Cultural practices include how we divide the day and our attitudes toward opening hours for shops or restaurants. Institutions, such as religious institutions, the media, and educational systems, will affect cultural patterns. Most religions, for example, seek to retain a special day for worship and hence are reluctant to sanction secularization of that particular day of the week, often in opposition to the promoters of tourism. Finally, most societies comprise a number of subcultures that exhibit variations of behaviour as a result of ethnicity or regional differentiation. Canadian culture consists of many diverse subcultures, and these subcultures have distinct lifestyles based on religious, racial, and geographic differences.

Age and Gender

As mentioned in Chapter 3, a traditional way of segmenting markets has been by age. For example, many travel suppliers today are targeting the growing senior market. This market is both lucrative and unique because it is less tied to seasonal travel, involves longer trips, and is not wedded to midweek or weekend travel, so it can boost occupancy rates for business and leisure travel opportunities. For the senior market, too, perceived value is much more important than price. After people retire, they may stay loyal to brand names they know best, but the price points will have to be suitable to a retirement income as well. Disney's recent push to attract visitors in their fifties and sixties to its theme parks is a good indicator that the baby boomer bandwagon is picking up momentum.

In some societies gender can influence consumer behaviour, in terms of societal expectations of the roles men and women should play. Gender segmentation has long been used in marketing clothing, hairdressing, cosmetics, and magazines. But more recently it has been applied to tourism and hospitality products and services. For example, the number of women travelling for work purposes has been growing steadily for decades, and vocal women travellers have influenced the introduction of better-lit parking garages, higher-quality soaps and lotions in hotel bathrooms, and improved room service fare. Travel industry experts say that women travellers are more demanding and discerning than their male counterparts. Their main concerns are safety and security, followed by comfort and convenience.

Social Class

social class

a position in society, determined by such factors as income, wealth, education, occupation, family prestige, value of home, and neighbourhood

Social class is still considered to be one of the most important external factors influencing consumer behaviour. **Social class** is a position in society, and it is determined by such factors as income, wealth, education, occupation, family prestige, value of home, and neighbourhood. Social class is closely linked to the existence of social institutions. The role and status positions found within a society are influenced by the dictates of social institutions. The caste system in India is one such institution. The election of a low-caste person — formally called an "untouchable" — as president in 1995 made international news because it was such a departure from traditional Indian culture. Decades ago, touching or even glancing at an untouchable was considered enough to defile a Hindu of high status. Even though the caste system has been outlawed, it remains a visible part of the culture in India, and it is difficult for people to move out of the class into which they were born.

In the West, it is easier for people to move into social classes that differ from their families'. However, most developed countries still have a class system consisting of upper, middle, and lower classes. In the UK for example, the middle class has been expanding and is forecast to overtake the working class by 2020 as the largest social group. A report published by the Future Foundation in 2006, titled "Middle Britain," found that 43 percent of Britons said they were in the middle class, a figure that is rising.[6] Unfortunately, that does not mean social inequality is on the decline — quite the opposite. By 2000, the gap between rich and poor was the highest it had ever been, and it continues to widen.

Marketers assume that people in one class buy different goods and services and for different reasons than people in other classes. As a rule, the higher the level of disposable income people have, the more likely they are to travel, and premium income earners tend to be those people who have studied at a higher educational level. In Canada, median wealth more than doubled between 1970 and 2005, and has grown by about 20 to 35 percent since 1984 (see Table 2.1). Thus, many Canadian families today are richer than their counterparts 20 or 35 years ago. However, there do exist major inequalities in the wealth structure of the country. In 2005, people in the top 10 percent of the wealth distribution, held 52 percent of household wealth. The *Profile* below shows how the backpacking segment has changed over the years, due to rising income and a higher disposable income among young people.

Table 2.1

Median and average wealth in Canada by age group, 1984–2005

YEAR	1984	1999	2005
Overall			
Median wealth	67 300	74 400	84 800
Average wealth	148 500	202 900	251 700
Under 25			
Median wealth	3 500	200	N/A
Average wealth	37 200	37 900	N/A
Age 25 to 34			
Median wealth	27 000	17 400	13 400
Average wealth	80 500	77 500	71 000
Age 35 to 44			
Median wealth	84 700	69 100	84 200
Average wealth	158 500	175 000	238 300
Age 45 to 54			
Median wealth	142 800	132 700	146 000
Average wealth	233 200	285 400	355 900
Age 55 to 64			
Median wealth	148 700	177 500	203 500
Average wealth	242 300	348 900	409 000
65 and over			
Median wealth	93 100	145 200	157 000
Average wealth	162 100	244 100	301 700

Source: Morissette, R., & Zhang, X. (2006). Revisiting wealth inequality. *Perspectives on Labor and Income,* 7(12). www.statcan.ca/english/freepub/75-001-XIE/11206/art-1.htm (September 2007).

PROFILE

BACKPACKERS WITH GOLD CARDS

Few modern social developments are more significant and less appreciated than the rise of backpacker travel. The tens of thou- sands of young Australians, Germans, Britons, Americans, and others who wander the globe, flitting from Goa to Costa Rica, from Thailand

PROFILE *continued*

to Tasmania, are building what may be the only example of a truly global community. Nobody has an accurate way of guessing the size of the backpacker market, but the growth of the Lonely Planet brand offers an approximation. The first Lonely Planet guidebook was stapled together on an Australian kitchen table in the early 1970s; 30 years later, the company publishes more than 600 destination guides from all over the world.

The backpacking market is a tourism market that doesn't get a lot of attention or coverage in Canada, and one that is not well understood by the industry. However, it appears that young Canadians are catching up with their counterparts from other cultures, such as the British, for whom a "gap year" spent travelling abroad is a rite of passage. Travel agents have noticed a huge increase in new customers willing to ditch the matching luggage and take on the challenges of living out of a backpack. In Canada, the average visiting backpacker spends $3366 during the course of a trip, and travellers who are 33 years old and younger generate about one third of overnight stays in Canadian accommodation properties.

Although the majority of backpackers are still aged between 18 and 25, and use inexpensive, communally oriented accommodations such as hostels, there is evidence that the traditional backpacker profile is changing. John Hughes, a British expatriate who runs a website for backpackers in Asia, says that young people taking breaks in schooling and those seeking temporary employment and learning opportunities abroad have largely replaced the travellers of old who wandered footloose and fancy-free as far and long as their money would take them. And there are some older ones who come back drawn by fond memories of their younger backpacking days. "It seems to me that a lot of backpackers have plastic in their back pockets

whereas they didn't before," says Hughes. "They're better organized and getting more packaged."

Hostel owners are also saying they are seeing a marked increase in the number of backpackers in their thirties and forties. As people marry later, make more money earlier, and switch careers more often, many are tapping into savings to have an extended adventure before going back to the grind. Moreover, companies that value their employees are bowing to their workers' wanderlust by granting travel sabbaticals. Those travel patterns are being catered to by specialized guidebooks that increasingly are giving more expensive options to the more grown-up market. Backpacker destinations are also attracting growing numbers of Koreans, Taiwanese, and Hong Kong citizens, and a vast potential market is seen in China and India. An example of a more sophisticated backpacking package comes from Vietnam. Ho Chi Minh City–based Linh Nam Travel Co. has a 79-day tour of Vietnam with an itinerary of 8000 kilometres through 59 cities and provinces nationwide. The program runs twice a year and tourists can chose to stay at hotels of one to three stars or take a home-stay.

"Flashpackers" is the name often given to those that prefer nice hotels to the backpacker's dormitory. They not only boast an adventurous spirit but also enjoy the safety net of a healthy bank balance when the going gets tough. "The twenty-something flashpacker accounts for around 20 percent of our overall bookings," says Nikki Davies, marketing manager for Trailfinders, a backpacking specialist in the UK. According to Dan Linstead, editor of the adventure travel magazine *Wanderlust*, the advent of the young flashpacker is blurring the distinctions between suitcase and backpacking holidays. "Conventional backpacking territories have broken down," he says. "While travellers are

PROFILE *continued*

still booking independent flights and exploring adventurous locations, they prefer to stay in upmarket hotels." The reason for this, according to Lonstead, is that today's travellers in their twenties are used to far higher standards of living than their predecessors on the original hippy trail. "A flashpacker pays in money rather than time," he says, "condensing what a backpacker spends in a year into a two- or three-week break."

These trends have brought new tensions to the adventure of the backpacker trail. Younger, more traditional backpackers say the sense of community they cherish in hostels is being lost as the richer backpackers use the accommodations only to sleep. "These new backpackers can take away from the communal aspect of what these backpacker hostels started out as," complains Lauren Roberts, manager of Whale House Backpackers in Hout Bay, near Cape Town. Traditional backpackers, she says, use hostels as one-stop

social outlets — inexpensive places to sleep and meet travellers from around the world to share adventures and travelling tips with. But older backpackers often rent cars and flash credit cards to ditch the hostel and fellow tourists for (in this case) camel safaris or white-linen wine-tasting evenings in Cape Town's excellent wine regions. "The double rooms people are building defeat the object of the backpackers: the dorm rooms get people talking to each other," she said. "It's sort of a fight in the industry now. You can lose the whole concept of the hostel."

Sources: Winston, A. (2006, August 13). The flash pack. *Independent on Sunday: The Compact Traveller,* 15; Backpackers lift an economy. (2002, September 25). *Vancouver Sun,* A15; Cousineau, A. (2002, November 2). Backpackers really do have more fun. *Calgary Herald,* TS04; Daley, B. (1999, September 29). Slumming it, with a gold card. *National Post,* B9; Gray, D. (2002, July 27). The new backpacker: Less scruffy and stinky, more moneyed and packaged. *Times-Colonist,* Victoria, D2.

Lifestyle

lifestyle analysis

examination of the way people allocate time, energy, and money

psychographic analysis

measurement of people's activities, interests, and opinions

VALS

a system for grouping consumers into eight categories according to factors such as self-image, aspirations, values and product choices, which drive consumer behaviour

Marketers are increasingly segmenting their markets by consumer lifestyles. **Lifestyle analysis** examines the way people allocate time, energy, and money. It tends to depend heavily on demographic and behavioural traits. Some researchers in marketing have combined demographic, behaviour, and psychological variables into a concept called psychographics. **Psychographic analysis** measures people's psychology, activities, interests, and opinions. By profiling the way groups of people live, it is possible to predict their travel motivations and future purchases. One of the best-known categorizations in this area is **VALS,** formerly known as the Values and Lifestyles program. The VALS framework divides consumers into eight groups: Innovators, Thinkers, Achievers, Experiencers, Believers, Strivers, Makers, and Survivors, as shown in Figure 2.4. Members of each group think and act differently. They have different travel preferences, different hobbies, and different communication styles. The position of a person in the VALS framework depends on the person's primary psychological motivation (ideas, achievement, or self-expression) and level of resources including income, education, self-confidence, health, eagerness to buy, and energy level. The VALS tool can be used to help businesses develop and execute more effective strategies. For example, a cruise company in the U.S. used VALS to identify and understand consumers most interested in its specialized tours. By designing direct mail marketing materials to appeal to targeted consumers and mailing to key zip codes, the cruise line increased reservations by 400 percent.

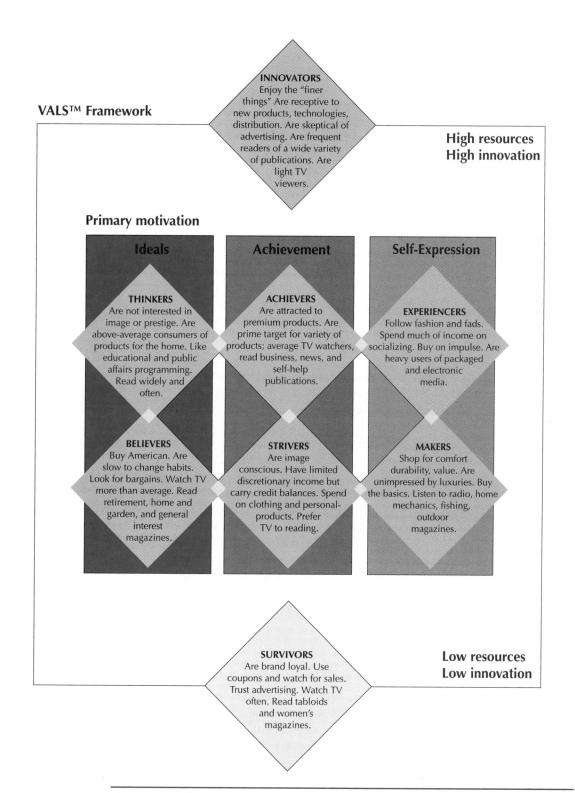

Figure 2.4 The VALS Typology Framework

Source: SRI Consulting Business Intelligence. (2007). www.sric-bi.com/VALS (September 2007).

Life Cycle

family life cycle

the stages through which families pass from marriage through children to retirement years

life cycle model

a model that predicts changes in travel patterns and destinations as people move through their life cycle

The concept of the **family life cycle** — the stages through which families pass from marriage through children to retirement years — is based on the premise that when people live together, their way of life changes. Single people are likely to behave differently from couples, and if couples subsequently have children, their lifestyle changes more radically, as does their level of financial and other commitments. Many authors have applied the **life cycle model** to tourism, suggesting that travel patterns and destinations vary as people move through their life cycle.[7] The model works well when investigating the traditional nuclear family composed of two parents and one or more children. It does not, however, purport to represent the increasing proportion of households that do not fall into this pattern, such as single-parent families, extended family networks, and those who remain single throughout their life. Tourists may also change their behaviour patterns over time, so if the life cycle model is used to predict behaviour, then trends in consumer behaviour need to be monitored. For example, the *Profile* on backpackers showed that this segment is no longer made up of young people aged between 18 and 25. They have been joined by an older, and wealthier, segment of backpackers who are changing the structure of the backpacker market.

Reference Groups

reference groups

groups that have a direct (face-to-face) or indirect influence on a person's attitude or behaviour

Learning also takes place through sharing values and expectations with others in a variety of social **reference groups**, including the family, college or university, workplace, or place of worship. This brings exposure to a normative set of values, i.e., those prescribe how we should behave morally in society. For example, experienced travellers, who have been exposed to other cultures and to people who are less fortunate than they, are influencing a new trend of volunteer tourism (see *Spotlight*). The United Nations World Tourism Organization (UNWTO) has noticed that there is "an increasing tendency among contemporary travel consumers to view travel as a means for enhancing the quality of their own lives by building on a philosophy of doing well while doing something good for society."[8] The UNWTO and other tourism organizations that monitor trends in the travel industry say it is precisely the growing number of well-heeled, well-educated older travellers — people who are indeed concerned with "doing something good for society" — that has been driving the demand for such developing niche markets as educational tourism, ecotours, agritourism, and cultural tourism. Travellers can take a "volunteer vacation" and give their time and expertise to help in projects in developing countries. These trips are not free, but they often cost less than conventional tours.

TYPOLOGIES OF TOURISTS

venturers (allocentrics)

travellers who prefer exotic destinations and unstructured vacations, with more involvement with local cultures, rather than packaged tours

The discussion so far has been about the variables that influence tourist behaviour. But many researchers have tried to explain tourist behaviour by developing typologies of tourists who carry out various roles. The tourist motivation model proposed by Stanley Plog is one of the most widely cited typologies of tourists.[9] According to Plog, travellers may be classified as venturers or dependables, formerly referred to as allocentrics or psychocentrics respectively. Those who are **venturers** or **allocentrics** are thought to prefer

dependables (psychocentrics)

travellers who prefer familiar destinations, packaged tours, and "touristy" areas

exotic destinations, unstructured vacations, with more involvement with local cultures, rather than packaged tours. **Dependables** or **psychocentrics**, on the other hand, are thought to prefer familiar destinations, packaged tours, and "touristy" areas. Figure 2.5 presents a visual picture of the old and new concepts, as applied to a normal population curve. Plog found that the majority of the population was neither venturer nor dependable, but "mid-centric" — somewhere in the middle. It has been argued, however, that Plog's theory is difficult to apply, as tourists will travel with different motivations on different occasions. There are many holidaymakers who will take a winter skiing break in a venturer destination, but will then take their main holiday in a dependable destination.

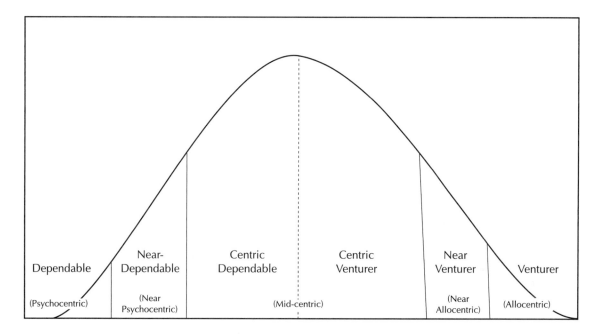

Figure 2.5 Plog's Psychographic Personality Types

Sources: Plog, S.C. (1974). Why destination areas rise and fall in popularity. *Cornell Hotel & Restaurant Quarterly*, 14(4), 55–58; Plog, S.C. (2002). The power of psychographics and the concept of venturesomeness. *Journal of Travel Research*, 40, 244–251.

In addition to Plog, other researchers have tried to explain tourist recreational behaviour by developing typologies of tourist roles. Most are based on empirical data obtained from questionnaires or personal interviews. Cohen's typology — one of the first — proposed four classifications of tourists: 1) the organized mass tourist, highly dependent on the "environmental bubble," purchasing all-inclusive tours or package holidays; 2) the individual mass tourist, who is more autonomous and free than those in the previous group; 3) the explorer, who seeks new areas but would sometimes opt to step back into comfortable accommodation, etc.; and 4) the drifter, who avoids any kind of "tourist establishment."[10] The accompanying *Snapshot* on Adventurer Annie takes a tongue-in-cheek look at the typology of modern-day "explorer."

SNAPSHOT

ADVENTURER ANNIE

Adventurer Annie gets around. In the last few years she's been heli-skiing in the Rockies, watched killer whales of the coast of British Columbia, climbed Everest, kayaked around Greenland, bungee-jumped in Queenstown, and been on a "Survivor Tour" in Thailand. In between, she is busy making big bucks in the city, trading stocks, and planning her trips. Next year she is off on a wildlife safari in Tanzania, hiking up Kilimanjaro, and rafting down the Zambezi. But Annie doesn't do any of this on a budget, and wouldn't compromise on comfort. Annie is part of a new breed of adventure tourists that many in the outdoor recreation business are referring to as "Bobos": bourgeois bohemians. They are looking for an escape to nature from their stressed-out urban lives, but they want the experience without the hassle of hauling a lot of gear into the backcountry, sleeping on lumpy ground, or hunting for kindling to cook smoky, second-rate meals.

So who is Annie? She's 45 years old and hence classified as a baby boomer. She is fit, is well educated, and is interested in novelty, escape, and authentic experiences. These days, she and her friends are opting for more physically challenging and "adrenalin-driven" activities. She is also rich monetarily but poor in time, and so wants to squeeze as much experience into as short a time as possible. What makes Annie tick? She is certainly motivated by the thrill and challenge of learning, and by the experience of nature and the environment. She is also health conscious and has realized that her travel experiences are a terrific stress reliever and make her more productive at work. However, she is also motivated by the physical and symbolic capital she can accumulate by purchasing these adventure tourism holidays.

She holds regular dinner parties in between her trips to let all her friends and family know where she has been and where she is going next. In return for being fed, guests have to gaze with awe and murmur appreciatively as Annie serves up a slide show for a main course and a portfolio of digital photos for dessert. Occasionally Annie gets too busy at work to get away for an adventure experience. Fortunately there is a new "dirt spray" on the market that she can use to discolour her SUV. She wouldn't want friends thinking she was becoming a suburban bore.

Adventure tourism is one of the fastest-growing segments of the tourism industry (growing 10–15 percent annually) and it is the experiential engagement that makes adventure tourism distinctive from other types of tourism. In the past, adventure was associated with uncertainty of outcome and any outdoor recreation undertaking that was *planned* could not be an adventure. Yet today this is precisely how adventure tourism is marketed. There exists, therefore, something of a paradox whereby the more detailed, planned, and logistically smooth an adventure tourist itinerary becomes, the more removed the experience is from the notion of adventure. Much as Annie would like to think she is engaging in a dangerous, unplanned adventure, in reality she is so dependent on her guides that if she was left to her own devices, she would kill herself within an hour!

As for the future, it is likely that Annie will continue her adventure tourism activities but will go from being a Bobo to a GRAMPIE, that is, people who are "growing, retired, and moneyed, in good physical and emotional health." It is estimated that by 2040 more than half the population in the developed world will be over 50. This means there will be more people in good health with a more informed global perspective — more GRAMPIES — thus more adventure tourists. The only change for Annie will be that her adventures will be softer, and she will be supported by an increasing number of massage therapists, chiropractors, and physiotherapists.

THE BUYING PROCESS

Before discussing the buying process, it is important to recognize that various buying situations influence this process. First of all, consumers likely display various levels of commitment, depending on the nature of the purchase. It has been suggested that there are three such levels.[11] These are:

1. **Extended problem solving**. In a situation such as the decision to take a long-haul holiday, the consumer is likely to have a deep level of commitment, to make a detailed search for information, and to make an extensive comparison of the alternatives.
2. **Limited problem solving**. The consumer has some degree of knowledge or experience already, but many factors are taken for granted and the information search is far more limited. A second holiday at a favourite skiing destination may be purchased in this way.
3. **Habitual problem solving**. This is a repeat purchase of a tried and tested short break or day excursion, which requires little or no evaluation. The decision is made primarily on the basis of a previous satisfactory experience and a good understanding of the destination or brand name of the tourism or hospitality offering.

Role adoption will also influence the buying process, and it is proposed that there are five roles.[12] They are:

1. **Initiator**: the person who starts the purchasing process and who gathers information;
2. **Influencer**: a person or persons who express preferences in choice or selection of information — this can be a group of friends, relatives, or a partner;
3. **Decider**: the person who has the financial control and possibly the authority within a group of people to make the purchase;
4. **Buyer**: the person who actually makes the purchase, visits the travel agent, and obtains the tickets, etc.; and
5. **User**: the person or persons who consume the purchase and actually go on the trip.

The consumer buying process for tourism is often regarded as being similar to that involved in the purchase of other products and services. The assumption is that a consumer moves through a number of stages leading up to a purchase. Figure 2.6 outlines these stages.

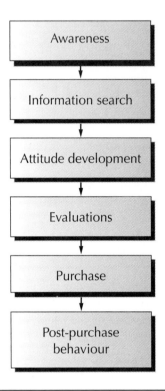

Figure 2.6   The Consumer Buying Process

The process begins with *awareness*, a stage that may be initiated by promotional efforts, by word of mouth, or by an informational search such as an online search. According to CanadaTravel.ca, most Canadians are unaware of the broad range of products and services offered in Canadian communities. This Internet company helps solve this problem by providing domestic and global consumers with a complete range of information and booking services for participating Canadian communities and local tourism businesses. CanadaTravel.ca sends regular newsletters that provide a variety of information on festivals, events, and getaways to more 60 000 consumers.

The next stage in the buying process involves the buyer *searching for more information*, and, as suggested previously, there are likely to be various levels of commitment depending on the nature of the purchase. Recent surveys show that the Internet plays a major role when Canadians research and book travel (see Chapter 10). This information search will result in the *development of an attitude,* perhaps reinforcing an existing attitude or bringing about a change on the part of the buyer. At the *evaluation* stage, the buyer will make more detailed comparisons. For example, a consumer may consider a number of destinations and will choose based on choice criteria such as price, recommendation, convenience, and convention. Many Canadians prefer to travel within Canada's borders, but a third of Canadian travellers are taking more exotic excursions to destinations such as the Caribbean, Mexico, Europe, South America, and Asia. Subject to time and financial constraints, the consumer will then make the *purchase*. The majority of travellers prefer to book their vacations months in advance, but an increasing number of consumers are booking their trips on the spur of the moment, facilitated by the growth of the Internet.

The purchase is followed by the final stage of the buying process, *post-purchase behaviour*. If the experience is satisfactory, the buyer may purchase the same type of holiday in the future. Often the importance of this stage is underestimated, but several studies have examined the association between service quality and more specific behavioural intentions, and there is a positive and significant relationship between customers' perceptions of quality and their willingness to recommend the organization or destination to others.[13]

ORGANIZATIONAL BUYER BEHAVIOUR

Decision Making for Organizations

Tourism marketers need to understand both the decision criteria used and the decision-making process undergone by groups and organizations in buying tourism services. The process is likely to be quite different for group buyers; for instance, there can be many individuals or groups involved in making decisions for the conference market. These players include the users, influencers, deciders, and buyers. It has been argued that in order to close a sale within the business-to-business market, the supplier must identify and satisfy all stakeholders in the decision-making unit and treat each accordingly.

A marketer will also need to understand the buying phases for organizations. The conference market, for example, follows a pattern of group decision making, and the "buy phase" has been described as follows: problem recognition, general need description, product specification, supplier search, proposal solution, supplier selection, order routine specification, and performance review.[14] These buy phases sometimes take a long period of time, depending on the size of the conference or the complexity of arrangements, with lead times of two or three years in some instances and longer ones for mega events such as the World Cup soccer tournament.

The process is also affected by the nature of the purchase, as it can be a new purchase, a modified re-buy, or a straight re-buy. A new purchase involves a high degree of risk, as the client is buying a facility or service for the first time. A modified re-buy is less risky, as the client has bought a service offering before, perhaps at another hotel or conference centre within the group, but now seeks to modify the purchase. This might mean a new venue or new specifications for service levels. The straight re-buy is the least risky purchase situation, as it involves, for example, reordering a service at the same venue.

Having identified the key decision makers and phases in the purchase process, the marketer must then establish which criteria the decision makers use to differentiate between suppliers. Frederick Webster and Yoram Wind suggest that four main factors influence the decision-making criteria of organizational buyers: environmental, organizational, interpersonal, and individual.[15] These factors are constantly changing, so it is essential to re-evaluate market trends frequently.

The Behaviour of Business Travellers

The behaviour of business travellers is significantly different than that of leisure travellers. In fact, according to experts, executives do not see travel as a perk but rather as another source of stress.[16] Executives feel that they have no proper balance between home life and work life, and that it causes problems in their relationships with partners and children. And it is not just the business traveller who suffers. One study found that people whose spouses travel frequently on business suffer more mental health problems than those whose partners remain at home.[17] Short, frequent trips away from home have a worse effect on people than longer, less frequent trips. The study recommended that workers travel no more than 90 days a year and that companies allow employees to decline making too many trips; it also suggested videoconferencing and flexible work arrangements as substitutes for travel. Unfortunately, few businesses pay attention to the damaging effect travel can have on their employees. The paradox is that travel costs the company money, and much business travel has been made redundant by modern communication technologies such as telephone conferencing and videoconferencing.

Airlines spend a lot of time and money trying to understand the needs of their business travellers. As the demographic gets wider for this group (as it has been doing for the last decade), zeroing in on which services and programs would most appeal is becoming more difficult. The group is not necessarily unified in terms of age or tastes, or in terms of what its members want to do or have when they fly. Whether a flight is inbound for business or outbound for home makes a difference in what a customer expects from an airline, and the key for airlines is to offer their customers the ability to work or play. Work-related technology — laptop power plugs and in-air phones — are obligatory for any airline interested in attracting the business traveller. For passengers' downtime, not much has changed: movies, food, and drink remain required staples. The selection in the last category has become much broader, due in part to the fact that 30 to 40 percent of frequent business passengers are women, and women don't always want a beer or a soft drink. One factor that is consistent among all passengers, however, is the need for space, and airlines are always looking for ways to increase personal space for passengers. Space is an equally important service consideration on the ground. It is standard to isolate first or business class passengers from those flying economy with special lounges and facilities devoted to their needs. Computer access, boardrooms, and entertainment centres are now standard requirements.

GLOBAL TRENDS IN CONSUMER BEHAVIOUR

As mentioned in Chapter 1, many major cultural trends affect the tourism industry, and the final section of Chapter 2 focuses on ten key trends (Table 2.2) or demands in consumer behaviour that are influencing tourism and hospitality marketing today.

Table 2.2

Key Consumer Behaviour Trends Affecting Marketing

Learning and enrichment travel	Convenience and speed
Ethical products	The unpredictable
Nostalgia	Spiritual enlightenment
Health consciousness	Service quality
Customization	Experiences

Learning and Enrichment

One of the major trends in tourism today is the desire of the tourist to have a learning experience as a part of the vacation. Educational travel has boomed over the past few decades. A recent survey found that half of North American travellers want to visit art, architectural, or historic sites on vacations, while one-third would like to learn a new skill or activity. Of course, the idea for self-improvement is nothing new. Young gentlemen of the 18th and 19th centuries who set out on the Grand Tour were looking for a dose of classical culture spiced with some pleasant debauchery as part of the package. But putting the label "educational" on vacation trips is becoming increasingly popular these days.

Today's travellers are seeking experiences that provide them with a greater insight, increased understanding, and a personal connection to the people and places they visit. Rather than choose their vacation by the destination, many are first determining the experiences they want, and then choosing the destination where these experiences are located. **Learning and enrichment travel** refers to vacations that provide opportunities for authentic, hands-on, or interactive learning experiences, featuring themes such as adventure, agriculture, anthropology, archeology, arts, culture, cuisine, education, forestry, gardening, language, maritime culture, mining, nature, science, spirituality, sports, wine, and wildlife — to name only a few!

An example of an attraction in Canada that is capitalizing on new consumer demand for enrichment and learning is "Dynamic Earth," in Sudbury, Ontario. The $14.35 million interpretive facility opened in 2003 on the former Big Nickel Mine site. The attraction offers an authentic northern experience, providing visitors with the opportunity to experience the unique geology and rich mining heritage of this northern Ontario city (see Figure 2.7). Interactive exhibits, multimedia theatre shows, and a unique site interpretation enable visitors to discover the geology of the Sudbury Basin and the strong connection between the

learning and enrichment travel

vacations that provide opportunities for authentic, hands-on, or interactive learning experiences mines and the community over the past 100 years. In addition to the high-tech displays, visitors hear real-life stories, told by real miners, about the difficulties early miners were forced to face and overcome. Through the tales of various other characters, visitors also learn how historical events have shaped the Sudbury community and have brought about some of the activities happening in the region today.

Figure 2.7   Example of an Enrichment and Learning Attraction

The Canadian Experience Travel Network, a national Canadian travel alliance representing members from a variety of tourism businesses in Canada, has created a business-to-business website (www.cetn.ca) that allows the user to easily find these segmented experiences as well as vacations incorporating multiple experiences in Canada. This website can be used to match vacation experiences with the interests of the user. Members of the travel trade and the media can research experiences in Canada by theme, season, supplier name, and destination. The site offers a free service to members of these two sectors who are interested in using the site for researching, generating story ideas, developing products, locating experiences by theme, finding an organization name or destination, accessing helpful information, sourcing prepackaged learning vacations, and accessing resources to assist in planning vacations for their clients. The *Case Study* on A Semester at Sea at the end of this chapter provides a closer look at a unique educational experience.

Ethical Products

social marketing

the use of marketing programs and marketing communication tools for the good of society

In the last few decades, responsible tourism has emerged as a significant trend in the western world, as wider consumer market trends in lifestyle marketing and ethical consumption have spread to tourism. Tourism organizations are beginning to realize that promoting their ethical stance can be good business as it potentially enhances a company's profits, management effectiveness, public image, and employee relations. **Social marketing** refers to the use of marketing programs and marketing communication tools for the good of society, and the

Spotlight at the beginning of the chapter mentioned responsibletravel.com, a UK company that promotes such a social marketing philosophy. In a recent survey, 26 percent of people aged 33 to 44 said they increasingly used their purchasing power to reward ethically, socially, and environmentally aware companies.[18] International leisure travellers are increasingly motivated to select a destination for the state of its environment and the diversity and integrity of its natural and cultural resources. Studies of German and U.S. travel markets indicate that environmental considerations are now a significant aspect of travellers' destination-choosing process, down to — in the case of the Germans — the environmental protection programs operated by individual hotels. It has also been suggested that 40 percent of Canadians consider the environmental track record of both holiday company and destination when booking a holiday. Certainly in the United States, the growth in special-interest, nature-oriented travel reflects an increasing concern for the environment. A recent study also showed that approximately 80 percent of American travellers believe it is important that hotels take steps to preserve and protect the environment. According to the study, 70 percent are willing to pay as much as $170 more for a two-week stay in a hotel that has a "responsible environmental attitude," and 55 percent are more likely to book a hotel that purports to be environmentally friendly.[19]

Even restaurants are taking the green route. Chanterelle Country Inn, on the Cabot Trail in Cape Breton, Nova Scotia, Canada offers a "green environment" and "Cape Breton fresh" cuisine. Besides recycling and precycling, the inn uses only organic and fragrance-free facial, bath, and laundry soaps, as well as cleaning products; linens and bedding of natural fibres; and solar power for water and space heating. Its water comes from a deep well fed by a spring. All dishes are prepared in the restaurant's own kitchens, using organic and locally produced ingredients. Its dining room also stocks organically grown wines.

Nostalgia

According to author Charles Leadbeater, we are in the middle of a nostalgia boom. The more rapidly people are propelled into an uncertain future, the more they yearn for the imagined security of the past. Not only have tourists become more interested in history, but the scale, richness, and diversity of the history they are interested in has also expanded enormously in the past 30 years. According to Leadbeater, Internet-linked, digital television–watching, brand-conscious, globally connected societies are in the middle of a nostalgia boom. "Globalization promotes a yearning for local roots and identities. Our immersion in the digital and virtual world creates a demand for tactile and tangible skills at home: cooking, gardening, and decorating. The growth of individualism makes us yearn for a time when we imagined that we lived in real communities, with a sense of shared memory and moral commitment," says Leadbeater.[20]

The outcome is an increase in nostalgia tourism, and the accompanying *Snapshot* shows how one nostalgia tourism attractions — Pier 21 in Halifax — is capitalizing on this trend.

SNAPSHOT

PIER 21 AND NOSTALGIA TOURISM

From films to music, from cars to architecture, we are using new technology to return us to the past, to deliver better versions of old experiences. Not only have we become more interested in history, but the scale, richness, and diversity of the history we are interested in have also expanded enormously in the past 30 years. Nostalgia tourism allows people to revisit the past, enabling them to come to terms with tragic historical events in order to put them into perspective, obtain closure, as well as keep good memories alive. One examples of a nostalgia tourism attraction is Pier 21 in Halifax, Nova Scotia.

A National Historic Site, Pier 21 is a unique tourism facility that offers the visitor the opportunity to understand the difficult early immigration process that many people had to withstand. Winner of a national award for Best New Attraction in 2001, Pier 21 operates as a learning facility and an informational and experiential tourism destination. It presents an experience that no other destination in Canada can provide: an in-depth look at what more than one million people went through to make a new life in a new country. It also provides a place to honour the members of Canada's armed forces who served in World War II.

First operational in 1928, Pier 21 was the gateway to Canada for more than one million immigrants until its closure in 1971. Ships would arrive, and immigrants would begin the final process leading to their new lives in Canada. As many as 250 people would disembark at a time and be led to the Assembly Room. From there, they filed into the Examination Room for a medical exam and an immigration interview. If successful, the immigrants could take trains to their final destination. During World War II, Pier 21 also operated as the departure point for the troops who sailed to Europe to engage in battle. Today, the Wall of Service, located on the World War II Deck, stands as a tribute to the sacrifices made by members of the Canadian military to ensure the freedom enjoyed by many nations.

Today, Pier 21 operates as a nonprofit society and offers a variety of services to special interest groups, visitors, and the local community. Pier 21 also has a comprehensive educational program that it offers to schools to give children the opportunity to gain first-hand knowledge of what it may have been like to be an early immigrant coming to Canada.

In March 2003, on the day of Pier 21's 75th anniversary, the Pier 21 Society announced a five-year strategic vision for a transformed museum. The objective of the vision was to expand Pier 21's existing immigration span of 1928–1971 to an all-inclusive heritage program. The future model will connect with most of Canadian society, instead of relating only to the 20 percent of Canadians who have a personal connection to the present Pier 21. The new plan was announced in Montreal at a fundraising gala dinner, "Footprints on the Pier." "The future Pier 21 will

SPOTLIGHT *continued*

speak to contemporary Canadians, reaching further than the immigrants during the Pier 21 era," says Pier 21 CEO Robert Moody. "There is a wonderful opportunity for Pier 21 to become Canada's national immigration heritage centre. Over the next five years, Pier 21 will evolve to tell the story of all immigrants to Canada; from the time of first contact with our First Nations people to present-day immigration, Pier 21 will celebrate how all our people have contributed to the building of our country. It will celebrate Canada's cultural diversity," says Sherry Porter, chair of the Pier 21 Society.

Sources: Leadbeater, C. (2002). Longing for the way we were. *Financial Times Weekend*, July 6–7, IV; Lowrie, M. (1998); Pier 21 promotional printed material; Pier 21 Education Kit; Pier 21. (2007). www.pier21.ca (September 2007).

Health Consciousness

The increased concern about health in today's society is often attributed to the influence of the baby boomer. Ian Patterson has examined the demographic characteristics of baby boomers and their growing interest in active tourism as they age.[21] Baby boomers are generally healthier, financially better off, better educated, and more interested in novelty, escape, and authentic experiences than were previous cohorts of older people. Many baby boomers and senior adult groups are consequently opting for more physically challenging and "adrenalin-driven" activities. The demographics of the baby-boom bulge are also having an impact on the health and wellness industry. Health and wellness centres are springing up in many tourism destinations, and spa tourism is seeing significant growth. The 2006 Canadian Spa Sector profile indicated that 29 percent of all spa visits to Canadian spas in 2005 were from people outside the spa's local market. The Canadian Tourism Commission (CTC) also suggests that 33 percent of Canada's leisure travellers plan their international, regional, and local vacations around access to spas.

Tourists are also looking to eat healthier foods on vacation. Marriott International, the world's largest hotel company, recently announced that it was going to eliminate trans fats from the cooking oil used by its restaurants at more than 2300 hotels in the U.S. and Canada. The hotel operator joins a growing number of fast food chains to drop the artery-clogging substance. Even brewers are catering for the more health-conscious consumer. In 2005, Scottish & Newcastle, which makes Foster's and Kronenbourg lagers, became the first brewer in the world to put general health warnings on beer bottles. The company said the initiative, similar to health warnings on cigarette packets, was just a part of being a responsible company, whereas critics argue that it was introducing the warnings as a way of avoiding potential lawsuits that could blame drink companies for health problems.[22] Either way, the move is responding to growing consumer pressures for a healthier lifestyle and for socially responsible companies, as mentioned previously.

Customization

Requests for customized and personalized vacations are also rising sharply, and both agents and traditional tour operators are changing their businesses to meet that demand. In addition to booking air and hotel reservations, agents and outfitters today are arranging customized wine tastings, visits to artisan workshops, and private after-hour tours of the British Crown jewels and the Vatican. Even at companies such as Butterfield & Robinson and Abercrombie & Kent — both of which have been primarily associated with pre-arranged tours — requests for customized trips are increasing. Kristina Rundquist, spokesperson for the American Society of Travel Agents, says that there are two parallel trends now: people who want personalized service and those who want highly specialized trips: "Many tourists have precious little time for vacations, so they like to make sure they get exactly what they want, whether it's a boutique hotel or a special kind of restaurant. They need someone who will listen and cater to their needs."[23]

An example of such customization can be found in Jamaica. During a stint as guest relations manager with the Holiday Inn in Montego Bay, Diana McIntyre-Pike (only 21 years old at the time) noticed there was nothing of the real Jamaica to be found at the hotel. "Even the so-called 'native show' had nothing to do with us. It was limbo dancing and fire dancing," she says. After studying hotel management in Germany, Diana returned to Jamaica and, in 1997, launched the Countrystyle Institute. She had two goals: to give visitors a real experience of Jamaican life and to get tourism dollars to areas where unemployment rates are high. Her seven-day all-inclusive tours cost about $1800, including airfare, food, accommodation, and entertainment. She customizes her vacations for her clients, depending on whether they have an interest in cooking, playing cricket, or golfing. Guest speakers visit to tell groups about the local economy, politics, and food. "What was drawing people to the Sandals and the SuperClubs was that they could pay one rate and get an experience," she says. "Now I'm offering the same thing but with a chance to see the real Jamaica."[24]

A Canadian travel company that has always been customer driven, with its "personal touch philosophy," is Nahanni Wilderness Adventures (NWA). Owned and managed by outfitters David and Wendy Hubbard, NWA has been operating river tours on the Nahanni River for more than 40 years. NWA has a wide range of trip packages and fashions each trip according to customer experience, type of activity, and time and price constraints. Despite the high level of variety, NWA also advertises private trips to "customize your dream adventure." Such trips could include a family vacation or a do-it-yourself package for which the company will rent out equipment and help arrange charter flights. "From the start, customizing trips has been our specialty," says David Hubbard.

Convenience and Speed

The increasing desire for convenience and speed is having its greatest impact on the restaurant sector in Canada. According to NPD Group Canada, drive-through sales are on the rise across the service restaurant category.[25] Since NPD began tracking these restaurants in 1994, drive-through sales have risen by a remarkable 250 percent. Other tourism sectors have been affected by this trend for convenience and speed. In transportation, self–check-in terminals are increasingly popular, and in accommodation, business travellers are seeking convenient rooms for shorter stays. An example of the latter is the new hotel concept introduced recently at Heathrow and Gatwick airports in the UK. Owing much to Japanese "capsule hotels," Yotel cabins are a cross between a hotel and a first-class airline seat. Each self-contained cabin has a double bed, and facilities include an ensuite bathroom with shower, a flat-screen television, and a pull-down desk. The first phase of cabins cost about £80 for an overnight stay, with the option of paying less for shorter periods, offering travellers the opportunity to stretch out and freshen up even on a short stopover. The company has plans to extend the concept into central London to compete with similar accommodation concepts such as Stelios Haji-Ioannou's easyHotel.

Theme parks are also responding to the desire for convenience and speed. At both Universal's Orlando theme parks (Islands of Adventure and Universal Studios), visitors can get priority access to all rides and attractions at no extra cost. In front of each attraction is a Universal Express Kiosk with a computer touch screen. Guests insert their park ticket or pass and choose from a selection of times to return later in the day. The distribution centre prints out a Universal Express Pass with the attraction name and return time, and guest can use this later to proceed directly inside, bypassing the regular lineups. The Universal Express Plus program, as it is called, allows customers to create their own schedule and maximize their Universal Orlando experience with shorter wait times at the attractions.

The Unpredictable

An increasing number of tourists are seeking experiences that have a sense of unpredictability. For example, during the October 2004 earthquake activity at Mount St. Helens, Washington captured worldwide attention as the volcano came back to life, spewing clouds of steam and ash. Thousands of tourists travelled to the area, determined to catch a close-up glimpse of North America's most active volcano. Local hotels, restaurants, and souvenir shops all enjoyed brisk business from the onslaught of tourists and the media. One expedition outfit offered helicopter rides over the volcano for $115 per person. Similarly, in Canada in 2003, firefighters battling British Columbia's forest fires said "fire tourists" in Kelowna made it increasingly difficult for firefighters to do their job. Tourists were travelling to suburbs to view the 200 homes destroyed by the fires and venturing into the woods to see the still-raging fires firsthand.[26]

Tour operators are beginning to cater to this new type of tourist. LIVE Travel in the UK specializes in tours to "inaccessible" or "obscure" countries. In 1997 Philip Haines became the youngest person to have visited all 193 sovereign countries in the world. He now offers packages to Iraq, Afghanistan, Iran, Vietnam, Cambodia, Bali, East Timor, Bolivia, and more. The company even had a trip to see the aftermath of Hurricane Katrina. Many of the destinations on LIVE's itinerary have strict warnings issued by the U.S. State Department against non-essential travel. At EcoAlberto Park in Mexico, visitors pay the equivalent of £8 to simulate an illegal journey across the U.S.-Mexico border.[27] The park, funded in part by the Mexican government, compares crossing the border to an "extreme sport" and tells participants that they, too, can "trick the *migra*," slang for the Border Control. Visitors are bounced around in the back of pickups racing along rock-strewn roads at high speeds and, as they crawl through tunnels, sirens blare and men dressed as Border Patrol agents pursue them. Some have criticized the organizers for profiting from an illegal and dangerous activity. Every year, some 500 000 Mexicans cross illegally into the U.S., a journey that has claimed more than 2000 lives over the past decade.

Spiritual Enlightenment

The desire for spiritual enlightenment on a vacation has led to a boom in religious tourism (see *Marketing in Action* on the Holy Land Experience). The Travel Industry Association of America (TIAC) says that one quarter of travellers in North America are interested in taking a spiritual vacation, and that the appeal of a spiritual vacation spans all age groups. In response to this demand for faith-based vacations, an increasing number of tourism companies are entering or expanding their presence within the $21 billion religious travel industry. Two of the most recognized faith-based travel authorities, Kevin J. Wright (president of the Religious Marketing Consulting Group) and Honnie Korngold (president of Christian Travel Finder), have launched the World Religious Travel Association, which is "the primary organization dedicated to leading, enriching, and expanding the global religious travel industry." With an initial focus on the North American religious market, the association plans to expand throughout the world as emerging religious markets mature and consumer demand increases.

Even monks are cashing in on this growing trend. Monasteries and temples provide the perfect backdrop for peaceful periods of mediation, prayer, and reflection for world-weary men and women. Often set in beautiful scenery, more religious institutions are jumping on the tourism bandwagon and opening their facilities for one to three day stays. Southern Koreans, for example, have approximately 36 different Buddhist temples to choose from for their retreats from everyday life. While the food can be very basic (vegetarian and lots of rice gruel), the peace and tranquility are priceless. Haein Temple, a World Heritage site, is in the idyllic Kaya Mountains and offers two-day stays for approximately $70 per night. Tourists have to don monkish robes, pray and meditate with the real monks, eat together, and even have lessons in calligraphy before an early bedtime of 9:30 pm. Wakeup call each day is 3:30 am and the day kicks off with an hour of silent meditation. Guests enjoy tours around the beautiful grounds and the hermitages after breakfast.

The notion of combining religion and tourism is also gaining momentum in other countries, notably Japan, where the Wakayama region is attracting day trippers from Kyoto and Nara. Visitors can also stay overnight in rooms ranging from simple to luxurious. With views of the Pacific from ancient forest trails, by day tourists learn about Shinto and Buddhist theory. By night, guests can enjoy sake and beer along with the vegetarian meals served by the monks. In Utah, Trappist-Cistercian monks are offering up to three-day trips for men at their Huntsville Monastery. Women are allowed to stay in the guest house if it's available. The Catholic monks lead prayer, reading, and hiking and there is also counselling available.

Service Quality

Service quality has been increasingly identified as a key factor in differentiating service products and building a competitive advantage in tourism. The process by which customers evaluate a purchase, thereby determining satisfaction and likelihood of repurchase, is important to all marketers, but especially to services marketers because, unlike their manufacturing counterparts, they have fewer objective measures of quality by which to judge their production. Many researchers believe that an outgrowth of service quality is customer satisfaction. Satisfying customers has always been a key component of the tourism industry, but never before has it been so critical. With increased competition, and with more discerning, experienced consumers, knowing how to win and keep customers is the single, most important business skill that anyone can learn. Customer satisfaction and loyalty are the keys to long-term profitability, and keeping the customer happy is everybody's business. Becoming customer centred and exceeding customer expectations are requirements for business success. Chapter 11 gives examples of individuals or companies that have succeeded in the tourism industry by being customer focused.

Experiences

experience

event created when an organization intentionally uses services as the stage and goods as props to engage individual customers

According to B. Joseph Pine II and James Gilmore, today's consumer desires what the service industry calls an "**experience**," which occurs when an organization intentionally uses services as the stage and goods as props to engage individual customers. More and more travel organizations are responding by explicitly designing and promoting such memorable events. As services, like goods before them, increasingly become commodified, experiences have emerged as the next step in the "progression of economic value." From now on, leading-edge companies — whether they sell to consumers or businesses — will find that the next competitive battleground lies in staging experiences.[28]

An experience is not an amorphous construct; it is as real an offering as any service, good, or commodity. In today's service economy, many companies simply wrap experiences around their traditional offerings to sell them better. To realize the full benefit of staging experiences, however, businesses must deliberately design engaging experiences that command a fee. While traditional economic offerings — commodities, goods, and services — are external to the buyer, experiences are inherently personal, existing only in the mind of an individual who has been engaged on an emotional, physical, intellectual, or even spiritual level. Thus, no two people can have the same experience, because each experience derives from the interaction between the staged event (like a theatrical play) and the individual's state of mind.

Experiences have always been at the heart of the entertainment business — a fact that Walt Disney and the company he founded have creatively exploited. But today the concept of selling an entertainment experience is taking root in businesses far removed from theatres and amusement parks. At theme restaurants such as the Hard Rock Café, Planet Hollywood, and the House of Blues, the food is just a prop for what is known as "eatertainment." And stores such as Niketown, Cabella's, and Recreational Equipment Incorporated draw consumers in by offering fun activities, fascinating displays, and promotional events (sometimes labelled "shoppertainment" or "entertailing"). But experiences are not exclusively about entertainment; companies stage an experience whenever they engage customers in a personal, memorable way. For example, WestJet and Southwest Airlines go beyond the function of transporting people from point A to point B, and compete on the basis of providing an experience. The company uses its base service (the travel itself) as the stage for a distinctive en route experience — one that attempts to transform air travel into a respite from the traveller's normally frenetic life (see *Case Study* in Chapter 11).

CHAPTER SUMMARY

Understanding the consumer's needs and buying process is the foundation of successful marketing. By understanding the buyer's decision-making process, the various participants in the buying procedure, and the major influences on buying behaviour, marketers can acquire many clues about how to meet buyer needs. The key factors that influence consumer behaviour are motivation, culture, age and gender, social class, lifestyle, life cycle, and reference groups.

It has been suggested that there are three levels of buying commitment, which depend on the nature of the purchase: extended problem solving, limited problem solving, and habitual problem solving. It is also proposed that there are five buying roles: initiator, influencer, decider, buyer, and user. A consumer moves through a number of stages leading up to purchase: awareness, information searching, development of an attitude, evaluation, purchase, and post-purchase.

A marketer will also need to understand the buying phases for organizations. The conference market, for example, follows a pattern of group decision making, and the "buy phase" has been described as follows: problem recognition, general need description, product specification, supplier search, proposal solution, supplier selection, order routine specification, and performance review.

The behaviour of business travellers is significantly different than that of leisure travellers. For example, business travellers do not see travel as a perk but rather as another source of stress. Hence some sectors of the tourism industry, such as airlines, spend considerable effort trying to understand the needs of their business travellers in order to satisfy them.

There are a range of trends or demands in consumer behaviour that are influencing tourism and hospitality marketing today. These include the desire for learning and enrichment travel, concern for the environment, a more health-conscious society, the desire for convenience and speed, requests for customized and personalized vacations, the increasing desire for convenience and speed, and the desire for experiences.

KEY TERMS

attitudes, p. 44	family life cycle, p. 54	perception, p. 45
beliefs, p. 44	learning, p. 44	perceptual mapping, p. 45
consumer attitudes, p. 46	learning and enrichment travel,	psychographic analysis, p. 52
consumer behaviour analysis,	p. 61	reference groups, p. 54
p. 42	life cycle model, p. 54	social class, p. 49
culture, p. 48	lifestyle analysis, p. 52	social marketing, p. 62
dependables (psychocentrics),	motivations, p. 43	VALS, p. 52
p. 55	needs, p. 43	venturers (allocentrics), p. 54
experience, p. 69		

DISCUSSION QUESTIONS AND EXERCISES

1. Using the *Profile* "Backpackers with Gold Cards" and all the material on consumer behaviour in this chapter, create a profile of a typical backpacker. How is this individual different in behaviour from other types of travellers, such as the packaged or the business traveller?

2. Where would you place the backpacker on Plog's continuum? What are likely to be the popular destinations for backpackers in the future? Are there some destinations that are not capitalizing on this market?

3. Why is the post-purchase behaviour stage included in most models of the buying process?

4. Consider the trends in consumer behaviour discussed at the end of the chapter. Can you think of any other trends that have emerged since this book was published?

5. Discuss the roles that each member of the family plays in the decision-making process when choosing a holiday. Is there any evidence that children have an influential role?

6. What motivates you to travel? Using the Internet, find a trip that excites you, and explain why this trip would meet your needs.

CASE STUDY

A SEMESTER AT SEA

Global education is not a recent innovation. It has its roots in the Grand Tour, a term first applied in England more than 300 years ago. This type of travel was seen as the best means of teaching wealthy young men about culture, taste, geography, art, and general worldliness in preparation for careers in military, government, and civil services. Today, more than 150 000 American university students every year go on their own international travels in the form of study-abroad programs. One of the most varied of such educational opportunities is provided by Semester at Sea (SAS), which twice annually takes approximately 650 students around the world in a single semester, visiting several different countries in a fusion of education and travel.

For more than 40 years, more than 40 000 students from the U.S. and elsewhere have experienced SAS programs, worth four credit courses in a comprehensive international curriculum. The Institute

for Shipboard Education, a nonprofit organization, has been administering these programs since 1976 in conjunction with various U.S. universities. The concept was inaugurated in 1926 with the University World Cruise, which later became the University of the Seven Seas, then World Campus Afloat, and, finally, with the help of the late C. Y. Tung (founder of the Orient Overseas Container Line), Semester At Sea.

Students, staff, and faculty from all over the world work, socialize, study, and travel together during a spring or fall semester, which lasts at least 100 days, or the summer program, which lasts about 65 days. Spring trips usually proceed eastward around the world and fall tours head west, with the shorter summer trips concentrating on Asia or Latin America. The focus is on non-western cultures with developing economies and diverse political and cultural systems. A multidisciplinary overview of the areas and issues encountered during the voyage is provided by a mandatory upper-level comparative studies course. Called Global Studies, it draws upon the experience and expertise of the whole faculty as well as specialized guest lecturers who provide a more personal insight into their nations' histories, cultures, and customs.

I was a Semester at Sea professor during the Spring 2006 voyage, and it really was a fulfilling experience. I could never normally afford to travel around the world for four months with my family (the cost for a 109-day cruise with Crystal Cruises is around US$50 000), so this was the perfect opportunity to combine travel with work in an affordable fashion. My two boys just loved every minute and still have not stopped talking about the experience. Interestingly, tourism had not been taught on the ship in previous voyages, although it seemed like an obvious choice for such a venture. I ended up with three full classes (about 36 students in each class) and a wonderfully eclectic group of students. For me, the most memorable countries we visited were Myanmar, India, and South Africa, but every port was a distinctive adventure.

It's not just undergraduates who are learning about the world on these trips. A small contingent of "Lifelong Learners" also pays to circumnavigate the world, joining in with classes, activities, clubs, lectures on board, and the Global Studies course. They form part of the extended family on the ship, acting us surrogate parents and grandparents for the younger generation. Students, too, volunteer as "Big Brothers" and "Big Sisters" for the younger kids on board — the children of faculty and staff are also educated while travelling around the world with their parents.

Subjects include anthropology, biological studies, business, economics, music, geology, philosophy, and theatre arts. among many others. Students with every major can apply and there are also grants available for those who qualify for financial aid. Fieldwork, which accounts for 20 percent of the hours needed for course credits, is geared to specific interests as well as different budgets. Day trips might include a tea ceremony in Japan or a Candomblé ceremony in Brazil; overnight excursions could take students to sites of significant cultural, historical, or political interest such as the Great Wall of China or Angkor Wat in Cambodia.

Other field experiences concentrate more on the local people and active involvement in the countries visited. Students and faculty can learn about local customs during a homestay with a Japanese or Indian family. There are overnight trips to "untouchable" villages where students work, eat, and sleep as the locals do. There are also opportunities to meet university students in each country during welcome receptions, sports competitions, and lectures. The ship, MV *Explorer*, includes all the luxuries of a regular cruise ship with the academic atmosphere and rules of a normal land-based campus. Thus there is an 8000 volume library and computer room as well as a gym and a wellness centre.

Hayley Angus from the University of Western Ontario was surprised there were so few Canadian passengers. She was fortunate to hear about SAS from a friend but lamented the lack of awareness back home. "I had never really thought about going on exchange, but I felt that my life at university was falling into a bit of a pattern," says Angus. "When I heard about SAS, it sounded like the ideal exchange as I would be able to go to multiple countries, instead of having to choose just one." Costing around US$30 000 all in, Angus says SAS is the "greatest thing so far" she has done with her life. Visas and immunizations, trips, purchases, bar bills, and travel expenditure nearly doubled the initial $16 000 academic fees. But she says it was well worth it, compared to paying "separately for a semester at university, plus food, and rent, as well as all of the travel expenses."

Ship life was almost as much fun as the travelling for Angus: "I loved the days on the ship when everyone was tanning or studying on the pool deck, drinking smoothies, and looking onto the never-ending ocean." And she found studying relatively easy despite social distractions. "The professors were some of the best profs I've had at university. I believe it is quite competitive to teach on SAS," she explains. She also valued the personal interaction with faculty: "When you have class, dinner, and travel with them, as well as tan next to them on the pool deck, you get to know them pretty well."

QUESTIONS

1. Why is it that demand for educational tourism has mushroomed in the last few decades?
2. Can Maslow's hierarchy of needs explain the motivation behind these trips?
3. Check out the SAS website. What is the profile of the student that SAS is trying to attract?
4. Do some research to find some examples of educational holidays offered around the world. Which one attracts you the most?

WEBSITES

www.voluntourism.org
Information on Volunteer Tourism

www.astanet.com
American Society of Travel Agents

www.pier21.ca
Pier 21

www.holylandexperience.com
The Holy Land Experience

www.semesteratsea.com
Semester at Sea

www.countrystylecommunitytourism.com
Countrystyle Community Tours

www.cetn.ca
Canadian Experience Travel Network

www.religioustravelassociation.com
World Religious Travel Association

ENDNOTES

1. Theme park roller coaster seminar helps people cope with their "weaker self." *National Post* (2004, May 13), A14.
2. Decima Research Inc. (2006, April 24). Consumer and travel trade research in China: Quantitative report. www.tourism.bc.ca/PDF/China%20Consumer%20Research%20(2006).pdf (retrieved September 2007).
3. Sutherland, S. (2002, May). Hospitality trends. *Alberta Venture*, 49–53.
4. Cateora, P. R., & Graham, J. L. (2005). *International marketing* (12th ed.). New York: McGraw-Hill Irwin, 119.
5. Hofstede, G. (1980). Motivation, leadership, and organization: Do American theories apply abroad? *Organizational Dynamics*, *9*, 42–63; Hofstede, G. (1983). National cultures in four dimensions: A research-based theory of cultural differences among nations. *International Studies of Management & Organization*, *13*, 46–75.
6. Brean, J. (2006, October 21). Where suburbia was born. *National Post*, A14.
7. Pearce, P. L. (1993). Fundamentals of tourist motivation. In D. Pearce & W. Butler (Eds.), *Tourism and research: Critiques and challenges,* 113–134. London: Routledge.

8. Mature travellers and volunteer holidays. (2002, February 2). *Edmonton Journal*, K2.

9. Plog, S. C. (1974). Why destination areas rise and fall in popularity. *Cornell Hotel & Restaurant Quarterly, 14*(4), 55–58; Plog, S. C. (2002). The power of psychogaphics and the concept of venturesomeness. *Journal of Travel Research, 40,* 244–251.

10. Cohen, E. (1972). Toward a sociology of international tourism. *Social Research, 39*(1), 164–182.

11. Howard, J. A., & Sheth, J. N. (1969). *The theory of buying behavior.* New York: Wiley.

12. Engel, J. F., Blackwell, R. D., & Miniard, P. W. (1990). *Consumer behavior.* Orlando: Dryden.

13. Zeithaml, V. A., Berry, L. L., & Parasuraman, A. (1996). The behavioral consequences of service quality. *Journal of Marketing, 60*(2), 31–46.

14. Radburn, D. (1997). Organizational buyer behaviour. In L. Lumsdon (Ed.), *Tourism Marketing,* 52–63. London: Thomson Business Press.

15. Webster, F., & Wind, Y. (1972). *Organizational buying behavior.* Englewood Cliffs, NJ: Prentice Hall.

16. Cohen, A. (2000, January 31). Business takes all the fun out of travel. *National Post*, C17.

17. Tong, T. (2002, March 8). Business travellers' spouses pay psychological price. *National Post*, A1.

18. Hickman, M. (2006, May 29). How ethical shopping is making business go green. *Independent*, 2.

19. Americans going green? (2002). *Tourism, 6*(8), 12.

20. Leadbeater, C. (2002, July 6–7). Longing for the way we were. *Financial Times*, IV.

21. Patterson, I. (2002). Baby boomers and adventure tourism: The importance of marketing the leisure experience. *World Leisure, 2*(4), 4–10.

22. Dennis, G. (2004, October 18). Brewer to put health warnings on beer bottles. *National Post*, A11.

23. Whitlock, S. (2001, September). The world on a platter. *Travel & Leisure*, 176–178.

24. Cornell, C. (2005, February 26). The culture is included: New packaged vacations. *National Post*, WP11.

25. Allossery, P. (2002, March 4). Fast food in high gear. *Financial Post*, FP6.

26. Skelton, C. (2003). Fire tourists get in the way. *National Post*, September 2, A5.

27. Lloyd, M. (2006, 1 September). Mexican tourist attraction simulates illegal border run. *Globe & Mail*, A1, 10.

28. Pine, B. J. II, & Gilmore, J. H. (1998). Welcome to the experience economy. *Harvard Business Review, 76*(4), 97–108.

Developing a Marketing Plan

3

Spotlight
FROM PRISON CELL TO TOURIST ATTRACTION: ROBBEN ISLAND, CAPE TOWN, SOUTH AFRICA

How to turn something associated with pain, suffering and evil into an attraction for tourists without modifying and sanitizing it — can it be done? Well, according to former inmate, political activist, and critic Dennis Brutus this is not possible. He thinks Robben Island, with its guided tours of the political prison where Nelson Mandela was incarcerated for 18 years, has been beautified and altered with flower gardens and murals to transform it from an "island of hell" in an attempt to rewrite history. However, another former inmate, poet, and prison guide, Modise Phekonyane claims that as long as ex-prisoners and former guards are still available to guide and educate the eager tourists flocking to the island near Cape Town, the prison will remain as an educational symbol of hope and unity for the future of South Africa.

Over the past 400 years, Robben Island has had a remarkably varied history, serving as a post office, fishing base, whaling station, hospital, mental asylum, military base, leper colony, and, most infamously, as a brutal penal colony and symbol of political oppression during apartheid in South Africa. Since the prison and island were opened to the public in January 1997, as the Robben Island Museum by Nelson Mandela himself, the number of annual visitors has risen from 100 000 in the first year to more than 400 000 in 2005. At peak times of the year, 2000 tourists a day take a three-and-a-half-hour tour, which includes a catamaran ride, a bus trip, and a guided tour of the prison. The bus ride encompasses famous sites such as political activist Robert Sobukwe's isolated house, the limestone quarry where Mandela and fellow prisoners slaved to cut stone to build prison facilities and ruined their eyesight in the glaring reflection, the leper's church and graveyard, wardens' village, and the habitat of the island's penguins, antelopes and other magnificent wildlife. The highlight of the prison tour is interaction with an ex-political prisoner and sometimes a prison guard, as well as a view and photograph of the tiny, ill-equipped cell where Mandela spent 18 years of his 27-year prison term, secretly writing and smuggling out illicit books and inspiring his fellow inmates in the revolutionary movement against apartheid.

There are many examples of prisons open to public view throughout the world. However, Robben Island differentiates its experience by offering an up-close-and-personal look at the suffering of its political prisoners by introducing the visitors to several actual prisoners who have now elected to be guides among an eclectic team of staff including artists, historians, environmentalists, and even ex-wardens. Robben Island, therefore, is not a museum of relics and photographs but an interactive, experiential, emotional, and educational facility that is striving to promote harmony, racial equity, and peace with its example of reconciliation and forgiveness. Its promotional brochure explains the philosophy behind the unique facility: "Those imprisoned on the island succeeded on a psychological and political level in turning a prison 'hell hole' into a symbol of freedom and personal liberation. Robben Island came to symbolize, not only for South Africa and the African continent, but also for the entire world, the triumph of the human spirit over enormous hardship and adversity."

Robben Island Museum thus offers a memorable experience rather than a monument or product that attracts tourists. With its poignant history and its designation as a World Heritage Site in 1999, together with its environmental attributes, such as the beautiful backdrop of prosperous Cape Town, a full view of Table Mountain, the colourful international harbour, and its abundant wildlife, it will always remain an important tourist destination as well as a physical symbol of South Africa's divided history. The primary challenge, however, will be to find ways in the future to keep the museum original and vital as the main attraction of its unique staff passes on. Many of the current guides met and associated with Mandela himself as well as with other famous political activists, making them a living part of history that could never be replicated with more remote guides, actors, or even recorded digital commentaries.

Sources: Robben Island Museum brochure. (2006); Personal interviews with D. Brutus and M. Phekonyane, Robben Island, February 14, 2006; Blond, R., Cornwell, J. & Fitzpatrick, M. (2004). South Africa, Lesotho, and Swaziland. Lonely Planet: London, 100–101.

Objectives

On completion of this chapter, readers should understand

- the eight key steps in the marketing planning process;
- the importance of the corporate connection;
- analysis and forecasting;

- setting goals and objectives;
- targeting and positioning;
- tactics and action plans; and
- how marketing planning is conducted in various sectors of the tourism industry.

Chapter Overview

The *Spotlight* highlights the importance of successful positioning in today's marketing environment, catering to the changing consumer described in the previous chapter. Positioning is an important part of marketing planning, which is the subject of Chapter 3. In its principles, marketing planning is no more than a logical thought process in which all businesses should engage. It is an application of common sense, as relevant to a small bed and breakfast as it is to an international airline. The chapter proposes that there are eight key steps in the marketing planning process. Each of these steps is discussed in turn, and practical examples are given from various sectors of the tourism industry.

INTRODUCTION TO MARKETING PLANNING

marketing plan

a written, short-term plan that details how an organization will use its marketing mix to achieve its marketing objectives

strategic marketing plan

a written plan for an organization covering a period of three or more years into the future

The term **marketing plan** is widely used to mean a short-term plan for two years or less. This chapter is devoted to the development of such plans. A **strategic marketing plan**, on the other hand, is different, as it covers three or more years. A marketing plan serves a number of purposes within any tourism organization: it provides a roadmap for all future marketing activities of the firm; it ensures that marketing activities are aligned with the corporate strategic plan; it forces marketing managers to review and think through all steps in the marketing process objectively; it assists in the budgeting process to match resources with marketing objectives; and it creates a process to monitor actual against expected results.

A systematic marketing planning process consists of eight logical steps, as outlined in Figure 3.1. For the strategic marketing plan, the first four stages may be more detailed, but any short-term marketing plan should also include an assessment of these steps. Each step feeds into the next one. A marketing plan is not a stand-alone tool, so the first stage is examining the goals and objectives of the organization as a whole and then developing a marketing plan that will support the organization's mission statement, corporate philosophy, and corporate goals. Once the corporate connection has been clarified, the next stage is defining the current situation, reviewing the effectiveness of current activities, and identifying opportunities. This is the "analysis and forecasting" stage. The third stage is concerned with defining marketing goals and objectives derived logically from the previous stages of the planning process.

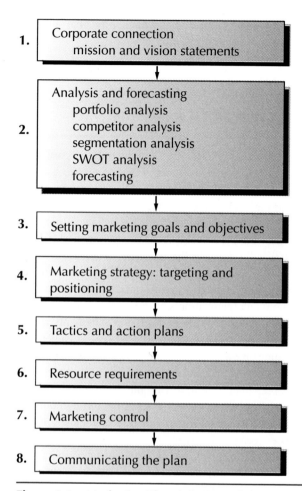

Figure 3.1 Marketing Planning: An Eight-Step Process

At the fourth stage, target markets should be selected from the previously developed list of available segments, and once the market has been segmented and a target market identified, the next step in the marketing plan is positioning. Market positioning is ultimately how the consumer perceives the good or service in a given market, and is used to achieve a sustainable competitive advantage over competitors. The fifth stage of the marketing plan involves selecting and developing a series of strategies that effectively bring about the required results. This part of the plan shows how the organization intends to use the seven P's. The marketing plan needs to address the resources required to support the strategies and meet the objectives, and resource requirements are the focus of the plan's sixth stage. The seventh stage of the marketing plan is concerned with marketing control and how objectives will be achieved in the required time, using the funds and resources requested. Finally, at the eighth stage, the marketing plan should be communicated both internally and externally to achieve maximum impact. Most marketing plans will contain an **executive summary** of the whole plan, and this should be no more than a few pages in length. *Marketing in Action* in this chapter provides an executive summary of the marketing plan for the Northwest Territories (NWT).

executive summary

a few pages, usually positioned at the beginning of the marketing plan, that sum up the plan's main sections

The role played by each section of the marketing plan will now be discussed in more detail.

1.   THE CORPORATE CONNECTION

A good marketing plan begins with the fact that the only purpose of marketing is to support the enterprise. Marketing planning should therefore reflect the goals and objectives of the organization as a whole. The mission and vision statement reflects the organization's philosophy, and the goals and objectives as set out in the business plan become the basis of planning for all departments. Marketing's responsibilities in relation to the corporate vision are usually outlined in one or more separate marketing-specific documents. A **vision statement** usually answers the question, What do we want to be, whilst the **mission statement** will answer the question, What business are we in? Whereas the vision describes where the organization wants to be in some future time, the mission is a broader statement about an organization's business and scope, goods or services, markets served, and overall philosophy. Vision and mission statements can vary. The Canadian Tourism Commission (CTC) has adopted a bold vision — "to become the leading destination marketing organization in the world." The mission of the CTC is "to increase awareness of and interest in Canada as a four-season tourist destination." G.A.P Adventures (see Chapter 1) has the following mission statement that focuses on service: "Our priority is to satisfy every customer, every time, through outstanding, personalized service! We are dedicated to the customer experience and are constantly evaluating how we can improve this experience."

Goals can be defined in terms such as sales growth, increased profitability, and market leadership, whereas **objectives** are the activities that will accomplish the goals. In the *Marketing in Action* in this chapter, one of Northwest Territories Tourism's (NWTT) goals is to increase tourism revenues to $145 million by 2010. One objective to achieve this goal is to establish a greater awareness and interest in NWT through key e-marketing promotions including the redesign of a comprehensive website.

In some sectors of the tourism industry, strategic and marketing planning faces many challenges. For example, in hotels and restaurants, major chains commonly do not own all the properties that they manage, and some owners show little interest in long-term planning. Strategic alliances between chains on a global basis may further complicate the planning process. In the hotel sector, owners themselves complain that hotel management companies are non-responsive and have no interest in planning. Managers have commonly been educated and trained to manage properties with concern for areas such as maintenance and front desk operations but have received little or no training in strategic planning. These unique management and ownership structures can complicate the process of strategic planning. Planning at the destination level also presents some fundamental differences and challenges, which are addressed in Chapter 12.

vision statement

a brief simple phrase or sentence that describes where the organization wants to be in some future time and usually answers the question, What do we want to be?

mission statement

a brief simple phrase or sentence that summarizes the organization's direction and communicates its ethos to internal and external audiences, and also answers the question, What business are we in?

goals

the primary aims of the organization

objectives

the specific aims that managers accomplish to attain organizational goals

MARKETING IN ACTION

CHALLENGES AND OPPORTUNITIES IN THE NORTHWEST TERRITORIES

The Northwest Territories possesses assets in tourism that are second to none in the world. It is home to four national parks, including one that is the largest in Canada, two UNESCO World Heritage sites, the greatest concentration of mounds of earth-covered ice known as pingos in the world, hundreds of thousands of barren ground caribou, spectacular mountain ranges, rolling tundra, thousands of rivers and lakes, the most northern highway in North America, rare and endangered species such as the whooping crane, peregrine falcon, and muskoxen, prime location in the auroral zone, nine official languages, seven aboriginal groups, and a population of only 41 000. Given some of its unique features and cultural diversity, there is much to build on to increase tourism. However, there are challenges. Some of these cannot be changed readily or at all,

such as distance, time, and the high cost to get to the NWT. Others will take time and investment to overcome.

Fortunately, there are many steps that can be taken to grow tourism in the NWT. The most immediate needs toward this end include:

- developing a distinct brand image to differentiate and create recognition of the NWT in key markets;
- enhancing key segment promotions (outdoor adventure, aurora promotions, general touring, fishing, and hunting) and developing new product and infrastructure to increase visitation and to extend visitor stays;
- reviving the NWT fishing program through increased promotions to key markets;
- establishing a greater awareness and interest in the NWT through key e-marketing promotions including the redesign of a comprehensive NWTT website;
- enhancing operator readiness by developing promotional campaigns that will feature market-ready products in key NWTT campaigns;
- providing tourism training that addresses all hospitality and management-related skill sets;
- undertaking more extensive market research to determine consumer trends and motivators; and
- increasing media exposure for the NWT through a series of support activities including increased media familiarization tours (FAM tours) and promotional materials.

MARKETING IN ACTION *continued*

In recognition of these needs, NWT's Department of Industry, Tourism, and Investment enhanced its 2005–2010 tourism plan to focus on the following goals:

- develop a unique brand image for the NWT as a travel destination;
- foster development of new tourism businesses, help existing businesses grow, and improve the profitability of tourism operations; and
- increase tourism revenues to $145 million by 2010 in conjunction with the private sector.

The Department of Industry, Tourism, and Investment's plan includes a tourism training component, a product development program, an infrastructure development program, and a marketing component.

NWTT role in meeting Industry Tourism and Investment's overall tourism goals is to develop, implement, and evaluate all marketing strategies and tactics as set out in this document.

Source: Department of Industry, Tourism, and Investment. (2006, October 12). In support of tourism. Marketing strategy and implementation plan for Northwest Territories Tourism, 2005–2010.

2. ANALYSIS AND FORECASTING

The next stage of the marketing plan is to define the current situation. It is essential that each component of the business be reviewed in order to ensure that resources can be allocated efficiently. Several models exist for reviewing effectiveness and identifying opportunities, but those proven by time and practical application across a range of industries include portfolio analysis, competitor analysis, segmentation analysis, SWOT (strengths, weaknesses, opportunities, and threats) analysis, and forecasting.

Portfolio Analysis

portfolio analysis

an approach to evaluating a diverse group of goods and services, based on long-term planning and economic forecasts

Boston Consulting Group (BCG) model

a technique designed to show the performance of an individual product in relation to its major competitors and the rate of growth in its market

Portfolio analysis first became popular in the 1960s, when many organizations sought to improve their profitability by diversifying their activities so as not to keep all their eggs in one basket. The **Boston Consulting Group (BCG) model** was one of the most popular approaches to evaluating a very diverse group of goods and services, based on long-term planning and economic forecasts. The model adopts the view that every product of an organization can be plotted on a two-by-two matrix to identify those offering high potential and those that are drains on the organization's resources.

In Figure 3.2, the horizontal axis represents **market share**, and the vertical axis represents anticipated market growth. High market share means that a business is a leader in that good or service; low market share indicates that either the marketplace is heavily competitive or a good or service does not have widespread market acceptance. A good or service can then take up one of four theoretical positions on the model. A **cash cow** is a product that generates cash and turnover, but the long-term prospects are limited. The company in Figure 3.2 operates two cash-cow businesses. A **dog** is a good or service that underperforms, providing neither revenue nor long-term opportunities and holding little promise for improved performance. In the illustration, the company has three dogs.

market share

an organization's sales expressed as a percentage of the sales for the total industry

cash cow

a service or product that generates a high volume of income in relation to the cost of maintaining its market share

dog

a service or product that provides neither cash flow nor long-term opportunities and holds little promise for improved performance

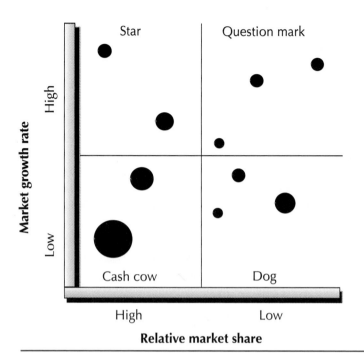

Figure 3.2 The Boston Consulting Group Model

stars

products or services that have a dominant share of a fast-growing market

question marks

speculative, potentially high-risk products or services that may be profitable and, because of their small market share, may be vulnerable to competition

Stars are products or services that have a dominant share of a fast-growing market. Although they may not generate a large amount of cash at present, they have potential for high returns in the future. **Question marks** are fairly speculative products that have high-risk potential. They may be profitable, but because they hold a small market share, they may be vulnerable to competition. Goods or services go through a product life cycle that can affect where they are positioned on the BCG model. A new product may start out as a question mark; as it becomes successful it moves into the star category, and then moves on to become a cash cow before it starts to decline and becomes a dog.

A good example of a tourism product that has taken up all four positions in the BCG model is the Concorde airplane (see the *Snapshot* in Chapter 5). Beginning as a question mark, the delta-winged marvel, a product of 1960s technology and optimism, quickly became a star as business executives and celebrities asserted their status by happily spending thousands of dollars to save a few hours of travelling time. The product soon became a cash cow, and more than 2.5 million passengers flew on British Airways Concordes after they entered service in 1976. However, filling the 100 seats became increasingly difficult, and, between 2000 and 2003, the Concorde could be classified as a dog. In April 2003 it was announced that the supersonic transport run by British Airways and Air France would be retired that year because of slumping ticket sales.

As part of a portfolio analysis, an organization should assess each good and service in terms of its position on the product life cycle. This concept is discussed in Chapter 5.

Competitor Analysis

competitor analysis

a review of competitors that allows the organization to identify market trends and the level of customer loyalty

direct competitors

organizations that offer similar goods and services to the same consumer at a similar price

product category competitors

organizations that produce the same product or class of products or the same services

general competitors

organizations that provide the same service or product

budget competitors

organizations that compete for the same consumer dollars

Information on the number and type of competitors, their relative market shares, the things they do well, and things they do badly will assist in the planning process. **Competitor analysis** will also highlight market trends and the level of loyalty of consumers. Competitors can be divided into four broad categories: **direct competitors** offer similar goods and services to the same consumer at a similar price; **product category competitors** make the same product or class of products or services; **general competitors** provide the same product or service; and **budget competitors** compete for the same consumer dollars. In addition to the existing competition, there is also the threat of potential competition in the form of new entrants. Figure 3.3 shows the forces that determine the competitive environment in an industry, as summarized by Michael Porter.[1] In China, a number of new foreign entrants has recently led to a very competitive hotel sector, particularly in the budget inn category. Ambitious players such as U.S.-based Wyndham Worldwide Corp.'s Super 8 chain entered the Chinese market in 2004, and by 2006 had 33 hotels. It plans to increase that to 110 hotels by 2009. Local players in this sector, such as Home Inns & Hotels Management Inc. and Jinjiang International, are also expanding aggressively.

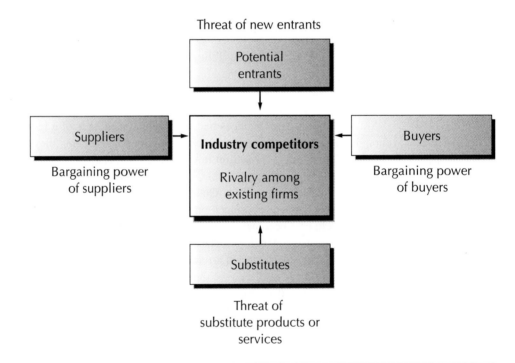

Figure 3.3 Forces Driving Industry Competition

Source: Porter, M.E. (1980). *Competitive strategy: Techniques for analyzing industry and competitors.* New York: Free Press, 4.

low-cost leadership

the simplest and most effective strategy for dealing with competition, requiring large resources and strong management to sustain

Porter suggests that there are only three generic strategies for dealing with competition: low-cost leadership, differentiation, and focus. **Low-cost leadership** is the simplest and most effective strategy, but it requires large resources and strong management to sustain. A low-cost leadership strategy is used when a firm sets out to become the low-cost producer in its industry. Low-cost producers typically sell a standard, or no-frills, product and place considerable emphasis on reaping scale or absolute cost advantages from all sources. The strategy may be short-lived, as it is easy for competitors to match a low price in an attempt to drive off the challenge. Low-cost airlines such as WestJet (see Chapter 11) that are springing up all over the world are examples of companies following such a strategy. These airlines are profiled in Chapter 6.

differentiation

a strategy that involves an innovative technological breakthrough, which can take competitors a long time to imitate, to gain a competitive advantage

Differentiation is a strategy that involves an innovative technological breakthrough, which can take competitors a long time to imitate. A competitive advantage can be gained by a product that is newer, better, or faster. The improvement can be in performance, durability, reliability, or service features. Airbus's new 560-tonne jet, the A380, carries up to 800 passengers and has differentiated itself from competitors by becoming the world's biggest commercial airliner. A **focus** strategy concentrates on designing a good or service to meet the needs of one segment of the market better than the competition does. Bruce Poon Tip from G.A.P Adventures follows such a strategy in the adventure tourism business (see Chapter 1). All three of these generic strategies are based on the organization's creation of a unique position for itself, which distinguishes its offerings from those of its competitors by price, product or service features, or the way in which it serves the needs of a particular segment. This process, known as positioning, is discussed later in this chapter.

focus

a strategy that concentrates on designing a good or service to meet the needs of one segment of the market better than the competition

Segmentation Analysis

segmentation analysis

the practice of dividing total markets up into groups on the basis of similar characteristics

Segmentation analysis refers to the way in which organizations identify and categorize customers into groups defined by similar characteristics and similar needs or desires. The concept of segmentation is widely adopted in tourism marketing, as few companies in the industry attempt to appeal to an entire market. The principles of segmentation are based on the premise that a market can be readily divided into segments for the commercial purpose of targeting offerings. The core advantage of segmentation is that customers will be more satisfied with the product or service because it has been designed with their needs in mind. Their social needs are also satisfied because they will be mixing with people like themselves and avoiding incompatible types. If an organization knows exactly which segments it wishes to reach, it can select the media most likely to be read, heard, or seen by those consumers, and so spend less on general mass-market advertising. If it knows the lifestyles and attitudes of that segment and the benefits its consumers are seeking from the product or service, the advertising message can be made more persuasive. The following *Snapshot* is an example of segmentation of domestic tourists within Canada. Research by Travel Alberta identified four key tourist segments, each with distinct lifestyles. Travel Alberta has since used the research to create marketing messages targeted to each specific segment.

SNAPSHOT

SEGMENTING THE DOMESTIC TOURISM MARKET IN CANADA

Between 2003 and 2005, Travel Alberta conducted market research to achieve a greater understanding of domestic tourists visiting Alberta. What they discovered was four key buying groups, each with distinct lifestyles. The four buying groups exist in differing proportions in each of the three western provinces, and Travel Alberta has used the research to create marketing messages targeted to each specific group. Using this marketing approach, Travel Alberta's in-province's 2005 summer campaign alone generated $142 million in incremental tourism revenues. Below is a summary of information about each segment.

Accomplishers

Your Adventure Awaits

Percentage of Population: Alberta 28 percent; British Columbia 31 percent; Saskatchewan 22 percent

Accomplishers want new, unfamiliar places to visit and new, active and exciting things to do, preferably outdoors. They spend more on travel than other buying groups, and are more likely married without children at home. Accomplishers spend the most time planning their vacations. Their primary source of information is the Internet. Accomplishers are a lucrative group, yet present a few challenges: Alberta Accomplishers also enjoy British Columbia, while British Columbia Accomplishers tend to stay at home. Take note: All Saskatchewan segments are Alberta-loyal.

Real Relaxers

Peace and Tranquility

Percentage of Population: Alberta 27 percent, British Columbia 26 percent, Saskatchewan 24 percent

Real Relaxers are "unwinders" — peace, rest, and tranquility take priority over specific activities. Nearly 40 percent are 50+ empty-nester couples. Real Relaxers are not planners; they book quick, easy, all-inclusive packages. Because they frequently return to the last place they visited, if you attract and please them, they're liable to return.

Alberta and Saskatchewan Real Relaxers enjoy Alberta, while their British Columbia counterparts stay in their home province.

Comfort Seekers

Home Away from Home

Percentage of Population: Alberta 24 percent, British Columbia 21 percent, Saskatchewan 25 percent

Comfort Seekers prefer familiar, relaxing, non-city locations. They're big on reconnecting with family and friends, and value for money is an important motivator for them. This group consists largely of budget-conscious parents who travel in summer and on school breaks. Comfort Seekers plan for a variety of activities that will collectively please the whole family. They research in detail, relying on the Internet (78 percent), word of mouth, and past experience. Alberta and Saskatchewan

SNAPSHOT *continued*

Comfort Seekers prefer Alberta, while British Columbia Comfort Seekers are loyal to their own province.

Urban Explorers

Savour the City

Percentage of Population: Alberta 21 percent; British Columbia 22 percent; Saskatchewan 29 percent

Urban Explorers prefer exciting city locations, cultural activities and events, dining, casinos, shopping, and "exploring" cities. Almost half are under 40, married without children. They spend the second most on travel, and enjoy going to large metropolitan centres in the United States. There is long-term growth potential for this market especially in Alberta and Saskatchewan with the Edmonton–Calgary Gateway Strategy. Festivals, events, shopping, and nightlife are strong attractions to Alberta and, particularly, Saskatchewan Urban Explorers.

The criteria used most often by tourism and hospitality suppliers to segment the market are as follows.

a) *Demographic segmentation* uses the primary variables of age, gender, family life cycle, and ethnicity to segment the markets. Bust Loose Holidays, for example, uses age and lifestyle stage variables to segment the holiday market by attracting singles who attend universities or colleges.

b) *Geographic segmentation* is the division of markets according to geographical boundaries, such as countries, provinces or territories, regions, cities, or neighbourhoods. In the past, for most destinations in Canada, market segmentation was often limited to understanding the more lucrative international tourist market. However, since the terrorist attacks of September 11, 2001, destination organizers have recognized the significance of local and provincial/territorial residents and the impact that they have on tourism revenues.[2]

c) *Benefit segmentation* divides customers based on the benefits they desire, such as education, entertainment, luxury, or low cost. Customers weigh different features of a service, and these are evaluated to form the basis of benefit segmentation. Customers of A&W (see *Snapshot*) would value benefits such as convenience and speed, whereas for other consumers these services would be irrelevant.

d) *Behaviour segmentation* divides the market into groups based on the various types of buying behaviour. Common bases include usage rate (light, medium, and heavy), user status (former users, non-users, potential users, first-time users, and regular users of a product), loyalty status (many people stay in five-star hotels as much for the status it confers on them as for the additional comfort), buyer-readiness stage, and occasions. On special occasions, people are prepared to pay more for special treatment, so many restaurants have deals for children's birthday parties, while hotels and cruise lines have special honeymoon suites.

e) *Psychographic segmentation* divides buyers into different groups based on social class, lifestyle, and personality characteristics. Pyschographics and lifestyle segmentation is based on personality traits, attitudes, motivations, and activities, and is discussed in more detail in Chapter 2. People in the same demographic group can have very different psychographic profiles.

In sum, the heart of any marketing plan is careful analysis of available market segments and the selection of the appropriate target market. A common mistake within tourism and hospitality is the selection of inappropriate segments (see the *Case Study* on Roots at the end of this chapter). The *Spotlight* in Chapter 8 mentions how Las Vegas tried unsuccessfully to re-brand itself as a family destination, providing pirate- and circus-themed hotels, funfairs, rides, amusement and games arcades, and animal attractions. It has since reverted to attracting more appropriate market segments, with the help of its "What Happens in Vegas, Stays in Vegas" advertising campaign.

When developing a marketing plan, marketers can gather information concerning market segments from two sources. Internal data can be analyzed by looking at business cards, guest registrations, credit card receipts, customer surveys, direct observations, and staff perceptions. External data can be gathered from published industry information, from marketing research, or by consulting competitors, vendors, and others in the industry.

Market segmentation is a dynamic process because customer trends are not static. It is thus important to carry out regular — preferably continuous — tracking studies to monitor changes happening in the market. One of the most recent trends in tourism and hospitality has been a "demassification" of the market, in which a greater number of niche markets are replacing the mass ones of the past.[3] As a result, **niche marketing** is increasing, whereby organizations offer products or services that are tailored to meet the needs and wants of narrowly defined geographic, demographic, or psychographic segments. In many areas of tourism and hospitality, technology has reduced the costs of creating a special product for each customer, making a degree of customization possible. For example, travel agents have access to electronic databases of accommodations, car rental companies, and airlines, so that they can quickly put together an itinerary and make bookings to create a customized package for a client.

niche marketing

focusing on the needs and wants of narrowly defined geographic, demographic, or psychographic segments

SWOT Analysis

SWOT analysis

a methodology for assessing strengths, weaknesses, opportunities, and threats for strategic purposes

SWOT is an acronym for strengths, weaknesses, opportunities, and threats. A **SWOT analysis** provides scope for assessing strengths (those things an organization does best and positive features of its products and services) and weaknesses (problems that affect its success). These factors are always internally focused. For hotels and visitor attractions, location may be a major strength, or the strength may lie in the skills of certain staff members. Strength may also lie in historical artifacts or architectural style, or it may reflect having a particularly favourable consumer image. Once identified, strengths are the basis of organizational positions and can be promoted to potential customers, enhanced through product or service augmentation, or developed within a strategic framework. In the *Profile* on Four Seasons Hotel and Resorts in this chapter, several strengths of the company can be identified, including its reputation, brand equity, and global positioning.

Weaknesses, such as aging products and services, declining markets or surly customer contact staff, must also be identified. Once identified, they may be subject to management action designed to minimize their impact or to remove them where possible.

Weaknesses and strengths are often matters of perception rather than fact, and might be recognized only through consumer research. Again, using Four Seasons as an example, weaknesses could include not being diversified enough and therefore being vulnerable to negative external environmental impacts.

Opportunities are events that can affect a business, either through its reaction to external forces or through its addressing of its own weaknesses. An opportunity identified recently by Four Seasons Hotels and Resorts is in private charters and general cruises, a move that may improve the group's weakness of not being diversified enough.

Threats are those elements, both internal and external, that could have a serious detrimental effect on a business. After September 11, 2001, the subsequent downturn in the economy had a devastating impact on tourism and by the end of 2002, Four Seasons had not recovered. The subsequent Iraq war and concerns about sudden acute respiratory syndrome (SARS) led to a huge number of cancelled trips to North America and to thousands of dollars in lost tourism revenue for all hotels, including Four Seasons properties.

A SWOT analysis is usually best undertaken early in the planning process, and in large organizations it is often carried out for each division. For example, a convention hotel would conduct a SWOT analysis on the property as a whole, but might also undertake a separate exercise for the functions area, restaurants, retail outlets, and recreation facilities. It is common practice in large market-oriented businesses for managers to commission consultants to carry out regular audits of all aspects of their business, including a SWOT analysis, to enhance their own foresight and bring to bear an independent, fresh vision. Table 3.1 is a SWOT analysis for Canada as a destination for Australians based on research conducted by the Canadian Tourism Commission.

Table 3.1

A SWOT Analysis of Canada as a Destination from Australia

STRENGTHS

- Cultural diversity of the destination — East / West, French Canada, First Nations
- Broad range to suit all demographics — natural attractions, soft adventure, ski, spa and wellness, shopping, food and wine, arts and culture
- A safe and clean environment, no language barriers
- Natural scenery, national parks, opportunities to see wildlife — strong nature-based tourism product offerings
- Welcoming locals, opportunities for travellers to interact socially to gain cultural insights
- Attractiveness to high yield niche consumer segments: wildlife viewing, adventure/trekking, gay and lesbian market, and non-ski winter
- Growing interest in independent travel and fly/drive packages
- Consistent top ranking among overseas ski destinations

TABLE 3.1 *continued*

- Resiliency to geo-political events and a strong economy that encourages spending on discretionary items such as travel

- Strong partner interest to expand resources in this market

OPPORTUNITIES

- Broaden the appeal of Canada as a holiday destination to a younger demographic by promoting niches (spa and wellness, food and wine, arts and culture)

- Target younger demographic interested in experiential travel

- Deliver a valueformoney message (against U.S. dollar and euro)

- Increase the number of in-market wholesalers

- Ensure Internet remains effective as a marketing and sales tool

- Strengthen partnerships with multiple airline partners

WEAKNESSES

- Consistent price barriers (especially air transportation costs)

- Low awareness of diversity of experiences and attractions available, including historical, cultural, shopping, spa and wellness, food and wine

- Requirement to clear U.S. customs and immigration during transit

- Limited accessibility by air

- Competition with the U.S. and Europe as long-haul destinations, both of which have greater air capacity and are therefore more price competitive

- Hesitancy by some tour and wholesale partners to include "new" product due to commercial viability

THREATS

- Continued concerns over terrorism, world events, and global health issues

- Fierce competition, increased promotional spending by competitors, especially for ski by Japan and U.S.

- Price competitiveness of Canada product

- Perception that Canada is only for older travellers on group tours

- Overall spending constrained, competing with household expenditures

- Limited awareness of all that Canada has to offer outside of iconic products

- Strengthening Canadian dollar

Source: Australia: A SWOT analysis. (2006, June). *Tourism Online, 3*(6).

Forecasting

forecasting

a process that uses market research to predict sales volume and revenue trends, consumer profiles, product profiles, price trends, and trends

Because information is never perfect and the future is always unknown, no one right conclusion can ever be drawn from the evidence gathered in the SWOT process. As a result, forecasting becomes an important stage in the planning process to support a SWOT. **Forecasting** uses market research to predict expectations, vision, and judgment, and to project factors such as sales' volume and revenue trends, consumer profiles, product profiles, price trends, and trends in the external environment. The *Marketing in Action* in Chapter 1 provided forecasts for the growing Chinese travel market based on reports by several market research companies. Because the future for tourism and hospitality products is subject to volatile, unpredictable factors and competitors' decisions, the goal of forecasting is not accuracy but careful and continuous assessment of probabilities and options, with a focus on future choices. Forecasting recognizes that most marketing mix expenditure is invested months ahead of targeted revenue flows. Since marketing planning focuses on future revenue achievement, it necessarily depends upon skill, judgment, foresight, and realism in the forecasting process.

There are two main sets of forecasting techniques: qualitative and quantitative. Qualitative techniques estimate future levels of demand based on detailed subjective analysis. They include sales staff estimates, senior management opinions, and buyers' intention surveys. Two more sophisticated qualitative techniques are the Delphi technique and long-term scenario planning. The Delphi technique involves obtaining expert opinions about the future prospects for a particular market without the experts actually meeting or necessarily knowing at any stage the composition of the panel. Long-term scenario planning is undertaken by larger organizations such as hotel or airline companies. It is a systematic attempt to predict the composition of the future market environment in 10 to 25 years' time and the likely impacts on the organization.

Quantitative techniques rely on analysis of past and current data. In some instances this involves the simple projecting of future demand in terms of past trends, and in other instances unravelling casual determinants needs to be considered. A number of well-tested methods are used; however, most require a degree of statistical ability. Time-series, noncausal techniques involve the forecasting of future demand on the basis of past trends. Causal methods attempt to show, by using regression analysis, how some measure of tourism demand is influenced by selected variables other than time. Finally, computer simulations are becoming more popular — trend-curve analysis and multiple regressions are combined mathematically to generate a computer model that simulates tourism demand.

3. SETTING MARKETING GOALS AND OBJECTIVES

Goals, the primary aims of an organization, can be defined in terms of sales growth, increased profitability, and market leadership. Objectives are the activities undertaken to accomplish the goals. For example, the goal of sales growth for a hotel could become an objective of a 20 percent increase in accommodation sales and a 30 percent increase in food and beverage sales. The goal of increased profitability could be translated into objectives of a 15 percent increase in profits across the board, and a goal of market leadership could be translated into objectives for each city in which a hotel chain operates.

Marketing objectives at the tactical level derive logically from the previous stages of the planning process. To be effective and actionable in practice, tactical marketing objectives must be:

- integrated with long-term corporate goals and strategy;
- precise and quantified in terms of sales volume, sales revenue, or market share;
- specific in terms of which products and which segments they apply to;
- specific in terms of the period in which they are to be achieved;
- realistic and aggressive in terms of market trends (revealed in the situation analysis) and in relation to budgets available;
- agreed to and endorsed by the managers responsible for the programs of activity designed to achieve results; and
- measurable directly or indirectly.[4]

If these criteria are not fully reflected, the objectives will be less than adequate for achieving the success of the business, and the marketing programs will be harder to specify and evaluate. The more thorough the previous stages of the marketing plan, the easier the task of specifying precise objectives. To ensure profitability and to remain competitive in today's marketplace, it has become necessary to establish several sub-objectives. For instance, a thousand-room hotel will undoubtedly have two broad objectives: average occupancy and average room rate. By themselves, these objectives do not serve as sufficient guides for developing marketing strategies. A set of sub-objectives might therefore include occupancy per period of time, the average room rate by type of room, and annual sales by each salesperson. Each marketing support area needs to be guided by a set of sub-objectives. This includes areas such as advertising, promotion, public relations, market research, and sales. It is important to acknowledge that objectives may not always be profit based. For many natural attractions, the objective may be to protect the fragile environment rather than to make money (see Chapter 13).

4.   MARKETING STRATEGY: TARGETING AND POSITIONING

Targeting

target market

a clearly defined group of customers whose needs the organization plans to satisfy

In terms of importance, no area of the marketing plan surpasses the selection of **target markets**, the clearly defined groups of customers whose needs the organization plans to satisfy. If inappropriate markets are selected, marketing resources will be wasted. High-level expenditures on advertising or sales will not compensate for misdirected marketing effort. Target markets should be selected from a previously developed list of available segments. These include segments currently served by the organization and newly recognized markets. A target market is simply the segment at which the organization aims its marketing message. Implicitly, the non-profitable customers should be given less attention. A target market generally has four characteristics. It should comprise groups of people or businesses that are well defined, identifiable, and accessible; members should have common characteristics; they should have a networking system so that they can readily refer the organization to one another; and they should have common needs and similar reasons to purchase the product or service.

The family market is a popular target market for many tourism organizations. Family travel is growing as more parents are choosing to share travel experiences with their children. Club Med is a good example. Once known for its ability to cater to young singles, it now has more than 60 family-friendly holiday villages worldwide. Adventure tours for families are also on the increase. A family-oriented, 13-day tour of South Africa offered by Explore is one example. The *Snapshot* on A&W highlights how the company has targeted baby boomers. This sector, born between 1947 and 1966, represents about a third of the Canadian population, and is a very attractive market for the tourism and hospitality industry. Another target market growing in attractiveness for the tourism industry is the gay and lesbian market. Montreal, for example, actively targets the "pink pound" (buying power of the gay and lesbian community), and hosted the Gay Games in 2006. Tourism Montreal estimated a $150 million economic impact from the games. Other destinations are targeting this segment. Evidence of the British Tourist Authority's campaign included the launch of the 2002 edition of its gay and lesbian travel guide and new strategies for building a market niche that the organization says has already produced "gratifying" results. The British Tourist Authority has subsequently expanded the campaign with the introduction of a larger travel guide and a dedicated gay and lesbian website.[5]

Evaluation of potential target markets involves examining the segment's size and growth, its structural attractiveness, and the firm's own objectives and resources. In terms of size, the American travel market is an important market segment for many Canadian tourism companies. The transformation of Canadian Pacific (CP) Hotels and Resorts into Fairmont Hotels and Resorts demonstrated this importance. The merger of these two companies, and the subsequent name change, was part of Canadian Pacific's targeting and positioning strategy. While the CP brand was relatively unfamiliar to many Americans, the Fairmont brand was very well known in the United States, and was associated with luxury, prestige, and high levels of service quality. Thus, in order to target the Americans, and to differentiate itself from other luxury accommodation providers in Canada, the company adopted the better-known brand name.

SNAPSHOT

A&W TARGETS THE BABY BOOMER

A&W isn't the only fast food chain trying to appeal to the ubiquitous baby boomers. But with a history that dates back to 1956, no other burger chain can claim to have raised boomers on fast food. Today, nearly empty nesters, boomers no longer have to eat where the kids want. And after all these years, it appears A&W still tops their list. "Some of our competitors might say they're going after the baby boomer market because it is such a big market, but they can't do what we do because we have a tremendous linkage to the boomer generation," says Jeff Mooney, chair and CEO of Vancouver-based A&W Food Services of Canada Inc.

For Mooney, the brand's strong heritage comes down to simple demographics. "We raised the boomers on fast food. They got older, got married, and got kids. Then McDonald's came along in the 1970s and bet that a four-year old screaming for a toy would win over an adult wanting a good hamburger. So as the boomers had children, that part of the market flourished. Now, the boomers'

SNAPSHOT *continued*

kids are grown and the adults are free to make their own choices about fast food." Some believe that despite being in a very competitive field, the fact that A&W is going after the older demographics as opposed to the younger adults or kids bodes well for its future because the boomer demographic is expanding. A&W president Paul Hollands adds, "Regardless of generations, A&W has a huge appeal and bridges right back to the incoming generations. The brand has broad appeal because we are true to what we are. We're really about good food."

A&W, which bills itself as Canada's first hamburger quick-service restaurant, has come a long way since first arriving in Canada nearly 50 years ago. The company was born in 1919 in Lodi, California, when Roy Allen and Frank Wright opened a sidewalk stand and later a drive-in, serving a creamy drink called root beer. A&W came to Canada in 1956 when two operators, Dick Bolte and Orval Helwege, opened their first drive-in on Portage Avenue in Winnipeg. The concept's popularity quickly grew, and by 1966, A&W operated more than 200 drive-in locations across Canada. Today, the company operates more than 660 restaurants across Canada, and it posted sales of $550 million in 2006. A&W is the country's third largest burger chain by sales volume, behind McDonald's and Wendy's, and it employs more than 17 000 people.

According to Mooney, A&W is a strategy-driven company. "That means everything that happens in our business — from major decisions about how the organization works to what goes on the placemats in our restaurants — is driven by this strategy," he says. A&W's current strategy involves a continued focus on the baby boomers, an expansion into the Ontario, Quebec, and Atlantic markets, and the development of a well-branded street presence. In 2002, the company began revitalizing its 300 free-standing restaurants with "retro" design and new exterior and interior signs.

Looking ahead, Mooney is confident that demographics will play a key role in the company's future success. "The two largest groups in the Canadian population right now are 35 to 44 and 45 to 54, and that's right where our customers are," he says. "And so the next 10 to 15 years are just a spectacular opportunity for growth for our company. We think we can have 1500 locations in this country, so we're excited about the future."

Interestingly, Mooney doesn't seem worried about the trend toward baby boomers choosing healthy options. The company's view is people taking a "cumulative approach" to diet. This means, as Mooney explains, if someone eats bran flakes with skim milk for breakfast, salmon for dinner, then what is wrong with eating an A&W burger with onion rings for lunch?

Source: Harris, R. (2002). Adult appeal. *Foodservice and Hospitality, 35*(10), 26–29.

Positioning

positioning

a communications strategy to establish an image for a product or service in relation to others in the minds of consumers

Once the market has been segmented and a target market identified, the next step in the marketing plan is positioning. **Positioning** is a communications strategy that is a natural follow-through from market segmentation and target marketing. Market positioning is ultimately how the consumer perceives the product or service in a given market, and is used to achieve a sustainable competitive advantage over competitors. Best Western recently changed its positioning strategy in China in the hopes of going beyond its traditional image as a purveyor of budget hotels. In 2006, the Phoenix-based chain scrapped plans to build a network of 100 three-star hotels in China by 2007. Instead, it plans to triple the number of its four- and five-star hotels in the country to 60 by 2009.[6]

Three steps are necessary to develop an effective position in the target market segment: product differentiation, prioritizing and selecting the competitive advantage, and communicating and delivering the position.

Step One: Product Differentiation

product differentiation

a technique that enables organization to seek competitive advantage by offering a product (or service) that has features not available from its competitors

Product differentiation, a phrase coined by Michael Porter, describes a technique that enables organizations to seek competitive advantage by offering a product or service that has features not available from their competitors. Product differentiation has the potential to assist companies in gaining a competitive edge and can distinguish them offering competitive advantages. A competitive advantage offers greater value to the consumer by providing benefits that justify a higher price. These advantages can be established through product attributes, features, services, level of quality, style and image, and price range. The key elements will shape how the consumer perceives the product. Physical attribute differentiation is achieved by enhancing or creating an image in the consumer's mind through tangible evidence. For example, Quality Inn offers a very simple physical appearance, communicating a clean, safe, inexpensive place to sleep. Fairmont Hotels and Resorts, on the other hand, combines an elaborate exterior with a luxurious interior to inspire feelings of comfort, relaxation, and prestige.

Service differentiation is an increasingly important way of gaining competitive advantage. Service quality has been more frequently identified as a key factor in differentiating service products and building a competitive advantage in tourism.[7] Several studies have examined the association between service quality and more specific behavioural intentions, and there is a positive and significant relationship between customers' perceptions of service quality and their willingness to recommend the organization or destination.[8] Likewise, research on service quality and retaining customers suggests that willingness to purchase again declines considerably once services are rated below good.[9]

Step Two: Prioritizing and Selecting the Competitive Advantage

Positioning is much like a ranking system, and an organization must decide where it wants to be in the hierarchy. Some companies have an image of high quality, service, and price — others, of being low budget. Neither image is better or worse. However, once the position is established, it is very difficult to change it in the consumer's mind. Therefore, companies must be very cautious in selecting the most effective combination of competitive advantages to promote and to contribute to building their positioning strategy.

unique selling proposition (USP)

a unique feature of a product or service that distinguishes it from all other products and services

It is important to promote not only one benefit to the target market, but also to develop a **unique selling proposition (USP)**, a unique feature of a product or service that distinguishes it from all others. The goal of a USP is for a organization to establish itself as the number-one provider of a specific attribute in the mind of the target market. The attribute chosen should be desired and highly valued by target consumers. If the marketing mix elements build the brand and help it to connect with the customer year after year, the total personality of the brand, rather than the trivial differences, will decide its ultimate position in the market. Although it is difficult in the tourism industry to find an effective USP in such a competitive and free market, it is essential to offer something new. Package holidays tend to offer similar deals, with only minor differences. Therefore, it is important for an organization to create a new good, service, or benefit that can be offered to consumers by it alone. Travel Cuts is an excellent example of a Canadian company that utilizes USP effectively. It offers student-discounted fares through its International Student Identity Card program — something that no other travel company offers. For Robben Island (see *Spotlight*) the USP was being able to offer tour guides who had actually been imprisoned on the island.

Step Three: Communicating and Delivering the Position

The final goal of an organization in the positioning process is to build and maintain a consistent positioning strategy. The overall aim of tourism providers is to attract attention from potential customers and to delight them with product offerings that cannot be beaten by competitors. Programs and slogans that support the organization's position must be continuously developed and promoted in order to establish and maintain the organization's desired position in the consumer's mind. Quality, frequency, and exposure in the media will determine how successful the positioning strategy will be.

branding

a method of establishing a distinctive identity for a product or service based on competitive differentiation from other products

Tourism and hospitality providers try to differentiate their products by using **branding**, a method of establishing a distinctive identity for a product or service based on competitive differentiation from other products. Branded products are those whose name conjures up certain images — preferably positive ones — in consumers' minds. These images may relate to fashion, value, prestige, quality, or reliability. Image is an important element of customer perception. If a hotel chain has an image of quality, staying at the hotel will provide benefits to business customers who want to project a successful image to their clients or colleagues. Some brands are recognized for their reliability. For example, it is comforting for many travellers to know that a Best Western property will meet certain standards, and that selecting one will be a reliable choice, even if the traveller is unfamiliar with the specific property or region. Hotels, in particular, brand-specific properties within their group to identify different categories of product. (See Chapter 5 for a more detailed discussion of branding.)

POSITIONING "FOUR" SUCCESS: FOUR SEASONS HOTELS AND RESORTS

Toronto-based Four Seasons Hotels and Resorts is an excellent example of distinctive positioning leading to global competitive success. In 2007 Four Seasons operated 74 luxury hotels and resorts in 31 countries around the world, with annual revenues of more than $290 million a year. It wins awards at an unprecedented level in industry publications as the leading player in the luxury hotel and resort business worldwide. Ten or more of

PROFILE *continued*

its hotels routinely make lists of the top 100 hotels in the world, and the company often appears on the *Fortune* list of best places to work. Its revenue per available room (RevPAR) in the highly competitive U.S. market is more than 30 percent higher than that of its closest chain competitor, Ritz-Carlton. Countries and cities around the world encourage Four Seasons to build hotels in their jurisdiction because the presence of a Four Seasons signals a high-quality location.

The success of the company has been derived from making an integrated set of choices that are highly distinctive from competitors'. Its goal was to develop a brand name synonymous with an unparalleled customer experience, and to meet these aspirations it chose to focus exclusively on serving high-end travellers. This is in direct contrast to large competitors such as Hyatt, Marriott, Hilton, and Westin, all of which compete across the spectrum of hotel classes, thereby struggling to establish consistent high-end service and branding.

Using high prices as a means of positioning, Four Seasons hotels raise their prices when competitors come near them. Even when September 11 2001, and the SARS outbreak of 2003 led to increased costs and lower occupancy levels, Four Seasons decided to maintain its room rates despite moves by competitors to slash prices. CEO Isadore Sharp believes the room rates are easily justified. "It isn't what you might call a discretionary expense, as most luxury items are," he says. "We provide a service. When travellers can rely on prompt room service, their suit being properly pressed, and their messages actually reaching them," says Sharp, "they realize this is a great value."

Another key early strategic choice for Four Seasons was to pursue a truly global strategy by developing an ever-growing portfolio of hotels and resorts in key destinations around the world. This distinguished Four Seasons from the bulk of smaller high-end competitors. The final key strategy was to specialize as a hotel manager, not a developer and owner. This was a distinct choice in the industry until Marriott divided its business into hotel ownership and hotel management companies. Because its business model means Four Seasons doesn't own most of its hotels, the capital risk is low, and the company boasts a sound balance sheet. Indeed, even in punishing economic cycles, the brand remains highly valued by investors — unusual for a place that often charges three or four times the price of a typical Sheraton.

An interesting development in the company's history is its movement into new territory with the launch of a luxury catamaran cruise in the Maldives. Called the *Four Seasons Explorer*, the catamaran offers a level of luxury not seen in this part of the world before. According to visitors, the boat lives up to its Four Seasons billing in terms of both service and activities. In fact, the *Explorer* is equal parts catamaran and luxury hotel; the staff of 25 includes not only a captain and several diving instructors, but also three chefs, a massage therapist, and an on-board marine biologist. Four Seasons' plan is to sustain equilibrium between private charters and general cruises.

Because the Four Seasons strategy is unique and involved in activities that would force competitors to make unacceptable trade-offs, its competitors have been disinclined to imitate Four Seasons, despite its obvious success. The result is a Canadian global leader with attractive growth prospects for the future.

Source: Sharp, I. (2000, April 27). The unseen precondition of long-term success. Presentation at the World Tourism Education & Research Centre's Air Canada Distinguished Lecture Series, University of Calgary, Calgary.

5.   TACTICS AND ACTION PLANS

Although no single strategy will be suitable for all organizations, marketing planning provides the opportunity to understand the operating environment and to choose options that will meet the organization's goals and objectives. Planning involves selecting and developing a series of strategies that effectively bring about the required results. Among the types of strategies that can be considered are,

- *Making good investment decisions.* Selecting the best, most effective use of financial resources is crucial. This will include reviewing the product's life cycle and doing a portfolio analysis.
- *Diversifying.* While it is important to ensure that resources are allocated to those markets showing the best potential yields, the possibility of disruptions to markets must also be taken into account. Diversification can provide an important cushion.
- *Planning for the long term.* Tourism marketing campaigns can have long lead times. The cumulative effect of promotions may take a while to produce measurable results. Building effectiveness over time is just as important as generating instant results.
- *Seizing new opportunities.* Being aware of consumer trends, fads, fashions, and attitudinal shifts will also help an organization to identify opportunities. Being flexible enough to respond to market developments will give an organization a strong competitive edge.
- *Developing strategic partnerships.* It is important to identify customers, suppliers, and competitors with which it is possible to develop an enhanced working relationship. Strategic alliances offer the opportunity to increase profits for all participants.

Applying the Marketing Mix

Marketing strategies are designed as the vehicle to achieve marketing objectives. In turn, marketing tactics are tools to support strategies. Action plans comprise a mix of marketing activities that are undertaken to influence and motivate buyers to choose targeted volumes of particular products. This part of the marketing plan shows how the organization intends to use the seven P's introduced in Chapter 1. Table 3.2 shows the activities that should be included in this section of the marketing plan. The third column lists the chapters in this book where these topics are covered in detail. A marketing mix program or marketing campaign expresses exactly what activities will take place in support of each identified product/service or market subgroup on a week-by-week basis.

6.   RESOURCE REQUIREMENTS

The marketing plan needs to address the resources required to support the marketing strategies and meet the objectives. Such resources include personnel, equipment and space, budgets, intra-organizational support, research, consulting, and training. A common error in writing a marketing plan is developing strategies that are probably highly workable but for which there is insufficient support. Generally, the most costly and difficult resource needed to ensure the success of marketing or sales

Table 3.2

Specific Strategies Included in the Action Plan

STRATEGIES	MARKETING MIX ELEMENTS (PS)	CHAPTER
Product strategies	Product Physical evidence Process	5
Pricing strategies	Price	6
Distribution strategies	Place	7
Advertising strategies	Promotion	8
Sales promotion and merchandising strategies	Promotion	8
Public relations strategies	Promotion	9
Sales strategies	Promotion	9
Direct marketing strategies	Promotion	9
Internet marketing strategies	Place Promotion	10
Internal marketing strategies (personnel, managing service quality, etc.)	People Process	11

strategies in tourism and hospitality businesses is personnel. Management commonly views the addition of personnel as unnecessary, impractical, or unwise, given budgetary restrictions.

Of prime importance in analyzing resource requirements is the budget. Setting a budget that provides the marketing department with sufficient resources to deliver its plan is essential. However, in most organizations, various departments compete for funds, and it is not always easy to convince management that the marketing budget should have a priority claim in limited funds. Although this is less of an issue in commercially oriented organizations, it can be a major problem in arts and entertainment organizations and non-profit groups. The idea of spending money on marketing (which is frequently not viewed as a core activity) at the expense of collections, maintenance, acquisitions, or expanding performance programs is often a very contentious issue.

7. MARKETING CONTROL

The penultimate step in the planning process is to ensure that objectives will be achieved in the required time, using the funds and resources requested. In order to measure effectiveness, evaluation programs have to be put in place and regular monitoring needs to occur. There is little value in preparing a one-year marketing plan and including an evaluation methodology that commences toward the end of the operating year, because it will not allow enough time to identify potential problems or initiate remedial action.

Because objectives have been set in quantifiable terms, regular reviews of sales forecasts and quotas, assessments of expenditure against budget, and data collection and analysis will provide guidance on how well objectives are being met. If a problem arises, contingency plans can be activated. Effective contingency plans are considered long before emergencies or problems arise. Reacting under pressure is rarely as effective as preplanning. If, as part of the original process, alternatives are considered, it is more likely that they will be successful. The most important reason for insisting on precision in setting objectives is to make it possible to measure results. Such results for a tourism business might be flow of bookings against planned capacity, inquiry and sales response related to any advertising, customer awareness of advertising messages measured by research surveys, sales response to any price discounts and sales promotions, sales response to any merchandising efforts by travel agents, consumer use of websites and flow of bookings achieved, and customer satisfaction measurements.

Most marketing plans are written to cover a one-year action plan in detail, with references made to the longer term — traditionally three years and five years. While the corporate goals may be longer term (often as long as 10 or 20 years), the actual objectives are usually defined in terms of a much shorter time frame. Some organizations base their marketing plans on their funding cycles. Some art organizations or government departments on three-year funding cycles prepare business and marketing plans that cover the full funding period. Even these, however, stress the importance of regular review and re-evaluate their action plan sections every 12 months.

Travel Alberta has developed a marketing planning model for the tourism industry based on four key questions: Where are we now? Where would we like to be? How do we get there? and How do we make sure we get there? The model guides the user through the planning process, helping to answer the four questions above. The model is outlined in Table 3.3.[10]

8.   COMMUNICATING THE PLAN

Involving as many staff members as possible in the process of setting objectives and drawing up plans that communicate well is an important aspect of motivating staff at all levels and securing enthusiastic participation in the implementation process. This involvement is a subject of increasing attention in many tourism and hospitality organizations.[11] It is especially important for service businesses, in which so many staff members have direct contact with customers on the premises. It is a good idea to time the stages in marketing planning so that managers and as many staff as possible in all departments can take some part in initiating or commenting on draft objectives and plans. Motivation can be damaged if objectives are continuously changed or if there is no opportunity to debate their practicality in operation. While marketing planning is conducted primarily to achieve more efficient business decisions, its secondary benefit is to provide a means of internal participation and communication, vital in creating and sustaining a high level of organizational morale.

Table 3.3

Readiness Checklist: Tourism Marketing Travel Alberta Model

	MY ORGANIZATION HAS WRITTEN THIS SECTION	MY ORGANIZATION HAS THE CAPACITY TO COMPLETE THIS, BUT HAS NOT WRITTEN THIS SECTION	MY ORGANIZATION NEEDS HELP ON THIS SECTION	I WOULD ATTEND A TRAVEL ALBERTA SEMINAR TO LEARN MORE ABOUT THIS SECTION
1. Executive Summary				
Where are we now?				
2. Situation Analysis				
2.1. Environment				
2.11. Economic environment				
2.1.2. Technological environment				
2.1.3. Political and legal environment				
2.1.4. Social and cultural environment				
2.1.5. Media environment				
2.2 The organization				
2.2.1. Mission				
2.2.2. History				
2.2.3. Product/service experience				
2.2.4. Current customers				

TABLE 3.3 *continued*

2. Situation Analysis (continued)									
2.2.5.	Value proposition								
2.2.6.	Competitive edge								
2.2.7.	Keys to success								
2.3.	Main competitors								
2.4.	SWOT analysis								
2.4.1.	Strengths								
2.4.2.	Weaknesses								
2.4.3.	Opportunities								
2.4.4.	Threats								
2.4.5.	Critical issues								
2.5.	Current marketing position and tactics								
Where would we like to be?									
3. Market Analysis									
3.1.	Market trends								
3.2.	Market opportunity types								
3.3.	Market segmentation								
3.3.1.	Behavioural								
3.3.1.1.	Demographic								
3.3.1.2.	Geographic								
3.3.1.3.	Psychographic								
3.3.1.4.	Purpose of trip								

TABLE 3.3 *continued*

3. Market Analysis (continued)					
3.4.	Marketing strategy rationale				
4. Marketing Strategy A					
4.1	Target market A				
4.1.1.	Market needs				
4.1.2.	Market growth				
4.2	Positioning statement				
4.3.	Marketing objectives				
How do we get there?					
4.4.	Marketing mix				
4.4.1.	Product				
4.4.2.	Partnership				
4.4.3.	People				
4.4.4.	Packaging				
4.4.5.	Programming				
4.4.6.	Place				
4.4.7.	Pricing				
4.4.8.	Promotion/Communication				
5. Marketing Budget					
5.1.	Sales forecast				

TABLE 3.3 *continued*

5. Marketing Budget (*continued*)				
5.2.	Break-even analysis			
5.3.	Expense forecast			
How do we make sure we get there?				
6. Implementation and Controls				
6.1.	Marketing organization			
6.2.	Milestones			
6.3.	Controls and expected results			
6.4.	Contingency planning			

Source: Travel Alberta. (2007). Readiness checklist: Tourism marketing, Travel Alberta model. (2007). Tourism Marketing Resource Booklet resource booklet, Travel Alberta.

Marketing plans must be "sold" to many people. Internally, these include members of the marketing and sales department, vendors and advertising agencies, and top management. Marketing plans are also important in communicating with stakeholders outside the organization. Approaching banks or other investors — for example, in tourism projects funded by government sources — invariably requires a business plan in which marketing is a primary component. Where money is granted, evidence of results will be required through a formal evaluation process. In terms of presenting the report, many readers, both inside and outside the organization, will be impatient and will want the conclusions immediately. The executive summary is therefore a key section of the report. Indeed, it can be assumed that some staff — and perhaps senior executives and board members — will read only the executive summary. In general, an executive summary should be between two and six pages. It should avoid the use of jargon, and it should highlight the key objectives and action aspects of the plan and budget, leaving the analysis of current situations and detailed market analyses for the main document.

CHAPTER SUMMARY

A marketing plan serves a number of purposes within any tourism organization: it provides a road map for all marketing activities of the firm for the future, it ensures that marketing activities are in agreement with the corporate strategic plan, it forces marketing managers to review and think objectively through all steps in the marketing process, it assists in the budgeting process to match resources with marketing objectives, and it creates a process to monitor actual against expected results. There are eight logical steps in a systematic marketing planning process:

1. *Corporate connection.* Marketing planning should reflect the goals and objectives of the organization as a whole.
2. *Analysis and forecasting.* This includes portfolio analysis, competitor analysis, segmentation analysis, and SWOT analysis. Forecasting becomes an important stage in the planning process to support a SWOT analysis.
3. *Setting marketing goals and objectives.* Goals are the primary aims of the organization, and objectives are the specific aims that managers accomplish to achieve organizational goals.
4. *Marketing strategy: Targeting and positioning.* Target markets should be selected from the previously developed list of available segments. Positioning is a natural follow-through from market segmentation and target marketing.
5. *Tactics and action plans.* This part of the marketing plan shows how the organization intends to use the seven P's.
6. *Resource requirements.* The marketing plan needs to address the resources required to support the strategies and meet the objectives.
7. *Marketing control.* This step in the planning process is to ensure that objectives will be achieved in the required time, using the funds and resources requested.
8. *Communicating the plan.* This is an important aspect of motivating staff at all levels and securing participation in the implementation process.

KEY TERMS

Boston Consulting Group
  (BCG) model, p. 82
branding p. 96
budget competitors p. 84
cash cow p. 83
competitor analysis p. 84
differentiation, p. 85
direct competitors, p. 84
dog, p. 83
executive summary, p. 79
focus, p. 85
forecasting, p. 91

general competitors, p. 84
goals, p. 80
low-cost leadership, p. 85
marketing plan, p. 78
market share, p. 83
mission statement, p. 80
niche marketing. p. 88
objectives, p. 80
portfolio analysis, p. 82
positioning, p. 94
product category
  competitors, p. 84

product differentiation, p. 95
question marks, p. 83
segmentation analysis, p. 85
stars, p. 83
strategic marketing plan, p. 78
SWOT analysis, p. 88
target market, p. 92
unique selling proposition
  (USP), p. 95
vision statement, p. 80

DISCUSSION QUESTIONS AND EXERCISES

1. Examine the mission statement for a local tourism or hospitality organization. Does it answer the question of what business the organization is in? If not, try to redefine the statement.

2. Choose a large tourism or hospitality enterprise in Canada and apply the BCG model to the various products and services on offer. Does the organization have a balanced portfolio?

3. Four Seasons Hotels and Resorts has achieved success through distinctive positioning. Think of another three examples of tourism organizations that have clearly understood the significance of positioning. Describe their target markets.

4. It is suggested in the chapter that competitors can be divided into four broad categories. Take an example from the tourism industry in Canada (a hotel chain perhaps) and list its competitors under the four categories.

5. The chapter highlights a number of target markets growing in attractiveness for the tourism industry. Segment the tourists that your region attracts. Are there any segments of the travel market that are not being targeted? Why not?

6. Go out and find a marketing plan from a tourism organization in your area. Does it follow the eight steps of the planning process outlined in this chapter? How is it different?

CASE STUDY

THE FAILURE OF ROOTS AIR

The story of Roots Air began early in 2000, with a cryptic voice mail message from Ted Shetzen, the man behind Roots Air, to Leo Desrochers, the chief operating officer of Skyservice Airlines Inc., a Toronto-based charter carrier that mostly ferried travellers south in the winter. Desrochers's acquaintance with Shetzen went way back, to the days when both worked at Air Canada. Shetzen's message was brief and to the point, saying only: "It's time."

From those two words emerged a plan to steal away a small portion of Air Canada's most profitable customers — business flyers — by enticing them with celebrity pitches and promises of great food, plush lounges, and excellent service, all at lower prices. A main attraction of the new venture was its branding agreement with Roots, the clothing empire founded by Michael Budman and Don Green. Roots invested $5 million for the right to put its name on the carrier and design the uniforms, lounges, and other promotional items. Trading on the trendy image of the apparel retailer, the timing of the new airline seemed encouraging. The merger of Air Canada and Canadian Airlines was not going well, and there was reason to believe there were a lot of disgruntled travellers looking for an alternative.

A key element of the Roots Air strategy was to use brand new A320 and A330 aircraft but exploit Skyservice's existing infrastructure to operate at low cost. "We basically saw an opportunity to carve a place out for ourselves in the business market, not with high expectations of market share, not competing with Air Canada everywhere, but enough to allow us an adequate return on capital," recalled Desrochers. Roots had two service tiers: gold and silver. Gold included luxury items such as leather-covered seats, whereas silver service was tailored for the more price-sensitive business traveller. In March 2001, a Roots silver-class fare was about $800 one-way from Vancouver to Toronto. Air Canada's fare was almost $2000 for the same journey.

As well as targeting the business traveller, Roots Air was looking to attract consumers who wanted to associate themselves with the cachet of the retailer, Roots Canada. But apart from outfitting its cabin staff and baggage personnel in the hip designs that have made Roots famous from Hollywood to the Olympics, Roots Air did not forge a clear marketing message. A major advertising campaign by Grey Worldwide of Toronto touted the Roots Air image, with a jazzy website, large banners inside and outside major airports, and print ads in major daily newspapers. The agency tried to entice customers and executives and travel agents with moody, black-and-white photos unconventional for the airline industry. This led to further criticisms that the Roots message was unclear.

As far as public relations were concerned, Budman and Green, co-founders of the Roots apparel phenomenon, were conspicuously absent in the airline's development phase, choosing not to play the Richard Branson role of playful, ubiquitous promoters — probably the only chance Roots Air had of making an impression on jaded air travellers. If they deferred to Russell Payson, CEO of Skyservice, it was perhaps with the knowledge that the Roots owners' previous non-retail fling with a Roots hotel in Colorado in the early 1990s was a flop.

But in general, the goals of the new airline were too ambitious. An offering circular was sent out in June 2000, by Research Capital Corp., to raise $35 million to fund the venture. It included a pro forma statement showing that Skyservice's revenue would increase to $548.3 million from $228.9 million in the first year of Roots Air's operation, starting with four planes and adding two more by the end of the year. By comparison, WestJet, arguably Canada's most successful airline ever, took five years to attain those numbers, reaching them only in 2000 after it had grown to 22 aircraft. "The expectations were not realistic, particularly for a start-up airline in its first year of operations," says Kobus Dietzsch, who worked in marketing planning and analysis in Roots Air. A more realistic expectation would have been for $175 million in revenue the first year, says Dietzsch.

Other assumptions made at the outset were also dubious. For example, the plan was based on a 50/50 mix of business and leisure customers, whereas 20 percent business class is considered good by most industry standards. In estimating traffic, the original plan was premised on having 71 percent of its silver and 78 percent of its gold business seats filled during August, a time when such traffic tapers off. "The real problem was that we had too many business-class seats on airplanes," says Skyservice's Payson.

Confusion was rampant within Skyservice leading up to and beyond its first Roots Air flight on March 26, 2001. "Despite the excitement of launching a new airline, there is a feeling of being overwhelmed by the enormity of the task and compressed timeline," said a consultant's study done by Marketing Matters for Skyservice in mid-January. Even basic scheduling decisions raised intractable problems. The airline did not know 11 days before March 26 whether or not it would be flying Calgary–Toronto on the first day. The flight was ultimately cancelled. Only one interline agreement (despite plans for many more) with other carriers to receive and hand off passengers was signed by the launch date. Even that deal with Air Tahiti fell apart after Roots Air announced on the first day that it would not fly to Los Angeles, where it was to connect with the Pacific Island carrier. This further hurt earnings projections, since initial expectations were that a significant portion of revenue would come from arrangements with other airlines. Desrochers states that it was difficult to negotiate such agreements because potential partners wanted to see Roots Air up and running before signing.

Perhaps the biggest fiasco came on launch day, when the carrier was forced to cancel two of its inaugural flights because one of its planes had not arrived on time. Compounding the problem was a mistaken entry in the travel agent computer reservation system, showing Roots Air operating a 316-seat Airbus A330 when in fact the plane was a 120-seat A320. As a result, the aircraft was oversold and Roots' Budman and his guests found themselves bumped.

Other problems ran deeper, and included internal disorganization and in-fighting between the low-end charter side of Skyservice, which operated the Roots Air scheduled flights, and the Roots Air people, who aimed to be high-end. Skyservice operational people began referring derogatorily to those in the Roots Air marketing arm as the "hangar people" because they were holed up in a different building. Cultural differences also had a negative effect on the advertising, which was crucial to attracting customers and of prime importance to the Roots clothing partners, for whom marketing has always been fundamental. Marc Stoiber, creative director of the Roots Air account at Grey Advertising says, "With two very different cultures coming together, understandably there was tension and the stakes were very high. Is it a price-driven thing or a style-driven thing?"

One month after launching, it was clear that a host of assumptions on which Roots Air had been based were incorrect. It was now clear that Air Canada did in fact have a hammerlock on corporate Canada, and business traffic was not materializing. Calgary passengers in particular were not as disaffected with Air Canada as had been believed, and the Roots Air brand was not resonating with the public as expected. Finally, the Roots Air's service aspirations were being thwarted by the charter culture of Skyservice. Having promised more legroom, shorter line-ups, better food, and real china in the promotional material, the airline found that it just could not deliver on promises.

There were simply too few passengers to sustain the business. During its short life, on average Roots Air flew less than 60 percent full. While some flights had 80 percent loads, others were much worse, such as the Calgary–Toronto run on May 3, 2001, the day the airline announced it would shut, when the 120-seat plane had only five people on board. The low loads overturned the economics of the operation, with the result that Roots Air lost money on virtually every flight. Payson says the carrier was losing $1 million a week, a significant expense for a company the size of Skyservice, which had revenue of about $110 million in the fiscal year ending April 30, 2000. In the end, having lost about $7.5. million, Skyservice opted for a deal with Air Canada that called for shutting down Roots Air on May 4, 2001, and for the two to collaborate on running a new low-cost carrier. The low-cost plan fell apart, but the deal allowed for an orderly closure with no passengers left stranded and no creditors left unpaid.

Sources: Bramham, D. (2001, March 27). Roots air: Not quite flight of fancy. *Vancouver Sun*, F1; Fitzpatrick, P. (2002, January 31). Up, up … and down: Roots, a short history. *Financial Post*, 1, 14; Laucius, J. (2001, May 5). Roots air couldn't compete with frequent fights. *Ottawa Citizen*, D1.

QUESTIONS

1. What went wrong with the Roots Air? Were there elements of the marketing plan outlined in this chapter that did not receive sufficient attention?
2. Since the writing of this case, several groups in Canada have started up new carriers. What can they learn from the experiences of Roots Air?
3. The text lists the criteria used most often by tourism and hospitality suppliers to segment the market. What particular segments was Roots Air trying to attract and what methods did it use to segment the market? Was it successful?
4. The Roots brand has never travelled very far beyond its established position in leisure apparel. Why do you think that is?
5. Other Canadian airlines have failed over the last decade or so (e.g., Harmony, CanJet, Jetsgo, Canada 3000). Do some research and find out why. Were there any similarities with Roots Air?

WEB SITES

---

www.fourseasons.com
Four Seasons Hotels and Resorts

www.robben-island.org.za
Robben Island

www.awrestaurants.com
A&W Restaurants

ENDNOTES

1. Porter, M. E. (1980). *Competitive strategy: Techniques for analyzing industry and competitors.* New York: Free Press, 4.

2. Hudson, S., & Ritchie, J. R. B. (2002). Understanding the domestic market using cluster analysis: A case study of the marketing efforts of Travel Alberta. *Journal of Vacation Marketing, 8*(3), 263–276.

3. Crawford-Welch, S. (1991). Marketing hospitality in the 21st century. *International Journal of Contemporary Hospitality Management, 3*(3), 21–27.

4. Middleton, V. T. C., & Clarke, J. (2001). *Marketing in travel and tourism.* Oxford: Butterworth-Heinemann, 209.

5. Canadian Tourism Commission. (2002). BTA launches 2002 edition of gay and lesbian campaign. www.canadatourism.com/en/ctc/ctx/ctxnews/search/newsbydateform.cfm (retrieved February 2002).

6. Fong, M. (2006, November 23). Best Western strategy in China goes upscale. *Globe & Mail,* B19.

7. Zeithaml, V. A., Berry, L. L., & Parasuraman, A. (1988). Communication and control processes in the delivery of service quality. *Journal of Marketing, 52*(2), 35–48.

8. Zeithaml, V. A., Berry, L. L., & Parasuraman, A. (1996). The behavioural consequences of service quality. *Journal of Marketing, 60*(2), 31–46.

9. Gale, B. (1992). *Monitoring customer satisfaction and market-perceived quality.* American Marketing Association Worth Repeating Series, No. 922CSO 1. Chicago: American Marketing Association.

10. Travel Alberta. (2007). Readiness Checklist: Tourism Marketing, Travel Alberta Model. Tourism marketing resource booklet.

11. Middleton, V. T. C., & Clarke, J. (2001). *Marketing in travel and tourism.* Oxford: Butterworth-Heinemann, 213.

Marketing Research

Spotlight

THE INTERNATIONAL TRAVEL SURVEY

importance of the tourism industry to the Canadian economy in terms of employment size and growth, foreign exchange earnings, tax revenues for all levels of government, and gross domestic product (GDP). The information the CTC provides has proved invaluable in gaining visibility for the tourism industry and drawing attention to some of the obstacles to its growth that are of a regulatory or financial nature (air transportation policy, taxation policies, customs practices, etc.).

While the CTC carries out regular market surveys regarding consumer perceptions, behaviour, and travel patterns in every major international market, it acknowledges that there is still a need for tourism organizations to get to know their customers better. One area that has seen significant improvements in recent years is in the collection of data from traffic flows across Canada's borders. The International Travel Survey (ITS) measures these flows and creates a profile of visitors' characteristics, travel habits, and spending while they are in this

The research program at the Canadian Tourism Commission (CTC) is fundamental to the success of the CTC. It establishes the country. In this way, trends can be spotted for international tourism traffic, predictions can be made for forecasting, and information can be produced for decision making. Conducted by Statistics Canada in partnership with the CTC, the ITS produces numbers that are released on a monthly, quarterly, and annual basis.

The ITS is an ongoing study and has been in process since the 1920s. It initially consisted of a simple form, requiring very little time to complete. As travel and tourism grew over the decades, so did the form's length — and the number of forms — required to keep track of visitors to Canada. But for many reasons, the survey had begun to yield data whose quality was eroding — partly because a smaller and smaller percentage of travellers' questionnaires were returned. So beginning in the late 1990s, the CTC research committee began to address the whole logic and design of the ITS, and to develop a new vision more suitable to the needs of the tourism industry, notably rationalizing it to focus on Canada's major ports of entry and key international markets.

Among the changes made is the supplementation of paper questionnaires (handed out by custom officers to overseas residents as they enter Canada) with personal interviews with some of these visitors as they leave. Also, the number of languages in which surveys are conducted has increased from two to ten, and sampling has been concentrated on the major and medium-sized Canadian airports. In addition to changing the way data are collected, the methods used to derive the estimates have been improved to better reflect the different characteristics of business and leisure travellers from some key overseas markets.

Rebuilding the ITS was not an easy task. Traditional surveys use a stable population, but the ITS involves millions of moving targets. The field work for the ITS also requires an enormous amount of effort and more than 3700 people to complete it each month. But the CTC is on the right track. Users of the new ITS numbers include the federal governments, provincial and territorial governments, the CTC, most large Canadian cities, and the U.S. government. Many private sector businesses, such as hotels, industry associations, and tourism organizations, use the data regularly for planning, developing marketing strategies, and measuring trends. The data are also used for reporting to international organizations such as the United Nations World Tourism Organization (UNWTO), the Organisation for Economic Co-operation and Development (OECD), and the Pacific Asia Travel Association (PATA).

Sources: Canadian Tourism Commission. (2002). Canadian Tourism Commission Strategic Plan, 2003–2005. Ottawa, 13; Meis, S. (2002). New era in research. *Tourism*, 6(8), 15.

Objectives

On completion of this chapter, readers should understand

- the meaning of marketing research;
- the types of applied marketing research employed in the tourism industry;
- the key stages in the marketing research process;

- the relative merits of the various methodologies available to researchers; and
- how marketing research can be used for effective decision making.

Chapter Overview

The *Spotlight* highlights some of the issues associated with collecting data, and this chapter focuses on marketing research in tourism and hospitality, beginning with an introduction to marketing research, its definition, and its role in the tourism and hospitality industry. A description of the type of applied research conducted in tourism is followed by a focus on the various stages in the research process. A section then describes the various methodologies available to researchers and discusses the relative merits of primary versus secondary research. The next part of the chapter looks at sampling, and five common research problems are then highlighted. The final section discusses effective use of research in decision making.

INTRODUCTION TO MARKETING RESEARCH

marketing information system (MIS)

a method of gathering, using, and disseminating research in the marketing context

Research should form the basis of an ongoing system for gathering data about an organization, its products and services, and its markets. Often, in the course of their everyday duties, managers gather intelligence informally and subconsciously by observing, listening to discussions, talking to colleagues in the industry, and reading trade journals and papers. Valuable as this process is, it should be supported by more formal procedures carried out in a systematic and scientific manner. The way in which an organization gathers, uses, and disseminates its research in the marketing context is generally referred to as the **marketing information system (MIS)**. The success of an MIS depends on the quality of the information, its accuracy and relevance, and the way it is collected, interpreted, and applied. A key component of the MIS is the marketing research process.

Researchers and managers seldom address the definition of what constitutes marketing research. To complicate the issue further, the terms "market research" and "marketing research" are often used interchangeably, sometimes within the same document. Paul Gerhold asserts that there is no difference between the two terms and that they can both be defined as "any scientific effort to understand and measure markets or improve marketing performance."[1] Thomas Kinnear and his colleagues distinguish

marketing research

the systematic and objective search for and analysis of information relevant to the identification and solution of any problem in the field of marketing

between the two terms, arguing that the focus of market research is on the analysis of markets, whereas marketing research extends the role and character of research and emphasizes the contact between researchers and the marketing management process.[2] This chapter adopts the term **marketing research** exclusively, defining it as the systematic and objective search for and analysis of information relevant to the identification and solution of any problem in the field of marketing.[3]

MARKETING RESEARCH IN TOURISM AND HOSPITALITY

According to Robert McIntosh, Charles Goeldner, and J. R. Brent Ritchie, there are six reasons for conducting tourism and hospitality research:

1. to identify, describe, and solve problems in order to increase the efficiencies of day-to-day tourism operations;
2. to keep tourism and hospitality organizations in touch with trends, changes, predictions, and so on, related to their markets;
3. to reduce the waste produced by tourists and tourist organizations;
4. to develop new areas of profit by finding new products, services, markets, etc.;
5. to help promote sales in situations where research findings are of interest to the public; and
6. to develop goodwill, as the public thinks well of firms that are doing research in order to meet consumers' needs.[4]

Unfortunately, in tourism and hospitality many smaller organizations feel that "real" marketing research is a costly and time-consuming luxury only available to large companies that have professional research staff, sophisticated computers, and almost unlimited budgets. Other organizations see marketing research as something to be undertaken when a major event is about to occur— the introduction of a new product, the acquisition of a new property, or a change in target markets. Its value at these junctures is recognized, but its ability to contribute to an organization's success daily is often overlooked. Another common problem in the tourism industry is that organizations do not make full use of the information that already exists and is easily accessed. Sometimes information is available and studies are done, but the results are either ignored or not fully considered in the final decision-making process. This lack of attention happens when the information is not in accord with the prevailing view of management or when the information has not been properly analyzed and clearly presented.

APPLIED RESEARCH IN TOURISM AND HOSPITALITY

Most marketing research is classified as applied research, which is undertaken to answer specific questions. It differs from pure research (done by scientists at universities or by government authorities), which is aimed at the discovery of new information. Applied research in tourism and hospitality can be grouped into eight categories: research on consumers, research on products and services, research on pricing, research on place and distribution, research on promotion, research on competition, research on the operating environment, and research on a destination. Table 4.1 lists some of the typical research programs undertaken within these categories.

Table 4.1

Applied Research in Tourism and Hospitality

RESEARCH ON CONSUMERS

- Identifying existing markets
- Identifying potential markets
- Identifying lapsed consumers
- Testing customer loyalty
- Developing detailed consumer profiles

- Identifying general trends in demographics and psychographics
- Identifying changes in attitudes and behaviour patterns (generally)
- Identifying changes in attitudes and behaviour patterns (product/service specific)

RESEARCH ON PRODUCTS AND SERVICES

- Measuring attitudes toward existing products or services
- Identifying products and services that may be at the end of their life cycle
- Identifying products and services that are considered acceptable substitutes/ alternatives

- Evaluating competitor's products and services
- Evaluating consumer attitudes toward decor, presentation, and packaging
- Evaluating consumer attitudes about combinations of products and services (bundles of product attributes)

RESEARCH ON PRICING

- Identifying attitudes toward prices
- Testing attitudes toward packages and individual pricing
- Identifying costs

- Identifying costing policies of competitors
- Testing alternative pricing strategies
- Testing payment processes (credit cards, electronic funds transfer, etc.)

RESEARCH ON PLACE AND DISTRIBUTION

- Identifying attitudes toward location
- Identifying attitudes toward buildings/premises
- Identifying attitudes on virtual sites
- Identifying potential demand for product or services at other locations
- Identifying cooperative opportunities for distribution of information or services

RESEARCH ON PROMOTION

- Testing and comparing media options
- Testing alternative messages
- Testing competitor's messages and their effectiveness
- Testing new communications options (Internet, e-mail, websites)
- Identifying cooperative opportunities
- Measuring advertising and promotion effectiveness

RESEARCH ON COMPETITION

- Measuring awareness
- Measuring usage
- Identifying levels of customer loyalty
- Identifying competitors' strengths and weaknesses
- Identifying specific competitive advantages (locations, suppliers, etc.)
- Identifying cooperative opportunities

RESEARCH ON THE OPERATING ENVIRONMENT

- Economic trends
- Social trends
- Environmental issues
- Political climate and trends
- Technological development and their impact

RESEARCH ON A DESTINATION

- Measuring residents' attitudes
- Benchmarking
- Measuring customer loyalty
- Identifying tourism activities
- Identifying spending patterns
- Branding research

A veritable explosion of new journals has been introduced as the outlet for academic publication of research in hospitality and tourism. A recent inventory, while neither exhaustive nor exclusive, yielded a count of 70, as listed in Table 4.2.

Table 4.2

An Inventory of Tourism and Hospitality Publications

GENERAL INTEREST	
Anatolia	Journal of Convention and Exhibition Management
Australian Journal of Hospitality Management	Journal of Convention & Event Tourism
Consortium Journal of Hospitality and Tourism	Journal of Gambling Studies
Cornell Hotel and Restaurant Administration Quarterly	Journal of Hospitality and Leisure for the Elderly
FIU Hospitality Review (Florida International University)	Journal of Hospitality & Leisure Marketing
	Journal of Hospitality and Tourism Research
Hotel and Motel Management	Journal of Hospitality Financial Management
International Journal of Contemporary Hospitality Management	Journal of Quality Assurance in Hospitality and Tourism
International Journal of Hospitality and Tourism Administration	Journal of Tourism and Hospitality Education
International Journal of Hospitality Information Technology	Praxis: The Journal of Applied Hospitality Management
International Journal of Hospitality Management	Scandinavian Journal of Hospitality and Tourism
Journal of Applied Hospitality Management	Tourism and Hospitality Research

TOURISM	
ACTA *Turistica*	Information Technology and Tourism
Annals of Tourism Research	International Journal of Tourism Research
ASEAN Journal on Hospitality and Tourism	Journal of Ecotourism
Asia Pacific Journal of Tourism Research	Journal of Human Resources in Hospitality and Tourism
China Tourism Research	
Current Issues in Tourism	Journal of Sports Tourism
Event Tourism	Journal of Sustainable Tourism

Journal of Teaching in Travel and Tourism	Tourism Intelligence Quarterly
Journal of Tourism Studies	Tourism Management
Journal of Travel and Tourism Marketing	Tourism Recreation Research
Journal of Travel and Tourism Research	Tourism Today
Journal of Travel Research	Tourism, Culture, and Communication
Journal of Vacation Marketing	Tourism: An International Interdisciplinary Journal
Pacific Tourism Review	Tourismus Journal
Tourism Analysis	Tourist Review
Tourism Economics	Tourist Studies
Tourism Geographies	Travel and Tourism Analyst
Tourism in Marine Environments	

FOODSERVICE

Journal of Agricultural and Food Information	Journal of Nutrition for the Elderly
Journal of College and University Foodservice	Journal of Nutrition, Recipe, and Menu Development
Journal of Culinary Science	Journal of Restaurant and Foodservice Marketing
Journal of Food Production Management	Journal of the American Dietetic Association
Journal of Food Products Marketing	NACUFS Journal (National Association of College and University Foodservices)
Journal of Foodservice Business Research	School Foodservice Research Review
Journal of Foodservice Systems	

consumer research

applied research focused on the consumer

Consumer research is one type of applied research, and cases in this chapter look at consumer studies in food services (see *Snapshot* on food research), consumer research (or the lack of) conducted by EuroDisney (see *Profile*), and a consumer behavioural study by Carton Donofrio Partners Inc. (see the other *Snapshot*). A word of caution about consumer research: Often consumers will tell researchers what they think they want to hear, or what the respondents want to believe about themselves. A decade ago, consumers told researchers that they wanted healthier fast-food options. Burger chains around the world responded by offering salads and fruit and fresh juices. Wendy's added a fresh fruit bowl to its menu; two years later they killed it, blaming a lack of demand. "We listened to consumers who said they wanted to eat fresh fruit but apparently they lied," a Wendy's representative said. Recent times have seen the launch of a rash of products that the fast-food industry calls "indulgent offerings" — foods marketed specifically on the basis of how much meat and cheese they contain and how few annoying vegetables they contain.

competitor intelligence

detailed information about the competition and how the organization is doing in comparison

Another important type of applied research is **competitor intelligence**. If an organization wants to keep track of competition, it requires a clear understanding of its competition, as well as knowledge of how it is doing in comparison to the competitors. Competitor intelligence is available from a variety of sources, including competitors' annual reports, local tourism authorities and state tourism departments, magazine articles, speeches, media releases, brochures, and advertisements. It is important, too, to recognize what is meant by "the competition" — see Chapter 3 for a discussion of four broad categories of competition. As previously noted, information about the number and type of competitors, their relative market shares, the things they do well, and the things they do badly will assist in the planning process. A review of the competition will also highlight market trends and the level of loyalty of consumers.

While some information is willingly shared, to get a true picture of how the competition is doing, an organization often needs to undertake research. The form of this research varies from business to business. For a tourist attraction or food operation, it could be as simple as counting the number of cars in the parking lot at various times, or actually going into the facility to see how busy it is. For a hotel, it might mean checking room availability at particular times or watching for advertisements of special offers and discounts. For tour operators, it may involve counting the number of competing coaches at major destinations and collecting tour brochures and schedules. Participant observation is also often used to gather competitor intelligence. For example, executives of airlines might travel with competitors, or hotel managers might check in to competitor hotels. These are effective ways of gathering valuable knowledge for research purposes.

SNAPSHOT

TRAVELLERS' NEEDS NOT BEING MET BY THE TRAVEL INDUSTRY

In 2002, a team of anthropologists in Tokyo, London, Israel, New York, Los Angeles, Chicago, Orlando, and Las Vegas gathered data from a global sample of travellers and identified basic needs that were not being met by the travel industry. These findings were used to locate and understand points within the travel experience where industries such as hotels, rental car companies, attractions, and cruises could better meet the needs of their customers. The report, published by Carton Donofrio Partners Inc., views "travel" as a brand. The collaborative nature of the travel industry makes it unique in that consumers come into contact with numerous products, services, and people each time they travel. The study examines the sum of all these interactions, which is one "travel" brand experience.

More specifically, the researchers found that consumers see travel as a process; they plan their trip, travel via some mode (air, train, ship, car), stay at their destination for a time, then pass back through the same mode to get home. They found that if one part of the process is in distress, the whole process suffers. The study concluded that this travel process is powered by three variables — the three needs that travellers seek to fulfill. The most basic is that of *control*

SNAPSHOT *continued*

over their travel experience. People also demand a consistent level of *service* throughout the whole process. And, ultimately, people want an experience that brings them the *joy* of travel. The needs of control, service, and joy must be satisfied throughout the planning, mode, and destination stages.

Figure 4.1 illustrates the differences between the ideal travel brand experience and that of today. The ideal model begins with a high level of control during the planning stage. Travellers, especially leisure travellers, slowly relinquish control as they move through their travel brand process. By the time they reach the destination, they want to turn a good deal of control over to someone else, whether it's to the leisure resort or the business lodging chain. They want things taken care of *for* them, not *by* them. Ideally, the service level remains consistent through every step of the travel brand experience. Travellers expect at least a satisfactory level of service at each stage of their trip. The joy level rises from planning to a peak at the destination part of the travel experience. In today's experience, however, these fundamental travel needs are often not being satisfied. The major source of this distress is the mode, or means of transportation, and people cannot easily plan their trip or truly enjoy their destination because of that disruption. Thus, needs are met minimally in this mode and this in turn lowers the level of satisfaction throughout the whole process.

The Carton Donofrio study suggests that the travel industry should focus on needs — on satisfying control, service, and joy — to balance today's travel brand experience. In sum, the study found that travel is no longer a fluid process, but is now broken up by anxieties that leave many consumers re-evaluating their reasons for travel. Organizations that, by the nature of their business, are able to touch a traveller only at one point in his or her experience should look to expand their influence to span many segments of the travel experience. By doing so, they will be recognized for increasing the level of customer service in unique ways that go beyond traditional measures and outside their usual boundaries.

Source: Carton Donofrio Partners Inc. (2002, April 15). Global study on travel examines consumer behaviours. www.cartondonofrio.com/news/archivecaster .cfm?id=289&cat=5 (retrieved September 2007).

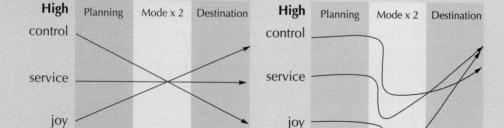

Figure 4.1 The Ideal Travel Brand and the Travel Brand Today

STAGES IN THE RESEARCH PROCESS

In undertaking research, there are a number of steps that should be followed, as outlined in Figure 4.2.

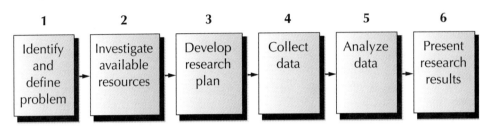

Figure 4.2 Stages in the Research Process

1. Identify and Define the Problem

Before the task of gathering information can be started, it is first necessary to identify the problem for which research is required. This step is crucial to ensure that any information collected is relevant. As well as formulating an aim, specific research questions (objectives) should be stipulated at the outset. These objectives will determine the type of information required. There are three types of objectives for a marketing research project:

1. *exploratory,* to gather information that will help define the problem and suggest hypotheses;
2. *descriptive,* to describe the size and composition of the market; and
3. *causal,* to test hypotheses about cause-and-effect relationships.

2. Investigate Available Sources

There is little point embarking upon a research program involving the collection of primary data if the information is already available. Seeking out available information involves a search of internal data generated and recorded by the organization as well as an examination of available secondary sources. Such information should then be assessed to establish the extent to which the research questions can be tackled using this information alone.

3. Develop the Research Plan

primary data

information collected for the specific purpose at hand

secondary data

information that already exists somewhere, having been collected for another purpose

Specific information should be determined from the research objectives. Research objectives must be translated into specific information needs. Two types of data can be used to meet the organization's information needs: **primary data**, consisting of information collected for the specific purpose at hand, and **secondary data**, consisting of information that already exists somewhere, having been collected for another purpose.

4. Collect Data

Upon development of a research plan, data should be collected using the method(s) selected. The data collection phase of the marketing research process is generally the most expensive and the one most frequently subject to error. Great care should be taken to avoid bias, which, if introduced, could render results meaningless. This is a particular problem associated with the interview and observation methods.

5. Analyze Data

The collected data must be processed and analyzed to pull out important information and findings. The methods used and the type of information collected will determine the analysis needed. Raw data taken from questionnaires, in-depth interviews, checklists, etc., need to be recorded, analyzed, and interpreted. Researchers are constantly searching for similarities and differences, for groupings, patterns, and items of particular significance. Commonly used statistical packages among tourism researchers are SPSS (Statistical Package for the Social Sciences), MINITAB, and NCSS (Number Cruncher Statistical System). These packages are continually being monitored, reviewed, and updated to reflect the process of continuous evolution in computer software.

6. Present Research Results

Information needs to be tabulated and interpreted, so that recommendations can be made regarding an appropriate course of action to take. This will almost certainly involve the presentation of a report that summarizes the results of the research. This report enables the management of the organization to make decisions based on the newly acquired information.

RESEARCH METHODOLOGY

The increased importance of tourism management decision making has caused more attention to be focused on the theories and methodologies of the tourism research process. A recurrent theme has emerged in the travel research literature concerning the appropriateness of specific types of tourism research and certain methodological applications. There are several approaches to collecting data, but two key decisions that have to be made are as follows:

- *Primary versus secondary data.* In planning a research project, it is sensible to consider whether it is worth going to the expense of collecting new information (primary data, where the researcher is the primary user) or whether existing data (secondary data, where the researcher is the secondary user) will be sufficient. In practice, it may be necessary to collect both types of information. The various types of primary and secondary research are explored later in this chapter.

qualitative research
research methods that use and give rise to subjective or interpretive information

quantitative research
research methods that produce numerical (empirical) data

- *Qualitative versus quantitative research.* **Qualitative research** methods give rise to subjective or interpretative information, whereas **quantitative research** methods produce numerical (empirical) data. There has been much debate recently about appropriate methods for leisure research, with some authors arguing for extended use of qualitative research over quantitative research. In tourism research, quantitative and qualitative research approaches seem to coexist without the sort of apparent rivalry seen in leisure studies. It is possible for research to be conducted entirely quantitatively, entirely qualitatively, or using a mixture of both. In fact, it is common for large-scale quantitative research to be planned on the basis of prior exploratory qualitative studies.

The distinction between the two methods is indicated in Table 4.3. Both research methods possess distinct limitations and weaknesses, but both also have redeeming characteristics. The choice between the two must be determined by the situation in which research takes place, not by some misguided search for rigor simply for its own sake.

Table 4.3

Qualitative versus Quantitative Research

COMPARISON DIMENSION	QUALITATIVE RESEARCH	QUANTITATIVE RESEARCH
Types of questions	Probing	Limited probing
Sample size	Small	Large
Information per respondent	Much	Varies
Administration	Interviewer requires special skills	Interviewer requires few special skills
Types of analysis	Subjective, interpretive	Statistical, summarizing
Hardware	Tape recorders, projection devices, video equipment, pictures	Questionnaires, computers, printouts
Ability to replicate	Low	High
Training of the researcher	Psychology, sociology, social psychology, consumer behaviour marketing, marketing research	Statistics, decision models, decision support systems, computer programming, marketing research
Types of research	Exploratory	Descriptive or causal

Source: McDaniel, C. D., Jr., & Gates, R. (1993). Contemporary marketing research (2nd ed.). Minneapolis–St. Paul: West, 126.

SNAPSHOT

RESEARCH IN THE FOODSERVICE INDUSTRY

Research in the foodservice industry is a subject that has received minimal attention in the literature on tourism. In a recent article, Nick Johns and Ray Pine reviewed the literature related to consumer studies in food service, organizing it into four sections representing different schools of research (see Table 4.4). "Survey research" includes studies of consumers as groups, while the work reviewed under "experimental research" involves test situations in which different factors have been manipulated. Studies under "economics and geography" represent alternative quantitative approaches to consumer research. Under "sociology and anthropology" is included a range of qualitative research that provides complementary insights into the restaurant experience.

Table 4.4

Summary of the Four Areas of Foodservice Consumer Research

AREA	PRACTICAL FOCUS	METHODS USED	THEORETICAL FOCUS	EXAMPLES OF AUTHORS
Survey research	• Segmentation targeting positioning	• Geodemographic, attitude and behavioural-based surveys • Modelling	• Attribute theory • Expectancy-disconfirmation • Repeat business	Nayga & Capps (1994) Binkley (1998)
Experimental research	• Customer preferences	• Control of specific variables	• Factors affecting food preference	Bruner (1990) Love (1995) Birch et al. (1984)

SNAPSHOT *continued*

AREA	PRACTICAL FOCUS	METHODS USED	THEORETICAL FOCUS	EXAMPLES OF AUTHORS
Economics and geography	• Spatial and socioeconomic location	• Analysis of secondary data	• Population flow and behaviour	Holm et al. (1995)
Sociology and anthropology	• Individual experience • Wider social context	• In-depth interview • Observation • Literature review	• Power relations • Social impacts • Semiotics	Jamal (1996) Finkelstein (1989) Smith (1985)

Sources: Binkley, J. K. (1998). Demand for fast food across metropolitan areas. *Journal of Restaurant and Foodservice Marketing, 3*(1), 37–50; Birch, L. L., Billman, J., & Richards, S. S. (1984). Time of day influences food acceptability. *Appetite, 5*(3), 109–116; Bruner, G. C. (1990). Music, mood, and marketing. *Journal of Marketing, 54*, 94–104; Finkelstein J. (1989). *Dining out: A sociology of modern manners*. Polity Press, Cambridge UK; Holm, F., Falkebo, M., Salmiovirta, T., Ramstad, A. H., & van Rooy, H. (1995). Analysis of retailing in the Nordic countries. *International Trends in Retailing, 12*(2), 3–31. Jamal, A. (1996). Acculturation: The symbolism of ethnic eating among contemporary British consumers. *British Food Journal, 98*(10), 12–26; Love, J. F. (1995). *McDonald's Behind the Arches*. Bantam Books, New York. Nayga, R. M., & Capps O. (1994). Impact of socio-economic and demographic factors on food away from home consumption: Number of meals and type facility. *Journal of Restaurant and Foodservice Marketing, 1*(2), 45–69. Smith, S. L. J. (1985). Location patterns of urban restaurants. *Annals of Tourism Research, 12*(4), 581–602.

Most quantitative studies in foodservice consumer research are concerned with some aspect of segmentation, e.g., characterizing segments, identifying needs, or positioning specific offerings relative to specific segments. A large amount of work in this field has established a coherent structure linking restaurant attributes to repeat business. Many studies use expectancy-disconfirmation theory (how well actual performance confirms or disconfirms expectations) and the relationship between the quality of the offering and likelihood of repeat business has been demonstrated using sophisticated multivariate techniques.

The experimental research tradition regards eating out as a function of the food itself and the situation in which it is eaten. Surprisingly, the physical surroundings in which food is eaten have been given comparatively little attention, despite offering very attractive targets for experiment. The effects of image, colour, and music were extensively investigated in retail settings in the 1960s and 1970s. More recently, it has been claimed that McDonald's uses colour and image to manage the behaviour of patrons. Taste experiments have shown that the time of day, and also the speed of a service, affect taste perceptions, and social context experiments reveal that the amount people eat increases with the number of people in a group.

Economic reports of the restaurant business appear frequently in the trade periodicals, but are generally limited in scope, are descriptive rather than analytical, and quickly become outdated. National statistics are offered by government publications in many countries, and deeper analyses of national data occasionally find their way into more permanent literature. No serious attention seems to have been paid to forecasting or to assessing the contribution of the restaurant business to local or national economies. Similarly, the geography of eating out seems to be a neglected area of research, apart from some work by Stephen Smith (1985) who analyzed restaurant location patterns in relation to geographical issues, such as the distribution of populations and industries.[5]

Social and anthropological studies have the potential to enrich consumer research in the foodservice industry by casting light on the individual experience that underlies consumer responses. Most studies have been more concerned with the societal effects of the foodservice industry, but a few researchers have used semiotics and discourse analysis to access consumers' deeper meanings. This approach may represent a way to understand perceptions of restaurant experiences.

In general, Johns and Pine see a need for studies to seek new techniques and to exchange ideas and perspectives between disciplines — particularly as many of the articles reviewed have been published outside the usual hospitality management journals. The eclectic approach of the review contributes in some measure to this process.

Source: Johns, N., & Pine, R. (2002). Consumer behaviour in the food service industry: A review. *International Journal of Hospitality Management, 21*(2), 119–134.

SECONDARY RESEARCH

Secondary data are data that already exists for an established purpose, and secondary research is also referred to as documents and desk research. It includes information collected from internal sources such as occupancy rates, sales figures, attendance figures, types of services sold, and so on. In-house surveys can also be valuable sources of data. As well, data can be collected from external sources. Government agencies such as the Canadian Tourism Commission (CTC) compile statistics on visitor arrivals, how much they spend, where they are coming from, and so on. Government is also responsible for a number of tourism-related publications (*Tourism*, a journal published monthly by the CTC, is one example), as well as for generating a considerable amount of statistical data at the macro level. Hotels, travel agents, tour operators, and airlines all have associated trade bodies that compile information on their members and the market. The trade press can provide a regular supply of information. In Canada, *Travel Week* claims to be the best-read trade publication. Research journals (see Table 4.2), periodicals, and special reports can be useful sources of information, as can conference papers, speeches, and annual reports. Searching the Internet, while sometimes a time-consuming process, can also reveal other potential sources of information, as can chat groups and online newsletters. It is worth noting, however, that the accuracy of such information is not guaranteed, so checking the reliability of the source is important.

Collecting secondary data is more cost-effective than starting from scratch to acquire the information. It may still be necessary to identify major gaps and fill them in by undertaking the required research, but using and incorporating information that already exists in the market research program can save significant amounts of time and money. However, the major disadvantage of secondary data is that it does not always meet the specific requirements or objectives of a research project. Because it hasn't been collected specifically to address the problem being studied, it may not include everything that would be useful. Research from the CTC may not break regional tourism statistics into precisely the units that are required, or it may have categories different from those that are really desired.

MARKETING IN ACTION

ONLINE SURVEY PROBES DESTINATION ACTIVITY RELATED TO FILM TOURISM

The study of film tourism is relatively new in tourism research. Sometimes called movie-induced or film-induced tourism, film tourism is defined as tourist visits to a destination or attraction as a result of the destination being featured on television, video, or the cinema screen. The main objective of this study was to find out what destination marketing organizations (DMO) around the world are doing in order to attract film tourists. An online survey was developed using Survey Monkey, an online tool for creating surveys, to achieve the research objectives (see Figure 4.3). Subjects were recruited by personal e-mail that directed them to a website to complete the survey. An e-mail address list of 490 DMOs worldwide that had attracted film tourists in the past was compiled from a variety of sources including *The Worldwide Guide to Movie Locations* by Tony Reeves, 10 copies of which were used as incentives for DMOs to complete the survey. The survey was "live" for two months, and two follow-up e-mails were sent during this time to encourage respondents to complete the survey. A total of 140 useable responses were collected, giving a response rate of 28 percent. The data were analyzed using SPSS.

The results showed that a large portion of destinations (42 percent) make a concerted effort to develop film tourism. This demonstrates the increasing focus on non-traditional marketing and sales for destination organizations experiencing increased competition in a message-heavy marketplace. Nonetheless, of the 140 respondents, 97 percent felt their organization could be more proactive in generating film tourism. Of those respondents making an effort to develop film tourism, 55 percent have seen an increase in visitor numbers as a direct result of their marketing efforts. However, more than half of these respondents (55 percent) are not taking steps to measure the impact of film tourism in the community.

Of those respondents making a concerted effort to develop film tourism, annual spending on film tourism was minimal, with 76 percent of respondents spending less than $11 500 per year. Most organizations having dedicated film tourism efforts spent very little per year on film tourism, with 58 percent of respondents spending under $5000. This suggests that film tourism is still a relatively new means of promoting a destination. The vast majority of DMOs (94 percent) that promote film tourism do so because they are aware of the benefits. A third have experience and expertise in promoting film tourism, and 41 percent have succeeded in previous film tourism initiatives.

Of those respondents not making an effort to promote film tourism, 58 percent cite budget constraints or lack of resources in their inability to focus on film tourism promotion. This information suggests that while many organizations feel there is potential in developing film tourism, the major barrier to its development is

MARKETING IN ACTION *continued*

Part 1 of 4: Destination Marketing Activities

We have identified four critical stages where activities may be undertaken by destination marketing organizations.

1. Before the production of a film
2. During the production of a film
3. During the release of a film
4. After the release of a film

The following questions have been designed to assess the importance of various activities in generating film tourism during these stages.

1. **Which of the following activities are more or less important to your organization in generating film tourism, BEFORE the production of the film? (please circle the appropriate number for each activity)**

	Not important				Very important
Appointing an executive or public relations specialist to deal with film studios directly	1	2	3	4	5
Actively promoting your destination to film studios	1	2	3	4	5
Offering grants and tax credits to encourage studios to your location	1	2	3	4	5
Being actively involved in location scouting	1	2	3	4	5
Planning carefully to maximize the impacts of post production exposure	1	2	3	4	5
Assessing a film's merit carefully in terms of its promotional value	1	2	3	4	5

2. **Which of the following activities are more or less important to your organization in generating film tourism, DURING the production of the film? (please circle the appropriate number for each activity)**

	Not important				Very important
Negotiating end credits for your destination	1	2	3	4	5
Negotiating and/or producing a "making of the film" feature	1	2	3	4	5
Engaging the film's actors/celebrities to promote the film location	1	2	3	4	5
Providing images for media and/or tour operators to use in promotions (for example, on CD or website)	1	2	3	4	5
Ensuring media coverage of the film mentions the film location	1	2	3	4	5
Inviting travel media to the filming location	1	2	3	4	5

3. **Which of the following activities are more or less important to your organization in generating film tourism, DURING THE RELEASE of the film? (please circle the appropriate number for each activity)**

	Not important				Very important
Inviting travel media to a special release of the film	1	2	3	4	5
Sponsoring the film directly	1	2	3	4	5
Providing images for media and/or tour operators to use in promotions (for example, on CD or website)	1	2	3	4	5
Ensuring media coverage of the film mentions the film location	1	2	3	4	5
Planning activities to promote other tourism sectors (e.g., art, crafts, food, wine, music, fashion)	1	2	3	4	5
Engaging the film's actors/celebrities to promote the film location	1	2	3	4	5

4. **Which of the following activities are more or less important to your organization in generating film tourism, AFTER THE RELEASE of the film? (please circle the appropriate number for each activity)**

	Not important				Very important
Posting signage and interpretative exhibits at the film location	1	2	3	4	5
Selling film memorabilia	1	2	3	4	5
Replicating or maintaining film icons/sites/scenes/sets to maintain authenticity	1	2	3	4	5
Hosting events that continue the pull of the film beyond its natural audience peak	1	2	3	4	5
Developing a dedicated website for potential tourists	1	2	3	4	5
Posting links on your website to film tours operated by local tour operators	1	2	3	4	5
Engaging in joint promotional activity with inbound tour operators	1	2	3	4	5
Packaging additional attractions to lengthen tourist stay	1	2	3	4	5
Working collectively with other public organizations and tourism authorities to promote film locations	1	2	3	4	5
Promoting hotels and guest houses that were used in the film	1	2	3	4	5
Engaging in joint promotional activities with film companies	1	2	3	4	5
Creating electronic links to your destination on the film's website	1	2	3	4	5
Offering guided tours and/or film walks	1	2	3	4	5
Producing film and site maps for tourists	1	2	3	4	5
Attracting continuous media attention to the location at each release window (e.g., theatre, DVD)	1	2	3	4	5
Creating exhibitions or displays of memorabilia from the film	1	2	3	4	5

Figure 4.3 Film Tourism Questionnaire

MARKETING IN ACTION *continued*

Part 2 of 4: Managing Film Tourism

5. How successful has your organization been in encouraging film tourism? (please circle the appropriate number)

	Extremely unsuccessful				Extremely successful
Success in encouraging film tourism	1	2	3	4	5

6. Could your destination be more proactive in encouraging film tourism?
   - ☐ No
   - ☐ Yes

7. Does your organization collaborate with the local film commission or film development office?
   - ☐ No
   - ☐ Yes

8. Is consideration given by your organization to the best film genres for disseminating a desired destination image to visitor groups?
   - ☐ No
   - ☐ Yes

9. Does your organization make a concerted effort to develop film tourism?
   - ☐ No *(if no, proceed to question 10 then to 15 below)*
   - ☐ Yes *(if yes, skip question 10 & proceed to question 11)*

10. If you answered no, why doesn't your organization make an effort to develop film tourism? (please check all that apply)
    - ☐ Lack of resources in general
    - ☐ Lack of knowledge
    - ☐ Low awareness of the potential for film tourism
    - ☐ Budget constraints
    - ☐ Low priority activity
    - ☐ Other (please specify)

    Now proceed to question 15

11. Has your organization seen an increase in visitor numbers as a result of your efforts in promoting film tourism?
    - ☐ No
    - ☐ Yes

12. Does your organization measure the impact of film-induced tourism on local communities?
    - ☐ No
    - ☐ Yes

13. How much does your organization spend annually on film tourism promotion, in US$? (please check one)
    - ☐ Nothing
    - ☐ $5,000 — $9,999
    - ☐ $10,000 — $49,000
    - ☐ $50,000 — $99,000
    - ☐ $100,000 — $499,999
    - ☐ $500,000 — $999,999
    - ☐ $1 million — $1,999,999
    - ☐ $2 million or more

14. Why does your organization make an effort to develop film tourism? (please check all that apply)
    - ☐ Experience and expertise in promoting film tourism
    - ☐ Awareness of the benefits of film tourism
    - ☐ Proven success in the past
    - ☐ Other (please specify)

Part 3 of 4: Other Factors Affecting Film Tourism   You have nearly finished the survey!

15. Apart from the promotional activities undertaken by your organization, what do you think are other success factors behind film tourism? (please circle the appropriate number for each factor)

	Not important				Very important
Film-specific factors (e.g., success of film, film actors, relevance of film to the location)	1	2	3	4	5
Government and regulatory factors (e.g., film permit regulations, tax incentives)	1	2	3	4	5
Destination specific factors (e.g., availability of film labour expertise, cost considerations, location availability)	1	2	3	4	5
Film commission efforts (e.g., attracting and working with producers, providing support)	1	2	3	4	5

Part 4 of 4: The Impacts of Film Tourism

The impacts of tourism can be both positive and negative for a destination. In this section, we are interested in examining the perceived benefits and drawbacks of destinations in promoting film tourism.

16. What do you think are the significant BENEFITS in attracting tourists to film locations? (please circle the appropriate number for each benefit)

BENEFITS	Not significant				Very significant
Increase in the number of visitors	1	2	3	4	5
Preservation of sites and locations	1	2	3	4	5
Improvements to infrastructure	1	2	3	4	5
Stronger destination image/brand	1	2	3	4	5
Increase in economic activity	1	2	3	4	5

MARKETING IN ACTION *continued*

17. What do you think are the significant DRAWBACKS from attracting tourists to film locations? (please circle the appropriate number for each drawback)

DRAWBACKS	Not significant				Very significant
Increased local prices	1	2	3	4	5
Location appears different than in the film leading to visitor dissatisfaction	1	2	3	4	5
Increased labour costs	1	2	3	4	5
Negative environmental impacts	1	2	3	4	5
Exploitation of local population	1	2	3	4	5
Increased traffic and crowding	1	2	3	4	5

About You and Your Organization

To allow us to interpret the results of the survey, please provide some general information about you and your organization.

18. What is the name of your organization?

19. What type of Destination Marketing Organization (DMO) is yours? (please check one)
 - ☐ National
 - ☐ City or town
 - ☐ National park, state park, or provincial park
 - ☐ State or province
 - ☐ Rural community
 - ☐ Other (please specify)

20. What position do you hold at your organization? (please check one)
 - ☐ President and/or CEO
 - ☐ Manager
 - ☐ Director
 - ☐ Coordinator
 - ☐ Other (please specify)

21. What is your organization's total operating budget (in US$)? (please check one)
 - ☐ $0 – $99,000
 - ☐ $1 million – $4.9 million
 - ☐ $20 million – $40 million
 - ☐ $100,000 – $499,000
 - ☐ $5 million – $9.9 million
 - ☐ Over $40 million
 - ☐ $500,000 – $999,999
 - ☐ $10 million – $19 million

End of Survey

You have completed all the questions in this survey. Please feel free to make any additional comments or notes here relating to film tourism that you may have considered during the course of the survey.

Thank you very much for taking the time to complete this survey!

If you would like results of this survey to be forwarded to you please enter your contact information below:

Name:

E-mail:

MARKETING IN ACTION *continued*

often financial in nature. For 47 percent of respondents, film tourism promotion is not a priority activity in their organization. A third of respondents did not make an effort to promote film tourism because of a lack of awareness of the potential for film tourism at the destination marketing level.

From the destination marketing perspective, the three main benefits of attracting film tourists are the positive economic impacts, a stronger destination image or brand, and more tourist visits. Preservation of sites and locations as well as improvements to infrastructure were also noted as important. Overall, the respondents indicated overwhelmingly that there were valuable benefits in attracting film tourists to their destination. The survey respondents were notably less concerned about the negative impacts of film tourism, such as difference in location appearance leading to visitor dissatisfaction, increased traffic and crowding, and negative environmental impacts.

Respondents from Canada and from around the world confirmed the importance of being involved with the film industry before a film is produced. Clearly, in order to generate film tourism, destinations must first promote and sell the location to producers, and be actively involved in location scouting. DMOs also felt that it was important to plan carefully in order to maximize the impacts of post-production exposure. Canadian respondents commented on their relationships with their film commissions, saying that they relied heavily on the pre-production activities of their film commissions to attract films, provide grants and tax credits, scout locations, and facilitate shooting sites.

Respondents of the survey felt that working closely with the media and in film tourism promotional activities were most important during production. The marketing activities most important during release of the film are ensuring that media coverage mentions the location of the film and providing images for media and others to use in promotions. After release of a film, marketing cooperation is perceived to be very important, as are the activities of packaging attractions and creating Internet links to the destination via the film's website.

Overall, the international DMOs were distinctly more proactive than their Canadian counterparts in using film as a marketing vehicle for their destinations. It appears that most of the Canadian organizations surveyed do not participate specifically in any kind of promotion or marketing based on destination placement via film or on film tourism. However, they do consider the notion to be sound and would be interested in the future in developing various promotional vehicles, both individually and collectively with other tourism partners such as associations, hotels, and travel companies. Funding could be a barrier, though, as very few tourism organizations can justify spending marketing budgets on what they still consider a long shot. It seems that in Canada, if the film commissions and local government are not already doing the marketing, then tourism organizations just don't have the funds or resources to support film tourism or destination placement.

Source: Adapted from Hudson, S., & Wall, R. (2005). "Film tourism: A marketing opportunity for destinations," In *The Three R's: Research, Results, Rewards: Proceedings of the Travel and Tourism Research Association Conference,* New Orleans, June 12–15.

PRIMARY RESEARCH

Qualitative Research Techniques

The term "qualitative" is used to describe research methods and techniques that use and give rise to subjective rather than empirical information. In general, the approach is to collect a great amount of "rich" information from relatively few people. Potential purposes of qualitative research include developing hypotheses concerning relevant behaviour and attitudes; identifying the full range of issues, views, and attitudes that should be pursued in large-scale research; and understanding how a buying decision is made. Qualitative research can be used in unstructured and structured situations.

Unstructured Situations

Participative observation falls into this category, in which a tourism field researcher may adopt one of four different roles. The first is the "complete participant," where the researcher becomes a genuine participant, and the second is the "participant as observer," where researchers reveal their intentions. Third, "observers as participants" also reveal themselves as researchers, and will participate in the normal social process but make no pretence of being participants. The fourth type, "the complete observer," simply observes without being involved. Just as Procter & Gamble researchers spend hours doing "shop-alongs" in retail outlets to understand their customers, so do Las Vegas conduct "tag-alongs" to observe the behaviour of visitors to the city (see *Spotlight* in Chapter 8).

Mystery shopping, the name given to participant observation in the commercial sector, has become a common market research technique in tourism and hospitality. In the services context, mystery shopping provides information about the service experience as it unfolds, and helps to develop a richer knowledge of the experiential nature of services. One example of such a study is that by Jonathan Boote and Ann Mathews, who were employed by Whitbread PLC to develop guidelines for the siting of middle-market restaurant outlets.[6] Part of their research involved participant observation of customers at lunchtime and in the evenings, in order to identify whether the actual clientele matched the intended market segment. Table 4.5 summarizes the various advantages and disadvantages of using this method of participative observation.

Table 4.5

Advantages and Disadvantages of Covert Participative Observation or Mystery Shopping

ADVANTAGES	DISADVANTAGES
Offers deep insights into feelings and motivations behind service and practice (Palmer 2000)	Raises ethical issues by observing people without their knowledge (Jorgenesen 1989)
Experience is natural and not contrived for the sake of the observer (Boote and Mathews 1999)	Based on assumptions that need to be made explicit and addressed (Savage 2000)
Serves as a management tool for improving standards in customer service by providing actionable recommendations (Erstad 1998; Cramp 1994)	Information collected may be biased as a result of arbitrary or careless selection of observation periods, or the observers' own prejudices (Smith 1995)
Ideal for investigating services (Crano and Brewer 1986; Grove and Fisk 1992)	In the long term, advantages for improving customer service can wear off if not integrated with other measures of service delivery process (Wilson 1998)
Serves as a management tool for enhancing human resource management (Erstad 1998)	Can be very costly and time consuming (Grove and Fisk 1992)

Sources: Boote, J., & Mathews, A. (1999). Saying is one thing, doing is another: The role of observation in marketing research. *Qualitative Market Research: An International Journal, 2*(1) 15–21; Cramp, B. (1994, August 18). Industrious espionage. *Marketing*, 17; Crano, W. D., & Brewer, M. B. (1986). Observational and archival data. In Crano, W.D. and Brewer, M.B. (Eds), *Principles and Methods of Social Research, 279–309*. Allyn-Bacon: Newton, MA; Erstad, M. (1998). Mystery shopping programmes and human resource management. *International Journal of Contemporary Hospitality Management, 10*(1)34–38; Grove, S. J., & Fisk, R. (1992). Observational data collection methods for services marketing: An overview. *Journal of the Academy of Marketing Science, 20*(3), 217–224; Jorgensen, D. L. (1989). *Participant observation: A methodology for human studies*. Sage Publications: Newbury Park, CA; Palmer, C. (2000). Heritage tourism and English national identity. In Robinson M., Evans N., Long P., Sharpley R., & Swarbrooke J. (Eds), *Tourism and heritage relationships: Global, national, and local perspectives*, 331–347. Business Education Publishers: Sunderland; Savage, J. (2000). Participative observation: Standing in the shoes of others? *Qualitative Health Research, 10*(3), 324–340; Smith, S. L. J. (1995). *Tourism analysis: A handbook*. Longman, Harlow; Wilson, A. M. (1998). The use of mystery shopping in the measurement of service delivery, *Service Industries Journal, 18*(3), 148–163.

Structured Situations

Qualitative research also permits more structured situations in which the researcher can play a more proactive role, although that role is more facilitative than directive. At the initial stages of tourism research, it may be necessary to follow up a conversation and, if the research is intended to generate quantitative data, to develop items for scales to be used on a questionnaire. Hence, there is a need to identify clearly the constructs that inform the attitudes toward

repertory grid technique

a structured research method that requires respondents to select from a group of three items

projection techniques

research methods that involve asking subjects to respond to hypothetical, or projected, situations; sometimes called "what if" techniques

focus group

a group of 8 to 10 people, representative of a wider population, whose views are elicited by a facilitator

specific destinations, behaviour, or experiences that are being surveyed. One effective method of identifying these constructs is the **repertory grid technique**, which requires respondents to select from a group of three items. In this research process, the question posed to respondents is along the lines of "looking at three destinations, which one do you think is different and why?" The object is to elicit the basis of comparison.

The constructs underlying an attitude can be revealed in other ways, one of which is the use of **projection techniques**. Sometimes called "what if?" techniques, they involve measures to get subjects to respond to hypothetical, or projected, situations. For example, subjects might be asked to indicate how they would spend a particular sum of money if given a free choice, or how they would spend additional leisure time if it were made available. Another projection technique is to show respondents a picture or cartoon representing a particular situation and to ask them to describe what they think is actually happening or what one cartoon character is saying to another. The concept behind many of these projection techniques is that respondents tend to give socially acceptable answers in normal interviews, whereas if they answer for another character, they are able to project on that character those unacceptable feelings that they may actually be feeling. The techniques are based on Freudian psychoanalysis, which posits that anxiety is easily dealt with if it is projected and attributed to some external part of the respondent's world.[7]

The idea of interviewing people in a group rather than individually is becoming increasingly popular in market research. In a **focus group**, the interviewer becomes the facilitator of a discussion rather than an interviewer as such, in order to obtain representative views of a wider population. A focus group is usually fairly homogeneous in nature and comprises 8 to 10 people. It is important that those selected have little experience of working in a focus group, as the researcher wishes to obtain views representative of a wider population, not from expert "opinion givers" who are used to the dynamics of a focus group.

Chris Ryan believes that the advantages of using focus groups for obtaining views arise from the social dynamics of the group. He categorizes those dynamics as follows:

- *synergism:* a wider range of ideas can result from a cumulative group effect, as opposed to individual interviews;
- *snowballing:* one comment can elicit a whole range of additional confirmatory or modifying statements;
- *security:* focus groups can generate a social ease, reducing the insecurity or defensiveness that often arise in an interview situation;
- *spontaneity:* focus groups will likely elicit more spontaneous views; and
- *stimulation:* the members of the group can stimulate each other to participate in group discussion.[8]

Focus groups are commonly used in commercial research, especially in developing and monitoring advertising campaigns. They are beginning to be widely used in the world of tourism, and are often used for obtaining feedback on holiday brochures. Groups are asked to respond to the layout, pictures, text, and typeface of brochures, in order to help companies find those that appeal most to various market niches. The Westin Hotels & Resorts brings in meeting planners for focus groups to find out more about their needs and wants. Mark Nisbett, former director of sales and marketing at The Westin Edmonton, described the feeling that he perceived in these buyers as "finally, someone is asking for our opinion." Nisbett continues: "Buyers were very excited to be involved, and we learned so much about what is going on in their industry today."

virtual focus groups

online sessions in which a limited number of pre-recruited respondents participate in a guided discussion electronically

in-depth interview

a qualitative research technique in which an interview lasts 45 to 60 minutes

Virtual focus groups are also becoming more common. Online "chat" sessions, in which a limited number of pre-recruited respondents participate in a guided discussion electronically, in real time, can be used effectively to bring together participants from virtually anywhere to discuss a client issue, activities, and experiences, or provide feedback on products. While virtual focus groups will not always be able to replace in-person interviews, the time- and cost-saving benefits of such groups make them a very useful tool for researchers — especially for gathering website feedback with participants when they are using the Internet.

In-depth interviews, which can last 45 to 60 minutes, tend to be used for three main reasons. First, they are used in situations where the limited number of subjects renders quantitative methods inappropriate. Second, they are used when information obtained from each subject is expected to vary considerably, that is when the question of "what percentage of respondents said what" is not relevant. Third, in-depth interviews can be used to explore a topic in the preliminary stages of planning a more formal questionnaire-based survey.

Interviews can be structured, unstructured, or a combination of the two. The unstructured interview differs from a conversation in the sense that both parties are aware of an agenda of question and answer. The structured interview involves a number of skills on the part of the researcher. For example, questionnaire-drafting skills, such as determining the sequence of questions and their precise content, are key. Other required skills are the interpersonal skills involved in conversation and being able to "lead" the interviewee. Also, the researcher must develop the skills of recording responses accurately; very often interviews are taped and a word-for-word transcription is prepared.

There are various ways of going about the analysis of interview transcripts, but it is imperative that the researcher returns to the terms of reference and statement of objectives and begins to evaluate the information gathered in relation to the questions posed. Recently, a variety of computer packages have become available to analyze interview transcripts.

Quantitative Research Techniques

Traditionally, most consumer research studies have been based on questions identified in market decision making, to be posed to random samples of existing or potential customers. The *Case Study* at the end of this chapter is typical of such research. This study found that many services were not meeting customer expectations. These findings are quantifiable dimensions that can be used for future decision making. This is quantitative research, meaning a study to which numerical estimates can be attached. Quantitative research is usually based on "structured" questionnaires, in which every respondent is asked the same questions. Because the range of possible answers is printed on questionnaires, variations to suit individual respondents are not possible.

However, quantitative data can also be collected via observations. Some researchers believe that this is one of the most effective ways to gain knowledge about consumers. Tracking studies, for example, are used in museums, galleries, and tourist attractions to monitor people's activities. Tracking studies provide information on what people do, the amount of time they spend on various activities, and the order in which they do things. Other types of observation include counting the number of people in a dining room at various times of the day, counting the number of cars in the parking lot, counting the number of people entering a casino, and even seeing which way people move through a museum or an art gallery.

The Questionnaire or Survey Method

A review of the methods used in collecting tourism and hospitality research data shows that the questionnaire technique or survey method is the most frequently used. The survey method includes factual surveys, opinion surveys, or interpretive surveys, all of which can be conducted by personal interview, telephone, mail, or by electronic means.

factual survey

a survey that asks the respondent to state certain facts, such as age or number of children

opinion survey

a survey that asks the respondent to express an opinion or make an evaluation or appraisal

interpretive survey

a survey that asks the respondent to act as an interpreter as well as a reporter

Factual surveys are by far the most effective: the respondent is asked to state certain facts, such as age or number of children. In an **opinion survey**, the respondent is asked to express an opinion or make an evaluation or appraisal. In **interpretive surveys**, the respondent acts as an interpreter as well as a reporter. Subjects are asked why they chose a certain course of action — why they chose a particular package, for example. While respondents can reply directly to "what" questions, they often have difficulty replying to "why" questions. Therefore, although interpretive research may give a researcher a feel for consumer behaviour, the usefulness of the results tends to be limited.

Personal interviews tend to be much more flexible than either mail or telephone surveys because the interviewer can adapt to the situation and the respondent. Typically, one can obtain much more information by personal interview than by other means, as personal interviewers can observe the situation as well as ask questions. A major limitation of the personal interview method, however, is its relatively high cost. An interview takes a considerable amount of time to conduct, and there is always the possibility of personal interviewer bias. Telephone surveys are conducted much more rapidly and at less cost than personal interviews. Speed and low cost are the primary advantages of telephone interviews; however, these interviews tend to be less flexible than personal interviews, and they also have to be brief. Computer-assisted telephone interviewing using random dialing is frequently used in North America. Mail surveys involve mailing the questionnaire to carefully selected sample respondents and requesting them to return the completed questionnaires. Advantages are that a large geographical area can be covered, respondents can fill out the survey at their own convenience, and personal interview bias is absent. The greatest problems with mail surveys are the lack of a good list and an inadequate response rate.

Finally, a relatively new way of conducting research is the use of electronic surveys that ask consumers questions and immediately record and tabulate the results. A computer terminal might be placed in a hotel lobby, mall, or other high-traffic location (for example, Tourism Whistler collects data from its skiers using electronic devices placed up and down the main street). Alternatively, respondents may be asked to complete a survey online. Internet-based survey methodology is gaining increasing popularity, and the *Marketing in Action* in this chapter provides an example of an online survey that used Survey Monkey. The questionnaire used in that study has been reprinted in Figure 4.3.

Questionnaire Design

The value of a survey questionnaire rests with its design. As there are so many ways in which a questionnaire can be formulated to perform its task, it is difficult to develop a set of rules. Each questionnaire is unique. Consequently, many refer to the design of questionnaires as an art that is influenced by the researcher's knowledge of the population, the subject matter, common sense, experience, and pilot work.

According to Sunny Crouch and Matthew Housden, questionnaires have four main purposes.[9] These are:

1. *To collect relevant data.* When drafting each question, the researcher should always ask, "What use will the answers be?" This relates back to the definition and purpose of the research, but also tests whether the question is phrased so as to produce the desired information.
2. *To make data comparable.* The wording of the questions and alternative answers should be clear and not open to more than one interpretation. The language should be simple so that it can be understood by all respondents. Sentences should be kept short and to the point. Carrying out a pilot survey on a small sample is useful for detecting any ambiguities.
3. *To minimize bias.* The phrasing of questions can bias the response given. For example, if a question begins with "you don't think, do you…," a negative response is likely to be given, and if a question begins with "shouldn't something be done about…," a positive response is the likely outcome. Care should be taken to avoid wording questions that lead respondents to feel that one answer will be regarded as more acceptable than others.
4. *To motivate the respondent.* The respondent must be made to feel that answering the question will be interesting, useful, and not time-consuming. If the questionnaire is too long, this can be demoralizing for the interviewer and respondent, thus affecting both refusal rates and the quality of the data. The survey should begin with interesting questions, not with requests for personal details about income or age. These questions can be placed at the end of the questionnaire, as in the film tourism questionnaire in Figure 4.3.

Traditionally, travel research has been conducted in-house, which reflects both narrow profit margins and an ignorance of the benefits that skilled independent researchers can offer. The result has been a proliferation of amateurishly designed questionnaires, many of which can be found in hotel rooms or are given to tourists on charter planes on the return journey home. There is also a tendency to distribute questionnaires to as many clients as possible, without worrying about what percentage will respond and whether there will be any built-in response bias among respondents. Furthermore, there has been very little research on the validity or accuracy of questionnaire data used in leisure and tourism studies. One study found that in a survey of tennis participation, respondents exaggerated their level of participation by as much as 100 percent. This suggests that the researcher and the user of research results should always bear in mind the nature and source of the data. Questionnaire surveys rely on information from respondents, and what respondents say depends on their own powers of recall, on their honesty, and, fundamentally, on the questions asked of them.

benchmarking

the process of tracking and comparing current performance with past performance or in relation to the competition

More recently, the practice of benchmarking has received attention from tourism market researchers. **Benchmarking** is essentially a technique that allows organizations to track and compare their current performance with past performance or in relation to their competitors. To date, the limited application of benchmarking within the tourism and hospitality industry has been confined mainly to hotels.[10] Benchmarking initiatives might include collecting guest satisfaction scores. For Sheraton Hotels and Resorts, measuring guest satisfaction is a crucial part of marketing research, and plays an important role in internal marketing. Guest satisfaction scores (GSS) are closely monitored by the research group, and results are shared with all hotels and all employees. To measure satisfaction, Sheraton Hotels has commissioned NFO Worldwide Group since 2002 to send out a questionnaire to every customer who stays in a Sheraton property in North America.

SAMPLING

Because of the expenses associated with research, managers often find themselves grappling with the question of how many people must be surveyed in order to obtain accurate responses. It is almost impossible — and not very cost-effective — to interview every product user or potential product user. Therefore, a company's decisions are based on the opinions and reactions of a sample of the population. The sample selection process is as follows:

1. *Define the population.* The first stage in the sampling process is to specify the target population. In the *Marketing in Action* on film tourism, the target population was destination marketing organizations (DMOs) worldwide that had attracted film tourists in the past.
2. *Specify the sample frame.* This is a detailed description of the listing, directory, or roster from which the sample will be chosen. In the film tourism example, the sample was taken from a book that listed DMOs that were promoting film tourism attractions.
3. *Select the sampling method.* The researcher must decide whether a probability or nonprobability approach will be applied to draw the sample and exactly how the sample members will be selected. There is a wide range of both probability and nonprobability sampling methods. The key difference between the two is that in probability sampling, a statistical evaluation of sampling error can be undertaken; such an assessment is not possible for samples drawn by nonprobabilistic methods. Therefore, the more accurate form of sampling is the probability method, in which each unit of the population has a known, but not necessarily an equal, chance of selection.
4. *Determine sample size.* The selection of sample size has received considerable attention from critics of tourism research. Kenneth Baker, George Hozier Jr., and Robert Rogers suggest that there are two basic approaches for the tourism researcher interested in accountability and efficiency: required size per cell and the traditional statistical model.[11] The required size per cell approach requires approximately 30 responses for each demographic cell of data. For example, two genders, four ethnic groups, and four age groups would require a sample size of 960 ($2 \times 4 \times 4 \times 30$). The traditional statistical model is based on a management specification of allowable error (e), the level of confidence in the sampling process (z), and the variance in the population (@). The sampling size is thus expressed as: $n = z@ / e$. One important aspect of the traditional statistical method of sample size determination is that the sample must be randomly selected; every member of the population of interest must have a known chance of being selected. This is a key to eliminating systematic bias. Another important point is that if questionnaire respondents are all basically alike, a small sample size is required, no matter how large the population. This is often a fundamentally difficult concept for researchers and managers alike to accept. Sample size is not a function of population size: it is a function of population variance. Large-scale data collection is very costly, and quite often not needed.
5. *Draw the sample and collect the data.* The final stage in the sampling process is the implementation stage, in which the sample is chosen and surveyed.

The sampling procedure adopted will have a direct impact on the validity of the results, so if the survey is to be the principal tool for data collection, careful consideration must be given to the technique employed and the sample size chosen.

PROFILE

LACK OF RESEARCH CONTRIBUTES TO EURODISNEY DISASTER

After the resounding success of Disney's first foreign expansion in Tokyo, where the U.S. theme park was transplanted in its entirety, the Paris experiment was initially an unprecedented disaster, partly due to ethnocentrism, partly due to insufficient cultural research, and partly to competition and adverse world economic conditions.

EuroDisney first opened in April 1992, right in the middle of a European recession that had begun at the end of the 1980s. Disney underestimated the economic results of this for tourists, aiming prices too high in both hotel accommodation and holiday packages. It had been banking on averages of three-day stays, whereas in reality Europeans were more likely to consider the theme park a one-day experience. Disney had projected it would attract 11 million visitors, generating over US$115 million in its first year in Paris. By summer 1994, however, it had lost more than US$900 million since opening. Visitor numbers were drastically down and so was spending on related purchases. This less-than-enthusiastic response to what French people saw as "American imperialism" was due to a innumerable errors in research, planning, and implementation. One of the first problems was lack of sufficient understanding of the customer. Researchers failed to understand both domestic tourists and those travelling from other parts of Europe.

Early advertising campaigns, which focused on "glitz" and "size" rather than the variety of rides and attractions, were unsuccessful in persuading the French to visit, although domestic visitors were initially predicted to make up 50 percent of the attendance figures. After the first year, a consulting firm summed the problem up as a widespread scorn for American fairy-tale characters in a land that already had its own cartoon favourites (such as Asterix), saying "The French see EuroDisney as American imperialism — plastics at its worst."

PROFILE *continued*

Right from the outset, Paris theatre director Ariane Mnouchkine had slated the theme park as a "cultural Chernobyl."

When researchers tried to understand why tourists were not visiting during the summer of 1992, they discovered that due to the combination of transatlantic airfare wars and currency movements plus domestic economic recession, it was actually cheaper for many Europeans to go to Disney World in Orlando than to take an equivalent trip to Paris. Why would tourists flock to the new, smaller park when they could just as easily go to the home of Disney, with all its other facilities plus guaranteed sunshine and beautiful beaches — and why did researchers not consider this? Moreover, the first Gulf War put the brakes on travel during 1991, and in 1992 the Olympics in Barcelona was heavy competition for the beleaguered Paris park.

There were many other miscalculations in the early stages of the Paris project. The original ban on alcohol at the park had to be lifted due to public demand, as no self-respecting French person could contemplate lunch without a glass of wine. Personal grooming rules also had to be bent to accommodate staff demands. And pets had to be accommodated as the French routinely take dogs and even cats on their road holidays. Other errors were made in the way visitors booked their Disney vacations. Reservations started out as direct bookings made by telephone or by Internet. This alienated British tourists, who usually booked holidays via travel agencies. Disney also expected European tourists to change their travel habits for their park. Traditionally French tourists travel in August during a one-month vacation period, when factories and offices shut down, and the British take two weeks sometime between the end of July and the first week of September. Disney predicted erroneously that both nationalities would take their children out of school for shorter periods outside of the main vacation periods.

The biggest change in the fortunes of EuroDisney came after the appointment in 1993 of a Frenchman, Philippe Bourguignon, as CEO. He took over financial negotiations and implemented wide-ranging improvements in marketing. In particular he changed marketing tactics to separate national identities of potential visitors throughout Europe. Individual marketing offices were opened in several capital cities in order to tailor campaigns to each national identity, taking into account cultural expectations. He also inaugurated price cuts, reducing park admission by 20 percent and cutting hotel room rates by some 30 percent.

Bourguignon spearheaded special promotional rates for the most inclement winter months. And he focused attention on an authentic Disney day out rather than on longer stay packages. In October 1994 the park's name was changed to Disneyland Paris to help focus on the American aspects of the experience rather than the European. Lessons were learned regarding food, weather fluctuations, language facilities, and continental cultural variations. Small details reflected attempts to get things right the second time around, such as providing covered seating to take into account the rainfall as well as a wider selection of different ethnic foods.

Sources: Roberts, K. (2004, August 8). Less a sleeping beauty, more a rude awakening at EuroDisney. *Independent on Sunday*, 6; Amine, L. S. (2006). The not-so-wonderful world of EuroDisney — things are better now at Paris Disneyland. *International Marketing* (12th ed.), 620–623.

COMMON RESEARCH ERRORS

There are many potential pitfalls in conducting research; the most common four errors are discussed here.

1. Not Including Enough Qualitative Information

Most surveys reported in trade magazines provide descriptive information. For example, an American Express survey of business people in 2002 reported that business travellers were using more online booking tools to make travel arrangements. However, to use this information, tourism suppliers and intermediaries need to know specifically what online tools these business travellers are using, what they believe is an effective website, how long they stay online per transaction, and so on. All these questions could be asked in face-to-face interviews or in focus groups with business travellers.

2. Improper Use of Sophisticated Statistical Analysis

It is possible for a multitude of errors to creep into the research process if collection, tabulation, and analysis are not done properly. Tabulation is likely done by computer and a number of excellent packages are available for this purpose. However, statistical conclusions must be interpreted in terms of the best action or policy for the organization to follow. The reduction of the interpretation to recommendations is one of the most difficult tasks in the research process.

3. Failure of a Sample to Represent the Population

A sample is a segment of the population selected to represent that population as a whole. Ideally, the sample should be representative, so that the researcher can make accurate estimates of the thoughts and behaviour of the larger population. In the *Spotlight*, the CTC acknowledged that the quality of the data provided by their International Travel Survey had begun to erode — partly because a smaller and smaller percentage of travellers' questionnaires were returned, thus not representing the population adequately. In the *Case Study* at the end of this chapter, the objective was to measure the service quality perceived by skiers, and the sample of skiers was drawn from the population of bookings taken for the upcoming winter season. A representative sample was chosen in terms of accommodation types and resorts in order to increase both the reliability and validity of the research program.

4. Problems with Interpretation

In many cases, results from research can be interpreted the wrong way. The *Case Study* at the end of the chapter shows how results can be interpreted in different ways. The results showed that there was no statistical difference among the four measurements of service quality and therefore any of them could be used to measure satisfaction. Such a finding would enable managers to employ the most straightforward test of satisfaction, so there would be justification in measuring performance only. But although the perceptions format offers the most predictive power — a finding that has consistently emerged in the literature — it offers little diagnostic potential and, indeed, may result in setting inappropriate priorities.

EFFECTIVE USE OF MARKETING RESEARCH IN DECISION MAKING

There is little doubt that in an industry as dynamic and expansive as tourism and hospitality, research must play a critical role in its development. Not only should research be undertaken by every organization, whether large or small, to assist in the task of practical decision making at a strategic level, but it should also be acknowledged as important at the academic level for shedding valuable light on the development of the industry on a global basis. For research to be worthwhile, it has to be acted upon. A good example of a company successfully using the results of marketing research is Marriott International.[12] When it was designing a new chain of hotels for business travellers (which eventually became known as Courtyard by Marriott), Marriott sampled 601 consumers using a sophisticated technique known as conjoint analysis, which asks respondents to make trade-offs among different groupings of attributes. The objective was to determine which mix of attributes at specific prices offers the highest degree of utility, so respondents were asked to indicate on a five-point scale how likely they were to stay at a hotel with certain features, given a specific room price per night. Features included room fixtures, food-related services, leisure facilities, and other services.

The research yielded detailed guidelines for the selection of almost 200 features and service elements, representing those attributes that provided the highest utility for the customers in the target segments, at prices they were willing to pay. Using these inputs, the design team was able to meet the specified price while retaining the features most desired by the target market. After testing the concept under real-world conditions, the company subsequently developed a large chain that filled a gap in the market with a product that represented the best balance between the price customers were prepared to pay and the physical and service features they most desired.

Research is never an exact science, but it can reduce the margins of error to which hunches on their own are subject. The feasibility study, for example, is an essential prerequisite to any new project, whether it is the launch of a new company, the introduction of a new logo, or the development of a new product. Above all, the success of research will be contingent on three conditions:

1. Sufficient resources must be allocated to do the job properly, in terms of both time and money.
2. Managers must be willing to believe the results of the research when they become available, even if they conflict with the management's own preconceived views.
3. The results should be used. All too frequently, research is commissioned in order to avoid making an immediate decision. Expensively commissioned research is then left in a drawer instead of being used to enable managers to make better decisions on the future direction of the organization's strategy.

CHAPTER SUMMARY

The way in which an organization gathers, uses, and disseminates its research in the marketing context is generally referred to as a marketing information system (MIS). A key component of the MIS is the marketing research process: the systematic and objective search for and analysis of information relevant to the identification and solution of any problem in the field of marketing.

In undertaking research, these steps should be followed: identify and define the problem, investigate available sources, develop the research plan, collect data, analyze data, and present research results. There are several approaches to collecting data, but two key decisions that must be made are whether to use primary or secondary data and whether to use qualitative or quantitative research. Quantitative research produces numerical estimates and is usually based on "structured" questionnaires, in which every respondent is asked the same questions. The questionnaire technique or survey method is most frequently used to collect tourism and hospitality research data. The survey method includes factual surveys, opinion surveys, and interpretive surveys, all of which can be conducted by personal interview, mail, or telephone, or by electronic means. Questionnaires have four main purposes: to collect relevant data, to make data comparable, to minimize bias, and to motivate the respondent.

The sample selection process is as follows: define the population, specify the sample frame, select the sampling method, determine sample size, and draw the sample and collect the data.

There are many potential pitfalls in conducting research. The most common four errors are not including enough qualitative information, improper use of sophisticated statistical analysis, failure of a sample that represents the population, and problems with interpretation. In addition, the success of research is contingent on three conditions: sufficient resources must be allocated to do the job properly, both in terms of time and money; managers must be willing to believe the results of the research when they become available; and the results should be used.

KEY TERMS

benchmarking, p. 138	interpretive survey, p. 137	projection techniques, p. 135
competitor intelligence, p. 120	marketing information system	qualitative research, p. 123
consumer research, p. 119	(MIS), p. 114	quantitative research, p. 123
factual survey, p. 137	marketing research, p. 115	repertory grid technique, p. 135
focus group, p. 135	opinion survey, p. 137	secondary data, p. 122
in-depth interview, p. 136	primary data, p. 122	virtual focus groups, p. 136

DISCUSSION QUESTIONS AND EXERCISES

1. Find an example of a local tourism or hospitality organization that has recently published research results. How has it used the results for decision making?
2. If you owned a high-class restaurant and wanted to improve the level of service offered by your staff, how could observational research help you accomplish your goal?
3. How do secondary data differ from primary data, and what are the main tourism sources of secondary data in your country?

4. Differentiate between qualitative and quantitative research and give specific examples of how each could be used by a hotel.
5. How would a tour operator go about collecting competitor intelligence on the success of tours in Asia?
6. As marketing research manager for a large destination-marketing organization, how might you use focus groups to collect information?

CASE STUDY

HOW WAS THE SKIING? FINDING THE BEST WAY TO MEASURE SERVICE QUALITY

Service quality in the tourism and hospitality industry receives increasing attention in the literature and yet confusion still exists about which measure offers the greatest validity. The two main research instruments are importance–performance analysis (IPA) and SERVQUAL. IPA is a procedure that shows the relative importance of various attributes and the performance of the firm, product, or destination under study in providing these attributes. SERVQUAL focuses on the notion of perceived quality and is based on the difference between consumers' expectations and perceptions

of service. However, both measures — IPA and SERVQUAL — have been questioned and some researchers have suggested a better measure of service quality is one that multiplies SERVQUAL by importance, or one that measures just performance (SERVPERF). This case reports on a research project that assessed these four main methods of measuring customer service quality.

The data were obtained in cooperation with a ski tour operator that was interested in measuring the service quality it provided to its skiers. Since the focus of the study was on aspects of the package holiday that were within the direct control, or at least the zone of influence, of the tour operator, a team of managers from seven departments — operations, overseas, product, reservations and agency sales, customer services, marketing and purchasing — was asked to brainstorm each individual aspect of the holiday that the customer might experience with the company. The resulting 146 elements were divided into 13 different dimensions reflecting various aspects of the holiday experience, from receiving the brochure through to contact with company after returning home (see Table 4.6).

Table 4.6

Ranking Service Quality Dimensions (1 = top service quality score; 13 = lowest service quality score)

RANKING	SERVQUAL (P — E)	IMPORTANCE-PERFORMANCE ANALYSIS (P — I)	SERVQUAL × IMPORTANCE (P — E) × (I)	SERVPERF P
1	Skiing/snowboarding	Company magazine	Skiing/snowboarding	Skiing/snowboarding
2	Departure	Skiing/snowboarding	Departure	Transfer to airport
3	Arrival at accommodation	Welcome	Arrival at accommodation	Meeting the rep
4	Meeting the rep	Meeting the rep	Transfer to airport	Departure
5	Transfer to airport	Departure	Meeting the rep	Brochure
6	Company magazine	Arrival at accommodation	Company magazine	Welcome
7	Transfer to accommodation	Accommodation	Transfer to accommodation	Waiting to go
8	Accommodation	Brochure	Welcome	Accommodation
9	Welcome	Transfer to airport	Accommodation	Resort activities
10	Resort activities	Waiting to go	Resort activities	Arrival at accommodation
11	Journey	Resort activities	Journey	Transfer to accommodation
12	Waiting to go	Transfer to accommodation	Waiting to go	Journey
13	Brochure	Journey	Brochure	Company magazine

One month before customers went on holiday, they were asked to complete a first questionnaire asking them:

1. *What is important to you?* Respondents used a five-point Likert scale (ranging from extremely important to not at all important) to rate 146 elements of their holiday. These elements represented the complete service delivery chain and included the usefulness of the brochure, getting to the airport, flights, representative, resort, accommodation, and contacts with the tour operator at home.

2. *What are your expectations?* Respondents were then asked to rate on a five-point Likert scale (ranging from definitely expected to definitely not expected) the same 146 elements of their holiday.

In a second questionnaire *towards the end* of their holiday, respondents were asked:

3. *How did you find your holiday?* This questionnaire asked respondents to rate on a five-point Likert scale (ranging from strongly agree to strongly disagree) the same elements of their holiday as measured in points 1 and 2 above.

The sample was drawn from the population of bookings taken for the upcoming winter season. Customers were asked in writing if they would like to participate in the panel and offered an incentive in the form of travellers cheque. A total of 250 people were asked to participate in the study and the response rate was 88 percent. After the respondents had completed the questionnaires, a service quality score was calculated for each question, using the following four formulas:

1. Performance (P) minus Importance (I)
2. Performance (P) minus Expectations (E)
3. [Performance (P) minus Expectations (E)] Multiplied by Importance (I)
4. Performance (P) only

Data were analyzed and a service quality score was calculated for each dimension of the holiday experience. Table 4.7 compares the mean scores for expectations and performance (SERVQUAL), and the results clearly show a negative service gap in all dimensions. To analyze IPA, a two-dimensional action grid was plotted, where importance values formed the vertical axis, while performance values formed the horizontal axis. Figure 4.4 identifies where each of the 13 dimensions fall in terms of those four quadrants. Significantly, the largest number of dimensions (eight) fell into the "Concentrate Here" (quadrant A) area of the action grid. Respondents rated these attributes high in importance but low in performance. These dimensions were the brochure, waiting to go, meeting the rep, transfer to accommodation, accommodation, resort activities, departure, and transfer to the airport.

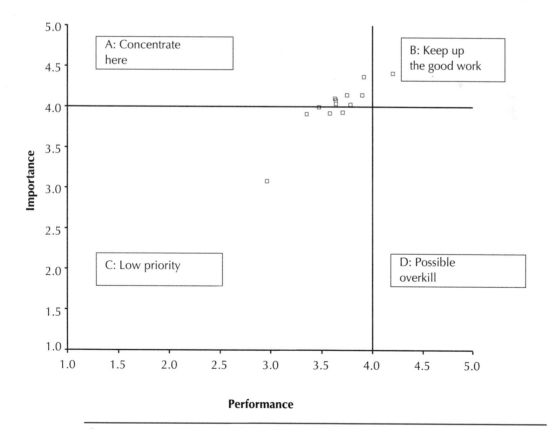

Figure 4.4 Importance-Performance Grid with Ratings for Holiday Dimensions

Table 4.7

Comparisons between Expectation and Performance in Holiday Dimensions (SERVQUAL)

Dimensions of the Holiday Experience	Expectations		Performance		Pair-Wise t-test	
	Mean	Std Dev	Mean	Std Dev	t-value	p-value
1. Brochure	4.254	.438	3.742	.575	−10.88	.000
2. Waiting to go	4.144	.427	3.640	.715	−9.35	.000
3. Journey	3.849	.428	3.358	.464	−12.20	.000
4. Meeting the rep	4.082	.515	3.894	.811	−2.80	.006
5. Transfer to accommodation	3.811	.563	3.471	.759	−4.93	.000
6. Arrival at accommodation	3.767	.521	3.582	.871	−2.46	.015
7. Accommodation	3.994	.416	3.645	.719	−5.86	.000
8. Welcome	4.053	.442	3.700	.882	−4.95	.000
9. Resort activities	4.009	.472	3.634	.600	−7.11	.000
10. Skiing/snowboarding	4.230	.493	4.208	.538	−.43	.666
11. Company magazine	3.250	.938	2.963	1.443	−2.38	.018
12. Departure	3.954	.484	3.784	.830	−2.41	.017
13. Transfer to airport	4.120	.584	3.912	.919	−2.59	.011

Service quality scores were then calculated by multiplying the SERVQUAL gap by importance. Finally the results of performance only (SERVPERF) were analyzed in order to compare with the other three formulas. Table 4.6 shows how each service quality dimension ranks according to the four models. It is interesting to note that factoring in importance actually makes little difference to the SERVQUAL rankings (the ranking of only four dimensions changes). The results of calculating performance only (SERVPERF) appear to produce very different rankings to the IPA for the dimensions, most noticeably for the company magazine, which is ranked highest using IPA, but lowest using SERVPERF. Similarly, SERVPERF and SERVQUAL formulas produce differing ranks for

each of the dimensions, although respondents show a reasonably high level of satisfaction with the overall level of performance. Yet, despite the many differences in rankings, the dimension skiing/snowboarding is ranked in the top two by all four tests, while the journey is ranked in the bottom three by all the tests.

As would be expected, SERVQUAL and IPA produced different rankings for each of the holiday dimensions. According to SERVQUAL, the largest gaps can be found in the brochure, waiting to go and the journey. Customers ranked the skiing, the departure arrangements, and the arrival at accommodation, as the top three in service quality. IPA, however, suggested that the biggest service quality problems were to be found in the journey, transfer to accommodation, and resort activities, with the smallest gaps being for the magazine, the skiing, and the welcome. Despite some differences in rankings, further statistical analysis revealed no significant differences among the four methodologies used for calculating service quality.

QUESTIONS

1. What do these results suggest? Since there were no differences in the methods used, would you recommend using performance only to measure service quality?
2. What are the implications of this research for management?
3. What are the limitations of this research?
4. If you were asked to measure service quality in a restaurant, how would you go about it?

WEB SITES

www.sheraton.com
Sheraton Hotels and Resorts

www.cartondonofrio.com
Carton Donofrio Partners Inc.

www.disneylandparis.com
Disneyland Resort Paris

END NOTES

1. Gerhold, P. (1993). Defining marketing (or is it market?) research. *Marketing Research, 5*(Fall), 6–7.
2. Kinnear, T., Taylor, J., Johnson, L., & Armstrong, R. (1993). *Australian marketing research.* Sydney, Australia: McGraw-Hill.
3. Green, P., Tull, D., & Albaum, A. (1988). *Research for marketing decisions* (5th ed.). Englewood Cliffs, NJ: Prentice Hall.
4. McIntosh, R. W., Goeldner, C. R., & Ritchie, J. R. B. (1995). *Tourism: Principles, practices, philosophies* (7th ed.). New York: Wiley.
5. Smith, S. L. J. (1985). Location patterns of urban restaurants. *Annals of Tourism Research, 12*(4), 581–602.
6. Boote, J., & Mathews, A. (1999). Saying is one thing; doing is another: The role of observation in marketing research. *Qualitative Market Research: An International Journal, 2*(1), 15–21.
7. Ryan, C. (1995). *Researching tourist satisfaction: Issues, concepts, problems.* London: Routledge.
8. Ibid.
9. Crouch, S., & Housden, M. (1986). *Marketing research for managers.* London: Heinemann.
10. Kozak, M., & Rimmington, M. (1999). Measuring tourist destination competitiveness: Conceptual considerations and empirical findings. *Hospitality Management, 18*(3), 273–283.
11. Baker, K. J., Hozier, G.C., Jr., & Rogers, R. D. (1994). Marketing research theory and methodology and the tourism industry: A non-technical discussion. *Journal of Travel Research, 32*(3), 3–7.
12. Lovelock, C. H., & Wirtz, J. (2007). *Services marketing: People, technology, strategy* (6th ed.). Englewood Cliffs, NJ: Prentice Hall.

5

The Tourism and Hospitality Product

Spotlight
CONCORDE: A JOURNEY THROUGH THE PRODUCT LIFE CYCLE

At a cost of $14 000 round trip, a supersonic Mach 2 speed, in the company of superstars and royalty, passengers used to be able to travel from London to New York in less than 3.5 hours. Since the demise of Concorde in 2003, however, emphasis has been on size rather than speed and on low-cost aviation rather than premium pricing.

After 27 years the legendary needle-nosed, delta-winged product of 1960s technology was finally grounded and the 14-strong fleet donated to museums around the world. The end of this supersonic aviation era was caused by a combination of soaring repair costs, declining global economy, rising fuel costs, confidence failure after a tragic crash in Paris in 2000, which killed 113 and the resultant downturn in bookings.

Concorde was first launched, amid both acclaim and criticism, in Toulouse, France in March 1969. It broke the sound barrier for the first time in October the same year. Eight years later, the first commercial flights began from London and Paris to New York. Since then, only 20 models were built, despite initial overseas orders for 200, because of high fuel and maintenance costs and noise protests from the environmental lobby.

By building Concorde, with its famous Rolls-Royce Snecma Olympus 593 engines (the most powerful jet engines in commercial use), Europe gambled on speed. It also targeted wealthy passengers, indulging stars of music and film, diplomats, and top business people, with the finest champagne and caviar during their transatlantic crossings. At the same time, having failed to make their own reliable supersonic rival, the Americans opted for size, which, in the long term, has proved to be the winner.

From the time of its inauguration, Concorde differentiated itself in its appearance (both beautiful and useful), its high pricing, its unmatched speed, and its luxury. Appealing to the rich and famous, it featured in the media constantly throughout its 27-year reign. Pop star Phil Collins performed for the Live Aid concert in London in 1985, then jumped on the Concorde and resumed his globally televised act in Philadelphia a few hours later.

Allying itself with such larger-than-life characters, whose lives were assiduously followed in all the glossy media magazines, Concorde became a household name synonymous with prosperity, fame, and technological innovation.

Concorde's death knoll was presaged by a fatal crash in Paris in 2000, which led to all planes being withdrawn for 15 months whilst being refitted at a cost in excess of $42 million. Subsequently, Concorde was unable to lure back former passengers in sufficient numbers.

Aviation today is being taken over by slower, roomier, steadier aircraft. The latest jet on the runway is the Airbus 380, a double-decker for 555 passengers, with sleeper cabins, crew quarters, and business centres.

Sources: Wallace, B. (2003, October 24). Concorde era on final approach. *Calgary Herald*, A3; Stokes, D. (2003, October 10). Farewell Concorde and thanks for the pearl caviar spoon. *National Post*, A5; Bertin, O. (2003, April 11). The Concorde: First the boom, now the bust. *Globe and Mail*, A1, A9; Fitzgerald, J. (2003, October 2). Thrill seekers pack Concorde. *Globe and Mail*, A7; Webster, B. (2003, April 10). Concorde may be retired by year-end. *Calgary Herald*, A17.

Objectives

On completion of this chapter, readers should understand

- the components of the tourism and hospitality product;
- the various levels of products or services;

- the tools used in product planning;
- the concepts of packaging and branding; and
- new product development in the tourism and hospitality sector.

Chapter Overview

tourism and hospitality products

selected components or elements of the hotel, restaurant, entertainment, and resort industries bundled together to satisfy needs and wants

The *Spotlight* provides a classic example of the journey of one tourism product — the Concorde — through the product life cycle (PLC), one of the most basic product analysis tools. This chapter begins by introducing the peculiarities of the tourism product and the idea that **tourism and hospitality products** are selected components or elements of the hotel, restaurant, entertainment, and resort industries bundled together to satisfy needs and wants. The next section looks at the three levels of tourism products — the core product, the tangible product, and the augmented product — and these product levels are then applied to theme parks. Product planning is the focus of the next section, which begins by describing the five basic market/product options and then discusses the usefulness of a features/benefits analysis. A critique of the product life cycle model is then followed by a discussion of various positioning strategies available to organizations in the tourism and hospitality fields. An in-depth analysis of branding in tourism is supported by a case discussing the growth of chefs as brands. The next section of the chapter considers the concept of packaging, and the final part of the chapter looks at new product development and the various theoretical stages a company can follow in developing a new product or service.

INTRODUCTION TO THE TOURISM AND HOSPITALITY PRODUCT

Product decisions, with all their implications for the management of tourism and hospitality operations, influence not only the marketing mix, but also a firm's long-term growth strategy and its policies for investment and human resources. Product specifications largely determine the corporate image and branding an organization is able to create in the minds of its existing and prospective customers.[1] Tourism constitutes such a wide span of products that it has to be considered in terms of sectors rather than as a single industry, as discussed in Chapter 1. These sectors include accommodations, attractions, transportation, travel organizers, and destination organizations, among others (see Figure 1.6). This diversity is matched by an even greater diversity of component features specific to each tourism product sector, which need to be considered and managed in providing individual products for particular markets. The conceptualization of tourism and hospitality products as a group of selected components or elements brought together in a "bundle" to satisfy needs and wants is a vital image for marketing managers.

From the standpoint of a potential customer considering any form of tourist visit, the product may be defined as a bundle or package of tangible and intangible components, based on activity at a destination. The package is perceived by the tourist as an experience that is available for a price. There are five main components in the overall product: destination attractions and environment, destination facilities and services, accessibility of the destination, images of the destination, and price.[2] Although these components are combined and integrated in the visitor's overall experience, they are capable of extensive and more or less independent variation over time. Intrawest, for example, has transformed the natural ski slopes of North America and created popular purpose-built tourist winter destinations (see the *Case Study* at the end of the chapter). But it is in the promotional field of images and perceptions that some of the most interesting planned changes occur, and these are marketing decisions (see Chapter 12 for examples).

PRODUCT LEVELS

For many years, marketing theory has differentiated between three levels of product offering. The three levels can be seen as a continuum, with the product's most basic benefit at one end, and a range of add-on benefits, not directly related to the product's essential purpose, at the opposite end. These three levels are:

core product

the basic need function served by the generic product

tangible product

the specific features and benefits residing in the product itself — styling, quality, brand name, design, etc.

augmented product

the add-ons that are extrinsic to the product itself but may influence the decision to purchase

- **Core product:** the basic need function served by the generic product. For an airline or train service, the core product is transportation; for a hotel, the core benefits offered are shelter and rest.
- **Tangible product:** these are the specific features and benefits residing in the product itself — styling, quality, brand name, design, etc.
- **Augmented product:** the add-ons that are extrinsic to the product itself but may influence the decision to purchase. Augmented features may include credit terms, after-sales guarantees, car parking, etc.

Although these levels were defined with manufactured products in mind, they do apply, with modifications, to tourism and hospitality goods and services. For example, John Swarbrooke has applied the three levels to theme parks (see Figure 5.1).

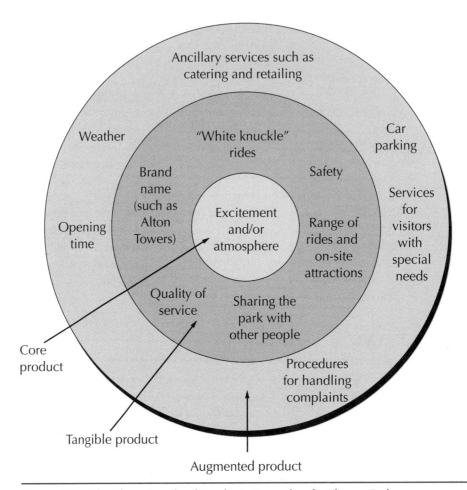

Core product

Tangible product

Augmented product

Figure 5.1 The Three Levels of Product: Example of a Theme Park

Source: Swarbrooke, J. (1995). *The development and management of visitor attractions.* Oxford: Butterworth-Heinemann.

Conceptualizing the product in these three areas allows the tourism marketer to appraise the comparative advantages and consumer appeal of his or her product versus those of others. In a highly competitive market, it is unlikely that any supplier will have an advantage in the core benefits, and differentiation is instead likely to reside in the second and third levels. For example, most theme parks offer excitement and thrills for consumers, but will compete with each other on the variety and quality of rides, or the quality of the surrounding environment.

PHYSICAL EVIDENCE AND THE SERVICESCAPE

An important part of the augmented product is the physical environment. Because many tourism and hospitality services are intangible, customers often rely on tangible cues, or physical evidence, to evaluate the service before its purchase and to assess their satisfaction with the service during and after consumption. As explained in Chapter 1, the physical evidence is the environment in which the service is delivered and in which the organization and consumer interact, and any tangible components that facilitate performance or communication of the service. The physical facility is often referred to as the "**servicescape**," and is very important for tourism and hospitality products such as hotels, restaurants, and theme parks, which are dominated by experience attributes. Disney, for example, effectively uses the servicescape to excite its customers. The brightly coloured displays, the music, the rides, and the costumed characters all reinforce the feelings of fun and excitement that Disney seeks to generate in its customers.

General elements of physical evidence are shown in Table 5.1. They include all aspects of the organization's servicescape that affect customers, including both exterior attributes (such as parking and landscape) and interior attributes (such as design, layout, equipment, and decor). Signage is also part of the physical evidence, and Beijing was attempting to stamp out embarrassingly bad English on bilingual signs before the 2008 Olympics. The municipal government issued translation guidelines for signs in hotels, shopping malls, public transport, and tourist attractions. The Park of Ethnic Minorities was identified as "Racist Park," while the emergency exits at Beijing's international airport read "No entry on peacetime."

servicescape

the environment in which the service is delivered and in which the organization and consumer interact, and any tangible components that facilitate performance or communication of the service

Table 5.1

Elements of Physical Evidence

SERVICESCAPE FACILITY EXTERIOR	SERVICESCAPE FACILITY INTERIOR	OTHER TANGIBLES
Parking	Layout	Uniforms
Landscape	Equipment	Business cards
Signage	Signage	Stationery
Exterior design	Air temperature	Invoices
	Interior design	Brochures
	Lighting	Websites
		Employee dress

Consumer researchers know that the design of the servicescape can influence customer choices, expectations, satisfaction, and other behaviour. Retailers know that customers are influenced by smell, decor, music, and layout. Arby's, a fast food chain in North America, uses the servicescape to position its restaurants as a step above other quick service outlets. The company asserts that the interior ambience of Arby's outlets, with carpeted floors, cushioned seating, and a decor "superior" to other fast food chains, contributes to attracting diners. Design of work environments can also affect employees' productivity, motivation, and satisfaction. The challenge in many tourism and hospitality settings is to design the physical space so that it can support the needs and preferences of customers and employees simultaneously. Employees and customers in service firms respond to dimensions of their physical surroundings in three ways — cognitively, emotionally, and physiologically — and these responses influence their behaviour in the environment. First, the perceived servicescape may elicit *cognitive* responses, including people's beliefs about a place and their beliefs about the people and products found in that place. For example, a consumer study found that a travel agent's office decor affected customer attributions of the travel agent's behaviour.[3] In addition to influencing cognition, the perceived servicescape may elicit *emotional* responses that in turn influence behaviour. The colours, decor, music, and other elements of the atmosphere can have an unexplained and sometimes subconscious effect on the moods of people in the place. Servicescapes that are both pleasant and arousing are considered "exciting," while those that are pleasant and non-arousing, or sleepy, are called "relaxing." Unpleasant servicescapes that are irritating are "distressing," while unpleasant, sleepy servicescapes are "gloomy."[4] Finally, the servicescape may affect people in purely *physiological* ways. Noise that is too loud may cause physical discomfort, the temperature of a room may cause people to shiver or perspire, the air quality may make it difficult to breathe, and the glare of lighting may decrease ability to see and may cause physical pain. All of these physical responses will influence whether people remain in and enjoy a particular environment. In 2004, Enhanced Air Technologies, based in Vancouver, developed Commercaire pheromone, a synthetic compound intended to mimic the maternal sense of comfort perceived by children when they are crying or unhappy. Filtered into a store, the odourless substance was meant to relax customers so they stay longer and buy more.[5] The firm claimed retailers could expect revenue growth of between 9 percent and 20 percent using the product. While Enhanced Air's sales-stimulating pheromone is no longer on the market, there is a long history of retailers using fake sawdust or fresh bread smells to foster favourable emotions in patrons.

In Chapter 2, the discussion of consumer trends pointed out that today's consumer desires experiences, and more and more businesses are responding by explicitly designing experiences with themed servicescapes. At themed restaurants such as the Hard Rock Café, Planet Hollywood, or the Rainforest Café, the food is just a prop for what's known as "eatertainment." Retailers are also creating themes that tie merchandising presentations together in a staged experience. A popular tourist attraction in Las Vegas is the Forum Shops at Caesars Palace, a mall that displays its distinctive theme — an ancient Roman marketplace — in every detail. The Simon DeBartolo Group, which developed the mall, disperses this motif through a panoply of architectural effects. These include marble floors, stark white pillars, "outdoor" cafés, living trees, flowing fountains — and even a painted blue sky with fluffy white clouds that yield regularly to simulated storms, complete with lighting and thunder. Every mall entrance and every storefront is an elaborate Roman re-creation. Hourly, inside the main entrance, statues of Julius Caesar and other Roman luminaries come to life and speak. "Hail, Caesar!" is a frequent cry, and Roman centurions periodically march through on their way to the adjacent Caesar's Palace casino.

Despite the increased emphasis on the servicescape in designing experiences, companies that fail to provide consistently engaging experiences, overprice their experiences relative to the value perceived, or overbuild their capacity to stage them will see pressure on demand, pricing, or both. The Rainforest Café and Planet Hollywood have both encountered trouble because they have failed to refresh their experiences. Guests find nothing different from one visit to the next. Advances in technology are allowing tourism providers to enhance the servicescape in order to create an interactive educational experience for visitors. An example is the Churchill Museum and Cabinet War Rooms, which opened in London in

February 2005 and has a unique electronic "Lifeline" table that allows visitors to journey through Winston Churchill's extraordinary life (see Figure 5.2). The 18-metre-long Lifeline is a computerized filing cabinet, with a virtual file containing items relating to each year and, in many cases, each month and day of Churchill's career. Touching the strip at the edge of the Lifeline brings up contextual data, documents, films, photographs, and even soundtracks that relate to his life while providing historical context. The Lifeline includes 4600 pages, 200 000 words, 100 documents, 1150 images, and 206 animations.

Figure 5.2 Example of an Interactive Educational Experience at Churchill Museum, London

Exhibit designers Casson Mann are proud of their technological and interactive advances, calling it "a 21st-century museum about a 20th-century giant." Casson Mann are exhibition, museum, and interior designers, responsible for, among other exhibits, the British Galleries at London's Victoria and Albert Museum. Their specialty is thoughtful communication that draws on all the senses by telling interesting stories in intelligent spaces. They aim, through design, to make people feel wanted and comfortable so that they can look at art, take in information, entertain the children, or have a discussion and do whatever it is they came to do.

PRODUCT PLANNING

Product Mix

product mix

the portfolio of products that an organization offers to one market or several

The most basic decisions a tourism organization must make are what business it is in and what product mix is appropriate to it. The **product mix** is the portfolio of products that an organization offers to one market or several. Five basic market/product options exist.[6] They are as follows:

1. several markets/multi-product mixes for each (e.g., mass tour operators that offer a wide range of multi-destination packages to a variety of market segments);

2. several markets/single product for each (e.g., airlines with a product for business and economy class travellers);
3. several markets/single product for all (e.g., a national tourist organization promoting a country);
4. single market/multi-product mix (e.g., a specialist tour operator with a range of cultural tours aimed at a wealthy, educated market); and
5. single market/single product (e.g., a heliskiing operator targeting the very rich).

The decision about which product mix option to adopt depends upon many factors, including the strength and value of consumer demand in the different markets, the level of competition in each market, and the distinctive competence of the organization to service the markets adequately. The starting point in product analysis and planning is thus an analysis of the consumer and competitive offerings in relation to the goals and product capacity of the tourism organization. The most successful products emerge when the marketing planning steps outlined in Chapter 3 are followed (see the discussion of portfolio and SWOT analysis). Another useful method of analyzing the tourism product is to consider its features and benefits. **Features** consist of the objective attributes of a product; **benefits** are the rewards that the product gives the consumer. The difference between the two is shown in Table 5.2. In 2005 Hong Kong International Airport was named the world's best airport in a survey of more than 50 000 frequent travellers.[7] Part of the reason is the features of the airport and the benefits these features offer passengers. Apart from shops offering everything from rare white tea to cellphones, there are free plasma televisions to watch, a children's play area, wireless access, Internet cafés, a prayer room, a pharmacy, nap rooms, a beauty salon, shower facilities, a medical centre (complete with onsite vaccinations and x-ray machines), and displays from Hong Kong museums.

features

the objective attributes of a product

benefits

the rewards that the product gives the consumer

Table 5.2

Features and Benefits Analysis for Tourism and Hospitality Products

TOURISM PRODUCT ITEM	PRODUCT FEATURE	CONSUMER BENEFIT
Low-cost airline	Low service, regional airports	Affordability
Purpose-built ski resort	All lifts near hotel rooms	Ski-in/ski-out facility allows easy access to slopes
Museum	Interactive facilities to learn	An entertaining as well as educational place to visit
River adventure tour	Quality kayaks and rafts	Reconnecting with nature in a safe environment
Five-star hotel	Quality beds	Comfort that offers a good night's sleep

Product Life Cycle

product life cycle (PLC) analysis

a way to identify the life-cycle stage of a product or service, review its past and current position, and predict its future

One of the most basic product analysis tools is the **product life cycle (PLC) analysis** (see Figure 5.3), and the *Spotlight* described the journey of Concorde through this life cycle. Plotting products or services to identify what stage they are at in their PLC is a valuable way of reviewing a product's past and current position and making predictions about its future. As part of a portfolio analysis (see Chapter 3), an organization should access each good and service in terms of its position in the PLC. *Product development* begins when the company finds and develops a new product idea. The *introduction* phase is a period of slow sales and low profits because of the investment required for product introduction. The *growth* phase is characterized by increasing market acceptance and substantial improvement in profits. The *maturity* phase is a period of slow sales but is marked by high profits as the product is well entrenched in the marketplace and has an acceptable market share. However, when sales begin to drop because competitors are moving into the marketplace, the product enters the *decline* stage. Profits and market share decline, and major costs may be involved in redeveloping, refurbishing, or maintaining the product.

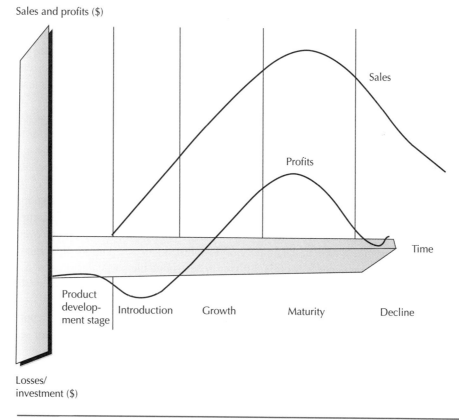

Figure 5.3 The Product Life Cycle

Using the PLC concept to develop marketing strategy can be difficult. Strategy is both a cause and a result of the PLC. At the introduction stage, promotion spending is likely to be high in order to inform consumers about the new product and encourage them to buy it. A company will focus on selling to buyers who are ready to buy, usually higher-income groups. Prices tend to be on the high side because of low output, production problems, and high promotion costs and other expenses. At the growth stage, the early adopters will continue to buy, and later buyers will start following their lead, encouraged by favourable word of mouth. Competitors will enter the market, attracted by the opportunity for profit, and they will introduce more features that will expand the market. In the growth stage, the organization faces a trade-off between high market share and high current profit. By investing heavily in product improvement, promotion, and distribution, it can capture a dominant position. But it sacrifices maximum current profit in the hope of making this up in the next stage.

When sales start to slow down, the product or service will enter the maturity stage, and this lasts longer than the previous two stages and poses stronger challenges to marketing management. Most products or services are in this stage, and it is a phase that is characterized by heavy competition. The only way to increase sales is to lure customers away from competition, and so price wars and heavy advertising are common. At this stage, an aggressive product manager will seek to increase consumption by modifying markets or products. The product manager may also try to improve sales by changing one or more of the marketing mix elements. In the decline stage, some firms will withdraw from the market. Those that remain may reduce the number of their product offerings or the number of market segments they are targeting. They may also reduce the promotion budget as well as prices. For each declining product, management must decide whether to maintain, harvest, or drop it.

However, the PLC is not as simple as it sounds in theory, and according to one writer "its supposed universal applicability is largely a myth."[8] The study of the PLC pattern for a particular product or service has to take into account the market it is in. For example, if a product or service is showing no growth or decline, it may still be very successful if the market as a whole is in decline. Another complication of the PLC is that a product or service in overall decline may be losing its customers from one market segment but increasing appeal or holding steady with another. Ski areas, for example, have been very successful in attracting an increasing number of snowboarders over the past decade, despite a drop in the number of downhill skiers. In addition, although the PLC concept is neat on paper, it is often difficult to determine the particular stage of a product or service. Finally, even assuming that a product life cycle position can be determined, it may not be obvious what action should be taken.

However, despite these problems, the PLC is a valuable concept to operationalize, because it forces the organization to analyze trends for its product or service in relation to the overall market and the segments within it, in order to assess future marketing requirements. Ski areas, for example, have adapted to the growth in snowboarders referred to above by changing the products and services they offer; most successful ski areas these days have designated areas for snowboarders (see the *Case Study* at the end of the chapter). A related concept for analyzing destinations is that of the tourism area life cycle (TALC), which is discussed in Chapter 12.

Positioning

Positioning is the bedrock of product management. Chapter 3 introduces the concept as the natural follow-through of market segmentation and market targeting, and highlights the three steps necessary to develop an effective position in the target market segment. The objective of positioning is to create a distinctive image in the minds of potential customers. Positioning in tourism should evoke visions of a destination or product in the customer's mind — images that differentiate the product from the competition and also convey that it can satisfy their needs and wants. Effective positioning should direct all of the marketing functions of a business. Advertising and promotions, as well as decisions on price, product, and distribution channels, must all be consistent with positioning goals. Often, these marketing functions will be driven by a **positioning statement**, which is a phrase that reflects the image the organization wants to create. The positioning statement for the Churchill Museum in London, for example, is "A benchmark for personality museums in the twenty-first century." This statement encapsulates what the museum stands for, the essence of what the museum does, and how it stands out from competitors.

positioning statement

a phrase that reflects the image an organization wants to create

There is an endless number of positioning strategies, and selection of the appropriate approach is vital to the success of a tourism organization. James F. Burke and Barry P. Resnick have identified four key positioning strategies that are not mutually exclusive and may therefore be used individually or in combination.[9] They are as follows:

- positioning relative to target market (e.g., business travellers, families with children under 10, etc.);
- positioning by price and quality (e.g., a premium product such as a room at a Four Seasons Hotel);
- positioning relative to a product class (e.g., a tour operator positioning its products within a winter sports tourism category); and
- positioning relative to competitors (e.g., the Hertz "We try harder" campaign, which drew attention to the fact that Hertz was not market leader among car rental companies but would work harder to catch up with its competitors).

Boutique hotels use a combination of positioning strategies to succeed in the very competitive hotel market. Loosely defined as small, specialized hotels, mainly in prime city locations, boutiques offer high standards of service, style, and comfort that suit the corporate jetsetter. An example in Canada is the new 10-room boutique property in Banff called Pension Tannenhof. The main challenge for boutiques is how to keep ahead in such a fiercely competitive market. Ian Schrager, owner of the Sanderson and St. Martin's Lane hotels in London, has managed to stay ahead of the game by attracting a celebrity clientele and introducing luxurious spas at his properties. Germany's Sorat Hotels and Spain's Sol Melia have tried to differentiate themselves by emphasizing the quality of their personal service, while the UK group Hotel du Vin has made its name with the high standard of food on offer at its stylish bistros.[10]

MARKETING IN ACTION

THE COOLEST PLACE IN TOWN: QUEBEC'S ICE HOTEL

Using 15 000 tonnes of snow and 500 tonnes of ice, a Canadian entrepreneur has created a fully functional luxury hotel that is attracting international attention as the hottest winter experience in North America. For Jacques Desbois, the man behind Quebec's coolest overnight lodging, sleeping in a snow shelter in winter is "a beautiful experience, a purification." As founder of the Ice Hotel, a concept he imported from Sweden, Desbois gave North Americans their first chance to purify in 2001. About 40 000 people visited the hotel's Montmorency Falls site, including 1500 who spent the night. Media coverage was worldwide, and the following year the hotel received 60 000 visitors, 3500 staying overnight.

Building on the runaway fascination, the promoters expanded the Ice Hotel in 2002 from 6 to 31 rooms. Ten of these are "suites" that have more than one bedroom and are decorated with ice sculptures. Ordinary rooms are furnished with just a bed and candleholder. To give guests something to do, the hotel site was moved to the Station Écotouristique Duchesnay northeast of Quebec City. Run by Sépaq, the organization that operates Quebec's parks and wildlife reserves, Duchesnay is an 89-square-kilometre forested area on a lake that offers opportunities for cross-country skiing, ice fishing, snowshoeing, dogsledding, or just walks in the woods.

Duchesnay is also a mini-village that Sépaq converted from structures belonging to a former forestry school. Guests eat breakfast and dinner in the reception and restaurant building. Three log pavilions contain 40 rooms, and the 14 fully equipped lakeside chalets can accommodate up to 12 guests. For people wanting it both ways, a package is available that includes one night at the Ice Hotel and one night in a warm room at the station.

The Ice Hotel itself, including meals and a welcome cocktail, cost from $199 per person in 2007, and the price of a public tour was $15 for an adult. A tour of the hotel provides both enchantment and shivers. On the enchanting side, two art galleries display ice sculptures of fish, swans, human figures, and more. One gallery honours nature and the municipality of Sainte-Catherine-de-la-Jacques-Cartier, in which Duchesnay is located, and the other, which includes a long house, celebrates Iroquois culture. A wedding chapel has an ice altar with a shining star in the background. Less encouraging are rooms with snow floors, no windows, and beds made of ice blocks. However, sleepers are separated from the ice by a wood frame, 8 centimetres of dense foam, and deerskins. The hotel supplies sleeping bags rated for Arctic conditions, which is more than enough protection as interior temperatures are unlikely to fall below 21°C. Humidity makes the indoor air seem chillier, however, and a tomb-like silence pervades the hotel, even the bar, which is named after sponsor Absolut Vodka. In the morning, a hotel employee comes by with a wake-up coffee or hot chocolate.

Peppered with questions about cold, Desbois replies that only 1 percent of guests leave the hotel without sleeping through the night. "Just follow the advice to change to dry clothes and don't drink much alcohol. Make sure to breathe outside your sleeping bag to avoid building up humidity." Guests are given a half-hour information session on how to keep warm before going to their rooms. As for

MARKETING IN ACTION *continued*

why anyone would sleep in an ice hotel, Desbois answers, "We're an adventure service, not a lodging service. There's a kind of pride you feel after surviving a night in the Ice Hotel. This is how we present the product." About 30 percent of the guests are American, said Desbois, who is known as Mr. Igloo around Quebec City, for the igloo villages he builds at carnival time. Canadians, account for 63 percent of guests. This unique success story has captured the attention of media worldwide with more than 3500 international reports recorded on the Ice Hotel since spring 2000. It has also been the recipient of numerous awards, including the Best Recreational Tourism Enterprise in 2006. Desbois himself was named Quebec's Tourism Personality of the Year for 2001. Year after year the Ice Hotel attracts an increasing number of visitors, and by the end of 2006, 343 000 people had visited the hotel, including 17 320 who stayed overnight. More than 20 000 people have held special events such as weddings, anniversaries, corporate celebrations, product launches, and film productions.

Source: Leney, P. (2002, January 19). Ice Hotel's aim is adventure not comfort. *Montreal Gazette*, G5.

BRANDING

The practice of branding developed in the field of marketing packaged goods as a method of establishing a distinctive identity for a product based on competitive differentiation from other products. It was commonly achieved through naming, trade marking, packaging, product design, and promotion. Successful branding gave a unique identity to what might otherwise have been a generic product. This identity produced a consistent image in the consumer's mind, which facilitated recognition and quality assurance. In the 19th century, products such as Beecham's pills, Cadbury's chocolate, and Eno's salts were early examples of branding. These days, the market in packaged goods is dominated by brands, and in the last few decades branding has also been widely recognized in services marketing. A brand, in the modern marketing sense, offers the consumer relevant added value — a superior proposition that is distinctive from competitors and that imparts meaning above and beyond the product's functional aspects. There is even the Museum of Brands, Packaging, and Advertising in London, where visitors can view 10 000 consumer products covering 200 years.

Branding in services offers a solution to some of the problems in services marketing discussed in Chapter 1 — in particular those of consistency and product standardization. Branding can be a way of unifying services, which is why it has been particularly developed in hotel marketing. Research shows that nearly 90 percent of bookings are made with branded hotel chains, and 9 out of 10 consumers can distinguish between chains, franchise operators, and independents.[11] For large hotel companies that have a wide variety of properties, grouping them into brands can:

- unify them into more easily recognizable smaller groups;
- enable each branded group to be targeted at defined market segments; and
- enable product delivery, including human resource management, to focus on creating a specific set of benefits for a specific market.

North America has more than 200 hotel brands competing for business, and many hotel chains offer a family of sub-brands or endorsed brands. For example, Hilton Hotels Corporation, Intercontinental, and Starwood each have seven sub-brands, while Marriott International has 12 (plus the Ritz-Carlton chain, which, to protect its exclusive image, is not normally identified for marketing purposes as part of the Marriott Group).[12] For a multi-brand strategy to succeed, each brand must promise a distinctive value proposition, targeted at a different customer segment. There are even branded hotel floors in some hotels. American Express and the Sheraton Vancouver Wall Centre Hotel have partnered to open a floor dedicated to business accommodations for American Express card holders. Located on the 27th floor, the American Express Club Floor features a private lounge with business service centre, direct access to boardrooms and fitness facilities, dedicated front desk check-in, and a 4:00 p.m. checkout. Club guests pay the same price for their room as American Express's negotiated standard room rate and benefit from a host of value-added services and amenities. These include complimentary continental breakfast, all-day coffee and tea, evening hors d'oeuvres, international and local newspapers, and 24-hour room service.

In the past, branding was often seen mainly as a matter of promotion and creating the right image through advertising and publicity. But marketing managers now recognize that successful branding involves the integrated deployment of product design, pricing policies, distribution selection, and promotion. The case for branding is stronger for tourism products that offer the possibility for differentiation in several areas of the marketing mix. This is why branding has been particularly successful in hotel and restaurant marketing. Branding of restaurants, hotels, and airlines developed extensively in the U.S. during the 1980s and '90s, and companies in the rest of the world are following suit. The momentum is driven mainly by large organizations that recognize that in order to remain competitive they need to offer several products to different markets instead of relying upon a monolithic presence in one main one.

Apart from the advantages already mentioned, Victor Middleton and Jackie Clarke suggest that branding in tourism offers other specific advantages.[13] These advantages include:

- Branding helps reduce medium- and long-term vulnerability to the unforeseen external events that so beset the tourism industry. Recovery time after an event such as a terrorist attack, or a natural disaster, is likely to be shorter for a well-established brand.
- Branding reduces risk for the consumer at the point of purchase by signalling the expected quality and performance of an intangible product. It offers either an implicit or explicit guarantee to the consumer.
- Branding facilitates accurate marketing segmentation by attracting some consumer segments and repelling others. For an inseparable product, onsite segment compatibility is an important marketing issue.
- Branding provides the focus for the integration of stakeholder effort, especially for the employees of an organization or the individual tourism providers of a destination brand.
- Finally, branding is a strategic weapon for long-range planning in tourism, as can be seen in the *Snapshot* on Four Seasons in Chapter 3.

It should be recognized that a competitive brand is a live asset and not a fixture, and therefore its value may depreciate over time if starved of investment and marketing and management skill. Brand decay may begin if a brand is overstretched into new products that damage its essence, or following a merger or takeover. Marketers sometimes use the term **brandicide** to describe the killing of a well-known brand by extending it into a new area without adequate management (Roots Air is an example — see the *Case Study* in Chapter 3) or by not maintaining it effectively.

Companies increasingly attempt to stretch their proven expertise into new areas. Walt Disney Inc., for example, has recently entered the produce business. Disney's cartoon characters are popping up on fruit and vegetable packaging across the U.S., as growers clinch licensing deals with entertainment companies hungry to cultivate positive images among health-conscious parents and children. A combination of factors has made companies more eager than ever to stretch their brands further and more boldly. Advances in technology have reduced barriers to entry in new sectors. Companies have developed stronger and more knowledgeable relationships with customers, and the cost and difficulty of developing new brands are encouraging companies to exploit the brands they already have. The *Profile* of Richard Branson in Chapter 11 shows how over the past 25 years, he has diversified his Virgin brand into an empire that includes a wide range of products and services beyond the original travel, including financial services, media and telecommunications, social and environmental enterprises, phone services, rail service, and even wedding dresses, as well as his music label and discount airline. Virgin's success has relied and benefited from Branson's youthful enthusiasm, entrepreneurial drive, and forward thinking, as well as his willingness to take risks with new projects, which he calls "brand stretching."

brandicide

the killing of a well-known brand by extending it into a new area without adequate management or by not maintaining it effectively

SNAPSHOT

CHEFS AS BRANDS: THE CASE OF JAMIE OLIVER

Some of the most successful and fastest-growing consumer brands today are chefs. Chefs used to be limited to working in the back of restaurants and creating great meals that consumers loved to eat. Since the 1990s, they have moved to the forefront, becoming brands in their own right. Many chefs today have their names attached to multiple product lines and have their hands in a wealth of restaurants and businesses. They are a new breed of chef — one that understands how powerful a brand name can be in the marketplace. And they are following popular marketing theory, which states that if you find a product that works, you should create brand extensions from it.

One celebrity chef has differentiated himself dramatically from all the others. Jamie Oliver, one of Britain's most loved TV personalities since his teenage debut as the "Naked Chef," is a prime example of branding success as well as innovative positioning. Traditionally, chefs were equated with the stereotype of older, portly men and women who appealed to an older demographic. Oliver, however, gives chefs a fresh, youthful, hip spin, appealing to young people with his casual clothes and no-nonsense cooking style. Moreover, he has aligned himself with underprivileged youth and also with school-children through his television reality shows and has even affected British politics with his successful campaign for healthy, government-funded school lunches.

From his early Naked Chef bachelor image, Oliver has developed his brand along-side his personal life. Since marrying and having two children, he has portrayed the image of the devoted family man and extended this to his professional life by taking on the job of improving nutrition throughout Britain among children. In 2004 he used his celebrity status to launch a nationwide Feed Me Better campaign along with a documentary TV series called "Jamie's School Dinners," which was aired in early 2005. His Feed Me Better petition secured more than 72 000 signatures, became front-page news, and inspired Tony Blair's govern-ment to respond with a vote-catching "children's manifesto" as well as a substantial increase in funding for school meals. Oliver also launched a set of Feed Me Better starter information packages for schools. In 2006 British education secretary Alan Johnson said the Children's Food Bill, passed as a result of Oliver's lobbying, was aimed at improving school pupils' nutrition and undoing decades of neglect. Now he is expanding the cam-paign in the United States.

Oliver understands how powerful his name can be both in the marketplace and in society. His brand expansion is not only making him very wealthy but also furthering his altruistic approach to national and inter-national healthy eating. He called his reform efforts "one of the biggest food revolutions England has ever seen," explaining that, having achieved so much personally, he had two choices: "I could go two ways at this point. I could give back or I could be

greedy." His chic restaurant, Fifteen London, combines his business acumen with his humanitarian tendencies. It is the result of another television show, in which he took a group of down-and-out youngsters and turned them into able kitchen staff. He has repeated this theme in Holland, too, at Fifteen Amsterdam.

The Internet is also extending the suc-cessful branding of celebrity chefs like Oliver. The medium brings chefs a wide-reaching sales channel that they couldn't find elsewhere. Oliver's website provides all the same marketing components traditionally found in direct marketing. There are elec-tronic updates of his shows and events plus information on recipes, new cookbook launch dates, and links to distributors of the Tefal cookware he sponsors. The site also serves as a customer service and relationship marketing tool, furthering brand loyalty. Fans can share ideas and information with him and with each other via an interactive mes-saging forum.

How far can you extend a chef's name as a brand without committing the ultimate brandicide? Jamie Oliver sensibly refused to pose naked for Nestlé and Coca Cola ad campaigns, both of which alliances would have compromised his healthy eating ethos. He has, amid some media criticism, agreed to promote the pro-organic British supermarket Sainsburys, which he considers more in line with his business principles. Oliver receives an estimated £1 million a year for his Sainsbury advertisements.

For celebrity chefs — as for many con-sumer products — marketing is all about con-necting with an audience. "These celebrity chefs are so hot because they are so touch-able," says industry publicist Lisa Ekus. "Consumers can see them, taste their food, feel like they are really getting something from them. That intimacy is invaluable when

SNAPSHOT *continued*

it comes to marketing. It allows them to turn themselves into successful brands."

Sources: Cohen, A. (2001, December). Look who's cooking now. *Sales & Marketing Management, 152*(12), 30–36; Turner, C. (2003, March 31). Edible peep show. *Globe & Mail*, R3; Fernand, D. (2006,

April 2). School meals revolution hits home. *Sunday Times*, Focus; Eckler, R. (2004, November 29). Bloody good. *National Post*, B12; Renzetti, E. (2005, March 22). St. Jamie serves up a cafeteria food fight. *Globe & Mail*, R1, R3; Fletcher, V. (2006, May 20). Junk food ban is lesson in health. *Daily Express*, 17.

PACKAGING

packaging

the practice of combining two or more related and complementary offerings into a single-price offering

In the tourism and hospitality industry, **packaging** is the practice of combining two or more related and complementary offerings into a single-price offering. A package may include a wide variety of services, such as lodging, meals, entrance fees for attractions, entertainment, transportation costs, guide services, or other similar activities. Travel packages have become increasingly popular over the years. They are attractive because they benefit both the consumer and participating organizations by providing convenience and value to the consumer and added revenue for the partner organizations.

More specifically, packaging provides several customer benefits, including,

- easier budgeting for trips: the customer pays at one time and has a good idea of the trip's total cost;
- increased convenience, which saves time and prevents aggravation;
- greater economy, as the cost to the customer is usually more economical than purchasing the package components individually;
- the opportunity to experience previously unfamiliar activities and attractions; and
- the opportunity to design components of a package for specialized interests.

For tourism operations, packages are attractive for the following reasons:

- They can improve profitability by allowing organizations to price at a premium by adding special good and services.
- They can streamline business patterns. Packaging during low-demand periods can add attractive features to the service or product, thus generating additional business.
- They allow joint marketing opportunities, which can in turn reduce promotional costs.
- They can be an effective tool for tailoring tourism products for specific target markets.

In Canada, the tourism industry is becoming increasingly sophisticated and innovative with its packaging. The *Marketing in Action* on Weekendtrips.com in Chapter 7 is an example of the growing number of companies catering to the demand for short-break tourism experiences sold via the Internet. Wine tourism packages are increasingly popular, as are packaging holidays that respond to the growing interest in wildlife tourism among older, more affluent tourists. In Manitoba, for example, Churchill attracts 2500 tourists a year who take trips in tundra buggies to see wildlife, primarily polar bears, but also ptarmigan, Arctic fox, Arctic hare, snowy owls, and lemmings. Tour packages range from $2200, for two nights including accommodation and transportation to and from Winnipeg, to $7000. A 2004 study found that 75 percent of Churchill's visitors were

American, and about 15 percent were from abroad, mostly Japan, Germany, and France. About 10 percent of visitors were Canadian.[14] The *Profile* on Vocation Vacations describes some unique tourism packages put together by the U.S. travel company.

PROFILE

VOCATION VACATIONS

Mixing business with pleasure is usually the ultimate "no no," especially when it comes to precious holiday time. However, one U.S. career change company has made this time-honoured cliché into an opportunity to make dreams come true by giving tourists the chance to experience firsthand the business or career they have always hankered for.

The first of its kind, Vocation Vacations was set up in 2004 in Portland, Oregon, by Brian Kurth. The company offers its customers the chance to combine travel with their dream job via a choice of more than 225 mentorships with experts in jobs as diverse as artist, cheese maker, vintner, fashion designer, comedian, and television producer.

It is more than just job shadowing; it's the chance to test-drive a career without financial risk or endangering a current form of employment. Kurth generally chooses smaller companies where owners tend to be particularly passionate about their specialization. "People who love what they do are more willing to share it," he explains. From this initial taste of the new career "vocationers" can then decide, with some experience as well as expert guidance, if they want to change their life or retreat to the safety of their chosen job.

The job choices, from horse trainer to pastry chef, are realistic options — "dream jobs, jobs anyone can learn to do with a little initiative," says Kurth. "Not fantasy jobs, such as rock star. You may not be qualified to be a rock star."

Inquiries are made via the company's website or by calling its toll-free number. The Vocation Vacations website includes extensive lists of media reviews as well as "vocationer" testimonials. Many journalists from TV, radio, and print have test-driven careers with Vocation Vacations in order to write about their real-life experiences. Packages range from US$399 for a basic day to US$1999 for three-day dream job experience with a Grand Am racing pit crew or a Wedding Coordinator Vocation Vacation with a celebrity wedding planner in Los Angeles. The company is partnered with credit card and hotel loyalty programs offering, for example, two-day Music Producer holidays for 150 000 points.

After being laid off in 2001 by a dot.com company, Kurth set up in this innovative new business following six months of travel around the United States. The statistics are in

Vocation Vacations' favour, with 55 percent of American workers disliking their jobs, 42 percent burned out, and 33 percent stuck in dead-end careers. These were the results of a survey of 7718 U.S. workers carried out by Harris Interactive Inc. in 2004. Kurth realizes that the market is huge for his unique concept and is working on a book on the Vocationing process for Warner Business Books and has signed with Al Roker Productions to create a career-change TV series.

"Work can be much, much more than just a four-letter word," claims Kurth and he works on the theory that people are ready for different experiences during their holidays, which he calls "adventures." The chance to learn something new was rated as "very important" by 64 percent of people polled in the 2004 RoperReports/NOP survey. This survey tracks vacation trends and found that relaxation was down slightly as a major motivation for holidaymakers, whereas the urge to learn was up from 51 percent the previous year.

Kurth rates the culinary, fashion, entertainment, hospitality, animal-related, and sports fields as the most popular to date of the Vocation Vacations offerings. But he counsels that people should see "beyond the glamour" and experience the job "warts and all."

Sources: Davis, A. (2006, January). Dream a little dream job. *Westjet.com Inflight Magazine*; Frazier, J. B. (2004, May 29). Test drive your dream job: Vocation vacation. *National Post,* PT6.

NEW PRODUCT DEVELOPMENT

According to the *Los Angeles Times*, 700 new products are introduced every day.[15] Many of them fail, and many new ideas take years before the idea becomes reality. The Bridge Climb in Sydney is a prime example of the latter. Climbing across the catwalk connecting two spans at the top of the Sydney harbor bridge (120 metres above Sydney Harbour) has become a successful tourist attraction. It is estimated that the Bridge Climb is a $9000-per-hour business that runs 12 hours a day, 363 days a year.[16] However, although Paul Cave conceived the idea in the late 1980s, it was not approved until 1998. Safety concerns and other issues kept the unique tourism product on hold for more than a decade.

Developing new products is different from maintaining existing ones, and planning for both kinds of product will differ according to whether the products are targeted at existing markets or new ones. Christopher Holloway and Ronald Plant provide a useful matrix to illustrate the permutations of possible market/product interaction and the product moves that might be suitable for each (see Figure 5.4).[17] According to the model, an organization has four alternatives.

Market

Existing   New

	Product development Introduce new product to present market	**Diversification (example)** Launch new product to new market
New		
Product	**Market penetration** Enter market with existing product	**Market development** Reposition present product to attract new market
Existing		

Figure 5.4   Product Options in New and Existing Markets

Source: Holloway, J. C., & Plant, R. V. (1992). *Marketing for tourism* (2nd ed.). London: Pitman, 73.

1. Market Penetration

market penetration

entering a market with an existing product or service and gaining competitors' market share

First, an organization can follow a **market penetration** strategy by entering a market with an existing product or service to gain competitors' market share. Improvements to an existing product can render that product or service so new as to make it seen by prospective purchasers as a genuinely new product. Starbucks, for example, has adapted its menu to local tastes in various regions in an attempt to increase patronage by current customers.

2. Market Development

market development

identifying and developing new markets for current products and services

The second strategy, **market development**, calls for identifying and developing new markets for current products and services. If an existing product is launched to a new market that is unfamiliar with it, it is, for all intents and purposes, a new product. When Banff's Mount Norquay introduced hourly tickets, it attracted a new market of skiers — local skiers who would not normally ski due to lack of time (see *Marketing in Action* in Chapter 6).

3. Product Development

product development

developing a new product or service to be sold to existing customers

The third strategy, **product development**, involves developing a genuinely new product or service to be sold to existing customers. Over the last few years, fast-food companies have developed new, healthier products for existing customers. Subway, for example, has positioned itself as a healthy fast food alternative, turning its low-fat and low-calorie food content into a marketing coup. When the company learned that Jared Fogel, a college student who once weighed 193 kilograms and lost 111 kilograms on a diet consisting mainly of Subway turkey and vegetable submarine sandwiches, it recruited him to endorse its products in numerous (successful) promotions.

4. Diversification

diversification

creating new products and services outside the present business

Diversification makes sense when good opportunities for new products and services can be found outside the present business. Three types of diversification can be considered. First, the organization could seek new products or services that have technological or marketing synergies with existing offerings, even though the product may appeal to a new class of customers (concentric diversification). Second, the company might search for new products or services that could appeal to its current target market (horizontal diversification). Third, the organization might seek new businesses that have no relationship with its current technology, products or services, or markets (conglomerate diversification). A unique new product in the United Kingdom comes in the form of a restaurant called the Clink. The restaurant, opened in 2006, is the first upscale eatery behind bars. Situated in Highdown Prison in Surrey, paying members of the public eat gourmet meals that are cooked and served by prisoners. Another example of diversification comes from Four Seasons Hotels and Resorts, which launched a luxury catamaran cruise in the Maldives in 2003.

An interesting new tourism product in the early stages of development is the Canadian Museum for Human Rights (CMHR). The *Snapshot* describes the project in more detail.

SNAPSHOT

THE CANADIAN MUSEUM FOR HUMAN RIGHTS

The late Izzy Asper, the Canadian media magnate, had a dream. It was to create a world-renowned museum in western Canada, one that would act as a centre for learning and history, where Canadians and people from other countries could experience Canada's human rights journey. That dream is coming to fruition with the new Canadian Museum for Human Rights (CMHR) scheduled to open in 2010.

The new national museum will be built in Winnipeg and will be devoted to human rights history and current issues. The vision of CMHR is to be a powerful symbol of Canada's unwavering commitment to recognizing, promoting, and celebrating human rights. Its mission is to enhance understanding and support for human rights in Canada and throughout the world.

According to Charlie Coffey, chair of CMHR's National Advisory Council, the museum "will honour Canada's human rights heroes and help us to better understand our human rights journey. Most importantly, however, it will enable tens of thousands of high school students — through a special endowment program — to participate in a life-changing experience and become human rights leaders and advocates in their own communities."

In 2003, the museum launched an international architectural design competition. With 60 firms from more than 21 counties responding, the winner was architect Antoine Predock, who presented his idea as "an architecture of dualities: light and shadow, ephemera and stone, gravity and weightlessness, reflection and opacity, earth and sky." He said: "It's a symbolic apparition of ice, clouds, earth, and stone set in a field of sweet grass." The CMHR's master plan will be executed by world-renowned exhibit designer Ralph Appelbaum. The project has been primarily promoted by Asper's daughter, Gail Asper, and the Asper Foundation, which has committed $20 million in funding. These parties envision the museum as a public-private partnership, to which the Canadian federal government would commit to a share of the development costs, estimated at $311 million, and the operational costs, estimated at $20 million annually. The Canadian government has already committed to provide $100 million in capital. The Province of Manitoba will provide $30 million and the City of Winnipeg $20 million. Much of the remaining funds are in the form of donations. For example, in February 2007, Leo Ledohowski, the president of Winnipeg-based hotel chain Canad

Inns announced a $1 million donation to the museum. He called it a "world-class facility capable of generating substantial tourism benefits."

Executive director Moe Levy stresses the importance of the educational component for the project. "Youth involvement is a key initiative of this museum," he said. "The Museum's elaborate interactive technology will ensure young people will be fully engaged in learning about our social history." Using dioramas, collections, audio-visual testimony, photographs, and dramatic re-enactments, the CMHR will feature never-before-told Canadian stories and document the experiences of groups such as Aboriginal peoples, women, French Canadians, Jews, Ukrainians, African Americans and Canadians, Acadians, people with disabilities, labour unions, Chinese, Japanese, Sikhs, and many more. The goal is to have a place where, for the first time, Canada's human rights stories will be documented so Canadians and people around the world can learn, benefit, and improve in the area of human rights.

Source: Kingstone, B., & McBlain, B. (2006). Reach for the stars: Canadian Museum for Human Rights, *Luxe Magazine, 1*(1), 46–51.

Approaches to New Product Development

A company must develop new products to survive. New products can be obtained through acquisition or through new product development (NPD). There is a reasonably established approach to NPD, but Eberhard Scheuing and Eugene Johnson have proposed a model for new service development (NSD), based on a review of other models and research into 66 U.S.-based service firms.[18] The model has 15 steps and four main stages (see Figure 5.5).

	Stage		Step	
New idea generation and development	1.	(1)		Objectives and strategy
		(2)		Structure
		(3)		Idea generation and screening
Go/no go	2.	(4)		Concept development
		(5)		Concept testing
		(6)		Business analysis
		(7)		Project authorization
Test design	3.	(8)		Service design and testing
		(9)		Process design and testing
		(10)		Marketing design and testing
		(11)		Personnel training
Evaluation	4.	(12)		Service testing
		(13)		Test marketing
		(14)		Launch
		(15)		Post-launch review

Figure 5.5   New Service Development Model

Source: Scheuing, E. E., & Johnson, E. M. (1989). A proposed model for new service development. *Journal of Services Marketing*, 3(2), 30.

The first stage (steps 1–3) of NSD focuses on how new ideas are generated and developed. The development process must begin with a precise formulation of *objectives and strategy*. A well-designed strategy drives and directs the entire innovation effort and imbues it with effectiveness and efficiency. The second step is for organizations to ensure that they have *structured* their plan in such a way as to enable innovation to take place. In large organizations, this may involve setting up a research and development (R&D) department. The third step consists of *idea generation and screening*. New ideas can be drawn from external sources, or be produced internally through consultation and brainstorming. Often the most powerful idea source is customer feedback.

The second stage of NSD is the "go/no go" stage, comprising four steps (steps 4–7) that enable the organization to decide whether it will proceed with the new development. *Concept development* requires that the surviving ideas be expanded into fully fledged concepts, especially if there is a significant service element. *Concept testing* is a research technique designed to evaluate whether a prospective user understands the idea of the proposed good or service, reacts favourably to it, and feels it provides benefits that answers unmet needs. The sixth step, *business analysis*, should represent a comprehensive investigation into the business implications of each concept. The *project authorization* step occurs when top management commits resources to the implementation of a new idea. In an industry such as tourism, which consists of many small organizations, it is likely that 90 percent of them have just one person or department to authorize all innovative projects.[19]

Once the go-ahead has been given, the third stage of NSD — test design — is reached, in which detailed design and implementation of the innovation is carried out (steps 8–11). At this point, the new concept is converted into an operational entity. This requires *service design and testing*, and should involve both the input of prospective users and the active cooperation of the operations personnel who will ultimately deliver the service. It may also be necessary to do *process design and testing* or develop new equipment. This stage also includes *marketing design and testing*. To complete the test design phase, all employees should undergo *personnel training* to become familiar with the nature and operational details of the new service. For instance, research into flight catering showed that 91 percent of airlines engaged in such training, whereas only 68 percent of food manufacturers did so.[20]

The final stage of NSD is the evaluation of the new innovation, involving four steps (steps 12–15). *Service testing* should be used to determine potential customer acceptance of the new service, while a pilot run ensures its smooth functioning. Chapter 4 described how the Marriott Corporation designed a new chain of hotels for business travellers — Courtyard by Marriott — but tested the concept under real-world conditions, before subsequently developing the large chain that filled a gap in the market.

The next step, *test marketing*, examines the saleability of the new service, and a field test should be carried out with a limited sample of customers. With the delivery system and marketing in place and with the service thoroughly tested, the organization should next initiate the full-scale *launch*, introducing the service or product to the entire market area. Different sectors tend to evaluate their new services or products in slightly different ways. For instance, fast food operators use market surveys, whereas foodservice contractors rely more on after sales for customer feedback. The final step, *post-launch review*, should be aimed at determining whether the strategic objectives were achieved or whether further adjustments are needed.

Sheuing and Johnson suggest that firms should not rigidly follow this model but instead consider it as a framework from which to select those activities they deem necessary for the specific development they are undertaking.[21] In fact, research studies have shown that tourism organizations do not follow a systematic NSD process.[22] It has been suggested that the systematic and formal approach to innovation is likely to be adopted only when one of the following is true: new products with major impact are developed, a number of interrelated innovations are being developed simultaneously, product life cycles are long, competitors are unlikely to enter the market with a similar product or service, the new product is protected by licence or patent, or the innovation is original or "new to the world."[23] The tourism and hospitality market clearly has few of these characteristics. Innovation is likely to follow a shorter, simplified development process when minor modifications are made to existing products or services; there is no licence protection; the "new" product is largely a copy of a competitor's product; innovation is not part of a major change program; and competitors are actively innovating.

An organization also creates internal conditions that either foster or hinder innovation. Often these are strongly influenced by the external environment. Conditions that may encourage a systematic but rigid approach to innovation are a bureaucratic culture, mature marketplace, the involvement of external consultants, and formal R&D departments. Conditions that encourage a dynamic and flexible approach to innovation are the following: growing supply chain integration, an organizational culture founded on innovation, industry association sponsorship, creative and entrepreneurial leadership, and deregulated markets. These conditions are likely to be more typical of organizations in tourism and hospitality, as there are many small, highly entrepreneurial firms, such as Weekendtrips.com (see *Marketing in Action* in Chapter 7), operating in a largely deregulated marketplace. However, large companies can also encourage innovation. Virgin, profiled in Chapter 11, for example, has always been innovative, largely because of the entrepreneurial leadership of Richard Branson.

CHAPTER SUMMARY

Tourism and hospitality products are a group of selected components or elements brought together in a "bundle" to satisfy needs and wants. There are three levels of tourism products: the core product, the tangible product, and the augmented product. An important part of the augmented product is the physical environment — often referred to as the "servicescape." This is very important for tourism and hospitality products such as hotels, restaurants, and theme parks, which are dominated by experience attributes.

The most basic decisions a tourism organization must make are what business it is in and what product mix is appropriate to it. The product mix is the portfolio of products that an organization offers to one market or several. Another product analysis tool is the product life cycle (PLC); an organization should assess each product and service in terms of its position on the PLC. The final product planning tool is positioning, its purpose being to create a distinctive place in the minds of potential customers.

Branding has developed in the field of packaged goods as a method of establishing a distinctive identity for a product or service based on competitive differentiation from others. The case for branding is stronger for tourism products that offer the possibility for differentiation in several areas of the marketing mix. This is why branding has been particularly successful in hotel and restaurant marketing.

In the tourism and hospitality industry, packaging is the practice of combining two or more related and complementary offerings into a single-price offering. Packaging provides several customer benefits, including easier budgeting for trips, increased convenience, greater economy, the opportunity to experience previously unfamiliar activities and attractions, and the opportunity to design components of a package for specialized interests.

Developing new products is different from maintaining existing ones, and planning for both kinds of product and services differs according to whether they are targeted at existing markets or new ones. Holloway and Plant suggest that an organization has four alternatives in developing new products: market penetration, market development, product development, and diversification.

KEY TERMS

augmented product, p. 153	market penetration, p. 170	product mix, p. 157
benefits, p. 158	packaging, p. 167	servicescape, p. 155
brandicide, p. 165	positioning statement, p. 161	tangible product, p. 153
core product, p. 153	product development, p. 170	tourism and hospitality
diversification, p. 171	product life cycle (PLC)	products, p. 152
features, p. 158	analysis, p. 159	
market development, p. 170		

DISCUSSION QUESTIONS AND EXERCISES

1. Give some examples of organizations that are responding to consumer desires for experiences and are not mentioned in this chapter. How are they using the servicescape to deliver these experiences?

2. Think of a particular tourism or hospitality organization in which physical evidence is particularly important in communicating with and satisfying customers. What information would you give to the manager of that organization to convince him or her of the importance of physical evidence in the organization's marketing strategy?

3. Apply the three levels of product to the Ice Hotel described in the *Marketing in Action*. Where would you place the hotel on the product life cycle (PLC), and how are the managers trying to position the hotel? How important is the servicescape for the Ice Hotel?

4. It has been suggested that companies can commit brandicide by stretching a well-known brand too far. Think of a brand that has done this. What killed it off? Take a tourism brand you are familiar with and keep stretching it. How far can you go?

5. Provide an example (not already given in the text) of each strategy from the tourism industry, referring to Figure 5-4, Product Options in New and Existing Markets.

6. Why have many research studies found that services rarely follow the new service development steps outlined in Figure 5.5?

CASE STUDY

CREATING AN ALPINE WINTER EXPERIENCE

"Create memories for our guests and staff as the best mountain, beach and golf experience ... again and again."

This is the mission statement of Vancouver-based Intrawest — perhaps the most successful ski resort company in the world. Its success has been achieved by developing resort destinations as opposed to ski resorts. "Experience" is a word used liberally by Intrawest in its marketing materials and by its staff. "Disney does an incredible job of delivering a terrific experience — they provide a consistent experience and that's what we strive for," says James Askew, director of marketing and sales for the Pacific Northwest region of Intrawest. According to Askew, people are looking for an overall vacation experience when they go skiing, a holiday that offers more than skiing down the mountain. So to meet the demands of ever fussier, more sophisticated winter enthusiasts, and to entice guests to stay longer, Intrawest offers a slew of services besides skiing. The resort village is at the core of this formula, and for Intrawest the most important ingredient of this has been the real estate at the base of the mountain. Such convenient access to the slopes attracts more guests and fuels further commercial development, creating a bustling off-slope atmosphere.

Intrawest is not alone in revolutionizing the ski industry. Other resorts have followed suit, with property development and management becoming an important part of the ski business. For the operators, the most desirable visitors are what the trade calls "destination skiers," the long-stay tourists. Resort operators are increasingly banking on these visitors to fill hotels, townhouses, and condominiums in the valleys below the slopes. The operators benefit not only from selling townhouses and condos, but also by helping the owners rent their properties to visitors. Destination skiers tend to spend more, and it has been suggested that to defeat seasonality, destinations should focus on yield, rather than volume. In the Banff region of Canada for example, the ski areas have been aggressively targeting European skiers over the last few decades. Although these destination skiers represent only 50 percent of the market, they account for nearly 80 percent of tourism expenditures.

There are many ingredients that combine to create a memorable alpine winter experience, but successful mountain operators appear to have followed one or more of three strategies to enhance the service experience: product diversification, product improvement, or product differentiation. Two factors drive the diversification of winter sports. First, winter resorts are losing customers. An analysis of market trends in North America and Europe suggests that an increasing proportion of those who regularly take winter sports holidays do not ski at

all. Second, even avid skiers are typically skiing less. On average they are somewhat older, and new high-speed lifts enable a skier to reach his or her physical stamina limit much more quickly. As a result, winter resorts have realized that they have to offer more activities, both on snow, and off snow. The more progressive resorts are now treating skiing as a form of entertainment by establishing more off-slope diversions. They are expanding the range of activities they offer, such as ice skating, snow scooting, sledging and dog sledding, ice driving, paragliding, snowmobiling, and tubing (the increasingly popular activity of sliding down the slope on the inner tube of a truck tire). Many resorts — Verbier in Switzerland is an example — are also looking to enhance the efficiency, quality, and profitability of their restaurants and shops.

Mountain resorts must also evolve continually and improve to meet the new demands of the consumer. The ski runs and related lift systems clearly represent a prime attraction of resorts and therefore have long been the object of continuous improvement. For example, the process of linking ski areas has now become commonplace in France, following the initial lead given by resorts such as Tignes and Val d'Isère, which combined to form "l'Espace Killy," and Courchevel, Méribel, les Ménuires and Val Thorens, which created the "Trois Vallées." With these changes, skiing areas have been expanded to higher altitudes, giving better snow conditions, increasing resorts' capacities and extending their season. The customer's experience can also be enhanced by the training of instructors and guides, and by offering authentic and natural experiences.

A third strategy taken by ski areas to enhance the service experience is differentiation. Despite the trend toward large resort alpine villages, there is a future for the small, independently owned resorts with comparatively shallow pockets. Some local hills are often more accessible, making them perfect for day trips, especially when they are close to large urban areas. Others can differentiate themselves from the large alpine resorts and gain a competitive advantage. Alberta's Lake Louise and Sunshine, for example, are based in a national park and cannot offer all the amenities of a bustling alpine village. However, the relative tranquility and beauty of the preserved environment set them apart from other more developed resorts. Smaller resorts can also differentiate on other aspects such as customer service as mentioned above. Crested Butte in Colorado, for instance, is attempting to differentiate on customer service and promotes its small size as a selling point. "You don't have to be a huge mega resort to offer a good ski vacation," says Tim Mueller, its owner. Tamarack, also in Colorado, is positioning itself as a "boutique" resort limiting the number of skiers and boarders to 3500 a day, despite capacity to accommodate 7000. The idea is to create a private resort, with a focus on yield rather than volume, catering for a more discerning customer. "This is not just a ski resort," says owner Jean-Pierre Boespflug, "but a unique place where homeowners, guests, and the public can take advantage of all there is to do here. We can send you into the wilderness, biking, skiing, golfing, or boating."

What is the future for the alpine winter experience? In most parts of the world, the ski industry has stagnated, with many resorts facing severe financial difficulties. If resorts are not to face inevitable decline, adaptation is essential. The trend to use winter sports as almost a loss leader to bring in revenue from base operations continues to be the dominant financial model for resort operations. All the signs suggest that successful resorts of the next decades will be custom designed to meet the needs of every type of winter sports lover.

Sources: Hudson, S. (2000). *Snow business: A study of the international ski industry.* London: Continuum International Publishing Group; Kadane, L. (2001, November 30). Lasting resort. *Calgary Herald*, SS1; Meyers, C. (2004, February). Crested Butte on the brink. *Ski*, 69–73.

QUESTIONS

1. The text suggests that companies that fail to provide consistently engaging experiences, overprice their experiences relative to the value perceived, or overbuild their capacity to stage them will see pressure on demand, pricing, or both. How can ski resorts avoid these pitfalls?

2. With reference to Figure 5.4, Product Options in New and Existing Markets, what strategies have ski resorts followed in order to attract visitors?

3. Take a look at Intrawest's website. Is it continuing to develop resort destinations or has it changed its strategy?

4. Take a look at the marketing strategies of a ski resort near you. Is the resort following any of the three strategies mentioned in the case in order to enhance the service experience?

WEB SITES

www.disney.com
Disney

www.vegas.com/shopping/forumshops.html
Forum Shops at Caesars Palace, Las Vegas

cwr.iwm.org.uk
Churchill Museum and Cabinet War Rooms

www.museumofbrands.com
Museum of Brands, Packaging, and Advertising, London

www.bridgeclimb.com
Sidney Harbour Bridge Climb

www.icehotel-canada.com
Ice Hotel, Quebec

www.canadianmuseumforhumanrights.com
Canadian Museum of Human Rights

ENDNOTES

1. Middleton, V. T. C., & Clarke, J. (2001). *Marketing in travel and tourism.* Oxford: Butterworth-Heinemann.
2. Ibid.
3. Bitner, M. J. (1990, April). Evaluating service encounters. *Journal of Marketing, 54,* 69–82.
4. Russell, J. A., Ward, L. M., & Pratt, G. (1981). An affective quality attributed to environments. *Environment and Behaviour, 13*(3), 259–288.
5. Brieger, P. (2004, July 14). The whiff of a shopping spree. *Financial Post,* 1, 10.
6. Seaton, A. V., & Bennett, M. M. (1996). *Marketing tourism products: Concepts, issues, cases.* London: Thomson Business Press.
7. Enough perks to make you hope for another flight delay. (2005, May 7). *National Post,* FW4.
8. Mercer, D. (1992). *Marketing.* Oxford: Blackwell, 295.
9. Burke, J. F., & Resnick, B. P. (1991). *Marketing and selling the travel product.* Cincinnati: Thomson South-Western.
10. Goff, S. (2003, February 3). The advantages of being small, intimate, and secure. *Financial Times,* IV.
11. Gilpin, S. (1994). Branding in the hotel industry. Where are we now? Paper presented at the Council for Hospitality Management Education conference, Napier University, Edinburgh, April 5–7.
12. Lovelock, C. H., & Wirtz, J. (2007). *Services marketing: People, technology, strategy* (6th ed.). Englewood Cliffs, NJ: Prentice Hall.
13. Middleton, V. T. C., & Clarke, J. (2001). *Marketing in travel and tourism.* Oxford: Butterworth-Heinemann.
14. Redekop, B. (2004, April 24). Bear facts about tourism. *National Post,* FT4.
15. What's New. (2005, January 3). *Globe & Mail,* A8.
16. Karlgaard, R. (2005, October 3). A can-do-country. *Forbes, 176*(6), 37.
17. Holloway, J. C., & Plant, R. V. (1992). *Marketing for tourism* (2nd ed.). London: Pitman, 73.
18. Scheuing, E. E., & Johnson, E. M. (1989). A proposed model for new service development. *Journal of Services Marketing, 3*(2), 25–34.
19. Jones, P., Hudson, S., & Costis, P. (1997). New product development in the UK tour-operating industry. *Progress in Tourism and Hospitality Research, 3*(4), 283–294.
20. Jones, P. (1995). Innovation in flight catering. In P. Jones and M. Kipps (Eds.), *Flight catering,* 163–175. London: Longman.
21. Scheuing, E. E., & Johnson, E. M. (1989). A proposed model for new service development. *Journal of Services Marketing, 3*(2), 25–34.
22. Jones, P., Hudson, S., & Costis, P. (1997). New product development in the UK tour-operating industry. *Progress in Tourism and Hospitality Research, 3*(4), 283–294; Easingwood, C. J. (1986). New product development for service companies. *Journal of Product Innovation Management, 3*(3), 296–312.
23. Jones, P., Hudson, S., & Costis, P. (1997). New product development in the UK tour-operating industry. *Progress in Tourism and Hospitality Research, 3*(4), 283–294.

Pricing

Spotlight

SPACE TOURISM: PRICED OUT OF THIS WORLD

Since 2001 when American millionaire Dennis Tito became the first space tourist, paying around $27 million for a week's trip, space tourism is gradually becoming a viable commercial industry. Virgin's Richard Branson is spearheading the private enterprise movement toward making space trips a reality via Virgin Galactic Airways, founded in 1991. A million would-be passengers are estimated to be ready and willing to pay for such cutting-edge tourism experiences.

Branson plans to start offering sub-orbital space flights as early as 2008 and 40 000 people are already registered. Around 100 reputedly paid the full $236 000 up front to become "astronauts" during their three-hour flight, at 4000 kilometres per hour, with a maximum of half an hour actually spent in space. "We priced the tickets to give us enough money to get off the ground, as well as to start looking into orbital flights, hotels in space, hopefully a hotel on the moon," said Branson. He first became interested in the project in the 1980s when he was outraged at a quote for $30 million to accompany Russian astronauts on a space voyage. He and various family members planned to be aboard the first Virgin Galactic flight.

Branson is not the only contender in the race to make commercial spaceflights routine. In 2006 Space Adventures announced plans to build a $313 million spaceport in the United Arab Emirates. Spacecraft for suborbital flights built by a Russian company were expected to be ready before 2008. Three telecommunications entrepreneurs (Hamid Ansari, his wife, Anousheh, and brother Amir) from Texas, decided to back Space Adventures in this challenge to Branson's plans. The United Arab Emirates government also invested in the project to the tune of $34 million.

Branson and Virgin have the advantage of brand recognition, connections, resources, and 20 years of airline experience. In 2005 Virgin Galactic announced an agreement with New Mexico for a state-built $225 million spaceport at Las Cruces near the White Sands Missile Range. Construction at Las Cruces was hoped to start in 2007, depending on approval from environmental and aviation authorities. Virgin would have a 20-year lease on the facility with annual payments of $1 million for the first five years, rising to cover the cost of the project by the end of the lease. New Mexico's steady climate, free airspace, low population density, and high altitude were all factors in choosing the site, factors that would also all significantly reduce the cost of the space flight program.

Surveys by the space industry show that at least half of Americans would like to see Earth from space — if they could afford it. In fact, demand for space travel is fairly elastic; in willingness-to-pay surveys, demand increases significantly when the price falls. By 2015, competition within the fledgling industry could cut prices to around $15 000 per head. And the Space Frontier Foundation, an industry group, is aiming even lower, to about $5000. In 2006 Space Adventures was already offering various space-related experiences at cheaper rates. Simulated lunar gravity flights could take passengers on parabolic rides, climbing and diving, giving a few minutes of weightlessness, for about $4000. Florida-based Zero Gravity offers similar experiences, marketed as the world's largest roller coaster rides, all available through travel agents. For those who would rather watch than experience such hair-raising rides, Planetspace was cashing in on voyeurism by providing paid public viewing of Canadian Arrow experiments at the Georgian Bay base in Ontario.

At the 55th Annual International Astronautical Congress in Vancouver in 2004, Haym Benaroya, a scientist from Rutgers University, presented a paper entitled "Doing Business on the Moon," describing a lunar landscape dotted with resorts and amusement parks. Benaroya noted that Hilton Hospitality Inc., owner of the Hilton hotel chain, had also jumped on the space tourism bandwagon, commissioning an architectural study of a surface lunar hotel. It seems that space tourism will soon become a reality.

Sources: Hutchinson, B. (2004, August 10). "Booking dreams at moon hotel." *National Post*, A3; Branson, R. (2005, August 1). "My final frontier." *National Post*, 33; Otis, P. (2004, October 11). "Please have your boarding pass ready at the launch pad." *Business Week, 3903*, 130–131; Wattie, C. (2004, June 22). "U.S. pilot makes space history." *National Post*, A11; Schwartz, J. (2006, February 18). "More enter race to offer space tours." *New York Times*, travel.nytimes.com/2006/02/18/science/18space.html (accessed September 2007).

Objectives

On completion of this chapter, readers should understand

- the key factors determining pricing decisions;
- the contribution of economics to pricing;
- the specific characteristics of the tourism and hospitality industry that affect pricing policy;

- the key approaches that companies take toward pricing in tourism;
- how prices are calculated for new products;
- yield management as it applies to tourism; and
- the difference between strategic pricing and tactical pricing in tourism.

Chapter Overview

The *Spotlight* looks at space tourism in relation to willingness to pay, as well as the elasticity of demand for a new tourism product. These two concepts are two of many pricing theories discussed in this chapter. It begins by looking at the impact of various corporate objectives on pricing. These objectives may be profit maximization, target rate of return, market share, survival, or growth. Even if these objectives are not explicit, they can have a significant impact on pricing. The second section highlights the key factors determining pricing decisions. As well as marketing objectives, these include costs, other mix variables, channel member expectations, buyer perceptions, competition, and legal and regulatory restrictions. The third part of the chapter focuses on the contribution of economics to pricing and includes a discussion of the interaction between supply and demand and of the importance of elasticity of demand. Generally, companies use pricing as part of their positioning of a product, employing one of three basic approaches: premium pricing, value-for-money pricing, and undercut pricing. These approaches are examined here, using hotels as examples. The next main section discusses the basic approaches to pricing, which fall into three general categories: cost-based methods, demand-based methods, and competition-oriented pricing. Pricing strategies for new products are the subject of the next part of the chapter, which discusses prestige pricing, market skimming, and penetration pricing. Other pricing techniques are then examined, followed by a discussion of yield management. The difference between strategic pricing and tactical pricing is then explained, and the final section of the chapter looks at the specific characteristics of the tourism and hospitality industry that affect pricing policy.

INTRODUCTION TO PRICING

price–quality trade-off

acceptance of the higher cost of a better quality of product or service

Pricing is crucial to the successful marketing of any product or service, but it is often the least understood of the marketing mix elements. The price that an organization charges for its product or service must strike a balance between gaining acceptance with the target market and making profit for the organization. Even in not-for-profit organizations, pricing is the key to encouraging consumption. The pricing element of the marketing mix is unique because it is the only one that directly affects an organization's revenues, and hence its profits. The fields of finance and economics have much to contribute in setting prices, but taken on their own they may not lead to the best pricing decisions. Other marketing mix decisions will often interact with pricing decisions. Quality (both real and perceived) needs to be considered in light of price. Decision makers should consider the **price–quality trade-off** made by consumers who are willing to accept a higher cost for a better quality of product or service. Similarly, with regard to brand image — often the consequence of marketing communications decisions — lesser-known brands might command lower prices. Furthermore, pricing decisions must take into account the needs of the distributor. Distributors will sell a product only if they will obtain a certain profit margin.

As with other elements in the marketing mix, pricing should be treated as a tool to achieve corporate and marketing objectives. If the target market has been clearly identified and a decision has been made about where a product or service is to be positioned, then pricing will become easier to determine. Organizations choosing to position their products or services in the mass market and to enter a field with many competitors will need to adopt a very careful pricing policy. Those seeking to appeal to niche markets may have slightly more price flexibility, since they have fewer competitors and perhaps more points of difference between their products or services and others in the niche.

FACTORS DETERMINING PRICING DECISIONS

Whatever the strategy of the organization, clear pricing objectives should be established before price levels are set. The key factors determining pricing decisions are shown in Figure 6.1.

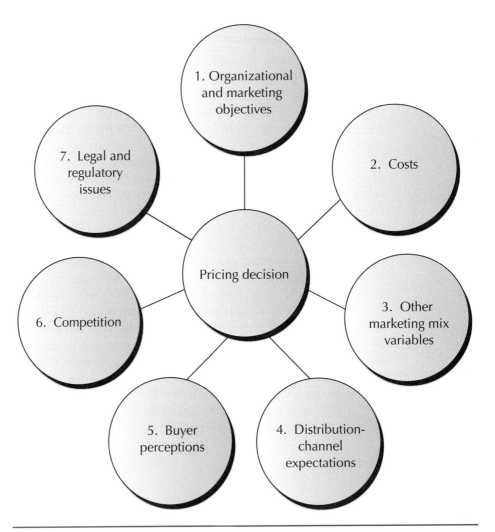

Figure 6.1   Factors Affecting Pricing Decisions

Source: Dibb, S., Simkin, L., Pride, W. M., & Ferrell, O. C. (1994). *Marketing: Concepts and strategies* (2nd ed). London: Houghton-Mifflin.

1. Organizational and Marketing Objectives

profit maximization

gaining the most profit possible by changing costs, prices, or volume

target rate of return

an intended rate of return on investment or expenses that determines the price

The most common objectives are **profit maximization**, which involves gaining the most profit possible by changing costs, prices, or volume; reaching a **target rate of return**, which involves setting an intended rate of return on investment or expenses that will determine the price; increasing **market share**, which involves increasing the percentage of sales for the total industry; and surviving. However, for some organizations, such as Parks Canada, the objectives are not only commercial in their nature, and pricing decisions are made for societal reasons — such as raising entry fees to reduce the social and environmental impacts of increasing numbers of visitors, or lowering fees to encourage more access. Other objectives may be being perceived as offering outstanding value for money, or being the brand leader in the marketplace. The first may be reflected in lower prices, whereas the second goal could lead to high prices in the long term.

2. Costs

Price setting should incorporate a calculation of how much it costs the organization to produce the product or service. If the company is profit-oriented, a margin will be added to the cost price to derive the selling price. An organization could also decide to sell below cost for a period of time, which is often referred to as a tactical price reduction, discussed later in this chapter.

3. Other Marketing Mix Variables

Pricing decisions always interact with the other elements of the marketing mix. Consider the example of Canadian Mountain Holidays (CMH), which sells heli-skiing holidays (see the *Case Study* in Chapter 7). The high price of this product must be reflected in other elements of the marketing mix. A high level of personal service is included as part of the promotional package, and the quality of the lodging must meet expectations that the high price has generated in the minds of the customers. Price usually gives the consumer the first indication of perceived product quality. Distribution of the holidays takes place via an exclusive channel system of overseas agents, reflecting the high-quality image and resulting high price.

4. Distribution Channel Expectations

A marketer must consider the potential cost of using intermediaries in the distribution channel when pricing a product or service. Travel agents, for example, will expect to earn commissions for their efforts. However, some stakeholders in the travel industry, such as airlines, car rental companies, and international hotel chains, have been quick to grasp the potential of marketing and selling their services online. They have recognized an opportunity to bypass agents and sell their basic products and services directly to the customer. Increasingly, package holiday tour operators are including direct sales on the Internet in their sales strategy, thus bypassing the travel agent.

5. Buyer Perceptions

The prices set for travel products and services must reflect customers' perceptions in the target market. The key is whether customers perceive that the price represents good value for money and matches their quality expectations. In tourism and hospitality, consumers expect a high level of service and special features if a high price is being charged. For example, after paying $7000, a CMH heli-skier will expect lodges to contain a fully stocked bar, a sauna, and jacuzzi, and even access to a resident qualified massage therapist. A survey of restaurant customers found that consumers perceive restaurants with higher menu prices with tip included to be more expensive than restaurants with lower menu prices and tipping. The authors of the study concluded that only restaurants with price-insensitive customers can adopt service-inclusive pricing without risking the loss of customers.[1]

6. Competition

In competitive markets, organizations try to win customers from competitors in two ways: price competition and non-price competition. Price competition involves offering the product or service at a lower price than the price charged by the competition. In a very competitive marketplace, organizations are likely to resort to intense price competition. The *Marketing in Action* on low-cost airlines in this chapter is an example. Non-price competition, on the other hand, is concerned with trying to increase market share or sales by leaving the price unchanged but persuading target customers that their offering is superior to that offered by the competition. Such a strategy is more typical in oligopolistic markets, in which there are few competitors. It is important for organizations to monitor the prices charged by competitors. A study of holiday costs in three different countries in 2006 (see Table 6.1) found that the UK was considerable more expensive that Spain or the U.S. for the same services.[2]

Table 6.1

Holiday Costs in Europe

SERVICE	PADSTOW, CORNWALL, UK	GERONA, SPAIN	NAPLES, FLORIDA
Hotel (three star)	$230	$92	$92
Rental apartment or cottage	$684	$393	$518
Cocktail	$5.75	$5.20	$3.68
Meal (three course)	$39	$23	$31
Coffee (espresso)	$2.60	$0.94	$1.84
Bike hire	$11.50	$9.20	$12.65
Car rental (three days)	$90	$63.25	$50.60

7. Legal and Regulatory Issues

There may be legal and regulatory restrictions that control the ways in which an organization fixes prices. For example, Robben Island (see *Spotlight* in Chapter 3), which is subsidized by the South African government, may be under pressure to keep prices low to encourage people to visit. Legal restrictions are often placed on the practice of price fixing and collusion. Additionally, there are a number of organizations, both quasi-governmental and industrial or trade, that exercise some influence on pricing policies and strategies, a fact that marketing managers must bear in mind.

CONTRIBUTIONS OF ECONOMICS TO PRICING

Economists contend that producers of a commodity are more likely to provide that commodity if the price for it in the marketplace is high. This principle is coupled with the suggestion that buyers are more likely to purchase more of the commodity if prices are low. From this comes the idea that the quantity produced and consumed and the price acceptable to each party will be in equilibrium at some point. This is shown in Figure 6.2.

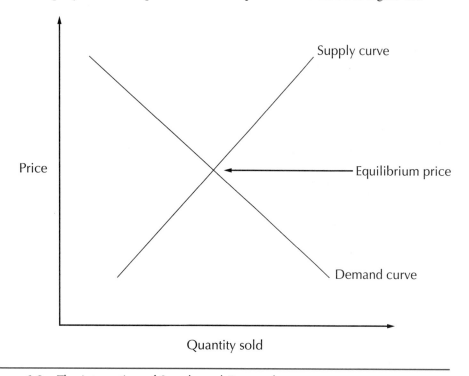

Figure 6.2 The Interaction of Supply and Demand

Unfortunately, this simplistic model is unlikely to be useful as a mathematical way of determining prices because it assumes that certain conditions need to be present for the process to occur. One of these is the assumption that consumers have perfect knowledge and know all the prices from all the producers. Despite consumers' increasing use of the

Internet, the likelihood of such wide knowledge is small in the travel industry. However, even though the model may not help pricing decisions in a mathematical or graphical way, the concept is useless. For instance, if a tourism organization suspects that the market is undersupplied, it may increase prices. This has happened in Las Vegas over the last few years as hoteliers have been able to charge premium room rates due to high demand. Similarly, if a buyer senses that the market is oversupplied, the buyer may try to negotiate lower prices — as happened in the hotel market after the terrorist attacks, the war in Iraq, and the outbreak of severe acute respiratory syndrome (SARS).

ELASTICITY OF DEMAND

elasticity of demand

the sensitivity of customer demand to changes in price

The increase and decrease of prices generally has an effect on the level of sales. The analysis of buyers' reactions to price change employs the concept of the **elasticity of demand**, the sensitivity of customer demand to prices. This is represented by the formula:

$$\text{Price elasticity of demand} = \frac{\%\ \text{change in quantity demanded}}{\%\ \text{change in price}}$$

If demand increases in line with price cuts, then the product or service is said to be elastic. But if demand remains relatively unaltered by price changes, the product or service is said to be inelastic. In the tourism and hospitality industry, many products are elastic — as prices fall, demand increases. However, there are many occasions when this is not true. Business travel is often inelastic, and popularity or fashion may render a destination or restaurant inelastic. In the *Snapshot* below, demand for the Burj Al Arab Hotel in Dubai would seem to be inelastic. The hotel can charge very high prices, as business travellers are willing to pay a high price for such luxury. Figure 6.3 shows two demand curves — one for an elastic product and one for an inelastic product. As with knowledge of the state of supply and demand, managers are not often in a position to know the mathematical value of elasticity for a product or service. They may not have access to all price and quantity data, or it may be new and there may therefore be no historical data from which to derive the slope of the demand curve.

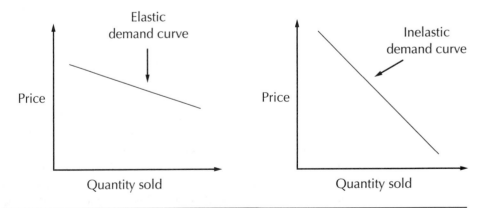

Figure 6.3   Elastic and Inelastic Demand Curves

Price elasticity can be affected by a number of factors, including the consumer's perception of the uniqueness of the product, the availability and awareness of substitutes, and how the consumer budgets. For example, a leisure traveller buying a holiday for personal use will have one perspective on price value; if the same person uses a company charge account, he or she may have another set of values. If consumers are purchasing something for someone else to use, they may be prepared to spend more — or less — than they would spend on themselves. Price elasticity of demand gives management a statistical method to measure whether the organization's prices are too high or low. In setting prices, a organization will want to know what levels of demand it is likely to experience at different prices. This can be done in two ways.

willingness to pay (WTP) assessment

a survey of potential customers to determine what they would be willing to pay for the product or service

The first method is often called **willingness to pay (WTP) assessment**. The *Spotlight* suggested that demand for space travel is fairly elastic; in WTP surveys, demand increases significantly when the price falls. The *Snapshot* below indicates how much skiers were willing to pay for environmentally friendly skiing. The difficulty with this method is that what people say they will do does not always translate into actual behaviour when the product or service is launched. Another way of assessing demand at different prices is test marketing, although it is difficult to control all the factors apart from price that will influence consumer decisions in different areas.

SNAPSHOT

WILLINGNESS TO PAY FOR GREEN SKIING

Conflicts between environmentalists and ski resort developers can be found around the world, and there is no better example than in Banff National Park in Alberta. The dilemma of balancing the protection of national park values while providing for their enjoyment is longstanding, and has become progressively more acute with the continued increase in recreation and tourist demand. It has been argued that an opportunity may exist for resorts to gain a competitive advantage by positioning themselves as being environmentally responsible, but little is known about skiers' environmental knowledge and awareness, or about their willingness to pay for "greener" tourism products. A proposed cap on the number of skiers permitted to visit Banff National Park and the huge increase in tourist numbers predicted by the World Tourism Organization make a rise in prices inevitable. It is therefore critical that tourism providers understand how much skiers are willing to pay to preserve the environment in the park.

In 2001, Simon Hudson and J. R. Brent Ritchie conducted research using the contingent valuation method (CVM) to find out how much skiers were willing to pay for a more environmentally friendly skiing product. This method involves presenting respondents with a questionnaire consisting of three parts:

1. Questions about the respondents' characteristics and their preferences with reference to the goods being valued.
2. A detailed description of the tourism product being valued (in this case an environmentally friendly ski destination).

SNAPSHOT *continued*

3. Close-ended questions that elicited the respondents' level of willingness to pay for the product being valued.

The quota-sampling method was used in the study to ensure that a representative sample was collected from three nationalities, to allow for cross-cultural comparisons. A target group of 300 skiers, divided evenly among visitors from Canada, the United States, and the United Kingdom, was set. The mean WTP, the standard error, and the median WTP were calculated for each population. These are shown in Table 6.2. Skiers on average were willing to pay $16 more per day to visit an environmentally friendly ski resort. However, univariate analysis of variance among the three countries indicated a significant difference across cultures. American skiers would pay $20.17 and British skiers $18.61, both of which were significantly higher amounts than the $10.39 that Canadians were prepared to pay. Taken as a whole, 65 percent of skiers would be prepared to pay more: 59 percent of Canadian and British skiers, and 67 percent of Americans, would pay more for an environmentally responsible ski destination. The mean WTP amount for the 217 skiers who would pay more was $25 per day.

Table 6.2

Willingness to Pay for Environmentally Friendly Skiing (in dollars)

| | INCREASED AMOUNT THAT SKIERS WERE WILLING TO PAY | | | |
	All Skiers Surveyed	Canadian Skiers	Skiers	American Skiers
Mean willingness to pay	16.41	10.39	18.61	20.17
Standard deviation	20.31	15.27	22.19	21.57
Median	10.00	5.00	12.00	15.00
Number of observations	332	111	105	116

Results of a regression analysis of the WTP amounts on relevant predictor variables indicated a strong correlation between WTP and the cost of the holiday. WTP amounts were also likely to rise with income, confirming previous WTP studies that found that people with higher incomes tend to exhibit higher WTP for the environment than those with lower levels. The third significant correlation was with the environmental consciousness level of skiers. As their perceived level of environmental consciousness went up, so did their WTP. Previous studies have shown that consumers who exhibit high levels of environmental awareness and consciousness make more green purchasing decisions than those exhibiting low levels.

Source: Hudson, S., & Ritchie, J. R. B. (2001). Cross-cultural tourist behaviour: An analysis of tourist attitudes towards the environment. *Journal of Travel and Tourism Marketing, 10*(2/3), 1–22.

PRICING AND POSITIONING

Generally, companies use pricing as part of their positioning of a product, employing one of three strategic approaches: premium pricing, value-for-money pricing, and undercut pricing.[3]

1. Premium Pricing

premium pricing

setting prices above market price, to reflect either the image of quality or the unique status of the product or service

In **premium pricing**, a decision is made to set prices above market price, to reflect either the image of quality or the unique status of the product or service. The product or service may be new, or it may have unique features not shared by competitors, such as the Burj Al Arab Hotel in Dubai (see *Snapshot*). Also, the organization itself may have such a strong reputation that the brand image alone is sufficient to merit a premium price. The Four Seasons hotel chain follows this strategy in setting prices. Promoted as upscale, full-service hotels, Four Seasons will, on occasion, raise prices to the highest level in the area. Disneyland's member-only Club 33 restaurant in Orlando follows a similar pricing strategy. The wait to join stretches nine years; most members are corporations willing to pay US$20 000 to join plus pay US$5825 in annual fees. Members must also pay a high price for meals, with the wine list offering a number of US$200 vintages.

Others may use premium pricing in order to generate publicity. In 2005, for example, the Hotel Jerome in Aspen started offering a 10-night holiday package that included unlimited ski tickets, private lessons, on-call massage therapists, a chauffeur, and a Maybach car that guests could keep. The price tag was $1.15 million.[4] Not to be outdone, the Marquis Los Cabos hotel in Baja, California, created a three-night stay with private jet and golf with Jack Nicklaus for $7 million.

2. Value-for-Money Pricing

value-for-money pricing

charging medium prices and emphasizing that the product or service represents excellent value at this price

In **value-for-money pricing**, the intention is to charge medium prices and emphasize that the product or service represents excellent value at this price. Organizations with well-established reputations for service generally do well with such a pricing strategy. According to *Travel & Leisure* magazine, guests staying at properties in Fairmont Hotels & Resorts are consistently maximizing the value of their money by receiving exceptional service, unique offerings, and renowned hospitality at an affordable price.

3. Undercut Pricing

undercut pricing

setting prices lower than the competition and using the price as a trigger to purchase immediately

The objective in **undercut pricing**, sometimes called "cheap value" pricing, is to undercut the competition by setting lower prices, so the lower price is used as a trigger for immediate purchasing. Unit profits are low, but satisfactory overall profits are achieved through high volume. This strategy is often used by organizations seeking a foot in or rapid expansion into a new market. EasyCruise, the cruise line owned by Stelios Haji-Ioannou, follows such a pricing strategy. Launched in 2005, EasyCruises (there are two of them now) sail around the hotspots of the French and Italian rivieras. Instead of emphasizing the shipboard experience (these are bare-bones cruise ships with just a bed, a shower unit, and a toilet in the cabins), Stelios makes the ports the main attraction. It is part of his strategy to attract a younger demographic — tourists in their 20s or 30s who might be leery of a week-long cruise. Sailing happens in the early morning for six hours or less, so that passengers can go on land, have a night of fun, then sleep it off in their cabins. Nightly rates are around £20 per person; the earlier one books, the lower the rate.

Any of these policies can be seen as "fair-pricing" policies. A fair price can be defined as one that the customer is happy to pay while the organization achieves a satisfactory level of profit. Thus a premium-pricing policy is acceptable, provided that the customer receives the benefits appropriate to the price. Only when organizations are able to force up prices against the consumers' will, such as in the case of monopolies, can it be said that fair pricing is inoperative. A **monopoly** is a supply situation in which there is only one seller.

monopoly
a supply situation in which there is only one seller

SNAPSHOT

PRICING FOR THE LUXURY MARKET: BURJ AL ARAB HOTEL, DUBAI

The United Arab Emirates may not be the first destination on many travellers' wish list, but Dubai's draw is undeniable. Described variously as the Gold City, the Artificial City, and the billionaire's playground, Dubai has been slowly shifting its attention away from energy over the years and into finance, commerce, transportation, and tourism. In short, Dubai is cash rich and resource poor, interested in doing business with the world and with money to pay for it. Construction has been more or less non-stop in Dubai over the last few decades, with a number of high-class hotels built to cater to the growing number of tourists. The sail-shaped Burj Al Arab Hotel is one such development.

Boasting seven stars, the Burj Al Arab Hotel caters to the millionaires and billionaires of the world with its luxurious and spectacular facilities. It provides exclusivity, security, and privacy for celebrities, in particular, and international business people for a high price tag — $690 for a basic room per night and $9200 for the Royal Suite. Voyeurs can also nose around the hotel's decadent public areas for $30, refundable against any purchase in the lavish bars, restaurants, or gift shops.

Working on the premise that people are willing to pay more for luxury, for the quality of service, and for the setting, the hotel

SNAPSHOT *continued*

opened in 1999 on a human-made island 280 metres offshore, to which guests are shuttled in Rolls-Royces on a causeway. Each of the 202 rooms has 42-inch plasma TV and Versace sheets on canopied beds, and is set on two floors connected by a spiral staircase. Every guestroom floor has its own check-in desk plus private elevators for the Royal Suites, ensuring both privacy and security. Butlers are available for guests' every need and they use separate entrances to guarantee the least disruption to the visitor. The two-bedroom Royal Suites are decorated in marble and gold, and have revolving beds, private cinema, and dressing rooms larger than the average hotel room.

No expense was spared on the hotel's design or its rococo furnishings, fit for a sheik's palace. The building is shaped like a ship's sail, soaring over 341 metres high, making it the tallest hotel in the world. The lobby is a massive atrium, stretching several hundred metres up, making it one of the largest in the world. Gold pilasters and enormous aquariums surround the escalators.

Restaurant facilities are equally luxurious, in particular the sealife-encircled Al Mahara seafood restaurant, reached by a short submarine ride from the lobby. The Skyview Bar, 200 metres above the Arabian Gulf, is reached by an express panoramic lift, travelling at six metres per second. During the day, only hotel residents can use the facilities but the restaurants are open to outside diners at night. Bills can soar into thousands of dollars but an average cost is between $200 and $500 for two people.

However, the emphasis on luxury in the Dubai market over the past decade has opened the door to budget travel, and a number of budget hotels are moving into this playground for the rich. For example, in 2007 Stelios Haji-Ioannou, the entrepreneur who founded the budget airline easyJet, broke ground on the first of six easyHotels to be built in the emirate. These budget hotels won't compete for the Burj Al Arab Hotel's customers and most hotel guests in Dubai continue to stay at high-end places. But statistics show a growing demand for lower-priced hotels.

Sources: Dalrymple, T. (2002, May 6). Gulf de luxe — luxury hotel in Dubai. *National Review*; Fannin, R. (2005, May). Desert luxury: A burgeoning oasis, Dubai is the new "in" place for the vacationing CEO. *Chief Executive*.

BASIC APPROACHES TO PRICING

Organizations involved in the marketing of tourism, leisure, and hospitality products and services use different methods of calculation to set prices. Pricing methods fall into three main categories:

1. Cost-Based Methods

cost-based pricing

adding a certain dollar amount or percentage to the actual or estimated costs of a product or service to arrive at a final price

Cost-based pricing — the addition of a certain dollar amount or percentage to the actual or estimated costs of a product or service to arrive at a final price — draws heavily on the accounting discipline of costing. To use this method, it is necessary to understand the differences in the nature of costs. At the simplest level, costs can be split into two types. **Fixed costs** are costs that do not vary with the amount of the product or service provided. Hence, a hotelier has to bear the fixed cost of owning the hotel, whether or not rooms are occupied. **Variable costs**, however, are those that do increase as more of a product or

fixed costs

costs that do not vary with the amount of the product or service provided

variable costs

costs that increase as more of a product or service is provided

break-even analysis

a pricing technique that considers fixed and variable costs, customer volumes, and profit margins

service is provided. For example, the energy and cleaning costs of a hotel will increase as more guests occupy the rooms. These two cost elements can be combined with revenue — which should increase as more of the service is sold — to give a picture of when an operation becomes profitable. Known as **break-even analysis** or cost/profit/volume (CPV) analysis, the interaction of these elements can be shown graphically. Figure 6.4 shows the break-even point for a hypothetical hotel that has high fixed costs.

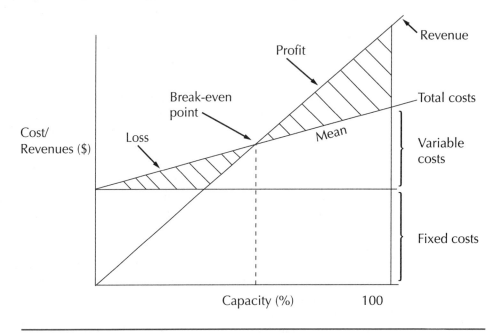

Figure 6.4   The Break-Even Point for a Hypothetical Hotel

cost-plus pricing

adding a standard mark-up to the cost of the product or service to arrive at the final price

Once the cost of doing business has been established, the simplest approach to pricing is to add next a standard mark-up to the cost of the product or service, known as **cost-plus pricing**. A restaurant manager might decide that all wines will be marked up by 100 percent and all food dishes will be marked up by 60 percent. For example, a bottle of wine purchased at $12 will be sold for $24, and a steak dinner that costs $10 (including both fixed and variable costs) will be sold for $16. Clearly, this approach to pricing takes little account of market forces, and while costs do have to be covered in the long run, policies have to respond more to changing market conditions and what the market will bear. However, the concept of marginal costing, which attempts to identify the cost of one or more unit of a product, is an important one in cost-plus pricing, since it offers the marketing manager a flexible tool for pricing. For example, in the case of an airline ticket for a flight across Europe, the additional cost of carrying one more passenger is extremely small: an added meal, a minute addition to fuel, etc. Therefore, once break-even is achieved, it becomes very attractive to price the "marginal seat" (any remaining seats over the number that have to be sold to break even) at a price that will attract market demand from those unwilling to pay regular fares.

2. Demand-Based Methods

buyer-based pricing (sensitivity pricing)

adjusting to high prices when the demand is high and lower prices when the demand is low, regardless of the cost of the product or service

Techniques in the demand-based category share the feature of giving major consideration to the consumer. **Buyer-based pricing** (or **sensitivity pricing**) allows for high prices when the demand is high and for lower prices when the demand is low, regardless of the cost of the product or service. Such pricing is common for accommodation in popular holiday beach resorts of Europe, where hotels tend to be more expensive in summer than in winter due to higher demand during the summer months. Buyer-based pricing allows an organization to charge higher prices and therefore to make higher profits as long as the consumers value the products or services above the cost price. Segmentation is often used to price travel and tourism products, using time (prices tend to be more expensive during school holidays) and age (children usually pay less for attractions), for example, as the basis for segmenting the market.

psychological pricing

using slightly lower prices to give consumers the perception of added value

price lining

pre-establishing price levels that the organization is confident will attract customers

Deeper understanding of the way consumers perceive prices can lead to **psychological pricing**, using slightly lower prices to give the perception of added value. This usually manifests itself as prices that avoid barriers. For example, a $1000 holiday may seem psychologically cheaper if offered at $999. Similarly, in order to present a simplified choice of product to the consumer, **price lining** — pre-establishing price levels that the organization is confident will attract customers — may be employed. For example, a whale-watching trip may be priced at $75 but may not include lunch. The same trip including lunch would be priced at $100: even though lunch can be provided at a low cost, the $25 is added to make the offer clearly distinct. As long as consumers perceive the gap as representing a clear difference of price and quality, they will likely accept the distinction. The mistake to avoid is to price many products with marginal differences and prices, as this may lead to consumer confusion.

One customer-driven pricing strategy that has increased in popularity due to the Internet is the reverse auction. Travel e-tailers, such as Priceline.com (see *Marketing in Action* in Chapter 10), Hotwire.com, and Lowestfare.com, act as intermediaries between prospective buyers, who request quotations for a product or service, and multiple suppliers who quote the best price they are willing to offer. Buyers can then review the offers and select the supplier that best meets their needs. Different business models underlie these services. While some are provided free to end users, most e-tailers either receive a commission from the supplier or do not pass on the whole savings. Others charge a fixed fee or one based on a percentage of the savings.

negotiating

a price-setting technique involving two or more parties with a conflict of interest regarding aspects of the product or service

Another important type of demand-based pricing, particularly in organizational buying, is **negotiating**, a technique used to establish prices when at least two parties are involved and have a conflict of interest regarding aspects of the product or service. Hotel space, exhibition services, and transport seats are all examples of tourism and hospitality products that are often the subject of price negotiation. And the negotiation of the pricing of holidays does not always have to involve hard currency. A Saskatchewan man who has waited more than two and a half years for surgery struck a novel deal with a U.S. surgeon who agreed to operate on his hernia in exchange for a free duck-hunting trip. The Nevada-based doctor performed the surgery in exchange for a duck-hunting excursion worth about $2300.

3. Competition-Oriented

competition-oriented pricing (going-rate pricing)

setting the price of a product or service in relation to competitors' prices

In **competition-oriented pricing**, an organization fixes the price of its product or service in relation to competitors' prices; this is often also called **going-rate pricing**. This method offers the advantage of giving the organization the opportunity to increase sales or market share, but it is a dangerous approach to pricing, as it does not focus on either costs or the consumer. The arguments for this approach are that the industry will have developed prices that are acceptable to the marketplace and there is little to be gained by offering different prices (so-called industry wisdom). The counter-argument is that there may be the opportunity to offer different prices (and therefore possibly to achieve better profits) that the majority of the industry has ignored.

Some organizations use competitors' prices as a target to be undercut. Those adopting this approach will need to be sure of their cost structures compared to others'. The danger is that competitors may have supply links that give them some type of cost advantage, or hold some kind of attraction for customers, such as a strong loyalty scheme. In this case, the prices may not be a true indication of either costs or price sensitivity. Generally, undercutting will be a difficult position to sustain if the price cutter does not have lower costs in the long term. It may also lead to price wars. Some tourism organizations, such as airlines, may be competition oriented to the extent that they use prices to try to drive out competition, perhaps to give themselves a long-term monopoly. Airlines have also been accused of price fixing in the past. For example, in 2006, several airlines including British Airways, American Airlines, and United Airlines, were at the centre of a criminal investigation into alleged price fixing on long-haul passenger flights across the Atlantic.[5] British Airways was eventually fined $300 million by the U.S. Department of Justice — one of the biggest U.S. anti-trust fines in recent years. The *Marketing in Action* below analyzes the growth of the low-cost airline sector around the world.

MARKETING IN ACTION

LOW-COST AIRLINES TAKE TO THE AIR

"No frills" is the latest buzzword for the airline industry around the world, where cut-price companies such as Ryanair are taking it to the extreme. The Dublin-based airline, the second biggest international carrier in the world, is spearheading the move toward very basic, cheap continental travel with no complimentary food and beverage services, very low luggage allowances, tight cabin space, high charges for excess baggage, and other surcharges for extras, such as

MARKETING IN ACTION *continued*

wheelchair service. Also, cut-price flights often use smaller, secondary airports, sometimes situated far from city centres (for example, instead of Heathrow, Ryanair uses Stansted, which is further from London). There is also limited compensation if flights are delayed. For example, in Europe passengers may not be eligible for food and accommodation since most cut-price airlines are not part of the European Union's Passenger Service Commitment.

Despite the disadvantages and potential discomforts of cheap travel, price is the bottom line and passengers are vying for seats sometimes offered as low as $25 for one-way European flights. This only covers the flight taxes and service charges, so basically the seats are sold for free. There are about 60 low-price airlines within Europe, including Geneva-based Flybaboo. Many have recently failed in this volatile, cut-throat market — such as JetGreen, Duo, JetMagic, V Bird, and Volareweb.com — giving customers some insecurity and no guarantees for advance reservations.

Similar price cutting is now also happening throughout India, Asia, and the Middle East. SpiceJet, an Indian low-fare airline, competes with Kingfisher Airlines and Air Deccan for the lucrative domestic market. Within India, with its increasingly prosperous emerging middle class, there has been a shift from train travel to the quicker and more efficient air travel. Air travel demand is expected to rise 25 percent per year up to 2010 with as many as 100 million people choosing air over travel by land, thanks to low fares and also improved in-flight amenities and service. This is partly due to government deregulation but also to the fierce competition between airlines, which has transformed the industry from its original reputation for poor service to an efficient and comfortable option. Low-cost air travel is mainly distributed via the Internet in India. SpiceJet sells about 70 percent of its

seats on the Internet and also reduces its overheads by utilizing its aircraft for a full 12 hours per day as well as aiming to fill up each flight with at least 80 percent loads.

In Southeast Asia, likewise, a fierce price war erupted in the budget airline market during 2004, in sharp contrast to its traditional high price flights. To gain market share and capture public attention, low-cost carriers offered one-way tickets from Singapore to popular destinations such as Bangkok for less than $1 each. The lowest price was 59¢, offered by Tiger Airways for one-way tickets to three different Thai destinations. In retaliation Thai Air Asia offered a 29¢ ticket to Bangkok, delighting consumers who would normally pay around $250 for Singapore to Bangkok return flights. In the Middle East, the region's air transportation sector is becoming increasingly segmented, as new start-up airlines emerge to challenge the incumbent Middle Eastern carrier Emirates, for a share of the global aviation pie. Low-cost carriers, such as Air Arabia and Jazeera Airways, launched in 2003 and 2005 respectively, were prompted by the success of low-cost pioneers in North America and Europe, as well as the opportunity to offer a wide choice of prices and options on intra-regional flights compared to legacy rivals.

In 2006, Brazilian carrier Varig offered free tickets for domestic flights in an effort to win back flyers after financial problems resulted in cancellations and stranded clients. However, most of these media-hitting promotions are short lived. Michael O'Leary, Ryanair's chief executive, is looking to push the boundaries in a bid to replace airfares with in-flight gambling. He planned to introduce gambling services by 2007 via passengers' mobile phones or via BlackBerries supplied by Ryanair, using a payment system that would debit a passenger's credit card before the plane lands. In 2005 subsidiary services such as car hire,

MARKETING IN ACTION *continued*

hotels, travel insurance, and in-flight sales accounted for approximately 20 percent of Ryanair's $200 million income and O'Leary predicted that non-ticket revenues could rise dramatically with the introduction of more in-flight entertainment.

Sources: Park, K. (2006, March 12). Flying high on low costs. *Hindu Business Line*, 11; Hutchinson, B. (2005, November 5). Citizens discover joys of air travel. *Financial Post*, FP1; Harrison, M. (2005, March 11). Onboard gambling may lead to free flights on Ryanair. *Independent*, 13.

PRICING STRATEGIES FOR NEW PRODUCTS

At the core of pricing is the consumer's perception of price in relation to quality and value for money. This perception can be influenced by the way in which a organization charges for its products or services. When a new product enters the market, it is vital to obtain market share and create the desired image for the product in the consumer's eyes. New products and services face unique problems. If it is truly new — something never before available in the marketplace — it will be extremely difficult for consumers to develop a sense of what price is appropriate. If there are no similar products or services with which to compare it, they may either undervalue the innovation or perhaps overvalue it. Detailed research on price sensitivity, clearly outlining the unique features of the new product and researching the best way to communicate this information to consumers, will be important.

Three strategies commonly used for the introduction of new products are prestige pricing, market skimming, and penetration pricing.

prestige pricing

setting prices high to position a product or service at the upper or luxury end of the market

1. **Prestige pricing**. This method sets prices high to position a product or service at the upper or luxury end of the market. For example, tourism and hospitality operators that wish to be seen as top-end operators or establishments must enter the market with high prices to reflect this quality image. The product itself will need to deliver this quality level (in terms of decor, menu, locations, fittings, etc.). A coach company introducing a new luxury vehicle with airline-style seats, individual light and air-conditioning controls, panoramic windows, onboard catering, and amenities can price the transportation as a prestige product. If consumers value these attributes, they will pay the additional premium price. A *Snapshot* in Chapter 13 discusses the new "love boat for millionaires" in China that is inviting China's growing number of eligible male millionaires to join a matchmaking boat cruise that promises "good-looking and desirable" women. Men had to be worth at least 2 million yuan ($275 000), and only women who are "attractive in every category" can participate.

market skimming

setting high prices at the launch stage and progressively lowering them as the product or service becomes better established

2. **Market skimming**. This policy of "skimming the cream" calls for setting high prices at the launch stage and progressively lowering them as the product or service becomes better established and progresses through its life cycle. The policy takes advantage of the fact that most products are in high demand in the early stage of the life cycle, when they are novel or unique or when supplies are limited. Demand can be managed by setting very high prices initially to attract those prepared to meet

them, and gradually reducing the price to meet different market segments' price elasticities. The particular value of this policy is that it provides a high inflow of funds to the company when the marketing costs are highest. If the product anticipates a very short life cycle — as in the case of major events such as the World Cup tournament — and organizing and marketing costs must be recovered quickly, market skimming is a sensible policy to pursue.

penetration pricing

setting low prices to get maximum sales and market share in the initial stages of the life cycle of the product or service

3. **Penetration pricing.** This strategy is the opposite of market skimming, as prices are set at a very low initial level. If an organization is trying to achieve maximum distribution for the product or service in the initial stages, it will probably price at a lower level to obtain maximum sales and market share. This method is commonly used in the marketing of fast-moving consumer goods, when rapid distribution stocking is essential to the success of the product. If the market is price sensitive (such as in the fast food sector), penetration pricing is an efficient way to gain a quick foothold. The intention is to set low prices only until this market share has been established and then to raise prices gradually to market levels. easyCruise, mentioned earlier, penetrated the cruise market with very low prices for its first ship, and then with its second, easyCruiseTwo, raised prices — justified by a more up-market restaurant and bar.

OTHER PRICING TECHNIQUES

Promotional Pricing or Discounting

promotional pricing

a temporary reduction in price

Promotional pricing is used by organizations when they temporarily sell products or services below their normal list price. Usually this is done for a short period of time, often to introduce new or revamped products. Promotional pricing is often used in the restaurant sector for these reasons. The assumption is made that consumers will buy other items at normal price levels along with the promotionally priced items. Promotional pricing is often used in conjunction with product-bundle pricing.

Product-Bundle Pricing

product-bundle pricing

grouping together products or services to promote them as a package

When an organization groups several of its products or services together to promote them as a package, it is using **product-bundle pricing**. The technique is often used to improve usage or sales during slow periods. An example is a hotel that offers a weekend special that includes a room, dinner in the dining room, valet parking, room service breakfast, and late checkout. In some cases the package will include products that customers might not normally buy (such as the valet parking). Package tours are also a popular type of product bundling. Wholesalers package airfare, ground transport, accommodation, sightseeing tours, and admission to attractions, and because of their bulk purchases they can negotiate significant discounts. These companies can then offer packages to customers that work out to be considerably cheaper than buying the individual components separately. Bundling therefore offers cost advantages to the organization as well as convenience to the consumer.

Price Spread and Price Points

price spread

a range of products
and prices that will
suit the budget of all
target markets

Organizations in tourism and hospitality try to offer a **price spread** — a range of products that will suit the budget of all target markets. A holiday park, for example, may offer camp-sites with tents, standard cabins, en suite cabins, and family units, each different from the other in terms of size, location, and types of fittings and furnishings. Table 6.3 shows the range of prices offered by Banff's Ski Norquay (see *Profile*). The range of prices that an organization can set is virtually unlimited. However, research in the restaurant sector has suggested that if the price spread is too wide, consumers will tend to order from among the lower-priced items.[6]

Table 6.3

Ski Norquay Lift Ticket Prices, 2007–2008

REGULAR TICKETS (NOT UPGRADABLE)

Categories	Adult 18+	Youth/Student	Child 6–12	Senior 55+
Full day	49.00	39.00	17.00	39.00
Afternoon	41.00	32.00	14.00	32.00
Night skiing	24.00	22.00	12.00	22.00
Last hour	15.00	15.00	10.00	15.00

HOURLY (NOT UPGRADABLE — VALID FROM TIME OF PURCHASE OR UNTIL CLOSING)

Categories	Adult 18+	Youth/Student	Child 6–12	Senior 55+
2 hours	29.00	25.00	11.00	25.00
2.5 hours	32.00	27.00	12.00	27.00
3 hours	35.00	30.00	13.00	30.00
3.5 hours	38.00	33.00	14.00	33.00
4 hours	41.00	35.00	15.00	35.00
4.5 hours	44.00	38.00	16.00	38.00
5 hours	47.00	40.00	17.00	40.00

MULTI-DAY (MUST BE USED ON CONSECUTIVE DAYS)

Categories	Adult 18+	Youth/Senior	Child 6–12
2 days	98.00	76.00	31.00
3 days	138.00	108.00	44.00
4 days	184.00	144.00	58.00
5 days	230.00	180.00	73.00

Source: Ski Norquay. (2007). Ski Norquay lift ticket prices
www.banffnorquay.com/rates/lifttickets.html (retrieved September 2007).

price points

the number of "stops" along the way between the lowest-priced item and the highest-priced item

Price points are the number of "stops" along the way between the lowest-priced item and the highest-priced item. Price points vary among industry sectors and types of business. In a restaurant, it is possible to create a menu with a wide range of dishes and to allot a different price to each dish. Restaurants will generally pick several price points and group dishes around those prices. There may be several dishes priced between $10 and 13, then several priced between $19 and $20, then others between $23 and $28. The idea here is to simplify costing and menu planning, and to create points of comparison for the consumer.

Some tourism organizations, notably from the transportation sector, have been accused of having convoluted systems of fare categories designed to confuse the consumer. The rail companies in the United Kingdom for example have come under fire for confusing passengers with their fare systems in order to charge more. Travellers are charged 34 different fares, from a $13 advance fare to a $700 business return, for the same route between London and Manchester.[7] A report by the UK's Transportation Select Committee in early 2006 suggested that the railways should develop a simple, user-friendly, and affordable structure of train fares that apply across the network to give passengers a fair deal. One rail company, First Great Western, reacted to the report by replacing its SuperSaver, Advance, Super-Advance, Apex, and First Apex fares with "leisure" and "business" class tickets.

PROFILE

"SAVE TIME, SAVE MONEY": SKI BY THE HOUR AT BANFF'S MOUNT NORQUAY

"Save time, save money." This is the slogan used by Ski Norquay in Alberta's Banff National Park to promote its skiing-by-the-hour concept. In 1995, the resort introduced the concept of hourly skiing, which has ultimately proved to be an extremely successful long-term pricing strategy. The resort decided to test the waters in 1995 by selling a mid-week-only, two-hour ticket called a "flex-time" ticket, targeted at the local market. Reaction to the flex-time ticket was extremely positive — skiers who had never been to Norquay were turning up for a couple of hours of skiing and then going back to work. Hourly skiing opened up a new market, so after two seasons Norquay decided to

PROFILE *continued*

expand the idea by introducing two-, three-, four-, and five-hour tickets, seven days a week. "We found it was not abused, and it did not cannibalize existing business," says Robert Coté, Ski Norquay's director of marketing. "People bought a two-hour ticket because they only wanted to ski for two hours — they wouldn't normally have bought a day ticket, and they wouldn't have bought a season's pass because they didn't ski enough to make it worthwhile."

According to Coté, hourly skiing takes down all the barriers to skiing that would normally prevent people from coming. "We knew everyone liked Norquay, but it wasn't accessible from a customer's point of view. If someone wanted to ski for the morning they had to buy a whole day's lift ticket, and if they wanted a half day, they had to wait until mid-day. This meant Norquay was imposing its timetable on customers. Now we have put customers in control of their own day."

Competitors have not followed Norquay's lead on hourly tickets, mainly because the competitors are not as close to Banff or Calgary, and also because the layout of their resorts is not conducive to hourly skiing. For hourly skiing to succeed, a close proximity to the client base is necessary. Norquay's proximity to Banff allows visitors to the city to snatch a few hours of skiing on arrival or departure day, or to put in a half-day of skiing before an afternoon at the hot springs or shopping. Locals can also come up just for a short period. "The way the lifts are laid out here, you can do a lot of skiing in two hours," explains Coté. "At other resorts it may not work because they are bigger and more spread out."

For Coté, the most significant advantage to skiing by the hour is that skiers now feel they are getting value for money. "There is a general perception that the sport of skiing is expensive. I don't think it is the actual money spent — I think it is a whole-value equation. Normally, if you don't make it by 9 a.m. for the first lift, you are not going to get full value for your lift ticket. You are going to leave with an unused portion and leave with the feeling of being ripped off. Our slogan is 'save time, save money.'" Coté adds, "The biggest thing here is saving time. In today's society with all the time demands placed on people, time is the most valuable commodity out there. People want to ski, but they don't necessarily want to commit so much time to it. Unfortunately, the full-day/half-day scenario of purchasing lift tickets just doesn't allow that. It all of a sudden puts a high demand on people's time." The hourly tickets have also led to fewer lines, as skier numbers are spread out through the day, and this puts less stress on the customers. Yield is also higher as it is proportionately more expensive to ski by the hour than by the day.

In 2002–2003, in response to customer demand for even more flexibility, Norquay decided to increase from hourly increments to half-hourly increments. The resort's ski-by-the-hour ticket options are shown in Table 6.3. The 2001–2002 season was the first winter in which gross sales from the different hourly tickets exceeded sales from full-day tickets — the three-hour ticket being the most popular, followed by two-hour and four-hour tickets. But full-day sales have remained steady, so hourly tickets have not adversely affected sales of full-day tickets. And skiing by the hour has become so popular at Norquay that Coté tags the skiing-by-the-hour concept onto many of its resort promotions. "After six years of it, people are really catching on to it, and it is becoming associated with us," he says.

Source: Personal communication with R. Coté, former director of marketing, Mount Norquay, January 2005.

Discriminatory Pricing

discriminatory pricing

selling a product or service at more than one price, despite the fact that its costs are the same

Organizations often alter prices to suit different customers, products, locations, and times. This **discriminatory pricing** allows the organization to sell a product or service at more than one price, despite the fact that its costs are the same. For example, many restaurants charge higher prices in the evening than they do at lunchtime, even if the food is identical, because of demand differences. Ski resorts may charge more for a weekend ski pass than during the week if the majority of their customers drive up on a Saturday or Sunday.

These are examples of time-based discriminatory pricing, but a market may also be segmented to encourage increased participation from special groups, such as senior citizens or students. In this case, the groups would be offered special concessions, as seen in Ski Norquay's lower prices for children, students, and seniors (see Table 6.3). The market must be capable of being segmented if discriminatory pricing is going to be an effective strategy. Segments will have highly distinct sensitivities, and being able to price differently to the various segments is key to success in maximizing profits.[8] Care should also be taken to ensure that the strategy is legal and that it does not lead to customer resentment.

Volume Discounting

volume discounting

offering special prices to attract customers who agree to major purchases

From time to time, most businesses will need to consider discounting their standard prices. Many tourism organizations engage in **volume discounting** — offering special rates to attract customers who agree to major purchases. Hotels and airlines, for example, offer special prices (or upgrades) to corporate clients to encourage volume business. A volume discount is really a wise move only if it increases demand, brings new users, or increases consumption by regular users. Organizations that discount key products but don't lower costs to offset the discount are taking an economic risk unless the discount is only for a very short period or is designed to overcome a very specific problem.

YIELD MANAGEMENT

yield

the profit made on the sales of products or services based on the number of customers, how much they spend, and the number of products or services they buy

yield management

maximizing opportunities for the sale of perishable products, such as airline seats, hotel rooms, and tour seats, and therefore improving long-term viability

Yield is the profit that is made on the sales of products or and services; it is calculated based on the number of customers, how much they spend, and the number of products or services they buy. **Yield management** is the practice of aopportunities for the sale of an organization's perishable products or services, such as airline seats, hotel rooms, and tour seats, and therefore improving its long-term viability. In other words, it has been defined as "lowering the price … according to expected demand, and relying heavily on computers and modeling techniques."[9] Yield management was initiated by the airline industry in the 1980s as a way to increase revenue from existing routes and aircraft. Computer technology made it possible for airlines to predict the number of seats that would be sold on a given flight — called the load factor. By analyzing costs, and also determining the price sensitivity of various types of airfares, airlines discovered that by offering seats at a variety of special fares they could boost load and revenues.

Many have argued in favour of yield management techniques, using price to balance the market conditions of supply and demand. Silvain Daudel and Georges Vialle, for example, distinguished between "'spoilage," the under-utilization of resources, and "spill," selling too low early, with the result that later, higher-yielding demand has to be denied.[10] The practice of yield management is now common in other sectors of tourism, from hotels to ski resorts. Different rates are offered for certain groups of customers, and restrictions are placed on the use of these rates by other groups. The Fairmont Palliser in Calgary, for example, has seen tremendous improvements in revenue per available room since its implementation of a new yield management program in 1997. The company's strategy is to charge a maximum price until demand at that level falls and then to lower the price until all available capacity has sold. This example shows that yield management systems, if used properly, can provide considerable extra revenue. A good system will benefit both the business and the consumer.

Even theatres are using yield management techniques to maximize revenue. The Stratford Shakespeare Festival, for example, offers a wide variety of ticket prices. There are more than 40 possible combinations of regular ticket prices and more than 30 different types of discount tickets, as well as special concessions for students, seniors, and families.

Sheryl Kimes has suggested that consumers seem to accept yield management in the airline industry, where they receive specific benefits if they accept certain restraints.[11] However, she raises the question of how customers react to it in other sectors, suggesting that a customer who pays more for a similar service and cannot perceive the difference in the service may view the situation as unfair. Kimes developed her argument on the basis of a **reference price**, derived from market prices and the customer's previous experience. At a normal (or reference) price, a high standard of service and amenities will please the customer, but these same standards will only satisfy those who are paying premium prices. Customers enjoying normal or superior standards on a holiday for which they paid low prices will be pleased or delighted. In contrast, customers receiving normal levels of service in return for high prices will feel at best exploited and at worst angry. This could result in complaints and negative word of mouth, undermining the credibility of the organization concerned.

Employing yield management, both hotels and airlines use overbooking to cover no-shows and late cancellations. Because overbooking is a risky practice, organizations using yield management must be prepared to offer inducements, such as free travel vouchers, in case overbooking occurs. In fact, some suggest that overbooking be avoided wherever possible because of potential ill will or even possible legal liability, or of additional costs such as having to relocate guests with confirmed reservations to another hotel. Hiemstra says that when hotels have significant problems with no-shows, they should develop overbooking strategies because it is costly to have rooms remain unused when they could be rented with better planning.[12] The first requirement in developing such a

reference price

a price derived from market prices and the customer's previous experience policy is to have good historical records of the occurrence of no-shows from which to calculate their probability. These records need to be carefully analyzed to determine seasonality, day of the week, or other patterns with which the practice may be associated. Costs associated with overbooking must also be determined and compared with the opportunity costs of not renting a room. Reciprocal arrangements with nearby hotels in the same quality segment can minimize the direct costs, but the cost of ill will is more difficult to estimate.

STRATEGIC AND TACTICAL PRICING

strategic pricing

setting prices early, in accordance with the long-term view of corporate strategy, product positioning, and value for money in the marketplace

tactical pricing

making short-term pricing decisions in response to changes in the marketing environment

Organizations in the tourism and hospitality industry operate pricing policies at the strategic and tactical levels. In **strategic pricing**, prices are determined early on in the planning of the marketing strategy, as the nature of the business means that prices must be set long in advance so that brochures and guides can be published. These pricing decisions are based on the long-term view of corporate strategy, product positioning, and value for money in the marketplace.

While strategic pricing is concerned with the overall plans for the implementation of pricing policy, **tactical pricing** relates to day-to-day, short-term pricing decisions that can be rapidly altered to suit changing conditions in the marketplace. Thus, a strategy of discriminatory pricing that involves setting different prices for different market groups (e.g., business travellers and leisure travellers) may be introduced, but the actual prices charged and the ways in which these prices are adjusted require tactical decisions. The fact that organizations cannot stock services means that if the planned supply exceeds demand in the marketplace for whatever reason, the organization must sell excess capacity. This often means resorting to tactical strategies, in the form of promotional pricing or discounting, for example. Hotels have become skilled at using last-minute tactical pricing methods to fill unoccupied rooms. Customers can often negotiate a substantial reduction on the rack rate if they phone the hotel the evening on which they want a room.

One strategic decision that must be taken is whether to price differently to different geographic areas. Should the price be common to all customers, or should it vary to reflect different market demand in various countries? It may be more costly to sell a package tour to the Japanese than to Americans, because of higher costs in Japan, or it may be necessary in one country to boost agents' commission levels to secure their support. According to Mercer Human Resource Consulting, Moscow, London, and Seoul were the most expensive cities in the world in 2007 (see Table 6.4). Tourism players who operate in an international market will have to be aware of such statistics when setting prices. In Canada, Toronto ranked 82nd, Vancouver 89th, Calgary 92nd, Montreal 98th, and Ottawa 108th.[13]

Table 6.4

The Most Expensive Cities in the World

Base city: New York (= 100).					
RANKINGS				COST OF LIVING INDEX	
March 2007	March 2006	City	Country	March 2007	March 2006
1	1	Moscow	Russia	134.4	123.9
2	5	London	United Kingdom	126.3	110.6
3	2	Seoul	South Korea	122.4	121.7
4	3	Tokyo	Japan	122.1	119.1
5	4	Hong Kong	Hong Kong	119.4	116.3
6	8	Copenhagen	Denmark	110.2	101.1
7	7	Geneva	Switzerland	109.8	103
8	6	Osaka	Japan	108.4	108.3
9	9	Zurich	Switzerland	107.6	100.8
10	10	Oslo	Norway	105.8	100

Source: Mercer Human Resource Consulting. (2007, June 18). Moscow tops Mercer's cost of living list; London is close behind. www.mercer.com/costofliving (retrieved September 2007).

all-in pricing (all-inclusive pricing)

a single price for all the various products or services on offer

Other popular strategies include **all-in pricing** or **all-inclusive pricing**. This type of pricing was used originally in holiday camps in the United Kingdom, where customers were provided access to every entertainment facility in the camp for a single price. The strategy proved highly successful, and Club Med built on this model for its chain of holiday resorts around the world. Club Med now advertises "total all-inclusive" holidays, so that consumers pay for no extras whatsoever (see Figure 6.5). Today, tourists are very familiar with booking all-inclusive holidays in resorts in the Caribbean and Mexico. Theme parks also normally adopt the all-inclusive strategy by charging just one fee for the use of all their attractions.

A contrasting strategy involves charging a low basic entrance fee and recouping profits through add-ons, which require that customers pay for each individual attraction. Organizers at the Calgary Stampede (see the *Snapshot* in Chapter 12) have used this strategy for the fun fair set in the middle of the Stampede grounds. Guests pay a small entrance fee but then pay for all of the rides. This is similar to **off-set pricing** or **bait pricing**, which sets a low basic price and adds charges for extra services. Casino hotels provide an example of bait pricing. Prices are often extremely reasonable for rooms, food,

off-set pricing (bait pricing)

charging a low basic price and charging for extra services

and drink because profits are reaped through gambling on the premises. Another example is an attraction that sets a very low admission fee, possibly even a loss leader at below cost, in order to attract visitors, who then pay extra for every event or facility.

Figure 6.5 Club Med Print Advertisement

TOURISM AND HOSPITALITY CHARACTERISTICS THAT AFFECT PRICING POLICY

Although this chapter already refers to some of the points that follow, a separate discussion of the particular features of the tourism and hospitality industry that affect pricing is warranted here.

1. High Level of Segmentation

The tourism and hospitality industry is highly segmented, with varying elasticities of demand in the segments. These demand segments may be associated with different income levels, age groupings, seasonality, and types of pleasure or business. Groups are also not homogeneous in their demands. Some may be business travellers with expense accounts and others may be pleasure travellers spending their own funds.

2. Variability of Demand

Different product or service offerings also face much variability in the level of demand within customer segments associated with different days of the week, holidays, different seasons of the year, and normal fluctuations in local personal or business situations. For hotels, this variability causes difficulty in forecasting normal room demands for an individual property, and requires that each day of the year be projected and priced differently.

3. Perishable Nature of the Product or Service

The tourism product or service is perishable: it cannot be stored and sold at a later date. In addition, suppliers may not wish the surplus to be sold through the same channel as the standard product, as this may affect future demand and pricing. This is why outlets exist that allow the supplier to remain anonymous. For example, the Internet provides an outlet for tour operators and airlines to offload surplus holidays or flights at reduced margins without changing their main brochures.

4. High Fixed Costs

High fixed costs in major tourism sectors exacerbate the perishable nature of the business of selling holidays, seats, or hotel rooms. This means that an organization saves little by not filling to capacity. In the hospitality sector, for example, variable costs associated with the rooms department account for only one-fourth of total room department income, while fixed costs associated primarily with paying for the building and overhead expenses account for a large share of the remaining revenue. This feature gives strong incentive to rent rooms at relatively low rates rather than leaving them vacant.

5. Cost Fluctuations

For many operators in the tourism and hospitality industry, there is a high probability of unpredictable but major short-term fluctuations in cost elements such as oil prices and currency exchange rates. A tour operator running packages to various European and South American destinations may, according to exchange rates and the general climate of tourism in each country, have to vary its prices. High oil prices in 2006 forced many airlines to cut costs. One Chinese airline, China Southern, calculated that it takes a litre of fuel to flush a toilet at 30 000 feet, so urged passengers to go to the toilet before they boarded.[14]

6. Vulnerability to Demand Changes

The industry is vulnerable to demand changes resulting from unforeseen economic and political events. Tourism worldwide suffered a downtrend between 2001 and 2004 due to the effects of terrorism, the Iraq war, low economies, and the SARS outbreak. Since September 11, 2001, there have been more than 3000 major terrorism attacks worldwide, most of which have affected the tourism industry.

7. High Level of Customers' Psychological Involvement

Customers display a particularly high level of psychological involvement in choosing vacation products, in which price may be a symbol of status as well as value.[15] They are therefore likely to invest considerable care in their choice. In the packaged holiday market, where the tour operators or travel agents emphasize prices rather than destination attributes in their promotions, the customers' attention is likely to focus on comparing prices rather than on what each destination offers, potentially resulting in a reduced commitment to the resort visited. Under these conditions, there is more likely to be a mismatch between the tourists' holiday expectations and their destination experiences, resulting in dissatisfaction and complaint.

8. Seasonal Demand

One of the most common ways of setting holiday price differentials is the seasonal banding that is typical of tour operators' brochures — and familiar to all who purchase inclusive holidays — in the form of price and departure date matrices. Seasonality of demand leads to differing price expectations. Commercial business demand for some hotels often declines in high summer. This leads to domestic consumers anticipating lower rates and higher availability in mid-week. Conversely, many tour operators and airlines are able to increase prices in high summer when demand is at its peak. An interesting pricing strategy was set by the Eden Roc Resort and Spa in Miami in the 1990s. The resort charged guests the same amount in dollars as the day's highest temperature. The idea was to give guest no cause for complaint even in the event of a cold snap!

9. Tactical Price Cutting and Price Wars

If supply exceeds demand, there is near certainty of price cutting by major competitors. This leads to the high possibility of price wars in sectors such as transport, accommodation, tour operating, and travel agencies, in which short-term profitability may disappear.

10. Low Prices

Price competition in many sectors has led to an industry characterized by low prices. Low prices have not only stimulated demand for holidays currently on offer, but have also altered the timing of demand — for example, by extending the holiday season — and have changed the demographic profile of holidaymakers to include all age groups and most socioeconomic groups of society. A lower price provides an increased access to the product, bringing the product to a new group of potential purchasers that have different behavioural characteristics. One example of this is the way that cruising holidays are now promoted to a broader market on the basis of reduced prices.

11. Fixed Capacity

Even though demand may be highly variable and unpredictable, in many sectors of the industry supply that is available in the short run tends to be relatively fixed. For a hotel, for example, it takes a long time to expand a building or to build a new one. Adding part-time or seasonal labour may be useful in improving service during periods of peak occupancy, but it can add little to available room inventory. As a result, pricing policies are largely restricted to allocating existing supplies among competing demands. This restriction adds importance to effective no-show policies.

12. The Customer's Total Purchases

Some sectors of the tourism and hospitality industry must consider the customer's total purchases when considering prices and profits. Hotels should not consider room rates and restaurant prices separately. Selling a room cheaply to a guest who will use the restaurant and bars extensively may be more profitable than selling it to someone who pays full rate for the room but purchases nothing else. For example, mixed-offering destinations such as those owned by Intrawest (see *Case Study* in Chapter 5) need not concern themselves too much with visitors who do not ski, as they can earn huge profits from selling other on-snow activities, as well as earn revenue from the restaurants and retail units.

13. Increased Use of the Internet

Many travel consumers are "empowering" themselves by learning the routines of Internet research and transacting for airfares. They are also increasingly aware of their ability to exercise more control over their purchases, and a large percentage of hotel customers attempt to negotiate lower prices on their rooms. In general, consumers have become more self-reliant, and the most adventurous are building their own holidays, many of them encouraged to make online purchases with Internet-only discount rates.[16]

14. Late Booking

Price reductions for late booking are a widespread holiday industry response to its unsold capacity, and are typically promoted by travel agents and tour operators shortly before departure. However, operators are increasingly using website pricing options to accommodate late bookers. It was not long ago that most businesses made only rack rates available online. Today, pricing is more complex, and many travel websites now have a whole menu of online pricing options. It is now typical to see last-minute discounts; Web-only offers; discounted pricing for groups; incentive rates for travel agents, tour operators, and reservation agents; and a variety of packages at different price points, including such add-ons as meals, activities, and transportation.[17]

CHAPTER SUMMARY

The key factors determining pricing decisions are marketing objectives, costs, other mix variables, distribution channel expectations, buyer perceptions, competition, and legal and regulatory restrictions. The analysis of buyers' reactions to price change uses the concept of elasticity of demand. If demand increases in line with price cuts, the product is said to be elastic. But if demand remains relatively unaltered by price changes, then the product is said to be inelastic.

Generally, companies use pricing as part of their positioning of a product, employing one of three strategic approaches: premium pricing, value-for-money pricing, and undercut pricing. Basic approaches to pricing fall into three main categories: cost-based methods, demand-based methods, and competition-oriented pricing. Three strategies commonly used for the introduction of new products are prestige pricing, market skimming, and penetration pricing. Other pricing techniques include promotional pricing, product-bundle pricing, price spread and price points, discriminatory pricing, volume discounting, and yield management.

Particular features of the tourism and hospitality industry that affect pricing include the high level of segmentation of industry, variability of demand, the perishable nature of the product, high fixed costs, cost fluctuations, vulnerability to demand changes, the high level of customers' psychological involvement, seasonal demand, tactical price cutting and price wars, low prices, fixed capacity, the customer's total purchases, increased use of the Internet, and late booking.

KEY TERMS

all-in-pricing (all-inclusive pricing), p. 206
break-even analysis, p. 194
buyer-based pricing (sensitivity pricing), p. 195
competition-oriented pricing (going-rate pricing), p. 196
cost-based pricing, p. 193
cost-plus pricing, p. 194
discriminatory pricing, p. 203
elasticity of demand, p. 188
fixed costs, p. 194
market skimming, p. 198
monopoly, p. 192

negotiating, p. 195
off-set pricing (bait pricing), p. 206
penetration pricing, p. 199
premium pricing, p. 191
prestige pricing, p. 198
price lining, p. 195
price points, p. 201
price spread, p. 200
price–quality trade-off, p. 183
product-bundle pricing, p. 199
profit maximization, p. 185
promotional pricing, p. 199

psychological pricing, p. 195
reference price, p. 204
strategic pricing, p. 205
tactical pricing, p. 205
target rate of return, p. 185
undercut pricing, p. 191
value-for-money pricing, p. 191
variable costs, p. 194
volume discounting, p. 203
willingness to pay (WTP) assessment, p. 189
yield management, p. 203
yield, p. 203

DISCUSSION QUESTIONS AND EXERCISES

1. What are the benefits and costs of a tourism operator providing discounts?
2. When would a new restaurant introduce a new product with premium pricing? When might it use undercut pricing?
3. What pricing strategy does Space Adventures use? How could the company find out about price sensitivity for its proposed new package?
4. Collect advertisements for hotels in your area and find examples of product-bundle pricing.

Explain how they work. Try to calculate the savings that the bundle offers.

5. Explain the differences between prestige pricing, market skimming, and penetration pricing, using examples from a sector of tourism and hospitality apart from hotels.
6. What type of pricing strategy does Ski Norquay follow? Can you see any disadvantages to this strategy?

CASE STUDY

SAFARI AND A FACELIFT: THE RISE OF MEDICAL TOURISM

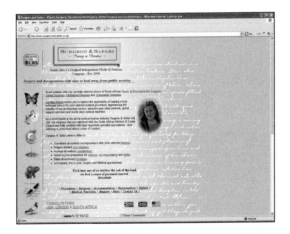

Medical tourism, whereby patients travel to a different country for either urgent or elective surgery, is fast becoming a worldwide, multibillion-dollar industry. Time, money, and anonymity are three reasons driving international medical queue-jumping. The rapid rise in this new industry is attributable to the exorbitant costs of medical care in developed countries, in conjunction with the comparative ease and affordability nowadays of international travel, rapidly improving technology and standards of care worldwide, and the proven safety records of medical care in many developing countries around the world.

Surgery wait times in particular can lead patients to seek alternative venues. North Americans are finding that trips abroad, combined with surgery can cost between four and ten times less than medical procedures at home. Also, by mixing surgery with pleasure, less time away from work is required. And, for everyone, foreign travel can disguise the primary purpose of the vacation so that friends and colleagues attribute their newly refreshed, youthful appearance to the benign effects of the holiday rather than the cosmetic surgeon's scalpel.

Dating back to Ancient Greece, pilgrims and patients travelled throughout the Mediterranean to the sanctuary of the healing god, Asklepios, at Epidarus. The healing waters at Bath, first established in Roman Britain, have been a shrine for more than 2000 years. Baden Baden in Germany was another traditional watering-hole for rich European patients seeking alleviation of arthritis and other debilitating ailments. Now, in the 21st century, cheap airfares and increasingly high standards of medical facilities and expertise worldwide have opened "medical tourism" up to a growing middle class market.

Countries that actively promote medical tourism include Cuba, Costa Rica, Hungary, India, Israel, Jordan, Lithuania, Malaysia, and Thailand.

India is currently considered the leading country promoting medical tourism, encouraging its expatriates from all over the world to return for cheaper and quicker access to medical attention for the past decade. Government and private sector studies there estimate that medical tourism, with a growth rate of 30 percent annually, could bring between $1 billion and $2 billion into the country by 2012. The Apollo Hospital Group is the largest of the outsourcing medical corporations in India, treating about 60 000 patients between 2001 and spring 2004.

Even South Africa, where medical advertising is still illegal, is joining in with medical safaris, dubbed "beauty and beast tours." South Africa is particularly attractive to cosmetic surgery patients because of its high-quality surgeons and prices, which are inexpensive in light of the currency rate rather than any deficiency in facilities or expertise. Surgeon and Safari is one Johannesburg-based company capitalizing on this growing demand, and has consultants located online and in South Africa, Britain, and the United States. Set up in 1999 by Lorraine Melvill, it circumvents advertising restrictions by providing a intermediary-type service between patients and doctors. Melvill, a marketing executive, saw that she could exploit the unusual synergy between the demand for tourism on one hand and for cosmetic surgery that is affordable, is high quality, and offers the client anonymity on the other.

Clients are informed by website about the medical and tourism aspects of their trip. Melvill makes all the arrangements for transportation, surgery, recuperation, and hotels and safari plans, meeting all her clients right off the plane. She attributes her success to this personal, hands-on, reassuring business approach. She even sits by their side during the lead-up to surgery. On offer are a range of cosmetic and reconstructive surgeries including plastic, ophthalmic, orthopedic, dentistry, hair transplants, and sports medicine as well as the non-surgical Botox and Restylane treatments. Almost half of the clients are from the UK and they opt mainly for reconstructive procedures. The other half, from the U.S., arrive with a shopping list of mainly cosmetic requests.

Costs vary according to the type of operation and the length of recuperation required. A seven-day package, including two surgical procedures (e.g., liposuction and tummy tuck), accommodation in a luxury resort, and some meals, would cost approximately $4300. If you tack a safari onto that package, then the overall cost would equal the price of having the surgery alone done back in the United States. A facelift in the U.S. costs around $10 000 compared to $5000 in South Africa. And Melvill assures her customers that the cost differential is purely due to the country's weak currency and represents value for money rather than low standards.

As with any surgery, there are risks associated with surgery abroad. The American Society for Aesthetic Plastic Surgery warns about the risks of sitting in the sun post-surgery, inconsistent follow-up care, drinking alcohol when on strong medications, flying too soon after surgery with the potential for deep vein thrombosis, and the possibility of insufficient credentials among foreign surgeons. Melvill counters all these criticisms, claiming that the South African surgeons are of the highest quality and expertly trained. The hospital's blood supply is screened for HIV, patients are tested for blood clots in their legs, and surgeons will refuse to operate on people who are mentally unstable, anorexic, or obese.

The future of medical tourism seems strong in light of the potential baby boomer market of more than 220 million people throughout the U.S., Canada, western Europe, Australia, and New Zealand. It capitalizes upon the fascination with vanity, agelessness, and beauty at any cost among an increasingly older population, as well as upon the globalization of tourism and medicine. "Come for the surgery, stay for the scenery" is a website advertising slogan attracting many people to South Africa to combine their elective surgeries with safaris, sightseeing, and even a round of golf. The following table shows the price of medical tourism for one American customer who travelled to South Africa to have excess skin removed, followed by a safari and a whale-watching trip.

Table 6.5

Plastic Surgery and Safari Tally

Round trip flight to South Africa	$1 125
Safari and whale watching	$247
Room and meals	$1 348
Tummy tuck and liposuction	$3 832
Private nurse and driver	$596
Total	$7 148
Average price of just surgery in the United States	$12 600
Source: Southern, E., & Rubin, C. (2006, March 27). Beauty and the beast. *People Magazine*.	

Sources: Marcelo, R. (2003, July 2). India hopes to foster growing business in "medical tourism." *Financial Times,* 10; Souter, E., & Rubin, C. (2006, March 27). Beauty and the beast, *People Magazine.*

QUESTIONS

1. Is demand for medial tourism price elastic or inelastic? Explain.
2. Explain how medical tourism in a developing country, such as India, involves a price-quality trade-off compared to a developed country, such as the United Kingdom or the United States.
3. What kind of pricing strategy is Surgeon and Safari following?
4. Account for the increase in demand for medical tourism. Where will the growth come from in the future for this particular sector of tourism?
5. What other tourism products could be bundled into the package detailed in Table 6.5?

WEB SITES

www.surgeon-and-safari.co.za
Surgeon and Safari

www.banffnorquay.com
Ski Norquay

www.spaceadventures.com
Space Adventures

www.burjalarab-hotel-dubai.com
Burj Al Arab Hotel, Dubai

www.easycruise.com
easyCruise

www.ryanair.com
Ryanair

ENDNOTES

1. Wang, S. & Lynn, M. (2007). The effects on perceived restaurant expensiveness of tipping and its alternatives. *Centre for Hospitality Research, 7*(3), www.hotelschool.cornell.edu/research/chr/pubs/reports/abstract-14373.html (retrieved September 2007).

2. Ungoed-Thomas, J. (2006, August 20). Tourists tell Britain: you're a rip-off. *Sunday Times*, 9.

3. Dickman, S. (1999). *Tourism and hospitality marketing*. Oxford: Oxford University Press.

4. A cool $1 million to ski at Aspen. (2005, November 5). *Calgary Herald*, G1.

5. Teather, D., Kundnami, H., & Clark, A. (2006, June 23) BA price-fixing turmoil: offices raided, executives suspended. *Guardian*, 1–2.

6. Carmin, J., & Norkus, G. (1990). Pricing strategies for menus: Magic or myth? *Cornell Hotel & Restaurant Administration Quarterly, 31*(3), 50.

7. Macfarlane, J. (2006, May 20). Rail bosses holding you to ransom. *Daily Express*, 8.

8. Hiemstra, S. J. (1998). Economic pricing strategies for hotels. In T. Baum & R. Mudambi (Eds.), *Economic and management methods for tourism and hospitality research,* 215–232. New York: Wiley.

9. Lundberg, D. E., Krishnamoorthy, M., & Stavenga, M. H. (1995). *Tourism economics.* New York: Wiley, 106.

10. Daudel, S., & Vialle, G. (1994). *Yield management: Applications to air transport and other service industries.* Paris: Institut du Transport Aérien.

11. Kimes, S. E. (1994). Perceived fairness of yield management. *Cornell Hotel & Restaurant Administration Quarterly, 43*(1), 21–31.

12. Hiemstra, S. J. (1998) Economic pricing strategies for hotels. In T. Baum & R. Mudambi (Eds.), *Economic and management methods for tourism and hospitality research,* 215–232. New York: Wiley.

13. Mercer Human Resource Consulting. (2007). Worldwide Cost of Living Survey 2007: City rankings.www.mercer.com/pressrelease/details.jhtml/dynamic/idContent/1268475 (retrieved September 2007).

14. Chinese airline urges passengers to go to the bathroom before they board to save fuel. (2006, December 1). *National Post,* A3.

15. Laws, E. (1998). Package holiday pricing: Cause of the IT industry's success, or cause for concern? In T. Baum & R. Mudambi (Eds.), *Economic and management methods for tourism and hospitality research,* 197–214. New York: Wiley.

16. Davis, T. (2002). Ski operators meet in Whistler to review "extraordinary" 2001. www.canadatourism.com (retrieved April 2002).

17. Hudson, S., & Lang, N. (2002). A destination case study of marketing tourism online: Banff, Canada. *Journal of Vacation Marketing, 8*(2), 155–165.

CHAPTER

Distribution

7

Spotlight
WHITE SPOT RESTAURANTS: A FRANCHISING SUCCESS STORY

In 1914, a 12-year-old boy named Nat Bailey left his home in Minnesota to make a living on his own. He crossed the Canadian border into British Columbia and settled in Vancouver, where for many years he sold peanuts, hot dogs, and hamburgers at sporting events. Recognizing that there was money to be made in the foodservice industry, he scraped enough cash together to buy a Model T Ford that he converted into a small restaurant on wheels. The success of Bailey's venture led to his establishment of the White Spot Barbeque, on Granville Street, where Bailey managed to woo the appetites and patronage of western diners by employing a simple, three-pronged recipe for success that endures to this day: quality, service,

and consistency. The intervening years of expansion eventually led to the development of today's White Spot Restaurants, a collection of family casual-dining spots that includes 58 full-service operations and 28 quick-service outlets. The family of corporately owned and franchised operations generated $120 million in system-wide sales in 2000. From the modest Granville Street cabin that functioned with three employees, the company's staff has grown to 3500, serving more full-service meals than any other restaurant in British Columbia.

In 1993, a full 65 years after the launch of the first White Spot restaurant, the company opened its first franchise location in Vernon, B.C. Today, Canada's two most westerly provinces are home to 38 franchised, full-service restaurants and 23 Triple-O franchises, the company's branch of quick-service operations. The remainder of White Spot's eateries are company owned and operated. White Spot management has a clear vision when it comes to the selection of new recruits. Company president Warren Erhart says potential franchises are not required to have a foodservice background, but a previous track record in the business field is a definite asset. Some of the core values sought by the franchiser mirror the principles held by the founder: integrity, innovation, a high energy level, communication skills, and a strong sense of community involvement.

Paul Gilley, one of White Spot's earliest recruits, represents a model example of what the company seeks in its franchisees. In 1994, he signed up for his first full-service franchise in Langley, B.C., and over the next five years purchased four additional operations, primarily in the Greater Vancouver Area. Gilley seemed ideally suited to join the White Spot family. He had spent a number of years in the retail sector, holding the position of head of Blockbuster Video for B.C., doing a stint in heavy equipment sales, and spending a few years as a Vancouver-based franchisee for AAMCO Transmissions. When Gilley learned that franchise opportunities with White Spot were available, the man who had grown up with the restaurant legend opted to invest. "White Spot was a highly respected name in the West and I had been a customer all my life," he says.

Gilley advises potential franchisees that being a people person is important, as is the willingness to work hard in a vibrant and challenging environment. "The expectations of White Spot customers are high, and you have to constantly work to maintain the level of quality and service the restaurant has become known for," he says. Although Gilley says that the process of growing a White Spot business requires long hours (restaurants operate from 6:30 a.m. to 11 p.m.) and a resolute focus, the opportunity for financial reward is unquestionable. While Gilley admits that several variables exist, his experience shows that it is entirely possible to discharge the capital investment required to purchase a full-service franchise in five years or less.

Depending on size and location, the cost to purchase a full-service White Spot franchise ranges from $610 000 to $845 000. An approved franchisee's investment portfolio incorporates a base franchise fee of $75 000, plus the costs of restaurant construction or renovation of existing retail space, fixtures and equipment, initial inventory and supplies, and start-up costs such as advertising. Erhart says that approved franchisees, who participate in a three-month training program, are not just buying a restaurant in which they can become independent and successful entrepreneurs; they are buying into a respected legend in the foodservice field. "The financial rewards possible are borne out by the number of existing franchisees who have been able to purchase a second or third restaurant," he says.

Company management is a reliable source of ongoing support for both new and seasoned White Spot franchises. Operating under the umbrella of the company's Vancouver-based head office, a staff of business consultants is available to provide franchisees with advice and assistance on everything from operational procedures to marketing, human relations, and financial matters. "Our business consultants are accessible to franchisees 24 hours a day, seven days a week," says Erhart. An important element in the franchisee/franchiser relationship is a two-way line of communication. "New franchisees bring fresh blood to the company, and their ideas for the advancement of White Spot restaurants are welcomed," says Erhart. Franchisees are invited to sit on various committees that examine all aspects of the business, from corporate direction to menu development.

Source: Carter, D. (2002). Success marks the Spot. *Franchise Canada, 2*(5), 26–31.

Objectives

On completion of this chapter, readers should understand

- the two main types of distribution channels used in tourism and hospitality;
- the key intermediaries involved in the tourism and hospitality distribution system;
- the main forms of channel conflict in tourism and hospitality;

- the two main types of channel organization in tourism and hospitality;
- the two major forms of vertically integrated marketing system — alliances and franchises; and
- how a company designs its distribution system and how and it ensures the effective execution of the distribution strategy.

Chapter Overview

The *Spotlight* provides an example of one form of distribution in tourism; franchising. This chapter examines the various ways in which tourism and hospitality products are distributed. It begins by looking at the nature and types of distribution channels. The key intermediaries involved in the tourism distribution system are then discussed, including travel agents, tour operators, convention and meeting planners, and travel specialists; the increasing use of the Internet as a part of the distribution channel is also analyzed. The next section of the chapter is concerned with channel conflict and organization; it explores the two main forms of channel conflict — horizontal conflict and vertical conflict — and the two main types of channel organization — the conventional marketing system and the vertical marketing system. Two major forms of vertically integrated marketing systems are alliances and franchises. Both have advantages and disadvantages, which are considered in detail and illustrated with several examples from the tourism industry. Finally, attention is given to how a company designs its distribution system and how it ensures the effective execution of the distribution strategy.

THE DISTRIBUTION SYSTEM

distribution system

the aspect of the marketing mix that relates to making a product or service available to the consumer

An organization's **distribution system** is centred on the "place" aspect of its marketing mix. The purpose is to provide an adequate framework for making a product or service available to the consumer; in the tourism industry, distribution systems are often used to move the customer to the product. The true rationale behind an organization's distribution system can be traced back to its specific needs and wants. Figure 7.1 shows that each distinct distribution participant has a unique set of needs and wants. The motivation for developing an effective distribution network, therefore, is to help the different members meet their individual needs. By choosing to combine the activities of the various members, participants in the distribution system can work together to identify opportunities to fulfill each other's needs.

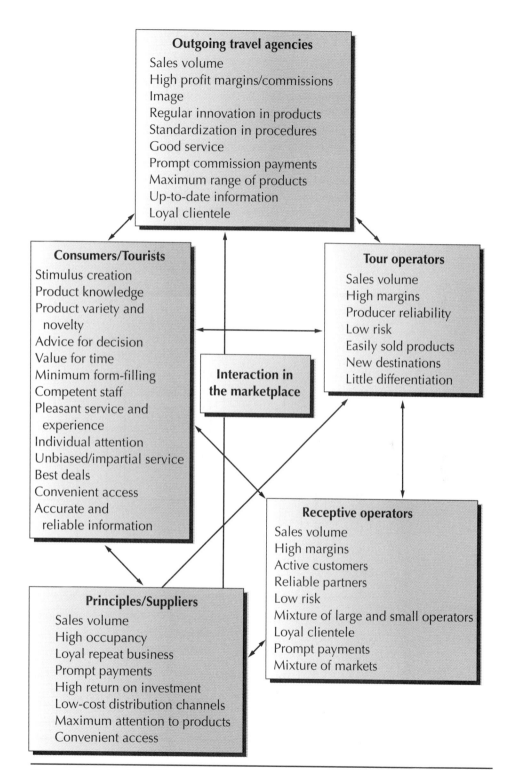

Figure 7.1   Needs and Wants of Tourism Distribution Channel Members

Source: Buhalis, D., & Laws, E. (2001). Tourism distribution channels: Practices, issues and transformations. New York: Continuum.

THE NATURE AND TYPES OF DISTRIBUTION CHANNELS

distribution channel

a direct or indirect delivery arrangement used by a supplier, carrier, or destination marketing organization

direct distribution channel

a channel through which an organization delivers its product or service to the consumer without any intermediaries

A **distribution channel** is a method of delivery used by a supplier, carrier, or destination marketing organization (DMO). There are two different types of distribution channels that can be used to deliver a product or service (see Figure 7.2). The first and most simple form of distribution is a **direct distribution channel**, a channel through which an organization delivers its product or service to the consumer without the outside assistance of any independent intermediaries. In such a case, the service provider is solely responsible for the delivery. Most bed and breakfasts in Canada use a direct distribution channel to market products to potential customers. They perform all of the necessary channel functions on their own, without relying on any assistance from intermediaries. The following *Snapshot* describes how Whistler is taking a direct distribution strategy in Japan in order to entice Japanese skiers to visit the B.C. resort.

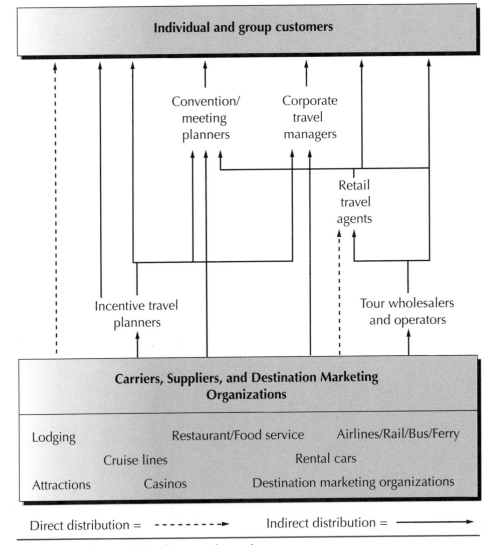

Figure 7.2   Types of Distribution Channels

Source: Morrison, A. M. (2002). *Hospitality and travel marketing* (3rd ed.). Albany, NY: Delmar Thomson Learning, 340.

indirect distribution channel

a channel through which an organization distributes its product or service with the assistance of intermediaries

The second type of distribution channel used to deliver a product or service is an **indirect channel**. In this case, the service provider makes use of independent intermediaries to help facilitate the distribution. Intermediaries such as travel agents, tour operators, and other tourism specialists assist the supplying company by helping to attract consumers to the product or destination. The *Case Study* on Canadian Mountain Holidays (CMH) at the end of the chapter explains how, in its early stages, the company used an indirect distribution system to market its holidays in Europe, using specialist agents.

SNAPSHOT

WHISTLER CHOOSES ONE-TO-ONE MARKETING IN JAPAN

新潟県・苗場スキー場ゲレンデに特製ドームテントが登場!!
冬季限定のカナディアンスタイルのカフェとして、
カナダ料理とウィンター情報を提供します。

「GOウィスラーキャンペーン」
1/20〜3/25 素敵な商品が当たる!

「金曜・土曜はCCナイト」
1/20〜3/24 の金曜・土曜
カナディアンクラブまたは
CCカクテルを1杯無料!!

Serving up distinctly Canadian food and drinks, the menu at Whistler Café reads like any popular Whistler après-ski hangout with chicken wings, nachos, and smoked salmon appetizers, and Whistler Premium Export Lager and Whistler Classic Pale Ale, wines from British Columbia's Okanagan region, Whistler Water brand bottled water, BLENZ coffee, Canadian Club Whisky, Calgary's Bernard Callebaut chocolate, and pure Canadian maple syrup. However, this particular café is situated on the slopes of Japan's Mount Naeba Ski Resort.

The café opened in February 2007 and serves double duty as both funky mountainside hotspot and Whistler information and sales outlet. Ongoing video presentations, special events, contests, and promotions such as "Canadian Club Whisky Fridays" and "Canada Heli-Ski Night" are planned throughout the season to promote Whistler tourism and other Canadian ski products, and attract a new generation of wintertime visitors across the Pacific. The staff are all Japanese locals who have spent time at Whistler, and can answer anyone's questions about the experience. About 24 000 Japanese come to Whistler every winter, making up about 4.3 percent of the area's visitors. The Japanese have always had a presence at Whistler, but visits fell during Japan's economic downturn in the 1990s. Now that the yen is stronger, Whistler wants to lure some of it across the ocean.

"This is a tremendous opportunity to bring the genuine Whistler après-ski experience directly to hundreds of dedicated Japanese skiers and boarders every day," says Karen Goodwin, Director of Sales, Tourism Whistler. "We're seeing a trend in the Japanese travel market towards more repeat visits to Whistler, which is very exciting," she says. "In addition, we're finding that more Japanese visitors are booking their own trips directly through airline, hotel, and tourism websites rather than utilizing the more traditional methods of tour operators and travel agents. These two important factors led us to support the concept of more direct-to-consumer marketing in Japan.

SNAPSHOT *continued*

The idea is that visitors to the Whistler Café in Naeba will enjoy the unique Canadian vibe and get excited about the Whistler product and will want to experience the real thing and come to B.C."

The café is not Mount Naeba's first Whistler connection. Each year, the Japanese resort hosts the Canada Cup Big Air Ski Competition in partnership with Tourism Whistler, Japan's *Bravo Ski Magazine*, and the Canadian Tourism Commission. Since its inception five years ago, the Canada Cup has continued to grow in popularity for spectators, media, and competitive athletes and has quickly become one the

resort's busiest weekends. First prize for the competition is an opportunity to compete in Whistler's Telus World Ski and Snowboard Festival Big Air Competition. Sponsored by Tourism British Columbia, Canadian Tourism Commission, Tourism Whistler, Whistler Blackcomb, Air Canada, and Naeba Ski Resort, the Whistler Café is open daily from 11.30 a.m. until 11 p.m. throughout the resort's ski season, ending in April.

Sources: Andrews, M. (2007, February 24). A little bit of Whistler on Japan's Mt. Naeba, *Vancouver Sun*; Personal communication with Louise MacDougall, Tourism Whistler, March 2, 2007.

INTERMEDIARIES

intermediaries

channels of distribution that operate between the organization and the consumer

In marketing, **intermediaries** are channels of distribution that operate between the organization and the consumer, such as travel agents, tour operators, travel specialists, and the Internet. Through the use of intermediaries, an organization is able to expand the strength of its distribution network and to reach a much larger portion of its target market. As a result, the combined marketing efforts of the entire distribution network will lead to an increase in the number of customers using the product or service, thus boosting overall revenues.

Travel Agents

travel agents

intermediaries that sell travel products and services

Travel agents offer the tourism customer a variety of travel-related products and services, including transportation, tour packages, insurance services, and accommodation. They are the most widely used marketing intermediaries in the tourism and hospitality industry. In Canada, there are approximately 3000 full-service travel agencies registered with the International Air Transport Association (IATA), down from a high of 4100 in the late 1990s. Despite the drop, Canada has the highest number of agencies per capita of any country, the result of a small population being spread over a huge land mass. Some of the major travel agency chains include Marlin Travel, Uniglobe, Algonquin, Maritime Travel, Thomas Cook, and American Express. An agency usually earns a commission for each sale, the amount depending on the type of product sold. The modern tradition of holiday packages started with the Industrial Revolution and the railways in the United Kingdom. In July 1841, a Baptist cabinet maker named Thomas Cook booked a party of 500 on a train from Leicester to a temperance rally in Loughborough. The future travel agent negotiated a price that included entertainment in local private gardens.

Today, the travel agency market is very competitive. Barriers to entry are low and as a result there are many new entrants, which is especially true for the rapidly growing segment of online agents. Independent travel agents are under pressure not only from e-agents but also from direct selling by tour operators. They therefore seek to differentiate themselves and add value to the product in order to justify their role in the value chain and retain market share. Travel agencies perform four distinct functions that pertain to an organization's distribution system.

1. *Distribution and sales network.* Travel agents are a key player in the distribution and sale of an organization's product or service under an indirect distribution system. Travel agents essentially act as brokers that bring the buyers and sellers of travel products together. The agents have access to an extensive network of suppliers and customers and are able to help facilitate interaction between the two by identifying the particular needs of each group.
2. *Reservations and ticketing.* Making reservations and issuing tickets are two of the more traditional roles of travel agents. Through the use of a global distribution system (GDS) such as Galileo, Abacus, or Sabre, travel agents can book reservations in numerous locations throughout the world. However, with the arrival of ticketless travel systems in the 1990s, the role of travel agents in issuing tickets (particularly airline tickets) is diminishing.
3. *Information provision and travel counselling.* Travel agents have a wealth of information at their disposal. They possess an extensive knowledge of tourism destinations and are well equipped to offer advice to the inexperienced traveller. Whether a customer is looking for a quick flight across the country or planning a major expedition around the world, travel agents can provide valuable assistance in planning a trip.
4. *Design of individual itineraries.* The person-to-person nature of the travel agent business allows the travel agent to gain an in-depth understanding of customers' travel needs. By identifying what a customer's specific needs are, the agent can put together a personalized itinerary that best suits those needs. Travel agents can arrange trip components including transportation, accommodation, insurance, activities, and tours, all with the intent of satisfying the traveller's particular needs and expectations.

Despite the benefits that travel agents can provide to an organization's distribution system, the emergence of new and cheaper distribution tools such as the Internet has placed the future role of travel agents in doubt. For this reason, a large number of travel agencies are seeking new positioning strategies to maintain their foothold in the tourism market. In the last decade, most airline carriers have eliminated base commissions for travel agents, so many agents are charging service fees to customers. Agents used to earn up to 10 percent on all airline tickets sold and approximately one-third of agency business came from the sale of scheduled airline tickets. Apart from charging fees to customers, agencies are now looking at other ways to make up for the loss of airline commissions, including selling more package tours and cruises and focusing on selling their expertise.

While traditional agents have lost market share to online purchasing, expert advice from travel advisors is likely to remain a vital service in the tourism marketplace. Travel agents are especially valuable to marketers of luxury travel. Nearly three in ten (28 percent) affluent leisure travellers report using a travel agent to gather information or book a leisure trip in 2005. Among these travellers, the majority report using an agent to book a hotel or resort or an airline reservation. One third used the services of an agent to book a cruise, and a slightly lower percentage used an agent to book a vacation package or tour.[1] Despite the decline in their number, travel agencies will continue to provide a valuable service to consumers. The availability of travel information has exploded, yet that explosion has created complexity and confusion. Thus, although traditional agents have lost market share to online purchasing, expert advice from travel advisors is likely to remain a vital service in the tourism marketplace. The *Profile* on Millennium Sun Travel below reinforces this theory.

PROFILE

JEANNIE HENKE MILLENNIUM SUN TRAVEL

I began my home-based travel agency approximately 11 years ago. I was in a unique position of working for an airline but at the same time building relationships with retail travel agencies in the community. For the next two or three years, I worked as a sales representative making referrals to "A" list travel agencies and making a small commission. At that time most suppliers (tour operators) did not recognize agents working on their own through their home. I retained my employment with the airline working as a casual employee and while on maternity leave, and was able to earn an income and maintain industry experience. As my children entered school I was able to devote more time building up my home-based business and expanded my marketing to referrals only from family and friends to corporate connections. I prefer to only work on a referral basis.

These days, I work directly with most tour operators, car agencies, and hotels for full commission, whereas, if I worked through a retail agency, I would be splitting an agreed commission. I specialize in group travel; therefore my target markets are the corporate and the leisure traveller. The most likely client would be the corporate group traveller taking clients on incentive trips. I also arrange executive corporate retreats and other such groups such as sports or school groups. I have about five key corporate accounts that I service and allow their personnel to have after-hours access to me for travel-related work. As a small business and sole proprietor owner, I provide my clients with the extra customer service that a lot of them feel is missing on the retail end. As one client said, "I book on the Internet or with a chain, but I need a little 'TLC'." I also offer a small referral fee to any of my clients who may refer someone from their company as an incentive to do their personal bookings. As the demographics of my clientele have changed to include more individuals with a higher disposable income, the travel demands have changed accordingly. This group of travellers is more interested in cruises, unique destinations around the world, including charitable tours that allow the client to contribute back. On a corporate level, there is a tremendous switch from scheduled airline trips to small charter planes with an annual share guaranteeing a fixed number of flights per year.

Throughout the year I attend product launches and trade shows put on by tour operators, tourist boards, and consulates. These provide me with current information regarding particular destinations that I then market to my clients. My competitors are retail agencies, the Internet, and, in some cases, the tour operators themselves. With the increase of travel-friendly booking engines on the Internet, most people feel that they can manage their own travel arrangements, but they don't realize the depth of price structures,

PROFILE *continued*

classes of services, and insurance restrictions of booking on the Internet. Quite often, I will receive a telephone call requesting a second opinion on a booking made by a friend of a client either for verification that they have done the right thing or for insurance, tour operator, or airline reconciliation. Also, I do not charge the service fee that most retail agencies are now charging; and some clients have expressed that they feel intimated when walking into an agency and are not satisfied they are getting what they paid for. I don't have the quotas that some "chains" have to meet and I do offer discounts, which can at times be against retail policies. The Internet also has its problems such as clients not being able to change flights or speak to an actual human being when a problem arises with their tickets. My

clients have come to trust my travel skills and knowledge, and this in turn allows them free valuable time.

Since bigger is not always better, I am not acquiring any more accounts and I am just servicing my existing accounts in order to provide them with the quality of service to which they have become accustomed to. Since I only work on referral, when I manage to secure a key account, it causes a chain reaction: they refer me to several of their colleagues in their professional field, assuming that I must be good in order for them to use me exclusively as an agent. As a result, over the past five years I have increased my business revenue up to approximately $500 000.

Source: Personal communication with Jeannie Henke, Millennium Sun Travel, author of *Compass Companions: A Collection of Canadian Travel Stories*.

Tour Operators

tour operators

organizations that offer packaged vacation tours to the general public

Tour operators are travel intermediaries that offer packaged vacation tours to the general public. These packages can include everything from transportation, accommodation, and activities to entertainment, meals, and drinks. Tour operators typically focus their marketing efforts on the leisure market, which represents the dominant buying group of travel packages. Some of the larger tour operators in Canada include Conquest Tours, Sunwing Vacations, Signature Vacations (owned by First Choice, based in the United Kingdom), Air Canada Vacations, Transat Holidays, World of Vacations, and Sunquest/Alba and its parent company, MyTravel. Like the travel agency industry, tour operators are concentrated in Ontario, Quebec, and British Columbia. Montreal-based Transat Holidays, for example, controls a third of the package holiday business in Canada. Major tour operators bringing tourists into Canada from other countries include Tauck Tours, Westours, JTB, Kintetsu, and Thomas Cook.

The tour operating sector has become increasingly concentrated. In Europe, for example, about 70 percent of the market is currently held by the two largest companies after Europe's four leading tour operators consolidated to two in 2007, with mergers of Thomas Cook and MyTravel and of Tui and First Choice. In the 1990s these tour operators followed a strategy of vertical integration. By controlling the value chain from sales and packaging through to transportation and hotels, tour operators sought to strategically secure their market share and shore up low profit margins in their core business with more profitable activities in downstream areas of the value chain. But a slowing and changing tourism market has exposed the lack of flexibility in this model. The "de-packaging" of travel — with customers building their own trips piece by piece using the Internet — has struck a blow at the heart of traditional tour operator products.

Tour operators have the ability to bring in large volumes of customers. They receive discounted rates from the various service providers in exchange for providing a large number of guaranteed visitors. They make their profits by providing low-margin travel packages to a large number of consumers. Typically, organizations that offer travel packages must sell between 75 percent and 85 percent of the packages available in order to break even. The majority of tour operators distribute their travel packages through travel agencies. Each travel agency represents an average of four tour operators, and has traditionally been an important player in the distribution of tour operator products. However, tour operators are increasingly selling their packages direct to customers, cutting out the intermediary by using their own outlets or websites.

With the rising use of the Internet as a distribution mechanism, a large number of tour operators are choosing to restrict their offerings to only a selected number of specialized travel packages. Companies profiled in this book such as G.A.P Adventures in Toronto, CMH in Banff, and Atlantic Tours Gray Line in Halifax are tour operators specializing in offering unique tour packages to different markets. G.A.P Adventures has chosen to target young, adventurous individuals interested in purchasing travel packages to the developing world, while CMH focuses on offering up-market heli-skiing packages in Canadian Rockies. Atlantic Tours specializes in escorted sightseeing tours throughout the Canadian Atlantic provinces. By reducing the scope of their operations, these companies have managed to differentiate themselves as specialized tour operators in each of their respective areas, and have thus been able to focus their efforts on appealing to particular niche markets.

Convention/Meeting Planners and Corporate Travel Managers

Convention and meeting planners plan and coordinate their organizations' external meeting events. These planners work for associations, corporations, nonprofit organizations, government agencies, and educational institutions. Some combine the task of convention planning with that of corporate travel management, whereas other organizations split up the tasks. Some are also involved in the marketing of conventions and exhibitions. An example is Reed Exhibitions, one of the world's leading organizers of trade and consumer events. Every year the company runs more than 460 events in 38 countries, bringing together more than 90 000 suppliers and more than 5.5 million buyers. With 2300 employees in 33 offices around the globe Reed serves 52 industries worldwide. Reed says that the company is not just about organizing trade shows. Its role is that of a relationship broker — identifying, targeting, attracting, and matching the needs of buyers and suppliers.

In Canada, approximately 15 percent of visitors from the United States and overseas come for business purposes, and many for meetings and conventions. To capitalize on this, the Canadian Tourism Commission (CTC) has created the Meetings, Conventions, and Incentive Travel Program (MC&IT) to target meeting and incentive travel decision makers with an integrated approach that has two main strategies: relationship building and advertising. Existing relationships are strengthened and new ones developed through direct mail, business development, familiarization tours and site inspections, trade shows, and special events. Another example of an organization involved in marketing conventions and exhibitions is the Canadian Management & Incentive Group (CMG), which assists in all event, meeting, travel incentive, and group needs. CMG is the Canadian partner of Global Event Partners, which is a network of 55 affiliated partners — 20 within the United States and 35 in other countries. CMG has positioned itself as the "one-stop shop" for all travel programs, domestic or international. The company can assist in everything from sight-seeing tours and ground transportation to entertainment, event coordination, and team-building exercises. Spousal and children's programs are also available. On the incentive side, CMG can arrange for travel packages, reward evenings and dinners, spa weekends, gift certificates, and merchandise rewards. For special events, the company arranges pre- and post-convention packages, city tours, dinners, concerts, theatre packages, fashion shows, and art and museum tours. Additional services available for special events include security, catering, photography and design, and staging.

Travel Specialists

travel specialists

intermediaries that specialize in performing one or more functions of an organization's distribution system

Travel specialists are intermediaries that specialize in performing one or more functions of an organization's distribution system. Hotel representatives, for example, specialize in providing contact with a hotel's customers in order to identify their specific accommodation needs. Advertising agencies can also act as specialists, performing the promotional aspect of a company's distribution system. By using travel specialists in its distribution system, an organization can designate particular functions to the intermediaries that are best equipped to perform them. Focusing on one specific operation within the distribution channel allows the travel specialist to carry out the function at hand effectively.

Other examples of specialist intermediaries are tour brokers, motivational houses, and junket representatives. **Tour brokers** act as intermediaries between sellers and buyers of tours, often selling motorcoach tours, which are attractive to a variety of markets. Such tours are important to hotels en route as well as to the attractions that the tours visit. **Motivational houses** provide incentive travel, offered to employees or distributors as a reward for their efforts. Incentive trips usually involve staying in high-end accommodation in resort areas, but not necessarily in warm destinations: winter sports incentives are becoming increasingly popular in North America. Finally, **junket representatives** serve the casino industry as intermediaries for premium players. Junket reps maintain lists of gamblers who like to visit certain gaming areas such as Las Vegas, Reno, or Atlantic City, and they work for one or two casinos rather than the whole industry. Junket reps are paid a commission on the amount the casino earns from the players or, in some cases, on a per-player basis.

tour brokers

companies that act as intermediaries between sellers and buyers of tours

motivational houses

companies that provide incentive travel as a reward for employees' or distributors' efforts

junket representatives

companies that serve the casino industry as intermediaries for premium players

An example of a travel specialist is Travelcare Sports, part of the Co-operative Group in the UK. Travelcare Sports manages the travel requirements of football (soccer) clubs such as Manchester United — players, players' families, club staff, press, and supporters. Over 15 years, the company has arranged official travel packages for more than 100 000 fans. In 2003, for instance, Travelcare Sports was appointed as the official ground operator for the Champions League final held in Manchester, and booked more than 30 hotels across northwest England for UEFA officials, sponsors, and both sets of fans. Through the Travelcare Sports website, fans can book packages to see their favourite teams. In 2006, for example, it was possible to book a Dreambreak Manchester United package that included a match ticket, one night's accommodation, museum and stadium tour, match program, and discount vouchers for various merchandisers. For many fans, this would be the only way of obtaining tickets for a match.

Marketing in Action focuses on a Toronto-based travel and leisure company that focuses on designing short-term getaways that are sold via the Internet.

MARKETING IN ACTION

WEEKENDTRIPS.COM

Travellers are turning in increasing numbers to the Internet to help them plan and book their travel. A parallel trend is an increasing number of people lacking the time for frequent, extensive holidays. The amount of time they spend working has been increasing steadily since 1992, and fast-paced work environments that place intense demands on individuals are the norm today. For many, time is at a premium, and people are often too busy to dedicate the time, energy, and imagination necessary to arrange all the elements of a comprehensive weekend getaway.

Responding to these trends is weekendtrips .com, a Toronto-based travel and leisure company that focuses on designing short-term getaways and sells them via the Internet. Building on its network of partners in the travel, hospitality, and recreation industries, the company uses its resources to package and market weekend experiences. In Canada, the development and marketing of weekend getaways is led primarily by hotels and inns, small leisure activity operators, and tourist trade associations. For the most part, these operators act independently, often with limited marketing resources. While a number of informative resource guides were already available to consumers, until weekendtrips.com came along there was no company that offered a comprehensive selection of pre-arranged weekend experiences.

The company was founded by two friends, Francesco Contini and Marawan El-Asfahani, who were sitting in a Toronto restaurant commenting on how uneventful their weekend had been and, for that matter, how routine every weekend had become. Both agreed that their lives were so hectic that it was hard to find the time to plan something eventful for the weekend. So they created weekendtrips.com, and now El-Asfahani, who has an extensive background in the hospitality industry and is a co-founder of Oxygen Design + Communications, runs the company on his own.

Weekendtrips.com offers a diverse range of weekend programs: multi-day cultural getaways in vibrant urban centres, adventurous canoeing excursions along remote northern rivers, guided nature appreciation day trips for children at conservation areas, and more (see Table 7.1). The variety of travel packages suits singles, couples, and families — people of all ages, interests, and budgets. There is a package for gliding over Southern Ontario and one for a four-day culinary spree in Bologna, Italy. Other options include sailing in Ontario's Prince Edward County, cycling tours in Mennonite country, photography workshops, cave exploration, gardening seminars, and off-road motorcycling, to name just a few. "We

MARKETING IN ACTION *continued*

recognize that our clients are busy, so we want to make it as simple as possible for them to take off for the weekend. For instance, when we develop a trip, not only do we provide accommodation and travel arrangements, but we also take care of any necessary gear and equipment," says El-Asfahani.

Table 7.1

Examples of Packages Offered by Weekendtrips.com

DAY TRIPS	WEEKEND TRIPS
Good Earth Cooking — $135	One Starry Night in Elora — $95
Cave Exploration — $ 110	Wine Country Getaway — $299
Introduction to Ice Climbing — $160	Sail & Stay — $240
Zipline Extreme — $150	Retail Therapy Package — From $260
Interactive Dinner Party — From $75	Spontaneous Country Getaway — from $149 per person per night
Tea at the Royal York — $25	Castles & Towers Package — from $199 based on double occupancy
Wrangler's Day — $139	Weekend Culinary Retreat — $299
Cycle and Winery Tour — $89	The "New" Bachelorette Party — $375 per person with 4-6 guests
Superhero Rappelling — $110	Stay & Play At Blue Mountain — from $418
Sail Escapes! — $189	Georgian Bay Getaway — from $280

Source: Weekendtrips.com. (2007). Our trips. weekendtrips.com/ourtrips.php (accessed September 2007).

The advent of the Internet has brought many new opportunities, and by allowing weekendtrips.com to deliver frequently changing product information to a mass market in a cost-effective way, the Internet has dramatically increased the economic viability of the company's business model. Consumers can browse the weekendtrips.com website and select from a variety of offers that change weekly. Because it centralizes the fragmented resources and expertise of its partners, the website becomes a point of reference as a reliable source of ideas for the weekend. By simplifying the decision-making process, the company encourages weekend travel and leisure, thereby creating new market opportunities for weekendtrips.com and all its partners. At the beginning of 2007, the company had booked more than 4000 packages and had amassed a database of 36 000 customers.

Source: Personal interview with Marawan El-Asfahani, weekendtrips.com, May 5, 2007.

The Internet

Canadians are turning in increasing numbers to the Internet to help them plan and book their travel. Some stakeholders in the travel industry, such as airlines, car rental companies, and international hotel chains, have been quick to grasp the potential of marketing and selling their services online. They have recognized an opportunity to bypass intermediaries and to sell their basic products and services directly to the customer. Online hotel bookings in Canada, for example, have doubled in the last few years. Companies such as Delta Hotels have developed web-based booking tools for both leisure and group sales. Increasingly, package tour operators are including direct sales via the Internet in their sales strategy, thus bypassing the travel agent. These travel companies are adopting both organic (internal) and acquisitive growth strategies. Many traditional companies have developed their own websites and interactive divisions, while others are acquiring Internet companies.

However, some critics have suggested that the tourism industry has traditionally been relatively slow on the uptake of new information technologies (IT), particularly in the travel agency sector.[2] Many researchers have focused on the impact of the Internet on travel agents and on the role of electronic intermediaries in the travel business.[3] Since the Internet encourages direct and immediate contact between suppliers and customers, together with a decrease in transaction and commission costs, there is a strong case for the elimination of intermediaries entirely. However, the last decade has witnessed the emergence of electronic brokers, an electronic version of the traditional model, whose role is that of aggregating and disseminating travel information to customers. Examples are Travelocity and Expedia, which offer information and reservations for flights, hotels, and car rental.

In contrast to the commercial sector, DMOs have been slow to adopt IT in their operations. Most DMOs did not start considering electronic distribution until public awareness of the Internet increased in the mid-1990s, and a key concern that DMOs have had to face about web development has been whether to field inquiries themselves or pass them on through links to member websites. Only a few DMOs have designed and developed their Internet sites to enable customers to move quickly and easily from travel planning to reservations. An expanding amount of research focuses on the challenges faced by DMOs in keeping pace with the evolution of new technologies. One study conducted by the World Tourism Organization (UNWTO), evaluated the websites of 25 DMOs and found great variations in sophistication and quality.[4] One DMO that has made a concerted effort to attract customers via the web is NYT & Company, New York City's official tourism marketing organization. In an effort to become a one-stop resource for travellers seeking information on the U.S.'s largest city, NYT expanded its accommodations section to include an online hotel reservation system with instant access to more than 160 hotels. Users can access property details, as well as up-to-date information on pricing and special packages. They can also book rooms online. The site features a comprehensive calendar of events, suggested itineraries, travellers' tips, and maps of all five boroughs.

Figure 7.3 shows a model of online distribution applicable to many destinations and illustrates the various ways customers can reach individual websites. The model places the browser window directly below the customer because it can have an impact on the ultimate message delivery, usability, and pathway to the operator websites.

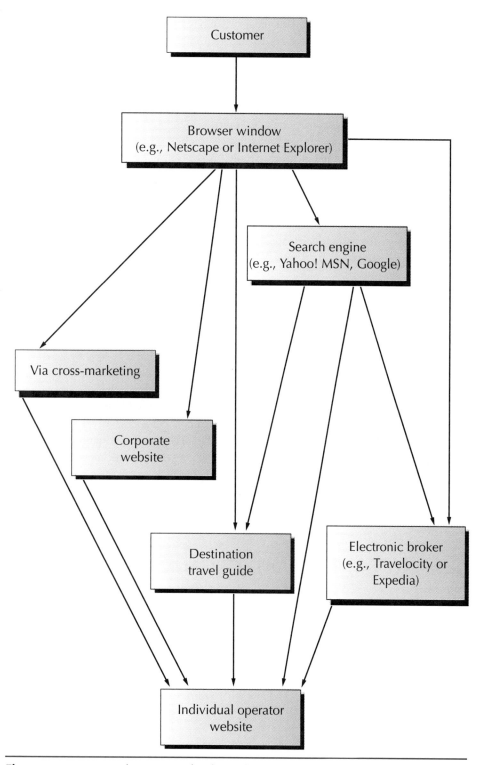

Figure 7.3 Intermediaries Involved in the Online Distribution of Destination Tourism Products and Services

The most common means of navigating through the online maze from customers to operator is typically for the customers to select the search engine or index service of their preference. For example, if they are looking for a hotel in the Banff area, they will type in, or funnel down through search categories to, something like "Banff Canada" or "Banff Canada hotels." Alternatively, they may go through an index structure by geography (North America, Canada, Alberta, Banff), by service type, or through a top-ical index that includes entries such as "travel," "accommodations," and "hotels." Another route they may take is to click on a link from a search engine to a destination travel guide or an electronic broker. These possible pathways are shown in Figure 7.3.

The diagram also indicates that some customers may book travel through a corporately managed website. These are sites operated by national companies, such as Howard Johnson, Sheraton, Marriott, Best Western, and Fairmont, that distribute hotel room reservations for the area via their corporate reservation systems. Customers may also book directly, through the various destination travel guides. An important part of the diagram in Figure 7.3 is the cross-link marketing, whereby complementary services supply each other with links to each other's websites. In this case, the user starts at a transportation website, for example, and then explores the links to a hotel and to an attraction, and ends up purchasing a hotel reser-vation and a sightseeing trip via the online systems on those other websites.

Obviously, individual operators would prefer to reach the customer directly, but the majority, especially the smaller operators, have to rely on electronic intermediaries to direct customers their way, in much the same way as they used to rely on travel agents. And while the Internet may be one of the most effective marketing channels for tourism companies, its costs are rising sharply. It is important, therefore, that operators keep track of the impact of websites on the bottom line. Michael Porter, a marketing strategy spe-cialist, has suggested that the Internet is not necessarily a blessing and that it tends to alter industry structures in ways that dampen overall profitability.[5] He predicts that many of the companies that succeed will be the ones that use the Internet to complement the traditional ways of competing. Porter says that to gain competitive advantage in such a climate, indi-vidual companies will have to set themselves apart from the pack: "As buyers' initial curiosity with the web wanes and subsidies end, companies offering products and services online will be forced to demonstrate that they provide real benefits."

CHANNEL CONFLICT AND ORGANIZATION

Channel Conflict

In order for organizations within a distribution channel to be successful, it is necessary that they cooperate. When every member in the value chain works together, the channel can combine its resources to perform in a more efficient and effective manner. The suc-cess of the entire channel will in turn benefit all of the individual members of that channel.

Unfortunately, many organizations in the tourism and hospitality industry tend to focus on their own, individual performance rather than on that of the entire chain. Thus a cooperative marketing system is often difficult to achieve, and a common occurrence is **channel conflict**, in which one member perceives another to be engaged in behaviour that prevents or hinders the first member from achieving its goals.

There are two main forms of channel conflict: horizontal conflict and vertical conflict. **Horizontal conflict** takes place between organizations at the same level of the distribution channel. An example is a conflict over territory between two Tim Horton's franchises. Due to the rapid growth of this company, it is common for two separate franchises to compete for the same market segment of customers. **Vertical conflict** occurs between organizations at different levels of the same channel, and it is more common. An example is the argument between travel agents and airlines over the latter's cutting of base commissions for the former. In the United Kingdom in the late 1990s, independent travel agents complained to the government about the practice of **directional selling**, which is a vertically integrated travel agent's sale, or attempted sale, of the foreign package holidays of its linked tour operator in preference to the holidays of other operators. The practice was facilitated by the lack of transparency of ownership links. It caused considerable conflict both among the large tour operators and between travel agents and tour operators.[6]

Conflicts may be caused by simple misunderstandings. For franchisees, for example, understanding the decisions made by the franchiser can sometimes be difficult. Dennis Murray, a Thrifty car rental franchisee, says, "It can be exceptionally challenging when a decision made by the franchiser seems undesirable to a franchisee's particular location, but it is better for the entire system in the end." Cooperating to achieve overall channel goals sometimes means giving up individual company goals. Although channel members depend on each other, they often act alone in their own short term best interests. They frequently disagree about the roles each should play or who should do what for which rewards. Such disagreements over goals and roles generate channel conflict.

Channel Organization

There are two main types of channel organization: the conventional marketing system and the vertical marketing system. The **conventional marketing system** has traditionally been adopted by organizations because the conventional hierarchical structure is consistent with the structure within individual organizations. It consists of a loose collection of independent organizations, each of which tries to maximize its own success (see Figure 7.4). For example, many small hotels pay a commission to travel agents, but no formal contract is signed between the hotel and the agent. The hotel simply communicates its policy and can, if it wishes, temporarily make rooms unavailable to travel agents. Although this system has worked in the past, trends of globalization and technological advancement have forced many tourism organizations to reorganize their distribution channel into a vertical marketing system in order to remain competitive.

---

channel conflict

conflict that occurs when one member of a distribution channel perceives another to be engaged in behaviour that prevents or hinders the first member from achieving its goals

horizontal conflict

conflict between organizations at the same level of the distribution channel

vertical conflict

conflict between organizations at different levels of the same distribution channel

directional selling

a vertically integrated travel agent's sale, or attempted sale, of the foreign package holidays of its linked tour operator in preference to the holidays of other operators

conventional marketing system

a distribution system that consists of a loose collection of independent organizations, each of which tries to maximize its own success

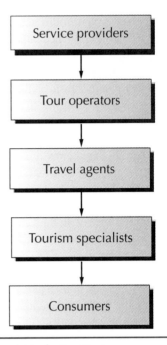

Figure 7.4   The Conventional Marketing System

vertical marketing system

a distribution system in which all members of the distribution channel work together as a unified whole

In the **vertical marketing system** all members of the distribution channel work together as a unified whole (see Figure 7.5). They become integrated vertically so that they can all work together to achieve a common goal. Usually, one member dominates the system and leads the entire channel toward its shared goal by reducing conflict within the system. This leader may be appointed either formally or informally. Formal leadership can

Figure 7.5   The Vertically Integrated Marketing System

be obtained through ownership control over the other members (e.g., Air Canada's ownership of Air Canada Vacations) or by forming contractual agreements with the other members in the channel (e.g., the Air Canada Vacations deal with Budget for specially priced car rentals). Informal control is usually given to the channel member with the most brand ownership or financial strength, or is simply designated on the basis of the role that the leader plays within the system.

The vertical marketing system has five main advantages over the conventional marketing system.

1. *It allows economies of scale.* The entire chain is able to produce goods or services less expensively than competitors can due to economies of scale (i.e., declines in unit costs of production as the volume of production increases), thus giving all channel members a competitive advantage.
2. *It makes managing conflict easier.* With just one member dominating the channel, the leader has the authority to punish those channel members that are creating conflict, as well as to implement solutions to resolve such situations.
3. *It eliminates duplication.* The vertical integration of the distribution channel allows all duplicated duties to be eliminated. This increases the efficiency of the chain.
4. *It levers bargaining power.* The vertical integration of the channel gives the system and its members more power to bargain than when channel members work individually.
5. *It creates shared goals.* The system allows for all the members of the channel to benefit from an achieved goal, rather than only one specific member benefiting.

There are two main forms of the vertical marketing system: alliances and franchises. Both carry with them advantages and disadvantages; which form an organization chooses depends on which one best matches that company's specific goals.

Alliances

alliance

partnership formed when organizations combine resources through a contractual agreement that allows them to overcome each other's weaknesses by benefiting from each another's strengths

An **alliance** is a partnership formed when two or more organizations combine resources through a contractual agreement that allows them to overcome each other's weaknesses by benefiting from each another's strengths. In this form of distribution channel, each organization shares everything from information to resources to strategies, but the key advantage to alliances is increased distribution. Those organizations joined through the alliance will enjoy access to new markets through new and diversified sales locations. Perhaps the most high-profile alliances in the tourism and hospitality industry are found in the airline sector. Star Alliance, of which Air Canada is a member, is the biggest airline network, with 17 members as of 2007. For passengers, the benefits of the alliances are faster check-in, shared airport lounges, and linked loyalty schemes. The member alliances are increasingly grouping together into single terminals at major hubs. Such benefits are most attractive to the frequent business travellers that all airlines are after. Those airlines that avoid the alliances are either fiercely protective of their brand, as is Virgin Atlantic, or keen to keep down costs, like the no-frills carriers.

Destinations and individual companies in the tourism industry also make alliances. For example, Tourism Vancouver joined together with Visa to create an alliance that would benefit both parties. The three-year marketing partnership was developed to promote both domestic and international travel to Vancouver, which in turn would increase the use of Visa cards. This alliance benefits not only Tourism Vancouver and Visa, but also the customer, who receives valuable package offerings. The *Snapshot* on South Africa's Game Reserves provides an in-depth analysis of marketing alliances. Another example is the Adventure Collection described at the end of this chapter in the *Case Study* on CMH, a group of nine adventure companies that have joined together. The alliance prints a collective brochure that is sent to guests of all nine companies, and the companies jointly promote each other's trips. They also combine itineraries to create new trips in order to give travellers more choices.

SNAPSHOT

MAKING ALLIANCES IN SOUTH AFRICA'S GAME RESERVES

The spirit of cooperation is thriving in South Africa's Greater Kruger National Park conservation area. Kruger, itself, has pulled down the fences on its lands, allowing animals freedom to roam in and out of the national park and the bordering private reserves. This open-fence policy even extends to its border with Mozambique where an ambitious multinational conservation program is opening up ancient wildlife trails, providing limitless grazing for large herds and thereby reducing devastation to vegetation in order to protect vital ecosystems.

At Motswari Game Reserve, one of six camps in the Timbavati Nature Reserve just west of Kruger, cooperative marketing is also the buzz word. The "White Lions of the Timbavati" made the area famous initially and Motswari was established in 1976 as a new, luxurious destination for tourists to view wildlife and witness the captive breeding program established there (*motswari* means to "keep and conserve"). The four-star operation has linked with its neighbours in a concerted marketing effort to attract international and domestic tourists. The range of accommodations at Timbavati are very varied, including a topnotch five-star lodge, where "dressing for dinner" is *de rigueur* and, at the other end of the scale, M'bali, a basic tented operation that offers safaris in the raw. Cooperation in marketing initiatives is also coupled with a collaborative approach to game spotting. All guides within the Timbavati area alert the others about animal sightings, kills, and activities, making their successes available to everyone.

The INDABA conference, held annually in Durban, is where Motswari marketers promote their lodge, safaris, and conference facilities. Over four days, the company entertains local agents as well as overseas clients, planting promotional "seeds" that often take up to a year to flourish in terms of bookings, according to Zalene, Motswari's reservations manager. She explains the cooperative marketing policy: "We market exclusivity for the whole area and cooperation with the other lodges. They all offer something intrinsically different, such as specialized packages including hot air ballooning or township visits." Manager Kathy Bergs confirms this marketing practice, saying that with such distinct offerings in terms of facilities and activities, the Timbavati lodges all

SNAPSHOT *continued*

recognized the validity of pooling their resources in order to compete with well-known safari rivals in the area.

Some of these competitors have become too "commodified," Bergs says, and have developed into larger hotel operations, taking away the original, exclusive feel of the safari. In response, Motswari is promoting its small size and one-to-one, attentive, personal service as its marketing differential. "Arrive as a visitor, leave as a friend" epitomizes Motswari's attitude toward personalized, high-quality service. Every member of the team, from housekeepers, cooks, to guides, spotters, and the management, welcomes and interacts with the guests, imbuing the luxurious but laid-back compound with a friendly, homey ambiance.

Via a website, newsletter, videos, and high-quality promotional written material, Motswari is targeting mainly northern Europe,

utilizing the intermediary services of Welcome Tours (based in South Africa), Kuoni (Switzerland), and African Pride (United Kingdom). Motswari is also trying to attract Australian tourists via the tour operator African Outpost. Domestic tourists make up the largest percentage of South Africa's tourists and Motswari is appealing to these short-haul tourists with its lower-cost fellow companies, which offer self-catering accommodations within the Timbavati, as well as shorter-stay safaris.

Sources: Personal interviews with Kathy Bergs, Frankie La Grange, and Zalene, at Motswari Game Reserve, February 17–18, 2006; Horner, S., & Swarbrooke, J. (2004). *International Cases in Tourism Management*. London: Elsevier, 198–211.

Franchises

franchise

a business established when it acquires the right to offer, sell, or distribute an organization's goods or services according to that organization's marketing format

A **franchise** is a business that is established when it acquires the right to offer, sell, or distribute an organization's goods or services according to that organization's marketing format. The *Spotlight* focuses on White Spot, a successful restaurant franchise in Canada. Franchising has become increasingly popular in tourism and hospitality, particularly in the hotel sector. Most investors in hotels today require some type of chain affiliation before they will consider becoming involved in a hotel project. They believe that the benefits of having an established brand image, a central reservations system, coordinated marketing, and a frequent traveller program are worth the cost of associating with a hotel chain. Hotel companies that have an established brand give independent lodging owners the right to use their brand logo, reservations system, and other programs by either granting a franchise or actually taking over the property's management through a management contract.

Globally, franchising has become the most popular method of obtaining brand identity because a franchise owner does not have to relinquish operational control. Normally the franchisee pays a fee to purchase a full-service franchise, as well as pays an annual percentage of sales. For example, in the car rental business, Thrifty Car Rental franchisees pay a monthly fee of 5 percent of their gross revenue from rental and parking activities, which helps pay for headquarters support and for select programs for franchises. There is also an advertising fee, but many services are provided to franchisees for free. Many people in the world of franchising claim that the relationship between franchiser and franchisee is one of the most important and challenging aspects of the hospitality and tourism business. Some of the advantages and disadvantages to both franchiser and franchisee are outlined below.

Franchiser Benefits

1. Increased distribution coverage, as franchises usually service markets nationally or globally — the main benefit, especially in this era of globalization.
2. Increased revenue through obtaining a percentage of the franchisees' sales.
3. Expansion of the brand, allowing access to new market segments.
4. Increased bargaining power with suppliers.
5. The creation of economies of scale in areas such as purchasing and advertising.

Franchiser Costs

1. Increased expenditure due to the need to monitor all franchisees' activities.
2. Limitation of the franchising organization's ability to expand other methods of distribution (such as alliances) due to territorial conflict.
3. Increased number of decision makers within the system leading to a higher likelihood of conflict.
4. Limitation of options for changing current operations because changes must occur throughout the entire franchise.

Franchisee Benefits

1. Reduced risk because of brand name recognition.
2. Methods of operation already decided, including everything from franchise layout and equipment to the entire marketing plan, reducing the amount of time and money to start the company.
3. Reduced costs due to economies of scale for aspects such as advertising and purchasing.
4. Free consulting on business issues.
5. Assistance with financing.

Franchisee Costs

1. Fees and royalties paid for benefits such as the use of brand name and advertising.
2. Limited decision making because franchiser does most of the planning.
3. Poor performance of one company affects every company in the franchise.

Some of the benefits that Thrifty Canada franchisees receive, for example, include world-wide consumer awareness of the brand name thanks to widespread advertising and access to frequency-based programs linked with internationally and nationally recognized airlines, hotels, and other organizations. Franchisees can receive help with purchasing cars, too, as car manufacturers will provide incentives for purchases when a company is part of a bigger system.

DESIGNING THE DISTRIBUTION SYSTEM

Tourism organizations must decide how to make their products or services available to their selected target market by choosing their distribution mix strategy. This can be a complex decision. They must select a mix that will provide them with the maximum amount of exposure to potential travellers as well as ensure that the strategy aligns with the company or destination image. In addition, the strategy should take full advantage of control over sales and reservations and should work within the organization's budget.

An organization can consider three broad choices of distribution strategies: intensive, exclusive, or selective.

intensive distribution strategy

a plan to maximize the exposure of products and services using all available outlets or intermediaries

exclusive distribution strategy

a plan to restrict the number of channels used to distribute products and service to customers

selective distribution strategy

a plan to use more than one but less than all of the possible channels to distribute products and services to customers

1. **Intensive distribution strategy**. In this case the organization maximizes the exposure of its travel services by distributing through all available outlets or intermediaries. This strategy is most useful for an organization that is trying to obtain high market coverage. An example of a Canadian tourism organization that uses this strategy is Air Canada.

2. **Exclusive distribution strategy**. Here the organization restricts the number of channels that it uses to distribute its products and services to its customers. Because only a limited number of intermediaries are given the right to distribute the product, the result is often a strengthening of the organization's image and an increase in the status of those who purchase the product or service. This strategy is an effective method for prestige tourism products and is used by companies such as Canadian Mountain Holidays, profiled at the end of this chapter.

3. **Selective distribution strategy**. In this strategy, between intensive and exclusive distribution, an organization uses more than one but less than all of the possible distribution channels. The Rocky Mountaineer, in the *Spotlight* in Chapter 9, employs selective distribution, using sales representation in 18 countries to sell more than a half a million tours each year.

Before an organization begins to design its distribution strategy, it is important that it consider the following five factors:

1. *Market coverage.* The amount of market coverage should be considered in coordination with the organization's goals and objectives, as this factor will directly affect the particular distribution mix that is best for it.

2. *Costs.* Only the most cost-effective distribution methods should be implemented, and they should make effective use of the organization's budget.

3. *Positioning and image.* The distribution strategy chosen should be consistent with the position and image that the organization wants to achieve and maintain.

4. *Motivation of intermediaries.* Intermediaries should be provided with appropriate incentives in order to motivate them to sell the product or service to consumers. The Quebec City Convention Bureau, for example, hosts about 700 tour operators and 400 meeting planners on customized itineraries each year. These trips provide an excellent promotional forum for giving intermediaries a first-hand appreciation of the facilities and services being offered.

5. *Characteristics of the tourism or hospitality organization.* Each organization has unique characteristics and needs that are specific to its operations. These needs must be considered when designing the distribution strategy. For example, if an organization operates in a manner that requires it to communicate directly with the consumer in order to be successful, then it must develop its distribution strategy to meet those needs.

The *Case Study* on Canadian Mountain Holidays at the end of the chapter shows how an exclusive distribution strategy worked well for the adventure tourism company. Cruise lines, too, have a carefully planned distribution strategy. These companies have traditionally used exclusive distribution, but are gradually moving toward selective distribution. Roughly 90 percent of cruises are sold through traditional travel agencies, and, in today's economy, suppliers are reluctant to jeopardize these firmly established, reliable relationships, despite the agency commissions involved. However, even though only 10 percent of cruises are predicted to be sold online by 2005, the Internet is now an important part of the equation, as many consumers will make their travel decisions online, even if they ultimately purchase offline. Cruise lines work with online travel agencies to sell discount and last-minute inventory, but they use their own websites for marketing purposes rather for than direct sales. Many companies don't even feature consumer booking engines on their sites.

DISTRIBUTION CHANNEL MANAGEMENT

channel management

the selection and motivation of individual channel members and evluation of their performance over time

Once the tourism organization has decided on its distribution mix strategy, it must implement and manage the chosen distribution channel. **Channel management** includes selecting and motivating individual channel members and evaluating their performance over time.

Selecting Channel Members

Tourism organizations must share information and work closely with the members of their distribution system. It is critical, therefore, that an organization selects the best-suited channel members in order to ensure an effective distribution system. When selecting channel members, the service provider should determine the characteristics that distinguish the most valuable marketing intermediaries from the others. Evaluation criteria may include such aspects as a channel member's number of years in business, the services and products it already carries, its past growth and financial history, its level of cooperativeness, and its reputation and image.

Motivating Channel Members

After an organization has selected its distribution channel members, it must continually motivate these members to perform their best. Three incentives are commonly used to motivate a company's intermediaries. The first one is financial, and includes commissions and bonuses. The second incentive often used in the tourism industry is the provision of educational trips for intermediary staff, during which they can experience the supplier's product for themselves. Such "familiarization trips" or "fam trips" are common in the travel agency sector. Another incentive, again quite common among travel agencies, is to provide intermediaries with reduced-price holidays. This type of incentive gives intermediaries greater knowledge of the product and enthusiasm for selling it to consumers.

Evaluating Channel Members

Tourism organizations must constantly monitor each channel member's performance in order to ensure the success of the channel as a whole. Performance can be measured through the generation of sales, customer delivery time, and the success of combined promotional efforts among intermediaries. Channel members that perform well should be recognized and rewarded, and assistance should be provided to those that are struggling to meet the organization's goals and objectives. The organization should also "re-qualify" its channel members periodically and replace the weaker members that harm the overall effectiveness of the distribution system. One reason that Best Western renew contracts annually is so that it can maintain control over the distribution channel. The company has also implemented a "quality assurance process," whereby a quality inspection team will use the same criteria to review every one of the member hotels around the world. In addition, the Best Western website gives customers the opportunity to provide online feedback regarding service quality.

CHAPTER SUMMARY

A company's distribution system is essential to delivering its product to the consumer. There are two different distribution channels that the service provider can pursue: direct or indirect channels. In a direct channel, an organization delivers its product or service to the consumer without the outside assistance of any intermediaries. In an indirect channel, the supplier makes use of several intermediaries in order to help distribute its product. These intermediaries are independent associations that are not under the organization's control, such as travel agents, tour operators, convention and meeting planners, travel specialists, and the Internet.

The conventional marketing system consists of a loose collection of organizations, each of which tries to maximize the benefits of the channel for its own best interests. However, under a vertical marketing system, organizations work together to achieve group objectives established by the channel as a whole, resulting in benefits for each independent party.

There are two main forms of vertical marketing systems: alliances and franchises. Alliances are partnerships formed when two or more organizations combine resources through a contractual agreement that allows them to overcome each other's weaknesses by benefiting from one another's strengths. Franchises are formed when a franchiser grants a franchisee the right to engage in offering, selling, or distributing the franchiser's goods or services under its marketing format.

When designing its distribution system, an organization can choose among three different types of strategy: an intensive distribution strategy, in which an organization maximizes the exposure of its products or services by distributing through all available outlets or intermediaries; an exclusive distribution strategy, in which an organization restricts the number of channels that it uses to distribute its product or service; and a selective distribution strategy, in which an organization uses more than one but less than all of the possible distribution channels. But before an organization begins to design its distribution strategy, it must consider the following five factors: market coverage, costs, positioning and image, motivation of intermediaries, and the characteristics of the tourism organization itself. In order for the organization to ensure the effective execution of its distribution strategy, it must select individual channel members, motivate these members, and monitor their performance over time.

KEY TERMS

alliance, p. 235
channel conflict, p. 233
channel management, p. 240
conventional marketing
   system, p. 233
direct distribution
   channel, p. 220
directional selling, p. 233
distribution channel, p. 220
distribution system, p. 218

exclusive distribution
   strategy, p. 239
franchise, p. 237
horizontal conflict, p. 233
indirect distribution
   channel, p. 221
intensive distribution
   strategy, p. 239
intermediaries, p. 222
junket representatives, p. 227

motivational houses, p. 227
selective distribution
   strategy, p. 239
tour brokers, p. 227
tour operators, p. 225
travel agents, p. 222
travel specialists, p. 227
vertical conflict, p. 233
vertical marketing system, p. 234

DISCUSSION QUESTIONS AND EXERCISES

1. How does the distribution system for the tourism and hospitality industry differ from that of other industries?

2. Explain the difference between the structure of a conventional marketing system and that of a vertical marketing system. Can you think of two tourism organizations that use these two different strategies?

3. Choose an organization within the tourism and hospitality industry of your country and explain how it uses its distribution strategy to attract customers to its product. Do you think that it is using the most effective distribution channel available? What do you recommend that the organization do to improve its distribution system?

4. Compare the different distribution strategies of two different tourism franchise organizations in your country. Which franchise do you think is more effective in distributing its product or service to consumers?

5. Give one example for each type of channel conflict that can arise in the distribution system of the tourism industry. How can these conflicts be resolved?

6. How would you evaluate the performance of a channel member as the manager of a large hotel franchise?

CASE STUDY

PROFITING FROM FUN: CANADIAN MOUNTAIN HOLIDAYS

Canadian Mountain Holidays (CMH), a helicopter tourism pioneer, was founded in 1965 and operates in 12 mountain areas of southeastern British Columbia. The Banff-based company has annual revenues of about $70 million and claims an 80 percent repeat-booking figure in the winter. CMH has the leasehold rights from the B.C. government to 15 765 square kilometres of remote territory in the Purcell, Cariboo, Selkirk, and Monashee mountain ranges. Boasting several times the number of heli-ski visits that its next competitor has, CMH has 21 helicopters and eight remote lodges — many accessible in winter only by helicopter. Lodges have been designed specifically to meet the needs of heli-tourists. Each lodge has a dining room and a fully stocked lounge, and each is equipped with a sauna and a Jacuzzi. There is even a resident qualified massage practitioner who can rejuvenate skiers' tired muscles. The company divides its business into three strands: heli-skiing, heli-hiking, and mountaineering.

According to director of corporate services Marty von Neudegg, "CMH is just a bunch of mountain guides taking people into the mountains to have fun, and the company philosophy reflects this attitude." But is having fun a good enough foundation for a successful business model? That was the principle that drove Hans Gmoser, the late founder of CMH. In 1965, after several years working as a mountain guide, he took a few friends up in a helicopter to go skiing in untracked powder. It didn't take long to catch on. "Demand literally exploded," he said, before his untimely death in 2006. "Suddenly there were no four- or five-hour walks and areas became so accessible. I was driven because I had such a good time myself, but it was infectious, and it rubbed off on the guests."

Since its inception, CMH has hosted more than 135 000 skier weeks. Each winter CMH sells 7000 holidays and keeps a waiting list of 3000. About 50 percent of customers are from the United

States and 40 percent are from Europe. A seven-day package costs about $6000 and includes 100 000 vertical feet of skiing and accommodation and food for seven nights. CMH invented heli-hiking (helicopter-assisted hiking) in 1978, and from June to September it runs excursions that depart from five mountain lodges. All-inclusive packages range from family adventures and photography workshops to alpine ecology. Stays can be at one or a combination of five lodges, and three-night heli-hiking packages cost approximately $2000. Helicopters transport guests to remote wilderness areas around B.C., where participants can decide from day to day whether they want to be mountaineers scaling steep ridges or to stroll leisurely along the glaciers and flower-filled meadows.

Marketing at CMH is unique. "We are often considered insular or aloof but we are deliberately unique. We don't want to follow traditional promotional or distribution paths — we position ourselves distinctly because we are distinct," says president Walter Bruns. The company's greatest marketing vehicle is "encouraged word of mouth" and CMH does very little advertising. Von Neudegg says that there are three marketing areas for the company: sales, advertising, and service. However, 90 percent of the marketing budget is spent on service, in order to encourage customer loyalty. CMH produces colourful brochures for each of its three activity strands (with winter brochures produced in six languages), expensive videos are made for all three products, and a website for each activity.

CMH also hosts marketing events called "An Evening with CMH" throughout North America, Europe, Japan, and Australia. These are invitation-only evenings at which CMH staff and guides entertain and provide information to past guests and their friends. These events are very successful, generating conversion rates in excess of 75 percent of all participants.

When CMH began marketing in Europe during the late 1960s and early 1970s, Europeans had no knowledge of Canadian heli-skiing opportunities. Rather than follow the normal route of mass media advertising, CMH chose to place no advertisements at all. Instead, the company found one person in each country to be the CMH agent, and this person had to know the product and its market intimately. These agents sold heli-skiing to one person at a time. This took place many years before the term "one-to-one marketing" had been coined. Although the distribution system has become more sophisticated over the years, these 12 agents still work in Europe and bring in 40 percent of the business. For the U.S. and Canadian markets, CMH employs its own travel agency, based in Banff. "The referral from a happy client to a new client is critical for CMH," says Bruns. "These relationships have evolved organically right from the beginning of the company — and our agents are seen as part of the family."

CMH is also part of the Adventure Collection, a group of nine adventure companies that joined together to form an alliance based on the principle that each company is deeply committed to the environment and culture through which it takes its guests. The alliance prints a collective brochure that is sent to guests of all nine companies, and the companies jointly promote each other's trips. They also combine itineraries to create new trips in order to give travellers more choices.

Although the company may not have changed much in culture over the years, the ownership structure has. Gmoser himself found the only way he could detach himself emotionally from the company was to sell it to Alpine Helicopters in 1995. Two years later, Intrawest of Vancouver purchased a 45 percent stake in Alpine, and in 2005 bought the remaining 55 percent. Involved in 15 mountain resorts in North America and Europe, Intrawest invests heavily in real estate developments and tourism infrastructure, adding retail, lodging, and restaurants to attract people to its resorts and keep them there.

Source: Personal interviews with Marty von Neudegg, Walter Bruns, and Hans Gmoser, Canadian Mountain Holidays, October 2005.

QUESTIONS

1. What particular distribution strategy is CMH following to sell its heli-skiing trips?
2. Should the company follow the same strategy for summer (heli-hiking) business?
3. Why is CMH able to distribute its heli-skiing holidays without using intermediaries such as travel agents or tour operators?
4. What are the advantages and disadvantages of relying on word of mouth to sell heli-skiing holidays?
5. What are the advantages and disadvantages to CMH's distribution channels as a consequence of being purchased by Intrawest?

WEBSITES

www.adventurecollection.com
The Adventure Collection

www.bestwestern.com
Best Western International

www.cmhski.com
Canadian Mountain Holidays

www.expedia.ca
Expedia.ca

www.iata.org
International Air Transport Association

www.thrifty.com
Thrifty Car Rental

www.travelocity.ca
Travelocity.ca

www.whitespot.ca
White Spot Restaurants

www.travelcareports.com
Travelcare Sports

www.reedexpo.com
Reed Exhibitions

www.tourismwhistler.com
Tourism Whistler

ENDNOTES

1. Travel agents: Do they still matter? (2006). *Travelweek, 34*(47), 1–2.
2. Christian, R. (2001). Developing an online access strategy: Issues facing small to medium-sized tourism and hospitality enterprises. *Journal of Vacation Marketing, 7*(2), 170–178.
3. Reinders, J., & Baker, M. (1998). The future for direct retailing of travel and tourism products: The influence of information technology. *Progress in Tourism and Hospitality Research, 4*, 1–15.
4. World Trade Organization Business Council. (1999). *Marketing tourism destinations online: Strategies for the information age.* Madrid: World Trade Organization.
5. Porter, M. E. (2001). Strategy and the Internet. *Harvard Business Review, 79*(3), 63–78.
6. Hudson, S., Snaith, T., Miller, G.A., & Hudson, P. (2001). Distribution channels in the travel industry: Using mystery shoppers to understand the influence of travel agency recommendations. *Journal of Travel Research, 40*(2), 148–154.

Marketing Communications: The Role of Advertising and Sales Promotions

Spotlight
"WHAT HAPPENS IN VEGAS STAYS IN VEGAS"

What happens here, stays here: Only Vegas
VisitLasVegas.com 1-877-VISIT-LV

The highly successful advertising campaign based around this slogan has succeeded in making Las Vegas one of the most powerful brands in the United States. The slogan, used extensively by Mayor Oscar Goodman, was coined by two advertising copywriters who were brainstorming for a new concept for Las Vegas in 2002. Jason Hoff and Jeff Candido have since developed a series of innovative television ads that do not dwell on the typical images of neon, showgirls, and gambling, but rather create an updated concept of Vegas as the place to realize your dreams, secret ambitions, and fantasies with no comeback.

Between 2001 and 2004 the two market researchers conducted a brand planning exercise. This involved qualitative research to understand consumer behaviour, including observational research and "tag-alongs" (following visitors around from the moment they arrive until the moment they leave). They used projection techniques, such as asking consumers questions like "If Las Vegas was an animal what would it be?"or "If Las Vegas was a person what type of person would it be?" (visitors often talked about themselves). They used other innovative research techniques such as asking people to write an obituary for Las Vegas. A sextant system was then used to segment guests. The sextant takes 40 000 people nationally, examines their psyches and behaviour, and neatly classifies them into 12 "tribes," such as Embittered Conservatives, Disaffected Escapists, and Gilded Gamesmen. It attributes 13 "glyphs"

— symbols that convey attitude or appearance such as "trendy," "shocking," "flirtatious," and "cool and hip" — to the tribes. Researchers then looked for one message that could resonate with the target tribes — one that had the Las Vegas brand personality: exciting, sexy, safely dangerous.

The resulting $69 million advertising campaign, launched by the Las Vegas Convention and Visitors Authority (LVCVA) to increase tourism in the famous casino city, resulted in visitor numbers increasing from 35 million in 2000 to a record-breaking 37 million by 2004. By 2005 there were 135 000 hotel rooms in Vegas, compared to 71 000 in 1955, and plans were being developed for an additional 155 000 rooms as well as 14 000 timeshare and condo hotel units in the near future. *USA Today* voted the television ads as most likeable ads in 2004. The sexually suggestive and humorous series of ads, appealing to both men and women and a variety of age groups, was aired during episodes of *Las Vegas* and *CSI*, both filmed in the city, heightening links between the advertising message and the product. The slogan's success was such that media outlets such as *The Tonight Show with Jay Leno*, *Saturday Night Live,* and *The Simpsons* exploited the concept, further increasing awareness for Las Vegas.

In alignment with the reimaging of Vegas via its food, shopping facilities, and entertainment, the ads drew attention to staying out late, spending more money, and eating well with none of the inhibitions or restraints of daily life at home. The website address is also provided at the end of each ad to facilitate access to more information and easy bookings.

Previous to the "Sin City" reimaging, some of the properties in Las Vegas had tried unsuccessfully to position themselves as family attractions, providing pirate and circus themed hotels, funfairs, rides, amusement and games arcades, animal attractions, and a dose of Disney at the MGM Grand. With the extra blow to visitor numbers provided by the fallout from September 11, marketers decided to recapture the original, raunchy glamour of Vegas, and the decadence of the past with a veritable explosion of topless shows and after hours clubs.

Sources: Banks, K. (2005, November). Vegas baby. *Westworld Alberta,* 49–55; Farhi, P. (2004, December 24). What Happens in Vegas Stays in Vegas. *Calgary Herald,* K4; Personal communication with Rob O'Keefe, R&R Partners, Las Vegas, 2006.

Objectives

On completion of this chapter, readers should understand:

- the role of promotion within marketing;

- the various marketing promotion tools used in tourism and hospitality;

- the communication process;

- the importance of integrated marketing communications;

- the stages involved in an integrated marketing communications campaign plan;

- the role of advertising in the promotional mix;

- sales promotion objectives and techniques used in tourism and hospitality; and

- types of joint promotions.

Chapter Overview

Effective communication with target customers is carried out by a variety of methods, referred to as "marketing communications." The *Spotlight* is an example of a highly successful advertising campaign, and this chapter focuses on the issue of advertising and sales promotions in tourism and hospitality. Chapter 8 begins with an introduction of the role and types of promotional tools used in tourism and hospitality. A section follows that focuses on the communication process. The chapter then discusses the rise of integrated marketing communications (IMC) as a result of the recognition that advertising can no longer be crafted and executed in isolation from other promotional mix elements. Consideration is then given to the communication techniques of advertising and sales promotion.

THE ROLE OF PROMOTION IN MARKETING

In many people's perception, marketing is promotion, for promotion is the highly visible, public face of marketing. However, promotion is only one element of the marketing mix, its role being to convince potential customers of the benefits of purchasing or using the products and services of a particular organization. Organizations use marketing communications — promotional tools used to communicate effectively with customers — for many reasons other than simply launching new products. They may, for example, be trying to encourage potential customers to try their product at the same time as encouraging their existing customers to purchase or use the same product again. Together with marketing, marketing communications dramatically increased in importance in the 1980s and 1990s, to the extent that effective, sustained communication with customers is now seen as critical to the success of any organization, whether in the private, public, or not-for-profit sector, from international airlines to tourism destinations and attractions.

MARKETING PROMOTION TOOLS

Promotions decisions will be determined by the overall marketing plan, as illustrated in Figure 8.1. Chapter 3 explains how marketing objectives are derived from the strategic tools of targeting and positioning. The marketing mix is then used to achieve these objectives, and promotions are just one part of this marketing mix.

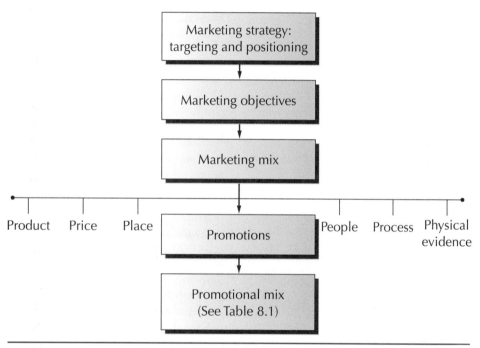

Figure 8.1   The Role of Promotions in the Marketing Strategy

promotional mix

an organization's total marketing communications program

The blend of promotional elements outlined in Table 8.1 is known as the **promotional mix**, the organization's total marketing communications program, which involves coordinating all the elements, setting objectives and budgets, designing programs, evaluating performance, and taking corrective action. Promotion can be a short-term activity, but considered at a strategic level it is a mid- and long-term investment aimed at building up a consistent and credible corporate or destination identity. Promotion, when used effectively, builds and creates an identity for the product or the organization. Brochures, advertisements, in-store merchandising, sales promotions, and so on, create the identity of the company in the mind of the consumer, and all aspects of the promotional effort should therefore project the same image to the consumer.

This chapter discusses the first two tools listed in Table 8.1 — advertising and sales promotion — and Chapters 9 and 10 discuss the remaining five promotional tools.

Table 8.1

The Promotional Mix Used in Tourism and Hospitality

PROMOTIONAL TOOL	TOURISM AND HOSPITALITY APPLICATION
Advertising	Television, newspapers, magazines, billboards, Internet, brochures, guidebooks.
Sales promotions	Short-term incentives to induce purchase. Aimed at salespeople, distributors such as travel agents, and consumers. Can be joint promotions. Include merchandising and familiarization trips.
Public relations	All non-paid media exposure appearing as editorial coverage. Includes sponsorship of events and causes.
Personal selling	Meetings and workshops for intermediaries; telephone contact and travel agents for consumers.
Word of mouth	Promotion by previous consumers to their social and professional contacts. Often perceived by consumers to be the most credible form of promotion.
Direct marketing	Direct mail, telemarketing, and travel exhibitions.
Internet marketing	Direct e-mail marketing, Internet advertising, customer service, and selling and market research.

marketing communications

communication via any and all of the marketing mix elements

It is worth clarifying that promotion management deals explicitly with the promotional mix. In contrast, **marketing communications** is an all-encompassing term (and activity) that includes communication via any and all of the marketing mix elements. How a product or service is packaged, priced, and distributed all communicates an image to a customer just as much as how it is promoted.

THE COMMUNICATION PROCESS

The communication process that takes place between the sender and receiver of a message is outlined in Figure 8.2. The diagram presents a scenario in which the message is prepared in a symbolic form by the sender (a cruise line, for example) for the prospective audience, perhaps as a visual representation. This process is referred to as "encoding." The message is then transmitted by way of a suitable medium such as a television advertising campaign. The receiver sees the message and decodes it; "decoding" is the method by which the message is filtered or internalized. The major concern of the sender at this stage is that the message is not distorted in the process by what is termed "noise." For example, a television advertisement promoting a cruise holiday that followed a news item referring to a cruise ship attacked by pirates (as happened off the coast of Africa in 2005) would fail to convey a convincing message. Likewise, the message might be distorted by "clutter," which means the audience may see an excessive number of commercial messages that just get in the way of the advertiser's intended message.

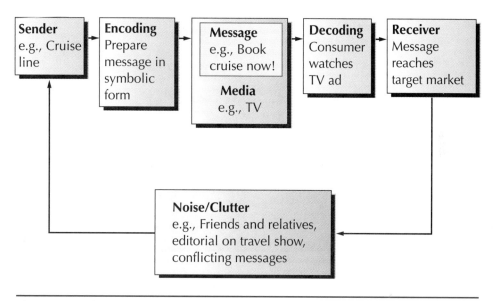

Figure 8.2 The Communication Process

How Communication Works

AIDA model

a checklist of the aims of advertising: attention, interest, desire, and action

There are a number of models that show how communication works, particularly in advertising. The models developed invariably assume that customers follow a number of predetermined stages, commencing with awareness and progressing to purchase. The most commonly cited model is that first proposed by Edward K. Strong, called the **AIDA model** (attention, interest, desire, and action).[1] The idea of this model is that communication should first attract the receiver's attention, then engage the receiver's interest, then create in the receiver a desire for the product or service, and then inspire action in the receiver. For example, in the print advertisement for Newfoundland and Labrador in Figure 8.3, the tail of a humpback whale with a giant iceberg in the background grabs the reader's attention. This visual image works with the print copy to gain the reader's interest and to provoke the desire to travel to that part of Canada. The website and 1-800 number are included in the ad to inspire action.

Figure 8.3   Print Advertisement for Newfoundland and Labrador

Though undoubtedly oversimplistic, the AIDA model is a memorable and useful checklist of the aims of advertising, and it provides a framework for other, more complex theories. All of the models of communication that have been developed are known as "hierarchies of effects models," as they assume a progression from one stage to the next (see Table 8.2).

All the hierarchies of effects models have as their basis the assumption that an effective advertisement makes the receiver think about the product or service, feel positively toward it, and do something to purchase it. Robert Lavidge and Gary Steiner label these the cognitive, affective, and conative stages of the response.[2] The cognitive stage involves the rational, conscious part of the brain; the affective stage involves the emotions; and the conative or motivation stage involves a resulting change in behaviour. Everett Rogers argues that the effect of advertising is to interest the consumer enough to evaluate the merits of the product or service and then to give it a trial before adopting it.[3] Simon Broadbent and Brian Jacobs go further, saying that it is often the trial and not the advertisement that convinces the customer to change an attitude toward a product or service.[4] Russell Colley presents the DAGMAR model (defining advertising goals for measured

Table 8.2

Hierarchies of Effects Models

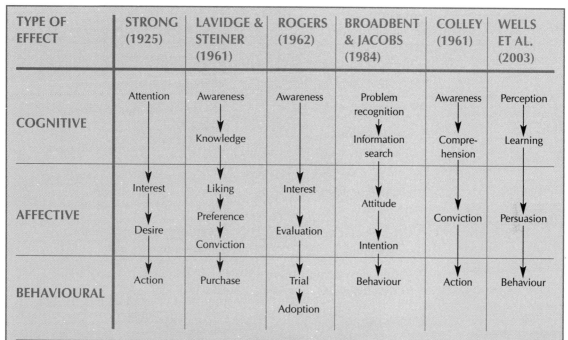

TYPE OF EFFECT	STRONG (1925)	LAVIDGE & STEINER (1961)	ROGERS (1962)	BROADBENT & JACOBS (1984)	COLLEY (1961)	WELLS ET AL. (2003)
COGNITIVE	Attention	Awareness ↓ Knowledge	Awareness	Problem recognition ↓ Information search	Awareness ↓ Comprehension	Perception ↓ Learning
AFFECTIVE	Interest ↓ Desire	Liking ↓ Preference ↓ Conviction	Interest ↓ Evaluation	Attitude ↓ Intention	Conviction	Persuasion
BEHAVIOURAL	Action	Purchase	Trial ↓ Adoption	Behaviour	Action	Behaviour

Sources: Strong, E. K. (1925). *The psychology of selling.* New York: McGraw-Hill; Lavidge, R. C., & Steiner, G. A. (1961, October). A model for predictive measurement of advertising effectiveness. *Journal of Marketing, 25*(6), 59–62; Rogers, E. M. (1962). *The diffusion of innovations.* New York: Free Press; Broadbent, S., & Jacobs, B. (1985). *Spending advertising money.* London: Business Books; Colley, R. H. (1961). *Defining advertising goals for measuring advertising results.* New York: Association of National Advertisers; Wells, W., Burnett, B., & Moriarty, S. (2003). *Advertising principles and practice.* Englewood Cliffs, NJ: Prentice Hall.

advertising results), which begins with awareness, moves to comprehension, then to conviction, and ends with action.[5] Finally, William Wells, John Burnett, and Sandra Moriarty suggest that there is a set of categories of typical effects that advertisers hope to achieve.[6] The first category is perception, which means the advertiser hopes the ad will be noticed and remembered. Then there are two categories of effects that are focused either on learning, which means the audience will understand the message and make the correct associations, or on persuasion, which means the advertiser hopes to create or change attitudes or touch emotions. The last major category of effects is behaviour: getting the audience to try or buy the product or perform some other action. These factors of message effectiveness are further illustrated in Table 8.3.

Table 8.3

Message Effectiveness Factors

KEY MESSAGE EFFECTS	SURROGATE MEASURES	COMMUNICATION TOOLS
Perception	Exposure	Advertising, public relations
	Attention	Advertising, sales promotion
	Interest	Advertising, sales promotion, public relations
	Memory: recognition/recall	Advertising, sales promotion, public relations
Learning	Understanding	Public relations, personal selling, direct marketing, advertising
	Image and association, brand links	Advertising, public relations, point-of-purchase ads
Persuasion	Attitudes: form or change Preference/intention	Public relations, personal selling, sales promotion
	Emotions and involvement	Advertising, public relations, personal selling
	Conviction: belief, commitment	Personal selling, direct marketing
Behaviour	Trial	Sales promotion, personal selling, direct marketing
	Purchase	Sales promotion, personal selling, direct marketing
	Repeat purchase, Use more	Sales promotion, personal selling, direct marketing

Source: Wells, W., Burnett, B., & Moriarty, S. M. (2003). *Advertising principles and practice*. Englewood Cliffs, N.J.: Prentice Hall, 9.

In the table, the key categories of message effects are listed down the left-hand side. The second column, surrogate measures, refers to the effects that advertisers seek to achieve and that they later use to evaluate how effective the advertisement was in achieving its objectives. The third column lists the communication tools that may be most appropriate for achieving the objective. The table illustrates that advertising is just one part of the communication mix, and that there are situations in which other communication tools may be more effective. For example, sales promotions are more effective in getting people to respond with a purchase or other types of actions.

THE GROWTH OF INTEGRATED MARKETING COMMUNICATIONS IN TOURISM

integrated marketing communications (IMC)

the unification of all marketing communications tools, as well as corporate and brand messages, so they send a consistent, persuasive message to target audiences

Perhaps one of the most important advances in marketing in recent decades has been the rise of **integrated marketing communications (IMC)** — the unification of all marketing communications tools, as well as corporate and brand messages, so they send a consistent, persuasive message to target audiences. This approach recognizes that advertising can no longer be crafted and executed in isolation from other promotional mix elements. As tourism markets and the media have grown more complex and fragmented, consumers find themselves in an ever more confusing marketing environment. Tourism marketers must address this situation by conveying a consistent, unified message in all their promotional activities. IMC programs coordinate all communication messages and sources of an organization. An IMC campaign includes traditional marketing communication tools, such as advertising or sales promotion, but recognizes that other areas of the marketing mix are also used in communications. Planning and managing these elements so they work together helps to build a consistent brand or company image.

Table 8.4 outlines an IMC campaign plan, and it can be seen that such a plan considers a variety of communications tools — not just advertising. The *Case Study* at the end of this chapter highlights how the Canadian Tourism Commission (CTC) used a number of promotional techniques to achieve campaign objectives. As well as traditional advertising techniques, the CTC used Smart cars wrapped in advertising, branded coffee sleeves, wrapped buses, and 3-D posters. *Marketing in Action* on Club 18-30 is another example of a company integrating different promotional tools as part of its marketing strategy. In 2004 Saatchi and Saatchi were given the task of eradicating sex and link from a United Kingdom tour operator's promotional material in order to change its image. Club 18-30, owned by Thomas Cook, sells overseas holidays to young British people but the company was looking to change its image. The new up-market, trendy image was disseminated online and via posters, magazines, and radio.

Table 8.4

An Integrated Marketing Communications Campaign Plan

STEPS IN THE CAMPAIGN	DETAILS
1. Situation analysis	Product and company research Consumer and stakeholder research Industry and market analysis Competitive analysis
2. SWOT (strengths, weaknesses, opportunities, and threats) analysis	Internal strengths and weaknesses External opportunities and threats Problem identification
3. Campaign strategy	Objectives Targeting Positioning
4. Communication strategy	Message development research The creative theme Tactics and executions
5. Media plan	Media mix Scheduling and timing
6. Other marketing communications activities	Sales promotion Direct marketing Public relations
7. Appropriation and budget	Based on the cost of reaching the target market
8. Campaign evaluation	Measure the effectiveness of stated objectives

MARKETING IN ACTION

CLUB 18-30 GROWING UP

In 2003, Thomas Cook had a crisis of confidence over its Club 18-30 brand, which sold overseas holidays to young people, due to dwindling bookings, bad press, and the daunting task of trying to reinvent the brand. However, by summer 2005 numbers were up

4. Message Strategy

concept testing

testing an idea with a group of target consumers to assess its consumer appeal

The message strategy (and the choice of what type of creative approach to use for the various stakeholder audiences) flows from an understanding of the key communication problems and objectives. The message, or creative strategy, outlines the impression the campaign intends to convey to the target audience. Variations on the creative approach are tested through **concept testing**, in which a simple statement of the idea (usually a sketch with a key phrase) is tried out on people who are representative of the target audience to get their reactions. The message strategy in a campaign includes this creative concept and its variations, known as executions, which carry the concept across different media, situations, stakeholder audiences, and times of year. Often an "umbrella" theme is used, as in the CTC's Keep Exploring campaign (see the *Case Study* at the end of the chapter). A strong umbrella theme not only holds the various ads in a campaign together but also creates synergy, meaning that the impact of the whole campaign is greater than the sum of the individual parts.

5. Media Plan

media mix

a combination of traditional media vehicles, nontraditional media, and marketing communication tools used to reach the target audiences

In the CTC campaign outlined at the end of this chapter, the media plan used TV, radio, brochures, newspapers, and other promotional vehicles to create awareness and motivate people to travel to Canada. All these media outlets are referred to as the **media mix**, the combination of traditional media vehicles (print, broadcast, etc.), nontraditional media (the Internet, cell phones, unexpected places such as the floors of stores or back of airline boarding passes), and marketing communication tools (public relations, direct marketing, and sales promotion) to reach the targeted audiences. If a product or service has an awareness problem, widespread mass media would probably increase the general level of awareness. If the problem is lack of trial, sales promotion may be the most important tool. If the product appeals to a very small market, then the Internet may be the best means of reaching that target audience. Media planners allocate media dollars to accomplish reach and frequency objectives. In a high-reach campaign, money is allocated to get the message to as many people as possible. In a high-frequency campaign, the money is allocated to fewer media, thus reaching fewer people, but message repetition increases.

6. Other Marketing Communications Activities

zero-based planning

the practice of analyzing the strengths and weaknesses of marketing communications tools to match them to the problem identified in the situation analysis

The concept of a communications mix in an IMC plan includes more than just traditional advertising media. In most cases, advertising campaigns are supported by other forms of marketing communications, such as sales promotion and public relations. An organization has to decide which IMC tool can best reach a mass audience (advertising), involve an audience (events), or build credibility and believability (public relations). This decision is made through **zero-based planning**, which is an analysis of the strengths and weaknesses of marketing communications tools to match them to the problem identified in the situation analysis, rather than just tweaking last year's plan.

7. The Appropriation and Budget

After developing the campaign plan, managers create a budget that estimates the costs of the various recommended campaign steps. If this budget exceeds the amount of funds available — the appropriation — either costs have to be reduced or the appropriation has to increase. Once the appropriation is set, the money can be allocated among the various communications activities. The budget size for communications has a tremendous range. A destination may have a communications budget of several million dollars, whereas a small attraction may only have a fraction of that to spend.

return-on-investment goals (or break-even analysis or payout planning)

the expected profit returns based on the costs of reaching a customer or group of customers

The budget should be based on the cost of reaching the target market rather than on the cost of certain kinds of marketing communication activities. Once the targets are identified, then it should be possible to quantify the value of the brand's customers and prospects, so that targets can be selected and prioritized based on what they are currently and potentially worth to the organization.[7] This makes it possible to set **return-on-investment goals** — that is, to calculate the expected profit returns based on the costs of reaching a customer or group of customers. This calculation is also called break-even analysis or payout planning.

8. Campaign Evaluation

The last stage in the development of a campaign plan consists of preparing a proposal on how the campaign will be evaluated. This important step determines whether the campaign effort was effective, and the key part of an evaluation is measuring an organization or brand's effectiveness against its stated objectives. However, advertisers need to consider many things, including whether the message reached the right people, the ads actually said what was intended, the ads achieved what was expected, consumer perceptions were changed, product sales increased, the media mix was effective, and if the campaign could be improved in the future. There are many evaluative research techniques available to marketers to measure effectiveness, and these are discussed later in this chapter.

PUSH AND PULL PROMOTIONAL STRATEGIES

One final factor to consider in the promotional strategy is the position of the organization in the distribution channel. For example, does a retailer (i.e., the travel agent or the venue) carry out its own promotion for the travel product, or does the producer (i.e., the tour operator or destination organization) have to promote the product in order to bring the public into the travel agency to buy it? This is known as the choice between push and pull promotional strategies. A **push strategy** uses the sales force and trade promotion to push the product or service through channels; the producer promotes it to wholesalers, the wholesalers promote to retailers, and the retailers promote to consumers. In contrast, a **pull strategy** spends a large amount on advertising and consumer promotion to build up demand; if successful, consumers will ask their retailers for the product or service, the retailers will ask the wholesalers, and the wholesalers will ask the producers. The two strategies are contrasted in Figure 8.4.

push strategy

a promotion strategy that uses the sales force and trade promotion to push the product or service through channels; the producer promotes to wholesalers, the wholesalers promote to retailers, and the retailers promote to consumers

PUSH Producer → Wholesaler → Retailer → End-user

PULL Producer ← Wholesaler ← Retailer ← End-user

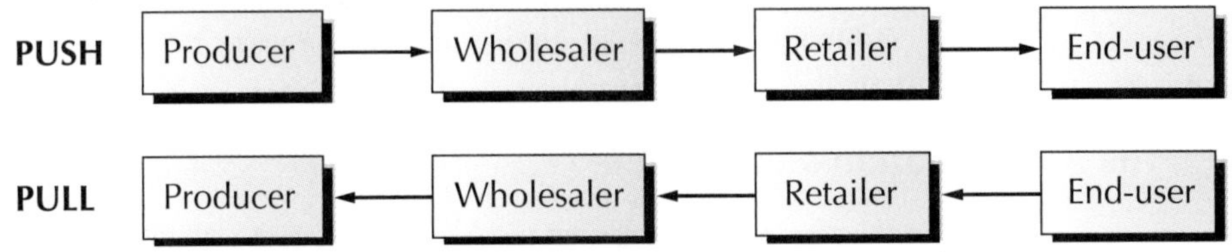

Figure 8.4 Push and Pull Promotional Strategies

pull strategy

a promotion strategy that spends a large amount on advertising and consumer promotion to build up demand so consumers will ask retailers for the product or service, the retailers will ask the wholesalers, and the wholesalers will ask the producers

The choice of strategy will depend on the degree of influence of each member of the distribution channel on the consumer's decision process and on the relative power of the producer's and the retailer's brand names. In most cases, a combination of the two strategies will be used, with each player in the channel marketing itself to the others and providing support for joint promotions. In 2005, Carnival Cruise Lines used a mix of pull and push strategies to entice consumers to purchase cruise vouchers as gifts. Capitalizing on recent consumer trends toward purchasing unique, experiential items as holiday gifts, Carnival launched an innovative IMC campaign to promote the concept of giving the line's "Fun Ship" vacations as holiday gifts. Created by Carnival's advertising agency, Cooper DDB, the multi-million dollar campaign debuted in October and included television commercials and consumer and trade print placements. The fully integrated campaign also included splash pages and banner ads on Carnival's website at carnival.com and point-of-purchase promotional items for gift shops on board the ships. A variety of other collateral materials tied to the campaign, including postcards, flyers, and e-cards, were created, and a virtual sales kit for travel agents was available on Carnival's travel agent Internet portal, bookccl.com.

The 30-second television commercial was an adaptation of Carnival's "Beyond the Sea" campaign, with the song modified to include sleigh bells and other traditional holiday musical accompaniments. It opens with images of shoppers carrying large boxes of foil-wrapped Fun Ships, recognizable by the cruise line's distinctive winged funnel, along a bustling Main Street during the holiday season. The commercial then cuts to a family window shopping; however, instead of traditional holiday gifts, a replica of a Carnival Fun Ship is shown behind the glass. The spot ends with the family driving away with the gift-wrapped Fun Ship tied atop their car, much like Christmas trees are transported home. The gift theme was also present in the consumer print campaign that included a shot of a foil-wrapped Carnival ship tied with a giant red ribbon and bow. Running across the top of the ad were the words "Give them a holiday to remember." Along the bottom of the ad, the copy reads: "How do you wrap togetherness? Can you put a bow on fun? It's easy when you give a Carnival Cruise. Nothing creates family togetherness and lasting memories like a Carnival vacation. It's a gift of fun everyone will treasure."

TOURISM ADVERTISING

Advertising has emerged as a key marketing tool in the tourism and hospitality industries. These industries require potential customers to base buying decisions upon mental images of product or service offerings, since they are not physically able to sample alternatives. As a result, advertising is a critical variable in the tourism marketing mix, and it covers a wide range of activities and agencies. Its role reflects that of promotion in general, which is to influence the attitudes and behaviour of audiences in three main ways: confirming and reinforcing, creating new patterns of behaviours, and changing attitudes and behaviour. Thus tourism and hospitality organizations use images to portray their products and services in brochures, posters, and media advertising. Destinations do the same, attempting to construct an image of a destination that will force it into the potential tourist's list of options, leading ultimately to a purchase decision. Whatever the tourism or hospitality product or service, its identity is the public face of how it is marketed, and the importance of advertising in tourism marketing should therefore not be underestimated.

Defining Advertising

advertising

any paid form of non-personal presentation and promotion of ideas, products, or services by an identified sponsor, using mass media to persuade or influence an audience

Advertising can be defined as paid non-personal presentation and promotion of ideas, products, or services by an identified sponsor, using mass media to persuade or influence an audience. This standard definition of advertising has six elements. First, advertising is a paid form of communication, although some forms of advertising, such as public service announcements, use donated space and time. Second, not only is the space paid for, but the sponsor is also identified. Third, most advertising tries to persuade or influence the consumer to do something, although in some cases the point of the message is simply to make consumers aware of the product or service or the organization. Fourth, the message is conveyed through many different kinds of mass media. Fifth, advertising reaches an audience of potential consumers. And sixth, because advertising is a form of mass communication, it is also non-personal.

Developing an Advertising Program

The process of developing an advertising program includes six important stages. These are illustrated in Figure 8.5 and discussed below.

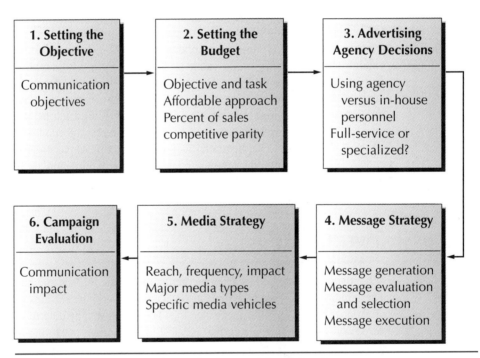

Figure 8.5   The Process of Developing an Advertising Program

1. Setting the Objectives

advertising objective

a specific communication task to be accomplished with a specific target audience during a specific period of time

In planning and managing advertising, a key factor is the setting of objectives. An **advertising objective** is a specific communication task to be accomplished with a specific target audience during a specific period of time. In general terms, advertising has four major tasks: informing, persuading, reminding, and selling. However, advertising in tourism and hospitality can have many uses. These might include creating awareness, informing about new products, expanding the market to new buyers, announcing a modification to a service, announcing a price change, making a special offer, selling directly, educating consumers, reminding consumers, challenging competition, reversing negative sales trends, pleasing intermediaries, recruiting staff, attracting investors, announcing trading results, influencing a destination image, creating a corporate image, soliciting customer information, improving employee morale, and contributing to cooperative or partnership advertising ventures.

In *Marketing in Action*, Club 18-30's advertising objective was to change the perception of the company and create a new up-market, trendy image. However, the *Snapshot* on Brazil in this chapter describes how the country's tourism industry used prevention ads to discourage unwanted behaviour — rather the opposite of normal behavioural responses sought through advertising.

2. Setting the Budget

Ideally, the advertising budget should be calculated on the basis of the objectives set in the first stage of the process. The media plan must reach sufficient numbers in the target market to produce the size of response that will achieve the sales target. Several methods can be used to set the advertising budget. The **objective-and-task method** involves developing the promotion budget by defining specific objectives, determining the tasks that must be performed to achieve these objectives, and estimating the costs of performing these tasks. Using this method requires considerable experience with response rates and media costs, as well as confidence in the accuracy of predictions. Cautious managers prefer to base the advertising budget on what they know from previous experience they can afford to spend. This **affordable method** sets the budget within the organization's existing available funds. The **percentage-of-sales method** involves setting the promotion budget at a certain percentage of current or forecasted sales or as a percentage of sales price. In the tourism and hospitality industry, the percentage of gross sales generally set aside for marketing is somewhere between 4 and 12 percent, with about a quarter of this amount allocated to advertising. The actual percentage will vary according to the position of the product or service in the its life cycle (see Chapter 5). For example, new products will require more advertising to launch them into the market. The budget size for communications can have a tremendous range. The Las Vegas Convention and Visitors Authority, for instance, spent $69 million on its "What Happens in Las Vegas Stays in Las Vegas" advertising campaign (see *Spotlight*), whereas the Calgary Zoo only had $35,000 to spend on the "No Substitute for the Zoo" campaign (see Figure 8.6).

Another way of setting the budget is the **competitive-parity method**, which sets the promotion budget at the level needed to match competitors's outlay. It may seem unwise to spend significantly less than competitors if an organization is aiming for a similar share of the same market. In markets with similar products, a high correlation usually exists between an organization's share of the market and its share of industry advertising.

3. Advertising Agency Decisions

Since advertising is usually considered the most important tool in the marketing communications mix, organizations must decide carefully whether they are going to do the work themselves or hire an outside agency. Only very small businesses, such as guesthouses or local visitor attractions, are likely to undertake their own advertising without professional help. At the very least, advertising agencies can help with the purchase of advertising

---

objective-and-task method

developing the promotion budget by defining specific objectives, determining the tasks that must be performed to achieve these objectives, and estimating the costs of performing these tasks

affordable method

setting the promotion budget within the organization's existing available funds

percentage-of-sales method

setting the promotion budget at a certain percentage of current or forecasted sales or as a percentage of price

competitive-parity method

setting the ppromotion budget to match competitors' outlay

space at discounted rates. The best advertising agencies create value for their clients, as seen in *Profile* on Tim Hortons. An agency can clearly interpret what the end user wants and then communicate information about its client's product or service so meaningfully, so effectively, and so consistently that customers reward that product or service with their loyalty. An agency can add perceived value to the client's product or service by giving it a personality, by communicating in a manner that shapes basic understanding of it, by creating an image or memorable picture of it, and by setting it apart from its competitors.

There are two main types of advertising agency: the full-service agency and the specialized agency. A **full-service agency** provides the four major functions: account management, creative services, media planning and buying, and account planning (which is also known as research). It will also often have its own accounting department, a traffic department to handle internal tracking on completion of projects, a department for broadcast and print production, and a human resources department. However, tourism and hospitality organizations often use the services of a **specialized agency**. This type of agency will focus on certain functions (e.g., writing copy, producing art, media buying), audiences (e.g., minority, youth), or industries (e.g., health care, computers, leisure), or on certain marketing communication areas, such as direct marketing, sales promotion, public relations, events and sports marketing, and packaging and point-of-sale.

full-service agency

an advertising agency that provides the four major functions: account management, creative services, media planning and buying, and account planning

specialized agency

an advertising agency that specializes in certain functions, audiences, or industries

PROFILE

TIM HORTONS PROVES THAT ADVERTISING DOESN'T HAVE TO BE FLASHY OR CONTROVERSIAL TO SELL

So there you are, a Canadian student, confined by the cold, clammy stone walls of Glasgow, away from the warmth and civilization of Canada. What are you going to do to bring a touch of home to these bleak environs? Perhaps a cup of Tim Hortons coffee would help. In this Tim Hortons television advertising campaign, a group of poor Canadian students at the University of Glasgow forced to survive on haggis and bannock appeal to Tim Hortons for help and receive a care package of coffee to keep their

spirits up. The campaign was based on a true human insight: it is nice to have the comforts of home when you can't be at home. The Tim Hortons product fits nicely into this insight.

The ads, part of the well-known "True Stories" campaign, were well received by critics. "It celebrates the incredible fact that a doughnut chain named after a hockey player has become a Canadian cultural icon. Tim Hortons has truly reached icon status as a Canadian brand, a positioning most clients would kill for," says Michael Clancy, director

PROFILE *continued*

of strategic and creative planning for Brandworks International. "The casting is especially good: real, earnest, Canadian, believable. And the mini-travelogue of Scotland is superb. The footage is beautiful and the sound of skirling pipes completes the effect."

Barry Campbell, senior creative director for Allard-Johnson Communications, is just as complimentary. "The staff of the agency must have thoroughly enjoyed working on this piece of business because of the partnership they enjoy with Tim Hortons," he says. "The agency clearly understands their customer and the business they are in. If it didn't, the agency could never have produced a spot that relies so heavily on credibility. We encounter testimonials every day but most of them roll by into obscurity even if we do believe their claims. This one entertains and informs after repeated viewings." The company's low-key approach reflects the fundamental brand character of Tim Hortons, which the marketing team sums up in one word: unpretentious. "In a way it is really how you would describe a Canadian," says Cathy Whelan Molloy, vice-president of brand marketing and merchandising. "We talk about it being unpretentious, friendly, honesty, caring, and dependable."

Enterprise Creative Selling, the Toronto-based agency behind the ads for Tim Hortons, may be one of the most influential advertising agencies in Canada, at least judging by the millions of Canadians who dutifully line up to purchase whatever product it features in its ads — whether it is coffee cake, bagels, or iced cappuccino. Although its commercials almost never win advertising industry awards, it has helped Tim Hortons achieve iconic status, proving that advertising doesn't have to be flashy or controversial to work. "We'd love to win an award or two," says Alison Simpson, general manager of the 43-staff agency, "but it is not our driving force. We define great creative [advertising] by the results it delivers."

Tim Hortons seems to be convinced. The doughnut chain has stuck with Enterprise for more than 14 years, an unusually long time in an industry in which clients and agencies are forever playing musical chairs. "Enterprise's advertising is not the only reason why we are where we are, but it has certainly helped us," said Bill Moir, executive vice-president of marketing for Tim Hortons. One of the biggest challenges for Enterprise has been trying to keep up with Tim Hortons' growth. The chain's sales have climbed steadily reaching nearly $1.5 billion in 2006. By mid-2007, there were 2733 outlets in Canada, and 345 outlets in the United States. This has put pressure on Enterprise to produce more ads to sustain Tim Hortons' double-digit growth.

The ads, like the products they promote, don't try to be overly sophisticated. That would alienate Tim Hortons' core customer. But the commercials are not afraid to be goofy or contrived. Sentimental music and sweeping shots of Scottish countryside with an emotional story of a Canadian who misses Canada — all of this works to sell an average cup of coffee. The ads are also simple, don't take themselves too seriously and, above all, focus on the product. Says Ken Wong, professor of marketing at Queen's University, "Their advertising in general is not brilliant, but it is disciplined. Essentially the agency is saying 'We don't care if we win creative awards. All we care about is what works for the client.'"

Sources: Heinzl, J. (2002, March 15). Enterprise finds that hokey sells. *Globe & Mail*, B7; Tim Hortons in Scotland mood piece stands up after repeated viewings. (2003, February 10). *Financial Post*, 12; Harris, R. (2005, February 7). Down-home smarts. *Marketing*. www.marketingmag.ca/magazine/current/marketer_year/article.jsp?content=20050207_66405_66405 (retrieved September 2007).

4. Message Strategy

The message strategy is the fourth stage in the process of developing an advertising program. Studies have shown that creative advertising messages can be more important than the number of dollars spent on the message. Creative strategy plays an increasingly important role in advertising success. Developing a creative strategy requires three message steps: generation, evaluation and selection, and execution.

Providers of tourism and hospitality products face an inherent barrier to effective communication with their customers: the intangibility of the product. A hotel or airline flight is experienced only at or after the time of purchase. This characteristic of services in general poses genuine challenges for message *generation*. Advertisers need to make tangible an intangible product, using emotion and experience. An example of a very creative and successful print ad produced on a low budget is the dog and sock ad for the Calgary Zoo (see Figure 8.6). It was developed through the zoo's advertising agency (Parallel Strategies, which is now Trigger Communications). Strategically, the zoo wanted something that would convey a very simple message but have a strong, funny visual that would appeal to both young and old and would work in all mediums. The budget was low at only $35 000 for the entire campaign, including creative design, fees, production, photography, and media buys. However, the campaign was so successful the zoo continued the campaign for another three years and now has 17 "No Substitute for the Zoo" ad executions. The campaign has won several awards, including the Trans-Canada Agency Network Award for Best in Show (2003), the Extra Award of Merit (Certificate of Excellence) in 2004, the Ad Rodeo Anvil 2004, and the International Association of Amusement Parks and Attractions Brass Ring for Best Outdoor and Best of Show for same in 2004.

Figure 8.6   Calgary Zoo Dog and Sock Ad

Although advertisers may create many possible messages, only a few will be used in the campaign, and the second step in developing a creative strategy — *evaluation and selection* — will determine the final message to be used. According to Philip Kotler, John Bowen, and James Makens, the advertiser must evaluate possible ads on the basis of three characteristics.[8] First, messages should be meaningful and should point out benefits that make the product or service more desirable or interesting to consumers. Second, messages should be distinctive. They should tell the consumer how the product or service is better than competing brands. Finally, messages must be believable. This goal is difficult to achieve, as many consumers doubt the truth of advertising.

In the third step of developing a creative strategy, *execution*, the creative staff must find a style, tone, words, and format for executing the message. Any message can be presented in a variety of execution styles. The following styles are commonly used in tourism and hospitality:

1. *Slice of life.* This style shows people in a normal 'real life' setting.. Most of Tim Horton's ads are "slice of life" ads (see *Profile*).
2. *Fantasy.* This style creates a wonder world around the product or service or its use. The human psyche is receptive to fantasy, and companies such as Disney have capitalized on this type of advertising, which is effective in an industry that appeals to one's desire to escape.
3. *Mood or image.* This style builds a mood or image around the product or service, such as beauty, love, or serenity. Destination marketers often attempt to create an emotional relationship between the destination and potential visitors. In this type of advertising, branding activities concentrate on communicating the essence or the spirit of a destination via a few key attributes and associations. The print ad for Newfoundland and Labrador in Figure 8.3 is an example of this style.
4. *Lifestyle.* This style shows how a product fits with a lifestyle. For example, British Airways, advertising its business class, featured a businessman sitting in an upholstered chair in the living room, having a drink, and enjoying the paper. The other side of the ad featured the same person in the same relaxed position with a drink and a paper in one of the airline's business class seats.
5. *Musical.* This style shows one or more people or cartoon characters singing a song about a product. Almost 30 years ago, Coca-Cola wanted to "teach the world to sing in perfect harmony," and the pattern was set for an important ingredient in successful advertising: the use of music. Airlines have used music to good effect. Delta Airlines used music effectively in its "We Love to Fly" campaign, as did British Airways in its "World Images" campaign. The association that various destinations have with music is often used in advertising campaigns. For instance, the haunting strains of Irish music are the background sounds in an ad for Ireland.
6. *Testimonial evidence.* In this style, celebrities, created characters (McDonald's Ronald McDonald, for example), experts, or people "just like us" whose advice one might seek out speak on behalf of the product or service to build credibility. An example is a print ad that appeared extensively in travel magazines in 2006 for Samsonite luggage, in which Richard Branson, chair of Virgin, endorses the products (see Figure 8.7). In 2005 Elton John appeared on 20 AirTran jets in a move to promote the Florida-based airline's launch of satellite radio at each passenger seat. In return the singer was given a $50 000 check for the Elton John AIDS Foundation.

Figure 8.7   Ad for Samsonite with Richard Branson

7. *Technical expertise.* In this style of advertisement, the organization shows its expertise
with the product. Hotels, for example, may use this style in advertising directed
toward meeting and convention planners, to show that they have the technical qualities to support the meeting planner. Airlines also sometimes make use of expertise to
reassure the consumer about the technical qualities of their pilots and mechanics.

ADVERTISING TO TOURISTS YOU DON'T WANT: SEX TOURISM IN BRAZIL

Most marketing programs are directed toward sales or positive actions of some kind. Prevention ads, however, discourage unwanted behaviour so are rather the opposite of normal behavioural responses sought through advertising. Deterring action or behaviour is a complicated process that involves counter-arguing by presenting negative messages about an unwanted behaviour and creating the proper incentives to stimulate the desired behaviour. Over the last few years, the Brazilian government has been using prevention ads to deter sex tourists from visiting the country. After the 2004 tsunami in the Indian Ocean, Brazil unwillingly replaced Thailand as the number-one destination for sex tourism. In response, Embratur, the agency responsible for marketing Brazil abroad, and the Brazil Ministry of Tourism, worked together to develop marketing programs to deter sex tourism. Tactics included ads that were shown on television in Brazil as well as on certain airlines within the country. An example is a television ad that begins with the usual pictures of beautiful beaches and spectacular Brazilian icons such as the Amazon and Iguassu Falls. However, the closing shot is of the rear view of a little girl, swinging happily in a playground, while the narrator talks about the prison sentences for child sex abuse. The ads brought to the forefront the campaign to eradicate sexual abuses of children and adults, which was inaugurated during carnival season in March 2005 to create maximum impact.

Print ads were also used in the campaign, placed in selected magazines and newspapers throughout Brazil. They were also distributed through travel operators and federal police officials at Brazilian air and sea ports. With an emphasis on improving the international image, postcards of scantily dressed women were banned, with retailers reporting that sales were not affected as tourists continued to buy more scenic postcards instead. In a press statement, tourism secretary Sergio Ricardo Almeida said: "Postcards that exploit photos of women in skimpy wear suggest sex tourism, a practice that stigmatizes us with undignified labels." Traditionally, Brazil has sold millions of such postcards, usually of women baring their almost naked buttocks in tiny bikinis. The World Tourism Organization (UNWTO) was also involved in this collaborative project, and details of the campaign were easily accessible on the UNWTO website.

In a country where the minimum wage is $155 per month and millions live under the poverty line, particularly in the rural areas, sex tourism is a growing concern. Uneducated and poverty-stricken parents in the Amazon region and northwest Brazil are even selling children into the trade via well-established child-trafficking routes. Both sexes are exploited, although the vast majority is female. According to the Brazil's Centre of Reference Studies on Children and Adolescents (CECRIA), the country was one of the major exporters of women for prostitution in the world in 2005, with around 70 000 15 to 25-year-old women being sent abroad annually via 131 trafficking routes to other South American countries. There are also travel services available internationally to organize child sex tourism to Brazil. In Italy in 2004 authorities arrested four people in a crackdown on travel agents engaged in

SNAPSHOT *continued*

Play your part.

TOGETHER AGAINST CHILDREN SEXUAL EXPLOITATION.

Brazil. Who loves protects.

Secretaria Especial dos Direitos Humanos   Ministério do Turismo

Figure 8.8   Brazilian Sex Tourism Prevention Ad

selling sex tourism to Brazil. They were allegedly sending tourists to bars, discos, and hotels in Fortaleza, where child prostitution was practised.

Sources: Vincent, I. (2005, December 12). No More Itsy-Bitsy. *Maclean's, 118*(50), 30; Finger, C. (2003). Brazil pledges to eliminate sexual exploitation of children. *Lancet, 361*(9364), 1196; Chesshyre, T. (2004, December 18). Sex tourism crackdown. *Times*, Travel, 2.

5. Media Strategy

The media plan section in an advertising plan includes media objectives (reach and frequency), media strategies (targeting, continuity, and timing), media selection (the specific vehicles), geographic strategies, schedules, and the media budget. The range of advertising media available to today's advertiser is increasingly bewildering and is becoming ever more fragmented. While these changes offer the prospect of greater targeting, they also make the job of the media planner more difficult. Table 8.5 provides a reference guide to the range of the main advertising media and lists their major advantages and disadvantages. In the Carnival Cruise campaign referred to earlier, the media plan included using TV, radio, newspapers, trade magazines, and other promotional vehicles to stimulate people to purchase cruise holiday gift vouchers.

Table 8.5

The Advantages and Disadvantages of the Major Advertising Media

MEDIA TYPE	ADVANTAGES	DISADVANTAGES
Print Media		
Local press	High market coverage Short lead time Easily laid out Frequency/immediacy Relatively inexpensive Allows for repetition of ads Creates local image	Audience reads selectively Short life span Low attention Media clutter Poor reproduction quality
National press	Large circulation Many creative options for layout Appeals to all income levels Relatively cheap for national coverage Frequency allows repetition Allows audience/geographical selectivity	Audience read selectivel Short life span Poor reproduction Low attention Clutter
Consumer magazines	Large circulation High pass on readership High-quality reproduction and colour Relatively long life and read in leisurely fashion Well-segmented audience High information content Allows sales promotion inserts	Expensive Distant copy dates Clutter
Specialist trade journals	Well-segmented audience Short lead times Potential for high information content ads	Clutter Competitors' ads may be featured

TABLE 8.5 *continued*

MEDIA TYPE	ADVANTAGES	DISADVANTAGES
Print Media continued		
Circulars	Low production and distribution costs Blanket coverage in target areas	Poor image Distribution abuse Short attention span
Inserts in free press and magazines	Relatively inexpensive Good for direct response ads	Short life span May be seen as having a poor image
Posters	Cheap Target specific areas/groups Longevity (especially on public transport — buses, etc.)	Short exposure tim Poor image Clutter Audience segmentation difficult
Broadcast Media		

Television	Opportunity for high creativity and
	    impact (sound, visual, etc.)
	Good for image
	Appeals to all income levels
	Relatively cheap for national coverage
	Frequency allows repetition
	Allows audience/geographical selectivity
	High attention gaining
		Relatively high production and
		    airtime cost
		Short life span
		Clutter
		Fleeting attention

Commercial radio	Large localized audience Gains local recognition Flexible deadlines Well-segmented audience Allows repeat messages	Production can be expensive Allows audio message only Clutter Short life span Fleeting message Low attention; high audience distraction

Cinema	Possibility to segment audience or
	    mass market
	Allows frequent exposure
	Potential for high creative impact of
	    colour and visuals — large screen
	    and sound
		Relatively high production and
		    airtime costs
		Competitors' ads may be featured
		Fleeting message
		Difficult to establish audience profile

Out of Home		
Billboards	High impact Low cost and large readership Longevity Ability to create awareness	Brief exposure Limited message — unsuitable for complex ads Needs large-scale distribution Creativity needed for impact

MEDIA TYPE	ADVANTAGES	DISADVANTAGES
Out of Home continued		
Transit	Can be targeted to specific audiences with high frequency Allows for creativity Can provide detailed information at a low cost	Brief exposure Image factors
Other Media		
Direct mail	Allows tracking Prepared mailing lists Allows audience/geographical selectivity High information content	Relatively high production costs of creating and maintaining databases Potential for poor image
Exhibitions/ trade fairs and shows	Large target audience Reach large numbers of customers simultaneously Good for attracting new, maintaining existing customers	Costs of set-up and staffing can be expensive Clutter
Sponsorship and events	Possibility to reach attractive segments or mass market Allows company to build credibility and benefit from reflected success Potential for unusual, attention-grabbing activity Builds company recognition	Relatively costly Transience of celebrity and lack of control over others' actions Time-consuming to build relationships and links with partners Difficult to evaluate impact
Point-of-sale displays, in-store merchandising	Relatively inexpensive Reinforces ad message Incentive for trade location to stock product	Reaches customers already likely to purchase
Ambient Media		
	Good coverage Good segmentation potential Many creative options	Creativity a constant challenge Targeting can be difficult Impact wears off quickly
Internet		
	Global impact Immediacy Many creative options for design Possibility of direct response and audience profiling	Short life span Creativity and web design costs Low attention Targeting can be difficult

Given cost constraints, media planners usually select the media that will expose the product or service to the largest target audience for the lowest possible cost. The way to measure this is to calculate the **cost per thousand (CPM)** impressions by dividing the cost of the unit (e.g., time on TV or space in a magazine) and the estimated number of impressions and multiply by 1000 ("M" is the roman numeral for 1000). Each **impression** is the viewing of an advertising message.

$$CPM = \frac{\text{cost of message unit}}{\text{number of impressions}} \times 1000$$

For example, if the TV show *Pilot Guides* has 92 000 target viewers and the cost of a 30-second ad during the show is $850, the CPM is $9.42 (CPM = $850/92 000 × 1000 = $9.24).

There are many components to the media mix, and how an organization blends them depends on a number of factors, particularly the nature of the product or service and the target audience. For example, tour operators and major destinations rely heavily on television advertising, but niche players such as special interest operators tend to focus their advertising in specialist publications. Decisions also have to be made about reach and frequency. **Reach** is the percentage of a medium's audience that is exposed to an advertiser's message at least once during a specific time frame. **Frequency** is the number of times an audience has the opportunity to be exposed to a media vehicle in a specified time frame. Nova Scotia, for example, relies heavily on reaching consumers via television advertising during the annual East Coast Music Awards. Viewers all over Canada with a predisposed interest in Atlantic Canada tune in to the program, and Nova Scotia tourism staff answer about 20 000 calls from across the country while it's on air. More than a third of those callers end up visiting the province, and officials claim that the advertising is worth about $8 million in economic activity.

While tourism and hospitality advertising makes use of all of the main media, the key vehicles are print and electronic media advertisements and brochures. In fact, the most popular medium used by tourism advertisers is undoubtedly the travel brochure. For many organizations, the design, production, and distribution of their annual tourism brochure is the single most important and most expensive item in the marketing budget. However, the position of the brochure as a major travel medium is being threatened by new technology, such as CDs, DVDs, and the Internet (see Chapter 10).

One of the fastest growing sectors of media is **ambient advertising.** This approach includes place-based advertising in non-standard, unconventional media. Examples include ads at the bottom of security trays in airports, on the back of grocery receipts, at gas pumps, in elevators, on ATM screens, on washroom walls, on toilet paper, on pizza boxes, on welcome mats, and on tickets. Such tactics might involve live advertising. The Golden Palace Casino has been advertising on the back of professional boxers for many years using large temporary tattoos. Sony Ericsson Mobile Communications hired actors to create buzz about a new mobile phone that was also a digital camera. The actors pretended to be tourists who wanted their picture taken, thus persuading consumers to try the product. The use of hypertag technology by Whistler and its partner in the UK, Neilson, referred to later in this chapter, is an example of ambient advertising. Another is the "talking urinal" developed by

cost per thousand (CPM)

the cost of the message unit divided by the number of impressions (ad views) multiplied by 1000

impression

one viewing of an advertising message

reach

the percentage of a medium's audience that is exposed to an advertiser's message at least once during a specific time frame

frequency

the number of times an audience has the opportunity to be exposed to a media vehicle in a specified time frame.

ambient advertising

place-based advertising in non-standard, unconventional media

Wizmark, which motion sensor to activate an attention-grabbing display of lights flashing in a pre-programmed pattern when someone approaches. This draws the eye to the graphics incorporated within the small, waterproof viewing screen at the base of the urinal.

In 1999, Virgin Atlantic made innovative use of ambient media in the tourism sector in the Hong Kong harbour when it painted the traditionally green and white Star Ferry bright red with its own logo. Another use of ambient advertising is the use of airfields as a context in which to view ads cut into crop fields. An example of such an attempt to capture the interest of the business traveller occurred at Munich airport, where arriving passengers saw a giant ad for Swissair growing in the fields below. A 250-metre-long aircraft, grown in green barley against a background of brown straw, depicted the red and white Swissair logo — the colours created by using pigments.

6. Campaign Evaluation

Managers of advertising programs should regularly evaluate the communication and sales objectives of advertising. The campaign evaluation stage is often the most difficult in the advertising cycle, largely because while it is relatively easy to establish certain advertising measures (such as consumers' awareness of a brand before and after the campaign), it is much harder to establish shifts in consumer attitudes or brand perception. Despite such uncertainties, the evaluation stage is significant not only because it establishes what a campaign has achieved but also because it will provide guidance to how future campaigns could be improved and developed.

There are many evaluative research techniques available to marketers to measure advertising effectiveness. Memory tests are often used, and are based on the assumption that an impression leaves a mental residue with the person who has been exposed to it. Memory tests fall into two major groups: recall tests and recognition tests. A traditional **recall test** involves contacting members of the audience and what they remember about the ad. For example, in an aided recall test, a commercial is run on television network and the next evening interviewers ask viewers if they remember seeing the commercial for the specific brand. Alternatively, in an unaided recall test, the interviewers may ask consumers what particular ads they remembered from the previous day. If the commercial fails to establish a tight connection between the brand name and the selling message, the commercial will not receive a high recall score. Another method of measuring memory, called a **recognition test**, involves showing the ad to the audience and asking them whether they remember having seen it before.

Another evaluative research technique is the **persuasion test**, which measures whether the ad affects consumers' intentions to buy the brand. In this technique, consumers are first asked how likely they are to buy a the product or service. Next, they are exposed to an ad for it. After exposure, researchers again ask them what they intend to purchase. The researcher analyzes the results to determine whether intention to buy has increased as a result of exposure to the ad. Persuasion tests are expensive and have problems associated with audience composition, the environment, and brand familiarity. However, persuasion is a key objective for many advertisers, so even a rough estimate of an ad's persuasive power is useful.

recall test

a test that evaluates the memorability of an ad by contacting members of the audience and asking what they remember about it

recognition test

a test that evaluates the memorability of an ad by showing members of the audience the ad and asking whether they remember having seen it before

persuasion test

a test that evaluates the effectiveness of an ad by measuring whether it affects consumers' intentions to buy a brand

INTERNATIONAL ADVERTISING AND THE GLOBAL VERSUS LOCAL DEBATE

In 2006, global expenditure on advertising worldwide was above $450 billion and is expected to rise to $511 billion in 2009. Of all the elements of the marketing mix, decisions involving advertising are those most often affected by cultural differences among country markets. Consumers respond in terms of their culture, value systems, attitudes, beliefs, and perceptions. Because advertising's function is to interpret or translate the qualities of products and services in terms of consumer needs, wants, desires, and aspirations, the emotional appeals, symbols, persuasive approaches, and other characteristics of an advertisement must coincide with cultural norms if the ad is to be effective. The *Case Study* at the end of this chapter explains how tourism marketers in Canada conducted 44 workshops and 18 focus groups in six countries, plus consultations with more than 500 travel professionals to give them an insight into how to market Canada internationally. Similarly, the *Case Study* in Chapter 10 highlights how in-depth research led to the success of Australia's "Where the Bloody Hell Are You" campaign. The television ads resonated with consumers in Japan, the UK, the U.S., Germany, China, New Zealand, and South Korea, even with subtitles. The phrase "bloody hell" was expressed in English by an Australian but caught the attention of all those cultures, while the local translation in subtitles, in colloquial language, conveyed the same sentiment and meaning.

Reconciling an international advertising campaign with the cultural uniqueness of markets is the challenge confronting the global marketer. A classic *Harvard Business Review* article by Theodore Levitt ignited a debate over how to conduct global marketing.[9] He argued that companies should operate as though there were only one global market. He believed that differences among nations and cultures were not only diminishing but should be ignored because people throughout the world are motivated by the same desires and wants. Other scholars such as Philip Kotler disagreed, pointing to companies such as Coca-Cola, PepsiCo, and McDonalds and arguing that they did not offer the same product everywhere.[10]

The outcome of this debate has been three schools of thought on advertising in another country:

1. *Standardization.* This school of thought contends, like Levitt, that differences between countries are a matter of degree, so advertisers should focus on the similarities of consumers around the world.
2. *Localization.* The localization or adaptation school of thought argues that advertisers must consider differences between countries, including local culture, stage of economic and industrial development, stage of life cycle, media availability, and legal restrictions.
3. *Combination.* The belief here is that a combination of standardization and localization may produce the most effective advertising. Some elements of brand identity or strategy, for example, may be standardized, but advertising executions may need to be adapted to the local culture.

The reality of global advertising suggests that a combination approach will work best, and most companies tend to use the combination approach or even lean toward localization. Starbucks, for example, offers more tea in the Far East, stronger coffees in Europe, and gourmet coffees in the United States. The company has standardized its product name, logo, and packaging to maintain brand consistency even though there is variation in its product line.

SALES PROMOTION

sales promotion

a technique to increase the value of a product or service by offering an extra incentive to purchase it

A marketer that increases the value of its product or service by offering an extra incentive to purchase it is creating a **sales promotion**. In most cases, the objective of a sales promotion is to encourage action, although it can also help to build brand identity and awareness. Like advertising, sales promotion is a type of marketing communication. Although advertising is designed to build long-term brand awareness, sales promotions focus primarily on creating immediate action. Simply put, sales promotions offer an extra incentive for consumers, sales reps, and trade members to act. Although this extra incentive usually takes the form of a price reduction, it may also be additional amounts of the product, cash, prizes and gifts, premiums, special events, and so on. It may also be a fun brand experience. A sales promotion usually has specified limits, such as an expiration date or a limited quantity of the merchandise.

The use of sales promotion is growing rapidly for many reasons: it offers short-term bottom-line results; it is accountable; it is less expensive than advertising; it speaks to the current needs of the consumer to receive more value from products or services; and it responds to marketplace changes. Sales promotions can also be extremely flexible. They can be used at any stage in the life cycle of a product or service and can be very useful in supporting other promotional activities. In a recent survey of marketers in North America, 82 percent said sales promotion was a part of the integrated effort and 31 percent of those marketers said it was the core component.[11]

Tactical promotional techniques designed to stimulate customers to buy have three main targets: individual consumers, distribution channels, and the sales force. Table 8.6 highlights the sales promotion objectives for each target market, along with typical techniques used to achieve these objectives in the tourism and hospitality industry. As the table shows, many tools can be used to accomplish sales promotion objectives. Some of the main tools used are discussed below, including samples, coupons, gift certificates, premiums and point-of-purchase displays (often referred to as merchandising), patronage rewards, contests, sweepstakes, and games.

Table 8.6

Sales Promotion Objectives and Techniques Used in Tourism and Hospitality

	OBJECTIVES	TECHNIQUES
Customer	Sell excess capacity — especially as the delivery date approaches Shift the timing of purchases/peaks and troughs Attract and reward regular/loyal customers Promote trial of products or services (new users) Generate higher consumption per capita Increase market share Defeat/pre-empt competitors' promotions	Price cuts/sale offers including Internet Discount vouchers/coupons Disguised price cuts Extra product/service Additional products/services Free gifts Competitions Passport schemes for regular customers Prize draws Point-of-purchase displays and merchandising materials Contests, sweepstakes, and games
Distribution channels	Secure dealer support and recommendations Achieve brochure display and maintain stocks Support for merchandising initiatives Improve dealer awareness of products and services Build room value Increase room rate	Extra commission and overrides Prize draws Competitions Parties/receptions Trade and travel show exhibits Educational seminars Recognition programs Flexible booking policies
Sales force	Improve volume of sales through incentives Improve display in distribution outlets Achieve sales "blitz" targets among main corporate accounts Reward special efforts	Bonuses and other money/incentives Gift incentives Travel incentives Prize draws Visual AIDS

An important dimension of sales promotion effectiveness is payout planning. There are many examples of poorly designed or performing promotions, and such failures hurt companies' reputations, waste money, and sometimes even hurt consumers. Chatper 1's *Snapshot* on Hong Kong Disneyland explains the consequences of poor payout planning. The overwhelming success of a discount-ticket promotion in 2006, in conjunction with the Chinese Lunar New Year, led to huge numbers of families being turned away at the gates despite having valid tickets. This resulted in a large amount of negative publicity for the newly opened attraction.

Samples

sampling

giving away free samples of a product or service, or arranging in some way for people to try all or part of it

Sampling involves giving away free samples of a product or service to encourage sales, or arranging in some way for people to try all or part of it. As many tourism and hospitality services are intangible, sampling is not always a straightforward process. However, restaurants and bars often give customers free samples of menu items or beverages. Sampling for the travel trade often comes in the form of familiarization trips. A familiarization trip (commonly referred to as a "fam trip") is a popular method used to expose a product to intermediaries in the channel of distribution. For example, a hotel might have a group of travel agents visit the facility to familiarize them with the features and benefits. If travel agents are impressed with a facility during a fam trip, they will convey their enthusiasm to customers, and bookings will increase. The trips are free or reduced in price and can be given to intermediaries by suppliers, carriers, or destination marketing groups.

Coupons

coupons

vouchers or certificates that entitle customers or intermediaries to a reduced price on a product or service

gift certificates

vouchers or checks that are selectively given away or sold to customers, who in turn give them to others

premiums

products or services offered either for free or at low cost as an incentive to buy a specific product or service

Coupons are vouchers or certificates that entitle customers or intermediaries to a reduced price on a product or service. In the U.S., the national coupon industry is estimated at more than $7 billion a year. Major companies such as Procter & Gamble, S.C. Johnson, General Mills, and Kraft continue to rely on traditional paper coupons, despite the increasing importance of the Internet and online coupons. Organizations issue coupons to encourage people to sample new products, to make impulse purchases, and to foster brand loyalty. Coupons are used extensively in the tourism and hospitality industries, especially among restaurants, hotels, rental car companies, tourist attractions, and cruise lines. Besides stimulating sales of a mature product or service, coupons are also effective in promoting early trial of new offerings. But many marketing professionals feel that too much promotional use of coupons creates a commodity out of a differentiated product or service. Overuse has also led to coupon wars and other forms of price discounting, all the while detracting from the intrinsic value of a organization's product or service. Figure 8.9 shows an example of coupon use: in this ad, an Alberta theme park offers two coupons for the summer for 2007. Calaway Park, positioned just outside Calgary, gains over 85 percent of its attendance through some form of promotions.

Gift Certificates

Gift certificates are vouchers or cheques that are either selectively given away or sold to customers, who in turn give them to others as gifts. Carnival Cruise Lines, for example, promoted the sale of gift vouchers for cruise vacations over the Christmas period.

Premiums

Premiums are products or services offered either for free or at low cost as an incentive to buy a specific product or service. There are several varieties of premiums, including self-liquidators (sold at a price to recover the sponsor's cost) and free premiums (distributed by mail, in or on packages). Most marketing professionals agree that, to be effective, premiums must be of an

Figure 8.9   Coupons for Calaway Park, Alberta

appropriate quality and durability, be appealing, and have high perceived value to certain customer groups. The danger of such promotions is that they can be expensive and — far from creating loyalty — they encourage consumers to switch brands constantly.

Point-of-Purchase Displays

point-of-purchase merchandising

a technique used to promote a product or service at locations where it is being sold

Point-of-purchase merchandising is a technique used to promote a product or service at the locations where it is being sold. The value of point-of-purchase merchandising has long been recognized in retailing and is making rapid inroads in restaurants, hotels, car rental companies, and travel agencies. In the food and beverage industry, menus and wine and drink lists are the key tools. Often, restaurants will display special ad cards that promote a feature wine or menu item; most wineries now offer free tasting in order to entice customers to purchase; and hotels also use a wide variety of merchandising techniques, including in-room guest directories, room-service menus, elevator and lobby displays, and brochure racks. In the travel agency business, brochures, posters, and window and stand-up displays are fairly common forms of sales promotion. A few years ago, Club Med designed a floor display for travel agents that featured a beach chair with a surfboard on one side and a pair of skis on the other to show that Club Med has both snow and sun destinations.

Patronage Rewards

Patronage rewards are cash or other prizes given to customers for their regular use of an organization's products or services. The intent is to encourage loyalty and to create a positive change in the behaviour of the consumer. Examples are the frequent flyer plans that award points for distance travelled. Many hotel chains also have frequent stay programs, and some restaurants have frequent diner programs. These are discussed in more detail in Chapter 11.

Contests, Sweepstakes, and Games

contests

sales promotions in which entrants can win prizes based on some required skill that they are asked to demonstrate

sweepstakes

sales promotions that require entrants to submit their names and addresses, with winners chosen on the basis of chance

Contests are sales promotions in which entrants win prizes based on some required skill that they are asked to demonstrate. **Sweepstakes** are sales promotions that require entrants to submit their names and addresses, with winners chosen on the basis of chance. **Games** are similar to sweepstakes, but they involve using game pieces, such as scratch-and-win cards. The use of contests, games, and sweepstakes has been shown to increase advertising readership. These promotional tools can be useful in communicating key benefits and unique selling points, and can be targeted at both consumers and members of the trade.

As mentioned above, promotional techniques designed to stimulate sales often target the trade. In 2005, Jumeirah, the Dubai-based hotel group, launched the "World's Most Luxurious Competition," offering travel agents worldwide the chance to win a stay at a Jumeirah property over the next 10 years. The competition was designed to promote the group's new private code, JT, among travel agencies using a global distribution system (GDS) to book reservations. Travel agents could register to participate by visiting a dedicated website. The first phase of the competition was an online memory game.[12]

games

sales promotions involving the use of game pieces, such as scratch-and-win cards

The *Snapshot* shows how Korean consumers who bought snowboard outfits at The North Face locations were given an opportunity to win a Canadian Rockies ski trip. Armed with a personal identification number given to them in the shops, they could visit the CTC-Korea's website or The North Face Korea's website, and then qualify for a lucky draw.

SNAPSHOT

CANADIAN TOURISM COMMISSION PARTNERS WITH THE NORTH FACE TO ATTRACT KOREAN SKIERS

Increasingly, the use of nontraditional partnerships (NTPs) is the norm rather than the exception for tourism marketing, just as it has become in other industries. The Canadian Tourism Commission (CTC) marketing teams have been very innovative in their use of these NTPs. In the United Kingdom, for example, a photo competition in 2006 raised the Canada brand profile through a partnership with Travel Alberta, Air Transat, and Nature's Path (a Canadian brand of organic cereal for children). These partners sponsored a children's photography competition at London city farms and community gardens. First prize was a holiday for a family of four to Alberta, including seven nights' accommodation, rental car, and return flights from London's Gatwick Airport to Calgary. Participants were asked to take a picture they believed captured the theme of "Nature in the City" at a city farm or community garden in London.

Another NTP example occurred in the winter of 2006/07, when the CTC partnered with outdoor-wear giant The North Face to promote Canada's ski and snowboarding experiences in Korea. The partnership, which included Travel Alberta International, specifically targeted Koreans, and aimed to feature Canada as a premium dynamic travel destination. The North Face — a well-established brand in Korea — launched a new line of snowboarding outfits in December 2006, and

this provided a hard-to-resist opportunity, according to CTC Korea's Anna Lee: "The North Face has 150 stores nationwide in Korea that are mostly located in upscale department stores, where high-end consumers come to shop. We have had a partnership with Arc'teryx to promote Canadian trekking products, and worked with canola oil producers to promote cuisine tours in Canada this year; both are Canadian products sold in Korea. We are putting a lot of faith in the kind of presence Canada will have thanks to this new partnership."

Customers who bought snowboard outfits at a North Face location before January 28, 2007, were given an opportunity to win a Canadian Rockies ski trip through the validation of a personal identification number they could enter when they visited CTC Korea's website or The North Face Korea's website, which then qualified them for a lucky draw. Each store displayed a highly visible pop-up poster of the promotion. The North Face also created advertising for their clothes that featured Canada, and these ads appeared in major Korean daily newspapers during the course of the campaign. At the end of the campaign, Canada appeared 16 times in these publications, providing exposure with an in-kind value of nearly $160 000.

"It is an effective way of trying to reach the right consumers while leveraging partners' budgets and networks," explained Lee. "There are almost 1.5 million skiers/snowboarders in Korea. It is huge market with great potential. Many Korean skiers and boarders go overseas to experience something different from what we have in Korea at the moment. Japan is number one, but we would like to see Canada become the next destination of choice, which is why we are investing much effort into increasing awareness of Canada as must-go ski destination."

Anna Lee points out that Canada has several competitive advantages when compared to Japan: "In Korea and Japan, the ski season ends in late February, while in Canada you can ski until late May. We are focusing more on spring skiing rather than winter skiing. We are encouraging Koreans to go to Canada in the New Year. Canada and Japan are already well-known ski destinations in Korea, even if fewer people go to Canada right now because it is farther away. Australia and New Zealand are also popular as ski destinations, although their seasons are totally opposite from ours."

Sources: Canadian Tourism Commission. (2007). CTC-Korea partnership reaches huge winter activity market. *Tourism Online* 3(12); Canadian Tourism Commission. (2006). Partnerships: Don't leave home without one! *Tourism Online* 3(9).

JOINT PROMOTIONS

joint promotion

a promotion in which organizations with similar target markets combine their resources to mutual advantage

In a **joint promotion**, two or more organizations with similar target markets combine their resources to mutual advantage. This collaboration can reduce the cost of the incentives offered, and it may be a one-off joint promotion or a long-term campaign such as a trade association campaign using an "umbrella" brand name. An example of a joint promotion is a partnership between Whistler ski resort and UK tour operator Neilson. In 2006, Tourism Whistler used hypertag technology in a UK Outdoor Advertising Campaign in attempt to bring more skiers to the Canadian resort. Hypertag is a way to provide access relevant information and content on a mobile phone or personal digital assistant (PDA, such as a Palm Pilot or Pocket PC) directly from a chip embedded in objects such as advertising panels, marketing, or exhibition displays. In the Whistler-Neilson campaign, Hypertag posters were placed in 25 key areas of central London. Interested consumers could download Whistler content directly onto their PDAs from the poster. Tourism Whistler used contests ("Win Your Dream Vacation to Whistler" and daily instant prizes) to encourage interaction. People would receive a "You're a Winner!" message onto their PDA for their instant prizes. All users (winners and losers) were given instructions to visit www.dreamskivacation.com to enter to win the grand prize.

Consumers interacting with poster were eligible to win one of 30 instant prizes (Whistler backpacks, jackets, t-shirts, etc.), including a seven-night/six-day Neilson trip to Whistler including airfare for two people. The campaign achieved 2601 downloads. In each interaction, a person stopped, read the poster, chose to devote time in downloading the Whistler message, and went away with a successful interaction. The download rate increased as the campaign progressed — by the end of the campaign the network was consistently achieving over 100 downloads a day.

CHAPTER SUMMARY

In marketing communications, the blend of promotional elements is known as the promotional mix; this includes advertising, sales promotions, public relations, personal selling, word of mouth, direct marketing, and Internet marketing. Perhaps one of the most important advances in marketing in recent decades has been the rise of integrated marketing communications (IMC) — the recognition that advertising can no longer be crafted and executed in isolation from other promotional mix elements.

Advertising can be defined as any paid form of non-personal presentation and promotion of ideas, products, or services by an identified sponsor, using mass media to persuade or influence an audience. There are six important stages in developing an advertising program: setting the objectives, setting the budget, advertising agency decisions, message strategy, media strategy, and campaign evaluation.

The use of sales promotion is increasing rapidly for many reasons: it offers the manager short-term bottom-line results; it is accountable; it is less expensive than advertising; it speaks to the current needs of the consumer to receive more value from products and services; and it responds to marketplace changes. Many tools can be used to accomplish sales promotion objectives; these include samples, coupons, gift certificates, premiums and point-of-purchase displays, patronage rewards, contests, sweepstakes, and games.

In a joint promotion, two or more organizations with similar target markets combine their resources to their mutual advantage. This collaboration can reduce the cost of the incentives offered, and it may be a one-off joint promotion or a long-term campaign such as a trade association campaign using an "umbrella" brand name.

KEY TERMS

advertising, p. 262
advertising objective, p. 262
affordable method, p. 263
AIDA model, p. 251
ambient advertising, p. 274
competitive-parity method, p. 263
concept testing, p. 259
contests, p. 281
cost per thousand (CPM), p. 274
coupons, p. 279
frequency, p. 274
full-service agency, p. 264
games, p. 282
gift certificates, p. 279
impression, p. 274

integrated marketing
    communications (IMC), p. 255
joint promotions, p. 283
marketing communications,
    p. 250
media mix, p. 259
objective-and-task method, p. 263
percentage-of-sales method,
    p. 263
persuasion test, p. 275
point-of-purchase merchandising,
    p. 281
premiums, p. 279
promotional mix, p. 249
pull strategy, p. 261

push strategy, p. 260
reach, p. 274
recall test, p. 275
recognition test, p. 275
return-on-investment goals,
    p. 260
sales promotion, p. 277
sampling, p. 279
situation analysis, p. 258
specialized agency, p. 264
sweepstakes, p. 281
SWOT analysis, p. 258
zero-based planning, p. 259

DISCUSSION QUESTIONS AND EXERCISES

1. Find an example of an advertisement from a tourism or hospitality organization. What execution style is it using? How effective is the ad? What changes would you make to improve its effectiveness?
2. What are the main factors that determine an airline's choice of advertising media? If possible, obtain details or examples of advertising from specific airlines to support your answer.
3. Which do you think is an effective advertisement: one that creates an emotional bond with consumers or one that is designed to inform consumers about the product's unique benefit? Why? Or do you have another definition and explanation?
4. How can sales promotions be used to support other elements of the marketing communications mix? Give examples to support your answer.
5. Do you think sales promotions create loyalty or encourage switching to competitors' products? Use examples from your own experience.

CASE STUDY

SPICING UP THE IMAGE OF CANADA

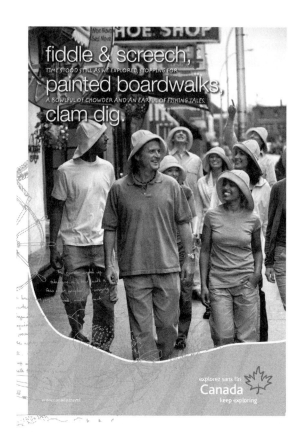

If you think Canada is all about mountains, moose, and Mounties, the Canadian Tourism Commission wants you to think again. Instead, the tourism commission wants you to imagine clam digs, painted boardwalks, and fiddles. It is all part of a new ad campaign, bearing the slogan "Canada. Keep Exploring," designed to entice foreigners to visit the Great White North.

The campaign is a response to a faltering Canadian tourism industry. The number of international tourists fell to 18.2 million overnight trips in 2006, a decline of 3 percent over 2005, and the World Tourism Organization (UNWTO) now lists Canada in 12th place when it comes to top tourist destinations, down five places in a decade.

"This campaign is designed to put us at top of mind for potential travellers," says Paul LaRue, communications advisor at the CTC. "People tend to look at Canada and say, 'Yeah, nice place, I'll think about it down the road.' We need to change that perception." One way the CTC is trying to accomplish that is with offbeat marketing designed to catch the attention of tourists, rather than to show off Canada's natural beauty. One ad features discarded clothes next to a hotel swimming pool, with intersecting lines labelled "midnight" and "mischief."

But not all Canadians are sold on the new campaign. Some people were confused by the ads, saying they don't represent the country Canadians know and love. Some said it was difficult to know the ads were even for Canada. One ad shows a broken kiddy ride at a shopping mall — complete with tire tracks — and the tag line, "We're all born explorers." But LaRue defendeed the new campaign. "We're not giving up on our geography and scenery," he says. "What we're doing is taking a different slant. We're appealing to peoples' emotional side; to make them a little more cognizant of their explorer nature, which is inherent in any human being."

The ads, which first appeared in Britain, France, and Germany in January 2006, are a departure from the typical Canadian icons. Instead, they are designed to show Canada as a unique travel destination, say officials at the tourism commission. Some of the ads, like one featuring the totem room at the Museum of Civilization in Gatineau, Quebec, seem to build on the accepted view of Canada while encouraging exploration. Other ads, which were run in European gyms, highlight the muscles used while enjoying various Canadian attractions, such as going to a comedy festival, visiting a spa, or raiding a mini-bar.

DDB Canada is the advertising firm behind the new campaign. DDB vice-president Yvonne van Dinther says her firm's challenge was to express the CTC's message in an interesting way. "What we need is to insert the ads into peoples' routines," she says. "We want to give new information — at the very least to get people to think differently, to look at things in a non-traditional way."

The CTC echoes that sentiment. "Tourism marketing in Canada … has been similar for 50 years. Basically the same message — 'Come to Canada, we have beautiful scenery and mountains," says LaRue. "We're the world's playground.' We used that phrase in 1945, and again in 2003. So we're not

hitting the people we need to hit." LaRue says the CTC has done extensive research to find out what potential tourists think about Canada. He points out that the CTC has held 44 workshops and 18 focus groups in six countries, plus consultations with more than 500 travel professionals, to gain valuable insight into how to market Canada. The research found that many people think of Canada as a classic novel that one should read, but never does.

In addition to Britain, France, and Germany, the new ads appeared in China, Japan, South Korea, Australia, the United States, and Mexico. Besides print ads, the campaign also featured Smart cars wrapped in advertising, branded coffee sleeves, wrapped buses, and 3-D posters in high-traffic locations. In Mexico, at key high-traffic locations and selected major shopping malls, a large black box or display was set up, playing on people's natural curiosity to discover and explore. A single challenge was posed to the shoppers: "Try your hand." Those daring enough to do so pulled out a branded "Canada. Keep Exploring" postcard with contact details on where to find information on travel to Canada. The same month, prior to movie theatre shows, an usher wearing a "Keep Exploring" t-shirt caught audience attention by peering out through the curtains and announcing something unexpected and out of the ordinary. On leaving the theatre, movie goers were provided with a unique take-home piece to pique their interest and drive them to the website. CTC-Mexico also sponsored radio programs — "Brought to you by the CTC — Keep Exploring" — with a message inspiring listeners to challenge their daily routine.

One of the goals of the campaign was to increase tourism revenues by 23 percent, or $7.5 billion, over the next five years. LaRue would not disclose the cost of the campaign, saying only that it comes out of the CTC's annual budget, which is roughly $80 million per year.

Sources: Tourism Online. (2007, January). Bring the brand to life: Mexico. *Tourism Online, 3*(1); Mandaro, M. (2005, December 2). Spicing up Canada's image. Capital News Online. www.carleton.ca/jmc/cnews/02122005/n4.shtml (retrieved September 2007).

QUESTIONS

1. Destinations are becoming increasingly aggressive in their marketing efforts to attract customers. Do you think this campaign from the CTC could be more aggressive, or do you think it is risky?

2. Do you think the ads discussed in the case represent the tourism product on offer in Canada?

3. Find out what ads the CTC is currently using in international markets. With reference to the theory in this chapter, what style of advertising are they using?

4. Do you think the promotional efforts in Mexico were particularly creative? What other techniques could have been used to raise awareness about Canada?

WEBSITES

www.club18-30.com
Club 18-30

www.braziltour.com
Brazil Ministry of Tourism

www.carnival.com
Carnival Cruises

www.visitlasvegas.com
Las Vegas Visitors Convention Bureau

www.canadatourism.com
Canadian Tourism Commission

ENDNOTES

1. Strong, E. K. (1925). *The psychology of selling*. New York: McGraw-Hill.

2. Lavidge, R. C., & Steiner, G. A. (1961, October). A model for predictive measurement of advertising effectiveness. *Journal of Marketing*, 25(6), 59–62.

3. Rogers, E. M. (1962). *The diffusion of innovations*. New York: Free Press.

4. Broadbent, S., & Jacobs, B. (1985). *Spending advertising money*. London: Business Books.

5. Colley, R. H. (1961). *Defining advertising goals for measuring advertising results*. New York: Association of National Advertisers.

6. Wells, W., Burnett, B., & Moriarty, S. (2003). *Advertising principles and practice*. Englewood Cliffs, NJ: Prentice Hall.

7. Hayman, D., & Schultz, D. (1999, April 26). How much should you spend on advertising? *Advertising Age*, 32.

8. Kotler, P., Bowen, J., & Makens, J. (2006). *Marketing for hospitality and tourism* (4th ed.). Upper Saddle River, NJ: Prentice Hall.

9. Levitt, T. (1983, May-June). The globalization of markets. *Harvard Business Review*, 2–11.

10. Kotler, P. (1988). *Marketing management*. Englewood Cliffs, NJ: Prentice-Hall.

11. Wells, W., Burnett, B., & Moriarty, S. (2006). *Advertising principles and practice*. Englewood Cliffs, NJ: Prentice Hall, 470.

12. GDS code promotion. (2005, December 1). *Travelweek*, 26.

Marketing Communications: *Public Relations, Personal Selling, and Word of Mouth*

Spotlight
MARKETING THE MOST SPECTACULAR TRAIN TRIP IN THE WORLD

Imagine a trip, by train, through the heart of the spectacular Canadian Rockies, specifically scheduled so that the breathtaking mountain scenery can be enjoyed entirely by daylight. This could be an ideal tourism product, one that would be easy to promote and easy to sell. Nevertheless, in the spring of 1990, the newly privatized Rocky Mountaineer passenger train service was facing many challenges, not the least of which was marketing this wonderful product on a minuscule budget.

The new company was headed by Peter Armstrong, who had previously turned Vancouver's Gray Line tour-bus business into a profitable operation. The marketing of the Rocky Mountaineer would be crucial, so Armstrong recruited the help of skilled marketers. Rick Antonson, formerly of the Edmonton Convention and Tourism Association, became the vice-president of sales and marketing. Murray Atherton, who had worked for Armstrong at Gray Line and had his own hospitality consulting firm, was brought in to reach the overseas tour companies, particularly those in the United Kingdom. Finally, Mike Leone, who had handled media relations in the United States for Expo 86, was entrusted with the company's public relations.

The company's first trip was for the Pacific Asia Travel Association (PATA), a booking committed to by VIA Rail. Despite the haste with which Rocky Mountaineer had to prepare for this trip, it was a great success. The company benefited from this initial trip in a number of ways. First, Tourism Canada (CTC's predecessor) had filmed portions of the trip for its own promotions and the company was able to get a couple of hundred copies of this video into circulation. Second, the PATA trip provided the company with first-hand knowledge provided by overseas tour operators on the best ways to sell travel products in their home markets. Finally, the then minister of external affairs for the federal government, Joe Clark, remarked during the trip that it was "the most spectacular train trip in the world." The company registered that quotation as a trademark and uses it in promotional materials.

A huge obstacle for the fledgling company was the media coverage of the "demise" of passenger rail in Canada. This was particularly troublesome in the U.S., where a PBS special and the evening news reported the end of passenger rail between Vancouver and Toronto. With such a limited marketing budget, it would be difficult to bring all the pertinent media on board for familiarization tours to promote the Rocky Mountaineer. However, Mike Leone's skill at public relations brought the Rocky Mountaineer press coverage and feature write-ups in the United States, all in an effort to overcome the public mindset that rail travel had disappeared.

The most important marketing task for that first year was to obtain the bookings to fill the trains. Given the financial constraints, very few dollars were available for marketing and the company had to make every one count. There were few tour operator contacts passed on by VIA, leaving only the very shell of an operator network. Murray Atherton was getting up at 2:00 a.m. to contact tour companies in the United Kingdom, trying to "paint the dream, paint the picture" for the tour operators. This personal selling was crucial, as the new company was building its tour contacts from scratch.

Marketing the second season was complicated by the fact that the company was well into the first season before it could confirm the schedule for the second year. It was also trying to develop offerings and contracts that would suit the needs of diverse markets, including Europe and Southeast Asia. As well, the company had no capacity at the time to arrange travel packages beyond its two-day service, and had to refer that business to other tour companies.

During a trip to London with Tourism Canada, a Mountain Vistas representative discovered that a Canadian tour operator had just cancelled a luxury train trip across Canada that had been arranged with Thomas Cook, and the cancelled trip was featured in a publication that had already gone to print. The company scrambled to have a Rocky Mountaineer brochure sent overnight to Thomas Cook for insertion into the publication. Its ability to capitalize on this opportunity led to a $10 000 deal and an eight-page feature in the Thomas Cook travel magazine.

For all their challenges, the people behind the Rocky Mountaineer knew they had a winning product to sell, and the company has gone from strength to strength. Today, media public relations plays a significant role in marketing the Rocky Mountaineer and Whistler Mountaineer, which debuted in 2006. Rocky Mountaineer Vacations employs two full-time travel media specialists to focus on attracting travel writers to travel on aboard the trains and write about their experiences. These travel media specialists are supported by public relations companies located in the U.S., England, and Australia that spend countless hours promoting the Rocky Mountaineer and Whistler Mountaineer in those countries to leading travel publications and media outlets. In 2006 this strategy paid big dividends with more than 200 travel writers from around the world travelling onboard and writing about both trains. This resulted in a media value of several million dollars.

Sources: Grescoe, P. (2000). *Trip of a lifetime: The making of the Rocky Mountaineer*. Vancouver: Hurricane; Personal communication with Ian Robertson, Executive Director, Corporate Communications and Public Affairs, Armstrong Group, April 2, 2007.

Objectives

On completion of this chapter, readers should understand:

- the roles and functions of public relations;
- public relations techniques;
- the roles and objectives of personal selling;
- the sales process and the staffing of sales personnel;

- the difference between direct marketing and direct response advertising;
- the key direct response advertising tools; and
- the importance of word of mouth in the promotional mix.

Chapter Overview

The *Spotlight* highlights how the Rocky Mountaineer used public relations (PR) as a key part of its communications program. This chapter begins by focusing on PR, examining the roles and functions of public relations and the main PRtechniques used in tourism and hospitality. Personal selling is the focus of the next section of the chapter, which discusses the roles and objectives of personal selling, the sales process, and the roles of a sales manager. The key advantages of direct marketing are discussed in the following section of this chapter, as are the major direct marketing tools. The chapter then concludes with a section on word-of-mouth communication — an important but often misunderstood form of promotion in tourism.

PUBLIC RELATIONS

Definition of Public Relations

public relations (PR)

the activities that an organization uses to maintain or improve its relationship with other organizations or individuals

publicity

attention received through news media coverage

Public relations (PR) includes all the activities that an organization uses to maintain or improve its relationship with other organizations or individuals. Although public relations has a distinguished tradition, people often mistake it for **publicity**, which refers to attention received through news media coverage. Public relations is broader in scope than publicity, its goal being for an organization to achieve positive relationships with various audiences (publics) in order to manage the organization's image and reputation effectively. Its publics may be external (customers, the news media, the investment community, the general public, government bodies) and internal (shareholders, employees). Figure 9.1 shows the different publics that may have an influence over the tourism or hospitality organization. Managing the relationships and communications with each and every public is essential to effective public relations.

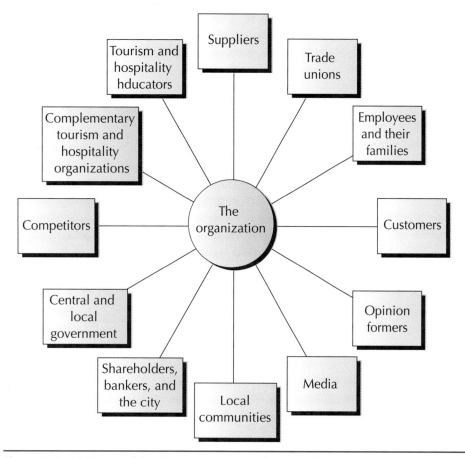

Figure 9.1   Various Publics in the Tourism and Hospitality Industry

Roles and Functions of Public Relations

The three most important roles of public relations and publicity in tourism and hospitality are maintaining a positive public presence, handling negative publicity, and enhancing the effectiveness of other promotional mix elements.[1] In this third role, public relations paves the way for advertising, sales promotions, and personal selling by making customers more receptive to the persuasive messages of these elements. Ultimately, the difference between advertising and public relations is that PR takes a longer, broader view of the importance of image and reputation as a corporate competitive asset and addresses more target audiences. The functions of the PR department include the following.

Establishing Corporate Identity

The objectives of establishing a corporate identity are similar to those of branding: to create an image of consistency, reliability, and professionalism that is easily recognized by the public. Everything that the organization owns or produces must project the same image. Richard Branson has created a clear corporate identity for the Virgin group. Over the past 25 years, Branson has diversified his Virgin brand into a far-reaching empire, encompassing mobile phone services, rail service, and even wedding dresses, as well as his original record label and discount airline. His personal image is one of unconventionality, youthful energy and enthusiasm, entrepreneurial spirit and thinking big and he imbues all his products with this brand distinction (see Chapter 11).

Government Relations

The organization's business may be affected by changes in the law or in government policy, and an organization may wish to ensure that politicians are aware of the impact of their decisions. For example, the ski areas of western Canada positioned in the national parks have been lobbying the government for many years to allow them to develop and upgrade in order to compete with ski areas outside of the parks. Lobbying can be done by individual companies, professional bodies, or specially formed groups such as the Tourism Industry Association of Canada (TIAC). Founded in 1930 to encourage the development of tourism in Canada, TIAC serves as the national private-sector advocate the industry, representing the interests of the tourism business community nation-wide. It attempts to influence government thinking and action on behalf of Canadian tourism businesses, promoting positive measures that help the industry grow and prosper. A recent example was its fight against the proposed cancellation of the GST/HST Visitor Rebate Program (VRP). TIAC urged the federal government to consider what eliminating this visitor incentive program would mean for working Canadians and the many small- and medium-sized businesses that make up Canada's tourism industry. However, TIAC's lobbying proved ineffective as the Foreign Convention and Tour Incentive Program became law on June 22/07.

Crisis Management

When a serious incident occurs, it is the PR department's job to take the pressure off operational managers by handling media enquiries and ensuring that the organization's version of events is presented. The organization needs to be seen to be acting swiftly, efficiently, and responsibly to deal with the problem. The *Snapshot* on Air Canada refers to the company's PR efforts in response to filing for bankruptcy. It is important that an organization has a crisis management plan in place before an incident occurs. In November 2005, a cruise ship — the *Seabourn Spirit* — was attacked by pirates off the Somalia coast. The ship's crew managed to prevent the hijackers from getting on board by increasing speed and changing course. Miami-based Seabourn Cruise Lines was quick to respond to the crisis. It gave the passengers vouchers for a free cruise in the future and quickly organized a day of activity in the Seychelles to buoy the tourists' spirits.

Internal Communications

Since staff plays an important role in creating the image of the company and the quality of the customer's experience, it is important that they are kept fully informed and made to feel part of the team. The PR function often includes producing staff newsletters and briefing presentations. Other employee relations techniques include employee recognition programs, cards or gifts that mark important dates such as birthdays, incentive programs, and promotions.

Customer Relations

Customers are the lifeblood of every organization, and techniques that improve relationships with them are very important to an organization's long-term survival. For example, answering customer complaints and claims promptly and fairly can limit the bad word-of-mouth publicity that dissatisfied customers can spread. The Sheraton

Suites Eau Claire in Calgary (see Chapter 11) produces a newsletter for customers, which includes profiles on top-performing employees, a schedule of events in and around Calgary, and the procedure for giving customer feedback.

Marketing Publicity

Marketing publicity is part of the wider PR function and is therefore part of the promotional mix. Its objective is to secure editorial space to achieve marketing goals. Editorial space in a newspaper, or indeed in a television show, can be extremely effective. In June 2006, the UK's Royal Shakespeare Company promoted its Complete Works Festival summer season by commissioning a flotilla of hot air balloons to drift over the town of Stratford-upon-Avon serenading residents with ambient music and readings from Shakespeare. The stunt generated a considerable amount of publicity, including a half-page feature in a major daily newspaper.[2]

SNAPSHOT

PUBLIC RELATIONS AT AIR CANADA

In a fiercely competitive airline industry, Air Canada uses an ongoing marketing campaign to communicate to customers its mission of offering value-added customer services, technical excellence, and passenger safety. In addition to the traditional channels used to communicate to the customer, such as television, print advertising, and direct mail, Air Canada is also placing an increasing emphasis on newer and more creative ways of reaching its audience, and public relations is now an integral part of its marketing mix.

Air Canada uses PR in a number of forms to promote its airlines, including communicating through the media via ongoing news releases and targeted interviews, and sponsorship programs, supporting charities and other non-profit organizations, and running contests. Its management of public relations helps to generate awareness about the company and creates a favourable image for the brand. It also helps to generate sales and control promotion costs.

The company is involved in sponsorship programs for a variety of organizations, each of which provides exposure to a different target market. The company sponsors a number of sport teams, including all six Canadian NHL teams and the Toronto Raptors of the NBA. Air Canada's sponsorship also plays role in the arts and culture community, including the Orchestre Symphonique de Montréal. Through its Kids' Horizons Program, Air Canada also sponsors many children-oriented charities, such as "Dreams Take Flight," an employee-led initiative. Through partnerships with organizations that offer effective and innovative programs, Kids' Horizons gives priority to children and youth health, the fight against child poverty, and children wish granting.

A major component of Kids' Horizons is the airline's Hospital Transportation Program. Through this initiative, Air Canada annually provides approximately 2700 flights to pediatric hospitals across Canada to help children reach medical treatment not available in their community. This kind of financial support to charities helps to create the image of Air Canada as being a company that cares about people and invests in the community. The company also sponsors awards such as the National Aboriginal Achievement Awards and the National Press Club of Canada's World Press Freedom Awards.

Air Canada continuously generates press releases that are picked up by national and local newspapers, magazines, and on television. Charities, sponsorships, and other forms of community involvement are the kinds of events that create a positive image for Air Canada in the news. The company's communications department is also keen to publicize information about new in-flight product offerings and company awards and achievements. Favourable news releases appear on the corporate website.

Air Canada uses *enRoute*, the company's in-flight magazine, as an important marketing communications tool. The magazine serves a broader public relations role as well: *enRoute* is a sponsor of the CBC Literary Awards, and the in-flight entertainment programming is used to promote Canadian film and music. Interestingly, Air Canada has the distinction of being the largest promoter of Canadian wines on an international scale.

In recent years, the communications department at Air Canada has been able to focus on proactive media relations and PR initiatives. Unfortunately, at the beginning of this century, the airline moved from crisis to crisis, and therefore much of the PR effort was directed toward crisis management issues. The adverse consequences of a declining economy compounded by the September 11, 2001, terrorist attacks and the 2003 outbreak of severe acute respiratory syndrome (SARS) led to the company filing for protection under the Companies' Creditors Arrangement Act (CCAA) in April 2003. The communications department worked extremely hard to persuade all stakeholders that business was operating as usual. For example, all e-mail subscribers to Destina.ca (Air Canada's online tour operator at the time) received a personally addressed e-mail informing them about the "restructuring" of Air Canada.

To mark the end of CCAA protection and to celebrate the official launch of a new era, major employee and media events were held on October 19, 2004, across Canada endorsed by Canadian superstar Céline Dion. Several initiatives were announced. A new look for the fleet, inside and out, new uniforms for front-line staff conveying contemporary sophistication, new leading edge in-flight enhancements, and a modernized brand image. The purpose was to show the world the re-energized Air Canada and signal a renewed focus on providing customers with value-driven products and services that place the carrier on the forefront of international carriers.

Simultaneously, Air Canada announced a cooperative brand advertising campaign with the Canadian Tourism Commission to jointly promote Canada as a travel destination in markets outside the country and featuring Dion's voice of Celine Dion. This ambitious project received positive world-wide attention and media coverage.

Source: Personal communication with P. Leblanc, senior director of communications, Air Canada, March 2, 2007.

Public Relations Techniques

A variety of PR techniques are available to tourism and hospitality organizations. Nine of the key techniques are highlighted in Figure 9.2 below and discussed on the following pages.

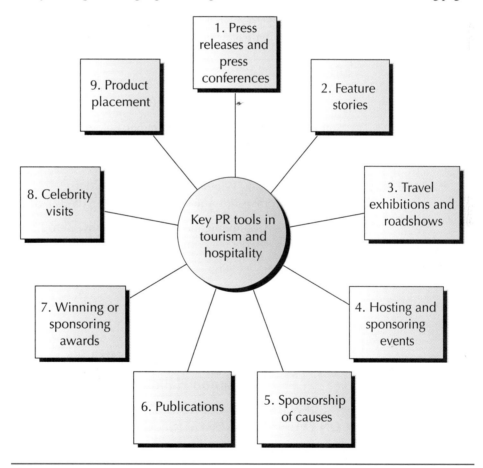

Figure 9.2 Selected Public Relations Techniques Available to Tourism and Hospitality Organizations

1. Press Releases and Press Conferences

press release (news release)

a short article about an organization or event written to attract media attention, intended to lead to media coverage

A **press release** or **news release** is a short article about an organization or event written to attract media attention, intended to lead to media coverage. Preparing press releases is probably the most popular and widespread PR activity. To be effective, the release must be as carefully targeted as an advertising media schedule. It should be sent to the right publications and be written in a style that those publications would use. The headline should give a clear idea of the subject. The release should then open with a paragraph that summarizes the main points of the news story by stating who did what, when, why, and where. The style should be that of a news report, and the story must be genuinely interesting to the publication's readers. Ideally, it should tell them something new that is happening and should contain a strong human angle. Other useful contents of a press release include a photograph and quotations, and it is essential to provide a contact name and telephone number in case journalists require further information. An example of a press release is given in Figure 9.3. Just as press releases can be effective media-attention grabbers, so can special press conferences. A press conference is a meeting at which a prepared presentation is made to invited media people.

Date: Dec. 21st, 2006

Source: Inniskillin Wines and Paintings Below Zero,
Niagara-on-the-Lake, Ontario, Canada

Contacts:
Deborah Pratt, Winery Public Relations Mgr.
dpratt@inniskillin.com 1-888-466-4754 x 310 Cell 905-327-5898

Caitlin Hicks, Communications-Paintings Below Zero
caitlinhicks@dccnet.com Cell-289-407-4759

Niagara Icewine Festival information
or
tickets www.niagarawinefestival.com
or
905-688-0212

PAINTINGS BELOW ZERO

by Gordon Halloran

ARTIST AND CREW DESCEND ON NIAGARA-ON-THE-LAKE TO BEGIN WORK ON EXTENSIVE INSTALLATION OF FROZEN PAINTINGS

during the 2007 Niagara Icewine Festival presented by Chrysler

---

continued

International artist Gordon Halloran arrived this week in Niagara-on-the-Lake to begin work on **Paintings Below Zero**, an extremely large installation of frozen paintings. The artist and crew were invited to be part of the **12th Annual Niagara Icewine Festival presented by Chrysler**. Halloran's unique frozen paintings here featured at the **2006 Olympic Winter Games** in **Torino, Italy**. His work is inspired by the vast Canadian winter landscape of ice and snow reflecting climate change and global warming as well as the ephemeral nature of existence.

Halloran invented this new art form — **frozen paintings** — and with each installation he develops the art form further. He is currently working in the **outside courtyard** at the Shaw Festival Theatre to create a completely new and unique installation of **Paintings Below Zero** using copper piping in addition to the freezer plate system which keeps the ice frozen. The circular copper piping will display colour and light, inspired by the grape vines of Ontario's many wineries. The natural process of these paintings is the movement of the crystal structure of the ice — freezing, melting, evaporating, re-freezing. About his work, Halloran says, "Everything is in motion."

The Icewine Festival is host to the premiere exhibition of the limited edition images from the Torino collection. These giclee prints are individually created by the artist and will be displayed **inside** at **The Donald and Elaine Triggs Production Centre at The Shaw Festival.** Throughout the exhibition the public can experience a café like setting featuring Inniskillin wine and food tasting.

This Exhibition is sponsored by

The Niagara Wine Festival, Ontario Cultural Attraction Fund, Inniskillin WinesAnd The Ontario Grape Growers of Ontario.

More information www.paintingsbelowzero.com

Current progress www.paintingsbelowzero.cominontario.blogspot.com

JANUARY 20–28, 2007

Shaw Festival Theatre

The Charles and Marilyn Baillie Courtyard and The Donald and Elaine Triggs Production Centre

10 Queen's Parade, Niagara-on-the-Lake

Daily 12:00 noon till 8:00 pm — $5.00

Tickets on arrival at the door at the Shaw Box Office
or
Niagara Wine Festival 905-688-0212.

Figure 9.3   Example of a Press Release

2. Feature Stories

feature stories

articles of human interest that entertain, inform, or educate readers, viewers, or listeners

Feature stories or features are articles of human interest that entertain, inform, or educate readers, viewers, or listeners. They are longer and have less immediate news value than news releases. However, such features can be extremely effective, and organizations in the tourism and hospitality sectors often encourage journalists to write stories about their products or services. The *Spotlight* describes how the Rocky Mountaineer benefited from an eight-page feature in the Thomas Cook travel magazine in its early days of business.

Familiarization tours or fam trips are an important part of many destination marketing initiatives. For example, during the summer of 2006, Northwest Territories Tourism hosted 21 different media fam trips for more than 40 media representatives. By hosting the media, the hope is that NWT Tourism products will be promoted in the media in magazines, television productions, websites, and newspapers, and on radio travel shows. Industry partners contributed $200 000 toward these fam trips. As an example of the value of such support, an article written by Chris Jagger, which ran in the UK's *Mail on Sunday* on April 2, 2006, was circulated to more than two million readers and was also available online. If NWT Tourism were to purchase one page of advertising in the same newspaper, it would cost $80 000.

3. Travel Exhibitions and Road shows

Many hospitality and travel organizations exhibit at travel trade shows, exhibitions, or conventions. Generally, these occasions bring together all parts of the industry (suppliers, carriers, intermediaries, and destination marketing organizations). Exhibiting at a trade show is similar to putting together a small promotional mix. Some exhibitors send out direct mail pieces (advertising) to intermediaries, inviting them to visit their booths. The booth displays (merchandising) portray the available services and may be tied in with recent advertising campaigns. Representatives working the booth hand out brochures and business cards and try to develop sales leads (personal selling). They may also give away free samples or vouchers (sales promotions). When the trade show is over, exhibitors often follow up with personalized mailings (direct mail) or telephone calls (telemarketing).

One of the largest trade shows in Canada is Rendez-vous Canada (RVC), an annual showcase organized by TIAC that puts Canada's export-ready tourism products in front of qualified international buyers. Another important annual event is Canada Media Marketplace, the cornerstone of the CTC's media relations program in the United States. In April 2007, Whistler hosted the Mountain Travel Symposium, the largest and longest-running annual gathering of mountain travel professionals in North America. The symposium brought 1000 delegates to Whistler, including North America's top buyers and sellers of mountain resort products. The event featured an educational forum, individual breakout sessions, and two separate trade shows with one specifically for tour operators and another for ski club and ski group organizers. A variety of social events and activities was scheduled throughout the week to provide additional network opportunities.

These trade shows are held in one place, but some trade shows take the form of roadshows that move from one city to the next. Each year, for example, the CTC's Roadshow visits various cities in Canada to present new partnering opportunities, market trends, and program updates developed by the commission and available to the industry. The CTC promotes the Canadian tourism industry by positioning Canada as a premier, four-season, world-class destination and works closely with the industry to achieve this. Partnering is an integral part of the CTC's strategy and is the essence of the Roadshow objectives.

4. Hosting and Sponsoring Events

event sponsorship

the financial support of an event (e.g., a car race, a theatre performance, or a marathon) by a sponsor in return for advertising privileges associated with the event

Event sponsorship is the financial support of an event (e.g., a car race, a theatre performance, or a marathon) by a sponsor in return for advertising privileges associated with the event. Sponsorships are usually offered by the organizer of the event on a tiered basis, which means that a lead sponsor pays a maximum amount and receives maximum privileges, whereas other sponsors pay less and receive fewer privileges. Investment in sponsorships is mainly divided among three areas: sports, entertainment, and cultural events. Sporting events attract the lion's share of sponsorship revenue. For example, the London 2012 Olympics are expected to attract over £100 million from just the top four to six main sponsors.[3]

Events are occurrences staged to communicate messages to target audiences. PR departments arrange press conferences, grand openings, public tours, and other events to create opportunities to communicate with specific audiences. Tourism and hospitality organizations or attractions can draw attention to themselves by arranging or sponsoring special events. The Empire State Building in New York, for example, has two annual events that generate large amounts of publicity for the 75-year-old attraction that draws more than 3.8 million visitors each year.[4] Valentine's Day weddings are the first event, with 14 couples chosen each year based on their strong attachment to the building. Then there is the Empire State Building Run-Up, when more than 100 runners from around the world race up 1576 steps to the 86th floor.

The sponsorship of events is also an effective way of gaining publicity, as it allows the sponsor to invite and host suppliers, journalists, distributors, and customers, as well as bring repeated attention to the company's name and products. The *Snapshot* on Air Canada referred to the airline's sponsorship of various events, such as such as the PGA Air Canada Championship. Companies should be careful however, in choosing the events that they sponsor. In 2005 there was some controversy over the decision by Eos, a luxury firm running business-class flights, to sponsor a performance by Sting in New York. The partnership was seen by some as incongruous as Sting is a self-proclaimed environmentalist, and Eos have been labelled "the world's worst" when it comes to pollution by Friends of the Earth.[5]

MARKETING IN ACTION

INNISKILLIN WINES

Wine tourism is hot. After a deep sleep of almost 50 years, the Canadian wine industry has experienced a dramatic rebirth over the last two decades, and Canadian wineries are capitalizing on the growth of wine tourism. The wineries in the Niagara region, for example, attract more than 300 000 visitors annually, and a push to develop regional cuisine has gained momentum. There are 17 wineries in the vicinity of the town of Niagara-on-the-Lake. They are all successful vintners, and they all offer tours, tastings, and special events featuring their wines. The challenge for these wineries is to combine a business focused on a consumer product with a successful tourist destination. As a group, they

MARKETING IN ACTION *continued*

successfully promote all the wineries under the prestigious Niagara-on-the-Lake destination, but each winery continues the challenge of marketing its own uniqueness in a cluster of competitors.

One winery attempting to differentiate itself is Inniskillin Wines. Founded in 1975 by Donald Ziraldo and Karl Kaiser, the company produces and bottles wines from select wine grapes grown in the Niagara Peninsula. Inniskillin's visitor facility is located among the vineyards at the winery site in view of the Niagara Escarpment. Renovations begun in 2006 have expanded the facility to create a major piazza connect the original restored Brae Burn Barn to a The Founders' Hall, a large hospitality space. The Founders' Hall contains a Culinary Corner within a larger space used for culinary events throughout the year. The open-concept kitchen allows easy interaction with chefs during demonstrations or dinners. This increases attention to the popularity of wine and culinary experiences that consumers are looking for. Inniskillin is well known for both table wines and icewines, but the strong international recognition of its icewines has led to an innovative Icewine Tasting Bar. Here visitors have a complete educational tasting exclusively dedicated to icewine. They can compare four styles while also seeing first hand the difference made by drinking out of a glass specially designed for icewine by Georg Riedel. Visitors learn about more than just the wine component. Food matches for icewine also are available, as this concentrated, expensive wine leaves many wondering what to pair it with.

Tour programs began as guided and self-guided. The innovative self-guided wine tour was developed in 1992, offering an easy alternative to guided tours and allowing flexibility within the visitors' arrival times. Commentary, illustrations, and photographs are set up at the stations, all of which have specifically designed windows that offer views into the winery facilities. This unique way of touring is evolving with the recent renovations.

The Inniskillin winery at Niagara-on-the-Lake hosts events, both public and private, year-round the Brae Brun Barn, the Piazza, and the Founders' Hall. Events range from tastings and sessions on wine and food pairings to events that are part of tours, festivals, and galas in partnership with the other wineries in the Niagara region. Most events are open to the public, and vary with costs, with some requiring reservations. Inniskillin clearly desires to make understanding wine and culinary a year-round experience for its consumers.

Inniskillin Wines uses public relations to maintain a consistent and positive public image and also to stay at the forefront of the minds of both those who purchase their product and those who visit the area around Niagara-on-the-Lake and who may visit their winery. The public image that Inniskillin wants to portray can be summed up by the statement that appears with the logo — One of the World's Great Wines.

Inniskillin ensures that any event of note related to the winery or the company's wines is communicated to the public through press releases. The following selected list of Inniskillin press releases provides an idea of the wide range of events that warrant the use of this PR tool. An example of such a press release was given earlier in the chapter.

December 10, 2003	Leading Wine Producer Announces Support of the Canadian Olympic Team
January 23, 2004	2004 Celebrity Icewine Picking & VIA Icewine Train
August 25, 2005	Inniskillin Launches Icewine Flavour Wheel

MARKETING IN ACTION *continued*

December 21, 2006	Inniskillin Launches Paintings Below Zero Exhibition during the Niagara Icewine Festival
September 17, 2007	VIA Rail and the Niagara Region Provide a Bounty of Wonders This Fall

Inniskillin wants the public to know about its current state of production, so the company publicizes its harvest, particularly the icewine picking. The company also forms partnerships with other companies, such as Riedel Glassware. Co-founders Ziraldo and Kaiser encouraged Georg Riedel to create an icewine glass within his portfolio of wine-specific glassware. The winery associates its products with celebrities when appropriate, such as with the event with the Food Network Canada, many wine and food programs and features, and its Celebrity Icewine Picking, which has featured Blue Rodeo's Jim Cuddy, CBC's Ron McLean, actor/singer Michael Burgess, Rush's Geddy Lee, and several Canadian Olympians.

Perhaps the most important idea that is communicated through Inniskillin's press releases is the recognition and renown that its wines receive at competitions around the world. Although Inniskillin enters many of its wines into competitions, its icewine is by far its signature product. The making of icewine requires a great deal of attention and skill and, not surprisingly, requires advantageous climatic conditions. In 1991, Inniskillin's 1989 icewine won Le Grand Prix d'Honneur at Vinexpo in Bordeaux, France — the fair's highest award — and, according to Inniskillin's website, "the greatest of international accolades for Canadian icewine."

Sources: Getz, D. (2000). *Explore wine tourism*. New York: Cognizant Communication Corporation; Inniskillin Wine. (2007). www.inniskillin.com (retrieved September 2007).

5. The Sponsorship of Causes

cause-related marketing

marketing that associates an organization with support for a good cause

The sponsorship of causes is part of the wider activity of **cause-related marketing**, a technique whereby organizations associate themselves with support for a good cause. An example is Transat A.T. Inc., which launched a program in 2007 to support sustainable tourism projects. Transat president and CEO Jean-Marc Eustache said that the company wanted to increase awareness of the importance of conservation among the general public and the tourism community. The company offers financial support of up to $50 000 per project. Another example comes from the restaurant chain White Spot (see the *Spotlight* in Chapter 7). Founder Nat Bailey's belief that a business that receives from the community should also give back to it remains a steadfast component of the company's corporate philosophy. A deep sense of community involvement is one of the core values the company seeks in potential franchisees. The White Spot family supports a variety of community-based sports teams and, off the playing field, the restaurant chain has a long history of helping organizations such as Vancouver's Children's Hospital, the Variety Club, United Way, Junior Achievement, and the White Spot Junior Pie Band, an award-winning musical group the company has sponsored for nearly four decades. Promoting driver safety has also been a high priority. Since the 1980s White Spot Restaurants has distributed tens of thousands of "If You Drink, Don't Drive" stickers.

Cause-related marketing is a rapidly expanding public relations trend, and is covered in more detail in Chapter 13.

6. Publications

publications

annual reports,
brochures, newsletters,
and magazines that
can draw attention to
an organization and its
products and services,
can help build its
image, and can convey
news to target markets

Organizations rely extensively on communication materials to reach and influence their target markets. **Publications** such as annual reports, brochures, newsletters, and magazines can draw attention to an organization and its products and services, and can help build its image and convey news to target markets. Audio-visual materials, such as films, videocassettes, and DVDs are coming into increasing use as promotion tools. Large companies such as Disney send promotional videos directly to consumers as well as to members of the travel trade. Smaller companies, such as Canadian Mountain Holidays (CMH) profiled in Chapter 7, will produce videos (CMH, for example, makes videos for heli-skiing, heli-hiking, and mountaineering in six languages) and then show them to specific audiences such as intermediaries or targeted audiences.

7. Winning or Sponsoring Awards

In many industries, such as the car industry, it has become common practice for organizations to promote their achievements. Automotive awards presented in magazines such as *Motor Trends* have long been known to carry clout with potential car buyers. Award winning has become increasingly important in tourism and hospitality sectors as well. For individual operators, the winning of an award is a campaign opportunity, a fact recognized by award-winning organizations such as Virgin Atlantic and Whistler Resort. These organizations will use the third-party endorsements in their advertising to build credibility and attract customers. Most of the awards in tourism and hospitality promote best performance and are often an indication of quality. They can therefore provide excellent publicity for winners.

An example of a successful awards scheme is the Alberta Tourism Awards (ALTO), which began in 2001. Contestants can enter one or more of eight different categories such as Marketing Excellence or Friends of Tourism, and independent judges review all submissions before deciding on the winner. Each award is sponsored by various organizations that in turn benefit from the publicity that the awards generate. All Alto finalists are recognized at an annual gala ceremony held in conjunction with the Travel Alberta Tourism Industry conference.

8. Celebrity Visits

Encouraging celebrities to use tourism and hospitality products or service can result in considerable media coverage, and can therefore help to promote that particular product or service. For example, Richard Branson built Virgin Atlantic Airways with the help of a strong public relations campaign that included inviting as many rock stars as possible to fly on his airline. Destinations, too, can benefit from celebrity visits. The ski resorts at Whistler have a reputation for attracting high-profile film and music stars, such as Arnold Schwarzenegger, Kevin Costner, and British singer Seal, as well as business magnates such as Microsoft's Bill Gates.

One popular destination in the Bahamas, Atlantis Resort, generates a considerable amount of publicity by attracting celebrities. With its aquatic and tropical decorated rooms costing up to $1000 per night for the fashionable Ocean Club facilities and the $25 000-per-day Bridge Suite, the resort attracts movie, music, and television celebrities from all over the world. For example, The Atlantis sponsored the film *After the Sunset,* which starred Pierce Brosnan, Salma Hayek, and Woody Harrelson. Joss Stone, Janet Jackson, Christina Aguilera, and Gloria Estefan have staged concerts there and Michael Jordan, who favours the Bridge Suite, regularly hosts his own celebrity golf tournaments at the island's onsite golf course.

9. Product Placement

product placement

the insertion of brand logos or branded products into movies and television shows

Product placement is the insertion of brand logos or branded products into movies and television shows, and it is another tactic for generating publicity. Since television viewers have a tendency — and now the technology — to zip through or avoid commercials, product placement has become increasingly popular with many organizations. In fact, product placement is now so blatant that the brand is often integrated right into the script of the movie. The movie *Castaway*, staring Tom Hanks, was little more than an extended commercial for FedEx courier company. In addition to featuring countless FedEx packages and logos, the film even managed to accommodate a brief history of the courier's corporate rise. *Survivor*, the popular reality TV show, has featured brands such as Reebok, Mountain Dew, Budweiser, and Doritos, and seemingly every movie starring Tom Cruise is loaded with product placements — even those that are set 50 years into the future!

Tourism and hospitality organizations have been quick to take advantage of this growing trend to generate publicity through product placement. British Airways was one of the first companies to be endorsed by James Bond in his movies, although Virgin were his airline of choice in the recent film *Casino Royale*. Virgin also paid a large amount for a promotional tie-in with the 1999 *Austin Powers: The Spy Who Shagged Me*. The movie contained a huge plug for "Virgin Shaglantic," and star and writer Mike Myers promoted the film in the U.S. by appearing on posters for Virgin Atlantic with the headline "There's only one virgin on this poster, baby." Hotels have also got in on the act. Mandalay Bay Hotel, Las Vegas took on the fictional role of the Montecito Resort & Casino in *Las Vegas,* one of NBC's top dramas between 2003 and 2005. The hotel also appeared in the popular reality show *Fear Factor*. No cash payments were involved in either placements, but NBC filmed free of charge in the Mandalay's gambling halls and other rooms. In addition, for *Fear Factor*, the crew and contestants received more than 820 room nights at Mandalay, Luxor, and the Monte Carlo resorts, as well as 2100 free meals. In return for the help, Mandalay gets the product placement, and the casino's Las Vegas-based ad agency, R&R Partners, estimates the one-hour *Fear Factor* was worth more than $10 million in paid advertising.

Often, product placement agencies are employed to broker the deals. Orbitz, one of the largest online travel companies in the world, is a client of the California-based Creative Entertainment Services Inc. (CES). CES has successfully placed Orbitz in a number of films and television programs, including the films *Single Santa Seeks Mrs. Claus, A Lot Like Love,* and NBC's *The Contender.*

Destinations, too, have begun to see product placement as an opportunity to gain exposure. In Canada, the film *Brokeback Mountain* inspired thousands of overseas visitors to visit Alberta where the film was made. *Budget Travel Magazine* listed the film in the top 10 films of 2005 that would inspire people to travel to the destination featured in the film. Alberta tourism officials capitalized on the success of the movie by linking the film to Alberta at every possible media opportunity. They even persuaded Oprah Winfrey to mention where the film was made as she interviewed the actors on her TV show. Travel Alberta advertised on an electronic billboard in Times Square New York emphasizing the fact that the spectacular scenery seen in the film was Alberta, and also sent 30 cowboys to downtown Manhattan to promote Alberta's cowboy culture. Officials estimated tracked media coverage linking the film to Alberta to be worth more than $1.3-million, far more than the original investment. The *Marketing in Action* in Chapter 13 shows how the Bahamas has been proactive in attracting films to be made in the Islands.

PERSONAL SELLING

personal selling

face-to-face interaction between a salesperson and the prospective consumer for the purpose of making a sale

Personal selling is face-to-face interaction between a salesperson and the prospective consumer (or prospect) for the purpose of making a sale. The high degree of personalization that personal selling involves usually comes at a much greater cost per contact than mass communication techniques. Organizations must decide whether this added expense can be justified, or whether marketing objectives can be achieved by communicating with potential customers in groups. And in this age of evolving technology and ubiquitous electronic communication, one element hasn't changed in the meetings and convention business: the industry is still driven by personal relationships. As Tony Pollard, president of the Ottawa-based Hotel Association of Canada likes to say, "You can't shake hands with a fax and you can't shake hands with an e-mail." Ralph Strachan, president and CEO of the Stronco Group of Companies and the former chair of the board of Tourism Toronto, adds, "Getting in the door, getting the attention of your client, and making an impression is the name of the game." Some tourism and hospitality organizations favour personal selling far more than others, as for them the potential benefits outweigh the extra costs. Companies such as MyTravel, parent company to Sunquest, AlbaTours, The Holiday Network, and Tours Maison, place a great emphasis on personal selling. For the Puerto Rico Convention Centre (see the *Case Study* at the end of the chapter), personal sales are an important part of its communications strategy.

Roles of Personal Selling

While the salesperson's job is to make a sale, his or her role goes well beyond this task. Personal selling plays a number of important roles in the tourism and hospitality industry, six of which are discussed below.

1. Gathering Marketing Intelligence

The salesperson must be alert to trends in the industry and to what the competitor is doing. Competitive knowledge is important when the salesperson faces questions involving product comparisons, and information on competitor's promotions can be very useful for the marketing department. Data collected by the salesperson is often reported electronically to the company's head office, where managers can retrieve the information and use it appropriately at a later date. Site inspections are a useful way of gathering market intelligence on competitors' properties, for example, and many hotels keep a file of their competition's promotional literature and rates.

2. Locating and Maintaining Customers

Salespeople who locate new customers play a key role in an organization's growth. Salespeople can identify qualified buyers (those most likely to purchase travel services), key decision makers (those who have the final say in travel decisions), and the steps involved in making travel decisions. This important information can be gathered effectively through inquiries by salespeople and from sales calls to an organization.

3. Promoting to the Travel Trade

Many organizations find personal selling to be the most effective communication tool in promoting to key travel decision makers and influencers in the travel trade, such as corporate travel managers, convention or meeting planners, tour operators, and retail travel agents. The purchasing power of these groups is impressive, and there are relatively few of them, which justifies the added expense of personal selling. Two significant opportunities for reaching those groups are the Canadian Meetings and Incentive Travel Show (CMITS) for the meetings and convention market and TIAC's Rendez-vous Canada for the tour and travel market.

4. Generating Sales at Point of Purchase

Personal selling can significantly increase the likelihood of purchase and the amount spent by customers at the point of purchase. Reservations staff at hotels and car rental desks have a great opportunity to persuade customers to buy a higher level of accommodations or category of cars (see up-selling, page 306), and staff in restaurants and travel agencies can have a major influence on the purchase decision of the customer. Increased sales are a result of the proper training of service and reservations staff in personal selling techniques.

5. Using Relationship Marketing

Sales representatives provide various services to customers: consulting on their problems, rendering technical assistance, arranging finance, and expediting delivery. These representatives are very important for building relationships with customers and maintaining their loyalty. Careful attention to individual needs and requirements is a powerful form of marketing for tourism and hospitality organizations. Key customers really appreciate the personal attention they receive from professional sales representatives and staff. This appreciation normally results in increased sales and repeat use, and the focus is always on creating and keeping long-term customers. This is just one part of a process that has become known as customer relationship management (CRM).

6. Providing Detailed and Up-to-Date Information to the Travel Trade

Personal selling allows an organization to pass on detailed information to the travel trade and provides an opportunity to deal immediately with a prospect's concerns and questions. This is especially important for an organization that relies on travel trade intermediaries for part or all of its business. Tour operators, for example, should have regular contact with travel agents in order to update them on changes in the marketing environment. In 2003, MyTravel merged its sales personnel into a single team to represent all of its brands. The move to consolidate and centralize inside sales meant that one representative of MyTravel replaced the three or more that a travel agency might have been accustomed to dealing with. Company reps were able to more readily explain the differences among the brands to help agents make the most out of the expansive product line.

Objectives of Personal Selling

Although sales objectives are customized for specific situations, there are general objectives that are commonly employed throughout the tourism and hospitality industry.

1. Sales Volume

Occupancy, passenger seats or miles, and total covers (restaurant seats) are common measures of sales volume within the industry. When it first opened, Calgary's Catch Restaurant and Oyster Bar, for example, employed two salespeople who were paid on the basis of the volume of covers that they generated for the establishment. An emphasis on volume alone, however, can lead to price discounting, the attraction of undesirable market segments, cost cutting, and employee dissatisfaction. Some sectors, such as exclusive resorts, unique adventure holidays, and upper-end cruises, restrict prospecting to highly selective segments, believing that price and profits will take care of themselves. Others may establish sales volume objectives by product lines to ensure a desired gross profit. This system is the basis for yield management (see Chapter 6).

2. Cross-Selling, Up-Selling, and Second-Chance Selling

cross-selling

persuading a customer to purchase additional allied products or services

Cross-selling occurs when a seller offers a buyer the opportunity to purchase additional allied products or services. Cross-selling is now integral to virtually every segment of the travel industry, travel insurance being one of the most profitable cross-sells in the industry. Good opportunities exist for tourism companies, such as hotels and resorts, to upgrade price and profit margins by selling higher-priced products such as suites through **up-selling**, which involves persuading a consumer to purchase a more profitable product or service. At the Ripley Ridge Retreat in Calgary (see Chapter 10), cross-selling and up-selling are tools used frequently in the sale of wedding packages. "We can turn a $300 wedding into a $3000 wedding just while the prospect is walking round the property," said Cara Ripley, marketing director. "We will try and satisfy needs as best we can, and we attempt to sell as many services as we can, from accommodation for the rehearsals to champagne breakfasts and brunches."

up-selling

persuading a customer to purchase a more profitable product or service

second-chance selling

trying to sell additional products or services to a customer who has already made a purchase

A related concept is **second-chance selling**, trying to sell additional products or services to a customer who has already made a purchase. For example, a salesperson may contact a client who has already booked an event such as a three-day meeting to try to sell services such as airport limousine pick-up or try to upgrade rooms or food and beverage services.

3. Market Share

Some sectors of the tourism industry are more concerned with market share than others. Airlines, cruise lines, major fast food chains, and rental car companies, for example, often focus more on market share than do restaurants, hotels, and resorts. As a consequence, salespeople are sometimes required to measure market share or market penetration and are held accountable for a predetermined level of either or both. As one hotel's director of sales says, it is useful to look at that the market share relative to other hotels in the vicinity to send back to the chain's regional office in order to prepare a report that tracks occupancies and revenues for each month.

4. Product-Specific Objectives

Occasionally, a sales force will be charged with the specific responsibility of improving sales volume for specific product lines. This objective may be associated with up-selling and second-chance selling, but may also be part of the regular sales duties of the sales force. Such objectives might be to sell more hotel suites, holiday packages to Mexico, honeymoon packages, or more premium car rentals. A common approach used to encourage the sale of specific products is to set objectives for them and to reward performance with bonuses or other incentives.

The Sales Process

The sales process consists of the following seven steps as outline in Figure 9.4.

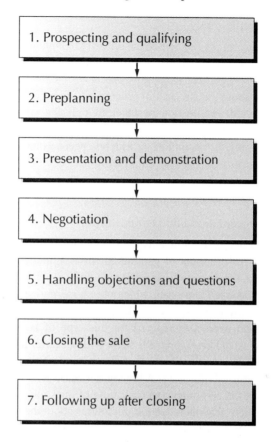

Figure 9.4   The Sales Process

1. Prospecting and Qualifying

prospecting

the process of searching for new customers

Prospecting is the process of searching for new customers. It has been said that there are three truisms about prospecting: most salespeople don't like to prospect; most salespeople do not know how to prospect; and most organizations are inept at teaching or training salespeople to prospect. There are two key elements to successful prospecting. The first is to determine positioning strategy, i.e., to whom you should prospect. The second is implementing a process to find and ultimately contact those prospects on a one-to-one basis. This might involve consulting a variety of directories or using telemarketing, or, for small organizations, it might mean waiting until customers make contact through word of mouth or through their website. For example, a couple planning their wedding may key in "Calgary weddings" on the Internet, find the Ripley Ridge Retreat website, and then call the company's 1-800 number.

2. Preplanning

A successful sales call, made either by telephone or in the field, requires careful preplanning and preparation. There are two elements to preplanning a sales call: the pre-approach and the approach. In the pre-approach stage, a salesperson needs to learn as much as possible about the prospect in order to be able to establish a rapport during the sales call and to have the foundation on which to build the sales presentation itself. The approach then follows and involves all the activities that lead to the sales presentation. These include arranging the appointments with prospects, establishing rapport and confidence at the start of a sales call, and checking preliminary details prior to the sales presentation. Sales representatives have three principal objectives in their approaches: to build rapport with the prospect, to capture a person's full attention, and to generate interest in the product.

3. Presentation and Demonstration

The salesperson now tells the product or service "story" to the prospect, often following the AIDA formula of gaining attention, holding interest, arousing desire, and inspiring action. Companies have developed three different styles of sales presentation. The oldest is the canned approach, which uses a memorized sales talk that covers the main points. The formulated approach identifies early the buyer's needs and buying styles and then uses an approach prepared for this type of buyer, which follows a general plan. The need/satisfaction approach starts with a search for the customer's needs by encouraging the customer to do most of the talking. This approach calls for good listening and problem-solving skills. A common method with the formulated approach in hotel sales is to ask the corporate client a variety of questions about their company and meeting needs and then show them a book of pictures about the property To illustrate how it can accommodate their needs.

According to experts, certain words make listeners take notice. Apparently, the 15 most persuasive sales words are discover, money, guaranteed, love, proven, safe, own, best, good, easy, health, new, results, save, and free.[6] It has been suggested that a salesperson needs to introduce a "wow" factor: an intangible element that causes an emotional response in potential buyers, making them take a second look, draw in breath, and say, "Wow, I have to buy that!"[7] There are two ways to create the wow factor. The first is by introducing a product that is unique. More often than not, this is impossible, so the second way is to add the factor to the sales personality by generating enthusiasm and delivering what is promised.

4. Negotiation

Much of selling to the travel trade involves negotiation skills. For meeting planners and hotel groups, for example, the two parties need to reach agreement on the price and other terms of the sale. The hotel salesperson will be seeking to win the order without making deep concessions that will hurt profitability. Although price is the most frequently negotiated issue, other factors may be taken into account, and numerous bargaining tools exist.

Sales force members should be taught to negotiate using services or bundled services as the primary negotiating tool rather than price. To follow with the example of the hotel, negotiations should begin with rack rates and price concessions should be given only when absolutely essential. Other negotiating tools, such as upgrades, airport pick-up, or champagne in rooms, can be employed. A hotel might package these amenities into bundles of services and brand them with names such as the Prestige Package, in order to entice buyers into making a booking.

At the Banff Rocky Mountain Resort, Shelley Grollmuss often provides complimentary upgrades or additional services that are of minimal cost to the hotel. "However, we try to make our proposal look as enticing as possible from the start. These days you are rarely given the opportunity to negotiate on the room rate — it has to be attractive and competitive from the start." At the Ripley Ridge Retreat in Calgary, prices for corporate retreats are usually competitive enough to win the business, but Cara Ripley will discount a maximum of 10 percent if a corporate customer requests it. "We find that most people don't ask because our prices are low enough already, but to be successful you have to understand how to negotiate in order to close a sale."

5. Handling Objections and Questions

When sales presentations are completed, most prospects ask questions and raise one or more objections. Objections come in all forms, even through body language. Resistance can be psychological (e.g., preference for rooms on a certain floor in a hotel) or logical (e.g., price). There are several effective ways to handle objections. One is to restate the objection and to prove diplomatically that it is not as important as it seems. Another is the "agree and neutralize" tactic or the "yes, but" approach. In this approach, the sales representative initially agrees that a problem exists, but goes on to show that the problem is not relevant or accurate. No matter which approach is used, objection must be dealt with directly.

6. Closing the Sale

Closing means getting a sales prospect to agree with the objectives of the sales call, which normally implies making a definite purchase or reservation. Closing the sale can be the most important stage of the sales process, and without it a sales call is unsuccessful. Every salesperson must ask for the business or at least some commitment to continue the dialogue, but many are not comfortable asking for the order or do not recognize the opportune moment to wrap things up. Knowing when and how to close are the keys to success. As with objections, this again requires careful attention to the prospect's words and body language. Closing techniques include actually asking for the order, offering to help write up the order, asking whether the buyer wants A or B, asking how the buyer would like to pay, or indicating what the buyer will lose if the order is not placed immediately.

At the Ripley Ridge Retreat, it is the job of Shawn Ripley to close the sale for a wedding. Asking for the business happens when the tour of the property finishes inside the reception room (which contains a cash machine), where Shawn will ask the couple if they would like to check availability, block a certain date off, and then leave a $100 deposit. According to the retreat's owners, 100 percent of prospective customers book on the spot.

7. Following Up after Closing

A salesperson's work is not finished until all the required steps and arrangements are made to deliver the promised services. In some cases, such as large conventions or incentive travel trips, delivery is extensive. However, the follow-up is essential if the salesperson wants to ensure customer satisfaction and repeat business. "Follow up or foul up" is the slogan of many successful salespeople. It is often advisable to give buyers some kind of reassurance that they have made the right decision. This reduces the buyers' level of **cognitive dissonance** — the customer's uncertainty after making a purchase (sometimes referred to as buyer's remorse). An important part of post-sale activity also involves immediate follow-up after buyers or their clients have actually used the services. Many travel agents use this effectively by telephoning clients soon after their trips to find out what they liked and did not like. Many hotel salespeople follow up with their clients directly after their functions to ensure that everything went as anticipated.

cognitive dissonance

a customer's uncertainty after making a purchase

SNAPSHOT

SELLING BEDS AT THE WESTIN EDMONTON

The Westin Edmonton is part of Starwood Hotels & Resorts, and the 4.5-star hotel has 416 guest rooms and suites, as well as 2230 square metres of meeting and banquet space. Selling to groups and business travellers is the main focus of the sales team at The Westin Edmonton. "Due to the strong economy in Alberta, we are experiencing a marked increase in leisure and business travel. We are also able to garner higher rates based on demand and our newly renovated guestrooms," says JoAnn Kirkland, director of sales and marketing.

Site visits are an important part of the sales process. When a buyer visits the hotel the staff do everything possible to impress. For example, they may put pictures up of the prospective buyers everywhere back of house prior to the visit, so that all members of staff can give the buyer personal attention. Preparation for the site inspection is very important. By finding out beforehand everything they can about the company and what their needs are, the Westin sales team can then tailor the site inspection to those requirements. However, not all selling takes place at the hotel. Sales managers travel three to four times a year to major Canadian cities for sales purposes, and occasionally to cities outside of Canada.

Sales planning is a key part of Kirkland's job. "What we do is forecast the entire year, based on existing bookings and historical data, and then plot a grid for our sales managers. We then work out a minimum target for each period, and the sales managers will be armed with this knowledge when they meet with a buyer." If a buyer or meeting planner is not prepared to pay this target room rate, then the sales personnel may negotiate by offering services such as free parking. Each sales manager has a room-night target and a revenue target. Food and beverage sales are also very important, and sales managers are encouraged to get buyers to commit to a certain amount of food and beverage sales, even if the event is three years away.

SNAPSHOT *continued*

Most of the training for The Westin sales team is web-based; it is live and interactive and contains about six different modules covering topics such as negotiating, handling objections, and making presentations. Salespeople can take them on their own, and each module takes about two and a half hours. Kirkland can see how well they have performed on each module, so if she sees one salesperson has not done well with presentations, she can offer extra training. Turnover is high among salespeople in the hotel industry, so the Starwood philosophy is to "pay for performance" to try to keep high-quality salespeople: sales managers can win incentive trips to luxury resorts by meeting pre-determined targets. Other incentives used by Kirkland include team-building exercises outside the hotel (such as a game of golf), reward points, and extra holidays. Kirkland also offers small cash incentives for good performance on the Starwood Mystery Shopping program. In this program, telephone calls are made by third-party researchers to various Starwood Hotels as well as to key competitors, and sales managers are scored on factors such as greeting, qualification of needs, presentation, handling of objections, attempts to close, and professionalism.

To encourage repeat business there is a loyalty program in place for meeting and event planners, called Starwood Preferred Planner. This program allows planners to earn one Starpoint for every $3 of group revenue spent. These points can be redeemed and put toward future hotel room nights, as a credit toward their group master bill.

Source: Personal correspondence with J. Kirkland, Director of Sales and Marketing, The Westin Edmonton, November 24, 2006.

Sales Management

sales management

the management of the sales force and personal selling efforts to achieve desired sales objectives

Sales management is the management of the sales force and personal selling efforts to achieve desired sales objectives. A sales manager has five key roles to play: recruiting salespeople, training them, motivating and rewarding them, sales planning, and sales performance evaluation.

1. Recruiting Salespeople

A sales manager's first job is to hire competent people to fill available positions. In tourism and hospitality, it is uncommon for field sales representatives to be hired without sales experience. The more established practice is for entry-level people to be order takers, who are eventually promoted to sales representative positions. Hiring salespeople from competitors and related outside organizations is also common. Research has shown that no one set of physical characteristics, mental abilities, and personality traits predicts sales success in every situation. Salespeople's success depends more on the actual tasks assigned to them and the environment in which they operate. Most customers say they want salespeople to be honest, reliable, knowledgeable, and helpful. Companies should look for these traits when selecting candidates. Another approach is to look for traits common to the most successful salespeople in the company. A study of high achievers found that high sales performers exhibited the following traits: they were risk takers, had a powerful sense of mission, had a problem-solving bent, cared about the customer, and engaged in careful planning.[8]

2. Training Salespeople

Sales training programs are very important to the continuation of success in personal selling. For example, every year, the Canadian Institute of Travel Counsellors (CITC) holds two Executive Certified Travel Manager retreats. Participants spend much of the program analyzing a travel agency case study. They deal with a range of issues and review the current obstacles and opportunities before the agency to determine what marketing and sales efforts should be employed, as well as what requirements agency staff have. At the close of the program, an individual strategic plan is drawn up for the case study agency that can then be used as a model to implement strategies for participants' agencies.

Many employers recognize the benefits of professional certification and give preference to certified individuals when hiring. The Canadian Tourism Human Resource Council (CTHRC) produces National Occupational Standards (in English and French) for the Canadian tourism industry under the "emirit" brand. The standards describe the skills, knowledge, and professionalism necessary in a sales manager in the accommodations sector. However, the standards also apply to other tourism sectors. They are the building blocks for achieving professional certification in the occupation, and are often used in training programs. To ensure that its certificate occupations remain current and relevant, the CTHRC brings industry representatives together for standards updates and revisions on a three- to five-year cycle, or as deemed necessary by the industry. Other national occupational standards have been developed for catering managers, banquet managers, banquet servers, and room service attendants. The emerit website (www.emerit.ca) lists the training tools available for nearly 50 occupations in the tourism and hospitality industry.

3. Motivating and Rewarding Salespeople

The majority of salespeople require encouragement and special incentives to work at their best level. This is especially true of field selling, as the nature of the job makes it open to frequent frustration: sales reps usually work alone, their hours are irregular, and they are often away from home. Even without these factors, most people operate below capacity in the absence of special incentives, such as financial gain or social recognition. Sales managers therefore need to understand motivation theories and to provide financial and nonmonetary incentives to keep sales force motivation at its peak.

Financial incentives include salary and commissions, as well as fringe benefits such as paid vacations, insurance programs, and medical programs. Often bonuses are given when predetermined volumes of sales and profits, or sales quotas, are achieved. In the tourism and hospitality industry, free travel is a very important fringe benefit, especially for travel agency and airline staff. Non-monetary compensation and motivators are reward/recognition programs and job advancement opportunities. Sales promotions can also be used to motivate a sales force. However, they tend to work best in achieving short-term objectives and are not advisable over the long term.

4. Sales Planning

The heart of sales planning is the sales plan, usually prepared annually and containing a detailed description of personal selling objectives, sales activities, and the sales budget. These selling objectives are frequently set as forecasts of unit or sales volumes or some other financial target derived from expected sales levels. This sales forecast is very useful to others outside the sales department and is a key planning tool for the entire organization. Expected sales levels influence the allocation of personnel and financial resources in many other departments. But the selling objectives may also be non-financial, such as the number of sales calls, new sales prospects converted to customers, or the number of inquiries answered successfully.

The sales department budgets are another part of the sales plan. Typically these include the sales forecast, the selling expense budget, the sales administration budget, and the advertising and promotion budget. Given the relatively high cost of personal selling, this budget plays a key role in planning and controlling the sales effort. The sales plan will also include the assignment of sales territories and quotas. **Sales quotas** are minimum sales volume goals, and may be set for individual sales representatives, branch offices, or regions. They help sales managers motivate, supervise, control, and evaluate sales personnel. The sales manager is likely to use a combination of past territory performance and market indices to allocate quotas for each territory.

sales quotas

minimum sales volume goal

5. Evaluating Sales Performance

The final function of sales management is the measurement and evaluation of sales performance, often referred to as sales analysis. This assessment can be done by considering total sales volume or by looking at sales by territory or customer groups. One of the most important methods of evaluation is to compare actual results against sales forecasts and budgets.

DIRECT MARKETING AND DIRECT RESPONSE ADVERTISING

direct marketing

a form of marketing that sends messages directly to consumers using addressable media, such as mail

Direct marketing is a form of marketing that sends messages directly to consumers using "addressable" media, such as mail. It is rapidly becoming a vital component of the integrated marketing communications mix. In Canada, direct mail advertising alone accounts for $1.5 billion annually, or 13 percent of net advertising revenues. As an advertising medium it ranks third, just behind television and daily newspapers, and ahead of magazines, radio, and outdoor advertising.[9] Direct marketing has increased in popularity as businesses have come to place more importance on customer satisfaction and repeat purchase. Direct marketing makes use of databases, which allow precise targeting and personalization, thus helping organizations build continuing and enriching relationships with customers. There are eight key advantages of direct marketing, which are listed in Table 9.1.

Table 9.1

The Key Advantages of Direct Marketing

1. Precise targeting	Aims at a specific individual and provides opportunities to target not only general groups of potential buyers but also specific buyers.
2. Personalization	Provides an opportunity to personalize messages with individuals' names and build stronger links between the organization and the consumer.
3. Flexibility	Contents of each message can be changed to suit the individual requirements of each consumer and can be delivered to specific geographic locations.
4. Privacy	Offers not readily visible to competitors and do not broadcast an organization's competitive strategy as widely as mass communication advertising.
5. Measurability	Offers the ability to measure the effectiveness of various response fulfillment packages sent out to prospects in terms of converting inquiries into sales, costs per booking, response by market segments, and so on.
6. Low cost	Generally lower costs per transaction than other forms of communication.
7. Detailed knowledge	Allow the gathering of valuable consumer information including names, addresses, lifestyle information, and purchasing behaviour.
8. Fast or immediate	Offers can be made quickly and can be quickly accepted, especially thanks to the Internet.

direct response advertising

advertising designed to generate a response by any means that is measurable

One segment of direct marketing is **direct response advertising**, which is designed to generate a response by any means that is measurable. It plays a major role in influencing consumer purchase patterns, and can use any medium such as direct mail, telephone (telemarketing), fax, or Internet. The message will include a toll-free telephone number, mailing address, or website where more information can be obtained. Another form is direct response television (DRTV).

Figure 9.5 presents some of the communication strategies of the four main forms of direct response advertising, discussed below.

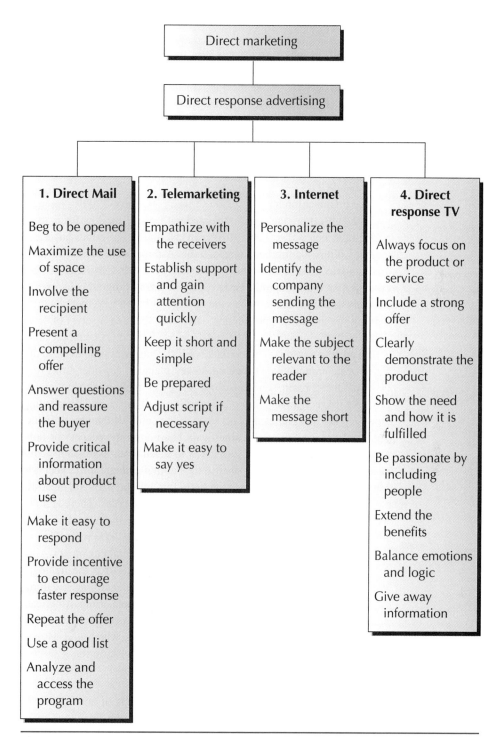

Figure 9.5   Strategic Considerations for Major Forms of Direct Response Advertising

1. Direct Mail

Direct mail, in which an offer is sent to a prospective customer by mail, is by far the most common form of direct response advertising. The use of mail is widespread due to its ability to personalize the message (the name can be included in the mailing), its ability to convey lengthy messages (printed sales messages can be sent with reply cards or contracts that can be returned by prospects), and its ability to provide a high degree of geographic coverage economically (the mailing can be distributed to designated postal codes anywhere in Canada). There are numerous options available to organizations wishing to use direct mail — examples include sales letters, leaflets and flyers, folders, brochures, DVDs, and CDs.

An organization has the option of using **solo direct mail** — sending a mail piece by itself and absorbing the costs associated with such a mailing (as in the postcard campaign highlighted below), or **cooperative direct mail** — sending an offer in a package that includes offers from other organizations. A direct mail campaign in 2006 by Edmonton Tourism was awarded a Mobius Advertising Awards Certificate of Excellence. A unique brochure for the Edmonton Festive City in a Box program was used to encourage event planners to choose Edmonton as the host city for their next meeting or convention by highlighting the theming opportunities. The piece featured a series of seven original illustrations, each highlighting a different facet of Edmonton's vibrant arts and culture scene across all four seasons. The booklet was 20 centimetres square with die-cut windows and flaps to accommodate text focused on key planning considerations for event planners.

The three basic steps involved in direct mail marketing are obtaining a proper prospect list, conceiving and producing the mail piece, and distributing the final version. However, the first step is the backbone of the entire campaign. Both the accuracy and definition of the list can have a significant bearing on the success or failure of a campaign. Organizations recognize that it costs six to seven times as much to acquire a new customer as it does to keep an existing one, so they compile databases to keep track of existing customers and form relationships with them through the mail and electronic means.

Lists are secured from internal and external sources. There is no better prospect than a current customer, so an organization's internal database must be monitored and updated routinely. In direct mail terms, an internal customer list is referred to as a "house list." As an alternative, organizations can form lists of potential customers. A list broker can assist in finding these prospects — those that perhaps mirror the demographic and psychographic profile of existing customers. Many hotels and airlines use third-party address lists from membership databases purchased, for example, from American Express or other credit card company databases. Such lists can usually be accessed at a cost per 1000 names. An organization can also purchase a response list, which is a list of proven mail-order buyers, or a circulation list, which is a magazine subscription list.

2. Telemarketing

One form of direct marketing that combines aspects of advertising, marketing research, and personal sales is **telemarketing**, which uses the telephone to reach customers or prospective customers. Telemarketing developed rapidly through the 1990s through the combination of technology-led development of consumer databases, telephone communications, and creation of call centres. A **call centre** is a central operation that handles inbound and outbound telemarketing programs. Inbound telemarketing refers to the reception of calls by the order desk, customer inquiry, and direct response calls often generated

direct mail

a type of direct response advertising in which an offer is sent to a prospective customer by mail

solo direct mail

a direct mail piece sent out by one organization

cooperative direct mail

a direct mail offer sent in a package that includes offers from other organizations

telemarketing

using the telephone to reach customers or prospective customers

call centre

a central operation that handles inbound and outbound telemarketing programs through the use of toll-free numbers. Outbound telemarketing, on the other hand, refers to calls that an organization makes to customers to develop new accounts, generate sales leads, and even close a sale. There are now more than 6000 call centres in Canada.

Telemarketing is becoming increasingly popular in tourism and hospitality industries. For example, in its first year of operation, Greenfield Hospitality Services Inc., a business-to-business telemarketing team of five agents, completed 25 projects and made more than 150 000 outbound phone calls for clients in the Canadian hospitality and tourism industry. Greenfield's clients include notables such as Resorts Atlantic, Rogers Media (*Meetings and Incentive Travel* magazine and *Marketing Magazine*), Kostuch Publications (*Hotelier* magazine, *Foodservice and Hospitality* magazine), Tourism Whistler, the Renaissance Toronto Hotel Downtown, the Ottawa Marriott Hotel, the Toronto Marriott Bloor Yorkville, and Meetings Prince Edward Island. In the future, its Teleservices Division will likely diversify operations with programs aimed at the publishing industry, government, and the association markets. The company also plans to venture into the U.S. marketplace.

The primary advantage of telemarketing is that it can complete a sale for less cost than is needed to complete a sale using such techniques as face-to-face sales calls or mass advertising. However, for this method to be effective, proper training and preparation of telemarketing representatives must be as comprehensive as it is for personal selling. Planning the message is as important as the medium itself. A drawback to telemarketing is the fact that consumers react negatively to it. The majority of Canadians consider telemarketing calls unwelcome and intrusive, and such calls are ranked as one of the least desirable sales techniques. Furthermore, half of the population thinks there are too many calls, and the same numbers of people react to them by hanging up. Despite this behaviour, organizations believe that the advantages of telemarketing, such as call reach and frequency and cost efficiency, outweigh the disadvantages.

3. Internet

The role of the Internet in direct response advertising is discussed in the Chapter 10. Needless to say, direct e-mail marketing, often eliciting direct e-mail response, is one of the most promising applications in online advertising.

4. Direct Response Television

DRTV is one of the fastest-growing segments of the direct response industry. Advertisers are attracted to this medium because it allows them to track response rates. Today, savvy advertisers such as American Express focus on advertising with a built-in response mechanism that allows them to judge results. There are essentially three forms of direct response television: 60-second (or longer) commercials that typically appear on cable channels, infomercials, and direct–home shopping channels. In all cases, the use of toll-free telephone numbers and credit cards make the purchase more convenient for the viewer.

Cable television lends itself to direct response because the medium is targeted to particular interests. The Shopping Channel (TSC), for example, has annual sales of $170 million, reaching millions of households. DRTV also makes good use of the infomercial format. An **infomercial** is a commercial, usually 30 minutes long, that presents the benefits of a product or service. Criticized in the past for being exclusively "get-rich-quick" concepts, many infomercials are now highly informative and well produced, although tourism and hospitality organizations have been slow to adopt this form of direct response advertising.

infomercial

a television commercial, usually 30 minutes long, that presents the benefits of a product or service

Digital television is likely to have a huge impact on the sale of tourism products and services, even though interactive television sets with computer capabilities are still a novelty. Digital television offers consumers travel services via digital travel agents or online tour operators, allowing them to make an immediate booking for the destination or tour featured on the television screen. This is an exceptionally effective sales tool. Many travel agents believe that digital television will be a greater threat to business than the Internet, precisely because it is an incredibly interactive medium facilitated by a very familiar tool — the television remote control. In 2004, VisitLondon launched a 24-hour digital TV channel to promote the British capital as a tourist destination. London TV appears on SkyDigital and provides reports and features on topics such as film, theatre, shopping, and tourist sites. Digital specialist Enteraction TV, the company behind Thomas Cook TV, runs the channel and produces content. Martine Ainsworth-Wells, general manager for marketing at VisitLondon, said the decision to launch the channel was made because it was more cost-effective than ploughing money into advertising.[10]

PROFILE

DENNIS CAMPBELL'S POSTCARD CAMPAIGN

At 18, Dennis Campbell believed he could build a successful tourism business based on Nova Scotia's Scottish history and heritage. To do this he registered a company in 1987 called Halifax City Guide Services and tagged it "The Company with the Kilts." By 1995, the company — now called Ambassatours Gray Line — was grossing $3.5 million and had become the number-one tour operator in Atlantic Canada after merging with Atlantic Tours. These days, the Atlantic Tours product is the company's main revenue generator, selling the four Atlantic provinces as a motorcoach destination to customers all over the world. To do this, Campbell, who is president of the company, markets through direct mail and aggressive web marketing aimed primarily at clients in Canada, the United States, the United Kingdom, Germany, Australia, and New Zealand, and has a marketing budget of $400 000.

PROFILE *continued*

However, when he was building his business in the early days, Campbell's best idea was the least expensive one. He called it the "postcard campaign": it was simple, creative, and possessed the boldness that only someone with nothing to lose would dare. Campbell was trying to attract the attention of his "dream client list." A dream client was a Holland America, a Carnival Cruise Line, a Cunard Cruise Line, a Tauck Tours — "someone who has the potential to give us a couple hundred thousand dollars worth of business," said Campbell. These companies were at the conventions, but Campbell was aware that "they were practically a fortress. They don't want to talk to you because they get bombarded — our dream client is everyone's dream client." He realized that mailing or phoning was not going to work, so he decided to start sending them postcards until he had their attention. "I sent one every month, and I wrote out for each month what the message would be."

He started with the cruise lines. He obtained the list of them and started writing postcards. For example, his first postcard to the head of shore excursions for Holland America at the time, Paul Stouffer, read: "Dear Paul, We are a shore excursion company that provides kilted guides, bagpipers, step dancers, and all kinds of neat things." The next month's read: "Dear Paul, Hope you got our postcard last month. We would like you to consider using us." Third month's read: "Dear Paul, We're not going to stop sending you postcards until we have your business." The next postcard read: "Dear Paul. Don't mean to sound pushy like the last postcard, but we really want your business."

After bombarding Holland America's Seattle offices with postcards, Campbell finally encountered his Stouffer at a Miami trade show. Campbell approached him and said, "Paul Stouffer? Dennis Campbell. Would you like a postcard?" Apparently, Stouffer laughed and said, "Dennis Campbell! Dennis, listen, I'll make you a deal. Stop sending me those damn postcards and I'll give you our business." The same thing happened with Cunard Cruise Lines. When Campbell called Cunard Cruise Lines and said, "It's Dennis Campbell, I'm going to be down in New York, can I meet with you?" the woman on the phone responded, "Dennis Campbell, I'd like anything more than a postcard! I'd love to meet with you!"

The postcard mailing worked with Carnival, Cunard, Holland America, Clipper, Renaissance, and Silver Seas. In the summer cruise seasons of 1994 and 1995, the unique campaign, which used about 200 nine-cent handwritten postcards and stamps, brought in $600 000 in sales from some of the world's leading cruise lines. The value of this simple but persistent campaign over many years has generated many millions of dollars in sales. A key part of the campaign was Campbell's insistence that each card be handwritten with a short simple but consistent message so as not to lose its effect. He even asked his mother to write them as she had much nicer handwriting than her son!

Ambassatours Gray Line now owns a group of companies: Atlantic Tours Limited, Nova Tours, Absolute Charters, Gray Line of Nova Scotia, Gray Line of New Brunswick, and Gray Line of Prince Edward Island. It is now not only the largest tour operator in Atlantic Canada but is now also the largest motorcoach tour operator in Atlantic Canada, having grown from 14 buses in 2003 to 53 buses in 2007. In 2006, the company had 45 year-round staff and just over 200 seasonal staff, with revenues in excess of $10.5 million. The company still uses postcard campaigns today as one of its most effective ways to get incremental business.

The company now uses technology to build on this persistent targeted approach by sending custom designed, personalized handwritten cards and postcards through the web using www.sendoutcards.com. Ambassatours

PROFILE *continued*

Gray Line uses the web to send a personalized handwritten thank-you card to each and every customer who has travelled on one of their multi-day tour packages. This personal touch is paying off. According to Dennis Campbell, "It's cheap, very cool, and it works — awesome! Personalized direct marketing at its finest."

Sources: Lynch, A. (1996). Ambassatours: Heritage drag pays off. In A. Lynch (Ed.). *Sweat equity: Atlantic Canada's new entrepreneurs* (181–194). Halifax: Nimbus; Personal communication with Dennis Campbell, March 12, 2007.

WORD OF MOUTH

word of mouth

communication about products and services among people perceived to be independent of the organization

Word of mouth is communication about products and services among people perceived to be independent of the organization.[11] It is a communication tool that works particularly well for the tourism and hospitality industry, and is worthy of special attention. Recommendations or advice from friends, relatives, peers, and influential persons are without doubt one of the most powerful communications media. Word of mouth can be controlled only to a degree, but it must be a priority nevertheless for tourism businesses, and it is indeed used in a variety of sectors of tourism. For example, Inniskillin Wines has recognized that even non-buyers are primary sources of communications about the winery and the wines tasted, and can have a potentially tremendous impact on future visits and remote sales. The Vancouver Convention and Exhibition Centre also values the power of word of mouth. Its "Be a Host" program assists local people to help sell Vancouver as a destination in their respective industries, and has helped to establish credibility and profile for the centre.

Word-of-mouth communications can be conversations or just one-way testimonials. They can be live or canned. They can be conveyed in person, by telephone, by e-mail, via a listserv group, or by any other means of communication. They can be one-to-one, one-to-many (broadcast), or group discussions. A growing trend is the reliance on user-generated online content (or blogs) as a way for consumers to become informed before travelling. This is discussed in more detail in the next chapter. The essential element is that such communications are from or among people who are perceived to have little commercial vested interest in persuading someone else to use the product and therefore no particular incentive to distort the truth in favour of the product. In contrast, advertising is the communication of a message that is chosen, designed, and worded by the seller of the product, in a medium that is owned or rented. A sales message is a "company line" delivered by a representative of the organization. On the other hand, word of mouth is originated by a third party and transmitted spontaneously in a way that is independent of the producer or seller, and can therefore have a high level of credibility.

In *The Anatomy of Buzz*, Emanuel Rosen takes a substantive look at creating word-of-mouth excitement about a product.[12] He suggests that the best starting points are "hubs," also known as influencers and opinion leaders. Some hubs are obvious, such as regional and national media outlets. For instance, if a local talk-show host discusses a restaurant on Monday, it will probably be full on Tuesday. Oprah Winfrey's book club is an example of this phenomenon. Other hubs are less obvious. They include fashion leaders in schools (for example, such a group in junior high schools made skinny scooters popular), gurus on college or university campuses (who may be technical leaders who spread the word via the Internet), and people on the boards of local charities (who may be community leaders who attend many social functions). The best hubs also span networks, in addition to influencing people in their own network. The leapfrogging of word of mouth from one network to another accelerates the rate of beneficial buzz.

Often generated within the hive of the Internet, "buzz" has become essential to a product's success in today's fast-paced business environment. As Rosen (a former marketing executive for Niles Software) explains, in pre-Internet days a new product would appear in stores, consumers would buy it or not, and the company would then take however long it wished to evaluate the launch. Today, however, consumers immediately voice their views — on blogs, message boards, review sites, company sites, complaint sites, via e-mail, or on their own websites — and so have a strong and immediate influence on whether a launch succeeds.

Rosen points out that hubs can be anywhere. Sometimes they present themselves. People who attend specialized conferences often are hubs for their organizations. Other times, they must be sought out. Good prospects are individuals who are considered experts and talk to a lot of people. People who are known by friends and colleagues as being interested in cuisine and fine wine, for example, are considered experts whose opinions are valuable when a new restaurant opens. Certain tourist segments can be more influential than others. For example, gay tourists, who attend events such as the Gay Games, are a minority of consumers, but they tend to be "hyperconsumers" who not only consume more but also influence the purchases of their gay and straight friends and colleagues, thus providing vital word-of-mouth endorsements for destinations, products, brands, and companies.[13] Word of mouth is also considered to be the main force of influence in the backpacker market.[14]

Silverman suggests that word of mouth is powerful for 10 key reasons.[15]

1. *It has independent credibility.* A decision maker is more likely to get the whole, undistorted truth from an independent third party than from someone who has a vested interest in promoting the company's point of view. It is this unique credibility that gives word of mouth much of its power. So someone thinking about backpacking around Australia is more likely to take advice from friends who have been there than from a travel agent.
2. *It delivers experience.* Lack of positive experience with a product or service is usually the single greatest factor holding it back from greater and faster acceptance. Again, hearing about other backpackers' experiences will act as the accelerator or the brake on booking that backpacking holiday.
3. *It is more relevant and complete.* Word of mouth is live, not canned like most company communication. When someone tells a friend about a country she thinks he would like, she is telling him because she thinks that he — not some anonymous stranger — would like it. She wouldn't tell him about it if she thought he wasn't interested in going.
4. *It is the most honest medium.* Because it is custom tailored, and because people participating in it are independent of the organization, it is the most honest medium. And customers know it. Advertising and salespeople can be biased and not fully truthful. The inherent honesty of word of mouth adds to its credibility.

5. *It is customer driven.* Closely related to the two reasons given above, word of mouth is driven by customers more than any other communications channel. Customers determine whom they will talk to, what they will ask, and whether they will continue to listen or politely change the subject.

6. *It feeds on itself.* Word of mouth tends to breed and is self-generating. Ten people have 10 experiences each while backpacking around Australia, making 100 direct experiences. If they each tell 10 people about their own experiences, that's an additional 1000 (indirect) experiences, which can be just as powerful as the direct experiences. It doesn't take long for everyone to hear about the wonders of Australia, often several times each, which provides additional confirmation (e.g., "everybody's talking about it").

7. *It has expert power.* The hubs referred to earlier have one overriding attribute that gives them their influence: trust. People trust them to filter, distil, and objectively evaluate the overwhelming amount of information, make sense of it, and present it in a recommendation that is most likely to be right. Tiers of experts and influencers tend to initiate word of mouth, sustain it, give it even more credibility, and supply the initial "bang" that can start the chain reaction of word of mouth.

8. *Influencers like to influence.* One of the reasons that the initial stages of word of mouth are sustained and can spread so rapidly is that influencers like to influence. That is one of the reasons that they are influencers. If they didn't enjoy the process, they would keep their mouths shut and their keyboards still.

9. *It saves time and money.* Word of mouth can be extremely efficient. If a person wants to visit a destination that is not very familiar, often the best way is to find a few people who have either been there or collected information about the place, and learn from them.

10. *It is an illusory force.* Word of mouth is an invisible, illusory force (sometimes even called "underground" communication, or the "grapevine," as well as the "buzz"). An organization can gain competitive advantage by making competitors think that increased sales are due to active promotional efforts, so the illusion is that the advertising, or the sales message, or the mailing caused the effects. In fact, many products or services succeed despite the marketing supporting them, for reasons different from the positioning of the product or the most emphasized benefits. Figure 9.6 explains this illusory force.

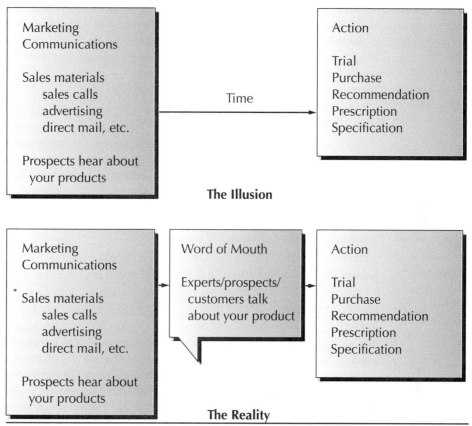

Figure 9.6　What Causes Sales? Illusion versus Reality

Source: Silverman, G. (2001, September). The power of word of mouth. *Direct Marketing, 64*(5), 47–63.

CHAPTER SUMMARY

Public relations includes all the activities that a tourism or hospitality organization uses to maintain or improve its relationship with other organizations or individuals. The functions of the PR department include establishing corporate identity, government relations, crisis management, internal communications, customer relations, and marketing publicity. The main techniques used in public relations are press releases and press conferences, feature stories, travel exhibitions and road shows, hosting and sponsoring events, sponsoring causes, publications, winning or sponsoring awards, celebrity visits, and product placement.

Personal selling is face to face interaction between a salesperson and a prospective consumer for the purpose of making a sale. In the tourism and hospitality industry, personal selling plays a number of important roles: gathering marketing intelligence, locating and maintaining customers, promoting to the travel trade, generating sales at point of purchase, relationship marketing, and providing detailed and up-to-date information to the travel trade. Objectives of personal selling include achieving sales volume, up-selling and second-chance selling, market share or market penetration, and product-specific objectives. The sales process consists of seven steps: prospecting and qualifying, preplanning, presentation and demonstration, negotiation, handling objections and questions, closing the sale, and following up after closing. A sales manager has three key roles to play. The first is to recruit salespeople, the second is to train them, and the third is to motivate and reward them.

Direct response marketing is rapidly becoming a vital component of the integrated marketing communications mix in the tourism industry. There are eight key advantages of direct marketing: precise targeting, personalization, flexibility, privacy, measurability, low cost, detailed knowledge of consumers, and fast or immediate response. Direct response advertising is one segment of the direct marketing industry, and plays a major role in influencing consumer purchase patterns. It can be defined as advertising designed to generate a response by any means that is measurable (e.g., mail, television, telephone, fax, or Internet).

Word of mouth is communication about products and services among people who are perceived to be independent of the organization that is providing the product, in a medium also perceived to be independent of the organization.

KEY TERMS

call centre, p. 316	event sponsorship, p. 299	publicity, p. 290
cause-related marketing, p. 301	feature stories, p. 298	public relations (PR), p. 290
cognitive dissonance, p. 310	infomercial, p. 317	sales management, p. 311
cooperative direct mail, p. 316	personal selling, p. 304	sales quotas, p. 313
cross-selling, p. 306	press release (news	second-chance selling, p. 306
direct mail, p. 316	release), p. 296	solo direct mail, p. 316
direct marketing, p. 313	product placement, p. 303	telemarketing, p. 316
direct response	prospecting, p. 307	up-selling, p. 306
advertising, p. 314	publications, p. 302	word of mouth, p. 320

DISCUSSION QUESTIONS AND EXERCISES

1. How important are public relations and publicity to tourism and hospitality organizations? Give examples to support your answer.

2. You have just won a tourism award and would like to publicize your achievements. Write a press release for the local newspaper in an attempt to get them to run a story relating to your win.

3. Which do you think is the most important step in the sales process? Explain your answer.

4. Think of some recent examples when someone has attempted to up-sell or cross-sell a product to you. Explain why they succeeded or failed. What are the disadvantages of these selling techniques?

5. Which direct response advertising technique do you think would be most effective for a growing ski resort attempting to attract new skiers?

6. What, in your opinion, are the disadvantages of the various direct marketing tools mentioned in this chapter?

7. Why is word of mouth considered the most neglected promotional tool in the marketplace?

CASE STUDY

PUERTO RICO TARGETS BUSINESS TRAVELLERS

An aggressive, international integrated marketing campaign culminated in 2005 in the grand opening of the Puerto Rico Convention Center, the centrepiece of a $415 million waterfront project development called Convention Center District in San Juan. The marketing plan was created and implemented by the Puerto Rico Convention Bureau, a non-profit, partially government-funded body, with an association of members from the hotel, tourism, and property industries. Its mandate was to promote and package the huge convention centre in conjunction with the resort facilities of Puerto Rico as a world class business tourism destination.

Gloribel Wachtel, director of marketing for the Convention Bureau, deems printed brochures her best marketing tool and the bureau spends much time, money, and creative thought on its leaflets, annual fiscal reports, presentation material, ads, and promotional postcards. Tactics over the past three years have included a dedicated website (www.meetpuertorico.com), direct mail, e-marketing, trade shows, site inspections, sales calls, special events including golf tournaments, client functions, orientations and reviews, publications, and e-newsletters, as well as printed news bulletins, media relations, and catalogues. The bureau has also been responsible for inaugurating data mining and strategic research with the aid of professional consultants and set up strategic partnerships within the industry and the community at large. It also has a feedback program for meeting planners to monitor service quality and has organized various sponsorships to help encourage groups that are more financially challenged.

However, the Puerto Rico Convention Center is not positioning itself as inexpensive. Wachtel explains, "One of the main challenges we face as a meetings destination is that it can be more costly to meet here than many other U.S. mainland and Caribbean destinations. The truth is that we are comparable in cost to many large U.S. cities. We offer a world-class meeting destination with top hotel brand names, a high level of service, and a full-range of amenities sought out by business travellers. In addition, we have a modern communications infrastructure, where cell phones work, high-speed Internet and wireless access are easily accessible, and business travellers can count on being able to stay in touch with the home office in a seamless fashion. In that way, you can't compare us to other destinations in the region." Higher prices are also offset by the ease of travel to and from the U.S. since Americans don't require visas or passports to visit Puerto Rico. The bureau is also working closely with air services to develop more regular direct flights from all over North America. Plus, of course, having English as the second language and the U.S. dollar as currency can be a plus for Americans. The bureau uses all these selling features in its promotional material — even the voltage is used to encourage visitors.

In January 2005 the Convention Bureau was accepted as a permanent member of the BestCities Alliance, the world's only convention bureau global alliance, which includes Cape Town, Copenhagen, Dubai, Edinburgh, Melbourne, Singapore, and Vancouver. The Puerto Rico bureau differentiates itself from its competition with a combination of reliable good weather, high technological standards, a packaged tourism/business service, and a colourful, ethnically rich culture, and history: "Our main selling feature is the weather because basically you can come here year round. Then, with the beautiful beaches, and having the regular good weather, you can do events outside. We have the 500-year-old fortified city, here so that's something very different from other destinations. And we are technologically advanced: we provide more infrastructure than many other islands in the Caribbean. There are upper-level facilities here that are as good as at your own house or your own city. So we package it that way. Good transportation helps, too, and we have also some major attractions on the island to visit alongside a business trip, such as the caves and the rainforest, which are a little bit different than other cities or destinations," says Wachtel.

Strategic priorities for the 2005/06 fiscal year included branding of the Puerto Rico Convention Bureau and also developing an integrated high-tech team with employee retention and motivation being top of the list. Wachtel explains, "Right now our objective is to continue spreading the word that the centre is finally open because it is something we have been talking about for 10 years. Three dedicated sales persons from the bureau are trying to sell it and get it full. But we all sell it because part of our contract is to include the centre in everything that the bureau is doing. So pretty much every time we make a presentation we mention the centre. The complete bureau is on 45 to 48 employees. And also the government does its part: it has the Convention Center District Authority, which is in charge of the convention centre. It is also mentioned at the airports and other government-run institutions. We have a close working relationship with not only the Puerto Rico Tourism Company, but also with the Convention Center District Authority and the Puerto Rico Hotel and Tourism Association, as we are all part of the destination team to sell and market Puerto Rico from our different perspectives. There is, of course, some variation in our efforts and marketing investment."

Trade shows are an important tool in spreading the word about the vast new convention centre, which covers 53 885 square metres of prime real estate in the downtown area of Isla Grande in San Juan. Representatives attended the Chicago trade fair in September 2005 and attracted the attention of numerous potential clients interested in revisiting Puerto Rico now that it has such an upbeat facility. Conventions tend to move location regularly in order to maintain interest among delegates, but after five or six years event planners can be attracted back to a destination, especially if it has improved facilities and infrastructure.

Hosting meeting planners, attending trade shows, and advertising in news and industry media have all been backed up by client events. So far pharmaceutical and medical companies plus insurance and banking have been the main groups attracted to the convention center. But sports and music are both markets that the bureau intends to corner. Wachtel says, "We are trying to educate people that the convention centre is suitable for sporting events both amateur and professional. There's one actual trade show for these sporting events called TEAMS, which we are participating in for promoting destinations, and we want to bring it here. Last year they did it in Fort Lauderdale in October. We can also do entertainment, for example the music awards, MTV, etc."

Once a group or event planner has decided to hold a conference or show at the convention centre, the bureau provides an array of free services. It will coordinate hotels and suppliers and provide links with its 500 local association members for all backup services. It also updates planners on local attractions, events, festivals, and entertainments. It will educate the planners and their clients in person by scheduling, accompanying, and transporting personnel to meeting sites and areas and by providing property inspections. The bureau will also offer creative ideas and marketing expertise in addition to its professionally produced promotional materials to help market the event. Plus the bureau has a broad regional sales network with offices in Chicago, Miami, New York, and Washington, DC.

Source: Personal communication with G. Wachtel, Director of Marketing, Puerto Rico Convention Bureau, January 2006.

QUESTIONS

1. What particular challenges face the marketers of convention centres (as opposed to marketing direct to consumers)?
2. How would you describe the target market of the Puerto Rico Convention Bureau?
3. Analyze the marketing mix currently used by the Puerto Rico Convention Bureau. Are there some communications tools you would put more or less emphasis on? Why?
4. Take a look at the websites of both the Convention Bureau and Puerto Rico Tourism Bureau. Would you say that they are positioning themselves as a world class business tourism destination? Why? What could they do differently?
5. Do some background research on a convention centre near you. How do does the centre promote itself to meeting planners and business travellers?

WEBSITES

www.rockymountaineer.com
Rocky Mountaineer

www.atlantis.com
Atlantis Resort

www.thewestinedmonton.com
The Westin Edmonton

www.meetpuertorico.com
Puerto Rico Convention Bureau

ENDNOTES

1. Morrison, A. M. (2002). *Hospitality and travel marketing* (3rd ed.). Albany, NY: Delmar Thomson Learning.
2. Britten, N. (2006, June 24). Is it a bard? Is it a plane? No, it's Shakespeare's flying circus. *Daily Telegraph*, 3.
3. London 2012 organizers expect record sponsorship. (2006, August 8). *Guardian Sport*, 2.
4. Perri, L. (2006, April 28). Celebrating 75 years on top, *USA Today*, 4D.
5. Tree-hugger Sting takes "worst" polluting airline's sponsorship. (2005, November 3). *Independent*, 10.

6. Brooks, B. (2002, June). Prospecting: How to stay in the mind of your prospect and win. *Home Business,* 40, 42.

7. Farber, B. (2001). That's a shocker. *HSMM Marketing Review*, Fall/Winter, 85–86.

8. Garfield, C. (1986). *Peak performers: The new heroes of American business.* New York: Avon.

9. Tuckwell, K. J. (2008) Integrated Marketing Communications: Strategic Planning Perspectives (2nd ed.). Toronto: Pearson Prentice Hall.

10. Sweney, M. (2004, March 11). VisitLondon plans digital TV channel. *Marketing*, 6.

11. Silverman, G. (2001, September). The power of word of mouth. *Direct Marketing, 64*(5), 47–63.

12. Rosen, E. (2000). *The anatomy of buzz: How to create word of mouth marketing.* New York: Doubleday Currency.

13. Pritchard, A., Morgan, N. J., Sedgley, D., & Jenkins, A. (1998). Reaching out to the gay tourist. *Tourism Management, 19*(3), 273–282.

14. Australian Tourist Commission. (2003, March 10). Australia a popular destination for back-packers.www.tourism.australia.com/NewsCentre.asp?lang=EN&sub=0360&al=299 (retrieved September 2007).

15. Silverman, G. (2001, September). The power of word of mouth. *Direct Marketing,* (5), 47–63.

Internet Marketing

10

Spotlight

TRAVEL BLOGS

Forget the brochures, and even destination websites. The latest, most up-to-date travel tips, stories, and experiences are now available as travel blogs (from the phrase "web logs"). Blogs are part of the latest trend in travel and destination decision making, giving the consumer a credible guide to tourism dos and don'ts without having to worry about advertising exaggerations. Often created by travellers, blogs are helping the tourist to become informed before travelling, taking the anxiety out of booking independent trips and also aiding with planning itineraries, booking accommodations, and transportation options. They can be very detailed — for example, even directing the consumer to the right meal choices in specific restaurants on the best nights — and are frequently modified and updated. The authors, or bloggers, are becoming de facto watchdogs and self-proclaimed experts in specific fields.

Websites such as MySpace, LinkedIn, and Friendster, as well as do-it-yourself blogging sites such as Blogspot, have inspired wild popularity among millions of Internet users who find friends, professional contacts, and also a forum for their own unvarnished opinions. With travel blogs, tourists can quickly access information, up-to-date prices, weather reports, and more, tapping into the combined experiences of the travelling public free of charge and at any time of the night or day rather than having to sift through advertising material, trying to sort the truth from the promotional chaff. Tripadvisor is a site that collects user testimonials on hotels and attractions worldwide, gearing itself toward vacationers rather than backpackers, and providing both glowing and scathing reports arbitrarily. The number of travel-oriented web magazines is also growing, ranging from HotelChatter, which focuses specifically on boutique hotels, and Cruise Diva, which reports on the cruise industry, to more narrow focuses such as pestiside.hu, which calls itself "The Daily Dish of Cosmopolitan Budapest." Access to most blogs and web magazines is free but some require a paid subscription. TravelPod, an Ottawa-based site that claims to be the web's original travel blog, is free but carries advertising, whereas My Trip Journal offers a premium service that requires a monthly fee but is ad-free.

Already sites are becoming more adventurous, linking photo albums to written pieces and also connecting bloggers to one another based on compatible travel interests and destinations. In theory one blog surfer could actually meet up with an assiduous blog writer during a trip, having exchanged notes on their similar travel experiences. Real Travel and TravelPod both fulfill this social purpose, catering primarily to adventure travellers. Also 43places.com links like-minded tourists by asking them to list the 43 places they would like to visit.

Blogs inspire much dialogue on the Internet as opinions rarely go unanswered. Criticisms from readers are often levelled at authors regarding reliability of information, alternative experiences, spelling, grammar, and writing ability. The author can choose whether the comments are included alongside the original. Many of the blogging websites are relatively ad free and the only guideline for contributors is that their work should be original. Newspaper travel guides are even giving editorial space to updated, recent blogs as a credible form of travel journalism.

Prompted by the success and popularity of blogs, some tourism operations have jumped on the internet bandwagon, eschewing conventional advertising for this more modern marketing tool. Carnival Cruise Lines created CarnivalConnections.com in early 2006 to provide a platform for cruise passengers to hook up with former shipmates, plan future sea trips together, and share experiences and opinions on cruise destinations and facilities. By mid-2006 this site had attracted 13 000 registered users, of which 2000 had already planned further trips with Carnival's 22 ships. These consumers were predicted to bring in around $1.9 million in revenue, which makes the relatively small investment a very high-yield marketing strategy for Carnival. According to the Miami-based cruise company's director of Internet and database marketing, Diana Rodriguez-Velasquez, there is no editing of subscribers' articles: "It doesn't have the makeup brush that the company would put on copy." Although initially this made marketers nervous regarding adverse comments, it seems that for every negative experience or opinion, there are many more positive reports in reply, giving an all round favourable flavour to this indirect form of advertising. Moreover, it provides valuable consumer opinion, giving marketers immediate market research and feedback for free.

Wikitravel is a website dedicated to amassing the collective wisdom of world travellers, one article at a time with carte blanche as to content. Wayfaring has taken Google's maps another stage further by allowing subscribers to add national guides, neighbourhood tours, and even their favorite watering holes. Also, Expedia and Yahoo! Travel have employed blogs to publicize their travel companies. Expedia allows consumers to compile itineraries of local attractions with personal reviews to complement its flights, hotels, and car rental facilities. It is cashing in on this by selling tickets in advance to recommended attractions alongside its regular travel services. Yahoo! has gone a step further by allowing travellers to draw upon fellow users' suggestions in planning their itineraries down to the smallest detail. It even allows details of free attractions and experiences, listing them in order of reader popularity, and is not in the business of booking tickets. Yahoo! Travel is, however, a smart strategy to gain consumers' confidence in a world where there are increasing options to regular advertising and tour information.

Sources: Personal correspondence with M. Mason, April 20, 2006; Tossell, I. (2006, January 3). Pack your blogs. *Globe & Mail*, R12; Tossell, I. (2006, January 3). Wikis let travellers create content from scratch. *Globe & Mail*, R12–13; Fass, A. (2006, August 5). TheirSpace.com. *Forbes*, 122–124.

Objectives

On completion of this chapter, readers should understand

- the role of the Internet as part of a communications strategy; and

- the ways in which the Internet is being used by the tourism and hospitality organizations for e-mail marketing, advertising, provision of information, distribution and sales, delivering customer service, building relationships, and for market research.

Chapter Overview

The *Spotlight* highlights a relatively new way that customers are obtaining travel information online — via travel blogs. Blogs are just one way the Internet is changing the marketing landscape and this chapter looks at an important and growing area of tourism and hospitality marketing: Internet marketing. The first section describes the growth of Internet generally and how it has affected the marketing of tourism. The tourism and hospitality industry is using the Internet to perform six key marketing functions: direct e-mail marketing, advertising, distribution and sales, information delivery, customer service and relationship marketing, and marketing research. These are discussed in turn.

INTERNET MARKETING

The world is going online in huge numbers. In Canada, 62 percent of the population regularly used the Internet in 2006, and in America, Internet users represented more than two-thirds of the population. Of these, 84 percent are travellers. In the United Kingdom, the average Internet user spends the equivalent of more than 50 days a year online, according a new survey that backs up claims that the net is replacing television as the public's medium of choice.[1] The study shows that Internet usage has risen dramatically over the past few years, with surfers spending an average of 23 hours a week online. In fact, in spite of the failure of some very high-profile companies over the past decade or so, the Internet is thriving and even transforming the tourism industry. The impact of e-marketing can be felt across all sectors in the industry, from large hotel chains to small outfitters. The advantage of this business model is that it is based on a sound foundation — consumer demand. Customers are looking to the Internet to research, plan, and even book their trips at rates that are increasing every year. The *Spotlight* describes how travel blogs are increasingly being used as a source of travel information. The *Snapshot* also shows how the brochure is slowly becoming redundant, to be replaced by travel "pods" that use Internet access and colour printers to give customers a streamlined hard copy of their travel options.

The Internet is changing the behaviour of consumers when they arrive at a destination, with many now demanding free Internet use. Wireless — or WiFi — provision is becoming quite common in bars, hotels, and airports. WiFi technology is no less secure than a regular (wire) Internet connection, and transmits a signal over a limited space that can only be accessed by people within that space and with a WiFi-enabled machine. Many Starbucks outlets around the world offer free WiFi access, for example, and some destinations such as Dubai have Internet access pretty much everywhere — even in gas stations. Marriott's

UK properties charge about $35 a day for WiFi whereas Marriott's Courtyard hotels in the U.S. do not charge because the service is cheaper to provide in the U.S., and there is more competition. However, a few hotels in the UK are offering WiFi on a free-for-all basis — not just for guests, but for anyone who wanders into the lobby or on to the terraces with a laptop. The City Inn chain, whose flagship hotel is in Westminster, estimates that 100 000 people used the service in 2005.[2]

Internet technology is also being used by travellers as a replacement for printed maps and guidebooks when they arrive at destinations. Consumers are using personal digital assistants (PDAs) — a small hand-held computer — to access digital maps or for satellite navigation. Podcasts are also widely available whereby tourists can download digital guides to attractions to their MP3 players, rather than having to be led by an audio guide. Podscrolls — lists of restaurant reviews stored as photographs — can also be downloaded onto personal media players. Internet postcards are also commonly available on destination websites where consumers can send an e-mail postcard to friends or family with a choice of pictures that usually promote the destination. The Internet is allowing travellers to watch their home TVs from anywhere in the world. Slingboxes, as they are called, are chocolate-bar–sized devices that sit on the top of a cable box and pump home TV signals across the Internet. By plugging it into a high-speed modem and connecting it to the cable box's audio and video ports, you can watch and control your TV from anywhere in the world you can get online.

The impact of the Internet does have some negative impacts for travel consumers. There has been an increase in the number of individuals and firms that buy up tickets for events or festivals in bulk and then sell them on websites such as eBay at vastly inflated prices. In the UK, there is growing concern about the behaviour of online agencies such as the now-defunct Getmetickets.net, and the use of Internet auction sites to sell overpriced and fake tickets. When tickets went on sale for the 2007 "T in the Park" festival in Scotland in July 2006, the entire advanced allocation of 35 000 was snapped up in just over an hour. Within five minutes of going on sale, they were on offer on eBay for up to five times face value. Officials are currently attempting to alleviate the problem, including recommending the creation of a website by the UK's Concert Promoters Association where people can exchange tickets at face value.[3]

SNAPSHOT

THE END OF THE BROCHURE AS WE KNOW IT?

Browsing through the new season's holiday brochures used to be a favourite pastime for travellers as they leafed through the pages until the perfect holiday caught the eye. However, the days of the travel brochure as we know it may well be numbered. In the UK in July 2006 the country's first "travel pods" — the brainchild of travel retailer First Choice — went on trial. Demonstration pods appeared in six of the company's supermarket concessions, four in Asda stores in Sheffield, Basildon, Milton Keynes, and Manchester, and an additional two in First Choice "Travel Centres" at Sainsbury's stores in Torquay and Liverpool.

SNAPSHOT *continued*

Occupying less than half the area of a standard concession, each travel pod is entirely brochure-free, using Internet access and colour printers to give customers a streamlined hard copy of their travel options. "The idea arose because supermarkets like the rent that concessions provide but don't like giving up the space shelves that brochures need," explained Cheryl Powell, managing director of First Choice Retail. Powell, who developed the idea after visiting her local shopping centre, believes that her new idea will benefit the environment, as well as sales. "The travel industry faces a huge problem with brochure wastage. With tons of brochures dumped every year, it is a genuine environmental issue."

First Choice is not the only company revisiting its marketing strategies to be prepared for a time when the digital formats could render brochures obsolete. British Airways Holidays, for example, has developed a range of destination-specific brochures that contain no prices, instead referring customers to dedicated online micro-sites that run "live pricing," regularly updating flight and package costs. "A problem with traditional hotel-led brochures is that the prices are out of date almost as soon as they hit the shelves," said Tracy Long from British Airways. BA is now moving toward "lifestyle brochures," booklets offering attractive content on a destination's various attractions. "On the accompanying micro-site for each destination prices are continually revised to reflect market forces, such as changes in exchange rates," said Long. "If people still want to talk to a human being we also provide a call-centre number," she said.

The technology behind recreating entire brochures online is relatively simple and is becoming more sophisticated. Downloading a brochure in digital format takes just a few seconds and rich media is increasingly available, which allows more dynamic content. Like many other sectors, travel websites are exploiting this technology and the prevalence of broadband means that most people can download video footage of a destination quite easily. However, a recent survey by Transversal, a company that helps businesses to communicate online with customers, found that travel companies have the least user-friendly websites of any service industry, at least in the UK. The research found that sites owned by Britain's most popular tour operators and airlines failed to answer even the most basic queries. For example, travel sites were e-mailed the question: "Will I get a refund if a natural disaster affects my destination?" First Choice took 43 hours to respond (and it was not the slowest!). Perhaps the travel industry has some work to do before the printed brochure can be ditched once and for all.

Sources: Mackenzie, M. (2006, July 30). Bin the brochure. *Independent on Sunday*, 19; Skidmore, J. (2006, June 17). Shocking online services. *Daily Telegraph Travel*, 4.

THE USE OF THE INTERNET IN TOURISM AND HOSPITALITY

The Internet is being used by the tourism and hospitality industry to perform six key functions: direct e-mail marketing, advertising, information delivery, distribution and sales, customer service and relationship marketing, and marketing research.

1. Direct E-mail Marketing

direct e-mail marketing (permission marketing)

marketing messages delivered by e-mail with permission from the recipient

One of the most promising applications in online advertising is **direct e-mail marketing**, which is messages sent by e-mail with permission from the recipient. E-mail marketing is one of the most effective communication and promotion vehicles in the Internet marketplace. High-quality e-mail campaigns can deliver effective messaging that drives action and manages customer relationships. This form of advertising is relatively inexpensive, has high response rates, and is easy to measure, and is targeted at people who want information about certain goods and services. Unlike banner advertising in its various forms, direct e-mail marketing seems quite acceptable to Internet users, since they agree to accept the message.

The success of an e-mail campaign — like that of a direct mail campaign — depends on the quality of the list, which can be created in-house or be bought from a list broker. Typically, these lists include opt-in names and addresses. "Opt-in" means that the people on the list have agreed to receive direct e-mail. E-mail sent to lists that are not opt-in are considered **spam**, which is unsolicited e-mail — including advertisements. Spam refers to the inappropriate use of a mailing list or other networked communications facility as a broadcast medium. It is junk e-mail. Because of the low cost of sending e-mail, users receive an increasing number of unwanted messages. The consequence is that more and more e-mail goes unopened, and gaining permission to send someone an e-mail is becoming more important. More than 70 percent of Internet users have made a purchase as a result of receiving a permission-based e-mail message.

spam

unsolicited e-mail, including advertisements

Establishing first contact is the toughest goal of any e-mail marketer. The most obvious places to find prospects may seem to be other websites, newsgroups, and mailing lists. This method of marketing still works, but many mailing lists and newsgroups have settled into their own set of experts. It is harder to penetrate market share this way. E-mail marketing is still in its infancy online, and many of the so-called lists are not tested or even targeted. The best means of survival is still endorsed mailings to a group of interested customers, which is why it is important to allow people to opt in or remove themselves from lists.

The goal is to have customers make first contact, and then have the marketer follow up. This can be done by giving customers something of real value, such as a good special report or newsletter, to encourage them to initiate contact. Yukon Tourism had major success reaching new audiences with an e-mail campaign promoting the "Yukon Alaska Ultimate Adventure Contest." Tourism Yukon rented two lists: one owned and operated by Telus, made up of Canadians who had previously requested other types of travel information, and the other, a Forge Marketing database of people who had already indicated an interest in Yukon travel. The "click thru" rate (rate of those who viewed the messages) was impressive at almost 19 percent, and about equal for both lists. The industry average for click-thrus on marketing messages is between 2 percent and 7 percent.

2. Advertising

These days, the Internet is an important part of the media mix, and Internet advertising is seen by some as the convergence of traditional advertising and direct response marketing (see Figure 10.1). In 2005, Canadian Internet advertising revenues reached $562 million, a 54 percent increase over the 2004 figure of $364 million. Online advertising holds four distinct advantages:

1. *Targetability.* Online advertisers can focus on users from specific companies, geographical locations, and countries, as well as categorize them by time of day, computer platform, and browser. They can target using databases, which are a tool that serves as the backbone of direct marketing. They can even target based on a person's personal preferences and actual behaviour.

2. *Tracking.* Marketers can track how users interact with their brands and learn what is of interest to their current and prospective customers. Advertisers can also measure the response to an ad (by noting the number of times an ad is clicked on, the number of purchases or leads an ad generated, etc.). This is difficult to do with traditional television, print, and outdoor advertising.

3. *Deliverability and flexibility.* Online, an ad is deliverable 24 hours a day, 7 days a week, 365 days of the year. Furthermore, an ad campaign can be launched, updated, or cancelled immediately. This is a big difference from print or television advertising.

4. *Interactivity.* An advertiser's goal is to engage the prospect with a brand or a product. This can be done more effectively online, where consumers can interact with the product, test the product, and, if they choose, buy the product.

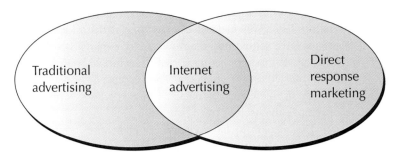

Figure 10.1 The Internet as the Convergence of Traditional Advertising and Direct Response Marketing

Source: Zeff, R., & Aronson, B. (1999). *Advertising on the Internet* (2nd ed.). New York: Wiley, 13.

Online marketers can advertise via e-mail (as discussed above) and by sponsoring discussion lists and e-mail newsletters. But still a common form of advertising on the Internet is the **banner ad** — an advertisement placed as a narrow band across a web page. In terms of appearance and design, banner ads are often compared to outdoor posters. The content of the ad is minimal. Its purpose is to stir interest, so that the viewer clicks the ad for more information. Once the banner ad is clicked, the viewer sees the advertisement in its entirety, usually via a link to the advertiser's home page. The design characteristics of the

banner ad

an advertisement placed as a narrow band across a web page

banner ad are critical, since the goal is to encourage clicking. The ad must link to a website that is be interesting, or the surfer will quickly return to the previous page. A recent study of Internet strategies used by resorts showed that well-placed and appropriate use of banner ads can be highly effective.[4]

Advertising money is also increasingly being spent on search engine advertising, which allows companies to target consumers as they research a holiday. The growth of search engine use for online travel research or booking is staggering, and has been facilitated by the introduction of newer "travel-specific" search engines such as Kayak, Sidestep, and Yahoo!'s Farechase. In Britain, seven out of ten people use Google when they trawl the Internet for flights, for instance. The search engine delivers the results and alongside them displays about a dozen "sponsored links" from companies that have paid to appear on the page. Each time a consumer clicks on one of these links, Google gets a fee. For a flight, this would be about $4.

Marketers are also using the Internet to place ads that may or may not be shown on television at a later date, taking advantage of Internet users' insatiable appetite for online content. The *Case Study* at the end of this chapter shows how an ad created by Tourism Australia was downloaded by more than 100 000 people in the UK alone before airing on television. BMW expanded the boundaries of advertising formats on the web where its short films featuring BMW automobiles were the attraction, not an advertising distraction. The company launched its first round of films online in the summer of 2001 and the short-film *The Hire,* featuring its Z4 and X5 models, also spawned its own comic book collection.

Advertising in online virtual worlds is another opportunity for marketers. An example is Second Life, an online world with a million registered users and a thriving virtual economy. Second Life allows its users to create a new, and improved, digital version of themselves. "Residents" can buy land, build structures, and start businesses. The service is fast becoming a three-dimensional test bed for corporate marketers, including Sony BMG Music Entertainment, Sun Microsystems, Nissan, Adidas, Toyota, and Starwood Hotels. Retailers have set up shops to sell digital as well as real world versions of their products, and even musicians can promote their albums with virtual appearances. In October 2006, performer Ben Folds promoted a new album playing at the opening party for Aloft, an elaborate digital prototype for a new chain of hotels planned by Starwood Hotels and Resorts. Projects like Aloft are designed to promote the venture but also to give its designers feedback from prospective guests before the first real hotel opens in 2008.

Table 10.1 offers ten tips for a better website, and, according to marketing experts, the success factors for marketing tourism on the web include the following: attracting users, engaging users' interest and participation, retaining users and ensuring that they return, learning about user preferences, and relating back to users to provide customized interactions.[5] Learning about user preferences would appear to be the most important element of this model, as it will affect the remaining elements, and yet very few studies have attempted to understand the online behaviour of tourists. Although statistical measures can be obtained through log files, it is difficult to ascertain the meaning behind the results (e.g., whether clicking on a link was an accident or an intended behaviour). Surveying visitors might be a better way to understand consumer preferences and to establish the effectiveness of a site.

Table 10.1

Ten Tips for a Better Website

1. Navigation	Keep it simple (KIS), and make sure it's consistent from page to page. No matter where you place your menu bar — either at the top or down the side — always include a small text menu at the bottom of every page. Make your domain name short, catchy, and memorable.
2. Privacy policy	With all of the concern over privacy on the web, if you collect any type of information from your visitors (even if it's just an e-mail address), you need to include a privacy policy. Post a link to it on every page.
3. Contact information	Post your contact information at the bottom of every page, along with the e-mail address. Don't make the user fill out a whole form just to send a simple comment.
4. Logos and graphics	Please keep your graphics down to a reasonable size. No one wants to wait two minutes while your huge, beautiful logo loads onto the screen.
5. Fonts	Stick to standards. Remember, if you stray from using the standard fonts that everyone has installed on their computers (such as Arial, Verdana, and Times New Roman) the user might not see your fonts as intended.
6. Make it sticky	Include interactive features if possible, such as live news feeds. Use chat rooms, discussion boards, etc. Create a sense of community — a place to which people will want to return.
7. Newsletter	Offer an e-mail newsletter, even if it's only about sale items, specials, or website updates, so you can build a list of your visitors' e-mail addresses.
8. Browsers	Check your website in as many browsers as possible. The display can vary from browser to browser, and what looks right on one platform might not look right on another.
9. Screen resolution	Although there is some question about what is best, norm these days seems to be 800 × 600, although there are still a people limping along in 640 × 480.
10. Index page	On the very first page of your website (the homepage), the first paragraph should answer the most basic questions: who you are and what you're offering. Surfers are a very impatient group. Stop them before they click away. Make sure you keep your website current. Nothing is more irksome to find the site was updated a year ago.

Sources: Ryval, M. (2005, March 17) Eight steps to a better website, *Globe & Mail*, C5; Ten tips for a better website. (2003). main.tourismtogether.com/inforesources (retrieved April 2003).

Research that has looked at content of websites suggests that it is crucial that content is accurate, attractive, and easily searchable.[6] Interactivity is also an imperative, as the very behaviour of consumers changes when they log onto the Internet. They not only search for information but also expect interaction and entertainment.[7] A positive experience on the website increases the time spent at the site and therefore increases the dollar amount spent by consumers.[8] Offering virtual tours is one way of providing interactivity, and many destinations offer potential visitors the ability to take virtual tours of an extensive selection of places. Tourism Vancouver, for example, provides customers with online virtual tours of Greater Vancouver's leading attractions and tourism products (see Figure 10.2). Through new interactive maps available on the website and syndicated through other sites such as Canada.com and MyBC.com, potential visitors to Vancouver can take virtual tours of an extensive selection of places, including Capilano Suspension Bridge, Stanley Park, and Vancouver International Airport. Virtual tours of hotels that potential customers have also proven to be a major sales asset for some hotel chains.

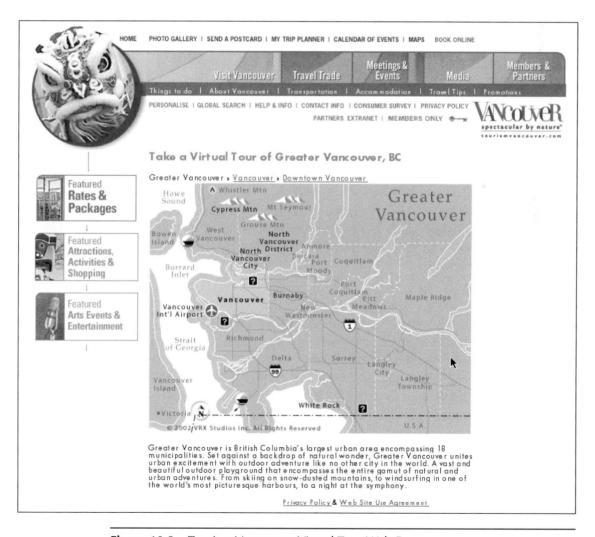

Figure 10.2 Tourism Vancouver Virtual Tour Web Page

Live video is another way of allowing visitors to interact with websites. For example, most ski resorts in Canada now have webcams on the hills so that skiers can check out conditions before they go skiing. Silver Star in British Columbia even has an interactive mountain tour that gives users a virtual experience of many of the resort's runs. Another website using interactive multimedia is that of Drumheller's, home of Alberta's hoodoos, fossils, and dinosaurs. In 2007, the destination launched a new state-of-the-art tourism website complete with its own online hotel reservation system. The website features a video section called "Meet the People of Drumheller," where local residents give visitors the inside scoop on things to do and see in the heart of the Canadian Badlands.

It is also important for tourism operators and destinations to consider the language of their online visitors. It was mentioned in Chapter 1 that the New York tourism bureau had added Chinese-language pages to its website in order to take advantage of the growing Chinese tourism market. Outrigger Hotels and Resorts has also recognized that it holds an international presence and needs to disseminate information about its properties in several languages. The company has realized how much business it gets from Korea and Japan for its locations in the Pacific and South Pacific, and has built portals to address these markets. In Canada, the Prince Edward Island tourism website now has more than 20 pages available in Japanese, allowing potential visitors from halfway around the world a chance to search for activities, transportation, or general information in their own language and at any time of day (which helps to reduce the barriers presented by time zones). The link is accessible from the website's homepage, where Japanese script directs visitors to a Japanese-language home page, and then to pages that outline "Things to Do" and "Places to Stay" and offers a "Vacation Planner" (see Figure 10.3). The text on the "Getting Here" page has been specially adapted to the needs of residents of Japan and will eventually include references to partner tour companies. Special attention is paid to the pages related to L. M. Montgomery and Anne of Green Gables, a favourite theme among many young Japanese women.

In recent years, there has been much discussion around the concept of Web 2.0. The term was first coined in 2005 by Tim O'Reilly, a web pioneer, as a way to mark a turning point for online development. It takes into account a fundamentally different point of view, where a website is based on a rich user experience, not a product or service. Customer-centric 2.0 websites require that an organization puts itself in the shoes of the user and sees itself as it appears on the website. A recent study of ski area websites concluded that those ski areas that take the time to design their website with the needs of their customers as the primary focus will not only be rewarded with more visitors on the web, but on the slopes too.[9] They found the most user-friendly ski area websites had four things in common:

1. They provided current information in a simple, clear, and attractive way.
2. They gave visitors a good reason to come back again (in technical web terms, they have "stickiness").
3. They involved the visitor. Not only did they provide interactive tools, but they also openly encouraged users to contribute comments, content, or images to their site.
4. They made sure the website matched other branding materials such as brochures and ads.

Figure 10.3   Prince Edward Island Tourism's Japanese Website

Finally, most experts tend to agree that a website site needs to look like it is a professionally produced website rather than an amateur one. This may involve employing web design specialists. In 2004, Tourism Barrie found itself plagued with a common dilemma — a website that consisted of 40 scrolling static pages that were difficult to maintain, did not show up in the search engines, and did not provide the proper analytics needed to determine whether or not what it was doing on its site was actually working. In December of that year, Tourism Barrie approached a company called Hot Banana, which completely revamped their web presence. Tourism Barrie's new online marketing program now offers over 250 pages of dynamic information, including an events calendar, restaurant and accommodation listings, things to do, and night life pages. They now show up on the first page of Google.ca for search terms such as "Barrie tourism" and "tourism attractions Barrie." One Calgary family business that has developed its own successful website is Ripley Ridge Retreat, as the *Snapshot* explains.

SNAPSHOT

RIPLEY RIDGE RETREAT

"Without the Internet, Ripley Ridge Retreat would not exist," says Cara Ripley, director of marketing for Ripley Ridge Retreat, a family-owned business run by Shawn and Cara Ripley in cooperation with Shawn's parents, Bill and Shirley Ripley. The retreat is located on seven and a half acres of beautiful aspen forest nestled in the Paskapoo Slopes on the western edge of Calgary, adjacent to Canada Olympic Park. Operations began as a one-room bed and breakfast (B&B) in the summer of 1997. Between 1998 and 2001, the accommodation choice grew to include another B&B suite, two cabins, and a guesthouse. A meeting facility was added in the fall of 2001, and a spa in January 2003. The names Ripley Ridge Retreat and Nature's Essence Spa became registered trade names in 2002. Food, lodging, and spa business licences were granted in January 2003.

Advertising for the retreat is primarily conducted online through various listings on websites servicing the target markets, such as BedandBreakfast.com and DiscoverCalgary.com. Print advertising is limited due to a small advertising budget and minimal return on investment. "We have had a few brochures in the past, but they don't seem to bring us any business," commented Cara. "Brochure costs are very high, as are distribution costs. The only place we can really distribute them is through Tourism Calgary and Travel Alberta, and we have found that they just haven't resulted in bookings."

Other promotional activities include direct mailings to target markets such as women's organizations, yoga studios, and past clients. Leaflets have been developed for the staff lounges at Air Canada and WestJet. Publicity is generated through prize giveaways for target market associations and for high-profile charities including the Canadian Cancer Association, Canadian Diabetes Association, and Planned Parenthood. A public relations campaign was also launched in the summer of 2003 to include disc jockeys from Alberta radio stations, travel writers, and television personalities.

However, the Internet remains the company's most powerful promotional tool, and all of its promotional activities drive people to its website. "Our primary marketing strategy is Internet based and the return on investment exceeds traditional marketing efforts 1000:1, at least," says Cara. "We were able to grow our business from a one-bedroom B&B with $4000 per year revenue to a retreat with three private cabins, two B&B suites, corporate meeting space with high-speed Internet, spa facilities, and over 1200 metres of interpretive nature trails with $150 000 annual revenue — in just four years. Revenue projections exceed $250 000. Over 95 percent of our current business comes from people who have visited our website."

The company has a very aggressive Internet strategy, driving qualified traffic to the website by using keyword strategies, portals, affiliates, link exchanges, and offline media. Ripley Ridge Retreat is located on strategic websites such as Bed & Breakfast Inns Online, BBCanada, and on other sites that list good-quality B&Bs and small inns. "We have a keyword strategy that we use. If you look us up using various keywords such as 'Calgary accommodations,' we are usually first, second, or third. People are always wondering how we get our name up there, but we don't tell them!" says Cara.

How does the company convert surfers into buyers? By using an "entertaining, informative, compelling, secure, and easy-to-use site," says Shawn Ripley. According to him, visuals are very important: "For accommodations, you have to enable the surfer to experience as much of the product as is possible. Beyond that, you have to make it easy for people to book." The website itself is divided into two main parts. One is designed completely using Flash (a high-graphics program) and is aimed at high-speed users and those who require a lot of sensory stimuli in the decision-making process. "It also shows a high level of investment and hopefully imparts an image of a serious business on the other end of the site," says Shawn. The other portion is designed in HTML (hypertext markup language) and allows users with a slower connection and those who are more information-driven to find information and make decisions quickly. "Both sections of the site use a lot of visuals that attempt to show how unique our product is. However, visitors do comment that the site undersells the real thing — an encouraging reaction showing that we still have a lot of room for improvement [of the website]."

The site itself is user friendly, and a toll-free number is provided for people who wish to speak to someone at the retreat. Reservations can be made online via a secure server. Shawn says it is rare to have a visitor come to the retreat who doesn't make a comment like "Your website is simply fantastic. It's really why I'm here." "I feel that although we have a very comprehensive Internet strategy at the moment, we've only just touched on the true potential of this venue for tourism products," says Shawn. "Take care of the fundamentals and then your imagination is really the only limitation."

Source: Personal communication with C. Ripley and S. Ripley, owners, Ripley Ridge Retreat, July 8, 2003.

3. Provision of Information

Online users are often divided between those who plan and those who book. In the U.S., some 78 percent of travellers can be described as online travel planners, since they consulted the Internet to get travel and destination information.[10] The most popular sources of travel information in 2005 for the Americans were online travel agencies such as Expedia and Yahoo! (67 percent), search engine sites (64 percent), travel company sites (54 percent), and destination sites (46 percent). One in three online planners checked websites and then called a supplier's toll-free number. The most popular planning activities conducted on the Internet are searching for maps and driving directions (50.6 million), searching for airfares (49 million), and looking for places to stay (48 million). The Internet is also the preferred method of obtaining travel information among Internet users in the UK, with some 65 percent of UK Internet users in 2005 using the web to research travel. A major trend affecting web usage for travel planning in this country is the arrival of such meta search engines such as www.kayak.com that enable customers to compare instantly details for flights, hotels and rental cars.

The Internet is also an important source of information for tourism practitioners. In 2003, the Canadian Tourism Commission (CTC) launched GoMedia Canada, a comprehensive, national travel portal for Canadian-based media. This unique resource is designed for media that need to access information about Canada as a tourism destination.

Journalists can now leverage essential resources to assist them with the research, writing, editing, and filing of assignments. Designed as a time-saving tool, GoMedia Canada provides the latest CTC media releases, links to the tourism industry, information on media tours, market research, and a comprehensive travel wire complete with still photography and video footage. Some of the most evocative travel stories, produced by some of Canada's best travel writers, are also available to Canadian media on a rights-free basis. The site allows journalists to store information and bookmark references for future use. And once their story is filed, they can ship the designed page, transcript, or photo electronically in universally accepted formats such as PDF or HTML.

A new international tourism portal set up for the travel trade is Tourism-Review.com. Launched in 2006, this website provides daily, weekly, and monthly tourism news as well as an online TV newscast that communicates relevant information among professional organizations and industry practitioners worldwide. Several directories list festivals, conferences, and travel destinations, as well as travel trade companies and organizations. "With so much information overloading travel trade professionals, there is a demand for more relevant and focused sourcing," said the site's project head Igor Fes. "Our final target is providing the users with customized information in all rich media formats available with the latest developing technology."[11]

Another online source of information for the travel trade, travel media, or researchers is World Tourism Directory. The site has detailed information on countries and territories listed and organized by following categories: government tourism agencies, tourism schools and institutes, travel associations and services, transport, outdoor and recreational activities, publications and information sources, immigration and foreign affairs, chambers of commerce, regional and local tourist information offices, miscellaneous information offices, information offices abroad, and embassies and consulates. Besides the comprehensive country directory there are also visitor's guides, country profiles, and maps.

Another trend is the importance of travel blogs in gathering travel information, as explained in the *Spotlight*. In a study completed by Compete, Inc., it was found that more than US$10 billion per year in online travel is influenced by consumer-generated content. Rather than passively viewing a collection of static pages, today's Internet user is becoming an active participant and, as the *Spotlight* highlighted, there is a growth in social networking — the creation and sharing of free content made by individual users. It is changing the way people consume media. For example, home video nights have been replaced by YouTube.com, and flipping through photo albums is now done via Flickr.com. The ease of use is the biggest factor driving this trend, both for users and creators. Jupiter Research in New York tracked a dramatic growth of Internet users who read blogs, from 11 percent in 2005 to 23 percent in 2006.[12] In September 2006, YouTube was recording 100 million views a day, and receiving 60 000 new videos a day.

An interesting new website providing information to travellers is IcebergFinder.com, a site created by Hospitality Newfoundland and Labrador that uses radar satellites to track the massive offspring of Greenland glaciers as the frozen chunks move south. In addition to maps that pinpoint the locations of icebergs, the website has an iceberg FAQ (frequently asked questions), links to iceberg tour operators, and e-mail alerts that provide "berg buffs" with sightings throughout the March to October iceberg season. Icebergs have become an important part of Newfoundland's $620 million tourism industry, as tourists flock to see the 10 000- to 15 000-year-old pieces of ice. Tour operators such as Northland Discovery Tours have seen their businesses grow steadily for the last five years, although they now face competition from drink manufacturers that are harvesting the icebergs to make iceberg vodka and other bottled drinks. However, the harvesting has become an attraction in itself, attracting media attention and TV crews from all over the world. So whichever way one looks at it, icebergs have become good business for Newfoundland tourism.

PROFILE

JENS THRAENHART: CANADIAN TOURISM COMMISSION

In a recent article in the *Tourism Daily*, Canadian Tourism Commission (CTC) president Michele McKenzie spoke about the attraction that Vancouver has for some of the world's best and brightest innovators and thinkers. The city's reputation as a place to live and work has allowed the CTC to choose its new staff from a list of rising stars in their respective fields. Jens Thraenhart, the CTC's executive director, marketing strategy and customer relationship management, is among them, having been recognized as one of the Top 25 Sales and Marketing Minds by Hospitality Sales and Marketing Association International (HSMAI) and one of the Top 100 Rising Stars by *Travel Agent Magazine*.

At the CTC Thraenhart oversees the development and implementation of approaches, programs, and initiatives to ensure the effective management and expansion of integrated solutions to e-marketing, e-business, campaign management, customer relationship management, and technology development initiatives aimed at increasing the penetration of Canadian tourism in targeted markets. He drives the

domestic Travel Canada portal strategy (www.canada.travel) to create synergies across Canadian destinations with the goal of generating targeted leads to travel and tourism providers.

He has more than 15 years of international hospitality experience that includes hotel and restaurant operations, revenue management, sales and marketing, e-business, strategic planning, and hospitality consulting. He has worked with such companies as Fairmont, Four Seasons, Ian Schrager Hotels, Kempinski, and Marriott, including founding and operating a successful food catering company and starting a New York–based Internet company focused on upscale leisure travel, as well as managing an independent luxury golf resort in Germany. He holds an MBA-accredited Masters of Management in Hospitality from the School of Hotel Administration at Cornell University and a joint Bachelor of Science in International Hospitality Management from the University of Massachusetts at Amherst and the University Centre "César Ritz" at Brig, Switzerland.

Speaking in early 2007, Thraenhart said: "The year ahead is a big one for the CTC, and for the industry as a whole. My job is to build and launch a new e-marketing platform that brings "Canada, Keep Exploring" to the new traveller. It has been said many times that consumers are changing. I will be working to ensure that these new, changing consumers have the content they need to make the travel decision to visit Canada. It is my intention to

PROFILE *continued*

incorporate my past experiences into my work at the CTC and create for the industry a web-based platform that will allow all of us in tourism to work together to bring more people to Canada. For the past few years the CTC has been operating with an array of websites. Our online presence was somewhat fractured: CanadaTourism.com but not .ca, TravelCanada.ca but not .com, for example. A customer searching for information on Canadian travel products would quickly become frustrated with this, and begin to search elsewhere. Now, we have been tasked with developing a strategy that brings together all of our knowledge, research, and marketing creative under one roof, on one platform. As brand awareness grows, we need to be able to leverage all of these attributes, and because the CTC does not have a product to sell, we need to engage the suppliers — the small businesses — in the process. Think of all this as a 'Canada' portal."

Outside of the CTC, Thraenhart is also very busy. He sits on HSMAI's Americas board as well as its global branch. He initiated and currently acts as the chair of the HSMAI Travel Internet Marketing Organization, and was the founding past chair of the HSMAI Hotel Internet Marketing Committee. He sits on the advisory boards for the International Hotel and Restaurant Association's Global E-Marketing Council and the Travel Industry Association of America's E-Business Committee, and is a former member of the advisory board of the Canadian Code of Practice for Consumer Protection. Thraenhart also co-founded WOWtraveller (www.wow.travel), which he successfully

merged with Vancouver-based publishing company Kiwi Collection. He is quoted frequently in consumer and trade media and is a frequent guest lecturer at universities and trade industry events. He served on the advisory board of TravelCom Expo and Conference and co-chairs the Online Revealed Canada conference.

Asked what type of skills a student needs to be successful in this environment, Thraenhart said: "The first thing for people looking at a career in e-commerce or Internet marketing is they need to have skills in marketing and branding, sales and distribution management, revenue management, database management and direct marketing, legal and business development, and design and publishing, as well as technology, in addition to a solid product knowledge, such as hotels, travel, and tourism. But even more important are financial skills, because you're always dealing with business models, so if you don't have the financial skills, it will be difficult to measure the return on investment. Because you're managing change in an organization, it is very important to have solid organizational behavioural and communication skills. Being able to convince executives of the value that new marketing mediums and new technologies may have for the organization, and as a result receive budgets to fund these initiatives, is very important, because for many people, the Internet is still a very confusing big black hole. So it's translating it so it's aligned to the corporate strategy and the marketing strategy. If someone can develop all those different skill sets, it's a very exciting career."

Source: Personal communication with J. Thraenhart, March 15, 2007.

4. Distribution and Sales

The share of online travel planners who book travel continues to grow worldwide. The purchase of airline tickets dominates the booking activity, closely followed by accommodation reservations. Ticket sales for all kinds of events and attractions are also showing steady growth. In 2005 in the U.S., while the major online travel agencies attracted the most online bookers (29.6 million Americans used either Expedia, Travelocity, or Priceline at least once in 2005), search engine sites experienced the fastest growth (from 11.6 million bookers in 2004 to 18.7 million in 2005), closely followed by destination sites — up to 12.6 million bookers.[13] U.S. online travel sales amounted to about US$94 billion in 2007, and are expected to grow at a 17 percent annual rate before reaching $146 billion in 2010 according eMarketer.[14] Canada's online travel market more than doubled between 2004 and 2006 to $6.5 billion, and is projected to nearly double again by 2009. Nearly one third of all leisure and unmanaged business travel by Canadians was booked online in 2007.

In Europe, fragmentation in the online travel agency market is high compared to the United States. Sixty percent of the European online travel agency market is in the hands of the top five agencies, whereas in the U.S., Expedia, Travelocity, and Priceline serve 93 percent of the online agency market. One growing competitor for these agencies is Orbitz.com, created when five airlines — American, Continental, Delta, Northwest, and United — came together to develop a state-of-the-art travel website. Orbitz is now one of the largest online travel companies in the world, selling airfares, lodging, car rentals, cruises, and vacation packages. Orbitz's inventory includes 455 airlines, 500 000 lodging properties, 25 car rentals, 30 vacation package providers, and 18 airlines. In North America, Travelocity.com continues to be the most popular place to purchase travel online by a two-to-one margin over any other travel site. The product depth of the Canadian version, Travelocity.ca, includes 700 airlines, more than 55 000 hotels, more than 50 rental car companies, direct booking of VIA Rail, and thousands of vacation packages and cruises. Online consolidators such as the Hotel Reservations Network (HRN) have also emerged as key distributors of the travel product. HRN's websites include hoteldiscount.com, TravelNow.com, and ca.hotels.com, plus more than 20 000 affiliate sites.

Hotels, in particular, are increasingly turning to the Internet to increase sales. High-tech investments in websites and other facilities already have paid off well for many participants in the hospitality industry. A survey of hotels in 2005 found that online sales represented 44 percent of business for those questioned.[15] The average amount they spent on online marketing was $60 000 per year, and respondents rated their own website as more effective than any other online channel of distribution. The greatest challenge for hotels was setting prices of optimized revenue and having consistency between prices in different distribution channels. Online agencies have also been building up their hotel business as a way to diversify from low-margin air sales. Non-hotel sites are also expanding into hotel reservations. Southwest, for example, launched a hotel reservations service in 2001 using the Galileo global distribution system. Expedia is also having tremendous success online. Through its Travelscape division, which operates on the merchant model, Expedia contracts for special room blocks to resell to consumers at a margin, thus guaranteeing revenue for the hotel. Hotels can sign on to become an "Expedia Special Rate Hotel" through Travelscape, to help fill unsold inventory. Travelscape helps hotels maximize revenue during peak, shoulder, and off-peak travel periods; it also offers hotels an Extranet tool that allows them to manage inventory and rates online. However, tensions between hotels and online agencies have led to some hotels pulling inventory from websites. For example, InterContinental Hotels Group (IHG) pulled its 3500 hotels from Expedia and hotels.com in 2004. IHG said the online agencies would not comply with business guidelines it had issued, and sought to have more control over how its rooms were sold.

Many companies are forming online partnerships in order to distribute their travel products. For example, World Wide Trails (WWT), a new northern Alberta–based company, has put together its Adventure Travel Affiliate Program for Canadian travel agents interested in making inroads into the adventure market. Describing itself as an "adventure library," the marketing firm has partnered with more than 50 adventure tour operators to offer more than 300 itineraries at www.worldwidetrails.com. Included in the program is an adventure travel online booking engine as well as incentives such as familiarization trips, monthly draws, and bonuses to top-selling agents and agencies on a regional, provincial, and national basis. Agents can also call for personalized service. There is no cost to join, although WWT splits commission on all tours booked.

Another example of a Canadian online partnership is an initiative between the Railway Association of Canada (RAC) and the CTC. Between them, these organizations have gathered a number of train-related tourist excursions and attractions under one umbrella, called Canada by Rail. The group has created a comprehensive, user-friendly, one-stop website resource for all rail-related leisure opportunities in every region in Canada. The site was officially launched in December 2002, and the offers information and links, by province and area of interest, to museums, rail excursions, historical societies, B&Bs, restaurants, hotels, and RAC members offering tourist services. The photographs in the photo gallery have proven very popular and can be downloaded.

An example of an international online partnership is Luxury Link. Following the lead of auction sites such as Priceline (see *Marketing in Action*) Luxury Link is an alliance of tourism companies around the world that lets visitors bid on sumptuous accommodations and vacation packages. Properties are sorted into nine geographic sections — such as the Caribbean or Europe — and can be accessed by browsing or by conducting a customizable search based on destination. Listings include photos and a thorough description of the package, as well as pricing and auction details such as "retail value," the minimum bid for the package, the starting and closing dates of the auction, and the smallest bid increments that the listing accepts. Before visitors can bid on listings that pique their interest, they must first register at the site. Winning bidders receive notification by e-mail, followed by a personal phone call within 20 minutes to collect payment information.

MARKETING IN ACTION

SHATNER STILL FLYING: THE PRICELINE MODEL

In May 2006, with gross bookings of $880 million reflecting a 33 percent growth rate for the year, Priceline declared its mission "to be the leading online travel business for value-conscious leisure travellers in North America" with similar goals for "unmanaged business travel" too. Priceline is the "Name Your Own Price" Internet service that specializes in booking online airline tickets, hotel rooms, and rental cars. It also has had rather more limited success with its subsidiary interests in finance (home mortgages, refinancing,

MARKETING IN ACTION *continued*

and home equity), cars, online groceries and long-distance phone calls. It was originally launched in early 1998 with a unique purchasing concept whereby prospective customers chose their merchandise via their own price and the service then offered possibilities within the price framework, enabling customers to bid for the products.

Since its launch, Priceline amalgamated with eBay after an agreement announced in February 2002 to combine forces and create a new travel booking service for eBay Travel, powered by priceline.com, combining the strengths and reputations of these two major online travel booking services. For booking airlines, hotels, cars, cruises, timeshares, and vacation packages, consumers compete in an auction style or "Buy It Now" format. Priceline is responsible for the technology, development, transaction processing infrastructure, and ongoing support of the booking service. Recent research at eBay had shown that 42 percent of eBay users had purchased online travel in the previous year, representing around $9.9 billion in gross merchandise sales.

In research results revealed in its seventh annual Internet conference in May 2006, Priceline noted that 61 percent of purchasers considered price to be key when choosing a travel website, compared to 52 percent in 2005. Moreover, 51 percent claimed that lower prices would be the primary reason for choosing to purchase travel merchandise by methods other than online. In order to capitalize on this "bottom line" attitude, the Priceline website is littered with slogans such as "More Ways to Save," "Best Deal," "Package and Save," and, of course, "Name Your Own Price." Its success has also been partly due to an aggressive and expensive ad campaign featuring a series of high-profile television commercials starring Star Trek's Captain Kirk, aka William Shatner. Mr. Shatner's self-mockery

and unique mixture of classical interpretations with today's lifestyle have attained cult status for him and, in turn, Priceline. In 2002, around $47 million was spent on an advertising campaign by Hill, Holliday, Connors, Cosmopulos, which had been directing the ad campaigns for the previous three years, including the Shatner ads. However, since then, Priceline has decided to dispense with the high-cost service and produce its own radio and television commercials internally, retaining Shatner as the figurehead.

The "Name Your Own Price" model seems to work well in the travel industry because accurate, timely information about travel prices is otherwise inaccessible to independent purchasers. Airlines' complex yield-management systems, designed to fill as many seats as possible at the highest prices, mean that seat prices fluctuate from minute to minute. Priceline helps consumers obtain the best information possible, which had hitherto been available only to industry insiders. However, it appears that Priceline lacks that edge in other markets. Despite its obvious travel market successes, it has had its share of failure and criticism since its launch. Its foray into the grocery business, where customers were able to shop and bid online for lowest price foods and gasoline, ended in 2000 after just two years. And plans to enter the life insurance and mobile telephone businesses were abandoned in 2000 as well.

Sources: Mullaney, T. J. (2000, November 20). Priceline should buy Priceline. *Business Week* msnbci.businessweek.com/2000/00_47/b3708119.htm (retrieved September 2007); Carter, B. & Rutenberg, J. (2002, May 15). Priceline cuts ties with Hill, Holliday. *New York Times*, C7; Jones, A. (2000, December 13). Can Priceline cling on to Captain Kirk? *Times*, 25; Priluch, R. (2001). The impact of Priceline.com on the grocery industry. *International Journal of Retail & Distribution Management, 29*(3), 127–134.

5. Customer Service and Relationship Marketing

The Internet is moving marketers much closer to one-to-one marketing. The web not only offers merchants the ability to communicate instantly with each customer, but it also allows the customer to talk back, and that makes it possible for companies to customize offers and services. The Internet also allows organizations to provide 7-day, 24-hour service response. For example, it is now relatively easy for customers to check on the status of their bookings or their frequent flyer/visitor programs at any time of the day. What is it that motivates the traveller to purchase online? According to experts, the main reason consumers have adopted the Internet is that it enables them to shop around the clock in the comfort of their home. Ease of navigation is thus the primary reason for variations in purchase decisions between different online products. In an attempt to simplify navigation, many sites provide one-stop shopping for travellers. This strategy has been extremely successful for such agencies as Travelocity and Expedia. Dynamic packaging, whereby web users create their own package while retaining a certain degree of flexibility, has added a new twist to the tourism landscape.

One study of North American travellers examined the top six factors that motivate consumers to make online purchases.[16] The first motivation factor was the opportunity to earn points through a customer loyalty program. Some sites have set up a special page for members to track their reward points (marriottrewards.com, for example). The second reason was the availability of the desired product, with the third being clear, detailed information that enables the user to make an informed decision. A simple reservation process is the fourth key factor in the online purchase decision, especially in the case of more complex travel products. The reputation of the organization or site's banner is also important as this reassures the purchaser and may positively influence the outcome of the transaction. Finally, consumers are more sensitive to the price of online products than they are to conventionally purchased products. This is partly due to aggressive advertising campaigns that have gradually led consumers to expect discount products.

Another study, by JupiterResearch in the U.S., found that best-rate guarantees would motivate the majority of online consumers to make more purchases online.[17] Consumers are highly interested in the ability to fix mistakes without penalty and cancel or change reservations on the website where travel was booked. Approximately one in four consumers would be more inclined to purchase more travel online if websites offered clearer wording regarding penalties and fees. Unlike their European counterparts, U.S. consumers are not as receptive to the idea of buying bundled products online, largely because they prefer to shop around. "Online travel consumers continue to be price sensitive and increasingly demanding," says Diane Clarkson, online travel analyst at JupiterResearch. "Best-rate guarantees have begun to benefit suppliers in increasing direct online bookings. If airfare prices are equal, consumers are more likely to use an airline site than any other type of site to book their travel," she adds.

Many consumers are looking to build relationships on the web. Seth Godin introduced the concept of **permission marketing**, in which consumers agree to be marketed to on the Internet. This type of marketing uses the interactivity offered by the web to engage customers in a dialogue and, as a consequence, in a long-term interactive relationship.[18] Permission marketing is based on the premise that the attention of the consumer is a scarce commodity that needs to be managed carefully. Its emphasis is on building relationships with consumers instead of interrupting their lives with mass marketing messages. About two thirds of hotels are using their online channels to collect information on their customers, and then use that information to drive marketing campaigns.[19] According to Carrie Harrison, director of sales for Forge Marketing, a permission-based e-mail direct marketing company, capturing customer data on organization websites is a crucial first step. Initial data capture is needed to build a database of customers who have given their permission to receive future marketing material on upcoming travel specials and tourism promotions. Vancouver's Wedgewood Hotel acquired 1600 e-mail subscribers within two months of adding data capture to its hotel website.

Selective marketing, whereby consumers are shown advertising and promotions related to their browsing interests, is also on the increase. For example, the use of online coupons is rising rapidly, by more than 50 percent a year, as Internet giant Google is joining companies such as ValPak and CoolSavings by bringing new technology to the business of marketing national or local coupons over the Internet. Digital coupons typically must be printed and physically turned in at a store so there is still some paper handling. The next stage, according to marketing experts, will come with the spread of digital cellphones with location tracking and automatic short-range communication technology. Electronic coupons will be delivered to cellphone owners on demand and redeemed by whisking the phone past a cash register, eliminating all the paper.[20]

6. Marketing Research

The Internet has introduced some exciting new ways of conducting surveys. The two main alternatives are using either e-mail or the web to deliver and receive questionnaires. Many hospitality and travel organizations have placed questionnaires on their websites to collect information from people visiting their sites. For example, resort company Intrawest runs regular surveys to collect data from past and prospective customers. The British Columbia Automobile Association (BCAA) uses direct e-mail marketing polls to survey the views of its membership. BCAA recently polled its e-mail subscribers and received a 12 percent response rate by offering an incentive of a chance to win a Samsonite Cabin Carry On suitcase. With the information BCAA gathered through its survey, the association can plan targeted e-mail direct mailings to its members based on their stated preferences.

Researchers are still experimenting with online surveys, and there are no conclusive guidelines about the strengths and weaknesses of online research. However, the relative speed and flexibility of online surveys are seen to be two major advantages. Additionally, there is the potential of reaching a large and growing audience of people on the Internet. Internet software is available to take the written survey and convert it into e-mail or web-compatible formats, to e-mail or administer online surveys, and then automatically collect responses, enter them into a database, and calculate descriptive statistics. By using this software on a busy website, it is possible to collect hundreds of responses in a short time period. However, Tierney has suggested that it may be increasingly difficult to get potential web surfers to become survey respondents.[21] Since the respondent must click on the link to find an online survey, an incentive is often necessary to get the user to do so. But the use of incentives with Internet surveys has been shown to cause at least three methodological concerns: response bias, multiple entry, and unwanted entries.

CHAPTER SUMMARY

In spite of the failure of some very high-profile companies over the past decade or so, the Internet is transforming the tourism industry. The impact of e-marketing can be felt across all sectors in the industry, from large hotel chains to small outfitters. The advantage of this business model is that it is based on a sound foundation — consumer demand. Customers are looking to the Internet to research, plan, and even book their trips at rates that are increasing every year. The Internet is being used by the tourism and hospitality industry to perform six key functions: direct e-mail marketing, provision of information, advertising, distribution and sales, customer service and relationship marketing, and marketing research.

KEY TERMS

banner ad, p. 336

direct e-mail marketing (permission marketing), p. 335

spam, p. 335

DISCUSSION QUESTIONS AND EXERCISES

1. After reading this chapter, explain how the Internet is affecting the marketing of tourism and hospitality products and services.
2. Explain how direct marketing and Internet marketing are related.
3. What are the main advantages and disadvantages of Internet marketing?
4. The Internet is being used by the tourism and hospitality industry in six key areas. In which area do you foresee the greatest future potential?
5. Take a look at an existing website for a particular tourism or hospitality organization. Do you think the site is customer focused? How would you improve it?

CASE STUDY

WHERE THE BLOODY HELL ARE YOU? AUSTRALIA AD CREATES "GLOBAL ONLINE TRAFFIC JAM"

In late February 2006, the Honorable Fran Bailey, Australia's minister for Small Business and Tourism, unveiled the $210 million "Where the Bloody Hell Are You?" marketing campaign in markets around the world. The campaign was developed specifically for international markets with the intention of showcasing the tourism assets of the entire country. Australia is well known for its personality and character, and this campaign was developed to extend an invitation to motivate people to visit Australia now. In an increasingly competitive and tough commercial environment, Tourism Australia felt its advertising must be "bold, aggressive, and distinctive" to grab consumer attention. But it must do this while remaining authentic and distinctively Australian. Tourism is very important to Australia. In 2005, tourism generated more than 500 000 jobs across Australia and delivered more than $17 billion to the national economy, from inbound tourists alone.

The ad, created by the Sydney office of the London-headquartered advertising agency M&C Saatchi, featured images of Australians "preparing" for visitors to their country. The televisions ad begins in an Outback pub with the barkeeper saying "We've poured you a beer." Further imagery to a similar effect is then shown, including a young boy on the beach saying "We've got the sharks out of the pool" and partygoers watching Sydney Harbour fireworks and saying "We've turned on the lights." The ad ends with bikini-clad model Lara Bingle stepping out of the sea and asking "So where the bloody hell are you?"

Almost immediately the ad was met with concern and criticism from consumers and media outlets alike; complaints ranged from the use of the words "bloody hell" to worries about age appropriateness and a scene in which one actor is taking a swill of beer. However, not only was Tourism Australia prepared for the backlash but it frankly welcomed it. According to Tourism Australia, the campaign created a "talkability" that marketers can usually only dream about. More than 180 destinations advertised on UK television in 2005 to attract tourists and only one of them, Australia, was now gaining cut-through. Even British prime minister Tony Blair asked "Where the bloody hell am I?" when speaking in Australian parliament and suffering from jet lag. The advertising also caused a stir in Canada, with the Canadian Broadcasting Corporation expressing concern over the TV spots. The CBC later opted to allow the ads, choosing instead to limit them to certain time slots. Regulators in Canada were not so much concerned about the language — it was more the implication of "unbranded alcohol consumption" by the opening line "We've bought you a beer."

With regard specifically to the UK market, the British Advertising Clearance Centre (BACC) initially chose to ban the TV spots. They would not allow the word "bloody" to be used in television versions of the commercial. This ban was seen as particularly pointless because accompanying print ads and cinema commercials for the campaign would not have been censored. Following lobbying by the Tourism Australia, including a visit to the UK by Bailey Australia's tourism minister and Lara Bingle, the ban was subsequently lifted. The controversy did, however, gain much media interest. Tourism Australia maintained that it had always factored in the prospect of such a decision in the UK. It decided to press ahead knowing that a ban would only increase interest in the campaign and give the public relations equivalent of "a free kick in front of an open goal." The destination marketing organization was careful to ensure that less "bloody" versions were prepared should they be required. Tourism Australia said that the tagline for the new campaign, "So where the bloody hell are you?," had been thoroughly tested in all of their major markets, in particular in Japan, the UK, the U.S., Germany, China, New Zealand, and South Korea, and was given the green light by their customers.

In the meantime Tourism Australia made the most of the opportunity created by the controversy. UK traffic to the campaign website quadrupled in the week following the BACC ban. According to Tourism Australia, the response to their new campaign was unprecedented, creating a global online traffic jam. Even before its official television debut the campaign was picking up momentum, with more than 100 000 people in the UK having viewed the ad online. A similar effect was achieved in the Canadian market. The campaign was soon viewed in nearly every country in the world and generated record levels of worldwide online traffic. A dedicated website was created by Tourism Australia — www.wherethebloodyhellareyou.com — whereby consumers could log in, view the ad, send a postcard, or download specific pictures from the ads. Despite only being launched in five countries (including Australia), the uncut advertisement was downloaded by around 700 000 people in nearly 200 countries, and Tourism Australia reported consumer and trade support in their top seven markets was "phenomenal." In the meantime, Tourism Australia's managing director joked in a press release: "We thank the UK authorities for the extra free publicity and invite them to have a 'bloody' good holiday in Australia. To show there are no hard feelings we are happy to extend them an invitation."

For Tourism Australia, there was a simple reason why the commercial had such impact. "It cuts through the clutter and conveys a distinct message that people find appealing and authentic." It was also no accident that the ad resonated with the target market. Tourism Australia invested $6.2 million profiling the target audience for the campaign, known as "Experience Seekers," to ensure the campaign worked. This audience is high-yielding travellers, who typically come from households that have higher than average income and are well educated. Tourism Australia constructed their message and tested it on experience seekers in their top seven markets and they gave it the thumbs up — saying it cut through, they got it, and it delivered a uniquely Australian invitation. According to Tourism Australia the commercial is all about the tone, the personality, the images and messages. "They all combine together to convey a feeling — in this case a warm, distinctive, and authentically Australian invitation that says we want you to come and get involved now. This in turn makes them more inclined to take the all important next step to come to Australia, rather than put it off for ever."

Sources: Tourism Australia extends a warm welcome. (2006). *Tourism Online 6*. www.corporate.canada.travel (retrieved September 2007); Australia Tourism. (2006). www.wherethebloodyhellareyou.com (retrieved September 2007); Morrison, S. (2006) It's a bloody tourism ad, and a good one! Tourism Australia. www.tourism.australia.com/NewsCentre.asp?lang=EN&sub=0327&al=2133 (retrieved September 2007).

QUESTIONS

1. Account for the success of the "Where the bloody hell are you?" advertising campaign.
2. Some people believe that the future of advertising lies in consumers being able to pick the ads they want to watch on television or on the Internet. Do you agree?
3. It would be very cost effective for a destination to advertise solely on the Internet. What would be the disadvantages of such a strategy?
4. Surf the Internet and find three examples of tourism advertisements that can be viewed online. Briefly explain each ad.

WEB SITES

www.tourism.australia.com
Tourism Australia

www.tripadvisor.com
TripAdvisor

hotelchatter.com
HotelChatter

www.cruisediva.com
Cruise Diva

www.travelpod.com
TravelPod

mytripjournal.com
My Trip Journal

www.realtravel.com
Real Travel

www.43places.com
43places.com

www.carnivalconnections.com
Carnival Cruise Lines social networking platform

www.wikitravel.org
Wikitravel

www.wayfaring.com
Wayfaring

www.kayak.com
Kayak search engine

www.priceline.com
Priceline

www.outrigger.com
  Outrigger Hotels and Resorts

www.tourism-review.com
  Tourism Review.com

www.worldtourismdirectory.com
  World Tourism Directory

www.secondlife.com
  Second Life

www.tourismvancouver.com
  Tourism Vancouver

www.icebergfinder.com
  Iceberg Finder

www.peiplay.com
  Prince Edward Island Tourism

www.tourismbarrie.ca
  Tourism Barrie

www.hotbanana.com
  Hot Banana

www.skisilverstar.com
  Silver Star Ski Resort

www.TravelDrumheller.com
  Drumheller, Alberta

www.bbonline.com
  Bed & Breakfast Online

www.bbcanada.com
  BBCanada

www.gomediacanada.com
  GoMedia Canada

worldtourismdirectory.com
  World Tourism Directory

www.canadabyrail.ca
  Canada by Rail

www.luxurylink.com
  Luxury Link

ENDNOTES

1. Johnson, B. (2006, August 8). British internet users spend 50 days a year surfing web, *Guardian*, 13.

2. Taylor, R. (2006, June 30). Check in, log on, fork out. *Guardian Travel*, 6.

3. Jones, R. (2006, July 22). New move to pull the plug on concert ticket touts. *Guardian*, 4.

4. Internet Marketing and Distribution Strategy for Resorts. (2006). *Hospitality Sales & Marketing Association International, 23*(1), A1–12.

5. Parsons, A. M., Zeisser, M., & Waitman, R. (1998). Organizing today for the digital marketing of tomorrow. *Journal of Interactive Marketing, 12*(1), 31–46; Gretzel, U., Yuan, Y. L., & Fesenmaier, D. R. (2000). Preparing for the new economy: Advertising strategies and change in destination marketing organizations. *Journal of Travel Research, 39*(2), 146–156.

6. Beirne, E., & Curry, P. (1999). The impact of the Internet on the information search process and tourism decision-making. In D. Buhalis & W. Schertler (Eds.), *Information and communication technologies in tourism* (88–97). Vienna: Springer-Verlag.

7. Schwartz, E. I. (1998). *Webonomics: Nine essential principles for growing your business on the World Wide Web.* New York: Broadway.

8. Hoffman, D. L., & Novak, T. P. (1996). Marketing in hypermedia computer-mediated environments: Conceptual foundations. *Journal of Marketing, 60*(July), 50–68.

9. Rufo, S. (2006). Ten things your website should have (but probably doesn't). *Ski Area Management, 45*(4), 31–35.

10. Pollock, A. (2006) Reaching travellers online. *Tourism.* 10(2), 5.

11. Newly launched international tourism portal focuses on travel trade professionals. (2006, October 19). www.worldtourismdirectory.com/news/213/newly-launched-international-tourism-portal-focuses-on-travel-trade-professionals.html (retrieved in September 2007).

12. Rocha, R. (2006, September 23). Internet's second coming gets users more involved. *Calgary Herald*, A14.

13. Pollock, A. (2006) Reaching travellers online. *Tourism*, 10(2), 5.

14. Wilkening, D. (2007, April 10). U.S. online travel slows frantic growth pace. *TravelMole News* www.travelmole.com/stories/1117281.php (retrieved September 2007).

15. Green, C. E. & Warner, M. M. (2006). Hospitality approach to online marketing: Survey of attitudes and approaches. HSMAI Foundation. www.hospitalitynet.org/file/152002476.pdf (retrieved September 2007).

16. Péloquin, C. (2005, October). Why purchase online? *Tourism*, 5.

17. Best-rate guarantees by travel suppliers help boost online bookings. (2004, September 9). *Travelweek*, 5.

18. Godin, S. (1999). Permission marketing. New York: Simon & Schuster.

19. Green, C. E. & Warner, M. M. (2006). Hospitality approach to online marketing: Survey of attitudes and approaches. HSMAI Foundation. www.hospitalitynet.org/file/152002476.pdf (retrieved September 2007).

20. Lohr, S. (2006, September 5). Still holding value. Financial Post, FP10.

21. Tierney, P. (2000). Internet-based evaluation of tourism website effectiveness: Methodological issues and survey results. *Journal of Travel Research, 39*, 212–219.

Service Quality through Internal Marketing

Spotlight

BEYOND THE CALL OF DUTY

In order to provide customer satisfaction and build loyalty in a highly competitive climate, tourism providers are going beyond the call of duty to wow their guests. The Fairmont Chateau Lake Louise in Canada, for example, recently sent a private car on a four-hour round trip to pick up a passport and ski pass left behind at a car hire desk. The Fairmont chain is also famous for providing a fire truck so that a young firefighter guest could propose to his girlfriend. There have been similar stories from many of the international hotel groups. In Britain, a Four Seasons Hotel concierge went the extra mile by becoming a private eye and tracking down a guest's long-lost friend on his day off work and reuniting the couple.

Hotels are not just relying on one-off incidents of exceptional service. Intercontinental Hotels are concentrating on making their guests' sleep more comfortable, not only by providing extra pillows both feather-filled and hypo-allergenic, according to preference. They hired a doctor to design a sleep program for jet-lagged guests. As a result, many of the rooms come equipped with drape clips to ensure darkness, CDs offering tips for good sleep, ear plugs, eye shades, scented oils, and a night light to make the bathroom easily accessible. Wake-up calls are also guaranteed by offering the guest free accommodation if the call doesn't actually come.

An innovative provision is the "Recovery Concierge" at Loews New Orleans Hotel. The concierge is head of a hangover cure program for guests who overindulge in the city's excesses of alcohol and rich food but need to bounce back in time for morning business meetings. After extensive research with nutritionists and experts, rooms now come complete with foot creams, face mists, Alka Seltzer, ginger tea, vitamins to replace electrolytes, painkillers, and soft rolls and smoothies to help settle upset stomachs. The Recovery Concierge also offers prevention ideas such as drinking water to avoid hangovers or what shoes to wear while touring the French Quarter to prevent sore feet. The idea is not new (the Ritz-Carlton has a make-your-own Bloody Mary bar in the spa, for example, for those who believe in the hair of the dog theory), but Loews has taken the concept one step further to differentiate its appreciation of guest needs and its pampering of guests.

Special treatment is not just dished out to two-legged customers. Delta is chasing families by encouraging them to bring along the family dog. At its Halifax property in Canada, for example, dogs get a registration kit including a food bowl, place mat, and treats. Other hotel chains, including Best Western, Howard Johnson Canada, and Loews

Hotels also allow guests to bring along their pets. Loews, in particular, treats pets as honoured guests, calling them "VIPs" (Very Important Pets). At check-in, guests are provided with a welcome letter for their pets outlining rules as well as local vet facilities, pet stores, and dog-walking routes. The chain's pet perks include a toy-filled bag, specialized bedding, and even gourmet room service with meals designed by chefs and approved by vets. Cats have a choice of salmon or tuna, dogs choose from "bow wow" burgers, chicken with rice or grilled filet, and there is even a vegetarian dish especially for jetlag. In the rooms, there are special place mats, water bowls, and toys for pets plus treats in the mini bar.

These examples are all part of a new superservice ethos that is extending to other sectors of the tourism industry, with companies such as Enterprise Rent-A-Car trying to make a difference to its service quality by offering "Good Samaritan" awards backed by financial prizes. Airlines, too, are improving service to woo customers. Family travel, in particular, is being encouraged by concentrating marketing tactics on the children. In order to reduce the rigours of travelling with kids, airlines are providing travel perks for the children, considering them "the consumers of tomorrow." Air Canada, for example, introduced a range of meals designed for children's appetites and tastes, including many healthy options, as well as souvenirs all wrapped up in a brightly coloured box. Also flight attendants distribute games and reading materials geared to different ages during the journey. British Airways provides family-oriented in-flight entertainment as well as giving kids a backpack or shoulder bag full of age-related goodies. Children can purchase an airline log book to record their travels that the captain will sign and certify.

Sources: Airlines, hotels woo "consumers of tomorrow." (2004, September 20). *Globe & Mail*, Travel Rewards II: Advertising Special Report, E5; Pet project. (2004, September 20). *Globe & Mail*, Travel Rewards II: Advertising Special Report, E7; Brieger, P. (2005, May 3). Hotels get personal with their perks. *National Post*, FW8.

Objectives

On completion of this chapter, readers should understand:

- The internal marketing process;
- The link between service quality and customer satisfaction;

- The measurement tools and the behavioural consequences of service quality;
- The link between customer satisfaction and loyalty;
- Relationship marketing strategies; and
- The importance of service recovery.

Chapter Overview

The *Spotlight* shows how tourism organizations are differentiating their service in order to attract and retain loyal customers. Having a service culture is one part of internal marketing, which is the focus of this chapter. The chapter begins by defining internal marketing and examining the four key steps in the internal marketing process. The next section focuses on delivering service quality, and includes discussions of the "gaps model" of service quality, the measurement of service quality, and the behavioural consequences of service quality. The third section of the chapter discusses loyalty and relationship marketing. Various customer retention strategies are introduced, as are the benefits of relationship marketing to both company and customer. The final part of the chapter analyzes service recovery and offers guidelines for tracking and handling complaints.

THE INTERNAL MARKETING PROCESS

internal marketing

marketing aimed the organization's own employees

Internal marketing was introduced in Chapter 1 as an integral part of the services marketing triangle (see Figure 1.5), and can be defined as marketing aimed at an organization's own employees. Internal marketing takes place through the fulfilling of promises. Promises are easy to make, but unless providers are recruited, trained, equipped with tools and appropriate internal systems, and rewarded for good service, the promises may not be kept. Internal marketing was first proposed in the 1970s as a way to deliver consistently high-service quality.[1] But despite the rapidly growing literature on internal marketing, very few organizations actually apply the concept in practice. One of the main problems is that a single unified concept of what is meant by internal marketing does not exist. Lack of investment in internal marketing may also be the result of corporate distraction. Companies that are busy trying to boost revenues and cut costs may not see why they should spend money on employees, thus missing the point that these are the very people who ultimately deliver the brand promises the company makes.

However, there is growing awareness that an effective internal marketing program will have a positive effect on service quality, customer satisfaction and loyalty, and eventually profits. Figure 11.1 illustrates the link between internal marketing and profits.

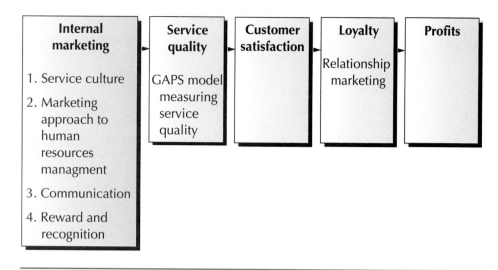

Figure 11.1   The Link between Internal Marketing and Profits

The main objective of internal marketing is to enable employees to deliver satisfying products to customers. This takes place through a four-step process.

1. Establishment of a Service Culture

Organizational culture refers to the unwritten policies and guidelines, to what has been formally decreed, and to what actually takes place in a company. It is the pattern of shared values and beliefs that helps individuals understand organizational functioning and thus provides them with norms for behaviour in the business. In the past few decades, researchers have begun to analyze the linkage between culture and the marketing of services. Due to the unique characteristics of services (i.e., intangibility, inseparability of production and consumption, perishability, and heterogeneity), the nature of the culture of a service organization is particularly important and worthy of attention.

Marketing culture refers to the unwritten policies and guidelines that provide employees with behavioural norms, to the importance the organization as a whole places on the marketing function, and to the manner in which marketing activities are executed. Since service quality is one dimension of marketing culture, it follows that the kind of marketing culture an organization has would be particularly important for a service organization, as the simultaneous delivery and receipt of services brings the provider and customer physically and psychologically close. Research has shown a strong positive relationship between the kind of marketing culture a service organization has and its profitability and degree of marketing effectiveness.[2]

service culture

a culture that supports customer service through policies, procedures, reward systems, and actions

A **service culture** is a culture that supports customer service through policies, procedures, reward systems, and actions. An internal marketing program flows out of a service culture. A services marketing program is doomed to failure if its organizational culture does not support servicing the customer. Such a program requires a strong commitment from management. If management expects employees to have a positive attitude toward customers, management must have a positive attitude toward the customer and the employees. The *Profile* in this chapter shows how Virgin's service culture is driven by CEO Richard Branson. The change to a customer-oriented system may require changes in hiring, training, reward systems, and customer complaint resolution, as well as empowerment of employees. It requires that managers spend time talking to both customers and customer-contact employees.

Turning potentially dissatisfied customers into satisfied customers is a major challenge for tourism and hospitality organizations, and empowering employees to go the extra mile in satisfying customers is recognized as one of the most powerful tools available to a service organization. **Employee empowerment** gives employees the authority to identify and solve customer complaints on the spot and to improve work processes when necessary. Often this will mean decentralizing decision making and flattening organization charts in order to give more power to the front-line employees who directly serve customers. It also means that managers must have greater levels of trust in their subordinates and must respect their judgment.

Empowerment is regarded as an essential aspect of internal marketing, and as essential for the operationalization of Christian Grönroos's interactive marketing concept, a part of the services marketing triangle introduced in Chapter 1. In order for interactive marketing to occur, front-line employees need to be empowered — that is, they require a degree of control over the service task performance in order to be responsive to customer needs and to be able to perform service recovery. However, the degree of empowerment is contingent on the complexity and variability of customer needs and the degree of task complexity. Also, empowerment does not suit all employees because of the extra responsibility that it inevitably entails. The *Case Study* at the end of this chapter highlights how WestJet staff members are empowered to think outside of the box to provide customers with exceptional service.

employee empowerment

the act of giving employees the authority to identify and solve customer complaints on the spot and to improve work processes when necessary

PROFILE

RICHARD BRANSON: DRIVING SERVICE QUALITY FROM THE TOP

A service culture is often driven by personalities within a business. It comes from the top and trickles down throughout the company. Sir Richard Branson, billionaire and self-styled world champion of adventure capitalism, personifies the best of everything. Through his personal "live life to the full" ethos, he drives industry in every area he expands, from his Virgin record business, to airlines, phones, and, more recently, space tourism with Virgin Galactic. However, despite his jet-setting lifestyle and the purchase of his own island, he does not fly on a private plane. He tries to remain "grounded" in reality and stay in touch with his customers by travelling on his own airline, spending six hours each flight at the bar, mixing with the passengers and valuing their feedback. In 2004, Virgin became the first airline to introduce double beds on board its planes. When Branson first floated the idea in 1999, he said: "The legitimate mile-high club is finally aboard."

PROFILE *continued*

Over the years, Branson has diversified his Virgin brand into a far-reaching empire, encompassing insurance and financial services, rail service, and even wedding dresses, as well as his original record label and discount airline. His personal image is one of unconventionality, youthful energy and enthusiasm, entrepreneurial spirit, and thinking big, and he imbues all his products with this brand distinction. In 2005 *Forbes* estimated his worth at over $4 billion despite many financial ups and downs over the previous decade. He now controls more than 200 mostly private companies and employs thousands of people worldwide. Branson equates entrepreneurialism with being "in the jungle learning the hard way, learning from your mistakes, learning your good points and learning the art of survival." His own career was launched at the age of 16 when he created a national magazine, *Student*.

Despite his personal riches, Branson has retained an "everyman" persona, marked by his casual dress, modest manner, and disrespect for convention. He understands the concerns and needs of his customers and his employees and acts as a conduit for fulfilling those needs. He may appear to plunge into new businesses just for fun, but there is much more calculation to it than that. "The time to go into a business is when it is abysmally run by other people," he says, and when he feels Virgin can provide a significantly better customer experience. "We look for the big bad wolves who are dramatically overcharging and under-delivering." For example before moving into cellphones, he realized that many young people couldn't afford the expensive monthly charges the big players were asking for. Instead, he envisioned a pay-as-you-go approach, so teenagers wouldn't need to lock themselves into yearlong contracts or pay for airtime they didn't use.

Always flamboyant and with an eye to exploiting his escapades for their advertising value, Branson's trademark is outlandish publicity stunts. In March 2005, he arrived at an outdoor downtown Toronto press conference wearing a superhero costume and rappelled down a four storey building into a group of models dressed as nurses. This was part of a promotion to introduce Virgin Mobile's phone service in Canada. Virgin Mobile earned $49 million in 2004 on revenue of more than $1 billion. The Toronto stunt celebrated the acquisition of a half interest for him in Virgin Mobile Canada in partnership with Bell Mobility. He reinforces such obvious publicity stunts with regular appearances on television shows. *The Rebel Billionaire* is an adventure-reality show, watched by six million viewers in England, in which Branson participates in outlandish adventure challenges alongside the contestants, consolidating his hands-on spirit. He explains his adventures as another facet of his entrepreneurship that has always led him to take on challenges, risks, and new projects, which he calls "brand stretching" — for example Virgin Cola, which specializes in cornering the market in countries where Pepsi and Coke have difficulties. He considers his daredevil activities "a double duty" for both personal achievements and effective, relatively cheap advertising.

Branson also inaugurated the ultimate loyalty scheme for Virgin Atlantic's frequent flyers in December 2005. He offered free space flights in 2008 for Flying Club members who can save their air miles until they have the requisite two million flying club miles to redeem them for a trip into space with Virgin Galactic. He also intended to put money earned in the early flights back into the venture in order to bring prices down for the future opening space tourism up to the masses — his goal: "A company that will

PROFILE *continued*

enable dreams to come true and, at the same time, will help put the Virgin brand on the map on a global basis."

In September 2006 Branson joined a growing list of billionaires contributing huge amounts to worthy causes by committing to spending all the profits from his airline and rail business — an estimated $3.5 billion over the next 10 years — on combating global warming. He said the money would be spent on renewable energy initiatives within his company and on investments in bio-fuel research, development, production and distribution, as well as projects to tackle emissions contributing to global warming. "I really do believe the world is facing a catastrophe and there are scientists who say we are already

too late, but I don't believe that is the case," he said. Branson's fuel bill for Virgin Airlines rose $1 billion between 2003 and 2006. The first investment project of Virgin Fuels will be in a California company called Cilion doing research on new kinds of ethanol production.

Sources: Restivo, K. (2005, March 2). Virgin Mobile serves industry wake-up call. *Financial Post,* FP3; Evans, M. (2005, March 2). Sir Entrepreneur. *Financial Post*; McCarthy, S. (2005, December 17). Can Branson trump the Donald? *Globe & Mail*, B4; Reuters. (2005, December 7). Virgin Atlantic offers its frequent flyers chance to soar into outer space. *Financial Post*, FP4; Banks, B. (2005, August). Life wish. *National Post,* 30; Branson, R. (2005, August). My final frontier. *National Post,* 33; Reiss, S. (2006, May). The original adventure capitalist. *Men's Journal.*

2. Development of a Marketing Approach to Human Resource Management

A marketing approach to human resources management (HRM) involves the use of marketing techniques to attract and retain employees. By 2010 there will be 1.95 million people working in the Canadian tourism industry, which means 300 000 tourism jobs will be created between 2007 and then. With the human resource crisis on the rise, employers need to think creatively about solutions. EasyJet, the UK-based low-cost airline, recently added a "come and work for us" plea to the address that greets passengers boarding its planes. The airline employs more than 2000 cabin crew across Europe, and this was an attempt to recruit staff by saving money on advertising. Taking a marketing approach to HRM also means using marketing research techniques to understand the employee market. Different employee segments look for different benefits, and it is important to understand what benefits will attract employees. Advertising for staff can then be developed with prospective employees in mind, building a positive image of the company for present and future employees and customers. Marketing can help by working with the human resources (HR) department to identify the key elements in employee motivation, including the effect of incentives and the development of training and improvement programs. Marketing can help most of all with research, working with HR to determine, internally, what can be done to improve the delivery of "customer-facing" people and to help understand what motivates employees, channel partners, and customer-service representatives. If marketers are good at understanding customers, consumers, and end-users of products and services, they should be able to lend those talents to HR to help them understand internal marketing conducted by internal marketers.

Such a marketing approach to developing positions and benefits helps to attract and retain good employees. Organizations should ensure that they recruit employees who are highly motivated, customer-oriented, and sales-minded because changing employee attitudes and behaviour is more difficult and costly once the employees have been recruited. Employees also need the right type and level of training to perform their jobs. This can help to reduce ambiguity surrounding their role and can help employees to meet the needs of customers more effectively.

More and more managers are trying to tap into the psyche of employees as the continuous turnover of staff takes its toll on the industry. Employee turnover in the hospitality industry is often 10 times that of other industries. Turnover in easyJet, mentioned above, for example, is about 20 percent annually. Some managers find that giving increased responsibility is improving retention and performance, a strategy that has proved successful for both WestJet and Fairmont, companies profiled in this chapter. Fairmont also offers employee exchange programs to boost staff loyalty. It is not, however, just entry-level positions that are difficult to keep filled. Turnover among hospitality industry sales and marketing professional is at almost 25 percent. A National Restaurant Association poll of more than 400 foodservice managers also found that about one-quarter of the respondents intended to leave their positions in the near future, with at least half of those planning to depart the foodservice business entirely.[3]

According to Jon Katzenbach, author of *Why Pride Matters More Than Money*, feelings of pride can motivate people to excel far more effectively than money or position.[4] He says that organizations such as Southwest Airlines and Marriott International, which manage to sustain the emotional commitment of a large proportion of their employees over good times and bad, seldom rely on monetary incentives. Instead, they find ways to inspire institution-building pride in what people do, in why and how they do it, and in those with whom they do it. Pride builders accomplish this by a) setting aspirations that touch emotions, b) pursuing a meaningful purpose, c) cultivating personal relationships of respect, d) becoming a person of high character, and d) injecting humour along the way. For the Sheraton Suites Calgary Eau Claire (see *Marketing in Action*), instilling pride in employees is a key motivator.

Continuous training can also help improve employee morale and reduce turnover of employees. The Canadian Tourism Human Resource Council (CTHRC) provides human resource development solutions for the tourism industry in Canada, and in 2002 it introduced the *Performance First HR Tool Kit*, a pragmatic guide to human resource management. The kit (which includes a manual and CD) provides the "ready-made tools" needed to recruit, select, hire, train, coach, and manage employees effectively. Several customizable, user-friendly templates and forms are available in the kit, including application forms, interview evaluations, job offer letters, training plans, and employee manuals suited to the position.

In Singapore, an unusual training program for taxi drivers is improving the service offered to tourists. Hundreds of taxi drivers have qualified as tourist guides, having spent more than 80 hours training over a three-month period. After sitting a written exam and taking practical assessments, drivers who make the grade are awarded a special Taxi Tourist Guide Licence.[5] Seok Chin Poh of the Singapore Tourism Board, which helped set up the scheme, said, "We are seeing a growth in independent travellers from Europe visiting Singapore who want to explore at their own pace but still benefit from the knowledge of a guide. The scheme offers visitors a refreshing and interesting alternative to touring Singapore."

SNAPSHOT

INTERNAL MARKETING AT FAIRMONT HOTELS AND RESORTS

Fairmont Hotels and Resorts is a good example of a company that aims its marketing efforts toward its employees. Fairmont is the largest luxury hotel management company in North America and has achieved great success since it opened in 1907. The company now operates 51 hotels in 12 countries with 20 in development. The company sees internal marketing as critical in achieving guest satisfaction, and consequently Fairmont is world renowned for its excellent guest service. The company measures the success or failure of its internal marketing programs through employee turnover rate — currently running at about 20 percent, with industry averages five or six times higher. Staff loyalty in turn encourages customer loyalty; repeat guests make up 60 percent of Fairmont's business.

Fairmont knows that it is important to segment the employee market as well as the guest market, and to develop a marketing mix to attract the best staff for its company. Attracting self-motivated, results-oriented staff for Fairmont is key to its employee marketing mix, which is why it has an extensive recruiting and hiring process to select the best employees to interact with its guests. Once hired, the employee participates in a mandatory two-day orientation offered by the Fairmont Learning Organization (FLO). New recruits learn Fairmont's service culture (policies, procedures, reward systems, and actions) and organizational culture (mission, vision, values, and history of the company).

Empowerment is about turning the traditional organizational structure upside down, with the customers and employees at the top of the structure and management at the bottom. Management and employees now work to serve the guest, versus serving the CEO or "boss." Focusing on the needs and wants of the customer and granting employees the power to achieve the ultimate guest service creates an atmosphere in which employees are not afraid to tell supervisors of a mistake in order to rectify it and satisfy the guest. The company-wide emphasis is on giving each employee — at both the corporate and the property levels — the tools, training, authority, and support they need in order to make informed decisions and take appropriate actions to deliver the highest level of service excellence to Fairmont guests. The goal is to empower employees to create customized experiences that make lifetime memories for guests — what Fairmont calls "wow" experiences.

Employee reward and recognition programs are an important part of the process of internal marketing. Once Fairmont has attracted and recruited the right employees, attention is focused on keeping employees satisfied and motivated to continue to impress the guest. Benefits and perks are important factors in compensating employees. Substantial discounts of up to 50 percent off food, beverages, and hotel rates are offered as employee incentives to encourage them to use these products and services, thus facilitating first-hand knowledge. Employees are part of the product, and encouraging them to be excited about Fairmont hotels and services will in turn make the customer more excited. Fairmont also has a number of recognition awards that are presented throughout the year. These benefits and awards market the company to the employees and install a positive attitude within the workplace. Internal communication at Fairmont is also taken seriously. A bi-monthly newsletter is distributed in each specific hotel, and a company-wide newsletter, *The Dialogue*, keeps staff up to date on new company procedures.

Sources: Cohen, S. (2001). Concierges go the extra mile to make visitors' stays memorable. *Business Journal*, Kansas City, *19*(50), 24; Liddle, A. J. (2002, January 28). Regional powerhouse chains. *Nations Restaurant News*, *36*(4), 100–102; Mueller, S. (2000). How do you set your hotel apart from others? *Business Journal*, Kansas City, *17*(51), 44; Fairmont Learning Organization. (2001, September). MyFairmont Serviceplus Training Binder.

3. Dissemination of Marketing Information to Employees

Managers need to pay significant attention to the communication of marketing (and other organizational) strategies and objectives to employees, so that they understand their own role and importance in the implementation of the strategies and in the achievement of the objectives. Research evidence suggests that the frequency, quality, and accuracy of downward communication moderates employee role ambiguity and hence increases job satisfaction. Such communication mechanisms may come in the form of company meetings, training sessions, newsletters, emails, annual reports, or videotapes. The *Snapshot* on Fairmont explained how the company distributed a bi-monthly newsletter in each hotel as well as a company-wide newsletter to keep staff up to date on new company procedures.

Unfortunately, many organizations exclude customer-contact employees from the communication cycle. The director of marketing may tell managers and supervisors about upcoming promotional campaigns, but some managers may feel that employees do not need to have this information. However, it is important that staff is informed about marketing promotions. They should hear about promotions and new products from management, not from external advertisements meant for customers. Changes in the service delivery process should also be communicated. In fact, all action steps in the marketing plan should include internal marketing. For example, when an organization introduces a new mass media campaign, the implementation should include actions to inform employees about the campaign. Because service advertising and personal selling promise what people *do*, frequent and effective communication across functions — horizontal communication — is critical. If internal communication is poor, perceived service quality is at risk. If company advertising and other promises are developed without input from operations, contact personnel may not be able to deliver service that matches the image portrayed in marketing efforts.

4. Implementation of a Reward and Recognition System

For employees to perform effectively, it is important that they know how they are doing, so communication must be designed to give them feedback on their performance. At the Sheraton Suites Eau Claire every effort is made to recognize the achievement of employees and to ensure that they are happy and proud of their jobs. In a Canadian survey, almost 90 percent of employees reported that "being made to feel like a valued employee is important in motivating them to achieve company goals."[6] The survey was conducted by Bob Macdonald, president of Maritz Canada Inc. Macdonald argues that in order to feed an employee's energy level and overall desire to perform, organizations need to clearly communicate performance objectives, as well as provide relevant training, feedback, and recognition in the form of non-cash rewards. However, the rewards should be tailored to the interests of the employees they are designed to motivate. Group excursions are popular with employees in the 18- to 29-age group, while older employees prefer individual trips. More men than women appreciate getting "company-logo merchandise" as a reward. For some, the ideal reward is the gift of a personal chef for the evening, and for others time off with pay is the perfect reward.

Some companies recognize superior performance with reward points that can be redeemed for an array of gifts. At the high end, the rewards can range from airline tickets to big-screen televisions. Sometimes recognition alone is enough. Macdonald says that 73 percent of the surveyed employees reported that receiving "recognition as top performer" was important. Furthermore, most employees want regular feedback. Macdonald found in his survey that only 15 percent of employees said that their companies offer that extra something for a job well done. He suggests that most employers do not offer non-monetary rewards because they are concerned about the cost or are not sure what their employees would value. Macdonald says that as the labour market tightens, retention of top performers will become an issue for employers. He adds that employees have made clear, in repeated surveys, that money is important — but it takes more than money to engage them in their jobs.

DELIVERING SERVICE QUALITY

Service quality has been increasingly identified as a key factor in differentiating products and building a competitive advantage in tourism. The process by which customers evaluate a purchase, thereby determining satisfaction and likelihood of repurchase, is important to all marketers, but especially to services marketers because, unlike their manufacturing counterparts, they have fewer objective measures of quality by which to judge their production. **Service quality** can be defined as customers' perceptions of the service component of a product, and these perceptions are said to be based on five dimensions: reliability, assurance, empathy, responsiveness, and tangibles.[7]

service quality

customers' perceptions of the service component of a product

customer satisfaction

the difference between the service that a customer expects and the perceived quality of what is actually delivered

Many researchers believe that an outgrowth of service quality is **customer satisfaction**, measured as the difference between the service that a customer expects and the perceived quality of what is actually delivered.[8] Satisfying customers has always been a key component of the tourism industry, but never before has it been so critical. In these uncertain times, and with increased competition, knowing how to win and keep customers is the single, most important business skill that anyone can learn. Customer satisfaction and loyalty are the keys to long-term profitability, and keeping the customer happy is everybody's business. Becoming customer centred and exceeding customer expectations are requirements for business success.

Well-publicized research shows that companies can increase profits from 25 to 85 percent by retaining just 5 percent more of their customers.[9] However, the newest research indicates that merely "satisfying" customers is no longer enough to ensure loyalty.[10] There is little or no correlation between satisfied (versus highly satisfied) customers and customer retention. This means that it is not enough just to please customers. Each customer should become so pleased with all elements of their association with an organization that buying from somewhere else is unthinkable.

"Customer-centred" is an exact term that connotes much more than focusing on or understanding the customer. The true customer-centred company has the willingness and ability to bring the customer to the very centre of its organizational being.[11] Customers' needs and expectations are communicated throughout, and every employee evaluates every process, every task, and every decision by considering how it will add value for the customers. All employees must be convinced that the customer really does come first. The issue of understanding needs and expectations is an important part of the quest for customer satisfaction. The "gaps model" of service quality (see Figure 11.2) provides a method of graphically illustrating these needs and expectations.[12] This conceptual model enables a structured thought process for evaluating and "designing in" customer satisfaction. The model begins with expected service as viewed by the customer. Every customer has certain expectations about a service, which may come from word of mouth, personal needs, group needs, past experience, or external communications. When the service is delivered and the customers' expectations are exceeded, the customers perceive the quality as relatively high. When their expectations have not been met, they perceive the quality as relatively low. Thus, as stated above, customer satisfaction can be defined as the difference between what the customer expects and the perceived quality of what is actually delivered. Often there is a gap between expected service and the actual service as perceived by the customer, and, in the model, this is gap 5. The magnitude of this gap is driven by four other possible gaps, each of which denotes failure in some aspect of service delivery. The five gaps are discussed below.

Gap 1: The Difference between the Customer's Expectations of Service and Management's Perception of Those Expectations

Many reasons exist for managers not being aware of what customers expect: they may not interact directly with customers, may be unwilling to ask about expectations, or may be unprepared to address them. The four key factors responsible for gap 1 are the service provider's inadequate marketing research orientation, lack of upward communication, insufficient relationship focus, and inadequate service recovery. The importance of both relationship marketing and service recovery is discussed later in this chapter. By building stronger relationships, understanding customer needs over time, and implementing recovery strategies when things go wrong, gap 1 — the customer expectations gap — can be minimized.

Gap 2: The Difference between the Management's Perception of Customer Expectations and How These Perceptions Are Translated into Specifications or Processes

Gap 2 occurs when managers know what their customers want but are unable or unwilling to develop systems that will deliver it. Some of the reasons that have been given for gap 2 are poor service design, absence of customer-defined standards, and inappropriate physical evidence and servicescape. One of the most important ways to avoid gap 2 is to design services clearly, without oversimplification, incompleteness, subjectivity, or bias. To do this, tools are needed to ensure that new and existing services are developed and improved in as

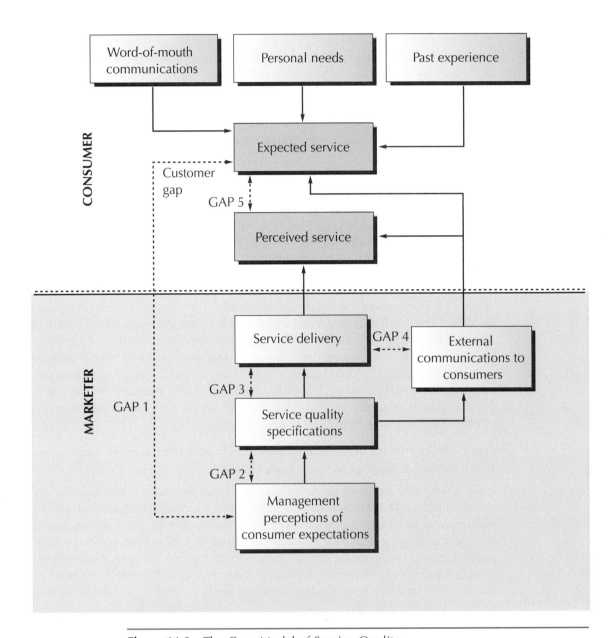

Figure 11.2   The Gaps Model of Service Quality

Source: Parasuraman, A., Zeithaml, V. A., and Berry, L. L. (1985). A conceptual model of service quality and its implications for future research. *Journal of Marketing, 49*(4), 40.

careful a manner as possible. Service blueprinting is often used as an implementation tool to address the challenges of designing and specifying intangible service processes. Service organizations must also explore the importance of physical evidence, the variety of roles it plays, and strategies for effectively designing physical evidence and the servicescape to meet customer expectations (see Chapter 5 for a discussion of the servicescape).

Gap 3: The Difference between Management's Specifications of Service and the Actual Service Delivered to the Customer

Even when guidelines exist for performing services well and treating customers correctly, high-quality performance is not a certainty. Research on customer experience has identified many of the critical inhibitors to closing gap 3. These include employees who do not clearly understand the roles they are to play in the company, employees who see conflict between customers and company management, the wrong employees, inadequate technology, inappropriate compensation and recognition, and lack of empowerment and teamwork. To deliver better service performance, these human resource issues must be addressed across functions. A second cause of gap 3 is the challenge involved in delivering service through intermediaries such as travel agents or franchisees. It is a huge task for organizations to attain service excellence and consistency in the presence of intermediaries who represent them, interact with their customers, and yet are not under their direct control. Other variables in gap 3 include the customers — who may not understand their roles and responsibilities and may negatively affect each other — and the failure to match supply and demand. Because services are perishable and cannot be inventoried, service companies frequently face situations of over- or under-demand. Marketing strategies for managing supply and demand should be used to reduce gap 3.

Gap 4: The Difference between the Delivery of the Service and External Communications about the Service

Gap 4 is created when promises do not match performance. Broken promises can occur for many reasons: over-promising in advertising or personal selling, inadequate coordination between operations and marketing, and differences in policies and procedures across outlets. There are also less obvious ways in which external communications influence customers' service quality assessments. Service companies frequently fail to capitalize on opportunities to educate customers in using services appropriately. They also frequently fail to manage customer expectations of what they will receive in service transactions and relationships. Therefore, in addition to improving service delivery, organizations must also manage all communications to customers, so that inflated promises do not lead to overly high expectations. Many companies profiled in this book — such as Canadian Mountain Holidays and WestJet — make it a policy to "under-promise and over-deliver." Unfortunately, there are too many examples of companies that do just the opposite. Aeroplan, Air Canada's frequent flyer program, for example, promises free flights for loyal customers. However, the reality is that those free flights are very difficult to book, and there is also a booking fee. This difference between what is promised and what is delivered can cause customer frustration, perhaps driving the customer to the competition.

Gap 5: The Difference between the Customer's Expectations and Perceptions

The central focus of the gaps model is gap 5, the customer gap: the difference between the service a customer expects and the service the customer perceives that he or she receives. Firms need to close this gap in order to satisfy customers and to build long-term relationships with them. To close this all-important customer gap, the four other gaps — the provider gaps — need to be closed.

Measuring Service Quality

importance–
performance
analysis (IPA)

an assessment of the
relative importance of
various attributes and
the performance of the
organization, product
or service, or destina-
tion in providing these
attributes

The two main research instruments that have been developed over the years to analyze the concepts of quality and consumer satisfaction in the service industry are SERVQUAL and **importance–performance analysis (IPA)**. IPA assesses the relative importance of various attributes and the performance of the organization, product or service, or destination in providing these attributes. Its use has important marketing and management implications for decision makers, and one of the major benefits of using IPA is the identification of areas for service quality improvements. Results are displayed graphically on a two-dimensional grid, and, through a simple visual analysis of this matrix, policy makers can identify areas where the resources and programs need to be concentrated. Introduced more than 20 years ago, IPA is well documented in the literature.[13]

Figure 11.3 shows the importance and performance mean scores of ski attributes from a study in Switzerland.[14] The action grid identifies where each of the attributes falls in terms of the four quadrants, with examples pinpointed in each quadrant. In this variation, the largest number of attributes (42 percent) was plotted into the "Concentrate here" area of the action grid. Respondents rated these attributes high in importance but low in performance. These attributes included the majority of services on the ski slopes, comfortable beds, value for money in bars and restaurants, and the prices in the ski shops.

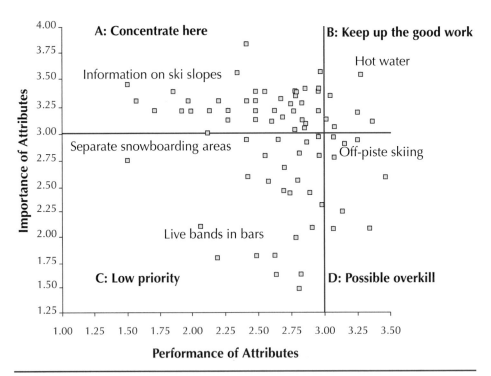

Figure 11.3 Importance–Performance Analysis with Attribute Ratings for a Ski Destination

Source: Hudson, S., & Shephard, G. (1998). Measuring service quality at tourist destinations: An application of importance–performance analysis to an alpine ski resort. *Journal of Travel and Tourism Marketing, 7*(3), 69.

SERVQUAL

an instrument used to measure the difference between consumers' expectations and perceptions of service quality

SERVQUAL is an instrument developed by A. Parasuraman, Valarie Zeithaml, and Leonard Berry, which is used to measure the difference between consumers' expectations and perceptions of service quality.[15] Exploratory research conducted in 1985 showed that consumers judge service quality by using the same general criteria, regardless of the type of service. Parasuraman and his colleagues capture these criteria using a scale composed of 22 items designed to load on five dimensions reflecting service quality. The dimensions are assurance, empathy, reliability, responsiveness, and tangibles. Each item is used twice: first, to determine customers' expectations about companies in general, within the service category being investigated; and second, to measure perceptions of performance of a particular company, within this same service category. These evaluations are collected using a seven-point Likert scale. According to the authors, the service quality is determined as the difference between customers' expectations and perceptions.

Other researchers have suggested that the mere fact of asking respondents to mark their perceptions of performance already leads them to compare mentally their perceptions and their expectations. In other words, the estimation of perceptions might already include a "perception minus expectation" mental process. They suggest that performance on its own, or SERVPERF (which stands for "service performance"), is the measure that best explains total quality. However, although the perceptions format offers the most predictive power — a finding that has consistently emerged in the literature — it offers little diagnostic potential and, indeed, may result in inappropriate priorities being established. From a managerial perspective, it would seem important to track trends of the extent to which expectations are met over time as well as trends in performance. The use of difference scores gives managers a better understanding of whether increasing expectations or diminishing performance might be responsible for declining service quality and customer satisfaction. An examination of minimum expectations may also be fruitful. Similarly, disregarding importance may mean losing useful insights. Without considering attribute importance, one has no indication of the relative importance that respondents attach to particular aspects of service performance. The *Case Study* in Chapter 4 expands on this discussion.

Service Quality Ratings

Measuring service quality has become an important consideration in many sectors of tourism and hospitality. In recent years, there has been evidence of "star inflation" throughout the travel industry. The seven-star Burj Al Arab hotel in Dubai profiled in Chapter 6 is an example of that. At present, no official rating system awards more than five stars — or diamonds in the case of the Canadian Automobile Association or the American Automobile Association (CAA/AAA) — and only a select few ever make the coveted grade. According to Mobil Travel Guides, a hotel garners a five-star rating if it "has consistently superlative service and expanded amenities in a luxurious, distinctive environment, making the establishment one of the best in the country." However, the sheer number of website rating systems means stars, diamonds, and other recommendations are becoming a confusing system that often means little to the average traveller. The confusion is increased in that while Mobil and CAA/AAA are the ranking kings in North America, many countries employ government-run rating programs that are more liberal and less stringent. In the Dominican Republic, for example, a four-star resort might boast a dozen, often crowded, eating venues and childrens' activities. Spas, however, are rare.

Every year, inspectors all over Canada travel to hotels, motels, inns, lodges, resorts, and bed and breakfasts to rate them for the Canada Select Accommodation Rating Program. It is a voluntary program in which inspectors arrive at the facility unannounced and rate the public areas as well as 10 percent of the rooms. They have a set of hard-and-fast criteria that they use to determine the amenities and services that are available, and they also assess the general quality of the surroundings, such as the furniture, walls, and floors. Overall cleanliness and the state of repair are factors in the rating. Properties are grouped into six categories based on shared characteristics such as general locations, facilities, services, and market appeal (rating criteria are different within each category).

Inspections cost about $180, with additional charges for larger properties. The inspectors usually sit down and discuss the inspection with the operator before they leave. Most people feel that the rating is fair, and more and more businesses are joining the program. Table 11.1 gives the star rating descriptions. Canada Select ratings are available on printed materials and on the Internet, and the benefits to the consumer include the ability to choose accommodation with confidence, knowing an independent authority has rated the property. All 10 provinces and Yukon participate in the program.

Table 11.1

Canada Select Accommodation Rating Program: Star Rating Descriptions

*	*Modest* accommodations meeting the Canada Select standards of cleanliness, comfort, and safety. At this level, guests should expect clean and well-maintained accommodations providing the necessary facilities for an enjoyable stay. Criteria includes standards such as room size, window screens and coverings, clothes storage, linens, door lock, smoke detector, and parking facilities.
**	*Moderate* accommodations with additional facilities and some amenities. This level equates to what is popularly considered "mid-range" accommodation. It exceeds the one-star level in quality of mattress, bed linen, floors/window/wall coverings, and in provision of bedside and seating area lighting, additional room furniture, and parking space.
***	*Above-average* accommodations with a greater range of facilities, guest amenities, and services available. These properties will offer larger units with additional room furniture, coordinated furnishings, better quality mattresses and linens, and will be equipped with clock/alarm, extra amenities in washrooms, etc. Private baths for all rooms is a requirement for a three-star and higher rating. Three-star properties offer above-average facilities and services.
****	*Exceptional* accommodations with an extensive range of facilities, guest amenities, and services. This rating indicates exceptional quality in all areas of facilities and services offering superior quality throughout the property in areas of guestrooms, bath, and common areas. The property typically provides laundry/valet service as well as many additional amenities.
*****	*Luxurious* properties; among the very best in the country in terms of their outstanding facilities, guest services, and quality provided.

Source: Canada Select. (2007). How is a property rated? www.canadaselect.com (retrieved September 2007).

MARKETING IN ACTION

"IT'S OUR PLEASURE!" — SERVICE EXCELLENCE AT THE SHERATON SUITES CALGARY EAU CLAIRE

The Sheraton Suites Calgary Eau Claire has a reputation for service excellence. The hotel was awarded the Sheraton Brand Highest Guest Satisfaction from 2001 straight through to 2006 continuously. This Sheraton award recognizes exceptional levels of hospitality, service, and attention to detail, as well as upscale facilities and variety of amenities. The Sheraton Suites was also the winner of the Alberta Tourism Award (Alto) for Service Excellence in 2002 and 2005. This particular award honours an organization in the tourism industry that demonstrates a commitment to service excellence, delivering outstanding customer service to their visitors, employees, suppliers, and other stakeholders.

But exactly what does it take to win awards like this?

Randy Zupanski was the hotel general manager from its opening and led this great team to terrific results, instilling a service culture and customer service focus for all the associates. In 2005 Ross Meredith was appointed general manager and in that year the hotel was awarded the Sheraton Hotel of the Year Award Worldwide from Starwood Hotels and Resorts. Meredith says there are two key reasons why the Sheraton Suites Calgary Eau Claire is so different from its competitors: customer loyalty and quality employees. First, a focus on customer loyalty is driven by the It's Our Pleasure program — a recognition and reward program for guests. On every fifth stay, each guest receives a gift, one that is meaningful to that guest, and the value of the gift increases the longer a customer remains loyal. For example, on the fifth stay a guest may receive a bottle of wine in the room, and by the 25th stay, a personalized bathrobe will be given as a loyalty gift. Meanwhile, the hotel collects valuable data on the personal preferences of customers and stores this in a database. For example, if a guest likes extra towels and feather pillows, then these will be waiting in the room when the guest arrives, with a note saying "It's our pleasure to provide you with these items."

Meredith suggests that the majority of hotels put in the customer service effort after the guest arrives, whereas the Sheraton Eau Claire takes care of preferences before arrival. A guest relations officer is employed for the sole purpose of coordinating the It's Our Pleasure program, and a room is not ready for a guest until this officer has ensured all preferences are taken care of.

Perhaps the most important reason that the Sheraton Eau Claire is an award winner is the quality of its employees. The hotel hires "nice people with great attitudes" and takes training very seriously. Training programs include a two-day hotel orientation, a full day spent on the "It's Our Pleasure" program, and the brand-specific "Building World Class Brands," an extensive Starwood training program that supports both the service delivery culture in that hotel and across the brand. The training programs use role playing to emphasize the meaning and importance of employee empowerment, and employees are trained in the art of service recovery and taught the

MARKETING IN ACTION *continued*

importance of customer contact. Energy is put into key contact areas, so that before a guest reaches his or her room, there has been plenty of opportunity for personal contact from the valet, bell staff, reception staff, and even the general manager. For Meredith, pride is the key, and every effort is made to recognize the achievement of employees and to ensure that they are happy and proud of their jobs. Loss of employees to other competitive set hotels is extremely low, he says, and if employees do leave, it is to go into other industries.

Sheraton Eau Claire's success has been a fascination and curiosity of a number of service companies and the hotel leadership team has been providing them with best practices and programs that supports service delivery. These include employee empowerment, celebrating success, managing key measurements and the benefits of goal setting, actions plans, and follow up.

The results of these efforts are not just manifested in the winning of awards. The hotel has occupancy rates 10 percent higher and room rates $40–50 above the competition, including the Hyatt, Fairmont, Westin, Delta, and Marriott. Since opening, the Sheraton Suites Eau Claire has led the market with an overall market share on revenue per available room of about 140 percent. This lengthy period of successful financial and guest service results clearly positions the Sheraton Suites Calgary Eau Claire as both the market leader and the service delivery leader. The challenge remains maintaining this position in a highly competitive downtown hotel market. In the meantime, the Sheraton Suites Calgary Eau Claire provides an excellent example of the value of internal marketing.

Source: Personal correspondence with R. Meredith, general manager, Sheraton Suites Calgary Eau Claire, 13 July, 2007.

The Behavioural Consequences of Service Quality

The issue of highest priority today related to service quality involves understanding the impact of service quality on profit and other financial outcomes of the organization. Executives of many companies in the 1980s were willing to trust their intuitive sense that better service would lead to improved financial success. They therefore committed resources to improving service prior to having documentation of the financial payoff. Some of these companies, such as Four Seasons and Ritz-Carlton, have been richly rewarded for their efforts. But executives in other companies have been reluctant to invest in service improvements without solid evidence of their financial soundness. However, research on the relationship between service quality and profits has begun to accumulate. Findings from these studies show that companies offering superior service achieve higher-than-normal market share growth[16]; that the mechanisms by which service quality influences profits include increased market share and premium prices[17]; and that businesses in the top quintile of relative service quality realize on average an 8 percent higher price than their competitors.[18]

Another fruitful area of research is that which examines the relationship between service quality and behavioural intentions. Zeithaml, Berry, and Parasuraman have developed a conceptual model that depicts the behavioural consequences of service quality as intervening variables between service quality and the financial gains or losses from retention or defection (see Figure 11.4).[19] The left portion of the model is at the level of the individual customer and proposes that service quality and behavioural intentions are related and, therefore, that service quality is a determinant of whether a customer ultimately remains with or defects from a company.

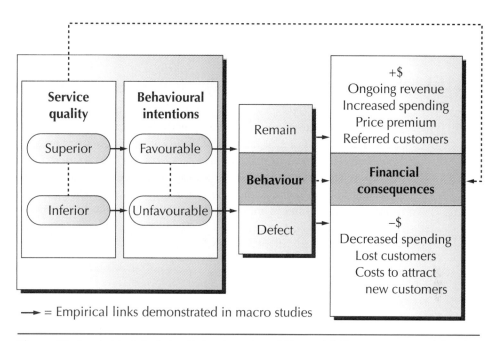

Figure 11.4 A Model of the Behavioural and Financial Consequences of Service Quality

Source: Zeithaml, V. A., Berry, L. L., & Parasuraman, A. (1996). The behavioural consequences of service quality. *Journal of Marketing, 60*, 31–46.

By integrating research findings and anecdotal evidence, a list of specific indicators of customers' favourable behavioural intentions can be compiled. These include saying positive things about the company to others, recommending the company or service to others, paying a price premium to the company, and remaining loyal to the company. Loyalty may be manifested in a variety of ways — for example, by expressing a preference for a company over others, by continuing to purchase from it, or by increasing business with it in the future. Customers perceiving service performance to be inferior are likely to exhibit behaviour signalling that they are poised to leave the company or spend less money with the company. This behaviour includes complaining, which is viewed by many researchers as a variety of negative responses that stem from dissatisfaction and predict or accompany defection.

After testing this model, the authors found strong empirical support for the intuitive notion that improving service quality can increase favourable behavioural intentions and decrease unfavourable intentions. The findings demonstrate the importance of strategies that can steer behavioural intentions in the right directions, including striving to meet customers' "desired-service" levels (rather than merely performing at their "adequate-service" levels), emphasizing the prevention of service problems, and effectively resolving problems that do occur. However, multiple findings suggest that companies wanting to improve service, especially beyond the desired-service level, should do so in a cost-effective manner.

LOYALTY AND RELATIONSHIP MARKETING

The Link between Satisfaction and Loyalty

customer loyalty

a measure of how likely customers are to return to an organization and of their willingness to build relationships with the organization

As Figure 11.1 shows, customer satisfaction is a requisite for loyalty. Customer satisfaction is a measure of how well a customer's expectations are met. **Customer loyalty**, on the other hand, is a measure of how likely customers are to return to an organization and of their willingness to build relationships with the organization. Customer expectations must be met or exceeded to build loyalty. As Figure 11.5 indicates, there is an important relationship between customer satisfaction and loyalty. The relationship is particularly strong when customers are very satisfied. Thus, businesses that simply aim to satisfy customers may not be doing enough to engender loyalty. They must instead aim to more than satisfy — or even delight — their customers.

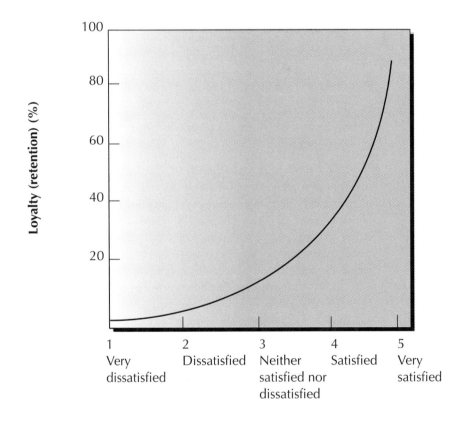

Satisfaction measure

Figure 11.5 Relationships between Customer Satisfaction and Loyalty in Competitive Industries

Source: Heskett, J. L., Sasser, W. E., Jr., & Schlesinger, L. A. (1997). *The service profit chain: How leading companies link profit and growth to loyalty, satisfaction, and value.* New York: Free Press, 83.

However, it is important to understand that there are several reasons why satisfied customers may not become loyal customers in the tourism industry. First, many travellers prefer to visit different places and may not return to the same destination or hotel even if they are extremely satisfied. Second, some travellers are very price sensitive and shop for the best deal they can get regardless of satisfaction measures. Third, customers expect to be satisfied with their purchase, so satisfaction ratings are often inflated. This underscores the need to have extremely satisfied customers in order to encourage loyalty.

Loyal customers are therefore more valuable than satisfied customers. A satisfied customer who does not return and does not spread positive word of mouth has no value to the company. On the other hand, a loyal customer who returns and spreads positive word of mouth has a very high value, and it is therefore important that companies identify those patrons who are likely to become loyal customers. Over the last few decades, loyalty reward programs have burgeoned as organizations seek to retain customers in an increasingly competitive market. Loyalty programs are popular because they are easy to enroll in and the consumer has the potential to earn rewards for products and services they already use. Loyalty programs have expanded to the extent that points can be earned in every consumer category, from groceries, to books, to car rentals and even phone bill payments. Travel rewards are the most prized rewards among consumers, and the *Snapshot* below looks at these rewards in more detail.

SNAPSHOT

TRAVEL REWARDS STILL A HOT TICKET

More than 25 years after frequent flyer miles sparked the current obsession with loyalty programs, public interest in travel rewards shows no signs of waning. In 2006, there were about 89 million participants worldwide in airline frequent flyer programs, and travel rewards — flights and accommodation — continue to be the most prized rewards among consumers, with cash rebates and merchandise running second and third. However, travel reward redemptions have moved from simple air flights to include vacation packages, hotel accommodations anywhere in the world, car rentals, cruises, train trips, bus tickets, attraction passes, and dining options for travellers once they reach their destination. For loyal business travellers, travel redemptions can be payback to their families for all the time they spend on the road.

Experiential rewards — rewards that involve creating an experience instead of handing over cash or a piece of merchandise — are part of a trend in the reward industry to keep consumer interest engaged in loyalty programs. "Travel is the ultimate experiential reward. It allows customers to dream," says Kelly Hlavinka, director of Colloquy, a U.S.-based loyalty program research firm. Of course, consumer satisfaction is only one half of the equation. Travel rewards for loyalty shown are also a big benefit to the travel industry, particularly in an era when the marketplace has become so competitive

SNAPSHOT *continued*

and soaring oil and insurance prices as well as terrorism threats have made the industry volatile.

As well as cultivating loyalty among consumers, loyalty programs provide detailed information about what these customers are looking for in services and give them a very direct means of communication — through e-mail newsletters and promotions for example. With growing competition to attract and retain customers throughout the tourism industry, loyalty programs are increasingly trying to outdo each other, offering more opportunities to build points, more ways to redeem them, and also a variety of rewards geared to personal preferences. Partnerships among travel, retail, and credit card companies are increasing the scope and sophistication of loyalty schemes in an attempt to persuade consumers that they can benefit from the system.

Car rental companies, for example, are differentiating their redemption options to cater for particular needs. Customers can choose between bonus miles, greater comfort, and upgrades or savings and free days, with increasingly more deals attached to online bookings. Restaurants are also jumping onto the bandwagon with points being gained by consumers eating in a particular individual venue and then paying the bill with a particular credit card. Movie theatres and golf courses are joining schemes, to give a wider scope for point or mile redemption. Hotel rewards schemes have recently adapted to erase the differences between business and leisure travellers, promoting the interchangeability of points gained in both forms of travel and also in redemption of the points. In response to customer complaints that while points are easy to gain, they are very difficult to redeem, the Holiday Inn chain now has no expiration dates for points and also no blackout periods for redemptions. Also, Days Inn offers redemption on hotel stays, car rental, and retail uses in order to make its scheme attractive to both leisure and business travellers. Hotels are getting the advantage of increased bookings from these schemes and are also tapping into a rich vein of data on their customers' preferences vital for marketing strategies.

Sources: Collis, R. (2006, March 10). Earning miles: Is it worth it? *International Herald Tribune*. www.iht.com/articles/2006/03/09/travel/trfreq10.php (retrieved September 2007); Schachter, H. (2005, November 30). Loyalty myths shredded like old air-miles statement. *Globe & Mail*, C5; Rewarding experience. (2004, September 20). *Globe & Mail*, Travel Rewards II: Advertising Special Report; Business, leisure lines blur in today's hotels. (2004, September 20). *Globe & Mail*, Travel Rewards II; Travel Rewards Still a Hot Ticket. (2006, September 19). *National Post*, JV2.

Relationship Marketing

relationship marketing

marketing that attracts customers, retains them, and enhances their satisfaction

Once an organization has identified potential loyal customers, the next stage is to create a relationship with these customers that will eventually lead to customer loyalty. This is called **relationship marketing**, a form of marketing that attracts customers, retains them, and enhances their satisfaction.[20] In the past, tourism and hospitality marketers have tended to put more emphasis on attracting new customers. More recently, the idea of nurturing the individual relationships with current and past customers has received greater attention. Most marketers now accept that it is less expensive to attract repeat customers than to create new ones, and this is the basic concept behind relationship marketing. The key outcome of all relationship marketing efforts is to make individual customers feel unique and to make them believe that the organization has singled them out for special attention.

Retention Strategies

There are four different levels of retention strategies that encourage relationship marketing: financial bonds, social bonds, customization bonds, and structural bonds.[21] These are illustrated in Figure 11.6.

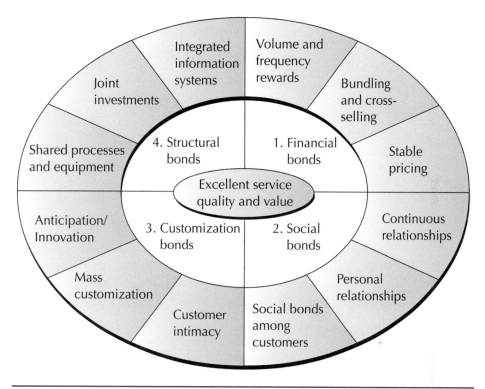

Figure 11.6 Levels of Retention Strategies for Relationship Marketing

Source: Zeithaml, V. A., & Bitner, M. J. (2000). *Services marketing: Integrating customer focus across the firm.* New York: McGraw-Hill, 153.

At level 1, the customer is tied to the organization primarily through financial incentives — often in the form of lower prices for greater volume purchases or lower prices for customers who have been with the company for a long time (e.g., frequent flyer programs). In other cases, firms aim to retain customers by simply offering loyal customers the assurance of stable prices, or at least smaller price increases than those paid by new customers. Other types of retention strategies that depend primarily on financial rewards are focused on bundling and cross-selling of services.

Level 2 strategies bind customers to the business through more than just financial incentives. Marketers using this retention strategy build long-term relationships through social and interpersonal, as well as financial, bonds. Services are customized to fit individual needs, and marketers find ways of staying in touch with their customers, thereby developing social bonds with them. Social, interpersonal bonds are common among professional service providers and their clients, as well as among personal care providers and clients. Sometimes relationships are formed with the organization due to the social relationships that develop among customers rather than between customers and the service provider. For example, people who vacation at the same place during the same weeks every year build bonds with others who vacation there at the same time.

Level 3 strategies involve more than social ties and financial incentives, and two commonly used terms fit within the customization bonds approach: mass customization and customer intimacy. Both of these strategies suggest that customer loyalty can be encouraged through intimate knowledge of individual customers and through the development of one-to-one solutions that fit the individual customer's needs. Ritz-Carlton, for example, maintains a computerized guest history profile of thousands of individual repeat guests. When guests visit any Ritz-Carlton property, members of staff already know about their likes and dislikes. Casinos also maintain sophisticated databases of guest preferences, as well as their wagering habits.

Level 4 strategies are the most difficult to imitate and involve structural as well as financial, social, and customization bonds between the customer and the organization. Structural bonds are seen mostly in business to business settings and are created by providing the client with customized services that are technology based and that serve to make the customer more productive. An example would be a reservations system installed in a travel agency by a tour operator. The agent is therefore structurally bound to that operator in its operations. Structural bonds can be created in a business to consumer environment, too. For example, some car rental companies offer travellers the opportunity to create customized pages on the firm's website, where they can retrieve details of past trips including the types of cars, insurance coverage, and so on. This simplifies and speeds the task of making repeat bookings.

Benefits of Relationship Marketing

Both parties in the customer–company relationship can benefit from customer retention. It is not only in the best interest of the organization to build and maintain a loyal customer base; customers themselves also benefit from long-term associations. Table 11.2 summarizes the various benefits of relationship marketing for both the company and the customer. Assuming they have a choice, customers will remain loyal to an organization when they receive greater value relative to what they expect from competing organizations. Value represents a trade-off for the consumer between what they give and what they get. Consumers are more likely to stay in a relationship when the "gets" (quality, satisfaction, specific benefits) exceed the "gives" (monetary and non-monetary costs). When organizations can consistently deliver what the customer considers to be value, the customer clearly benefits and has an incentive to stay in the relationship.

The benefits to an organization of maintaining and developing a loyal customer base are numerous, but they are linked directly to the bottom line. Among service organizations, reducing customer defections by just 5 percent can boost profits by 25 to 85 percent.[22] Retained customers are much more profitable than new ones because they purchase more and they purchase more frequently, often at a price premium, while at the same time requiring lower operating costs. They also make referrals that cost the business nothing. And, of course, their acquisition cost is nothing, which is significant because it costs a company five to seven times more to prospect for new customers than it does to maintain the current ones.[23]

Table 11.2

Benefits of Relationship Marketing to the Organization and the Customer

BENEFITS TO THE COMPANY	BENEFITS TO THE CUSTOMER
Increased purchases	Social benefits
Lower costs	Confidence and trust
Employee retention	Special treatment
Increased profits	Reduced risk
Less customer defection	Increased value
Free advertising through word of mouth	Customized services

lifetime value of a customer

a calculation that considers customers from the point of view of their potential lifetime revenue and profitability contributions to a organization

To understand the financial value of building long-term relationships with customers, companies sometimes calculate lifetime values. The **lifetime value of a customer** is a calculation that considers customers from the point of view of their potential lifetime revenue and profitability contributions to a organization. This value is influenced by the length of an average lifetime, the average revenues generated in that time period, sales of additional products and services over time, and referrals generated by the customer. For example, Disney has estimated that each loyal customer has a lifetime value to the company of US$50 000. But it is not just the lifetime value of consumers that is important to tourism providers. In the Bahamas, where diving is a multimillion dollar industry, and sharks are an ever increasing draw, experts have calculated that a single shark in a healthy habitat is worth as much as $200 000 in tourism revenue over its lifetime![24]

Focusing on the "Right Customers"

The idea of targeting the "right customers" for relationship marketing has emerged in the literature and in practice over the last few decades. Reichheld, for example, stresses that companies aspiring to relationship marketing should make formal efforts to identify those customers who are most likely to remain loyal, and should develop their overall strategy around delivering superior value to these customers.[25] Targeting profitable customers for relationship marketing involves studying and analyzing loyalty- and defection-prone customers, searching for distinguishing patterns in why they stay or leave, what creates value for them, and who they are.

Innovative service organization today are beginning to recognize that not all customers are worth attracting and keeping. Many customers are too costly to do business with and have little potential to become profitable, even in the long term. To build and improve upon traditional segmentation, organizations are now trying to identify segments that differ in current or future profitability to the organization. After identifying profitability bands, the organization offers services and service levels in line with the identified segments. Virtually all organizations are aware at some level that their customers differ in profitability — in particular that a minority of their customers account for the highest proportion of sales or profits. This has often been called the 80/20 rule: 20 percent of customers produce 80 percent of sales or profits. This 80/20 customer pyramid is shown in Figure 11.7.

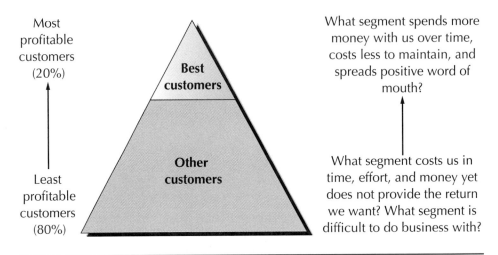

Figure 11.7   The 80/20 Customer Pyramid

Source: Zeithhaml, V. A., & Bitnen, M. J. (2000). *Services marketing: Integrating customer focus across the firm.* New York: McGraw-Hill, 470.

A few years ago, Thomas Cook Travel divided its customers into three categories: A (those who bring in $900 or more in annual revenues), B (those who bring in $300 to $900), and C (those who bring in less than $300). The company found that 80 percent of its customers fell into C. By focusing in on the more profitable customers (A and B), and by charging C for their time-consuming demands (a $25 deposit was taken for researching any trip), the company increased its profits considerably. The growth of the company's A- and B-level clients also increased by 20 percent.[26]

However, a customer's unprofitability may not be the only reason an organization chooses to refuse or terminate a relationship. For various reasons, the belief that "the customer is always right" does not always apply in service industries. It would not be beneficial to either the organization or the customer for the organization to establish a relationship with a customer whose needs it cannot meet. Every server in the restaurant business has met the "customer from hell," a paying guest whose behaviour is beyond rude and who seems determined to ruin the evening for everyone concerned. These disruptive customers have even been segmented in some research articles, into classifications such as "Egocentric Edgars," "Freeloading Fredas," and "Dictatorial Dicks."[27] Such customers are often impossible to satisfy, and may place too much stress on employees and the organization.

Similarly, it would not be wise to forge relationships simultaneously with incompatible market segments. In many tourism businesses, customers experience the service together and can influence each other's perceptions about the value received. For example, a conference hotel may find that mixing executives in town for a serious training program with students in town for a sporting event may not be wise. If the student group is a key long-term customer, the hotel may choose to pass up the executive group in the interest of retaining the students' business.

Although the idea of firing customers is catching on in the West, it appears that in Asia, service providers are still doing all they can to satisfy their awkward customers. One bar in China is allowing its stressed patrons to unleash pent-up anger by allowing them to attack staff, smash glasses, and generally make a ruckus.[28] The Rising Sun Anger Release Bar in Nanjing, capital of the eastern province of Jiangsu, employs 20 muscled young men as "models" to be punched and screamed at. Since it opened in April 2006, most of the patrons have been women, especially those working in karaoke bars and massage parlours.

Service Recovery

service recovery

rectifying a service delivery failure

Service delivery failure is likely to occur at some point for organizations in the service industry. Although it is unlikely that businesses can eliminate all service failures, they can learn to respond effectively to failures once they do occur. This response is often referred to as **service recovery**, defined simply as rectifying a service delivery failure. An effective recovery will retain customer loyalty regardless of the type of failure. In one study, customer retention exceeded 70 percent for those customers who perceived effective recovery efforts.[29] Another study reported that customers who experienced a service failure told nine or ten individuals about their poor service experience, whereas satisfied customers told only four or five individuals about their satisfactory experience.[30] Therefore, an effective recovery process may lead to positive word of mouth, or at least diminish the negative word of mouth typically associated with poor recovery efforts. Figure 11.8 shows the various ways that a customer can respond following a service failure.

Such advantages of effective service recovery efforts display the importance of these efforts in satisfying current customers and reducing defections. The average business does not hear from 95 percent of dissatisfied customers, and every complaining customer represents 26 dissatisfied but non-complaining customers.[31] As was mentioned above, reducing customer defections can boost profits, and retained customers are much more profitable than new ones because they purchase more and they purchase more frequently, while at the same time requiring lower operating costs. It is therefore critical that organizations attempt to reduce customer defections, and they must therefore take a strategic look at customer complaints.

The events that actually wind up irritating and frustrating customers are the end points of a process that needs to be fixed immediately. Airlines around the world are often criticized for poor service and tend to receive more complaints than most sectors of the travel industry. In a 2005 survey of airline complaints, delays, cancellations, and waiting were the top irritants for air travellers, followed by cramped seating and crowding. According to one report, complaints about airlines jumped 50 percent in 2005, but the industry ignored many of those complaints and refuses to compensate passengers, despite regulations protecting rights.[32]

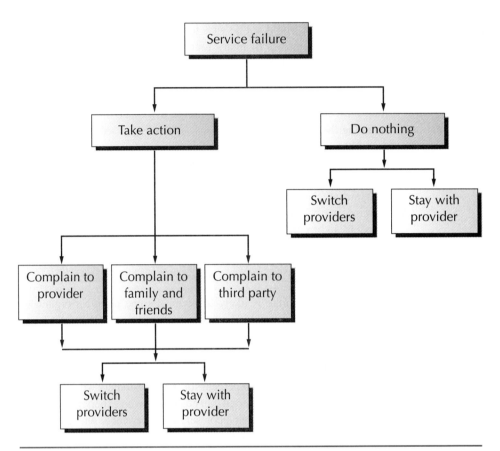

Figure 11.8　Customer Response Following Service Failure

Source: Zeithaml, V. A., & Bitner, M. J. (2000). *Services marketing: Integrating customer focus across the firm.* New York: McGraw-Hill, 168.

In a provocative article called "Thank Heavens for Complainers, by Oren Harari, eight guidelines for tracking and handling complaints were presented.[33] These guidelines are discussed below.

1. Make It Easy for Customers to Complain

Create survey cards that are easy to fill out and that have return postage. Include these with all products, at all sites, and with invoices or other correspondence. Position suggestion boxes in as many sites as possible. Establish electronic accessibility to central terminals. Make sure that home phone numbers are on all business cards. Proactively solicit complaints. Call customers and ex-customers with a list of specific questions. Carefully probe what didn't work, what didn't go well, or what could have been done better. Every manager should be responsible for making at least five calls per month. Hold regular small focus groups; solicit specific, even "minor," sources of hassle and irritation. Every manager should be a part of at least one focus group per month. The Sheraton Suites Calgary Eau Claire (see *Marketing in Action)* hosts a weekly cocktail party at the hotel, which gives guests the opportunity to offer suggestions for how service could be improved.

2. Respond Quickly to Each and Every Complaint

This is where empowerment comes in. If clerks, salespeople, service representatives, account representatives, brokers, accountants, housekeeping, maintenance, and all other employees of an organization are not given the information and authority (including spending authority) to resolve problems quickly, then the organization's concern about complaints is not commitment, but rather lip service. Empowerment also implies responsibility. Somebody in the organization has to "own" each complainer — that is, see that the problem is fixed, follow up to ensure customer satisfaction, and champion appropriate changes in the organization. Every manager's job description should include being such a "somebody" regularly, if not frequently.

3. Educate Employees

Teach employees about the strategic and financial value of complaints, about the need for urgency in responding and, perhaps most important, teach them that everyone owns the problem — not just the "customer service" people. This can be done in orientation, in management-development sessions, in memos and briefings, and in meetings and speeches.

4. Approach Complaints as Operational Problems and Strategic Opportunities

Approaching complaints as opportunities means putting complaints in the category of research and information, not of personal attacks. It means replacing blame analysis with problem analysis. It means viewing complaints in the sense of a critic being an ally who has helped the object of the criticism to focus better on reality.

5. Make Complaints and Complainers Visible

Publish quantitative complaint data publicly (for employees and for customers). Post raw, unedited letters, e-mail messages, and phone call transcripts on bulletin boards. Reprint them in newsletters. Read and discuss them in meetings. Publicize responses to the complaints. Identify and applaud the employees who did the responding. Invite complainers to address people in the organization and to work with them on improvements. Pay them if necessary. Include a "customer panel" in every management retreat.

6. Adjust Quality Measures, Performance Reviews, and Compensation Accordingly

What gets measured and rewarded gets done. Quality measures should always incorporate pervasive customer complaints. Key questions for managers' performance evaluation and pay might include the following: How many complaints have you solicited? How many "firefighting" teams have you been on? How have you used the input of complainers to improve this organization? Rewarding managers for discovering and acting on complaints should be encouraged. Winners of the Nova Scotia Pineapple Awards for service excellence, for example, are often employees whose service recovery goes above and beyond what is expected to enrich a visitor's stay in Nova Scotia.

7. Reward Complainers

Complainers can help a business prosper, and their advice is often priceless. Visible displays of gratitude not only make good common sense but also send a signal to complainers and to the organization. Consider thank-you notes and phone calls, small cash rewards, plaques and certificates, gifts, "consultant of the month" awards, feature stories in company newsletters, and periodic celebrations with complainers as guests of honour.

8. Stop Calling Them "Complainers"!

Don't call them "difficult customers" or "jerks"! These people are critics, allies, consultants, or guests of honour. Call them anything as long as it reflects their contribution to the success of the organization.

CHAPTER SUMMARY

Internal marketing can be defined as marketing aimed internally at an organization's own employees. The main objective of internal marketing in the service industry is to enable employees to deliver satisfying products to guests; it is a process that involves four steps: the establishment of a service culture, the development of a marketing approach to human resource management, the dissemination of marketing information to employees, and the implementation of a reward and recognition system. A solid internal marketing program will lead to good service quality, defined as the customer's perception of the service component of a product. Such perceptions are said to be based on five dimensions: reliability, assurance, empathy, responsiveness, and tangibles.

An outgrowth of service quality is customer satisfaction. The issue of understanding needs and expectations is an important part of the quest to achieve customer satisfaction. The "gaps model" of service quality provides a method of graphically illustrating these needs and expectations, and this conceptual model enables a structured thought process for evaluating and "designing in" customer satisfaction. The two main research instruments that have been developed over the years to analyze the concepts of service quality and consumer satisfaction in the service industry are importance–performance analysis (IPA) and SERVQUAL.

An issue of high priority today involves understanding the impact of service quality on profit and other financial outcomes of the organization. This has led in turn to a focus on customer loyalty and relationship marketing, which involves attracting customers, retaining them, and enhancing their satisfaction. It has been suggested that there are four different retention strategies that encourage relationship marketing: financial bonds, social bonds, customization bonds, and structural bonds.

Finally, service failure is apt to occur at some point in time for businesses in the service industry. Although it is unlikely that organizations can eliminate all service failures, they can learn to respond effectively to failures once they do occur. This response is often referred to as service recovery, defined as the process by which a firm attempts to rectify a service delivery failure. Harari offers eight guidelines for tracking and handling complaints: make it easy for customers to complain, respond quickly to each and every complaint, educate employees, approach complaints as operational problems and strategic opportunities, make complaints and complainers visible, adjust quality measures, performance reviews, and compensation accordingly, reward complainers, and stop calling them complainers.

KEY TERMS

customer loyalty, p. 378
customer satisfaction, p. 368
employee empowerment, p. 362
internal marketing, p. 360

importance–performance
    analysis (IPA), p. 372
lifetime value of a
    customer, p. 383

relationship marketing, p. 380
service culture, p. 361
service recovery, p. 385
service quality, p. 368

DISCUSSION QUESTIONS AND EXERCISES

1. Apart from those organizations discussed in the chapter, name a tourism or hospitality organization that has an outstanding service culture. What is the evidence of this culture?
2. If you were the manager of a hotel and wanted to apply the gaps model to improve service, which gap would you start with? Why? In what order would you proceed to close the other gaps?
3. Think about a service organization that retains you as a loyal customer. Why are you loyal to this provider? What would it take for you to switch?
4. With regard to the same organization, what are the benefits to the firm of keeping you as a customer? Calculate your "lifetime value" to the organization.
5. Why is it important for a tourism organization to have a strong service recovery strategy?
6. Think of a time when you received poor service from a tourism or hospitality organization. Was any recovery effort made? What should or could have been done differently? What was your response (refer to Figure 11.8)?

CASE STUDY

The Airline with a Sense of Humour: WestJet Airlines

WestJet Airlines is a company that has, so far, beaten the odds to become a favourite of both travel agents and consumers in Canada. It is, after all, the airline that boards passengers by sock colour or zodiac sign, concocts promotions that enable passengers with names such as "Love" and "Heart" to fly free on Valentine's Day, and has seen gate agents break out flutes to entertain stranded passengers during an ice storm. And compared to rigid, often humourless Air Canada, WestJet earns raves from the travel trade. "They'll do almost anything for you," one Ontario agent gushed to *Canadian Travel Press*. In fact, WestJet recently placed first in "Canada's Most Admired Corporate Cultures" for the second year in a row.

Bob Cummings, Executive Vice-President, Guest Experience and Marketing, for WestJet, says the formula is simple: "We foster a caring culture."

While employees earn industry averages, they also take part in profit sharing and share purchase plans which has WestJet matching 100 percent of WestJetter's contributions for share purchase on up to 20 percent of their salary. This evokes "a strong sense of ownership" in every WestJetter in the company, says Cummings. "When someone picks up the phone, they're an owner. The person at the gate is an owner." Another key ingredient of WestJet's success is its underlying philosophy to emulate and "Canadianize" the model of successful U.S. discount carrier, Southwest Airlines.

WestJet has evolved to become more of a hybrid model within the airline industry. It is moving away from the no-frills, discount airline reputation with the addition of live seat-back satellite television at every seat and pay-per-view movies as well as buy-on-board services. WestJet also has the most modern fleet of jet aircraft in North America with the average age of its fleet being only 2.5 years. "What won't go away is our focus on the guest and on our people. The way we interact with our guests is really what sets us apart," says Cummings. And after a decade, this core strategy of a focus on people has been wildly successful. In an industry that has seen the majority of airlines fail in Canada, WestJet has been consistently profitable. Apart from a small loss in 2004, WestJet has been profitable every year and led North American airlines in percentage operating margin and percentage net earnings in the third quarter of 2006. People want to be a part of this success — WestJet receives more than 1000 unsolicited résumés each week.

Clive Beddoe, former president and CEO of WestJet, was one of Canada's Entrepreneurs of the Year in 2000 because of his willingness to take risks. He was already a wealthy and successful businessperson (in plastics), but was willing to risk everything to move into an industry in which the failure rate is extremely high. WestJet's entry into the marketplace in early 1996 was a watershed in the Canadian airline industry, as it was the first true low-cost, low-fare, short-haul scheduled carrier. What has enabled this airline to make money for its owners in each year of its existence while many others fight to simply survive? Some suggest it is the fact that WestJet operates an airline in a nontraditional manner and achieves nontraditional results. WestJet has been praised by guests for its service and light-hearted humour, which starts from the first booking call — if you're put on hold, you will hear a message full of corny jokes, as well as helpful information. In the airport, passengers may be boarded by the colour of their hair or shoes. At other times the pilot may sing, or attendants will offer prizes for the passenger with the most lipstick in her purse or the one with the biggest hole in his socks. Invariably, at least one WestJet passenger leaves the aircraft with a smile. As WestJet spokesperson Richard Bartrem says, "We take our job seriously, but not ourselves."

WestJet says empowerment is more than a buzzword because it wants its front-line staff to be able to make the right decision in a given situation. The idea is that the goodwill generated by resolving a complaint will translate into repeat business. Top managers often send handwritten notes to recognize top-performing employees. These sometimes include small rewards such as a movie pass or a $10 gift certificate. Praise is also made public. WestJet issues a monthly newsletter called Kudos Corner, containing a selection of 10 or so letters from passengers giving praise for good service. It also carries three or four internal kudos.

But the airline industry is extremely vulnerable to changes in the environment. In 2001, as a result of September 11, air traffic fell off as much as 50 percent. International air carriers such as Swissair, Sabena of Belgium, and Canada 3000 crumbled. Airlines across North America called for government bailouts and compensation packages as 100 000 people lost jobs in the industry. The domestic airline industry in Canada went through a consolidation process with only two players — WestJet and Air Canada — left standing. Despite the drop in passenger numbers and fares around the world after September 11, WestJet managed to continue growing by adding new destinations and airlines to its fleet, and was well positioned to fill the competitive void left by the grounding of Canada 3000. "We just continued to do what we'd set out to do from the beginning of the year. We had a plan for the year and we sustained it," said Beddoe. "We felt confident that travel would come back. We saw what happened after the Gulf War in the early 1990s. It was short-lived, but there was a catastrophic reaction within the industry when people stopped travelling."

Beddoe says it was WestJet's culture that brought the airline through tough times after September 11. "We were the first airline in North America to be fully operational, with every one of our scheduled flights flying," he said. "On the 12th of September we were given the rules by which we were going to operate and our people worked through the night to figure how we were going to apply those rules and how to disseminate those operating procedures and standards out to all of our bases. By four o'clock in the morning we were able to be up and operational and ready to go." The display of excellence in leadership, corporate performance, innovation, focus on customer relationships, and human resource practices was truly evident around this single catastrophic event. "It was probably the most extreme example of how well this culture of teamwork can work and how it can be applied to create extraordinary results," says Beddoe.

However, Beddoe is aware that additional terrorist attacks, the fear of such attacks, or increased hostilities could further affect the airline industry and WestJet, and could cause a decrease in travel and an increase in costs to airlines and airline travellers. In the aftermath of the terrorist attacks, the availability of insurance for airlines has decreased and the costs of such insurance have increased. In the event that the Canadian government does not renew its indemnity regarding war and terrorism insurance, it is possible that such insurance will not be available to the Canadian airline industry, including WestJet.

Industry watchers argue that WestJet's expansive growth will make it difficult for the company to keep its distinctive culture alive. Beddoe argues that Southwest Airlines, on which WestJet has been based, has kept its culture alive for more than 25 years even as its workforce swelled to 30 000. Having said this, Beddoe realizes that protecting the culture is essential. "It's focus number one. Our risk, in my view, is internal, not external. And that's why we put so much emphasis on it." However, Beddoe is cautious about becoming too arrogant and conceited. "It's not me who made all this happen; it's 6000 people here who make it happen. The focus is on the teamwork and that no matter how good we are at what we're doing, we can always be better." In September 2007, Beddoe stepped down as CEO, but observers say he will be remembered as a Canadian aviation pioneer who gained a competitive advantage by building a very strong corporate culture.

Sources: Jang, B., & Grant, T. (2006, October 17). Fuller planes, cost cuts propel airlines, *Globe & Mail*, B12; Baginski, M. (2002). WestJet celebrates sixth anniversary. www.canadatourism.com (retrieved February 2002); Fitzpatrick, P. (2001, October 16). Wacky WestJet's winning ways. *National Post*, C1; Quinn, P. (2001, September 12). Success stories. Flying in the face of adversity. *Financial Post*, E1; Welner, C., & Briggs, D. (2002). Reaching for the skies. *Alberta Venture, 6*(5), 26–27; WestJet annual information form, March 20, 2002.

QUESTIONS

1. The case study highlights several reasons for WestJet's success. In your opinion, which one is the most important?
2. Is the culture at WestJet as important to the success of the organization as its management team believes it to be?
3. How serious is the threat from conventional airlines that want to imitate the WestJet culture? What does it take to imitate organizational culture?
4. As WestJet continues to expand, will it be more difficult to sustain its culture?
5. How does WestJet's culture affect customer service?

WEBSITES

www.fairmont.com
Fairmont Hotels & Resorts

www.sheratonsuites.com
Sheraton Suites Calgary Eau Claire

www.westjet.com
WestJet Airlines

www.virgin.com
Virgin

www.virgin-atlantic.com
Virgin Atlantic

www.loewshotels.com
Loews Hotels

ENDNOTES

1. Berry, L. L., Hensel, J. S., & Burke, M.C. (1976). Improving retailer capability for effective consumerism response. *Journal of Retailing, 52*(3), 3–14.
2. Webster, C. (1995). Marketing culture and marketing effectiveness in service firms. *Journal of Services Marketing, 9*(2), 6–22.
3. Sutherland, S. (2002). Hospitality trends. *Alberta Venture, 6*(4), 49–53.
4. Katzenbach, J. (2003). *Why pride matters more than money*. New York: Crown Business.
5. Skidmore, J. (2004, July 31). Singapore cabbies wheel out the knowledge. *Telegraph Travel*, 4.
6. Galt, V. (2003, February 12). Can't pay more? Try some little extras. *Globe & Mail*, C2.
7. Parasuraman, A., Zeithaml, V. A., & Berry, L. L. (1988). SERVQUAL: A multiple item scale for measuring consumer perceptions of service quality. *Journal of Retailing, 64*, 12–20.
8. Cronin, J., & Taylor, S. (1994). "SERVPERF versus SERVQUAL: Reconciling performance-based and perception-minus-expectations measurements of service quality." *Journal of Marketing, 58*(1), 125–131.
9. Reichheld, F. F., & Sasser, W. S., Jr. (1990). Zero defections: Quality comes to services. *Harvard Business Review, 68*, 105–111.
10. Heskett, J. L., Sasser, W. E., Jr., & Schlesinger, L. A. (1997). *The service profit chain: How leading companies link profit and growth to loyalty, satisfaction, and value*. New York: Free Press, 83.
11. Hauck, M. (2001). How to ensure the satisfaction of your meeting planner customers. *Hospitality Sales and Marketing Association International Marketing Review,* Fall/Winter, 50–52.
12. Parasuraman, A., Zeithaml, V. A. and Berry, L. L. (1985). A conceptual model of service quality and its implications for future research. *Journal of Marketing, 49*(4), 41–50.
13. Martilla, J. A., & James, J. C. (1977). Importance–Performance Analysis. *Journal of Marketing, 41*(1), 13–17.
14. Hudson, S., & Shephard, G. (1998). Measuring service quality at tourist destinations: An application of importance–performance analysis to an alpine ski resort. *Journal of Travel and Tourism Marketing, 7*(3), 61–77.
15. Parasuraman, A., Zeithaml, V. A. and Berry, L. L. (1985). A conceptual model of service quality and its implications for future research. *Journal of Marketing, 49*(4), 41–50.
16. Buzzell, D., & Gale B. T. (1987). *The PIMS principles*. New York: Free Press.
17. Phillips, L. D., Chang, D. R., & Buzzell, R. (1983). Product quality, cost position and business performance: A test of some key hypotheses. *Journal of Marketing, 47*(Spring), 26–43.
18. Gale, B. (1992). *Monitoring customer satisfaction and market-perceived quality*. Chicago: American Marketing Association.

19. Zeithaml, V. A., Berry, L. L., & Parasuraman, A. (1996). The behavioural consequences of service quality. *Journal of Marketing, 60,* 31–46.

20. Berry, L. L. (1983). Relationship marketing. In L. L. Berry, G.L. Shostack, & G. Upah (Eds.), *Emerging perspectives on services marketing* (25–28). Chicago: American Marketing Association.

21. Zeithaml, V. A., & Bitner, M. J. (2000). *Services marketing: Integrating customer focus across the firm.* New York: McGraw-Hill.

22. Reichheld, F. F., and Sasser, W. S., Jr. (1990). Zero defections: Quality comes to services. *Harvard Business Review, 68,* 105–111.

23. Zeithaml, V. A., & Bitner, M. J. (2000). *Services marketing: Integrating customer focus across the firm.* New York: McGraw-Hill.

24. Holland, J.S. (2007). An Eden for sharks. *National Geographic, 211*(3), 116–137.

25. Reichheld, F. F., & Sasser, W. S., Jr. (1990). Zero defections: Quality comes to services. *Harvard Business Review, 68,* 105–111.

26. Rasmusson, E. (1999). Wanted: Profitable customers. *Sales and Marketing Management, 151*(5), 28–34.

27. Withiam, G. (1998). Customers from hell. *Cornell Hotel & Restaurant Administration Quarterly, 39*(5), 11; Zemke, R., & Anderson, K. (1990). Customers from hell. *Training, 27*(2), 25–33.

28. Reuters. (2006, August 8). Bar aims for smash hit by letting customers run riot. *Guardian,* 16.

29. Kelley, S. W., Hoffman, K. D., & Davis, M. A. (1993). A typology of retail failures and recoveries. *Journal of Retailing, 69*(4), 429–452.

30. Collier, D. A. (1995). Modeling the relationships between process quality errors and overall service process performance. *Journal of Service Industry Management, 64*(4), 4–19.

31. Tax, S., & Brown, S. W. (1998). Recovering and learning from service failures. *Sloan Management Review, 49*(1), 75–88.

32. Brignall, M. (2006, July 29). Airlines cleared for rip-off, *Guardian Money,* 3.

33. Harari, O. (1997). Thank heavens for complainers. *Management Review, 86*(3), 25–29.

Destination Marketing

Spotlight
MARKETING FIRST NATIONS TOURISM IN THE YUKON

According to many tourism experts, First Nations communities in Canada are sitting on a gold mine of tourism potential. Studies have revealed a potential of up to 18 million international visitors over the next five years. The United Kingdom alone is home to 13.5 million potential long-haul pleasure travellers, and of those, 4.1 million have expressed high levels of interest in aboriginal tourism. Germany has 9 million potential tourists interested in aboriginal culture, France has 1.5 million, the Netherlands has 1.7 million, and Italy has 4.9 million.

But marketing and promoting First Nations tourism is not always the responsibility of traditional destination marketing organizations (DMOs). For example, in the Yukon it is the Yukon First Nations Tourism Association (YFNTA) that is dedicated to promoting and maintaining the cultural integrity of native tourism in that region. The YFNTA was incorporated in 1994 and has First Nations tourism-business owners on its board of directors. The association has the following guiding principles:

- *Marketing and Promotion.* To market and promote the growth of First Nations tourism in a manner that maintains the cultural integrity of each Yukon First Nation.
- *Networking and Communication.* To develop positive working relationships between the YFNTA and communities, industry, and government.
- *Product and Entrepreneurial Development.* To assist in the development of Yukon First Nations tourism products that promote cultural awareness and maintain cultural integrity.

- *Human Resource Development.* To provide First Nations tourism training and education in a manner consistent with cultural requirements and national standards.
- *Lobbying and Advocacy.* To represent the interests of the YFNTA openly, honestly, and with integrity.

The positioning of the YFNTA puts the First Nations people, history, and culture central to an understanding of the Yukon. The organization's mission statement makes this very clear: "The Yukon First Nations Tourism Association is dedicated to promoting and maintaining the cultural integrity of native tourism." By bringing together tourism businesses and attractions that are run by the First Nations, the YFTNA strives to bring the visitor to an understanding of not only the landscape of the Yukon Territory but also of the people who have lived there for thousands years as well as those who are more recent arrivals.

The YFTNA's *Welcome: Visitor Guide 2001/02* and website do more than list tourist attractions, accommodations, and shopping. They have been carefully crafted to provide a wealth of information that goes beyond directions and maps. In fact, the bulk of the *Visitor Guide* provides information under such headings as "Our History," "The Land Gives Us Life," "Our Cultural Heritage," and "Yukon First Nations Arts." The facts in these sections are fascinating and cover topics ranging from ancient trade routes and traditional remedies to modern land claims and cultural gatherings. Everything is written so that it is easily understood by non-natives, and unfamiliar terms are explained for the visitor. Throughout the *Visitor Guide* are explanations of etiquette and cultural differences, and how best to respect the traditions of the First Nations.

There are several maps provided in the guide, one of which is a typical tourist guide map that shows major roads, towns, and cities, and tourist attractions. However, the other maps provide a division of the Yukon by culture groups and by nations. Each of the First Nations is located and described for visitors, so they can have at least a moderate understanding of the people that are their hosts. The attractions and business listings at the back of the guide focus on the attractions that have First Nations content and on First Nations businesses.

Visitors are encouraged to seek out cultural tourism experiences that are often paired with popular wilderness/adventure experiences. There are also many events hosted by Yukon First Nations that are open to visitors. Through the YFNTA, visitors are invited to learn more about the cultures of the First Nations and to participate in appropriate ways. That said, both the *Visitor Guide* and the website remind visitors that many in the Yukon still practice a traditional lifestyle, and their privacy, seasonal campsites, and burial grounds are to be respected.

The YFNTA provides businesses that are part of the association with a way to differentiate themselves from other tourism businesses in the Yukon. The association has strongly positioned itself to convey to the visitor that an understanding of the First Nations peoples is vital to an understanding and appreciation of the Yukon. In early 2007, the YFNTA hosted the Gathering of Northern Nations, Aboriginal Tradeshow, and Cultural Expo. The event took place over four days and saw over 5000 people come and do business with the Northern Territories under one roof.

Sources: Yukon First Nations Tourism Association www.yfnta.org; Personal correspondence with M. Williams, executive director, Yukon First Nations Tourism Association, March 21, 2007; Aboriginal tourism in Canada. (2003, February 5). *Winnipeg Free Press*, B2; Yukon First Nations Tourism Association. (2001). Yukon First Nations Tourism Association. (2001). *Welcome: Visitor Guide 2001/02*, Whitehorse.

Objectives

On completion of this chapter, readers should understand:

- the principles of destination marketing;
- the role of destination marketing organizations (DMOs);

- the principles of destination branding;
- strategies used to promote destinations;
- the marketing of events and conferences
- the marketing of all-inclusive resorts.

Chapter Overview

The *Spotlight* provides an example of an emerging destination basing its positioning on its cultural tourism and its wilderness and adventure experiences. In the Yukon, tourism is now the territory's top private sector employer. More than 300 000 visitors each year spend upward of $180 million, creating an estimated 2000 jobs. As tourism expands around the globe, it brings new opportunities for destination marketing, such as the high levels of interest in aboriginal tourism. But at the same time, this globalization leads to a dilution of established destination identities and to increased competition among emerging tourism destinations. This chapter looks at both the opportunities and challenges inherent in marketing destinations. It begins by discussing the principles of destination marketing and defining, characterizing, and classifying destinations. A small section also examines the scope of visitor attractions. A summary of the objectives and benefits of destination marketing is followed by a more in-depth look at the role of destination marketing organizations (DMOs). The next two sections focus on destination branding and destination promotion. Finally, the chapter looks at the marketing of two particularly important sectors for destinations: events and conferences, and all-inclusive resorts.

THE PRINCIPLES OF DESTINATION MARKETING

Characteristics of a Destination

destination

place that has some form of actual or perceived boundary, such as the physical boundary of an island, political boundaries, or even market-created boundaries

To understand the principles of destination marketing it is important to comprehend what is meant in the tourism industry by the term "destination." A **destination** is a place that has some form of actual or perceived boundary, such as the physical boundary of an island, political boundaries, or even market-created boundaries. The tourism destination can comprise a wide range of elements that combine to attract visitors to stay for a holiday or day visit, but there are four core elements that make up the destination product: prime attractors, built environment, supporting supply services, and socio-cultural dimensions, such as atmosphere or ambience (see Table 12.1).

Table 12.1

Characteristics of a Destination

CHARACTERISTICS	DESCRIPTION	EXAMPLES
Prime attractors	The main attractors that appeal to visitors and that differentiate one destination from another	Rocky Mountains in Canada; Niagara Falls in the United States and Canada; Angkor Wat temples in Cambodia
Built environment	The physical layout of a destination, including waterfronts, promenades, historic quarters, and commercial zones. Major elements of infra-structure such as road and rail networks, plus open spaces and commercial facilities	London Docklands in the United Kingdom; Canals in Venice, Italy; bullet train in Japan, West Edmonton Mall in Edmonton
Supporting supply services	Essential facilitating services such as accommodation, communications, transport, refreshment and catering, entertainment, and amenities	Essential at most destinations
Socio-cultural dimensions	Cultural attributes: bridges between past and present, the mood or atmosphere — ranging from sleepy to vibrant. The degree of friendliness and cohesion between the host community and visitors	The friendliness of Canadians; chaotic transport in China; the music in Ireland; the laid-back attitude of Fijians

Source: Adapted from Lumsdon, L. (1997). *Tourism marketing*. Oxford: Thomson Business Press.

It would be misleading to define the destination as a composite product, for this implies that it can be marketed as a packaged bundle of benefits in the same way that a fast-moving consumer good can. As the prime attractors and cultural attributes of the host community are a major appeal to the visitor, the offering is far more complicated than that of a composite product. Since many of these elements are inherited from previous generations, the marketer has little control over such external factors. Furthermore, the mix of public and private sector provision makes traditional approaches to branding and marketing planning difficult to apply. The other main difference between a destination and other types of product is that the visitor becomes part of the overall appeal and forms an integral part of the contemporary destination.

Classifications of Destinations

Philip Kotler, John Bowen, and James Makens distinguish between macro-destinations such as the United States and micro-destinations such as the states, regions, and cities within the United States.[1] However, there are many different types of destinations, including those listed in Table 12.2.

Table 12.2

Classifications of Destinations

DESTINATION TYPE	DESCRIPTION
Major international destinations	Destinations on "must see" lists. Examples are places such as Paris, New York, London, and Vancouver, which have mass appeal to large numbers of international travellers.
Classic destinations	Destinations where the natural, cultural, or historical appeal encourages long-stay holidays. Examples are Saint-Tropez or Lourdes in France, or Banff National Park in Canada.
Human-made destination resorts	Destinations where visitors view the resort as the destination itself and rarely venture outside the perimeters. Examples are the all-inclusive resorts in the Caribbean or Mexico, or the Hilton Hawaiian Village in Honolulu.
Natural landscape or wildlife tourism destinations	Destinations that have high natural appeal and are habitats of rare species of flora, fauna, or wildlife. Examples are the Galapagos Islands in Ecuador, the Serengeti wildlife reserve in East Africa, and the Queen Charlotte Islands in British Columbia.
Alternative destinations	More contemporary destinations such as cruises, theme parks, massive shopping centres such as the West Edmonton Mall, and time-share properties.
Business tourism destinations	Destinations where retailing and entertainment sectors encourage longer stays by business executives and partners. This is often accompanied by a thriving hospitality sector and a desire to heighten the destination's image through events marketing.
Stopover destinations	Destinations that are situated between generating areas and holiday destinations. Often characterized by having a wide-ranging budget accommodation sector and a strong mix of restaurants and cafés.
Short-break destinations	Destinations that have national appeal — and often international appeal if suitable attractions exist. Niagara Falls is a classic example.
Day-trip destinations	Destinations that attract primarily regional, day-visitor demand — the most common of all destinations. They range from seaside ports to major retailing centres in all parts of the world.

There is an increasing grey area in the distinction between attractions and destinations. Some human-made attractions such as Disney World in Florida, while technically attractions, appear to have more in common with destinations than with most other attractions. In terms of the area they cover and their visitor numbers, especially if they have on-site accommodation, they appear to be more like destinations. However, the fact that they are usually single-ownership rather than multiple-ownership operations confirms that they are not like other destinations, as does the fact that they usually have a single core product or theme, unlike most destinations. But attractions like West Edmonton Mall in Alberta (see below) are often seen as shopping destinations as well as being labelled as major attractions.

ATTRACTIONS

Attractions are one of the most important components in the tourism system, often being the main motivator for a trip. There is a strong link between destination and attractions, and it is usually the existence of a major attraction that stimulates the development of destinations, whether the attraction is a beach, a temple, or a theme park. As with other sectors of the tourism industry, attractions are increasingly polarized between a few large attractions and thousands of small and micro-sized enterprises.

Tourist attractions can also be classified as natural or human-made. An example of a popular natural attraction is the Volcano National Park on the Big Island of Hawaii, which is Hawaii's number-one attraction. However, increasingly tourists are drawn to human-made attractions that offer entertainment, and West Edmonton Mall in Alberta is a major attraction in Canada, drawing 21 million visitors a year. The more than 800 stores and services and 110 eating establishments within its 49 hectares make the mall a shopper's paradise. But "hanging out at the mall" takes on a whole new meaning there, where the 3700-square-metre Galaxyland (the world's largest indoor amusement park) offers 25 rides, including Mindbender, the world's largest indoor triple-loop roller coaster, and Space Shot, one of the world's tallest indoor tower rides. The enormous World Waterpark contains the world's largest indoor wave pool and the world's tallest indoor bungee jump. The full-size skating rink inside the mall is the second home of the Edmonton Oilers hockey team and offers public skating and rentals throughout the week. Other attractions include the Sea Life Caverns and Dolphin Lagoon, the Ice Palace, Professor WEM's Adventure Golf, Go Karts, and the Palace Casino. Tour operators have recognized that the West Edmonton Mall is the destination of choice for many people and have partnered with the mall to provide vacation getaway packages to customers that include return airfare, accommodation at one of the mall's two hotels, and value-added incentives such as coupon books.

There are a number of key factors that influence the marketing of visitor attractions.[2] The first are the marketing objectives of attractions, as they may vary considerably. For private attractions, like most theme parks, the objectives are often profit, market share, or achieving a satisfactory return on investment. Public sector attractions, on the other hand, may have wider and fewer financial objectives, such as encouraging participation from people who are socially disadvantaged. The *Spotlight* in Chapter 1 explained the objectives behind the Hong Kong government investing in Disneyland Hong Kong. It was seeking to re-position the island as a tourism leader in Asia, enhancing its international image and creating a stronger leisure tourism destination in line with its established success in business tourism. Other goals were to add quality to the life of residents, provide a model for staff training and human resource management for fellow tourism organizations, and fill a gap in its tourism product.

Another important factor in the marketing of attractions is that they are often marketed by other agencies as well as by themselves. Using the previous example, inbound tour operators in Hong Kong would use Disneyland in their brochures to encourage tourists to take their packages, whilst the government will promote the theme park to persuade people to visit the country. The level of competition will also vary drastically between different types of attractions. For example, the theme park and seaside amusement arcade business in the UK is highly competitive in its bid to outdo all other genres of attractions. However, local authority museums may simply be competing with other council-run museums. The Association of Leading Visitor Attractions reported in 2005 that the most visited attraction in the UK was Blackpool Pleasure Beach (5.9 million visitors), followed by the British Museum (4.5 million), the National Gallery (4.2 million), and the Tate Modern (3.9 million). However, many theme parks did not disclose their arrivals figures.

The attraction market is particularly volatile and fashion-led, with many factors in the visitor experience outside the control of attraction operators. The *Profile* in Chapter 4 showed how Disney's entry into Paris was thwarted by factors beyond the company's control, such as domestic economic recession, and the Gulf War of 1991. Visitor usage rates also vary dramatically from occasional purchases, perhaps just once in a lifetime, to those who may visit the same attraction time and time again. Attractions will often create and promote special exhibitions to increase visitor numbers during the off-peak seasons. For example, in the U.S. the Rock and Roll Hall of Fame and Museum in Cleveland opened "Revolution Rock: The Story of the Clash," an exhibit to honour the 1970s English punk band that was open to the public from November 2006 to April 2007.

Furthermore, marketers of attractions need to be sensitive to the fact that some attractions are extremely fragile and therefore need to be protected and not exploited. The UNESCO World Heritage List consists of sites considered globally important either because of their natural heritage or their significant human-made contribution to world culture. An example of a listed cultural site is the Parque Nacional Rapa Nui Easter Island, home of the famous Easter Island statues (the moai), which date back some 1000 years. Each year, between 20 000 and 40 000 travellers visit Easter Island, most coming to see these massive stone statues, which are spread across the Chilean island. Each statu is unique, differing in expression, height or weight, representing carved images of the island's ancestors. In 2005, a major conservation project effort began to restore the statues. Made of pressed volcanic ash, the stones are particularly susceptible to erosion, a process that may erase clues to their origins and endanger the local tourism industry. These attractions are threatened by environmental factors, but some are under threat from the tourists themselves. Apparently booming tourism is having a catastrophic effect on Egypt's antiquities, too, with the number of people visiting famed sites such as the Valley of the Kings causing serious damage in a way that centuries of weather has failed to do.[3] Chapter 13 looks at the relationship between tourism and environmental damage in more detail.

SNAPSHOT

THE GREATEST OUTDOOR SHOW ON EARTH: THE CALGARY STAMPEDE

The Calgary Stampede is an annual ten-day celebration of western Canada's values and heritage. It started from humble beginnings as an agricultural fair in 1884, with attractions and attendance growing each year, until the first rodeo was added in 1912. Nowadays, more than 1.2 million people attend annually, including some 400 000 foreign tourists, helping to generate more than $400 million in direct revenue within the City of Calgary, and another $50 million across Alberta.

Dubbed "The Greatest Outdoor Show on Earth," the Stampede has now become an intrinsic part of the city's identity, an international symbol even, just like Mardi Gras has for New Orleans and Carnival has for Rio de Janeiro. Calgary is now known around the world for its values of integrity, commitment to community, pride of place, and western hospitality. The Stampede organizers are committed to preserving and promoting western heritage and values while ensuring that it remains relevant to the community. The cowboy hat is the major icon associated with the event, as well as with the city itself. It is almost a crime against society not to wear one during the whole of the ten-day summer fair and cowboy boots, jeans and other appropriate apparel and paraphernalia proliferate among audience members, competitors and vendors.

The Stampede parade starts the festivities off each year with around 400 000 spectators lining the downtown area to watch 55 appropriately themed floats, 750 horses, 1000 band members, celebrity rodeo clowns, street sweepers dressed as "critters," and an oxen train. There is no entry fee for floats but there is heavy competition to attain one of the coveted spots. Local celebrities and families of former pioneers are also honoured at these occasions. By that time, most visitors will have experienced their first Stampede Breakfast. These began in 1923 when a chuckwagon driver decided to cook up breakfast in his wagon in the core of the downtown area. Since then the theme has developed to encompass all major corporations, church groups, schools, community associations, city attractions, retail and restaurant outlets, car lots, as well as the Stampede ground itself. These breakfasts are traditionally free for all who attend and are used to promote businesses.

Another cultural spin-off from the Stampede phenomenon is the Young Canadians School of Performing Arts, a musical, dancing, and drama facility for students from age 8 to 22. Scholarships worth

SNAPSHOT *continued*

$7500 each were established to provide free training in music performance, all forms of dance, and gymnastics to create a yearly line-up for the Stampede Grandstand Show. Nowadays, there is even training in a Cirque de Soleil–style circus program as well as hiphop, in keeping with contemporary trends. With audiences of 20 000 each night, the 500 cast members produce a visual spectacular in 1200 specially designed costumes and a variety of elaborate sets. The show culminates in a dazzling firework display.

Stampede Park has multiple stages and marquees for Nashville-style music as well as more modern singers and bands. There is also an extensive funfair in the Midway, and many restaurants and kiosks selling food, an Indian village with daily shows, farm animal enclosures with entertainments and competitions, as well as all the rodeo and chuckwagon events. Many local businesses use it as a team-building, corporate opportunity to host

events among the festivities. The whole of Calgary participates, dressing up store fronts with old straw bales and rickety pieces of wood to simulate old-style pioneer buildings; restaurants, bars, and nightclubs, all themed accordingly, host Stampede events with internationally famous country and western singers and bands as well as more mainstream stars. Doing the rounds of these night spots is now called "stampeding" and many locals save up all year to be able to throw themselves into the stampeding spirit with a vengeance.

Sources: McGinnis, S. (2003, July 4). Stampede brings boom. *Calgary Herald*, B1; MacGregor, R. (2005, July 5). The greatest outdoor show on Earth. *Globe & Mail*, A2; Partridge, J. (2006, August 7). A great big birthday bash. *Calgary Herald*, AA4; Knapp, S. (2005, July 8). Pioneer's progeny part of centennial salute. *Calgary Herald*, AA4; Personal communication with Calgary Stampede corporate communications, March 2007.

OBJECTIVES AND BENEFITS OF DESTINATION MARKETING

A fair proportion of destination marketing tends to be carried out by public sector bodies, and hence it is quite complicated. These public bodies are often involved in destination marketing for a wide range of reasons other than just attracting tourists. These objectives might include:

1. improving the image of an area in the hope that this will encourage industrialists to relocate their factories and offices to the area;
2. providing jobs for local residents;
3. increasing the range of facilities that are available for the local community;
4. giving local residents more pride in their local area, which can happen when people see that tourists want to visit their region;
5. providing a rationale and funding for improvements to the local environment; and
6. trying to make the destination politically more acceptable.

However, public sector bodies can earn income from tourism in a number of ways, so economic benefits are just as important. Revenue may come in the form of sales taxes or hotel room taxes, and from admissions to publicly owned attractions. A large tourism benefit comes from the multiplier effect, as tourist expenditures are recycled through the local economy. Recently, for the first time, the Singapore government began to promote gambling because of its economic benefits. Governments use economic impact models to estimate overall employment gains in goods and services consumption resulting from tourism multipliers. Tourism is often used to shift the burden of taxes to nonresidents. Taxation of tourists has, in fact, become very popular, and it includes taxes on airline tickets, hotel taxes, and other user fees. Many in the tourism industry have suggested that these taxes should go back into promoting tourism and developing the infrastructure to support tourism.

Not all tourism marketing campaigns are directed at potential tourists. In some cases, DMOs need to convince residents that tourism is an important sector and worth supporting. For example, in Alaska in 2007, the Kenai Peninsula Tourism Marketing Council (KPTMC) developed a print advertisement that ran in a special section of the local paper that focuses on the peninsula's three biggest industries: oil and gas, commercial fishing, and tourism (see Figure 12.1).

Figure 12.1 KPTMC Print Advertisement

The KPTMC is a non-profit membership-based organization that receives partial funding from local government, the Kenai Peninsula Borough. As is the case with many Alaskan communities, tourism is very important to the local economy. Twenty-five percent of licensed businesses on the peninsula are involved in tourism, and a conservative estimate is that 30 percent of sales tax revenue is directly related to the visitor industry. "Unfortunately, many of our residents believe that our visitors are a nuisance and the dollars they bring to the area only benefit a small group of people. Many also take issue with our resource allocation," said Shanon Hamrick, executive director of the KPTMC. "Residents don't want outsiders catching all of their fish and crowding the rivers and commercial fishermen feel like they are unfairly restricted because of the sport fisheries. A favourite debate is the value of a salmon caught in a commercial net versus one caught at the end of a fishing line by a visitor."[4] The advertisement generated a lot of interest. "We had several people contact us and congratulate us on taking such a "bold stance' in support of tourism," said Hamrick. "As we are a tourism marketing organization, I didn't feel like our statement was all that bold, but I think our tourism business owners are tired of being treated as unimportant and were pleased to see someone make a public statement in support of the industry. We will continue running similar ads throughout the year. I will stick with the theme of businesses that aren't considered a tourism business and how they benefit from the industry. My ultimate goal is to make people understand that tourism is an important renewable resource that generates money for our local economy and improves our quality of life. If by doing that we have an easier time getting increased funding for marketing each year, I have really done my job."

THE ROLE OF DESTINATION MARKETING ORGANIZATIONS

destination marketing organizations (DMOs)

government agencies, convention and visitors bureaus, travel associations, and other bodies that market travel to their destination areas.

The role of national tourist boards in proactively marketing and advertising destinations that they represent has changed substantially in the last few decades.[5] A major development of the 1980s and 1990s was the appearance of private–public sector **destination marketing organizations (DMOs)** or national tourist organizations (NTOs), which are government agencies, convention and visitors bureaus, travel associations, and other bodies that market travel to their destination areas. These organizations complement and sometimes replace the advertising and marketing activities of conventional, fully state-funded tourism offices. This trend is being reinforced by the very rapid expansion of the Web and the Internet as media that give the tourism industry the ability to market, promote, advertise, sell, provide information, and accept reservations. The appearance of regional tourist boards with an agenda to promote and advertise only their own attractions in foreign markets is another trend that is likely to develop. Meanwhile, the world's leading names in travel have moved pronouncedly to the use of advertising and promotions that create brand awareness.

The growth in tourism has lured many government agencies and other groups into marketing their destinations to pleasure and business travellers. Nearly every state, province, and territory now has a separate body that is responsible for marketing.

Nationally, organizations such as the Australian Tourist Commission, the British Tourist Authority, and the Canadian Tourism Commission invest millions of dollars in tourism marketing and development. At the state or province level, marketing agencies also spend millions of dollars promoting tourism. Their marketing programs target both individual travellers and travel trade intermediaries. Often they enter into cooperative marketing with suppliers, carriers, intermediaries, and other destination marketing organizations. Many agencies also provide seed money to other DMOs for their individual marketing programs.

convention and visitor bureau (CVB)

a regional or city-level organization specialized in developing conventions, meetings, and conferences as well as responsible for marketing a specific destination

In North America, at the regional or city level, **convention and visitor bureaus (CVBs)** have been created to be responsible for destination marketing. In the U.S., nearly every community with a resident population of more than 50 000 now has a CVB. Approximately 500 of the larger bureaus belong to Destination Marketing Association International (DMAI), which provides educational resources and networking opportunities to its members and distributes information on CVBs. The individual bureaus divide their attention between the travel trade — particularly convention/meeting planners and tour operators — and individual travellers. Their goal is to bring more conventions, meetings, and leisure travellers to their communities. These bureaus represent a broad group of suppliers in their destination areas and are often funded through local accommodation and restaurant taxes.

TOURISM DEVELOPMENT

The tourism marketer is likely to be involved in the process of developing a destination, in terms of either building new resorts or rejuvenating old ones. Part of the process involves estimating future demand, as in a feasibility study, but increasing emphasis is being placed upon evaluating the likely impacts — such as the economic, social, or environmental impacts — of any development. These issues are discussed in more detail in the next chapter.

tourism area life cycle (TALC)

the stages a destination goes through, from exploration to involvement to development to consolidation to stagnation to rejuvenation or decline (also known as the "tourism destination life cycle')

It has been argued that the nature of the marketing strategy adopted by a destination is often dictated by the tourism destination life cycle, also known as the **tourism area life cycle (TALC)**.[6] Like the product life cycle (see Chapter 5), the tourism area or destination life cycle moves from exploration to involvement to development to consolidation to stagnation to rejuvenation or decline, as indicated in Figure 12.2. The assumption is that at each stage the tourism marketer will plan the marketing effort to fit the next predicted phase of development, or possibly in the later stages, to suit the resort's ultimate decline. One Canadian destination that has moved rapidly through the life cycle in the last few decades is Newfoundland and Labrador. In 1996, Newfoundland and Labrador's tourism industry was little more than a footnote on the province's economic statement. Today, it is a powerhouse of the economy. With more than a 40 percent increase in nonresident visitation since 1996, more and more hoteliers, restaurateurs, and tour companies are entering the industry. One could therefore argue that Newfoundland and Labrador is in the consolidation stage of the TALC.

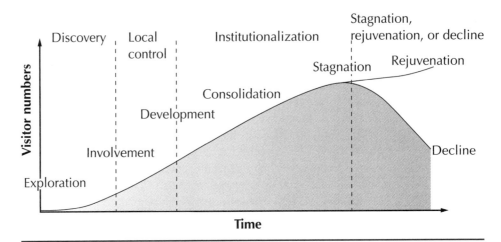

Figure 12.2   The Tourist Area Life Cycle

Source: Adapted from Butler, R. W. (1980). A tourism area cycle of evolution. *Canadian Geographer*, *14*(1), 7.

The life cycle also suggests that the destination will appeal to different markets as it matures. This fits with Plog's consumer typology framework, introduced in Chapter 2, which suggests that the adventurous, outgoing (allocentric) visitor seeks unfamiliar and unspoiled destinations.[7] Those who are more passive and like the familiar (psychocentrics) prefer mature destinations. Midcentrics (a mixture of the two extremes) head for resorts that are more developed, or are becoming mature.

DESTINATION BRANDING

destination branding

a method of establishing a distinctive identity for a destination based on competitive differentiation from others

The subject of **destination branding**, establishing a distinctive identity based on competitive differentiation from others, has received increased attention over the last few decades. In an increasingly competitive global marketplace, the need for destinations to create a unique identity — to differentiate themselves from competitors — has become more critical than ever. As suggested in Chapter 5, a brand in the modern marketing sense offers the consumer relevant added value, a superior proposition that is distinctive from competitors, and imparts meaning above and beyond the functional aspects. Today, most destinations claim to have spectacular scenery, superb attractions, friendly people, and a unique culture and heritage. However, these factors are no longer differentiators, and successful destination branding lies in its potential to reduce substitutability.

Destinations will often "re-brand" or reinvent themselves to broaden their appeal. Hong Kong, for example, having established itself as a mecca for shopping, great food, and other adult pleasures, is pursuing the family market. Building on the success of its "Live it. Love it" campaign, the Hong Kong Tourism Board launched "Discover Hong Kong Year in 2006." Three new attractions headlined this campaign, all of which targeted the family market: Hong Kong Disneyland, Hong Kong Wetland Park, and the Ngong Ping historic village. India is also heading in a new direction — away from backpackers and toward well-heeled tourists. With five-star hotels and resorts spreading throughout the country, some built from former maharajas' palaces, India is moving up-market. And Taiwan declared 2004 the "Visit Taiwan Year" as part of its efforts to remake its long-standing image and boost tourism. Often seen as a manufacturing hub and a place under constant military threat from neighbouring China, Taiwan is trying to change its image. The government is seeking to attract five million tourists by 2008, double the numbers of 2004. The plan is to bring people to the less populated, hard-to-reach areas that comprise 80 percent of the island by promoting attractions such as the 17-year-old theme park called the Formosan Aboriginal Culture Village and the Taroko Gorge, a 19-kilometre-long canyon with deep gorges and long trails for hikers.

SNAPSHOT

POSITIONING THE CAPITALS OF CANADA

Marketers of Canada's capitals are working harder than ever to broaden their appeal by packaging innovative new themes and historical, cultural, and geographic attractions to sell their cities as exciting four-season travel destinations. Many have branded themselves with slogans designed to impress and attract. Here is how they are positioning themselves:

- Charlottetown: Birthplace of Canada
- Edmonton: Canada's Festival City
- Fredericton: New Brunswick's Riverfront Capital
- Halifax: The City that Touches Your Soul
- Iqaluit: Canada's Newest and Most Northern Capital City
- Ottawa: Canada's Capital
- Quebec City: The New Capital
- Regina: The Queen City
- St. John's: The City of Legends
- Toronto: Diversity Our Strength
- Victoria: Full of Life
- Whitehorse: Our People Our Strength
- Winnipeg: Embrace the Spirit
- Yellowknife: Diamond Capital of North America

Many of the cities have capitalized on their cultural assets. Winnipeg invites visitors to "Embrace the Spirit" of the city by experiencing unique historical and cultural attractions such as the Circle of Life Thunderbird House — a focal point for aboriginal art, dance, music, and theatre among Winnipeg's aboriginal population, the largest of any city in Canada. Prince Edward Island's capital, Charlottetown, has built on the city's image as the birthplace of Canada to promote its unique historical and cultural assets. And St. John's is using its popular "City of Legends" theme to market its rich mix of history and Newfoundland culture.

Other capitals have used rivers, oceans, or ports to differentiate themselves. Fredericton, capital of New Brunswick, is a good example. Three hundred years of development at Fredericton is tied to the majestic Saint John River, which runs through the heart of the capital. When Fredericton re-branded itself in 2002, it chose "Atlantic Canada's Riverfront Capital" as a theme to build on this unique setting and create a more active and experiential interpretation of the city for visitors. Canada's northern capitals are successfully

SNAPSHOT *continued*

packaging their culture, climate, and geography to build a unique brand of adventure tourism. They are increasingly popular destinations for European visitors looking for "hard" adventure — canoeing, camping, hiking, and wildlife spotting — in the wide open spaces of the Yukon. Yellowknife, the "Diamond Capital," is synonymous with exploration and adventure, from the tales of the early bush pilots to current mining initiatives. And Iqaluit, Canada's smallest capital, on the shores of Koojeesee Inlet at the head of Frobisher Bay, is a centre of Inuit culture and a starting point for adventure on Baffin Island or other areas of Nunavut.

Some capitals are basing their positioning on festivals and special events. World-class festivals, such as the Toronto's Caribana, the Edmonton Fringe Festival, and the Halifax Busker Festival, are slowly becoming known throughout the world as high-quality attractions.

Edmonton has successfully billed itself as "Canada's Festival City" for many years, thanks to a stable of 15 annual festivals and events.

Finally, destinations are following the example of the Canadian Tourism Commission (CTC) and branding themselves around experiences. Victoria's recently introduced "full of life" tagline celebrates the city's old and new world heritage, and invites visitors to experience everything from the city's historic sites to its outdoor adventure activities, arts and culture, culinary tourism and luxury resorts. Halifax has also undergone a re-branding process, discovering that defining Halifax involved defining the Halifax experience. "The City That Touches Your Soul" tagline was the result of extensive research with both tourists and residents.

Source: Higgins, G. (2003). Sharing the capital experience. *Tourism, 7*(3), 10–12.

Challenges of Destination Branding

But destination branding has its challenges. Nigel Morgan and Annette Pritchard suggest that there are five key challenges faced by destination marketers: limited budgets, politics, external environment, destination product, and differentiation.[8] Each is discussed below.

1. Limited Budgets

The first challenge facing destination marketers is that compared to marketers of consumer goods and services, their budgets are extremely limited. Combine this problem with evidence that tourism promotion does not persuade uncommitted vacationers (but rather acts to confirm the intentions of those already predisposed to visit), and destination marketers have genuine cause for concern. As a result, they have to outsmart rather than outspend the competition — and that means creating innovative, attention-grabbing advertising on a budget and maximizing the amount spent on media. In Uganda, due to a pitiful marketing budget, high school students were recruited to help choose the African country's first-ever slogan "Gifted by Nature." In Bangladesh, tourism officials are attempting to re-brand the country with a budget of just $84 000. Inspired by India's success with the "Incredible India" campaign (see *Marketing in Action*), they dropped the decades-old "Visit Bangladesh Before the Tourists Come" in 2004, and are now promoting "Bangladesh — Beautiful Surprise." However, insufficient funding means that the slogan is unlikely to be very successful. "Until and unless we have an aggressive marketing plan, the slogan doesn't really matter," said Mahfuzul Haque, chair of the Bangladesh Tourism Organization.[9]

2. Politics

Public sector destination marketers are hampered by a variety of political pressures and have to reconcile a range of local and regional interests and promote an identity acceptable to a range of constituencies. Destination brand building is frequently undermined by the short-term mindset of the tourism organization's political masters. It was not until 2002 that India's decision makers began to take tourism seriously and invest money in promoting the country (see *Marketing in Action*). Effective advertising can also be confounded by bureaucratic red tape. For example, political considerations within a province or country can often dictate the range of photographs that are included in a campaign. Politics in other countries can also affect the success of a branding campaign. Singapore, for example, refused to air the edgy Australian "Where the bloody hell are you?" ads (see *Case Study* in Chapter 10), and even British regulators initially objected to the word "bloody."

3. External Environment

It has become evident at the beginning of the 21st century that destinations are particularly vulnerable to external forces such as international politics, economics, terrorism, and environmental disasters. September 11, the war in Iraq, and the outbreak of severe acute respiratory syndrome (SARS) were just some of the crises that have derailed destination promotional planning in the past few years. Even the best branding effort can unravel because of political unrest, rampant crime, or disease. The deadly SARS virus, which caused fever and respiratory distress, brought Hong Kong's economy to a virtual standstill in 2003, striking just after the city had launched a tourism campaign under the slogan "Hong Kong Will Take Your Breath Away." Similarly, Israel's new 2006 branding campaign called "Who Knew?" fell on deaf ears when the country began hostilities with Lebanon.

4. Destination Product

The tourism destination comprises a number of elements that combine to attract visitors to stay for a holiday or day visit. These elements include accommodation and catering establishments, tourist attractions, the natural environment, arts, entertainment, and cultural venues. Destination marketers have relatively little control over these different aspects of their product, and a diverse range of agencies and companies are partners in the task of crafting brand identities. While packaged goods normally have an obvious core — so that their advertisements can anchor themselves to product performance and attributes — with destinations the situation is much less clear. Many destination branding efforts have foundered for lack of focus. The Philippines has branded itself many times over the past 30 years, with slogans ranging from "Pride of the Orient" to "Fiesta Islands" to "Philippines: The Last Bargain in Asia." Its most recent slogan, "WOW Philippines," was intended as much to instil national pride as to attract overseas visitors. Even Las Vegas, prior to the "What Happens in Vegas Stays in Vegas" campaign, was sending mixed and confusing messages to consumers. Previous to the "Sin City" re-imaging, some of the properties in Las Vegas had tried unsuccessfully to position themselves as family attractions, thus deviating from the core brand attributes.

5. Differentiation

The final challenge of destination branding is that of creating differentiation in spite of the pressures on destination marketing. Countries often promote their history, their culture, and their beautiful scenery in their marketing, but most destinations have these attributes, and it is critical to build a brand on something that uniquely connects a destination to the consumer now or has the potential to do so in the future. Australia's $210 million "Where the bloody hell are you?" campaign (see *Case Study* in Chapter 10) had an incredible impact, cutting through the clutter and conveying a distinct message that people found appealing and authentic. According to the creators, the commercials were all about the tone, the personality, the images, and messages. "They all combine together to convey a feeling — in this case a warm, distinctive, and authentically Australian invitation that says we want you to come and get involved now. This in turn makes them more inclined to take the all important next step to come to Australia, rather than put it off for ever," said Scott Morrison, managing director of Tourism Australia. Other suggestive or in-your-face slogans have broken out before. Las Vegas for example has succeeded with "What Happens in Vegas Stays in Vegas" (see *Spotlight* in Chapter 8).

Brand Building

Morgan and Pritchard suggest that there are five stages in the process of building a destination brand: market investigation, analysis, and strategic recommendations; brand identity development; brand launch and introduction; brand implementation; and monitoring, evaluation, and review.[10] These are each discussed below.

1. Market Investigation, Analysis, and Strategic Recommendations

The first stage is to establish the core values of the destination and its brand. This stage should consider how contemporary or relevant the brand is to today's tourism consumer and how it compares with key competitors. Destinations tend to retool their messages more frequently than in the past. Australia's "See Australia in a Different Light" was only a few years old before Tourism Australia hired M&C Saatchi to come up with something different that would resonate with the target market. After conducting focus groups for six months, they found that people liked Australia not so much for Australia but for the Australians. The recommendation was to come up with a campaign that would capture the real Australia and who the people really are. The result was the "Where the bloody hell are you?" campaign that proved so successful. The objective behind the "Discover Hong Kong Year in 2006" was to show off the island's hidden treasures, and so the campaign highlighted the contrast between the urban centre of the city and the green space found on nearby islands.

2. Brand Identity Development

Once this market investigation is complete, the next stage is to develop the brand identity. Of importance here is the brand benefit pyramid (see Figure 12.3). Critical to the success of any destination brand is the extent to which the destination's brand personality interacts with the target market. A brand's personality has both a head and a heart: its head is its logical features, while its heart is its emotional benefits and associations. Brand propositions and communications can be based on either. Brand benefit pyramids sum up consumers' relationships with a brand and are frequently established during the consumer research process, in which consumers are usually asked to describe what features a destination offers and what the place means to them. Using their answers, it should then be relatively easy to understand what particular benefit pyramids consumers associate with the destination in question. In 2005, Canada re-branded itself with the slogan "Canada. Keep Exploring." The campaign attempted to look beyond Canada's clichéd brand attributes of mountains, Mounties, and moose to depict a more vibrant tourist destination (see *Case Study* in Chapter 8). One ad used intersecting lines labelled "midnight" and "mischief" to highlight discarded clothes by a pool. The ad suggests a more risqué tourism destination than previous ads. "Overall, the brand positioning is designed to bridge the gap between the consumers' historical perspectives of what Canada is — a place of beautiful geography — and connect that with our emerging international reputation of being more progressive, welcoming society," said Michele McKenzie, president and CEO of the Canadian Tourism Commission (CTC).[11]

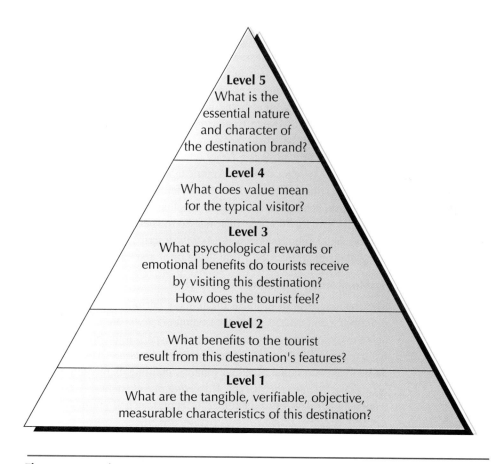

Figure 12.3   The Destination Brand Benefit Pyramid

Source: Morgan, N., & Pritchard, A. (2002). Contextualizing destination branding. In N. Morgan, A. Pritchard, & R. Pride (Eds.), *Destination branding* (11–41). Butterworth-Heinemann: Oxford, 31.

3. Brand Launch and Introduction

The third stage in brand building is to communicate the vision and launch the brand. This may be done through a single announcement or as a part of huge international advertising campaign. For the "Where the bloody hell are you?" campaign, a dedicated website was created by Tourism Australia where consumers could view the ad, and this created tremendous publicity for the ads before they appeared on television and in print. Australia's tourism ministry planned to spend about $160 million over a two-year period to promote their fresh tagline in commercials aired all over the world. In 2006, the Tourist Authority of Thailand (TAT) presented its new marketing slogan, "Thailand Unforgettable," as a key component of a strategy to achieve a target of 13.8 million arrivals in 2006 and 15 million in 2007. TAT also set a target of 82 million domestic trips for 2007. The branding strategy was decided upon after extensive consultation with the private sector and launched at the annual marketing meeting in August 2006.

4. Brand Implementation

The implementation stage involves translating the brand personality and proposition into deliverable messages. A logotype or brand signature and a design style guide, which ensures consistency of message and approach, should also reinforce the brand values. The vision should be expressed in the brand's core values, which are consistently reinforced through the product and in all marketing communications. Every execution in all media contributes to maintaining brand presence. When Canada re-branded itself in 2005 with the slogan "Canada. Keep Exploring," the slogan appeared not only on televisions and print ads around the world, but also on coffee sleeves, branded bakery bags, and in the London Underground. When Israel introduced the "Who Knew?" campaign, tourism ads appeared in a number of North American newspapers while the trade were encouraged to attend educational seminars and offered familiarization trips to the country. The answer to the question behind the new slogan was that Israel had more to offer than religious tours and walking in the footsteps of Jesus. So the new ads promoted beaches, ski slopes, and a thriving night life. *Marketing in Action* describes how the "Incredible India" campaign was rolled out all over the world using print and television, and outdoor ads.

5. Monitoring, Evaluation, and Review

The final stage is to evaluate the brand's performance in the marketplace. Continuous monitoring and evaluation of the communications are key here, as are open-mindedness and a willingness to embrace change on the part of the brand managers. Any change must be managed with the overall consistency of the brand. The secret is to evolve continually and enrich the original brand personality, building on the initial strengths to increase their appeal and broaden the market. *Marketing in Action* describes how the "Incredible India" campaign has developed a number of themes such as spirituality, festivals, and wildlife.

MARKETING IN ACTION

THE INCREDIBLE INDIA CAMPAIGN

ntil the end of 2002, India was being promoted differently in different countries. Tourism was not promoted in an organized fashion and the wealth of historic sites that India has to offer were not made known to potential tourists. In comparison, countries such as Thailand, Malaysia, China, and Singapore were attracting increasing numbers of tourists. However, in 2002, the Indian government's attitude to tourism changed, and a new advertising campaign, launched in December of that year, focused on showing the numerous facets of India's cultural heritage and geographical diversity, all under the umbrella tag line of "Incredible India."

The following year, $5.9 million was spent on the campaign, in print (see Figure 12.4), and television, targeting Southeast Asia, Australia, Britain, France, Italy, and Germany. Promoting a kaleidoscope of experiences including yoga, wildlife, and festivals, the "Incredible India" campaign also placed ads outdoors, choosing popular sites such as Times Square in New York, and international airports. The campaign focused on various themes, but one successful print campaign focused on the popular spiritual amenities that the country offered. "Body, mind, and soul are a big thing for tourists opting for India as a destination," said V Sunil of Ogilvy and Mather. "In Singapore the focus is on shopping, fun, and entertainment. Similarly, most people come to India for spiritual reasons. That is the big differentiator for India, in comparison with other countries."

In 2003, India's tourism inflow rose 15.3 percent mostly because of this campaign, with foreign exchange earnings through tourist

Figure 12.4 Incredible India Print Advertisement

arrivals rising as much as 20 percent. Foreign tourist arrivals increased a further 25 percent in 2004. The campaign continues to be successful. In 2006, advertising agency Grey Worldwide India won a bronze Euro Effies award for its "Incredible India" campaign that ran from December 2005 to March 2006 across most big European markets. Since the beginning of "Incredible India," as many as 10 ad agencies have worked on the campaign. While the original print campaign was created by Ogilvy and

MARKETING IN ACTION *continued*

Mather in Delhi, the television commercials were created by Enterprise Nexus in Mumbai. "We focused on the fact that India has plenty to offer. India is one country with thousands of places worth visiting and is a country of tremendous contrasts," said Enterprise Nexus executive director Anil Sanjeevan.

The Internet has also been used as a platform for the "Incredible India" campaign. In 2002 the first online campaign was launched, with the communication objective "to project India as a unique opportunity for physical invigoration, mental rejuvenation, cultural enrichment, and spiritual elevation." The website — www.tourismindia.com — was revamped to make it attractive, functional, and resourceful to help a user plan a trip to India. More than 100 different creative pieces were designed for the campaign across 12 themes, and innovations such as contests were used to increase user interaction. The campaign resulted in more than 13 million hits to the website per month. Since then, the website has been relaunched as www.incredibleindia.org, designed to be a showcase of all good things in India — colours, technology, vastness, diversity, and depth. By April 2005, the website was receiving more than 25 million page views per month.

The "Incredible India" campaign continues to attract tourists to India. In 2005/06 the campaign was given a different look and was targeted at more affluent tourists who saw the country as a destination suited to their thirst for interests such as yoga, ayurveda, spirituality, and wildlife. Responsibility for the 2007 campaign was handed to A Advertising and creative director V Sunil, who had moved from Ogilvy. Sunil said, "The new campaign will again be a visual campaign, and thus a reflection of India. However, this time the focus will also be on creating an unapologetic, confident, and growing India. Thus it combines spectacular images of India with a wry, self-assured tone — a far cry from the bowing and scraping of the past." The media mix will include print and outdoor executions, the two media that "Incredible India" had used extensively in the past. The campaign placed ads in many major international publications, including *National Geographic,* the *New York Times, Condé Nast Traveller, Time Magazine,* and the *Wall Street Journal.* Outdoor locations include Times Square in New York and airports in London, Paris, Singapore, and Dubai.

Sources: Neelakantan, S. (2004, January 22). *Far Eastern Economic Review, 167*(3), 44; Indiatelevision.com (2003, October 28). Tourism ministry sells Incredible India with generous dose of spirituality. www .indiatelevision.com (retrieved September 2007).

DESTINATION PROMOTION

Identifying Target Markets

Chapter 3 discusses in detail the importance of segmentation and targeting, and a lengthy discussion on this subject is therefore unnecessary here. However, it is worth underlining the importance of destinations understanding what motivates tourists, how they make their decisions, and how they evaluate and perceive destinations. Having gained such understanding, destinations must then segment the market — whether it is into subcategories such as business travellers, conference and convention delegates, incentive travellers, and tourists, or into classifications such as the typologies proposed by Stanley Plog.[12] There are also growing tourism markets that destinations need to court, such as the baby boomer market, the gay and lesbian market, the senior market, and the family market. But there are also others, such as those travellers interested in sport tourism and those looking for environmentally friendly tourism.

A destination can identify its natural target market in two ways. The first is to collect detailed information about its current visitors in order to determine which visitors should be targeted. The second approach is to audit the destination's attractions and select segments that might logically have an interest in these attractions. Marketers should not, however, assume that current visitors reflect all the potentially interested groups. After a destination identifies its natural target markets, tourism planners should conduct research to determine where these tourists are found. If many segments are identified, the relative potential profit from each should be evaluated. The potential profit of a target tourist segment is the difference between the amount the tourist segment is likely to spend and the cost of attracting and serving this segment. Ultimately, potential tourist segments should be ranked and selected in order of their profitability.

Whatever tourist segments a destination seeks, it needs to be very specific in its targeting. A ski area attracts skiers, yet even with such givens, potential visitors must be segmented by additional characteristics. For example, Lake Louise in Banff National Park appeals to image-conscious, upper-income, and professional skiers, whereas Banff Mount Norquay, just an hour away, attracts a more price-conscious family market. Marketing organizations need to be aware of these subtle differences. Likewise, destinations must closely monitor the relative popularity of their various attractions by determining the number and type of tourists attracted to each. Information should be collected continuously on the changing needs and wants of existing markets, emerging markets, and potential target markets. The research conducted by Tourism Whistler, for example, has contributed considerably to the unprecedented growth and rising stature of Whistler as a world class year-round destination. By identifying and targeting potential target markets such as British and South American skiers, Whistler has become North America's most acclaimed recreational destination. Tourism Whistler regularly conducts customer surveys to gauge satisfaction levels, to identify areas that need improvement, and to formulate strategies.

Destination Promotion Strategy

promotion strategy

a plan to reach prospective visitors using a promotional mix to achieve destination awareness and influence attitudes and purchasing behaviour

A destination's **promotion strategy** plans to reach prospective visitors using a promotional mix to achieve destination awareness and influence attitudes and purchasing behaviour.[13] The promotional campaigns of most DMOs fall into three main categories: traditional image or brand-building campaigns, which aim to build or maintain awareness of the destination; strategic campaigns, aimed, for example, at attracting visitors in the shoulder season; and "damage control" campaigns typified by Thailand's promotional campaign that followed the tsunami in 2004 (see the *Case Study* in Chapter 13). Media investment in attracting tourists has grown rapidly in recent years, and most DMOs are involved in a range of promotional activities. These include six types: brochures, advertisements, the press and public relations, personal selling, sales promotions, and trade fairs and exhibitions. Each is discussed here in turn.

1. Brochures

Brochures are produced for both promotional and informational purposes, although both functions may be served by a single brochure. As well as a general brochure covering the whole destination, a range of other brochures may also be offered. These may cover smaller geographical entities within the overall destination region. Alternatively, they may be targeted at specific market segments. An example is the magazine launched by Tourism Montreal in 2001 to attract the gay market. *Gay Destination Montreal* is distributed to gay industry decision makers in North America and contains articles on the various pride events, nightlife, fashion, and the gay village in Montreal. Canada is perceived as a gay-friendly destination, with the top three cities for the gay traveller being Montreal, Toronto, and Vancouver. Each city has developed, supported, and marketed its gay spaces and events to great success.

2. Advertisements

Due to the challenge of limited budgets referred to earlier in the chapter, most destinations' ads are placed in print media rather than in the more expensive, but more effective, medium of television. The "Incredible India" media mix, for example, consists mainly of print and outdoor media. Most resort advertising is seasonal and takes place when it is thought potential visitors will be making their holiday decisions. The majority of ads seek to encourage potential consumers to request a copy of the destination's brochure, although more recently ads have been created to drive the audience to a destination website.

3. The Press and Public Relations

The press and public relations play a significant role in the marketing of destinations, and Chapter 9 provides many examples of destinations using familiarization trips, celebrity visits, press releases, product placement, and television broadcasts to attract attention and improve their image with the general public. For agencies that have limited budgets, this low-cost form of promotion is particularly attractive. Promotional videos are often used as a sales tool by destinations. For example, in 2005, the Kenyan Tourist Board commissioned a British filmmaker to film Kenya's rich attractions and wildlife. The promotional video was sponsored in part by industry players in Kenya, including Nairobi's Holiday Inn and Heritage Hotels as well as SafariLink, Kenya's safari airline. Targeted mainly to potential travellers in the UK, the objective of the video was to promote the diversity of the country.

4. Personal Selling

Relatively little personal selling is carried out by DMOs. However, some destinations find personal selling to be the most effective communication tool in promoting to key travel decision makers and influencers in the travel trade, such as corporate travel managers, convention or meeting planners, tour operators, and retail travel agents. The purchasing power of these groups is impressive, and there are relatively few of them, which justifies the added expense of personal selling. In 2005, the Kenya Tourist Board launched the Fall 2005 Roadshow in order to increase awareness of the destination across the United States. Along with 20 tour operators from Kenya, members of the tourist board visited travel agents in Arizona, Florida, Los Angeles, New York, and Texas in order to educate them on the virtues of travelling to Kenya. At the same time, an extensive network of newly appointed global market representatives were employed in Kenya's key markets in Europe, the U.S., and Asia. Their role was to raise the profile of Kenya among trade representatives and consumers by emphasizing the quality and diversity of Kenya.

5. Sales Promotions

Due to the lack of control over the destination product and pricing, sales promotions are used relatively little in destination marketing. However, "added value" promotional offers may be made available, featuring elements of the destination product over which the DMO does have control. One example of a destination using sales promotion comes from the UK, where VisitBritain partnered with Columbia Pictures in 2006 to plan a series of events that capitalized on the release of the film *The Da Vinci Code*. Promotional campaigns relied heavily on an online code-breaking competition to tie in with the book's plot and locations in London and Scotland. VisitBritain also provided incentives for tourists to write blogs about their experiences for its website.

6. Trade Fairs and Exhibitions

Many DMOs exhibit at travel trade shows, fairs, exhibitions, or conventions. Generally these occasions bring all parts of the industry together. Such events may be annual, or used as a short-term tactic to boost tourism interest. In October 2006, Zimbabwe opened an international tourism fair to promote its once booming resorts, largely deserted because of President Robert Mugabe's controversial politics. The southern African country's tourism revenues had collapsed in the face of a crumbling economy, chronic fuel shortages, and Mugabe's standoff with Britain and other western nations that oppose his politics. Although the country has some of Africa's most popular tourism destinations, including the famous Victoria Falls and some of the continent's largest game reserves, promoters have found it hard to sell Zimbabwe overseas.

Marketing Cooperation

Considering the fact that DMO budgets for marketing purposes are equivalent to an average of 0.5 percent or less of tourism expenditure, as well as the fact that most DMOs cannot influence more than around 10 percent of all prospective visitors, the question of the effectiveness of many DMO marketing campaigns in practice is a valid one. DMOs will therefore often cooperate with other members of the tourism industry. These cooperative strategies create marketing bridges between a DMO and individual operators in the tourism industry, and between "umbrella" campaigns and industry marketing expenditure. One of these strategies is the participation in joint marketing schemes. Many destinations have formed partnerships with travel, recreational, and communication businesses on joint promotional efforts. They advertise in national magazines and travel publications and do vertical marketing with business travel promotions to link to the business-leisure segment of the travelling public, and they target intermediaries such as travel agents.

A recent example of marketing cooperation in Canada occurred in 2007, when the Government of Yukon launched a multi-million–dollar national marketing campaign in partnership with the governments of Canada, the Northwest Territories, and Nunavut, as well as the 2007 Canada Winter Games Host Society. The $5 million campaign, launched during the Canada Winter Games, included promotional spots for national television and movie theatres, along with national print advertising and magazine supplements. A new website, www.lookupnorth.ca, was also created to support online advertising and to centrally manage interest generated by the advertising. The website linked to territorial tourism and economic development sites.

Another effective way to attract potential travellers is to offer them convenient packages that not only include the basic necessities but also contain visits to the iconic attractions in the destination. Packaging destinations either for the general mass tourism market or for niche specialist markets can significantly increase a destination's appeal. Inbound operators are usually responsible for packaging the destinations: putting together the combination of stopovers, attractions, accommodations, and tours; deciding the best transportation to use along the way; and allocating the amount of time to be spent at each destination. These operators, working with DMOs and provincial tourism offices, as well as with regional tourism groups and individual suppliers, create tours and promotional materials that will help to win business in the highly competitive international marketplace.

As part of the 2007 joint marketing campaign between the Yukon, the Northwest Territories, and Nunavut, a promotional contest gave entrants the chance of winning three separate northern packages, one from each territory: a Tatshenshini River trip in the Yukon, provided by Nahanni River Adventures, a fishing expedition provided by Peterson Point Lodge in the NWT, and a wildlife viewing/ecological vacation provided by Bathurst Inlet Lodge in Nunavut. The trips were all-inclusive, including round-trip airfare for two from one of Air North's gateway cities.

MARKETING EVENTS AND CONFERENCES

For business and leisure travellers, events and conferences often play a key role in bringing people to destinations. These can vary from conventions and exhibitions for the business market to huge sporting events such as the Olympics or the World Cup, which attract millions of sport tourists. From the destination's perspective, event tourism is the development and marketing of events to obtain economic and community benefits. To the consumer, it is travel for the purpose of participating in or viewing an event. The *Snapshot* shows how marathon runners have become a huge draw for destinations. New races are starting up all around the world, and even successful, long-established marathons are diversifying into new options such as shorter runs, concerts by big-name musical acts, elaborate fitness expos, and hotel discounts.

One example of a Canadian destination that has successfully attracted events and conferences over the last decade is Saint John, New Brunswick. In 2005, Saint John hosted more than 300 meetings and sport events, attracting 43 000 delegates to the city. Sporting events were worth $14.5 millon to the local economy, and conventions were worth $32 million in economic spinoffs in 2005. Much of the credit for this success is due to Venue Saint John, a strategic private/public sector alliance of 15 organizations whose goal is to attract and host events in Saint John. Noted for its creative approach, increased productivity, cost savings, and improvement of the economy of the city, Venue Saint John was named the grand prize winner in the industry category of the 2002 Tourism Innovation Competition. Table 12.3 provides a list of events that Venue Saint John assisted with in 2005 and shows that the organization's impact is wide-ranging.

Table 12.3

Major Events Hosted by Venue Saint John in 2005

January	Maritime Speed Skating Championships (160 participants)
February	Equine Canada National Conference (300)
March	Canadian Water Wastewater Conference (400)
April	Early Childhood Conference (450)
May	Canadian Museums Association Conference (400)
June	Maritime Lumber Bureau (500)
July	Canadian Physiotherapy Association (650)
August	Kinsmen & Kinette Clubs of Canada Convention (1000)
September	Canadian Country Music Awards (2000)
October	Canadian Soccer Nationals under 16 (620)
November	Canadian Institute of Traffic & Transportation AGM (125)

Source: Tourism Saint John. (2006, January 19). 2005 Venue Saint John Wrap Up and Outlook for 2006. Press release. www.sjwaterfront.com/saint_john_waterfront_development_newsroom/news_releases.html (retrieved September 2007).

Events and Festivals

Events and festivals are often introduced to cope with seasonality and to boost tourism receipts during normally quiet times of year. For example, in April 1995 Whistler held its first World Ski and Snowboard Festival in order to increase occupancy rates at the end of the winter season. Now the event is North America's largest snow-sport and music event, attracting thousands of enthusiasts from all over the world. Hotel rooms are fully booked during the event, which spans two weekends in order to maximize occupancy rates. In addition to ski and snowboard competitions, film events, parades, and a lively club scene at night, more than 50 acts are booked for the Outdoor Concert Series. The concerts usually attract audiences of up to 10 000 revellers. According to an independent research study commissioned by the organizers, the 2006 festival resulted in a $37.7 million impact on the province, including nearly $21.3 million for the resort. The staging of major events in Whistler is not a new experience, and although the destination lost the World Cup skiing competition to Lake Louise, it was successful in its bid to be the host city for the 2010 Olympic Winter Games. The estimated cost of the joint Vancouver/Whistler Olympic bid was about $20 million, but hosting the games is expected to generate $1.3 billion in revenue from ticket sales, sponsorships, and television rights.

Whistler is not alone in aggressively marketing sporting events. There is an increasing popularity among destinations for hosting sporting events in order to increase future visitation, improve the image of the city or country, or to disperse tourism activities in a wider region.[14] In 2007, Whitehorse played host to the 16-day Canada Winter Games, and nearly 4000 athletes, coaches, media, and fans descended on the territorial capital. The games were used to kick off the $5 million tourism campaign by all three northern territories referred to above. Yukon also re-branded itself around the "larger than life" slogan with a new website (www.largerthanlife.com) that offers a year-round travel guide.

Destinations are becoming more skilled in event leveraging to obtain desired impacts from an event. The success of previous sporting events such as the Barcelona Olympic Games has drawn attention to the strategic value of events. For example, in the Bahamas, an events management company has been given the task of developing events that show the natural beauty of the islands to the world. Australian tourism organizations implemented a series of strategies and tactics designed to leverage the tourism benefits to be obtained from the 2000 Olympic Games. The Australian events sector now has a very high profile as it is seen to be of national, strategic importance for developing tourism in the country. In 2006, the Irish government spent $24 million to stage and market the Ryder Cup golf tournament, in an effort to reverse a five-year decline in North American visitors.[15] Television ads appeared on U.S. channels such as CBS and the Golf Channel. The Ryder Cup was expected to generate about $110 million in business through TV rights, merchandise, tickets, and sponsorship.

Events do not necessarily have to involve sport. To commemorate the best-known date in British history, 1066, when the Norman William the Conqueror defeated the Anglo-Saxon King Harold, the re-enactment of the Battle of Hastings is held every year at Battle Abbey in Battle, East Sussex. The event typically attracts up to 7000 spectators, but 21 000 people turned up in 2006. The reason for this was a specially extended script that attempted to imitate the original battle as closely as possible. More than 3000 fighters massed in full war dress for the event. Men marched from Yorkshire and Kent and from Cambridge and Leicester. But in a revisionist twist, the ranks of the Norman, Breton, Flemish, and Saxon armies were swelled on the 1040th anniversary by "actors" from 18 countries worldwide. Performances took place on both Saturday and Sunday, and 30 000 people attended the fireworks display in Hastings that followed Saturday's re-enactment. The *Snapshot* describes the Calgary Stampede, an annual ten-day celebration of western culture and heritage, which is another good example.

Some destinations may be known for just one event or festival. In the north of China, for example, Harbin is well known for its International Ice and Snow Festival held every January. Being one of the few tourism attractions in the city — an otherwise bleak industrial city of four million people where temperatures drop below –30°C during winter — even an environmental disaster in 2005 did not deter the organizers from hosting the event. Water supplies were cut for more than a week when toxic chemicals were poured through the city's water supplies. The event went ahead as scheduled. Tens of thousands of visitors from around the world travel to Harbin for the month-long festival, which is famous for its dazzling array of ice sculptures. World historical monuments such as the Eiffel Tower, the Great Wall and Egyptian pyramids are replicated in ice.

Other destinations such as Hong Kong have hosted a number of traditional festivals that take place throughout the year. Hong Kong has 20 public holidays per year, many linked to Chinese festivals and each with its own identity. These religious, mythical, and historical celebrations are open to non-Chinese locals and tourists. Examples include the Dragon Boat Festival at Stanley Beach, which is an annual event that attracts large crowds to watch the fierce competition amongst teams of rowers, kept in rhythm by pounding drums, in sleek dragon-prowed racing boats. The Bun Festival on the Cheung Chau waterfront features a procession of colourfully dressed children on carnival floats along with 16-metre high bun-studded bamboo towers traditionally erected for the occasion. The island's population triples during this cultural event. As the luxury retail capital of Asia, Hong Kong naturally has to host a Shopping Festival during the summer months when sales, late shopping hours, and special restaurant menus encourage consumers to adopt the "shop 'til you drop" culture. Sporting events attracting international audiences include the Champions Challenge tennis tournament in January, the Hong Kong Marathon in February, and the most famous event of them all, the Hong Kong Sevens. This is a rugby tournament, celebrating its 30th anniversary in 2007, is a magnet for rugby fans from all over the world, particularly Australia, New Zealand, South Africa, and Britain.

In Canada, several organizations are involved in the marketing of events and festivals. For example, Festivals and Events PEI, a federation of more than 80 festivals, events, and suppliers, promotes events on Prince Edward Island. Festivals get little exposure outside of their own home province or territory. And despite the millions of visitors who attend Canadian festivals across the country every year and the substantial revenues they generate for the tourism industry, marketing for the festival sector has been relatively taken for granted. World-class festivals such as the Montreal Jazz Festival and the Edmonton Fringe Festival remain relatively unknown outside of their own home provinces. Smaller community events and celebrations also have much to offer and would interest visitors touring through a particular province or region.

The *Case Study* at the end of this chapter focuses on a popular music festival in Ontario, and the Ministry of Tourism in Ontario is a great supporter of events and festivals. In 2007, the ministry invested $3 million to help organizations develop and market festivals and events in communities across Ontario. Ontario's Tourism Event Marketing Partnership Program also invested $500 000 to enhance the marketing of festival and events in the province. The program provides financial support to events and festivals to cover the costs of advertising in a targeted tourism market. The average large festival in Ontario generates more than $11 million in taxes and creates nearly 700 full-time jobs, mostly in the hospitality sector.[16]

Conferences

The convention and exhibition market, another lucrative market for destinations, has experienced unparalleled growth during the past 20 years. However, the period between 2000 and 2002 saw significant declines in demand for convention centres. During that time, several technology events associated with the "dot-com" era ceased to exist and many others downsized as a result of general economic conditions and the reduction of travel following the vents of September 11. The market has now recovered, and conventions centre events experienced an increase of more than 2 percent from 2005 to 2006, following a significantly higher increase of 16 percent in the prior year. Convention and trade show occupancy rates at the largest halls were strong in 2006, at 44.9 percent, topping the previous year's 43.9 percent, with other sized centres also showing improvement.[17]

Chapter 7 provides information on the convention market in Canada. In 2007, *M&IT Magazine* recognized Niagara-on-the-Lake's White Oaks Conference Resort and Spa as the top conference facility in Canada for the sixth consecutive year. The 5574-square-metre conference centre also has 220 guest rooms, a spa, and dining facilities, and provides consistently excellent service. The entire complex was designed with state-of-the-art audio and visual equipment, and specializes in providing small to medium-sized groups a productive and comfortable meeting environment. The magazine had asked meeting planners to select the conference centre, meeting facility, resort, or hotel in Canada that exceeded expectations and best catered to their needs in the past 12 months.

High-quality convention and exhibition centres can be found in virtually every city around the world, and Chapter 9's *Case Study* showed how Puerto Rico is attempting to position itself as a world class business tourism destination with its new convention centre. An aggressive, international integrated marketing campaign culminated in 2005 in the grand opening of the $490 million Puerto Rico Convention Center. Puerto Rico is a member of the BestCities Alliance, a convention bureau global alliance, which includes Cape Town, Copenhagen, Dubai, Edinburgh, Melbourne, Singapore, and Vancouver. Other countries, such as Jordan, are also positioning themselves as convention-friendly destinations. In 2006, the Jordan Tourism Board, the kingdom's official marketing organization, launched a sales drive and communications campaign to promote Jordan as a business and meetings, incentives, conventions, and exhibitions destination for Gulf Cooperation Council members.

SNAPSHOT

DESTINATION MARATHONS

The image of the long-distance runner has been overhauled and remade in the image of modern society. In the past, marathon winners hailed from the traditions of the great long-distance runners from small African villages. The majority of participants these days are white, middle-aged, urban professionals, and are often given the label of destination marathoners. Destination marathoners are runners who combine the physical and spiritual rush of completing a 42-kilometre (26.2-mile) road race with the pleasures of a vacation. Every one of the 50 U.S. states now caters to these travellers who follow their passion — whether it is to Alaska's Midnight Sun Marathon, New York City's beloved five-borough block party, or races at Disney World, Mount Rushmore, and Nashville (where country music bands play at each mile along the race course). London, Berlin, Athens, and Paris play host to a few of Europe's top races, and even the Great Wall of China has its own marathon, held each May. Table 12.4 provides a sample of some of the marathons from around the world.

Table 12.4

International Marathon Calendar from around the World

MONTH	MARATHON
January	Hong Kong Island Mountain Marathon, Hong Kong, China; ING Miami Marathon, Miami and Miami Beach, FL
February	International Egyptian Marathon, Luxor, Egypt; BMW Malta Marathon, Malta
March	Marathon Catalunya, Barcelona, Spain; City of Rome Marathon, Rome, Italy
April	Flora London Marathon, London, UK; Boston Marathon, Boston, MA
May	Great Wall Marathon, Beijing, China; Fiji Bula Marathon, Fiji
June	Safaricom Marathon, Lewa Wildlife Conservancy, Kenya; Edinburgh Marathon, Edinburgh, Scotland
July	Swiss Alpine Marathon, Davos, Switzerland; Gold Coast Airport Marathon, Gold Coast, Australia
August	Loop the Lake, Invermere, BC; Reykjavik Marathon, Reykjavik City, Iceland
September	New Mexico Marathon, Albuquerque, NM; Warsaw Marathon, Poland
October	Augrabies Extreme Marathon, Augrabies, South Africa; Toronto Marathon, Toronto, ON
November	New York City Marathon, New York, NY; Athens Marathon, Athens, Greece
December	New Las Vegas Marathon, Las Vegas, NV; Reggae Marathon, Negril, Jamaica

Source: International Marathons, 10/01/07–12/02/07. (2007). www.marathonguide.com (retrieved September 2007).

The marathon is one of the most storied races of all time, dating back to the ancient Greeks. But once the exclusive domain of Olympic athletes and hard-core fitness fiends, today's marathon is geared toward people who compete not to win, but to finish. In the U.S. alone in 2006, an estimated 397 000 runners finished marathons, with the average age of runners being 41 for males and 36 for females. The top three marathons in the U.S. are New York (38 000), Chicago (33 600), and Honolulu (24 500). New races are springing up all around the world, and even successful, long-established marathons are diversifying into new options such as shorter runs, concerts by big-name musical acts, elaborate fitness expos, and hotel discounts. To cater to these marathon travellers, Honolulu puts on a luau with guest musicians such as Brian Wilson and Van Morrison, and on race day holds a 10-kilometre walk for runners' families and friends.

Destination marathons have also become popular in Canada. A growing number of Canadians — especially those in the baby boomer bracket — are planning their holidays

SNAPSHOT *continued*

around marathon events. Popular marathons include Woody's RV World Marathon, in Red Deer, Alberta; Casino Niagara Marathon, in Niagara Falls, Ontario; and the Royal Victoria Marathon, in Victoria, B.C. One that has received recent accolades is Marathon by the Sea, in Saint John, New Brunswick (see Figure 12.5). The event has been attracting runners and their families since 1995, and has become the largest participative sport event in the province's history, with runners and walkers of all ages and physical ability completing a 12-kilometre race, a half marathon, or a full 42-kilometre marathon.

Marathon by the Sea's purposes are to test people's limits, to encourage them to take part in an event that motivates a healthy lifestyle, and to create pride in the community. The event has attracted a growing number of entrants from across Canada and the United States. About 270 people attended the first year, and 565 participants took part in 2006. The event also involves more than 300 volunteers and has grown to become a three-day

event with a festival-like atmosphere. Total revenue brought into the city for this weekend-long event is estimated at $300 000.

The 2000 Ultimate Guide to Marathons rated Marathon by the Sea the seventh Top Summer Destination in North America, and the following year race director Lori Weir won the Venue Saint John Sport Planner of the Year Award, an award that recognizes sport event leaders who bring recognition and business to Saint John and the Venue Saint John partnership. The same year, Marathon by the Sea caught the eye of *Runners World*, the most widely read running magazine in the world, and Saint John was a featured destination in a subsequent issue.

Sources: Cummings, S. (2002). Sport Planner of the Year Award, Saint John. www.canadatourism.com/en/ctc/ctx/ctx-news/search/newsbydateform.cfm (retrieved May 2002); MarathonGuide.com www.marathonguide.com; Mate, S. (2002, September 4). The marathon tourist. *Globe & Mail*, R10; Winik, M. (2003). Going the distance. *Travel + Leisure, 33*(4), 124–128; Blackwell, T. (2006, October 14). The new opiate of the middle-class masses. *National Post*, A14.

Figure 12.5 Print Advertisement to Promote the Marathon by the Sea

MARKETING ALL-INCLUSIVE RESORTS

The concept of all-inclusive resorts is not new. As mentioned in Chapter 6, this type of package holiday originated in holiday camps in the United Kingdom, where customers were provided access to every entertainment facility in the camp for a single price. The strategy proved highly successful, and Club Med has built on this model for its chain of holiday resorts around the world. However, over the past few decades, there has been a huge increase in the development of new all-inclusive resorts, as well as an adaptation of a number of older traditional hotels into all-inclusive properties. All-inclusive packages were originally designed for resorts situated in the isolated tourist destinations where the absence of tourism infrastructure and the insufficient supply of tourist services were limiting the consumption possibilities for a tourist. The concept became popular as it decreased the uncertainty of the tourist about the total amount of money to be spent during a holiday. It also offered value, as it normally involved the sale of different products as a unique package at a price lower than the total price of its components sold separately. "All-inclusives" normally supply a room, three meals daily, unlimited beverages, sports, and entertainment for one fixed price. Sol Meliá is the world's largest resort operator, running more than 300 hotels with 80 000 rooms, mostly located in Europe and the Caribbean. In 2006 profits were expected to be about $172 million, a gain of 24 percent on the previous year. All-inclusives are very popular with honeymoon couples, but another trend is all-inclusive nudist or *"au naturel"* resorts. SuperClubs Hedonism II was so popular in Negril, Jamaica, that Hedonism III was opened in Ocho Rios, and promotes itself as a beach resort for "uninhibited singles or couples."

The market for this type of holiday has grown steadily over the last few decades, and has also become increasingly competitive. Resorts are not just competing on price, and continue to add new services and components to provide more choices. Today, it is hard to find an all-inclusive resort that has only buffet meals; most resorts now have à la carte restaurants. Resorts are also improving facilities and services. Royal service at Sol Meliá's Paradisus Riveria Cancún, for example, includes private check-in and check-out, access to a private lounge for club members, a private buffet, private beach club, a pool butler service, and free Internet access. Like golf, spas are very popular, and more all-inclusive resorts are adding them. For example, Sandals Resorts have full-service, state-of-the-art European spas offering a variety of both rejuvenating and fitness services. Some resorts like SuperClubs are providing "No Hurricane Guarantees" year-round. Should a hurricane happen to strike, the resort will issue a voucher for the same number of disrupted nights for use for a stay during the same month of the following year. The same applies with the "Jamaica Sunshine Guarantee" should one encounter a sunless day — a rare occurrence in Jamaica.

Despite the success of all-inclusives, they have been criticized on a number of fronts in terms of their social, economic, and environmental impacts.[18] Socially, they are accused of creating ghettos, segregating tourists and locals, and discouraging the mixing of the two. Economically, they often provide little income for the local communities. Many all-inclusives are internationally owned and much of the money spent in the resorts leaks outside of the country where the resort is situated. In Mallorca, Spain, for example, where all-inclusive accommodation grew sharply from 9.6 percent in 2002 to 16.3 percent in 2004, some government representatives have complained that such hotels do not generate significant revenues for the island. Finally, all-inclusives are accused of negatively affecting the local environments as they are often complexes on a very large scale. As well as harming the visual amenity of sites, they often use valuable water and damage wildlife habitats. In a video titled *Thailand for Sale* produced in the 1980s, Club Med was strongly criticized for the negative environmental and social impacts of its developments. In terms of the future, all-inclusive resorts could be a permanent feature, or they may prove to be part of a transition phase which new destinations go through until their local infrastructure has developed to the point where facilities and quality are on a par with the all-inclusive resort.

CHAPTER SUMMARY

Destinations are places that have some form of actual or perceived boundary, such as the physical boundary of an island, political boundaries, or even market-created boundaries. There are many different types of destinations, including major international destinations, classic destinations, human-made destination resorts, natural landscape or wildlife tourism destinations, alternative destinations, business tourism destinations, stopover destinations, short-break destinations, and day-trip destinations.

There is a strong link between destination and attractions, and it is usually the existence of a major attraction that lends to stimulating the development of destinations, whether the attraction is a beach, a temple, or a theme park. As with other sectors of the tourism industry, attractions are increasingly polarized between a few large attractions and thousands of small and micro-sized enterprises. Tourist attractions can also be classified as natural or human-made.

Destinations promotion is concerned with reaching prospective visitors via expenditure on a promotional mix intended to achieve destination awareness and influence prospective customers' attitudes and purchasing behaviour. The subject of destination branding has received increased attention over the last few decades. Destination brand builders face five key challenges: limited budgets, politics, the external environment, the destination product, and differentiation. The destination brand building process comprises five stages: market investigation, analysis and strategic recommendations, brand identity development, brand launch and introduction, brand implementation, and monitoring, evaluation, and review.

For business and leisure travellers, events and conferences often play a key role in bringing people to destinations. From the destination's perspective, event tourism is the development and marketing of events to obtain economic and community benefits. To the consumer, it is travel for the purpose of participating in or viewing an event. Events are often introduced to cope with seasonality and to boost tourism receipts during normally quiet times of year. The convention and exhibition market is another lucrative market for destinations, and has experienced unparalleled growth during the past 20 years.

Over the past few decades, there has been a huge increase in the development of new all-inclusive resorts, as well as an adaptation of a number of older traditional hotels into all-inclusive properties. All-inclusive resorts could be a permanent feature, or they may prove to be part of a transition phase which new destinations go through until their local infrastructure has developed to the point where facilities and quality are on a par with the all-inclusive resort.

KEY TERMS

convention and visitor bureau (CVB), p. 405	destination branding, p. 406	promotion strategy, p. 415
destination, p. 396	destination marketing organizations (DMOs), p. 404	tourism area life cycle (TALC), p. 405

DISCUSSION QUESTIONS AND EXERCISES

1. Considering the characteristics and classifications of destinations, do you think Disneyland Florida is an attraction or a destination?
2. Research the marketing activities of a local destination marketing organization. What promotional tools is it using?
3. Apply the tourism area life cycle (TALC) to a destination you are familiar with. What does its position on the life cycle tell you about the target market?
4. Apply the Destination Brand Benefit Pyramid (Figure 12.3) to a local destination. What does the exercise tell you about the destination's brand?
5. Find an example of a destination that is attempting to attract tourists through events and festivals. Is such a marketing strategy sustainable?

CASE STUDY

"CATCH THE TROUT, IT'S MUSIC IN THE WOODS": THE TROUT FOREST MUSIC FESTIVAL

"Catch the Trout" is the invitation. The logo is a trout in a fedora playing the banjo. If that's not enough to catch a person's attention, the Trout Forest Music Festival (TFMF) certainly is. In August 1996, 106 guests gathered in Pakwash Provincial Park in northwestern Ontario for the first TFMF, also known as "Troutfest" and "Music in the Woods." The festival was moved in its second year to Ear Falls Waterfront Park in the town of Ear Falls, Ontario. By 2001, attendance at the festival was so high as to almost double the population of Ear Falls during the festival — quite a feat, as the town's population is 1316 people. Only 1500 adult tickets to the festival are available, and guests come primarily from the local region, northwestern Ontario, and southern Manitoba.

TFMF relies heavily on grants and donations that come from a wide range of sources, including Canadian Heritage, the Canada Council for the Arts, the Ontario Trillium Foundation, the Ontario Arts Council, Ontario Council of Folk Festivals, Red Lake Touring Region, CKDR 1450 Ear Falls, CBC Radio One Thunder Bay, Q104, Weyerhaeuser, Industry Canada, and the Township of Ear Falls, as well as from at least 88 other large and small organizations. The Trout Forest Music Festival has six stated objectives, which are critical, as the support of the Department of Canadian Heritage is contingent upon the fulfillment of these objectives. They are as follows:

1. To provide a quality music experience for festival goers of every age, in an intimate outdoor setting.
2. To promote the development of regional artists by providing an appropriate venue to showcase their talents and provide opportunities to interact with and learn more from more experienced musicians.
3. To showcase new types of music experiences to promote a wider appreciation of music by the regional audience.
4. To promote local First Nations music and artists.
5. To unite people of various ages and walks of life from across the region as volunteers sharing a common love of music and sharing in a common task.

The overall purpose of the festival is clearly stated by its organizers: "The Trout Forest Music Festival organization is a grassroots, nonprofit collective of folk music enthusiasts who are committed to providing quality live entertainment to their audiences." The artists are drawn from the pool of talented musicians across Canada. The TFMF has assembled a team of directors, crew, and volunteers that continue to make the festival a success. The theme varies each year: in 2001, the festival had a bi-coastal theme, with many performers from the East Coast; in 2002 the theme was "Latin Music in the Woods"; and the theme in 2003 was an "East Coast Kitchen Party."

By 2005, festival organizers had raised enough funding and support to build a permanent main stage and band shelter at the Ear Falls Waterfront Park. Live music is also performed in the beer garden area that becomes the Jam Pit in the evenings. Consistent with their goals of encouraging interaction between performers and guests, festival organizers have designated an area around the bonfire in the evening, after the stages close, for performers and guests to gather with their instruments and join in the music and share the experience. In addition, the festival features creative arts that are for sale, a family area, and camping that is reserved for out-of-town guests.

The TFMF has close connections with some other well-known folk festivals across Canada. In its second year, when it was experiencing many difficulties in planning, the director of the Winnipeg Folk Festival offered assistance and expertise on behalf of the Winnipeg Folk Festival, which is the largest folk festival in the country. TFMF is also a member of the Ontario Council of Folk Festivals. In 2001, Lloyd Romaniuk, the executive director of the TFMF, was a guest of the Stan Rogers Folk Festival in Canso, Nova Scotia, with the assistance of the Canada Council for the Arts. Canso is a similar-sized community that supports and benefits from a similar-sized festival. Both festivals want to support local and Canadian culture and provide a new level of economic benefits to their communities. It is these connections with the folk music community that allow TFMF to find the performers for Troutfest. Romaniuk attends events such as the East Coast Music Awards and the Atlantic Scene Festival to find the best talent for the festival in August.

The festival is not confined only to Ontario. In April 2003, for the first time, TFMF took its spirit on the road to put on a benefit concert in Winnipeg, called the Trout Forest Mini-Festival. Thirty percent of attendees at the TFMF were residents of Manitoba, so this was part of an outreach program to increase attendance at the Troutfest in Ear Falls. In 2004, TFMF reorganized and hired some full-time staff to complement the vast numbers of volunteers. The festival began strategic operational planning and uncovered a need to increase audience support. The outreach program is part of this forward-thinking planning. The TFMF's commitment to folk music in Canada includes supporting other festivals and making efforts to build a "network of festivals that can assist each other." It also brings together communities across northern Ontario for a common purpose, and the board of directors now includes members from Kenora, Red Lake, and Winnipeg, to complement those from the local community.

Sources: Amory, R. (2001, August 25). Catch the trout in the forest. *Saturday Miner and News*; Canadian Heritage continues to support Troutfest. (2003). www.troutfest.com (March 2003); History of the Trout Forest Music Festival. (2006). www.troutfest.com (September 2007).

QUESTIONS

1. Using only the stated objectives of the TFMF, describe the demographic profile of its main target markets.
2. Given these target markets, what has the TFMF changed to accommodate these groups?
3. What additional features has the TFMF added to connect the guests with the music?
4. Why are connections with other folk festivals in similar-sized communities beneficial to the TFMF?
5. Find some information on a festival in your area. How does it compare to the TFMF?

WEB SITES

www.marathonguide.com
A guide to marathons around the world

www.rockhall.com
Rock and Roll Hall of Fame and Museum

www.incredibleindia.org
Incredible India

www.calgarystampede.com
Calgary Stampede

www.visitsingapore.com
Uniquely Singapore

www.newzealand.com
The Official Site for New Zealand Travel & Business

www.troutfest.com
Trout Forest Music Festival

www.festivalspei.com
Festivals & Events PEI

www.marathonbythesea.com
Marathon by the Sea

www.venuesaintjohn.com
Venue Saint John

www.yfnta.org
Yukon First Nations Tourism Association

ENDNOTES

1. Kotler, P., Bowen, J., & Makens, J. (2003). *Marketing for hospitality and tourism.* Upper Saddle River, NJ: Prentice Hall.
2. Swarbrooke, J. (1995). *The Development and Management of Visitor Attractions.* Butterworth-Heinemann: Oxford.
3. Booming tourism taking terrible toll on Egyptian antiquities, experts say. (2006, November 2). *National Post*, A14.
4. Personal communication with S. Hamrick, executive director, Kenai Peninsula Tourism Marketing Council, March 19, 2007.
5. Gauldie, R. (2000). Advertising and promotion in the travel industry. *Travel & Tourist Analyst, 4*, 71–84.
6. Butler, R. W. (1980). The concept of a tourist area life cycle of evolution: Implications for management of resources. *Canadian Geographer, 24*(1), 5.
7. Plog, S. C. (1974). Why destination areas rise and fall in popularity. *Cornell Hotel & Restaurant Quarterly, 14*(4), 55–58.
8. Morgan, N., & Pritchard, A. (2002). Contextualizing destination branding. In N. Morgan, A. Pritchard, & R. Pride (Eds.), *Destination branding* (11–41). Butterworth-Heinemann: Oxford.
9. Stanley, B. (2006, March 10). Australia throws another tourism advertising slogan on the barbie. *Wall Street Journal*, B1.

10. Morgan, N., & Pritchard, A. (2002). Contextualizing destination branding. In N. Morgan, A. Pritchard, & R. Pride (Eds.), *Destination branding* (11–41). Butterworth-Heinemann: Oxford.

11. McArthur, K. (2005, November 15). Rebranding campaign unveils a new, more risqué Canada. *Globe & Mail*, B13.

12. Plog, S. C. (1974). Why destination areas rise and fall in popularity. *Cornell Hotel & Restaurant Quarterly, 14*(4), 55–58.

13. Middleton, V. T. C., & Clarke, J. (2001). *Marketing in travel and tourism*. Butterworth-Heinemann: Oxford.

14. Hudson, S., Getz, D., Miller, G.A., & Brown, G. (2004). The Future Role of Sporting Events: Evaluating the Impacts on Tourism. In K. Weiermair & C. Mathies (Eds.), *The tourism and leisure industry: Shaping the future* (237–251). Haworth Press: Binghampton, NY.

15. Cole, C. (2006, September 20). Ireland has never been greener. *National Post*, B8.

16. Travel Press (2007). Ontario invests $3 million more to promote festivals, events. *Tourism Daily*. www.tourismexchange.com (retrieved January 2007).

17. PriceWaterhouseCoopers reports increase in demand for convention centres. (2006, October 25). www.hospitalitynet.org/news/4029207.search?query=pricewaterhousecoopers+reports+increase+in+demand+for+convention+centres (retrieved September 2007).

18. Horner, S. & Swarbrooke, J. (2004). *International cases in tourism management: All-inclusive resorts.* Elsevier Butterworth-Heinemann: Oxford, 226–232.

13

Contemporary Issues in Tourism and Hospitality Marketing

Spotlight
SECOND LIFE AND THE VIRTUAL HOTEL

It is October 2006 and performer Ben Folds is promoting his new album by playing at the opening party for Aloft, a new Starwood hotel. People wander in, sit down, and discuss the music. Everything seems normal, but the whole scene exists only on the Internet. The audience is made up of virtual representations of real people.

The real people are sitting at their computer screens around the world, living their lives through avatars, the characters that appear on the screen. Ben Folds is real but he is selling his music in a virtual world, his music company believing that releasing his album to this "virtual listening party" is the marketing strategy of the future.

Welcome to Second Life, an online world with millions of registered users and a thriving virtual economy. Second Life allows its users to create a new, and improved, digital version of themselves. They then guide their avatar wherever they choose: down streets, into nightclubs, and into stores. When they meet another avatar they can start a conversation, developing friendships, love affairs, and entire sub-cultures. "Residents" can buy land, build structures, and start businesses, and the service is fast becoming a three-dimensional test bed for corporate marketers, including Sony BMG Music Entertainment, Sun Microsystems, Nissan, Adidas, and Toyota. Retailers have set up shops to sell digital as well as real world versions of their products, and even musicians can promote their albums with virtual appearances.

The demographics of Second Life users are interesting. The average age is 33, half of the users are women, and a very large number have not played online games before. "It's the best combination of social networking, chat rooms, and a 3D experience," said Justin Bovington, chief executive of Rivers Run Red, a London branding agency helping shape Second Life. "It's such an immersive experience that people get it quicker than anything else. We'd been looking for the broadband killer application, and Second Life is it." Linden Labs, the San Francisco company that operates Second Life, makes most of its money leasing "land" to tenants. A company like Nissan or its advertising agency can buy an "island" for a one-time fee of about $1500 and a monthly rate of about $230. Programmers can then be hired to create a driving course and design digital cars that people "in world" could drive, as well as some billboards and other promotional spots throughout the virtual world that would encourage people to visit Nissan Island.

Starwood Hotels is the first real-world hospitality company to open in Second Life, featuring its new line of moderately priced, loft-style hotels called Aloft. Projects like Aloft are designed to promote the venture but also to give its designers feedback from prospective guests before the first real hotel opens in 2008. Starwood will observe how people move through the space, what areas and types of furniture they gravitate toward, and what they ignore. Consumers are encouraged to post comments about the hotel on a blog, which features regular updates on the virtual hotel's design, along with detailed screen-shots. The ultimate goal is to attract trendy, youthful, tech-savvy customers to the Aloft brand, and the plan is to keep the virtual hotel as an interactive marketing tool, even after the real world buildings open.

The prototype being built in Second Life is based on a physical prototype under construction in a warehouse in New York. Starwood hired two New York–based companies to build the digital model and then to market it within Second Life and beyond: Electric Artists, a marketing firm, and the Electric Sheep Company, which specializes in designing goods for sale within Second Life. Both the physical prototype and the digital model feature clean architectural lines, high ceilings, and minimalist couches, tables, and beds that characterize the Aloft brand as efficient yet stylish. This is the first time the company has created a complete mock hotel, and it is unusual for the industry. Hotel prototypes usually don't amount to more than a single-room model that might be shown at a trade show. But the company says that both prototypes made financial sense. "We're saving money," said Starwood vice president Brian McGuiness. "If we find that significant numbers of people don't like a certain feature, we don't have to actually build it." Starwood predicts that, by 2012, there will be 500 Aloft properties worldwide.

Whether or not this innovative approach to marketing lures Second Lifers and, more importantly, real-life guests, toward the Aloft brand, remains to be seen. Meanwhile, why not check into the hotel and see for yourself?

Sources: Jana, R. (2006, August 23). Starwood Hotels explore second life first. *BusinessWeek Online*. www.businessweek.com/innovate/content/aug2006/id20060823_925270.htm?chan=innovation_innovation+%2B+design_innovation+and+design+lead (September 2007); Siklos, R. (2006, October 16). A virtual world but real money. *New York Times*, C1.

Objectives

On completion of this chapter, readers should understand:

- trends in tourism and hospitality marketing;
- how tourism should be marketed in the experiential economy;
- the growing importance of responsible marketing;

- the application of cause-related marketing in tourism;
- the marketing of sport and adventure tourism; and
- the marketing of tourism at times of crisis.

Chapter Overview

The *Spotlight* is an example of an organization harnessing the potential of the Internet to test and promote its services, a growing trend in tourism and hospitality marketing. This chapter is mainly concerned with marketing trends and focuses on some key contemporary tourism marketing issues. An analysis of tourism marketing trends is followed by a discussion about tourism marketing in the experiential economy. The next section looks at the responsible marketing of tourism, and then examples of cause-related marketing in tourism are outlined. The final two sections of the chapter look at the marketing of sport and adventure tourism, and marketing tourism in times of crisis.

TOURISM MARKETING TRENDS

General Growth Trends

Tourism is expected to grow 4.5 percent annually over the next decade, with the World Travel and Tourism Council (WTTC) predicting that, by 2014, tourism will amount to a market of more than 11.2 trillion, adding $8 trillion to the world's gross domestic product (GDP). By 2020, according to the WTTC, 100 million Chinese tourists will fan out across the globe replacing Americans, Japanese, and Germans as the world's most numerous travellers. China will soon be the most popular destination as well, with 130 million arrivals in 2020. Also, by 2020, 50 million Indians are expected to tour overseas. Business travel from, and among, developing countries will grow much more rapidly than the business market in general, as industries migrate from countries with a shrinking, expensive labour force to those where more skilled personnel are available at lower cost. Two obvious growth areas are China and India.

Certain sectors of the tourism industry will grow faster than others. The world's airlines are expected to report a profit in 2007 for the first time in six years, but they will remain constrained by the rising costs of fuel, government taxes, and airport service fees.

Cruises, a favourite vacation for older travellers, have grown by 50 percent in recent years; they now attract some 12 million travellers each year, and growing numbers of business meetings occur on board cruise ships. Cruise ships themselves are also expected to get larger, as the *Snapshot* in this chapter testifies.

In Canada, domestic travel is expected to continue to increase, underpinned by the ongoing strength in consumer confidence and solid economic fundamentals. However, global competition for travellers will continue to erode Canada's traditional travel markets, particularly the U.S. market. The combination of more and more countries developing their tourism industries, growing investments in marketing, and improving air access will continue to draw an increasing number of travellers to international destinations other than Canada. As the border tightens between Canada and the U.S., the number of Americans entering Canada will continue to decline and industry sector profits are expected to fall or be stagnant until 2010. At that time, a gradual recovery from the effects of the Western Hemisphere Travel Initiative (WHTI), rising travel spending from new markets such as China, and the 2010 Olympics will all contribute to rising profit levels.

Unfortunately, the growth of the tourism industry does have some pitfalls. Increased international exposure includes a greater risk of terrorist attack. Even before September 11, 2001, American-owned hotels experienced several major bomb attacks, in part because American government facilities overseas have been effectively hardened against terrorist assault. Such attacks are likely to continue as the amount of terrorist activity in the world is likely to increase in the next 10 years. The "World of Travel in 2020" study, commissioned by Cendant Travel Distribution Services, suggests that the perception of danger that is generated by our culture of fear has created two contrasting consumer groups with very different attitudes and purchasing behaviour.[1] They are New Puritans, who let their worries prevent them from living a full life, and Hyperlifers, whose response to fear is to try to live life to the full to avoid acknowledging risks. These groups represent opposite ends of the behavioural spectrum, whereas in reality, most people fall somewhere in between, or change groups depending on the circumstances.

SNAPSHOT

CRUISING TRENDS: BIGGER IS BETTER!

Cruise ship holidays are attracting more tourists these days and appealing to different sectors. In 2006, 12.1 million people around the globe took a cruise in this $47 billion industry, up from 11.2 million in 2005 and 10.6 million in 2004. Bigger and better equipped ships are being built in order to provide more varied facilities for the different age groups and cultures and also to appeal to wider income brackets. Royal Caribbean International's *Freedom of the Seas*, for example, is longer than three football fields and 15 stories high with a pool area featuring a stationary "wave" big enough to surf on for its 4370 guests. Most Caribbean island docks are not big enough to accommodate it so it has to anchor offshore and send passengers to land in smaller boats.

Traditionally, cruises were the preserve of the rich and famous who travelled in luxury with no financial or time restraints on such vessels as the *Lusitania* and the *Queen Elizabeth II*. Nowadays, bigger ships can improve company profits, since economies of scale in purchasing and operating expenses reduce overhead costs. Thus, cruise lines with the latest 3000 passenger mega-ships can offer all-inclusive fares for about $100 per person per day, less than half the cost on most small ships and comparable to resorts on shore. This new trend toward

SNAPSHOT *continued*

bigger ships is not just about transporting tourists from one port to the next. It is about providing a complete floating resort, with simulated "town squares," huge pools, activities and hobbies, kids' clubs and entertainment, spas and gyms, and diverse restaurants and bars, as well as a variety of standards of accommodation to suit every pocket. Carnival Cruise Lines' latest 3100 passenger ship, *Carnival Valor*, for example, boasts a shopping centre commensurate with an affluent urban neighbourhood with cocktail lounges and coffee shops, sushi bar, dance club, and a casino.

Cruise lines are differentiating, too, in featured activities, competing with entertainment favoured by land-based resorts. Cirque du Soleil has performed on Celebrity Cruises ships; MSC Cruises has employed Toronto Blue Jays manager Cito Gaston, to lead the lineup in a seven-night baseball theme cruise; and Princess, Silversea, offer "healthy" cruises with special low-fat, low-calorie menus as well as keep-fit activities such as yoga, pilates, aerobics, kickboxing, and generous gym and spa facilities.

Huge capacities lead to problems, of course, especially when more than 3000 passengers want to disembark simultaneously at port. Traffic control, with tickets issued specifying each passenger's docking time, has now been implemented by most large ships to limit such bottlenecks. Environmental concerns are also increasing with a mega-ship's waste equalling that of a small city, yet not governed by the same anti-pollution laws as land-based municipalities.

Future plans are for even bigger, super-mega ships holding more than 5000 passengers. Carnival Cruises has projected that its "Pinnacle Project" will double its top capacity to date and outstrip Royal Caribbean's *Freedom*-class ships. The Cruise Bowl, an imaginative project designed by John McNeece, envisages a self-sufficient floating resort, convention centre, and sports arena that would never have to dock on land. Up to 12 000 passengers would arrive and leave by smaller boats and stay long or short term. However, such projects are not in development yet due to huge upfront costs in engineering and building.

Utilizing cruise ships to solve the shortage of nursing-home beds for North American baby boomers is another recent trend. Royal Caribbean has social programs catering to seniors on its year-long Caribbean packages. And several cruise lines have begun selling shipboard condominiums where seniors can enjoy travel, varied food, and entertainment while also having round-the-clock care. While 90 percent of cruises are still sold through travel agencies, many of those tickets are now sold over the Internet using websites such as CruiseCompete.com, where consumers pick a ship and a sail date, get quotes from agents online, and then book the best deal. CruiseCompete sold 24 000 cabins in 2006.

Furthermore, the Chinese cruise industry is looking towards the future. A new "love boat for millionaires" is inviting China's growing number of eligible male millionaires to join a matchmaking boat cruise that promises "good-looking and desirable" women. The love boat service was launched in Shanghai in November 2006 and sails along Shanghai's Huangpu River. Organizer Xu Tianli said that the men had to be worth at least 2 million yuan ($265 000) and only women "who were attractive in every category" could participate.

Sources: Cruise industry looking toward record year in 2007 with 12 new ships. (2007, January 25). *TravelWeek*, 2; Columbus Travel. (2005). *Columbus cruise and port review*. Columbus Travel Publishing: Kent, UK; Staples, S. (2004, 27 October). Cruise ships touted as future old-age homes. *National Post*, A11; China love boat for millionaires. (2006, 14 November). BBC News. news.bbc.co.uk/go/pr/fr/2/hi/business/6146776.stm (September 2007).

Demographic Trends

In terms of demographics, the world population is forecast to reach 8.9 billion people by 2050, with the most populous nations being India, China, Pakistan, Indonesia, and Nigeria. Although this population growth will be driven by Asia and Africa, over the next 20 years the key markets for outbound travel will remain Europe, Asia, and the Americas. One of the most significant implications of demographic change in this century is the aging of the world's population. The world median age is projected to rise from 26 years in 2000 to 44 years by 2100.[2]

Table 13.1 shows the forecast changes in the age structure of Canada. The figure indicates the rise in the retirement-age population, from 13 percent of the population in 2000 to 21 percent by 2026 and 24.5 percent in 2051. In Canada, as well as in Europe, the United States, and Japan, the aged also form the wealthiest segment of society, and this will have a positive impact on the travel industry. Off-season tourism by seniors will help to smooth out the annual cycle in cash flow for hotels, motels, resorts, and other travel businesses. However, this segment will also require special amenities, such as extra help with transportation and baggage, faucet handles that can be operated by arthritic hands, and larger signs and menus with easier-to-read type. Boomers' health problems mean there will be an increasing demand for diabetic, salt-free, lactose-free, and other specialized diets.

Table 13.1

Forecast Age Structure of the Canadian Population (000s)

YEAR	0–14	15–64	65+	TOTAL
1996	5992 (20.2%)	20 098 (67.7%)	3582 (12.1%)	29 672
2000	5869 (19.1%)	21 018 (68.3%)	3863 (12.6%)	30 750
2006	5527 (17.1%)	22 400 (67.7%)	4302 (13.3%)	32 229
2016	5241 (15.2%)	23 477 (68.2%)	5702 (16.6%)	34 420
2026	5382 (14.9%)	23 056 (63.7%)	7753 (21.4%)	36 191
2036	5203 (14.0%)	22 765 (61.5%)	9067 (24.5%)	37 035
2051	5053 (13.7%)	22 440 (60.9%)	9366 (25.4%)	36 860

Source: Statistics Canada. (2001, March 13). Population Projections. *The Daily.* www.statcan.ca/Daily/English/010313/d010313a.htm (September 2007).

An aging population does not mean that tourism marketers should ignore other cohorts. According to the World Youth Student and Educational Travel Confederation (WYSE), young travellers are the travel industry's fastest growing sector, representing more than 20 percent of all international visitors. WYSE say that these adventurous young backpackers stay longer, spend more, seek out alternative destinations, and enjoy a wider mix of travel experiences compared with average tourists. In 2007, WYSE launched a partnership with the World Tourism Organization (UNWTO) to promote and develop this multi-million dollar industry by encouraging governments to actively support and develop youth tourism products and services.

Changing family structures will also have an effect on tourism products and cost structure. Over the next 15 years there will be more flexible travel format and cost structures to suit different family compositions. However, family travel (adults with children) is expected to grow at a faster rate than all forms of leisure travel, as both parents and grandparents continue to look at travel as one way in which to "reunite" families in a contemporary world that is increasingly dominated by the demands of work.

Behavioural Trends

life caching

desire of individuals to convert experiences into images and stories

The desire for experiences has been mentioned in Chapter 2 and is expanded on in a separate section in this chapter. But, in addition to collecting experiences, there is the phenomenon of **life caching**, the increasing desire of individuals to convert those experiences into images and stories, which in return enable them to engage others — whether to please, convince, or gain status. Rapid improvements in technology are allowing consumers to capture, store, collect, and display their holiday experiences to friends or family — or even the entire world. Digital scrapbooking is one way that consumers can capture moments and create layouts and art that transforms experiences into memories (see www.digitalscrapbookplace.com).

Technology is also affecting the way travel is purchased. As the Internet grows internationally, so will its use by the tourism industry. By 2011, 38 percent of travel revenue sold in the U.S. will be done online, according to a report by JupiterResearch.[3] The company predicts that $150 billion in travel will be sold online in the U.S. in 2011, growing from $100 billion in 2006. Factors that will spur online spending are greater discretionary income, increasingly sophisticated products available online, and improved security for online bookings. Higher fares and an increase in people flying have driven total air revenue to $162 billion in 2006, with $58 billion of that sold online. JupiterResearch predicts that this figure will grow to $85 billion in 2011. Online bookings for hotels will also rise. In 2005, Internet sales represented 18 percent of Best Western's total business, and that percentage can only grow in the years ahead.[4]

The "World of Travel in 2020" study, referred to above, gives some insight into the consumer of the future. It suggests that the "one size fits all" approach will no longer work and, in their pursuit for individualism, consumers will look for new experiences such as controlled danger, unusual environments and cultures, personal or physical improvement, and emotional development. They will not wish to revisit the same place. Loyalty to a travel supplier will be driven by an intermediary's ability to deliver a fresh stream of one-time experiential vacations. The twin goals of individualism and experience will present growing demand from European and North American consumers for increasingly specialized holidays that combine unusual experiences and the potential for personal development. For example, a visit to the turtle sanctuary in Brazil, described in the *Snapshot*, will be typical of the niche offers that experience-seeking travellers will be purchasing.

The study points to a trend toward inconspicuous consumption in the developed world with a desire by people to express their identity in more subtle ways than in the past. Visible expressions of status are becoming less important and, instead, a more fluid and less elitist concept of luxury is emerging that is driven by consumer concerns about authenticity, experience, and individualism. Increasingly, luxury is about the pursuit of authentic and exotic experiences and services, rather than scarcely available, high-value goods. Intangibles such as time and experience will therefore define the luxury holiday of the future, creating challenges for companies that currently offer more traditional luxury holidays that focus on exclusivity and price.

Hand in hand with the shift toward inconspicuous consumption is a greater awareness of issues such as sustainable development, ecotourism, and ethical consumption. It is expected that ethical initiatives will enter the mainstream and take on a different dimension as consumers demand more responsible behaviour from tour operators and airlines. In a 2007 survey of Canadian consumers, two-thirds said they were likely to change their shopping habits to purchase more environmentally friendly goods and services, even if it means paying a premium price.[5] British Columbians were the most likely to change, at 83 percent, followed by Ontarians at 78 percent and Albertans at 75 percent.

In the coming decades, the world needs to develop and adopt new, low-emission and low-carbon energy resources. Transport and accommodation account for a significant proportion of energy consumption by the tourism industry. As a result, it is likely that there will be some innovative alternative-energy solutions for tourism, likely to begin appearing in the world's more environmentally minded countries, such as Sweden and Germany. The airline industry, in particular, is being encouraged to minimize its environmental impact through better technology, operations, and infrastructure. Many airlines now offer consumers the chance to offset the environmental impact of their flights. In Canada, Air Canada offers consumers the choice to reduce the environmental impact of their travel in cooperation with Zerofootprint, a non-for-profit organization that operates carbon offset programs. WestJet does things a little differently. When customers book WestJet tickets via Offsetters, WestJet gives a small amount to Offsetters, which invests the cash in renewable energy efficiency projects.[6]

Other sectors are likely to adopt green policies in an effort to operate in an environmentally friendly manner. In 2006, Starwood Capital announced plans to develop a new hotel chain called *1*. Hotels will be designed from the inside out to be as eco-friendly as available technology can make them. The Hotel Association of Canada (HAC) has the Green Key Eco-Rating Program, and by the end of 2007 had between 1200 and 1500 hotels participating in the program. Furthering its commitment to environmental responsibility, Fairmont has made it easy to stage green events with its Eco-Meet program. Designed to help organizations reduce the environmental footprints of the business travel industry, Eco-Meet showcases four areas where companies can reduce their impact on the environment and raise the awareness of attendees. Eco-service provides "disposable-free" food and beverage services and recycling stations in the meeting rooms. Eco-cuisine provides menus that incorporate local, seasonal, and organically grown foods. Eco-programming features team-building activities and guest speakers and eco-accommodation offers a greener place to stay after the meeting is over.

Destinations will also become more responsible. The *Profile* in this chapter shows how Machu Picchu in Peru is limiting access to preserve the environment, and more destinations are likely to follow suit. The Kenya Tourism Board, for example, has launched a program to curb visitor numbers and preserve the fragile environment of the Masai Mara National Reserve. This is known as demarketing, using advertising to slow the demand for products or services.

Finally, the "World of Travel in 2020" report suggests that streamlining the travel process to minimize travel stress will hold much higher appeal to the time-poor traveller of the future. Consumers will demand more convenient flight schedules, the ability to check in and have a boarding pass before getting to the airport, better connections, online visas, and a waiting private car transfer or a "good to go" rental car. The study also suggests that personal service will increasingly outweigh price as the key differentiator.

SNAPSHOT

TARGETING THE GREEN TOURIST: PRAIA DO FORTE IN BRAZIL

Historically, when a type of rural subsistence (agriculture, mining, fishing, for example) becomes obsolete in the modern world, communities collapse and towns dwindle as the work force moves elsewhere. However, there are some cases where preserving what used to be destroyed can actually regenerate a community way beyond its

origins. Praia Do Forte, on the northeast coast of Brazil, is such a case. Turtle eggs, meat, and shells used to be the mainstay of their village economy via a significant fishing industry. The same items are still prized commodities today, but now they must be in their original pristine condition — i.e., alive and thriving — in order to satisfy environmental concerns about endangered species as well as tourism needs.

With international pressure from turtle conservationists developing through the 1970s, a two-year survey launched in 1980 identified the crucial situation regarding sea turtles along the Brazilian coastline. The Tamar Project was established in the Bahia village of Praia Do Forte, along with other bases in Espirito Santo and Sergipe, to learn vital turtle nesting and reproductive habits from residents and fishers, to educate the locals environmentally, and to hire fishers to protect their former prey. The empiric knowledge of the locals, together with the science of the researchers, created today's conservationism whereby thousands of baby turtles are released each year and the females are able to complete their reproductive cycles without harm.

Despite initial suspicion, alarm, and distrust from local populations, the Tamar Project has led to a fruitful partnership and alliance

SNAPSHOT *continued*

between conservationists and locals in saving the sea turtles in Brazil as well as creating new ways of subsistence, preserving local culture, and offering jobs. Nationwide, the Tamar Project has 20 stations, with visitor centres, shops selling themed merchandise, and onsite restaurants, providing 1200 jobs, 85 percent of which are filled by fishers and their relatives. It is administered by the Instituto Brasileiro do Meio Ambiente e dos Recursos Naturais Renováveis (IBAMA) in partnership with the Pro-Tamar Foundation, monitoring 1000 kilometres of beach across eight Brazilian states. Tamar also supports cultural activities to preserve village traditions and values, providing an ongoing educational program and promoting information services to further job creation and alternative sources of income.

Tamar staff live in the village centres year round, reflecting their status as pivotal members of the local communities. Integrating the project and its personnel into the everyday life of the regions has been intrinsic to its success both in conservation efforts and in improving the lives of local residents. Community outreach projects, such as school presentations of videos and slides, hatchling release ceremonies (popular among locals and tourists), and festivals, all help in allying preservation of the healthy marine ecosystem with more personal materialistic goals.

Praia Do Forte, just 72 kilometres from Salvador, has become the eco-friendly tourist resort most favoured by Bahian weekenders and the local tourist market as well as an international tourism destination. Today the "Projecto Tamar" is the resort's biggest attraction resulting in a burgeoning beach resort of quaint *pousadas* (small inns), eclectic restaurants, stylish boutiques, and lively bars all lining the three main cobbled streets. Boasting a beautiful sandy, coconut palm–lined beach with great swimming and snorkeling in the warm azure and turquoise waters, Praia Do Forte is now a source of far greater levels of income than in its previous incarnation as a fishing hamlet.

The turtle sanctuary at Praia Do Forte is set right on the sand with a large shop, several themed restaurants, and a visitor information centre. Tourists can view between 15 and 30 turtles of various species in different stages of maturity for a small fee. There is a hatchery, video information, and a "Mini Guide" program providing environmental education and experience for the young people of the village. Alongside the turtle preservation schemes, the resort has the Reserva De Sapiranga, where rare orchids and bromeliads are protected within 1482 acres of secondary Atlantic forest. This is also a sanctuary for endangered animals, with more than 187 species of native birds, as well as various indigenous monkeys. Limited jeep, raft, and canoe tours are permitted in the nature reserve.

Sources: Marcovaldi, M. A., & Marcovaldi, G. G. (1999). Marine turtles of Brazil: The history and structure of Projecto TAMAR-IBAMA. *Biological Conservation 91*, 35–41.

TOURISM MARKETING IN THE EXPERIENTIAL ECONOMY

According to many marketing experts, marketing in the 21st century is all about delivering the customer experience. Future generations of consumers will have more discretionary income, less time, and more choices, and will display wholly new spending patterns, depending on age, geography, and wealth. Customers will be looking for an experience, and not just a product. The "World of Travel in 2020" study predicts that travellers of the future will seek, on average, up to four very different experiences a year. A passion for "doing" rather than "having" will double the number of consumers flying by 2020. Over the next 15 years people will increasingly want to be differentiated by what they do, not what they buy, and this will drive a desire for experience-driven travel.

This book contains many examples of such experience-driven travel, such as war tourism in Vietnam, volunteer tourism, space tourism, nostalgia tourism, VocationVacations, and film tourism. Another example comes from Cape Town, South Africa, where township tourism has increased hugely in popularity since South Africa's multiracial elections of 1994. More than 80 percent of Cape Town's 250 licensed tour operators take tourists into the sprawling settlements that were set up by the old apartheid government and that are still home to the majority of the population. In 2006, 320 000 people went on a township tour for the "cultural experience."

In a recent survey of 362 firms by Bain & Company, 80 percent believed they delivered a "superior experience" to their customers. When customers were asked, it was a very different story: they said that only 8 percent of companies were really delivering.[7] To close that gap, companies need to put customers at the heart of the organization, and engage in experiential marketing. **Experiential marketing** gives consumers in-depth experiences to provide them with sufficient information to make a purchase decision.[8] It is widely argued that, as the science of marketing evolves, experiential marketing will become the dominant tool of the future. The difference between traditional and experiential marketing can be highlighted in a number of ways. First, the focus is on customer experiences and lifestyles, which provides sensory, emotional, cognitive, and relational values to the consumer. Chapter 2 described how organizations such as Walt Disney are explicitly designing and promoting experiences. Second, there is a focus on creating synergies between meaning, perception, consumption, and brand loyalty. Third, it is argued that customers are not rational decision makers, but rather are driven by a combination of rationality and emotion. Finally, it is argued that experiential marketing requires a more diverse set of research methods in order to understand consumers.

In order to promote tourism experiences, tourism marketers will have to think beyond traditional advertising techniques. Promoting experiences via the Internet, through channels such as Second Life (see *Spotlight*), is one new way tourism providers can introduce products to consumers. Product placement (see Chapter 9) is another promotional tool growing in significance for tourism and hospitality providers. *Marketing in Action* in this chapter shows how the Bahamas Ministry of Tourism fully supports the use of film locations as part of its publicity and as an effective communications tool to attract tourists.

One emerging variation on product placement is **tryvertising**, the practice of making consumers familiar with products and services by trying them out, so they can make a purchase decision based on experience.[9] Hotels, for example, are partnering with luxury car makers to offer high-end model test drives to guests during their stay. The Ritz Carlton offers the Key to Luxury program in cooperation with Mercedes Benz. Hotels are also making deals with furniture companies. Sweden's IKEA has partnered with France's ETAP Hotels to equip all 60 of their budget hotels in Germany with an IKEA room and a public quiet space, also furnished by IKEA. One company that has responded to this growth area is Vacations Connections, which offers an organized approach to in-room placement of samples targeted at vacationers. Carnival Cruise Lines is one of their clients. As an extension of this trend, in the future there will likely be "lifestyle" hotels built around themes and co-branded with large companies, for example, an athletic-themed Nike hotel brought to you by Starwood.

experiential marketing

marketing initiatives that give consumers in-depth experiences to provide them with sufficient information to make a purchase decision

tryvertising

the practice of making consumers familiar with products and services by trying them out, so they can make a purchase decision based on experience

Experiential advertising requires more creative expression on the part of advertisers. Campaigns of the past were built on bricks and mortar, whereas today advertisers are trying to touch emotions and get into the consumer's psyche. Advertising now is more about reasons why people do things and less about rational things that people factor into their decision making. An example was given in Chapter 8 with Las Vegas promising "What Happens in Vegas Stays in Vegas," but another comes from Hilton Hotels, which won a 'Best of Show' award in the 2006 HSMAI Adrian Awards Competition for its 'Travel Should Take You Places' ad campaign. Instead of trying to entice guests through rational product attributes, Hilton decided to engage them at an emotional level, winning their hearts rather than their heads. The big idea was that the very nature of travel is transformative, and that transformation should be an enriching experience, changing you for the better. The ads (see example in Figure 13.1) remind the consumer that travel is more than A to B if we open our eyes to travel's possibilities and opportunities. The campaign resulted in increased brand differentiation and brand energy, and translated into concrete business results for Hilton Hotels.

Figure 13.1   Hilton Print Advertisement

Beyond the creative expression, other influences have altered the course of tourism advertising. The 1980s was all about broadcast and mass advertising, and the 1990s was the decade of the Internet. However, in today's age of MP3 players, personal digital assistances (PDAs), digital recorders, remote controls, podcasts, blogs, wikis, and video on demand, the audiences are narrower and fragmented, and tune in or out as they please. Advertising has to capture an audience in mere seconds. One hotel label that has experienced success with podcasts (downloadable audio recordings) is Desires Hotels operated by Tecton Hospitality. About 70 percent of guests at Desires Hotels are in the post–baby boom demographic of Generation X and executives had noticed that they were responsive to social media, or social networking, via the Internet on sites such as MySpace and TripAdvisor. Desires properties in Miami, San Juan, and Atlanta began to record a podcast each week about that week's upcoming events in nightlife, restaurants, and concerts. In the three-month period following the start of the podcasts, more than 100 000 people visited the podcast section of the hotels' websites and the click-through rate to the reservations booking engine from the podcasts was a healthy 5 percent.[10]

As for the future, perhaps the movie *Minority Report* (set in 2054) provides a glimpse of advertising to look out for in the not-too-distant future. Projecting out from today's marketing and media technologies — Web cookies, global positioning system (GPS) devices, Bluetooth-enabled cell phones, personal video recorders, and barcode scanners — the Steven Spielberg film gives shape to an advertising-saturated society where billboards call out to you on a first-name basis, cereal boxes broadcast animated commercials, newspapers deliver news instantly over a broadband wireless network, and holographic hosts greet you at retail stores where biometric retina scans deduct the cost of goods from your bank account. So tourists of the future may be walking past a travel agent and a radio frequency identification (RFID) scanner will check their credit cards, link to their travel history, and text message, or even call out, an invitation tailored precisely to their interests. Similarly, people may be driving near a theme park or other tourist attractions, and the car's navigation system will light up with an offer for discount tickets. Already, Chicago's O'Hare International Airport has interactive billboards where people can touch a screen to obtain weather in their destination city or get up-to-date news.

MARKETING IN ACTION

PROMOTING DESTINATIONS THROUGH FILM: THE CASE OF THE BAHAMAS

Placing a destination in a film is the ultimate in tourism product placement, and the Bahamas Ministry of Tourism fully supports the use of film locations as part of its publicity and as an effective communications tool to attract tourists. The Bahamas realized the potential of promoting tourism through films after the Beatles filmed *Help* there in 1964. Now the ministry gets actively involved immediately it receives a script. For example, $18 million was invested on the recent film *After the Sunset,* starring Pierce Brosnan, in order to ensure maximum exposure for the island. "We consider tourism as our main

MARKETING IN ACTION *continued*

business and we hold it up as our core industry. Filming is part of the communication and publicity drive and tourism is the engine that powers it all," explains Basil Smith, communications director for the Ministry of Tourism.

"The year 2004 was a great one for the film industry in the Bahamas," says Craig Woods, the Bahamas film commissioner. "We had three movies back to back: *After the Sunset, Into the Blue,* and *Pirates of the Caribbean II.*" Woods is keen to land television series as well as films. Landing a weekly TV show such as *Triangle* or *Troubadour* means longer commitments than are typical in movie productions, which are usually one-shot deals.

A number of film tourism attractions exist on the islands for film tourists to visit. For example, the Hilton in Nassau boasts a "Double-O" Suite, stocked with James Bond movies, soundtracks, posters, movie stills, and memorabilia from the filming. There are also Bond books, a special bathrobe, and, of course, a martini. The hotel has a "Live and Let Dive" package, which includes dive visits to the 36-metre freighter that was sunk for the movie *Never Say Never Again* and the Vulcan bomber airplane from *Thunderball.*

In fact, dive sites are the most popular film tourism attractions in the Bahamas. Stuart Cove, who is a regular stunt diver for the Bond movies, takes 50 000 divers and snorkellers every year to his diving/film location on the south coast of New Providence Island. He says, "Production of film, TV, and commercials is a very important part of our business, and very important for marketing. We emphasize the connection to film and television in all of our marketing material — in the brochures and on the website. Divers just love the connection to the James Bond movie sites, and our monthly news releases consistently refer to films and TV programs being made here."

Cove attempts to keep movie locations and memorabilia to attract more tourists and also to add to the quality and differentiation of their diving experience. The film *Flipper* was based at his site and he manages to keep his dock much as it was in the movie: "We have learned our lesson with the movie sets. The producers destroyed the set for *For Your Eyes Only,* but since then we have tried to negotiate right from the start to keep any sets used in movies." Photographer Claudia Pellarini says that about 90 percent of divers purchase photographs and some spend hundreds of dollars. "Some of the most popular photographs are those of divers in the film sets. For example, they just love their photo taken in the *Thunderball* set." The photo shop itself turns over $500 000 a year.

Movie producers were attracted to the Bahamas initially for various economic reasons and environmental exigencies. Cove

·**MARKETING IN ACTION** *continued*

claims that "the main reason is that we have the perfect location. The natural beauty of the Islands is a terrific pull — the Bahamas sells itself — and we are very close to the mainland. There is also a beneficial tax situation, and we can supply labour very easily and very cheaply. In fact, the producers can get much better value all round by coming here than they could on mainland U.S." The Atlantis Resort gives free rooms in exchange for exposure in films. An example was *After the Sunset,* where the resort gave three months of rooms to the crew in exchange for very favourable shots in the film.

Most of the film and television business is generated through word of mouth, according to Cove, and these days there is normally no charge for his assistance: "We are very aware that the exposure these films and TV programs give Stuart Cove is critical for our business."

Morgan O'Sullivan, film commission consultant, says that the Ministry of Tourism is now looking at the possibility of producing movie maps related to locations particularly in relation to *Pirates of the Caribbean* and also movie tours. The James Bond genre, especially, draws large numbers of tourists to the Bahamas, so a Bond tour would be the first one launched.

Sources: Personal correspondence with Basil Smith, director of communications, Bahamas Ministry of Tourism, January 1, 2006, Craig Woods, film commissioner, Bahamas Film and Television Commission, January 1, 2006, Stuart Cove, Stuart Cove's Dive Bahamas, January 13, 2006, Claudia Pellarini, Stuart Cove's Dive Bahamas January 13, 2006, Opal Gibson, director of business development, British Colonial Hilton, January 11, 2006, & Morgan O'Sullivan, co-managing director, World 2000 Entertainment Ltd., January 11, 2006.

RESPONSIBLE MARKETING OF TOURISM

The tourism marketer is likely to be involved in the process of developing an attraction or a destination, in terms of either building new resorts or rejuvenating old ones. Part of the process involves estimating future demand, as in a feasibility study, but increasing emphasis is being placed upon evaluating the likely impacts — such as direct or indirect economic impact — of any development. Techniques have also been developed to monitor other impacts, such as the environmental and social impacts of tourism. Common analytical frameworks include an environmental audit, environmental impact analysis, carrying capacity, and community assessment techniques. It is beyond the scope of this book to cover these techniques in detail, but the tourism marketer needs to have knowledge of the most current models and techniques applied to the evaluation of environmental and social impact.

sustainable tourism

tourism that can maintain its viability in an area indefinitely and does not damage the environment

A tourism marketer must also have an understanding of the principles of **sustainable tourism**, which can maintain its viability in an area indefinitely and does not damage the environment. Richard Butler describes sustainable tourism development as "tourism which is developed and maintained in an area in such a manner and at such a scale that it remains viable over an indefinite period and does not degrade or alter the environment (human and physical) in which it exists to such a degree that it prohibits the successful development and well-being of other activities and processes."[11]

The *Profile* in this chapter shows how officials in Peru are taking measures to ensure that tourism at Machu Picchu is sustainable. The *Snapshot* on Praia Do Forte also shows how a destination is preserving the natural environment — in this case, turtles — in order to be sustainable. Similarly, it was mentioned in Chapter 11 that the Bahamas have calculated the lifetime value of a healthy shark to be $200 000 to the tourism industry. That is certainly an incentive to keep them alive, regardless of the shark's value to the ecosystem.

The theory of sustainable tourism emphasizes the critical importance of environmental stewardship. Similarly, a common thread running through all of the existing literature on competitiveness suggests that, to be competitive, an organization must be sustainable from an environmental perspective. However, tourism organizations and destinations are generally still inexperienced in handling environmental issues creatively. A substantial fraction of environmental spending relates to the regulatory struggle itself and not to improving the environment, particularly in the tourism sector. But corporate managers in certain industry sectors have begun to consider environmental management as a critical component for sustaining competitive advantage, and in the tourism industry it is time for managers to start recognizing environmental improvement as an economic and competitive opportunity, rather than an annoying cost or inevitable threat.

If environmental improvement is to provide a competitive opportunity, an organization must consider **responsible environmental marketing**, which balances environmental initiatives and environmental communication to achieve a sustainable competitive advantage. Unfortunately, there has been no consistent approach to environmental marketing practices in tourism. Some companies neglect their environmental obligations, perhaps because of a lack of guidelines and examples of best practice, or perhaps because they don't understand the benefits. Others exploit environmental communication for short-term gains or fail to tell visitors about their environmental initiatives. Many studies indicate that environmental considerations are now a significant element of the destination-choosing process, and much of what first-time visitors learn about a destination's environmental qualities that may influence their choice depends on the effectiveness of information and the motivation stimulated by commercial brochures or websites.

Figure 13.2 is model of responsible marketing that managers in the tourism industry can use to improve their environmental marketing practices. The model is based on previous literature in marketing and in strategic and environmental management, and it adopts the view that an organization or destination can be plotted on a two-by-two matrix to identify its position regarding responsible marketing. The vertical axis represents environmental action and the horizontal axis represents communication of these activities. Organizations can take up one of four theoretical positions within the model. They can be classified as *inactive* when they tend not to see the benefits of allocating any resources toward environmental activities and when they have a low level of commitment to both environmental improvement and communication of environmental activities. Those that see the benefits of environmental action (perhaps for regulatory purposes) but fail to communicate these efforts are *reactive*. Organizations that exploit consumer interests in environmentally friendly products without considering resource characteristics, environmental ethics, or a long-term perspective are

responsible environmental marketing

marketing that balances environmental initiatives and environmental communication to achieve a sustainable competitive advantage seen as *exploitive*. The position in the model most likely to remain sustainable (and competitive) is that in which both environmental action and environmental communication of this action are high, and these organizations are labelled as *proactive*. In the proactive position, products and services are developed sensitively, with regard to their long-term future, and consumers are aware (both before purchase and during the visit) of the concern for the resources involved.

Environmental Communication

		Low	High
Environmentally Responsible Action	**Low**	**Inactive** No support or involvement from top management Environmental management not necessary No environmental reporting No employee environmental training or involvement	**Exploitive** Some involvement of top management Environmental issues dealt with only when necessary External reporting but no internal reporting Little employee training or involvement
	High	**Reactive** Some involvement of top management Environmental management is a worthwhile function Internal reporting but no external reporting Some employee environmental training or involvement	**Proactive** Top management involved in environmental issues Environmental management is a priority item Regular internal and external reporting including an environmental plan or report Employee environmental training or involvement encouraged

Figure 13.2   A Model of Responsible Marketing

It is important to recognize that an organization's position in the model may only be temporary, as it may be in transit between one place in the model and the next. Furthermore, there is likely to be a variety of contingency factors that will affect the position on the model. Previous research suggests that these influences include the level of environmental pressures from stakeholders, managerial interpretations of environmental issues, the level of environmental regulations, and the size and the financial position of the organization.

PROFILE

MACHU PICCHU IN PERU LIMITS ACCESS

Over-popularity as a tourism attraction can often lead to a destination becoming the environmentally unsustainable victim of its own success. Machu Picchu, Peru, an Inca site rediscovered in 1911, is fast seeing the detrimental impacts caused by its international popularity. The Peruvian government is keen to market the UNESCO World Heritage site in order to generate tourist dollars. However, if the destination is to remain intact and therefore viable for the future, the government needs to look at sustainability that involves limiting access.

Back in 1992 only 9000 tourists visited the ruins all year, but by 2002 the figure had risen to 150 000 and reached around 400 000 by 2005. There was little restriction to either access or visitor behaviour within the sacred sites, which reportedly generates $47 million annually for the Peruvian economy. Aguas Calientes, the village at the base of Machu Picchu, mushroomed in size, garbage lined the banks of the nearby Urubamba River, and the Inca Trail had deteriorated due to many years of unrestricted over-use. Overcrowding, erosion, and the exploitation of local people as guides and porters were all endemic before January 2001, when the government finally intervened and initiated a system of regulations and permits.

Increasing pressure from UNESCO, the World Tourism Organization (UNWTO), and numerous nongovernment agencies has encouraged a limit on the number of visitors to the ancient Inca ruins. Laws limit numbers on the trail to 500 per day and visitors must join guided tours with registered companies to ensure adherence to conservation regulations. In 2000 the World Monuments Fund, a conservationist group in New York, numbered the ruins among the 100 most endangered sites, but removed them from the list when the Peruvian government regulated the Inca Trail. UNESCO continually threatens to put Machu Picchu on its list of World Heritage in Danger list, a designation meant to encourage immediate corrective action. Archeologists and preservationists alike regularly bemoan the deterioration caused by overuse.

Since the 2001 regulations were introduced, conditions are better for trekkers, porters, and the Inca Trail itself, despite the continued rise in numbers. As a result of lobbies from the Inka Porter Project, a nongovernmental organization (NGO), wages for porters have increased and work conditions, first aid provision, and language tuition have all improved. Moreover, tour operators must use assigned campsites with proper toilet facilities, remove all garbage, use only propane for fuel, maintain a ratio of one guide per seven tourists, and limit weight loads to 25 kilograms per porter. Prices are rising to visit the site — general admission is now $35 per person and the Inca Trail permit has gone up from $20 to $70 in order to pay for trail maintenance, monitoring of regulations and better facilities.

Machu Picchu is promoted by Peruvians as an intrinsic part of Peru on the official destination website Peru Tourism. Responsible tour operators, such as G.A.P Adventures and Trek Holidays, include tours to Peru's most famous destination. G.A.P promotes Machu Picchu by appealing to travellers who are aware of ecotourism and sustainability. Published literature plays a key role in promoting Machu Picchu as a tourist destination.

Nonfiction literature about the ruins also encourages visitors as well as films, such as Alberto Granado's screenplay *The Motorcycle Diaries,* which eulogized Machu Picchu and the land of the Incas and has had a huge and continuing impact on international visitor numbers. A 2003 music video for Gloria Estefan's song *Wrapped* was such a good advertisement for both Machu Picchu and Peru as a whole that it appeared, mistakenly, to be a government-sponsored project. The site is also projected positively in many documentaries and educational videos focusing on its history and its dramatic rediscovery.

However, even filming can further the deterioration of the ancient ruins while at the same time paradoxically promoting tourism success. Recent media attention in the form of commercials and music videos has helped boost tourist numbers but during actual filming of a Cusquena beer commercial in 2001, a sacred sundial was damaged accidentally, resulting in criminal charges against the production company for using a prohibited crane.

Sources: Rachowiecki, R. & Beech, C. (2004). *Lonely Planet: Peru*, 5th ed. Lonely Planet Publications: London, 209; Leffel, T. (2005). *Saving Machu Picchu: Responsible tourism is a 3-way deal.* www .transitionsabroad.com/publications/magazine/0511/ saving_machu_picchu.shtml (September 2006); Roach, J. (2002, April 15). Machu Picchu under threat from pressures of tourism. *National Geographic News.* news.nationalgeographic.com/news/2002/04/0415_ 020415_machu.html (September 2002).

CAUSE-RELATED MARKETING IN TOURISM

Cause-related marketing, said to be "corporate philanthropy organized to increase the bottom line," is a rapidly expanding trend in marketing communications.[12] It is growing at a time when the public is increasingly cynical about big business. It is basically a marketing program that strives to achieve two objectives — improve corporate performance and help worthy causes — by linking fundraising for the benefit of a cause to the purchase of the organization's products or services.

It was an American Express campaign that signified the inception of cause-related marketing in 1981. American Express joined with a nonprofit group to promote fine arts in San Francisco. Profits from increased use of American Express cards were donated to the organization. The success of this campaign led to the first national cause-related marketing campaign in 1983 between American Express and the Statue of Liberty–Ellis Island Foundation. The results were $2 million donated to the foundation and an increase in American Express card usage of 28 percent. American Express called its link with charity "cause-related marketing" and registered the term as a service mark with the U.S. Patent Office.

Cause-related marketing has spread rapidly over the last two decades and is not only used by product-oriented corporations. Other industries such as education, health care, human services, and community and civic affairs are becoming active users of the practice. Organizations use cause-related marketing to contribute to the well-being of society and to associate themselves with a respected cause that will reflect positively on their image. Companies, and their brands, can benefit from strategic alignments with causes or with not-for-profit organizations. It is hoped the emotional attributes associated with cause-linked brands differentiate them from their rivals (sometimes referred to as "cause branding").

Cause-related marketing efforts can be categorized into autonomously branded, co-branded, house-branded, and industry-branded approaches. The distinctive features of each are summarized in Table 13.2 and discussed below.

Table 13.2

Branding Approaches to Cause-Related Marketing

Features	Autonomous	Co-Branded	House Branded	Industry Branded
Charity reputation	Established/ independent of organization	Tied to organization and charity	Company dependent	Established/ independent of industry
Organization's involvement in charity administration	None	Partial to jointly administered	Company controlled	None
Organization control over charity use of funds raised	Limited	Some influence	Complete	Limited
Strategic opportunity	Leverage external brand	Leverage brand congruence	Support existing organization/ product brand	Leverage industry brand
Cause-related marketing promotional objective	Demonstrate organization- charity congruence where not obvious	Demonstrate organization- charity brand congruence	Promote organization's commitment	Promote industry's commitment

1. Autonomously Branded Cause-Related Marketing Initiatives

Autonomously branded philanthropic collaborations are characterized by an arm's length relationship between the sponsor's brand and the brand of the charity or cause that it supports. These are the quickest and easiest kind of relationships to arrange and are the dominant form of philanthropic activity. An example is the American Express initiative described above. Generally those organizations in the tourism industry that embrace autonomous cause-related marketing are those that offer a wide range of destinations to their clients. In recent years there has been an increasing number of travel companies that collect funds to distribute to established charitable concerns. These include Abercrombie and Kent, Bales Worldwide, Intrepid Travel, and Ultimate Travel — the latter adding a "voluntary £25 contribution" to each customer booking that has resulted in an 85 percent take-up. With some of these philanthropic programs there is a link, if only a subtle one, between the program and the purchase of holidays. The Galapagos Conservation Fund created by Lindblad Expeditions provides guests with a direct solicitation envelope the night before landing, and they are offered a discount coupon of $300 on future Lindblad excursions in return for charitable contributions of $300 or more. Since 1997, guests have contributed close to $1.2 million. Early in 2007, the Metropolitan Hotel Vancouver ran a cause-related marketing initiative called "Room for Charity." The hotel donated the entire value of one night's stay to the guest's Canadian charity of choice.

2. Co-Branded Cause-Related Marketing Initiatives

In co-branded collaborations, the organization and the charity form a new brand co-sponsored and marketed by both organizations. An example of this type of branding approach is when CIBC sponsors the Run for the Cure in partnership with the Canadian Breast Cancer Foundation. Collaborations of this type are more strategic than autonomously branded programs because the organization can differentiate itself by becoming the sole category sponsor of an event or cause and co-ownership implies increased commitment and effort. In their simplest form, co-branded cause-related marketing initiatives might best be demonstrated by a tour operator and a charity jointly marketing a holiday in a chosen project area with a proportion of the money generated being used to fund the project. Wildlife conservation projects on Kenya's Masai Mara, in the Galapagos Islands, and at India's Ranthambhore Tiger Park have benefited from jointly marketed holidays with tour operators. Similar arrangements are in place elsewhere between Save the Rhino Trust Namibia and the UK tour operator Discovery Initiatives. The relationship between Born Free and Kuoni benefits additionally from both partner organizations being located in the same town, so aiding local links and marketing.

3. House-Branded Cause-Related Marketing Initiatives

With the house-branded approach "the firm takes ownership of a cause and develops an entirely new organization to deliver benefits associated with the cause."[13] Similar to private label products, house-branded charities are by definition differentiated from other charities, and in the increasingly crowded marketplace for philanthropic program partners, the organization has unfettered access to its own charity. McDonald's has a house-branded charity benefiting children — Ronald McDonald House — achieving true charitable status in the minds of consumers. In general the organizations using this strategy are well established and have a mission focused on the cause they support. Ad Terrae Gloriam (ATG) Oxford is a UK walking and cycling tour operator founded in 1979 on principles of conservation and sustainable tourism, "long before these concepts became fashionable."[14] Ten percent of its pre-tax profits are donated to its ATG Trust. The ATG Trust works with local communities to identify, develop, and complete conservation projects in areas where ATG clients travel.

4. Industry-Branded Cause-Related Marketing Initiatives

Industry-branded initiatives are those that involve contributions to a cause from the industry as a whole, rather than separate organizations. As with the house-branded cause-related marketing initiatives, few examples exist in tourism of industry-branded initiatives, but the Travel Foundation in the UK fits this typology. It was established in 2004 as a partnership among government, NGOs, and the travel industry to acknowledge the awareness of tour operators' responsibility to help protect the places that tourists visit and to ensure that the benefits of tourism reaches the local communities. The Travel Foundation is mostly funded by the commercial tourism industry, which, engages in various cause-related marketing programs, but the foundation is firmly the industry's charity. The disadvantage of the shared benefits of industry-dependent brands and the difficulty of individual organizations in leveraging those benefits may explain why only a small number of tour operators are actively committed to the Travel Foundation: many prefer to that their cause-related marketing is directed by the interests of their own staff and clients rather than by the foundation.

The Future for Cause-Related Marketing in Tourism

Despite the examples above, and research that shows travel organizations can gain competitive advantage by adopting ethical policies, the use of cause-related marketing in the tourism industry is still not widespread and remains in its infancy. However, there is evidence that tourism organizations are beginning to wake up to the threat of legislative intervention should the industry fail to address its negative impacts. For example, in 2005, British Airways encouraged passengers to offset the environmental impacts of their flights by donating a "green fee" to a partner organization that planted trees to neutralize the carbon emissions according to the distance travelled. Suspicion surrounded the introduction of the scheme, with one newspaper reporting that it was intended to "persuade the Government that it takes the issue of pollution seriously. The airline fears that ministers will seek to impose taxes on flights unless the industry is seen to act to mitigate emissions."[15] Players in the industry are also starting to recognize that taking, and then promoting, an ethical stance can be good business as it potentially enhances profits, management effectiveness, public image, and employee relations. The tourism industry also affords an excellent example of brand fit where the charitable causes supported often bring direct benefits to the company and its travelling clients.

One weakness of cause-related marketing is that it is often short term, opportunistic, and seen by some as self-serving and exploitive. It is therefore important that tourism organizations adopt a cause and make the cause an important part of the their business by integrating a non-commercial, socially redeeming value system into the their business plan and operations. Considerable attention also needs to be paid to the role of fit between the organization and the charity in philanthropic efforts. Which approach an organization adopts will often depend on the size of the organization and resources available. While the autonomously branded programs can be effective for specialist operators, co-branded approaches to cause-related marketing offer an opportunity to move away from just making donations and toward a more collaborative partnership with charitable organization partners. Industry-branded initiatives have the advantage of benefiting the industry as a whole (as well as the cause), but not individual organizations. For players in the tourism industry, the house-branded philanthropic initiative may be the most strategic of the four branding approaches because its development, promotion, and administration are entirely within the control of the sponsor.

MARKETING SPORT AND ADVENTURE TOURISM

Sport Tourism

One of the fastest growth areas in the tourism sector is sport tourism, and many destinations are seeking to capitalize on this growth. Although sport tourism is a relatively new concept, its scope of activity is far from a recent phenomenon. The notion of people travelling to participate and watch sport dates back to the ancient Olympic Games, and the practice of stimulating tourism through sport has existed for more than a century. Within the last few decades, however, destinations have begun to recognize the significant potential of sport tourism, and they are now aggressively pursuing this market niche. Broadly defined, **sport tourism** includes travel to participate in a sporting activity for recreation or competition or to observe sport or to visit a sport attraction, such as a sports hall of fame or a water park. Five major areas of sport tourism have been identified: attractions, resorts, cruises, tours, and events, each of which is discussed below.

Recent data suggest that sport tourism is a high-impact and growing segment of the Canadian tourism industry. The Canadian Sport Tourism Alliance (CSTA) estimates that sport travel generates more than $2.4 billion in domestic spending in Canada. Currently, about 200 000 sport events occur annually in this country, and nearly 40 percent of travellers participate in or attend a sport event every year. Many destinations are investing in this profitable sector of tourism. For example, in September 2002, the government of Ontario announced that it was investing $15 million in snowmobiling over four years to strengthen recreation and northern Ontario tourism. Tourism plays a key role in the economy of many rural and northern communities, and snowmobiling contributes $1 billion annually to the Ontario economy. In the same province, Brantford is branded as the "Tournament Capital of Ontario" and hosts a growing number of regional, provincial, national, and international sporting events each year that attract thousands of participants, coaches, and spectators. London, in southwestern Ontario, also considers sport to be one of the most significant contributors to the city's promotion and growth.

sport tourism

travel to participate in a sporting activity for recreation or competition or to observe sport or to visit a sport attraction

Sport Tourism Attractions

Sport tourism attractions are destinations that provide the tourist with things to see and do related to sport. Attractions could be natural (parks, mountains, wildlife) or human-made (museums, stadiums, stores). This core area of sport tourism also includes visits to a) state-of-the-art sports facilities or unique sports facilities that generally house sports events, such as stadiums, arenas, and domes; b) sport museums and halls or walls of fame dedicated to the sport heritage and to honouring sport heroes and leaders; c) sport theme parks, including water slides, summer ski jumps, and bungee jumping; d) hiking trails developed for exploring nature; and e) sport retail stores.

An example of a popular hall of fame in Canada is the Hockey Hall of Fame, founded in 1943 to establish a memorial to those who developed Canada's great winter sport — ice hockey. On June 18, 1993, the Hockey Hall of Fame opened the doors of its current home in BCE Place in Toronto. The new $35 million facility comprises 5300 square metres, including 930 square metres in the magnificently restored Bank of Montreal building located at the corner of Yonge and Front streets, with the balance housed in the concourse level at BCE Place. The new Hockey Hall of Fame quickly established a reputation as a world-class sports and entertainment facility and one of Toronto's prime tourist attractions, bringing in more than 500 000 visitors in its first year alone.

Sport Tourism Resorts

Sport tourism resorts are well-planned and integrated resort complexes that have sport or health as their primary focus and marketing strategy. In many situations, these vacation centres have high-standard facilities and services available to the sport tourist. The sport tourism resort category includes amenity and destination spas, golf and tennis resorts, and water and snow sport resorts, as well as nature retreats offering outdoor adventure and exploration. Generally speaking, these resorts have leading-edge sport equipment and facilities and offer visitors various levels of activity opportunities and educational programs led by instructors who have a great deal of expertise and personal visibility. These resorts do vary in their focus, however, ranging from those that have high-level international standards and specialize in specific and highly developed skills to campground services specializing in recreational sporting activities.

An extension of the sport resort category is sport camps. An example of such a sporting complex is Canada Olympic Park (COP) in Calgary. Since its construction in 1986, the COP has hosted thousands of sports enthusiasts from all over the world at sport camps for both amateur and professional sports participants.

Sport Tourism Cruises

The sport tourism cruise category incorporates all boat-related trips that use sports or sporting activities as their principal market strategy. Many ships built today resemble hotels and resorts and have unique sport installations. They also use guest sport celebrities as a marketing tool. To satisfy the sport tourist even further, cruise ships often arrange special transportation to provide guests with opportunities to participate in activities such as snorkelling and water skiing in unique and varied water environments. Other planned activities include provision of onboard sport competitions or modified games (e.g., a golf driving range on deck) and special presentations or clinics from invited sport celebrities. "Cruise-and-drive" programs allow tourists to board their own vehicles to facilitate transportation to desired sport destinations. Private yachts may also be chartered, which may be sailed directly to the sport destination of the sailor's choice. The use of watercraft for sporting activities (e.g., recreational and competitive sailing or jet skiing) is also an important dimension to this category.

Sport Tourism Tours

Sport tourism tours bring visitors to their favourite sport events, facilities, or destinations around the world. These tours may be self-guided or organized, depending upon access, location, and nature of the activity. For example, many ski tour packages provide air travel, accommodation, local transportation, and ski-lift tickets with no special guide or amenities. At a more organized level, some organizations specialize in travel packages that fly fans to a sports event — such as a hockey game — in another city, put them up in a hotel for a couple of nights, provide tickets to the game, arrange for a cocktail party and pre-game briefing with media as well as a post-game reception with players and coaches, and then return them safely home. This type of tour is especially appealing to sport aficionados who want to follow their team on the road or take in a major event such as the Grey Cup or Indianapolis 500, and for those whose dream is to walk the fairways of Augusta National during the Masters golf tournament. The major Canadian company in this market is Roadtrips, which boasts that it can take fans to just about any sport event in the world, from Formula One car racing to the Masters golf tournament to World Cup soccer to the Beijing Olympics. Another niche operator in the sport tourism business is The Vacation Station. The company has a retail office in Sault Ste. Marie and a wholesale office in Ancaster, Ontario. The Vacation Station offers an extensive program of ski vacations to Europe and New Zealand, and numerous cycling programs in the summer to Europe, Australia, and New Zealand. While sport devotees are the most passionate customers, corporations form the biggest part of the sport tourism tour business, since companies often reward their best employees with trips to the biggest sporting events in the world.

Sport Tourism Events

Finally, the sport tourism event category includes sport activities that attract a sizable number of visiting participants and spectators. The type of visitor depends on the sport event: some are obviously more spectator-driven than others (e.g., the Olympic Games versus the National Amateur Shuffleboard Championship). Furthermore, these sport tourism events have the potential to attract nonresident media and technical personnel such as coaches and other sports officials. High-profile sport events such as the Stanley Club playoffs, Olympic Games, or World Cup are often referred to in the literature as "tourism hallmark events" or "mega events." Of the five categories of sport tourism, the sport event category has the most significant economic impact on host destinations. It is increasingly common for organizers to calculate the amount of new dollars or hotel room nights that are generated by an event. Events designed to attract large numbers of spectators can bring thousands, or even millions, of dollars into a local economy. The 2007 Florida Super Bowl for example, generated an estimated US$463 million in spending for the Florida economy. However, smaller participatory events, such as tournaments or marathons, can also bring benefits, particularly to smaller cities or less populated regions.

The *Snapshot* in Chapter 12 described some of the marathon events around the world, but a new one is the Running Safari in Kenya that includes morning and evening runs with Kenya's top runners, and visits to training camps including one run by 1968 Olympic winner Kip Keino. Since participatory events often make use of existing infrastructure and volunteer labour, they can be relatively inexpensive to host, thereby yielding high benefit-to-cost ratios. Furthermore, participatory sport events have been shown to be an effective way to attract new visitors and to generate return visits.

The mission of the CSTA is to increase the capacity and competitiveness of communities across Canada in hosting sporting events. Its objectives are to provide the sport tourism industry with a credible image and profile; to facilitate networking, educational, and communication opportunities between sport and tourism partners; to facilitate access to national tools and best practices; to ensure the delivery of high-quality services in the sport tourism industry; to build investment in sport tourism from the public and private sectors; and to set targets for expansion of the industry and monitor their achievement. All cities and sport-friendly businesses and organizations are invited to join the CSTA.

Adventure Tourism

Adventure tourism brings together travel, sport, and outdoor recreation, and, like sport tourism, is one of the fastest-growing segments of the tourism industry. The Adventure Travel Society classifies adventure tourism according to activity, distinguishing between "hard" and "soft" adventure tourism activities. Mountaineering is classified as a hard adventure activity, along with activities such as white-water rafting, scuba diving, and mountain biking. Soft adventure activities include camping, hiking, biking, animal watching, horseback riding, canoeing, and water skiing.

The Travel Industry Association of America estimates that 10 percent of North Americans have taken an adventure travel vacation, and that the market is growing 10 percent a year.[16] According to the first annual "2006 Adventure Travel Industry Survey, Practices and Trends," released in 2007 by the Adventure Travel Trade Association, women comprise the majority of adventure travellers worldwide (52 percent). The highest participating age group is 41–60 year olds, and South America ranks highest in terms of increasing destination interest among consumers.[17]

As the adventure tourism bug has spread to the masses, adventure companies are attracting a growing number of people who are not necessarily passionate about one particular activity, and there is a strong trend in the industry toward multi-activity soft adventure tourism packages in nature-based environments. In fact, what is sold as the ultimate multi-sport adventure is the "Survivor" tour. The incredible success of the TV series of the same name has encouraged companies to launch Survivor-themed trips that offer participants multiple challenges.

Adventure tourism companies tread a careful line between selling adventure as an idea and delivering adventure as an experience. In this respect, adventure is socially constructed and has been subjected to a process of commodification. Three key factors have facilitated this commodification: a deferring of control to experts, a proliferation of promotional media, and the application of technology in adventurous settings.[18] These factors have combined to create a cushioning zone between the normal home (often urban) location of everyday life and the extraordinary experience of an adventure holiday.

To explain the rise of this commodification, consider Spirit of the West Adventures, a Vancouver Island outfitter that takes small groups of guests on camping and kayaking trips to see the killer whales in B.C.'s Johnstone Strait. The company provides a wilderness camping experience without the inconvenience of having to "rough it." Travellers are housed in a four-person tent kept high and dry on cedar platforms. Guides and cooks prepare snacks and meals such as barbequed sockeye salmon and prawn shish kebab, followed by wine and chocolate-dipped fruit. "We sometimes jokingly call it 'float and boat,' an eating trip with some kayaking thrown in between meals," says Spirit of the West owner John Waibel. "What out guests want is a chance to have an outdoor adventure without the risk of being uncomfortable."

Waibel's customers are among a growing number of aging North Americans who many in the outdoor recreation business are referring to as "bobos": bourgeois bohemians. They are looking for an escape to nature from their stressed-out urban lives, but the catch is that they want the experience without the hassle of hauling a lot of gear into the backcountry, sleeping on lumpy ground, and hunting for kindling to cook smoky, second-rate meals. Alberta-based Pure West Lifestyles & Adventures is another company catering to this group. It offers camping adventures along the foothills of the Rocky Mountains "without the hassles of packing in tents and equipment." In fact, participants don't even have to walk much. The company's website promises access by all-terrain vehicles "so you and your family can enjoy the remote wilderness without the exhausting long hikes on foot usually required to get to such secluded and pristine backcountry locations."

THE ROLE OF MARKETING IN CRISIS MANAGEMENT

Destination Crisis

destination crisis

the result of external factors beyond the control of managers and authorities negatively affecting the appeal and marketability of a destination

A **destination crisis** is normally the result of external factors beyond the control of managers and authorities negatively affecting the appeal and marketability of a destination.[19] Such factors may be acts of terrorism, national disasters, health issues, crime, or international conflict. Since September 11, 2001, there have been more than 3000 major terrorist attacks, most of which have had an impact on the tourism industry. Although terrorism is not a new phenomenon, what is new is its use to attain political ends and the global attention media coverage gives to terrorist incidents. The continuous publication by the media of the horror of terrorist attacks and their subsequent responses and highly publicized results are often enough to sway many international travellers toward reconsidering their vacation plans.

Nepal exemplifies this situation, a country where global terrorism, coupled with the ongoing domestic Maoist war, wrecked its image as a popular adventure tourism destination between 2000 and 2003. Security concerns sapped the vitality of the country as a desirable destination, especially for those from the West, as they seemed to be the target of terrorist acts in international hubs.[20] In Turkey too, terrorists have made a point of targeting tourism. In 2006, after bombings in two Turkish resort towns, Kurdish militants warned tourists not to come to Turkey as it was not safe. Worth nearly $24 billion in 2005, tourism is Turkey's second most lucrative sector. In other parts of the world, terrorism and conflict continues to have a negative effect on tourism. In the wake of the military coup in Bangkok in 2006 and a series of deadly bomb blasts in tourism hot spots, thousands of travellers cancelled holidays in Thailand.

Natural disasters can also have a devastating impact on tourism. The *Case Study* at the end of this chapter focuses on the impact of the 2004 tsunami on Thailand. In 2005 New Orleans in the U.S. was hit by Hurricane Katrina that devastated the city. Prior to Katrina, New Orleans received about 10 million visitors a year, but a year after the disaster, hotel bookings were still down by 26 percent. The hurricane damaged 80 percent of the city, and killed 1836 people. In response to the threat of hurricanes, hurricane guarantees are now offered by many tour operators and travel agents. In 2005, resorts such as Beaches, Sandals, SuperClubs, and Club Med were promoting policies that allowed travellers to rebook for another time without penalty if a hurricane ruins their vacation.

Responding to Crisis

Once a destination has identified and acknowledged it is facing a crisis, it has been suggested that there are three steps to marketing management of a destination crisis.[21]

1. Establish a Crisis Management Team

The first step is establishing a crisis management team and assigning key roles, such as media and public relations, relations with the travel industry in source markets, and destination response coordination with the local tourism industry. In theory, the middle of a crisis is not a good time to formulate a strategy for managing image or reputation, but for many organizations it is precisely when the conservation begins. Businesses and destinations that are serious about their reputation need to manage risk as an ongoing issue, and plan for unfortunate events. In 2006, the Caribbean Tourism Organization (CTO) and the Caribbean Disaster Emergency Response Agency (CDERA) agreed to develop a disaster risk management strategy for the tourism sector that would help minimize negative impacts from any crisis in the region. Under the agreement, CDERA will make an immediate and coordinated response to any disastrous event as required by participating CTO members.

2. Promote the Destination During and After the Crisis

Promotional campaigns following a crisis are often the only way a destination can persuade visitors to travel. Initiatives can include offering incentives to restore the market, and ensuring that opinion leaders in source markets visit the destination to see that recovery is in place. After September 11, the challenge for many tourism organizations was to encourage people to travel again with creative marketing campaigns. An example was Choice Hotels who saw the challenge as two-pronged: to persuade people to travel again while appearing compassionate and selfless and to provide travellers with a compelling reason to stay at a Choice Hotel property. The promotional strategy came together with the central idea "Thanks for Travelling," which was emblazed on 15 000 banners outside Choice Hotel properties and alongside highways, bridges, and tollbooths. A fully integrated ad campaign followed using TV, print, out-of-home, interactive, point-of-purchase and collateral, direct response, event marketing, and international communications. The campaign was effective and its slogan "Thanks for Travelling" became a rallying cry for the entire travel and tourism industry generating more than $6 million value in consumer and trade public relations. Choice Hotels CEO Chuck Ledsinger was invited to appear before the U.S. Congress in support of new tourism legislature and the White House invited him to attend the signing of the Airport Security Bill. The success established Choice Hotels as the industry leader without making the company appear to be opportunistic.

For countries with an image problem, such as Israel after its 2006 war with Hezbollah in Lebanon, promoting to the trade, media, and consumers is often more effective within a regional framework than if they chose to market their destinations alone.[22] Regional organizations also serve as a cost-effective umbrella under which to continue marketing a destination. An example is the Eastern Mediterranean Marketing Association (EMTA) that markets the entire region (from Italy to Jordan) to Australia. The EMTA was established based on the realistic perspective that travellers from long-haul source markets such as Australia and New Zealand are likely to combine several destinations in the eastern Mediterranean, and consequently a joint marketing exercise (especially to the trade but also to consumers and the media) would be more cost effective and attractive to sellers and consumers than single-destination marketing exercises.

Destinations can also seek marketing support from the public sector. In 2006, the United Nations World Tourism Organization worked closely with the Lebanese government to help restore the country's tourism industry following the conflict with Israel. The

UNWTO offered marketing, branding, and media support, with a particular focus on trade fairs. It also assisted Indonesia in recovering from the earthquakes that damaged the country's tourism industry that same year.

3. Monitor Recovery and Analyzing the Crisis Experience

The final stage in marketing in times of crisis involves monitoring statistical trends and the duration of both the crisis and recovery process. Analysis of source markets to determine which under- or over-performed during the crisis assists the destination marketers in determining the allocation of marketing resources to each market. Market research will gauge the effectiveness of marketing campaigns on source markets and segments within those markets.

CHAPTER SUMMARY

Trends in tourism marketing include a general growth in tourism, with certain sectors, such as cruises, growing faster than others. It is predicted that there will be increased competition, and many more mergers among hotel chains, cruise lines, and other segments. One of the most significant implications of demographic change in this century is the aging of the world's population. The world median age is projected to rise from 26 years in 2000 to 44 years by 2100.

The consumer of the future is likely to be seeking experiences, and there is an increasing desire of individuals to convert them into images and stories. In their pursuit of individualism, consumers will look for new experiences and loyalty to a travel supplier will be driven by an intermediary's ability to deliver a fresh stream of one-off experiential vacations. There will be a shift toward inconspicuous consumption and a greater awareness of issues such as sustainable development, ecotourism, and ethical consumption. Consumers of the future will also demand more convenience, and personal service will increasingly outweigh price as the key differentiator.

If environmental improvement is to provide a competitive opportunity an organization must consider responsible marketing, which is the balancing of environmental initiatives and environmental communication in order to achieve sustainable competitive advantage. Cause-related marketing is also a rapidly expanding trend in marketing communications, and is being adopted by some players in the tourism industry. Cause-related marketing efforts can be categorized into autonomously branded, co-branded, house-branded, and industry-branded approaches.

Once a destination has identified and acknowledged it is facing a crisis, it has been suggested that there are three steps to marketing management of a destination crisis: establishing a crisis management team, promotion of the destination during and after the crisis, and monitoring recovery and analyzing the crisis experience.

KEY TERMS

destination crisis, p. 458	responsible environmental marketing, p. 447	sustainable tourism, p. 446
experiential marketing, p. 442		tryvertising, p. 442
life caching, p. 438	sport tourism, p. 454	

DISCUSSION QUESTIONS AND EXERCISES

1. The text states that one of the most significant implications of demographic change in this century is the aging of the world's population. What are the implications for the tourism industry in Canada?

2. This chapter suggests that marketers can expect to see growing demand for increasingly specialized holidays that combine unusual experiences and the potential for personal development. Research some vacations on offer today that would fulfil these criteria.

3. Apply the model for responsible marketing to a tourism organization or destination you are familiar with. What position does the organization take, and how could it become more sustainable?

4. Find a current example of a tourism or hospitality organization that is engaged in cause-related-marketing activities. Which of the three approaches to cause-related marketing discussed in the text is the organization following?

5. Find an example of a destination that is attempting to attract sport tourists. Which of the five areas of sport tourism discussed in the chapter is the destination focusing on?

CASE STUDY

MARKETING AFTER A CRISIS: RECOVERING FROM THE TSUNAMI IN THAILAND

Warning came too late or not all on December 26, 2004, when an earthquake off the coast of Sumatra triggered a tsunami in the Indian Ocean that struck more than a dozen countries. The tsunami had an overwhelming human and physical impact. A total of 223 492 people lost their lives, a further 43 320 are still missing, some 400 000 homes were reduced to rubble, 1.4 million people lost their source of livelihood, and more than 3000 miles of roads and 118 000 fishing boats were damaged or destroyed. The disaster caused $12 billion in damages in barely 24 hours. The world responded to the plight of the tsunami's victims on a massive scale and with unprecedented generosity. In the weeks following the disaster, multi-agency assessment teams calculated that approximately $12 billion would be needed to reconstruct the destroyed communities. In response, official and private pledges reached $16 billion.

Before the tsunami, tourism in Thailand was at an all-time high, continuing its strong growth with a 20 percent rise from the previous year, reaching visitor numbers of 12 million. However, the tsunami had devastating affects on Thailand's Andaman coast, leaving more than 8000 people — about half of them foreign tourists — dead or missing. Damages and losses were close to

$2.6 billion, hitting the tourism sector particularly hard. On Ko Phi Phi Island for example, the tsunami killed more than a thousand people, wiped out many restaurants and rooms, shattered coral reefs, and moved white sand beaches into coconut groves. For Phuket, tourism is a very important source of income and employment. The industry employs about 300 000 people, many from other Thai provinces.

However, although the United Nations said the tsunami affected more than 500 Thai villages in six provinces, many popular beaches were relatively unscathed or have been quick to recover their natural beauty, if not their usual number of visitors. "People watched TV news and thought that everything was damaged. But that wasn't true," said Suwalai Pinpradab, the southern regional director of the Tourism Authority of Thailand (TAT). But Thailand needed to get the word out that it was open for business. Potential tourists were cancelling their bookings because they assumed that all the hotels had been destroyed, and this was not the case. For example, only 12 percent of Phuket's hotel rooms were damaged by the tsunami.

To combat the problem, tourism experts representing 42 countries, the private sector, and several international organizations drew up the Phuket Action Plan, which spelled out a comprehensive series of activities intended to restart the region's economically vital tourism industry, stalled after the tsunami struck. The main objective was to restore travel confidence in the region, with marketing and communications playing a key role. Soon after the tsunami, marketing campaigns began to attract tourists back to the Thailand. Phuket's hotel occupancy rates, which dipped below 10 percent in January, rose to 40 percent in February, helped by the first plane-loads of package tourists from Scandinavia, which landed in Phuket on February 2 to much local media fanfare. In 2005 Phuket received 2.5 million visitors, compared with 4.8 million in 2004. Pinpradab said that because there were fewer tourists, everybody wanted to serve those who came. "We've realized that tourism is very important for us. So we treat tourists much better than before."

To combat the loss of tourism at a local level, Phuket's tourism board partnered with local businesses to offer lower airfares, two-for-one deals, and extra meals included in the price of hotel rooms. Laguna Phuket Resorts and Hotels, which owns five hotel properties in and around Phuket, cut hotel rates by 50 percent to entice tourists to return. Managing director James Batt said, "We are trying to position Phuket as a summer destination for the British. In addition to offering special packages and lower room rates, we have launched a $245 000 campaign with UK operators to revive business."

At an international level, the Thai cabinet approved a $150 million project to rebuild and market the tourism industry in Thailand. The Thai government partnered with Thai Airways International (TAI) and others to promote its "Best Offer" — three days and two nights at any of 11 different resorts for as little as $90 for the whole stay. In addition, a highly publicized series of events was planned, beginning with a religious ceremony where monks and priests freed the souls of those lost during the tsunami and gave permission for the tourists to return to southern Thailand. This took place on the first anniversary of the tsunami. The TAT even found something positive to say about the effects of the tsunami. Juthamas Siriwan, TAT governor, said that environmental studies showed that the tsunami actually cleansed the water and beaches, improving quality and helping the ecosystem. The TAT planned to capitalize on this by restoring and improving tourist hot spots.

TAT also partnered with TAI and the Tourism Council of Thailand (TCT) to organize two "Mega" familiarization trips to the south of Thailand. The second trip that took place in July 2005 hosted 270 tour operators and travel journalists from visitor-generating countries in North East Asia and the Middle East, while the first trip was targeted at the remaining international market. The fam trips were part of the Andaman recovery plan to promote Thailand as a safe and beautiful destination, and designed to show tour operators that Thailand was safe and open for business. TAT also contacted corporations to offer incentives to stage conferences in Phuket. TAT was hoping that business travellers from Thailand and nearby Singapore, China, and Japan would occupy beaches and pools vacated by westerners. This strategy of focusing on regional tourism helped Bali recover from the 2002 bombing that killed more than a hundred foreigners and emptied resorts for months.

Longer-term recovery efforts are still underway, but the tourism sector suffered revenue losses of about $1.6 billion, and the rebound in arrivals has been slower than expected. The government continues to support measures to speed up the recovery with packages and incentives to encourage tourists to return to the affected areas. The government has also invested in the establishment of an early warning system and in disaster preparedness planning.

Sources: Johnson, C. (2005, March 26). Thai beaches bounce back — but where are the tourists? *Globe & Mail*, T6; Tourism sector hopeful about tsunami recovery. (2005). *WTO News, 4*, 1, 3; Solidarity overcomes competition. (2005). *WTO News 1*, 1, 3, 7; United Nations. (2006). Tsunami recovery: Taking stock after 12 months. United Nations, Office of the Secretary-General's Special Envoy for Tsunami Recovery.

QUESTIONS

1. Overall, would you say that the tourism authorities in Thailand responded well to the tsunami and its impact on tourism?
2. What more could have been done to promote Thailand after the tsunami?
3. Restoring travel confidence is often the major marketing challenge for a destination after a crisis. How did tourism officials in Thailand cope with this challenge? Is there more they could have done to restore consumer confidence?
4. Tourism in Thailand has more recently been impacted by political instability and terrorism. How should (or how did) the Tourism Authority of Thailand respond to the latest crisis?

WEB SITES

www.peru.info/perueng.asp
Peru Tourism

www.machupicchu.org
Machu Picchu Gateway

www.bahamas.com
Official Tourism Website of the Islands of The Bahamas

www.tourismthailand.org
Tourism Thailand

www.purewest.com
Pure West Lifestyles & Adventures

www.kayakingtours.com
Spirit of the West Adventures

secondlife.com
Second Life

www.thevacationstation.com
The Vacation Station

www.adventuretravel.biz
Adventure Travel Trade Association

www.offsetters.ca
Offsetters Climate Neutral Society

www.hacgreenhotels.com
Hotel Association of Canada's Green Key Eco-Rating Program

ENDNOTES

1. Future Foundation. (2005). The World of Travel in 2020. Commissioned by Cendant Travel Distribution Services.

2. Future Foundation (2005). The World of Travel in 2020. Commissioned by Cendant Travel Distribution Services, 16.

3. JupiterResearch forecasts online travel spending to reach US$128b in 2001. (2006). *Travelweek, 34*(46), 2.

4. Cetron, M. (2005). An updated report on ten trends impacting the hospitality industry. *HSMAI Marketing Review, 22*(2), 19–25.

5. Bullfrog Power Inc. (2007, February 26). Companies that commit to green policies will attract consumer spending. bullfrogpower .com/news/Consumers%20looking%20for%20 green%20options.pdf (September 2007).

6. Riga, A. (2007, September 22). Fly with a little clearer conscience. *Calgary Herald*, F1.

7. Allen, J., & Markey, R. (2006, May). Seven things you need to know about marketing in the 21st century. *World Business*, 81.

8. Williams, A. (2006). Tourism and hospitality marketing: Fantasy, feeling and fun. *International Journal of Contemporary Hospitality Management, 18*(6), 482–495.

9. Tryvertising. (2005, April). www.trendwatching .com/trends/TRYVERTISING.htm (September 2007).

10. Schneider, T. (2006). Travel advertising today. *HSMAI Marketing Review, 23*(3), 25–26.

11. Butler, R. (1993). Tourism: An evolutionary perspective. In R. W. Butler, J. G. Nelson, & G. Wall (Eds.), *Tourism and sustainable development: Monitoring, planning, managing.* Department of Geography, University of Waterloo, 29.

12. Barnes, N. G., & Fitzgibbons, D. (1991). Is cause-related marketing in your future? *Business Forum, 16*(4), 20.

13. Hoeffler, S., & Keller, K.L. (2002). Building brand equity through corporate societal marketing. *Journal of Public Policy & Marketing, 21*(1), 84.

14. Ad Terrae Gloriam Oxford. (2006). The company. www.atg-oxford.co.uk/about.php (September 2007).

15. Webster, B. (2005, October 20). Call for air fuel tax after flyers ignore green levy, *The Times*, 26. www.timesonline.co.uk/tol/news/ uk/article580476.ece (retrieved September 2007).

16. Jackson, K. (2005, May 20). Going semi-wild on adventure tours. *Seattle Times*.

17. Adventure Travel Trade Association (2006). "Adventure Travel Industry Survey, Practices and Trends." Seattle.

18. Beedie, P., & Hudson, S. (2003). The commodification of mountaineering through tourism. *Annals of Tourism Research, 30*(3), 625–643.

19. Beirman, D. (2003). *Restoring destinations in crisis: A strategic marketing approach.* Wallingford, UK: CABI International.

20. Bhattari, K., Conway, D., & Shresta, N. (2004). Tourism, terrorism, and turmoil in Nepal. *Annals of Tourism Research, 32*(3), 669–688.

21. Beirman, D. (2003). *Restoring destinations in crisis: A strategic marketing approach.* Wallingford, UK: CABI International, 23.

22. Beirman, D. (2001). Marketing of tourism destinations during a prolonged crisis: Israel and the Middle East. *Journal of Vacation Marketing, 8*(2), 167–176.

Glossary

advertising: Any paid form of non-personal presentation and promotion of ideas, products, or services by an identified sponsor, using mass media to persuade or influence an audience.

advertising objective: A specific communication task to be accomplished with a specific target audience during a specific period of time.

affordable method: Setting the promotion budget within the organization's existing available funds.

AIDA model: A checklist of the aims of advertising: attention, interest, desire, and action.

alliance: Partnership formed when organizations combine resources through a contractual agreement that allows them to overcome each other's weaknesses by benefiting from each another's strengths.

allocentrics: See venturers.

all-in pricing (all-inclusive pricing): A single price for all the various products or services on offer.

ambient advertising: Place-based advertising in non-standard, unconventional media.

attitudes: Ingrained feelings about various factors of an experience.

augmented product: The add-ons that are extrinsic to the product itself but may influence the decision to purchase.

banner ad: An advertisement placed as a narrow band across a web page.

beliefs: The thoughts that people have about most aspects of their life.

benchmarking: The process of tracking and comparing current performance with past performance or in relation to the competition.

benefits: The rewards that the product gives the consumer.

Boston Consulting Group (BCG) model: A technique designed to show the performance of an individual product in relation to its major competitors and the rate of growth in its market.

brandicide: The killing of a well-known brand by extending it into a new area without adequate management or by not maintaining it effectively.

branding: A method of establishing a distinctive identity for a product or service based on competitive differentiation from others.

break-even analysis: A pricing technique that considers fixed and variable costs, customer volumes, and profit margins.

budget competitors: Organizations that compete for the same consumer dollars.

buyer-based pricing (sensitivity pricing): Adjusting to high prices when the demand is high and lower prices when the demand is low, regardless of the cost of the product or service.

call centre: A central operation that handles inbound and outbound telemarketing programs.

cash cow: A service or product that generates a high volume of income in relation to the cost of maintaining its market share.

cause-related marketing: Marketing that associates an organization with support for a good cause.

channel conflict: Conflict that occurs when one member of a distribution channel perceives another to be engaged in behaviour that prevents or hinders the first member from achieving its goals.

channel management: The selection and motivation of individual channel members and evaluation of their performance over time.

cognitive dissonance: A customer's uncertainty after making a purchase.

competition-oriented pricing (going-rate pricing): Setting the price of a product or service in relation to competitors' prices.

competitive parity method: Setting the promotion budget to match competitors' outlay.

competitor analysis: A review of competitors that allows the organization to identify market trends and the level of customer loyalty.

competitor intelligence: Detailed information about the competition and how the organization is doing in comparison.

concept testing: Testing an idea with a group of target consumers to assess its consumer appeal.

consumer attitudes: A consumer's enduring favourable or unfavourable cognitive evaluations, emotional feelings, and action tendencies toward some object or idea.

consumer behaviour analysis: The study of why people buy the products or services they do and how they make decisions.

consumer research: Applied research focused on the consumer.

contests: Sales promotions in which entrants can win prizes based on some required skill that they are asked to demonstrate.

convention and visitor bureau (CVB): A regional or city-level organization specialized in developing conventions, meetings, and conferences as well as responsible for marketing a specific destination.

conventional marketing system: A distribution system that consists of a loose collection of independent organizations, each of which tries to maximize its own success.

cooperative direct mail: A direct mail offer sent in a package that includes offers from other organizations.

core product: The basic need function served by the generic product.

cost per thousand (CPM): The cost of the message unit divided by the number of impressions (ad views) multiplied by 1000.

cost-based pricing: Adding a certain dollar amount or percentage to the actual or estimated costs of a product or service to arrive at a final price.

cost-plus pricing: Adding a standard mark-up to the cost of the product or service to arrive at the final price.

coupons: Vouchers or certificates that entitle customers or intermediaries to a reduced price on a product or service.

cross-selling: Persuading a customer to purchase additional allied products or services.

cultural environment: Institutions and other forces that affect society's basic values, perceptions, preferences, and behaviour.

culture: The norms, beliefs, and rituals that define a group of people or a way of life.

customer loyalty: A measure of how likely customers are to return to an organization and of their willingness to build relationships with the organization.

customer satisfaction: The difference between the service that a customer expects and the perceived quality of what is actually delivered.

demographics: Statistics that describe the observable characteristics of individuals.

dependables (psychocentrics): Travellers who prefer familiar destinations, packaged tours, and "touristy" areas.

destination: Place that has some form of actual or perceived boundary, such as the physical boundary of an island, political boundaries, or even market-created boundaries.

destination branding: A method of establishing a distinctive identity for a destination based on competitive differentiation from others.

destination crisis: The result of external factors beyond the control of managers and authorities negatively affecting the appeal and marketability of a destination.

destination marketing organizations (DMOs): Government agencies, convention and visitors bureaus, travel associations, and other bodies that market travel to their destination areas.

differentiation: A strategy that involves an innovative technological breakthrough, which can take competitors a long time to imitate, to gain a competitive advantage.

direct competitors: Organizations that offer similar goods and services to the same consumer at a similar price.

direct distribution channel: A channel through which an organization delivers its product or service to the consumer without any intermediaries.

direct e-mail marketing (permission marketing): Marketing messages delivered by e-mail with permission from the recipient.

direct mail: A type of direct response advertising in which an offer is sent to a prospective customer by mail.

direct marketing: A form of marketing that sends messages directly to consumers using addressable media, such as mail.

direct response advertising: Advertising designed to generate a response by any means that is measurable.

directional selling: A vertically integrated travel agent's sale, or attempted sale, of the foreign package holidays of its linked tour operator in preference to the holidays of other operators.

discriminatory pricing: Selling a product or service at more than one price, despite the fact that its costs are the same.

distribution channel: A direct or indirect delivery arrangement used by a supplier, carrier, or destination marketing organization.

distribution system: The aspect of the marketing mix that relates to making a product or service available to the consumer.

diversification: Creating new products and services outside the present business.

dog: A service or product that provides neither cash flow nor long-term opportunities and holds little promise for improved performance.

economic forces: Those forces that affect consumer purchasing power and spending patterns.

elasticity of demand: The sensitivity of customer demand to changes in price.

employee empowerment: The act of giving employees the authority to identify and solve customer complaints on the spot and to improve work processes when necessary.

ethnocentrism: Notion that one's own culture knows best how to do things.

event sponsorship: The financial support of an event (e.g., a car race, a theatre performance, or a marathon) by a sponsor in return for advertising privileges associated with the event.

exclusive distribution strategy: A plan to restrict the number of channels used to distribute products or services to customers.

executive summary: A few pages, usually positioned at the beginning of the marketing plan, that sum up the plan's main sections.

experience: Event created when an organization intentionally uses services as the stage and goods as props to engage individual customers.

experiential marketing: Marketing initiatives that give consumers in-depth experiences to provide them with sufficient information to make a purchase decision.

factual survey: A survey that asks the respondent to state certain facts, such as age or number of children.

family life cycle: The stages through which families pass from marriage through children to retirement years.

feature stories: Articles of human interest that entertain, inform, or educate readers, viewers, or listeners.

features: The objective attributes of a product.

fixed costs: Costs that do not vary with the amount of the product or service provided.

focus: A strategy that concentrates on designing a good or service to meet the needs of one segment of the market better than the competition.

focus group: A group of 8 to 10 people, representative of a wider population, whose views are elicited by a facilitator.

forecasting: A process that uses market research to predict sales volume and revenue trends, consumer profiles, product profiles, price trends, and trends.

franchise: A business established when it acquires the right to offer, sell, or distribute an organization's goods or services according to that organization's marketing format.

full-service agency: An advertising agency that provides the four major functions: account management, creative services, media planning and buying, and account planning.

games: Sales promotions involving the use of game pieces, such as scratch-and-win cards.

general competitors: Organizations that provide the same service or product.

gift certificates: Vouchers or cheques that are selectively given away or sold to customers, who in turn give them to others.

goals: The primary aims of the organization.

horizontal conflict: Conflict between organizations at the same level of the distribution channel.

importance–performance analysis (IPA): An assessment of the relative importance of various attributes and the performance of the organization, product or service, or destination in providing these attributes.

impression: One viewing of an advertising message.

indirect distribution channel: A channel through which an organization distributes its product or service with the assistance of intermediaries.

infomercial: A television commercial, usually 30 minutes long, that presents the benefits of a product or service.

integrated marketing communications (IMC): The unification of all marketing communications tools, as well as corporate and brand messages, so they send a consistent, persuasive message to target audiences.

intensive distribution strategy: A plan to maximize the exposure of products and services using all available outlets or intermediaries.

intermediaries: Channels of distribution that operate between the organization and the consumer.

internal marketing: Marketing aimed at the organization's own employees.

international marketing: Business activities designed to plan, price, promote, and direct the flow of a organization's goods and services to consumers in more than one country for profit.

interpretive survey: A survey that asks the respondent to act as an interpreter as well as a reporter.

in-depth interview: A qualitative research technique in which an interview lasts 45 to 60 minutes.

joint promotion: A promotion in which organizations with similar target markets combine their resources to mutual advantage.

junket representatives: Companies that serve the casino industry as intermediaries for premium players.

learning: The way in which people receive and interpret a variety of stimuli.

learning and enrichment travel: Vacations that provide opportunities for authentic, hands-on, or interactive learning experiences.

life caching: The desire of individuals to convert experiences into images and stories.

life cycle model: A model that predicts changes in travel patterns and destinations as people move through their life cycle.

lifestyle analysis: Examination of the way people allocate time, energy, and money.

lifetime value of a customer: A calculation that considers customers from the point of view of their potential lifetime revenue and profitability contributions to a organization.

low-cost leadership: The simplest and most effective strategy for dealing with competition, requiring large resources and strong management to sustain.

macroenvironment: The larger societal forces that affect the microenvironment: competitive, demographic, economic, environmental and natural, technological, political, cultural and social, and legal forces.

market development: Identifying and developing new markets for current products and services.

market penetration: Entering a market with an existing product or service and gaining competitors' market share.

market share: An organization's sales expressed as a percentage of the sales for the total industry.

market skimming: Setting high prices at the launch stage and progressively lowering them as the product or service becomes better established.

marketing: The process of planning and executing the conception, pricing, promotion, and distribution of ideas, goods, and services to create exchanges that satisfy individual (customer) and organizational objectives.

marketing communications: Communication via any and all of the marketing mix elements.

marketing information system (MIS): A method of gathering, using, and disseminating research in the marketing context.

marketing plan: A written, short-term plan that details how an organization will use its marketing mix to achieve its marketing objectives.

marketing research: The systematic and objective search for and analysis of information relevant to the identification and solution of any problem in the field of marketing.

media mix: A combination of traditional media vehicles, non-traditional media, and marketing communication tools used to reach the target audiences.

microenvironment: Forces close to the organization that can affect its ability to serve its customers: the organization itself, marketing channel firms, customer markets, and a broad range of stakeholders or publics.

mission statement: A brief simple phrase or sentence that summarizes the organization's direction and communicates its ethos to internal and external audiences, and also answers the question, What business are we in?

monopoly: A supply situation in which there is only one seller.

motivational houses: Companies that provide incentive travel as a reward for employees' or distributors' efforts.

motivations: Inner drives that cause people to take action to satisfy their needs.

needs: The gaps between what people have and what they would like to have, seen as the force that arouses motivated behaviour.

negotiating: A price-setting technique involving two or more parties with a conflict of interest regarding aspects of the product or service.

niche marketing: Focusing on the needs and wants of narrowly defined geographic, demographic, or psychographic segments.

objective and task method: Developing the promotion budget by defining specific objectives, determining the tasks that must be performed to achieve these objectives, and estimating the costs of performing these tasks.

objectives: The specific aims that managers accomplish to attain organizational goals.

off-set pricing (bait pricing): Charging a low basic price and charging for extra services.

opinion survey: A survey that asks the respondent to express an opinion or make an evaluation or appraisal.

packaging: The process of combining two or more related and complementary offerings into a single-price offering.

penetration pricing: Setting low prices to get maximum sales and market share in the initial stages of the life cycle of the product or service.

percentage of sales method: Setting the promotion budget at a certain percentage of current or forecasted sales or as a percentage of price.

perceptual mapping: Technique used to identify the relationship between the level of perceived importance of certain aspects of a product or service on the part of the consumer and the actual performance on the part of the supplier.

personal selling: Face-to-face interaction between a salesperson and the prospective consumer for the purpose of making a sale.

persuasion test: A test that evaluates the effectiveness of an ad by measuring whether it affects consumers' intentions to buy a brand.

point-of-purchase merchandising: A technique used to promote a product or service at locations where it is being sold.

portfolio analysis: An approach to evaluating a diverse group of goods and services, based on long-term planning and economic forecasts.

positioning: A communications strategy to establish an image for a product or service in relation to others in the minds of consumers.

positioning statement: A phrase that reflects the image an organization wants to create.

premium pricing: Setting prices above market price, to reflect either the image of quality or the unique status of the product or service.

premiums: Products or services offered either for free or at low cost as an incentive to buy a specific product or service.

press release (news release): A short article about an organization or event written to attract media attention, intended to lead to media coverage.

prestige pricing: Setting prices high to position a product or service at the upper or luxury end of the market.

price lining: Pre-establishing price levels that the organization is confident will attract customers.

price points: The number of "stops" along the way between the lowest-priced item and the highest-priced item.

price spread: A range of products and prices that will suit the budget of all target markets.

price–quality trade-off: Acceptance of the higher cost of a better quality of product or service.

primary data: Information collected for the specific purpose at hand.

product category competitors: Organizations that produce the same product or class of products or offer the same services.

product development: Developing a new product or service to be sold to existing customers.

product differentiation: A technique that enables organization to seek competitive advantage by offering a product (or service) that has features not available from its competitors.

product life cycle (PLC) analysis: A way to identify the life-cycle stage of a product or service, review its past and current position, and predict its future.

product mix: The portfolio of products that an organization offers to one market or several.

product placement: The insertion of brand logos or branded products into movies and television shows.

product-bundle pricing: Grouping together products or services to promote them as a package.

profit maximization: Gaining the most profit possible by changing costs, prices, or volume.

projection techniques: Research methods that involve asking subjects to respond to hypothetical, or projected, situations; sometimes called "what if" techniques.

promotion strategy: A plan to reach prospective visitors using a promotional mix to achieve destination awareness and influence attitudes and purchasing behaviour.

promotional mix: An organization's total marketing communications program.

promotional pricing: A temporary reduction in price.

prospecting: The process of searching for new customers.

psychocentrics: See dependables.

psychographic analysis: Measurement of people's activities, interests, and opinions.

psychological pricing: Using slightly lower prices to give consumers the perception of added value.

public relations (PR): The activities that an organization uses to maintain or improve its relationship with other organizations or individuals.

publications: Annual reports, brochures, newsletters, and magazines that can draw attention to an organization and its products and services, can help build its image, and convey news to target markets.

publicity: Attention received through news media coverage.

pull strategy: A promotion strategy that spends a large amount on advertising and consumer promotion to build up demand so consumers will ask retailers for the product or service, the retailers will ask the wholesalers, and the wholesalers will ask the producers.

push strategy: A promotion strategy that calls uses the sales force and trade promotion to push the product or service through channels; the producer promotes to wholesalers, the wholesalers promote to retailers, and the retailers promote to consumers.

qualitative research: Research methods that use and give rise to subjective or interpretive information.

quantitative research: Research methods that produce numerical (empirical) data.

question marks: Speculative, potentially high-risk products or services that may be profitable and, because of their small market share, may be vulnerable to competition.

recall test: A test that evaluates the memorability of an ad by contacting members of the audience and asking what they remember about the advertisement.

recognition test: A test that evaluates the memorability of an ad by showing it to members of the audience and asking whether they remember having seen it before.

reference groups: Groups that have a direct (face-to-face) or indirect influence on a person's attitude or behaviour.

reference price: A price derived from market prices and the customer's previous experience.

relationship marketing: Marketing that attracts customers, retains them, and enhances their satisfaction.

repertory grid technique: A structured research method that requires respondents to select from a group of three items.

responsible environmental marketing: Marketing that balances environmental initiatives and environmental communication to achieve a sustainable competitive advantage.

return-on-investment goals (or break-even analysis or payout planning): The expected profit returns based on the costs of reaching a customer or group of customers.

sales management: The management of the sales force and personal selling efforts to achieve desired sales objectives.

sales promotion: A technique to increase the value of a product or service by offering an extra incentive to purchase it.

sales quotas: Minimum sales volume goal.

sampling: Giving away free samples of a product or service, or arranging for people to try all or part of it.

secondary data: Information that already exists somewhere, having been collected for another purpose.

second-chance selling: Trying to sell additional products or services to a customer who has already made a purchase.

segmentation analysis: The practice of dividing total markets up into groups on the basis of similar characteristics.

selective distribution strategy: A plan to use more than one but less than all of the possible channels to distribute products and services to customers.

self-reference criteria (SRC): an unconscious reference to one's own cultural values, experiences, and knowledge as a basis for decisions.

service culture: A culture that supports customer service through policies, procedures, reward systems, and actions.

service quality: Customers' perceptions of the service component of a product.

service recovery: Rectifying a service delivery failure.

services marketing mix: The original four P's of the marketing mix — product, place, promotion, and price — plus the people, the physical evidence, and the process.

services marketing triangle: A model that illustrates the three interlinking groups that work together to develop, promote, and deliver services: the company, the customer, and the provider.

servicescape: The environment in which the service is delivered and in which the organization and consumer interact, and any tangible components that facilitate performance or communication of the service.

SERVQUAL: An instrument used to measure the difference between consumers' expectations and perceptions of service quality.

situation analysis: A summary and assessment of all the relevant information available about the product or service, the organization, the competitive environment, the industry, and the consumers.

social class: A position in society, determined by such factors as income, wealth, education, occupation, family prestige, value of home, and neighbourhood.

social marketing: The use of marketing programs and marketing communication tools for the good of society.

solo direct mail: A direct mail piece sent out by one company organization.

spam: Unsolicited e-mail, including advertisements.

specialized agency: An advertising agency that specializes in certain functions, audiences, or industries.

sport tourism: Travel to participate in a sporting activity for recreation or competition or to observe sport or to visit a sport attraction.

stars: Products or services that have a dominant share of a fast-growing market.

strategic marketing plan: A written plan for an organization covering a period of three or more years into the future.

strategic pricing: Setting prices early, in accordance with the long-term view of corporate strategy, product positioning, and value for money in the marketplace.

sustainable tourism: Tourism that can maintain its viability in an area indefinitely and does not damage the environment.

sweepstakes: Sales promotions that require entrants to submit their names and addresses, with winners chosen on the basis of chance.

SWOT analysis: A methodology for assessing strengths, weaknesses, opportunities, and threats for strategic purposes.

tactical pricing: Making short-term pricing decisions in response to changes in the marketing environment.

tangible product: The specific features and benefits residing in the product itself — styling, quality, brand name, design, etc.

target market: A clearly defined group of customers whose needs the organization plans to satisfy.

target rate of return: An intended rate of return on investment or expenses that determines the price.

telemarketing: Using the telephone to reach customers or prospective customers.

tour brokers: Companies that act as intermediaries between sellers and buyers of tours.

tour operators: Organizations that offer packaged vacation tours to the general public.

tourism: The activities of persons travelling to and staying in places outside their usual environment for not more than one consecutive year for leisure, business, and other purposes not related to the exercise of an activity remunerated from within the place visited.

tourism and hospitality products: Selected components or elements of the hotel, restaurant, entertainment, and resort industries bundled together to satisfy needs and wants.

tourism area life cycle (TALC): The stages a destination goes through, from exploration to involvement to development to consolidation to stagnation to rejuvenation or decline (also known as the "tourism destination life cycle").

tourism market: A market that reflects the demands of consumers for a wide range of travel and hospitality products and services.

travel agents: Intermediaries that sell travel products and services.

travel specialists: Intermediaries that specialize in performing one or more functions of an organization's distribution system.

tryvertising: The practice of making consumers familiar with products and services by trying them out, so they can make a purchase decision based on experience.

undercut pricing: Setting prices lower than the competition and using the price as a trigger to purchase immediately.

unique selling proposition (USP): A unique feature of a product or service that distinguishes it from all other products and services.

up-selling: Persuading a customer to buy a more profitable product or service.

VALS: A system for grouping consumers into eight categories according to factors such as self-image, aspirations, values and product choices, which drive consumer behaviour.

value-for-money pricing: Charging medium prices and emphasizing that the product or service represents excellent value at this price.

variable costs: Costs that increase as more of a product or service is provided.

venturers (allocentrics): Travellers who prefer exotic destinations and unstructured vacations, with more involvement with local cultures, rather than packaged tours.

vertical conflict: Conflict between organizations at different levels of the same distribution channel.

vertical marketing system: A distribution system in which all members of the distribution channel work together as a unified whole.

virtual focus groups: Online sessions in which a limited number of pre-recruited respondents participate in a guided discussion electronically.

vision statement: A brief simple phrase or sentence that describes where the organization wants to be in some future time and usually answers the question, What do we want to be?

visitor: Any person travelling to a place other than that of his or her usual environment for less than 12 months and whose main purpose for the trip is other than exercise of an activity remunerated from within the place visited.

volume discounting: Offering special prices to attract customers who agree to major purchases.

willingness to pay (WTP) assessment: A survey of potential customers to determine what they would be willing to pay for the product or service.

word of mouth: Communication about products and services among people perceived to be independent of the organization.

yield: The profit made on the sales of products or services based on the number of customers, how much they spend, and the number of products or services they buy.

yield management: Maximizing opportunities for the sale of perishable products or services, such as airline seats, hotel rooms, and tour seats, and therefore improving long-term viability.

zero-based planning: The practice of analyzing the strengths and weaknesses of marketing communications tools to match them to the problem identified in the situation analysis

Index

TEXT ACKNOWLEDGMENTS

p. 4: Sourced from: Statistics Canada "Characteristics of International Travellers," *The Daily*, Catalogue 11-001, May 29, 2007, http://www.statcan.ca/Daily/English/070529/d070529a.htm. **p. 5:** UN World Tourism Organization News, 2006, Issue 3, page 4. ©UNWTO, 2007, #92844/13/2007. **p. 6:** UN World Tourism Organization News, 2006, Issue 3, page 5. ©UNWTO, 2007, #92844/13/2007. **p. 7:** From *Tourism Snapshot Year Review*, 2005 Facts & Figures, published by the Canadian Tourism Commission. **p. 7–8:** Canadian Tourism Commission, *Tourism Snapshot* February 2007. **p. 9:** From *Tourism Snapshot Year Review*, 2005 Facts & Figures, published by the Canadian Tourism Commission. **p. 13:** From *International Marketing*, 12th Edition, Cateora, PR & Graham, JL, 2005, p10. © 2005, The McGraw-Hill Companies, Inc. **p. 16:** From *Services Marketing: Integrating Customer Focus Across the Firm*, Zeithaml, V & Bitner, MJ, 2000, p16. © The McGraw-Hill Companies, Inc. **p. 17:** Booms, B. H., & Bitner, M. J. (1981). "Marketing strategies and organizational structures for service firms." In J. H. Donnelly & W. R. George (Eds.), *Marketing services* (pp. 47–51). Chicago: American Marketing Association. **p. 45:** From *Consumer Research in China: Quantitative Report*, July 2006, published by the Canadian Tourism Commission. Reprinted with permission. **p. 50:** Sourced from Statistics Canada "Perspectives on Labour and Income," Catalogue 75-001, December 2006, vol. 7 no. 12. Released December 13, 2006, URL: http://www.statcan.ca/english/freepub/75-001-XIE/75-001-XIE2006112.pdf. **p. 53:** Source: SRI Consulting Business Intelligence (SRIC-BI); www.sric-bi.com/VALS. **p. 55:** Used by permission of *Cornell Hotel and Restaurant Quarterly*. **p. 64–65:** Courtesy of Pier 21. **p. 84:** Reprinted with the permission of The Free Press, a Division of Simon & Schuster Adult Publishing Group, from COMPETITIVE STRATEGY: Techniques for Analyzing Industries and Competitors by Michael E. Porter. Copyright © 1980, 1998 by The Free Press. All rights reserved. **p. 101–104:** Courtesy of Travel Alberta. **p. 81–82:** Courtesy of Northwest Territories Tourism. **p. 89–90:** Reprinted with permission from the Canadian Tourism Commission. **p. 93–94:** Reprinted with permission from *Foodservice and Hospitality* magazine, 2002. **p. 121:** Courtesy of Context-Based Research Group. **p. 125–127:** This article was published in *International Journal of Hospitality Management*, 21 (2), N. Johns and R. Pine, "Consumer Behaviour in the Food Service Industry: A Review" pp119–134, Copyright Elsevier 2002. **p. 129–131:** Adapted from: Hudson, S., & Wall, R. (2005) "Film Tourism: A Marketing Opportunity for Destinations," in 'The Three R's: Research, Results, Rewards,' Proceedings of the Travel and Tourism Research Association Conference, New Orleans, June 12–15, pp. 288–300. **p. 154:** This article was published in *The Development and Management of Visitor Attractions*, Swarbrooke, J. "The Three Levels of Product - Example of a Theme Park," p147. Copyright Elsevier 1995. **p. 162:** Reprinted with permission from the author. **p. 170:** Holloway, J.C. and Plant, R.V. (1992) *Marketing for Tourism*. London: Pitman, 73. © 1992. Reprinted with permission from Pearson Education UK. **p. 173:** Republished with permission from Emerald Group Publishing Limited. **p. 184:** Dibb, Sally, Lyndon Simkin, William Pride, and O.C. Ferrell, MARKETING: CONCEPTS AND STRATEGIES, European Second Edition, Copyright © 1994 by Houghton Mifflin Company. Used with permission. **p. 206:** Reprinted with permission from Mercer Human Resource Consulting Limited. Copyright 2007 All rights reserved. **p. 216–217:** Used by permission of Franchise Canada. **p. 219:** From *Tourism Distribution Channels: Practices, Issues and Transformations* by BUHALIS, D and LAWS, E. Reprinted with permission of Thomson UK, a division of Thomson Learning: www.thomsonrights.com. Fax 800 730-2215. **p. 220:** From *Hospitality and Tourism Marketing* 3rd Edition by MORRISON. 2002. Reprinted with permission of Delmar Learning, a division of Thomson Learning: www.thomsonrights.com. Fax 800 730-2215. **p. 231:** From Hudson, S. & Lang, N. "A Destination Case Study of Marketing Tourism Online: Banff, Canada," *Journal of Vacation Marketing*, 8(2), pp 155–165, 2002. **p. 243–244:** From *Sport and Adventure Tourism*, Hudson, S. The Haworth Press, Binghampton, NY, 2003. Used by permission. **p. 254:** WELLS, WILLIAM D; BURNETT, JOHN; MORIARTY, SANDRA, ADVERTISING PRINCIPLES AND PRACTICE, 6th Edition, © 2003, p9. Reprinted by permission of Pearson Education, Inc., Upper Saddle River, NJ. **p. 280:** Courtesy of Calaway Park. **p. 282–283:** From "CTC-Korea partnership reaches huge winter activity market," from *Tourism Online*, December 2006. Canadian Tourism Commission, retrieved February 12, 2007. Reprinted with permission. **p. 296–297:** Reprinted by permission of Inniskillin Winery. **p. 318–320:** Reprinted by permission of A Lynch. **p. 323:** Reprinted by permission of George Silverman, President, Market Navigation, Inc. **p. 336:** Reprinted by permission of the Zeff Group. **p. 361: 370:** From "A Conceptual Model of Service Quality and its Implications for Future Research," Parasuraman, A, et al. *Journal of Marketing*, 49(4), pp 41–50, 1985. Reprinted by permission of the American Marketing Association. **p. 372:** Hudson, S & Shephard, G. (1998) "Measuring Service Quality at Tourist Destinations: An Application of Performance-Importance Analysis to an Alpine Ski Resort." *Journal of Travel and Tourism Marketing*, 7(3), p69. Used by permission of Haworth Press. **p. 374:** Courtesy of the Hotel Association of Canada. **p. 377:** From "The behavioural consequences of service quality," Zeithaml, VA, Berry, LL and Parasuraman, A. *Journal of Marketing*, 60, pp 31–46, 1996. Reprinted by permission of the American Marketing Association. **p. 378:** Reprinted with the permission of The Free Press, a Division of Simon & Schuster Adult Publishing Group, from THE SERVICE PROFIT CHAIN: How Leading Companies Link Profit and Growth to Loyalty, Satisfaction and Value, by James L. Heskett, W. Earl Sasser, Jr., Leonard A. Schlesinger. Copyright © 1997 by The Free Press. All rights reserved. **p. 381:** From *Services Marketing: Integrating Customer Focus Across the Firm*, Zeithaml, VA & Bitner, MJ, 2000, p153, used by permission of the McGraw-Hill Companies. © The McGraw-Hill Companies, Inc. **p. 384:** From *Services Marketing: Integrating Customer Focus Across the Firm*, Zeithaml, VA & Bitner, MJ, 2000, p470, used by permission of the McGraw-Hill Companies. © The McGraw-Hill Companies, Inc. **p. 386:** From *Services Marketing: Integrating Customer Focus Across the Firm*, Zeithaml, VA & Bitner, MJ, 2000, p168, used by permission of the McGraw-Hill Companies. © The McGraw-Hill Companies, Inc. **p. 406:** Reprinted from *The Canadian Geographer*, Vol. 24, No. 1, 1980, article by Butler, R. **p. 407–408:** From "Sharing the Capital Experience," (2003), Higgins, G., *Tourism*, 7(3), published by the Canadian Tourism Commission. Reprinted with permission. **p. 411:** This article was published in *Destination Branding*, Morgan, N., et al. "Contextualizing Destination Branding," page 31, Copyright © Elsevier (2002). **p. 419:** Courtesy of Venue Saint John. **p. 437:** Sourced from Statistics Canada (2001) "Population Projections," *The Daily*, Catalogue 11-001, March 13, 2001. http://www.statcan.ca/Daily/English/010313/d010313a.htm. Retrieved March 26, 2007.

PHOTO/SCREEN CAPTURE ACKNOWLEDGMENTS

Photos used on *Cover* Jacobs Stock Photography/Photographer's Choice/Getty Images and Steve Craft/Masterfile.

Photo used in *Profile* box features: © Pep Roig/Alamy. Photo used in *Snapshot* box features: © Peter Guess/ShutterStock. Photo used in *Marketing in Action* box features: © emin kuliyev/ShutterStock.

p. xxii and p. 27: Courtesy of G.A.P. Adventures. **p. 2:** Courtesy of the Canadian Tourism Commission. **p. 24:** Reprinted with permission. **p. 36:** Courtesy of Simon Hudson. **p. 40:** Courtesy of Responsible Travel. **p. 62:** Courtesy of Science North/Dynamic Earth, dynamicearth.ca, © Science North. **p. 64:** Courtesy of Pier 21. **p. 71:** Courtesy of Semester at Sea®. **p. 76:** © david sanger photography / Alamy. **p. 81:** Courtesy of Northwest Territories Tourism. **p. 107:** CP/Aaron Harris. **p. 112:** Sourced from Statistics Canada. Reprinted with permission. **p. 140:** © mediacolor's / Alamy. **p. 145:** Courtesy of Simon Hudson. **p. 150:** © Graham Bloomfield/Shutterstock. **p. 157:** IWM / John Maclean, © IWM. **p. 176:** Randy Lincks/www.coastphoto.com, Tourism Whistler. **p. 180:** Courtesy of Space Adventures. **p. 192:** © Karen Kean/Shutterstock. **p. 196:** © vario images GmbH & Co.KG / Alamy. **p. 201:** Courtesy of Ski Norquay. **p. 207:** Courtesy of Club Med. **p. 212:** Courtesy of Surgeon and Safari, www.surgeon-and-safari.co.za, Email – info@surgeon-and-safari.co.za. **p. 216:** © Al Harvey, The Slide Farm **p. 221:** Courtesy of Tourism Whistler. **p. 228:** Courtesy of Weekendtrips.com. **p. 243:** Courtesy of Canadian Mountain Holidays. **p. 246:** Courtesy of R&R Partners. **p. 252:** Courtesy of Newfoundland and Labrador Tourism. **p. 266:** Courtesy of Calgary Zoo and Trigger Communications. **p. 268:** Image courtesy of The Advertising Archives. **p. 270:** Courtesy of Instituto Rio Branco/Tourism Brazil. **p. 285:** Courtesy of the Canadian Tourism Commission. **p. 288:** Courtesy of Rocky Mountaineer Vacations. **p. 293:** Courtesy of Air Canada. **p. 318:** Courtesy of Atlantic Tours Gray Line. **p. 325:** © 2005 Puerto Rico Convention Center. **p. 330:** Courtesy of Carnival Cruise Lines. **p. 339:** Courtesy of Tourism Vancouver. **p. 341:** Courtesy of Prince Edward Island Tourism. **p. 345:** Courtesy of www.TourismInternetMarketing.com. **p. 353:** Courtesy of Tourism Australia. **p. 358:** Courtesy of Pets Can Stay, www.petscanstay.com. **p. 375:** Pascal Desjardins, Calgary, AB photographer. **p. 389:** Courtesy of WestJet. **p. 394:** Courtesy of the Yukon First Nations Tourism Association. **p. 401:** Courtesy of the Calgary Stampede. **p. 403:** Courtesy of the Kenai Peninsula Tourism Marketing Council. **p. 413:** Courtesy of India Tourism. **p. 424:** Courtesy of Marathon by the Sea. **p. 427:** © manuel velasco / iStock. **p. 432:** ©2007 LINDEN RESEARCH, INC. All Rights Reserved. **p. 440:** Courtesy of Simon Hudson. **p. 443:** Courtesy of Hilton Hotels. **p. 445:** Courtesy of Stuart Cove's Dive Bahamas. **p. 461:** Courtesy of Sebastian Bordage.